Teach Them Well

Teach Them Well

An Introduction to Education

George F. Madaus
Boston College

Thomas Kellaghan
St. Patrick's College, Dublin

Richard L. Schwab
University of New Hampshire

1817

HARPER & ROW, PUBLISHERS, New York

Grand Rapids, Philadelphia, St. Louis, San Francisco,
London, Singapore, Sydney, Tokyo

Sponsoring Editor: Alan McClare
Project Editor: Susan Goldfarb
Text Design: Keithley and Associates, Incorporated
Cover Design: Brand X Studio
Text Art: Fineline Illustrations, Inc.
Photo Research: Inge King
Production Manager: Jeanie Berke
Production Assistant: Beth Maglione
Compositor: ComCom Division of Haddon Craftsmen, Inc.
Printer and Binder: R. R. Donnelley & Sons Company
Cover Printer: Lehigh Press

Picture credits begin on page 519.

TEACH THEM WELL: An Introduction to Education

Library of Congress Cataloging-in-Publication Data

Madaus, George F.
    Teach them well : an introduction to education / George F. Madaus,
Thomas Kellaghan, Richard L. Schwab.
        p.   cm.
    Bibliography: p.
    Includes index.
    ISBN 0-06-044186-0
    1. Education—Study and teaching—United States.   2.Education—
United States.   I. Kellaghan, Thomas.   II. Schwab, Richard Lewis.
III. Title.
LB17.M28   1989   88-32679
370′.973—dc19   CIP

89 90 91 92   9 8 7 6 5 4 3 2 1

BRIEF CONTENTS

Preface   *xiii*

Part One: Foundations   *3*
   1: Philosophical Foundations of
     Education   *7*
   2: Historical Foundations of Education   *39*
   3: Social Science Foundations of
     Educational Policy and Practice   *57*

Part Two: The System   *83*
   4: The American System of Public
     Education   *85*
   5: Key Positions in the Educational
     System   *109*
   6: Alternatives to the Public Schools   *130*
   7: Legal Rights and Responsibilities of
     Teachers and Students   *145*

Part Three: The Teacher   *175*
   8: The Career of Teaching   *177*
   9: Careers in Education   *210*

Part Four: The Student   *231*
   10: Student Pluralism   *233*
   11: Characteristics of Individual
     Students   *255*

Part Five: Teaching and Instruction   *279*
   12: The Moral and Social Contexts of
     Teaching   *281*
   13: Preparing for Class   *307*
   14: Classroom Instruction   *337*
   15: Teacher Evaluation of Students   *357*
   16: The Effective School   *383*

Part Six: Current Issues   *405*
   17: Computers in Education   *407*
   18: Accountability   *428*
   19: The Role of Testing in Education   *448*
   20: The Reform Reports   *476*

References   *505*

Picture Credits   *519*

Index   *521*

CONTENTS IN DETAIL

Preface   *xiii*

Part One: Foundations   *3*

   **1: Philosophical Foundations of
      Education   *7***
   What Is Education?   *8*
   Education and Schooling   *12*
   Philosophical Bases for Different Views
      About Education   *14*
   Basic Approaches to Educational
      Practice   *19*
   Education and Society   *28*
   Conclusion   *37*
   Questions and Activities   *38*

   2: Historical Foundations of Education   *39*
   The Need for an Institution Devoted to
      Education   *40*
   The Colonial Period   *42*
   The Revolutionary Period   *43*
   The Nineteenth Century   *46*
   The Twentieth Century   *51*
   Conclusion   *56*
   Questions and Activities   *56*

   **3: Social Science Foundations of
      Educational Policy and Practice   *57***
   Scientific Enquiry and Education   *58*
   Child Development   *61*
   Learning   *67*
   Testing   *75*
   The Classroom as a Social System   *77*
   Home and School   *79*
   Conclusion   *81*
   Questions and Activities   *82*

Part Two: The System   *83*

   **4: The American System of Public
      Education   *85***
   The Complexity of the American System
      of Public Education   *86*
   The Local Government's Role in American
      Education   *87*
   The State Government's Role in American
      Education   *94*
   The Federal Government's Role in
      American Education   *96*

The Role of External Nongovernmental
    Groups in American Education   99
Financing Education   103
Conclusion   107
Questions and Activities   107

**5: Key Positions in the Educational
    System   109**
State School Board Members   110
Chief State School Officer   112
Local School Board Members   113
Superintendent of Schools   115
Assistant Superintendent for Curriculum
    and Instruction   117
Assistant Superintendent for
    Personnel   118
Assistant Superintendent for Pupil
    Personnel Services   119
Assistant Superintendent for Finance and
    Budget   121
The Principal   122
Department Chairperson   124
Guidance Counselors and Other Support
    Staff   125
Conclusion   128
Questions and Activities   128

6: Alternatives to the Public Schools   130
The Current State of Private
    Schooling   131
Historical Origins   132
The Legal Test of Private Schooling   135
Government Aid to Private Schools   137
The Organization of Private Schools   137
The Publics Served by Private
    Schools   138
Choice of School   139
Religion and Values in Education   140
Competition in Education   141
Conclusion   143
Questions and Activities   144

**7: Legal Rights and Responsibilities of
    Teachers and Students   145**
Legal Foundations   146
School Attendance and Programs   148
Student Records   151

School Discipline *153*
Procedural Due Process Protections in
 School Discipline *158*
First Amendment Guarantees in
 Education *159*
Religion and the Schools *161*
Discriminatory Practices *163*
Education of Students with Handicapping
 Conditions *166*
Employment of Teachers *169*
Tort Liability *171*
Conclusion *172*
Questions and Activities *173*

Part Three: The Teacher *175*

8: The Career of Teaching *177*
Teaching as a Profession *178*
The Demographics of Teaching *181*
Preservice Training *183*
Professional Growth *189*
Professional Development Programs *189*
Teacher Burnout *204*
Should I Teach? *206*
Finding a Job *206*
Conclusion *209*
Questions and Activities *209*

9: Careers in Education *210*
Roles and Life Patterns *212*
Career Alternatives in Traditional
 Educational Settings *213*
Career Alternatives in Other Settings *223*
Conclusion *229*
Questions and Activities *229*

Part Four: The Student *231*

10: Student Pluralism *233*
Students from Disadvantaged
 Backgrounds *234*
Bicultural and Bilingual Students *237*
Talented and Gifted Students *240*
Students with Handicapping
 Conditions *245*
Gender *249*
Conclusion *252*
Questions and Activities *253*

**11: Characteristics of Individual
Students** *255*
Historical Background of Individual
Differences *257*
Dimensions of Individual Differences *258*
Coping with Individual Differences *272*
Conclusion *276*
Questions and Activities *278*

Part Five: Teaching and Instruction *279*

**12: The Moral and Social Contexts of
Teaching** *281*
The Moral Dimension of Teaching *282*
Expectations for Teachers *285*
The Social Context of Teaching *296*
Conclusion *305*
Questions and Activities *305*

13: Preparing for Class *307*
Preactive Teaching *308*
Planning the Physical Environment of the
Classroom *309*
Planning the Psychological Environment of
the Classroom *312*
Planning the Intellectual Environment of
the Classroom *318*
Planning a Safe Classroom *320*
Grouping for Instruction *321*
Curriculum Planning *323*
The Context of Lesson Planning *328*
Conclusion *334*
Questions and Activities *335*

14: Classroom Instruction *337*
Lesson Structure and Practice *338*
Mastery Learning *347*
Motivation *349*
Types of Lessons *350*
Conclusion *355*
Questions and Activities *355*

15: Teacher Evaluation of Students *357*
Formal and Informal Evaluation *358*
Public and Private Evaluation *360*
The Functions of Classroom
Evaluation *361*

Teachers' Expectations   *363*
Constructing a Classroom Test   *368*
Record Keeping   *378*
Conclusion   *381*
Questions and Activities   *381*

16: The Effective School   *383*
The School Effectiveness Debate   *384*
Effective Schools: What Do We
   Mean?   *387*
The Characteristics of Effective
   Schools   *391*
Conclusion   *403*
Questions and Activities   *404*

Part Six: Current Issues   *405*

17: Computers in Education   *407*
Computer Basics   *408*
The Computer as a Tool   *414*
The Computer as Tutor   *416*
The Computer as Tutee   *420*
The Computer as Trouble   *422*
The Future of Computers in
   Education   *424*
Conclusion   *426*
Questions and Activities   *427*

18: Accountability   *428*
Reasons for Demands for
   Accountability   *429*
Expectations for Accountability
   Programs   *434*
Basic Questions About
   Accountability   *437*
Accountability Mechanisms   *442*
Conclusion   *446*
Questions and Activities   *447*

19: The Role of Testing in Education   *448*
What Is a Test?   *450*
Different Kinds of Standardized Tests and
   Their Uses in the School   *453*
How Tests Are Used in Schools   *461*
The Misuse of Test Results   *463*
Criticisms of Standardized Tests   *465*
The Use of Tests in Setting Education
   Policy   *469*

Conclusion   *475*
Questions and Activities   *475*

20: The Reform Reports   *476*
The Background to the Reports   *478*
A Profile of the Reports   *479*
The Political Dimension of the
    Reports   *483*
Common Beliefs in the Reports   *486*
The Reports' Recommendations   *492*
Conclusion   *503*
Questions and Activities   *504*

References   *505*

Picture Credits   *519*

Index   *521*

PREFACE

We wrote *Teach Them Well* in order to introduce students who are considering teaching as a career to the field of education. This book is designed for survey courses in the field and covers what are traditionally regarded as the foundations of education in philosophy, history, and the social sciences; the system's structure; its key participants (teachers, students, and administrators); and its central activities (teaching, instruction, and learning). The text reflects the current interest in improving education in America, as well as new developments in educational practice.

In writing this book, we were influenced by the belief that research in education has an important contribution to make to teaching. There is a wide range of topics about which research evidence is available, all of potential use to the teacher. We examine the most recent findings in several chapters. The application of research by teachers should help contribute to their professional development and improve the way they teach. Research also provides a body of advanced knowledge that is characteristic of professional activity.

However, we do not think that teaching is merely the application of theoretical or scientific knowledge. Even a superficial examination of teaching indicates that it is an extraordinarily complex activity, carried out in a complex social situation characterized by the immediacy and unpredictability of classroom events. Teachers have to respond quickly to many different kinds of situations, from an unruly student to the failure of a class to understand a concept. In making these decisions, they need to be able to combine information from a variety of sources quickly and decisively. Since new teachers will find it helpful to have established basic procedures and rules, we have provided practical guidelines to help them prepare for class and manage the classroom environment.

We consider teaching to be a moral undertaking that sets out to achieve moral objectives and is based on moral relationships between teachers and students. We believe that it is important for teachers to be familiar with the rules of conduct and social norms that govern the schools they teach in and to be aware of what parents and the society at large expect from schools. Since teaching takes place in particular cultural and historical contexts, new teachers should understand some of the elements of those contexts. For this reason, parts of the book are devoted to the philosophical and historical foundations of education, the structure of the American school system, and the legal rights and responsibilities of teachers and students. We also address a number of current issues in education, including the use of computers in schools, the idea of accountability, the role of testing, and the ongoing debate about reform in American education.

The choice and organization of topics for an introductory course in education are to some extent arbitrary. Because people will differ in their views about the best order in which to study those topics, and because different teacher-preparation programs have different emphases, some instructors might decide to skip some chapters, or to start with one of the later chapters and then backtrack. We believe that the book allows for both these possibilities. The list of references at the end of the text offers suggestions for further reading.

The authors are indebted to a number of people for their assistance in the preparation of this book. Chapter 6 was written by George Elford, Educational Testing Service; Chapter 7 by Dianna Pullin, Boston College; Chapter 9 by Carol Kehr Tittle, City University of New York; and Chapter 17 by Walt Haney, Boston College. Material for other chapters was provided by Clare Cejer, Bridgewater State College, Massachusetts; John Donovan, Boston College; and Helene Skrzhiarz, Middleborough Public Schools, Massachusetts.

Reactions to sections of earlier drafts of the manuscript were provided by Andrew Burke, Simon Clyne, and Mark Morgan, St. Patrick's College, Dublin; John McDonagh, Mater Dei Institute of Education, Dublin; Thomas McIntyre, Atlanta Public Schools, Georgia; and faculty and students at the University of New Hampshire.

Mary Rohan, with the assistance of Mary O'Brien, was responsible for preparing the manuscript. The manuscript was typed by Nuala Flynn, Hilary Walshe, Teresa Bell, and Kay Munson. Other assistance was provided by Michele Ryan, Sharon Masterson, Myra Noonan, and Kristin Schwab.

We also want to thank the following reviewers for their thoughtful comments and suggestions:

J. Bruce Burke, Michigan State University
John Lenssen, Oregon State University
Bill Rutherford, University of Texas at Austin
W. Ross Palmer, University of Alabama
Harold H. Jaus, University of North Carolina at Charlotte
Richard Pratte, Ohio State University

Finally, we wish to express our appreciation to Alan McClare, sponsoring editor in the College Division of Harper & Row, for his unfailing support while we were preparing this book.

Teach Them Well was written at a time of great interest and change in education in America. This is reflected in current writing about education as well as in new developments in educational practice. Above all, current debate in education is focused on its improvement. It is our hope that this text will make a contribution toward that goal and that our readers will become highly competent professionals teaching tomorrow's children well.

GEORGE F. MADAUS
THOMAS KELLAGHAN
RICHARD L. SCHWAB

Teach Them Well

PART ONE

Foundations

An educational system can be described in terms of the general structure of its schools (elementary, secondary, advanced) and of the system's roles and legal arrangements. These things can be described as the body of the system. But an educational system also has a less obvious component—a spirit that gives life to the body. The spirit encompasses a range of factors that can be divided into three main categories. First, there are beliefs and values that characterize the behavior of parts of the system (classrooms, schools, school districts) and of persons who relate to those parts (students, teachers, parents, administrators, employers) (Green, 1980). A study of these beliefs and values falls within the field of philosophy. Second, the particular kind of spirit that an educational system exhibits at any point in time has its roots in history—events and values in the past that have shaped the aims, values, structure, and extent of the system today. Third, the education system's spirit is also influenced by the findings of empirical research in the social sciences that relate to the functioning of the system, its major participants (particularly students), and its major activities (teaching and learning). To understand the system, it is necessary to study not only its structure and roles (its body) but also the philosophy, history, and social sciences (its spirit) that give it life.

Each of the areas of philosophy, history, and the social sciences (the three areas dealt with in the three chapters in this section) has its own unique contribution to make to the study and understanding of education. Each area views education from a particular perspective and has its own characteristic conceptual structure and its own characteristic way of obtaining evidence and coming to conclusions. Certain questions can be answered only on the basis of philosophical, historical, or social science evidence. This is most clear in the case of history. If we want to know how the size of the educational enterprise developed over time or how many students went to high school during different periods, we obviously have to turn to historical evidence to find the answer.

It may be less obvious, but it is equally true, that certain questions can be addressed only from a philosophical perspective. When we ask about the aims of education or about the attributes of an educated person, we are asking questions that cannot be answered without reference to values—the belief that some things are better than others and are hence desirable. Philosophy studies such values, tries to make them explicit, and examines how they are justified by those who hold them.

While these issues are the province of philosophy, there are other issues to which philosophers have addressed themselves in the past but that in more recent times have been addressed by social scientists. For example, philosophers have had much to say about human nature, about the nature of knowledge, and about the nature of learning. However, their views have not usually been based on systematic examination of people's behavior. For this reason, philosophers have differed markedly in their views on these issues: for some, children are born "cognitively empty"; for others, the child exemplifies an internal pattern of development that education should help realize. Social scientists have adopted the methodology of the physical sciences to examine these issues. Their aim has been to provide an accurate picture of human nature, and particularly of the nature of children, that is based on the careful observation of how people behave. In their studies, they have examined how children learn, how they develop, the ways in which they perceive and conceptualize the world, and how those ways change as the child grows. Information from studies of this kind is to a large extent replacing the speculations of philosophers. As we shall see, however, social science itself is based on basic philosophical assumptions about human nature, and these assumptions color the way problems are investigated and consequently the findings of studies. Further, as we shall see in Part One, the older speculative views of philosophers still influence what happens in classrooms.

CHAPTER 1

Philosophical Foundations of Education

This chapter introduces you to how beliefs about the nature of individuals and society influence the ways in which people define the methods and purpose of education, what is taught, and how it is taught.

• In general, education is an activity based on some intervention designed to produce some desired changes in individuals.

• The exact nature of the activity and the form and extent of intervention will differ according to each person's belief system.

• Views about education, schools, the curriculum, and teaching are in turn a function of beliefs about the nature of knowledge, the organization of knowledge, the nature of the learner, and the roles of teachers and students.

• Approaches to the organization of schools and the curriculum and approaches to teaching are influenced by the extent to which education is viewed as transmitting culture or developing the person.

• The extent to which people believe the schools should promote the national interest, prepare students to take their place in society, or reconstruct society influences educational policy and practice.

• Equality of educational opportunity is an important concept in American education. However, there are different ways in which equality can be defined. These different definitions influence the organization of schools and the delivery of instruction.

Of all the professions, teaching is probably the one you feel you know most about. You have sat in classrooms for many years—sometimes interested, sometimes bored, sometimes indifferent—watching teachers go about their daily work. From this experience, you probably are able to say that teachers vary a good deal in their styles of teaching, in their attitudes toward students, and in the aspects of education they think are important. No doubt some of the variation that exists among teachers is due to basic differences in their personalities. But teachers also are exposed to a range of diverse influences in their everyday lives, during their teacher-education programs, and in the course of their experience in schools—influences that might contribute to differences in their approaches to the task of teaching. Some influences may be fairly specific, such as the content of programs in educational psychology or the suggestions for managing a class given in courses on teaching methods. Other influences, however, are almost like the air we breathe. They are all around us, but we rarely pay attention to them. Indeed, when we try to isolate and study them, we find that they are very elusive.

In this chapter, we will be concerned mostly with these elusive influences on teaching which arise from different views about education and what education should be about. The chapter can be divided into two major parts. The first part deals with the education of the individual. For centuries, people have expressed a variety of views about the nature and purpose of education, and these views still influence what goes on in our schools. We will consider some of these views, which in turn depend on other more basic views about the nature of the individual and the nature of knowledge and how it is acquired. There are four sections in this part, dealing with the nature of education, with the difference between education and schooling, with philosophical bases for different views about education, and with basic approaches to educational practice. The second major part of the chapter deals with the relationship between education and society, in particular with how education has been conceived as serving the needs of society.

What Is Education?

We start by asking: What is education? This fundamental question raises a series of other important questions:

- Why do schools exist?
- Why are children and adolescents required to spend so much time in them?
- Which is more important, the individual or society? Should the aim of education be to contribute to the personal development of the student or to the improvement of society?
- Why are some things taught in school and others not?
- Among the things that are taught, why are some regarded as more important than others?
- Are some aspects of behavior more important than others? For example, is moral development more important than intellectual develop-

ment? And if it is, how should that be reflected in what goes on in schools?

These questions may not seem to be of great practical importance. However, answers to the questions, although they may not be explicit, affect both what the teacher does in the classroom and general educational policy. As far as the teacher in the classroom is concerned, what is taught and how it is taught reflects views about what is important to teach and learn and what the best ways of learning and teaching are. From a policy point of view, educational decisions are constantly being made about such matters as what should be included in the curriculum, academic excellence, minimal competency, and teacher performance. (We will consider some of these issues in later chapters.) A decision about any of these matters cannot be made without answering (or assuming an answer to) at least two basic questions: What is the aim of schooling (what should it be trying to achieve)? and, as a consequence, What kind of student performance is important and of value (Ebel, 1972)?

Issues such as these have occupied the minds of many people over the centuries, certainly since the time of Plato (427–347 B.C.), which was long before mass education developed. In attempting to answer them, we face the task of setting out a *philosophy* of education. This involves deciding what the goals or purpose of education should be and then making recommendations to achieve those goals. The recommendations will have to deal with what is taught (the curriculum), how it is taught (methods of education), who should be taught, and how the educational system should be organized.

To define what education is, and especially to outline a whole philosophy of education, is not easy to do. That is partly because a philosophy of education reflects basic ideas about humanity and society, about the purpose of existence, and about what is and what is not important in life. Since people do not agree on these things, we cannot expect agreement on a philosophy of education. For example, in considering the purpose of education, some regard the individual—his or her needs and interests—as the most important consideration; others see the needs of society as being of primary concern. Your own choice in this matter will affect the kinds of experiences that you believe individuals should be exposed to when you teach.

A Dictionary Definition

One way you might attempt to find out what is meant by education is to examine how the word has been defined in various standard dictionaries. If you do this, what we said about the difficulty of defining the term will be confirmed, for you will find that the concept is fairly fluid and has been used in different senses in different periods in history. Latin usages of terms related to the English word *education* sometimes refer to physical development *(educere)* and in other cases to the rearing of plants and animals as well as children *(educare)*. In earlier English usage, education was also used to describe bringing up animals as well as children. Today we restrict the word *education* to humans, though we still apply the word *training* to plants and animals as well as to humans. With the development of schooling in the nineteenth century, the use of the term *education* was largely restricted to what went on in schools (Hirst & Peters, 1970).

Characteristics of Education

People may differ in their definitions of what they think education should achieve and how teachers should go about teaching, yet most would probably agree that if we are to call something education, it should possess a number of characteristics. First, education is *an activity;* it is something that happens. Second, it brings about *change.* We expect a person who has been educated to be different from one who has not been educated. Third, the change we expect is in a *desired direction.* That is, we expect the change to be an improvement, not a regression; for example, after being educated a person should have a wider range of skills or behavior at his or her disposal than before being educated. The idea of improvement implies that norms or values (what is good and desirable) are built into the educational process. Fourth, educational activities are *intentional;* that is, they are designed to assist the change that has taken place. Thus, change that takes place spontaneously or as a result of maturation is not regarded as education. Some people restrict the term *education* to the formal kind of intervention that takes place in schools; others, however, regard informal activities outside the school as contributing to the educational process. Finally, there is disagreement among people on the extent to which schools should emphasize the development of cognitive and intellectual skills (for example, the ability to speak and write correctly, the ability to think creatively) or other aspects of an individual's development (for example, emotional, moral, social, or aesthetic behavior) (Gallup, 1985b).

Toward a Fuller Definition of Education

If we accept these characteristics as essential to education, we can now define education as *an activity based on some intervention which is designed to produce desired changes in individuals* (Marler, 1975). Note that this definition avoids the difficult issue of deciding which characteristics *should* be changed or how they should be changed. It does not say what kinds of achievements, knowledge, character, or skills we would wish an educated person to possess. A consideration of this issue leads us to the question of the *aim* of education: What does education try to achieve? A simple answer to this is that education tries to produce a person who meets various criteria of intellectual, moral, and aesthetic development (Moore, 1982). There are a number of points that we can make about this definition. First, it does not refer to any benefit outside education. Education is an end in itself; the development of a person is regarded as something intrinsically good. Second, to give an aim substance, it is necessary to place it in some particular social, political, economic, or religious context. Although the aim of education may be to produce an educated person, this notion will vary in content in different times, places, and cultures (Moore, 1982). Third, this definition of education does not specify the criteria we should apply to determine whether or not we would regard a person as educated. Is an educated person one who is familiar with the great classical works of literature or music, or one who knows a lot about science and technology, so important in our modern world? Is the educated person one who has skills that are useful in everyday living and work, one who is well adjusted and who has a sense of personal fulfillment?

Because of the different values people hold, we are not likely to reach a general agreement about the aspects of development that education should foster. If we consider what actually happens in schools (how time is spent there and how the work of schools is often assessed and judged—on the basis of student test performance), it would seem that particular attention is paid to the development of intellectual skills. But few people would say that other aspects of development are not important.

Close to the question of aim is the question of *purpose.* Concern with purpose leads us to ask: What is education for? Why do we want people with well-developed minds? For Herbert Spencer (1820–1903), an English philosopher who has had considerable influence on the way we think about education, the purpose of education was "to prepare us for complete living" (Spencer, 1891, p. 7). He classified the areas of life for which preparation is necessary: activities related to self-preservation (health), activities that secure the necessities of life (earning a living), activities related to rearing children (family life), activities that maintain proper social and political relations (life in society), and activities devoted to the gratification of tastes and feelings (aesthetic areas of life).

Since Spencer, many definitions of the purpose of education have adopted the basic view that education should prepare students for life (and particularly for working life). The details and terminology may vary, but the general thrust remains the same. A few examples of the purpose (often described as goals) posited for American education will illustrate this. The Commission on the Reorganization of Secondary Education in its *Cardinal principles of secondary education* in 1918 listed seven areas of life for which education should prepare a student: health, command of fundamental skills needed for life in a modern society, family life, work, life in the community and nation, leisure activities, and ethical behavior (U.S. Bureau of Education, 1918). Later, a report of the Educational Policies Commission (1944), entitled *Education for all American youth* identified the need for education to develop skills, knowledge, and attitudes required to make the worker an "intelligent" and "productive" participant in economic life. It also, in the Spencerian tradition, identified needs in social, moral, aesthetic, and cognitive areas.

The need to prepare students for work achieved a new relevance in the 1970s with the realization that schools were prolonging adolescence and isolating students from the reality of life outside the school. As more and more students stayed longer in school, the ability of the school to provide the kind of experiences that more mature students needed was questioned and proposals were made to supplement the school's work with skills development and job-training programs in the community (Coleman, 1974). The need to prepare students vocationally is mentioned in several of the recent reports on the state of American education.

While the idea that education should prepare people for living is a central one in American education, in itself it is inadequate as a recipe for educational practice. There are many possible ways in which one might be prepared for life, and the statement of an aim or purpose does not help us decide which of these possible ways one should choose. Some further guidelines or signposts for educational activity are required. What we are talking about here is not a conscious effort to operationalize general aims by stating specific and concrete objectives for classroom activities (Tyler, 1949); this will be described in Chapter 14. In this chapter, we will be dealing with a more general and largely subconscious adoption of broad strategies that pervade the whole educational endeavor. Two traditions can be identified in these strategies. In one, the aims of education are to be achieved through the transmission of the accumulated traditions of the culture to the student; in the other, students' experience of the world around them is regarded as the basis of knowledge which will be useful in later life. We will outline these traditions after we have considered the distinction between education and schooling.

Education and Schooling

Although our views of education derive primarily from the experience of schooling, education and schooling are not the same thing. The point that education is much broader than schooling was made by the Greek philosopher Plato. Indeed, in his *Republic*, perhaps the most complete analysis of education ever written, he pays little attention to schools. That is not surprising, since formal schooling was not a major feature of the society in which he lived. But there may have been a more fundamental reason for Plato's lack of concern with schooling: Plato believed that the community—its laws, drama, art, music, athletics—has a major impact on the development of the young. Today, it is recognized that the family has the principal responsibility for child rearing. The school has been designed by society to complement the work of the family in those areas with which the family cannot cope (Coleman, 1987). In our concern with the formal educational system, and in particular with the failure of the system to live up to people's expectations, we sometimes lose sight of the fact that factors outside the school to which the child has been exposed from birth onward have a major influence on development.

If we pause to reflect for a moment, it is obvious that a lot of the achievements of children have nothing to do with the school. Just consider what children can do before they even enter school. Apart from basic motor skills (for example, walking, tying shoes, buttoning a coat), children will also have learned a lot of social behavior (for example, to share with others). Emotions will have developed so that many children can cope with fear, aggression, and frustration. The extent of psychosexual development can be seen in preschool children's sex-role behavior (behaving in stereotypical ways like boys or like girls). Of particular interest (because it so directly applies to the context of school) is the enormous development that takes place in preschool children's language and thinking skills.

All these developments take place in the informal atmosphere of the home or, for many children nowadays, in a day-care facility. Not all, of course, are the result of educational intervention (even in the broadest sense). Some may be due to the "maturation" of the child; that is, they depend primarily on the inherited characteristics of the individual rather than on stimulation from outside and practice in response to that stimulation. However, while many aspects of behavior are dependent on genetic inheritance (for example, only humans learn to speak), it is also true that the quality and extent of a child's development is very much affected by the environmental conditions in which he or she develops. Although most of children's early experiences are in the home, as children grow they are more and more influenced by the neighborhood, broadening the range of their experience.

Despite the educational importance of nonschool factors referred to by Plato, Americans, since the time of the Puritans, have put great store in the school's ability to achieve important objectives. And, as we have seen, these objectives have been not only academic ones, but also ones related to preparation for work and life. Perhaps Americans have come to expect too much from their schools in making them take on educational functions that were previously the province of the community, church, or family. In this expectation they were supported by the ideas of John Dewey, who had a great influence on thinking about education in America in the twentieth century (see Box 1.1). Dewey recognized in his important book *Democracy and education*, published in 1916, that deliberate education (in the school, the home, or the church) represents only a part of the child's total education; however, he also believed that traditional institutions (the home, the church, the local community), under the pressures of industrialization and urbanization, were no longer fulfilling their educational roles. In this situation, he felt that it was necessary for some institution to take on these functions and the appropriate institution in his view was the school. This obviously places a heavy burden on the school.

For most of this text, we shall consider the institutionalized aspect of education known as schooling, since this is the context in which teachers in this country work. However, occasionally we shall refer to out-of-school influences, insofar as these impinge on the work of the school.

Philosophical Bases for Different Views About Education

We have already noted that different views about education, about the purpose and type of education offered to individual students, and about the way the educational system should work raise important issues that have occupied the minds of philosophers and, no doubt, of many other people. These issues give rise to a number of more specific questions. What kind of knowledge is more important—the knowledge we receive from the past or that which we find out for ourselves; academic knowledge (for example, a knowledge of literature) or practical knowledge (for example, a knowledge of weaving)? How do we acquire knowledge? By reading books, by sitting and listening to someone who "knows" more than we do, or by going out and experimenting with things in the world and finding out in a trial-and-error fashion what "works" and what does not? Do children and adolescents differ greatly from adults in their personalities and in the way they learn? What should govern relationships between adults and children in the learning situation?

In this section, we shall consider how people's views about four major issues can affect practice in the classroom and general educational policy. The four issues are the nature of knowledge, the organization of knowledge, the nature of the learner and of learning, and the roles of teacher and student. Views relating to these issues will be set out in fairly stark terms. In the process, we may, by ignoring their complexity, tend to oversimplify them. Within any view it is possible to find considerable variation of opinion and qualifications of the points we make. Our aim is to represent general positions.

The Nature of Knowledge

THE OBJECTIVITY OF KNOWLEDGE Over the centuries, much educational practice has been strongly influenced by the thoughts of Greek philosophers, particularly Plato (427–347 B.C.) and Aristotle (384–322 B.C.), about the nature of knowledge. The Greeks had a dual conception of knowledge. One type was based on reason, the other on the information we obtain through our physical senses of hearing, seeing, and touching.

Plato came to this distinction having noticed that our conversations are based on absolute notions or ideas. For example, we can judge honesty, or loyalty, or even the "straightness" of a line only by reference to some *absolute idea* we have of these things. Plato concluded that these absolute ideas are eternal and unchanging and have an independent existence of their own outside space and time. While the color of a leaf may change from green to red, "greenness" or "redness" does not change. True, we obtain everyday information through our *sense activities* (Plato's second type of knowledge), but this does not give us the kind of knowledge that is immutable and timeless. It can form the basis of our "opinions" or "beliefs" that in our daily affairs might be satisfactory enough to act on, but unlike "real" knowledge, our opinions or beliefs are always subject to revision in the light of criticism or conflicting evidence. The task of education is to produce a "rational" mind, capable of grasping, perhaps only in an intuitive way, knowledge of absolute ideas ("real knowledge"). This, Plato tells us, is achieved through intellectual effort, often through debate.

Aristotle, who was a student of Plato, did not accept his teacher's view that "real" knowledge exists outside the individual in an eternal and unchanging form. Neither did he regard our senses as unreliable sources of knowledge. On the contrary, for Aristotle, all our knowledge comes through our senses. Such knowledge takes the form of concepts that reflect the reality that exists around us and is experienced through our senses. Further, because we are rational beings, we are able to discover the laws that govern the natural events we perceive. Although Aristotle differed from Plato in his view of what knowledge is and how it is attained, like Plato, he also thought of knowledge as something objective with an existence outside the individual, consisting of facts, laws, and procedures that can be discovered in nature.

John Dewey (1859–1952) believed that schools should assume some of the functions previously served by the home, the church, and the community.

Plato's emphasis on rational thought as the way to establish certain and necessary truths about the world provides the basis of what have become *rationalist* and *idealist* traditions in philosophy. These traditions can be found in the works of later philosophers, especially René Descartes (1596–1650), Baruch Spinoza (1632–1677), Gottfried Wilhelm Leibniz (1646–1716), and Immanuel Kant (1724–1804).

Aristotle's approach, on the other hand, because of the importance it attached to our ability to find out about the world through the direct experience of events, is often regarded as providing the basis of *empiricist* and *realist* traditions in philosophy. These traditions, like rationalist and idealist ones, have attracted adherents throughout history. Among their strongest champions were John Locke (1632–1704) and David Hume (1711–1776); the latter, although a strong supporter of the empirical approach in the quest for knowledge, did not believe that the approach could lead to a knowledge of absolute or necessary truths about reality (Marler, 1975; Power, 1982).

The emergence of modern science during the Renaissance (a cultural movement that began in Italy in the middle of the fourteenth century) gave rise to many doubts about existing philosophical positions about the nature of knowledge. For example, it cast doubt on the kind of Platonic knowledge that was arrived at on the basis of intellectual activity, and it challenged the basis of religious beliefs. However, the new science did not challenge the value of intellectual activity, and initially, it did not challenge the idea that knowledge is objective. Rather, it sought to replace one kind of objective knowledge (religion) with another (science).

Thus, the notion that knowledge is objective—something outside the individual waiting to be discovered—was a dominant idea in Europe up to the eighteenth century. At first educated Europeans attached great esteem and authority to ancient (often sacred) texts, studying and copying them with great care, memorizing them, and analyzing their contents in great detail. The emphasis of the Protestant Reformation on the absolute truth of sacred texts reinforced this tradition. As scientific studies became more widespread and successful in helping people understand the world, reverence for the authority of revealed texts and the church's teaching was replaced by reverence for the authority of objective and rational natural facts (Cohen, 1987).

French philosopher René Descartes (1596–1650) believed that society could solve all problems through new knowledge generated by scientific method and rational inquiry.

CHALLENGES TO THE OBJECTIVITY OF KNOWLEDGE A challenge to the idea that the world is governed by natural laws, which exist completely independently of us and which we find in nature, did not attain prominence until relatively recently in the history of thought. This challenge finds expression in the thinking of such philosophers as David Hume, who argued that we impose laws on nature rather than discover laws which already exist there. This position implies, as later philosophers have pointed out, that even scientific knowledge (which might appear to be the most "objective" kind of knowledge) contains elements that are imposed by the investigating scientist and so cannot be said to delineate the constituent structure of nature itself (Hubner, 1983).

The notion that knowledge is something that the individual builds for him- or herself through experience also contributed to undermining the idea that knowledge is objective and exists outside the individual. Among those associated with this view was the American philosopher Charles S. Peirce (1839–1914), who argued that our conception of a thing is determined by our anticipation of its practical applications. Thus, meaningfulness is really a question of practical utility. This view is associated with a philosophical position known as pragmatism. William James endorsed the pragmatic position, maintaining that the test of the truth of a belief is its fruitfulness. John Dewey

(1859–1952) also joined this tradition and applied many of its ideas to school learning.

Pragmatic views of knowledge reflect the society in which they were developed. First, it is significant that the ideas were developed in nineteenth-century America, in which society was becoming increasingly industrialized and technological. In that context, many problems were regarded as technical or methodological rather than as substantive. Viewing problems in this way led to an emphasis on the pragmatic aspects of living at the expense of traditional knowledge. Second, individualism and the practical ability to explore and develop the country were highly regarded at the time. It is not surprising that many Americans in that situation had little regard for "book learning," which was associated with the idle lives of the rich. Third, the evolutionary theory of Charles Darwin, who published his book *The origin of species* in 1859 (the year of Dewey's birth), provided a rationale and support for ideas of change, evolution, development, and improvement.

It would seem that philosophical views that question the objectivity of knowledge have had relatively little impact in scientific practice, in educational practice, and on popular belief. This is clear if one considers the most popular methods of teaching in family life (in which parents are more likely to simply tell children what to do rather than explain reasons for doing things) as well as those prevailing in most schools (in which it has proved extremely difficult to alter teaching methods, texts, the kind of things taught, and instructional organization) (Cohen, 1987).

The Organization of Knowledge

DIFFERENT TYPES OF KNOWLEDGE In Greek philosophy, knowledge was regarded as being highly organized. For example, Plato envisaged two levels of education corresponding to different types of knowledge; each level was considered appropriate for a different group of students. Those who could benefit from it should study philosophy, science, and mathematics. For others, a system of public education should be available to teach them to read, write, count, appreciate poetry and drama, and exercise physically.

Aristotle reinforced the distinction between levels of education by distinguishing among three types of knowledge: theoretical, productive, and practical. Knowledge pursued for its own sake (by the philosopher, for example) is theoretical. Knowledge pursued for the sake of making or producing something (for example, the potter's knowledge) is productive. Knowledge pursued for the sake of action (as exemplified in politics) is practical. In the history of Western education, Aristotle's practical knowledge has received little attention.

For Aristotle, theoretical knowledge was the highest form of knowledge, and education that concerned itself with its development was more highly valued than manual or vocational education. The more highly valued types of knowledge were considered appropriate for the more "talented" children, the future leaders of society. The less valued types were regarded as being appropriate for the rest of the population.

Aristotle provided the basis for the division of knowledge into disciplines—for example, philosophy, science, mathematics—each with its own basic concepts, structure, rules of inquiry, and organization. With the growth of knowledge, disciplines divided and sub-divided so that today we find a host of specialized areas of knowledge. Curricula in schools reflect this division, and the Greek philosophers' view that some kinds of knowledge are superior to others has not entirely disappeared either.

KNOWLEDGE AS A PRAGMATIC SKILL The hierarchical organization of knowledge in schools exists despite a number of contrary views about the nature of knowledge. In one such view, knowledge is not a bank acquired through education, but a tool for action. This view actually is to be found in Platonic philosophy. Later, Friedrich Froebel argued that what the child needs to develop is not a store of remembered facts but habits which would enable him or her to acquire knowledge when necessary. John Dewey adopted a similar position and regarded the logical structure of subject matter as irrelevant to the student. What is important is how subject matter, which might be drawn from a variety of disciplines, contributes to the solution of problems. In this view, there is no hierarchy of value among studies.

Marxist views of education also deny that there is a hierarchy of values in knowledge. In Marxist pedagogy, knowledge should not be partitioned into subjects or otherwise hierarchically organized, since such partitioning or organization is likely to be used to create an elitist frame of reference in which the kinds of knowledge possessed by people with political power are regarded as superior to the kinds possessed by people without such power (Whitty & Young, 1976). An interesting feature of the Marxist view of knowledge is that it accords a high value to Aristotle's type of practical knowledge pursued for the sake of action.

The Nature of the Learner and of Learning

LEARNING AS A PASSIVE PROCESS In some views of learning, the learner is considered to be a relatively passive person and learning involves the accumulation of information and knowledge. The idea is to fill the student's mind with knowledge. Such a view has strong roots in medieval Europe and continued into the eighteenth century. It went hand in hand with a view of knowledge as objective and residing outside the individual. The available evidence indicates that children learned by listening, reading, reciting, and recalling material presented to them by teachers or in books (Ariès, 1965; Cohen, 1987). "To study was to imitate: to copy a passage, to repeat a teacher's words, or to memorize some sentences, dates, or numbers" (Cohen, 1987). This approach received support from John Locke's description of the infant's mind as a *tabula rasa* (or blank slate) that passively reacts to the world and acquires content and structure through the impact of sensation and the crisscross of associations. German philosopher and psychologist Johann Herbart (1776–1841) applied these views systematically to education and exercised considerable influence on school practice in the last century. Much school teaching in Germany and in this country was based on his prescription that the student should be presented with information or ideas which he or she should then "associate with," or "relate to," other ideas.

LEARNING AS AN ACTIVE PROCESS There is a view contrary to this, one that says that children should be active agents in their own learning. Jean-Jacques Rousseau (1712–1778) made the point that growth is the outcome of interaction between the individual and the natural and social world. Other educators and philosophers, such as Friedrich Froebel (1782–1852), Johann Pestalozzi (1746–1827), William James (1842–1910), and John Dewey, also argued that it is through their own activity that children transform perceptions and experience into knowledge. Far from being passive, then, children mold, arrange, and interpret their world. They learn best by acting on their natural impulses to inquire, to express themselves, and to construct their own knowledge of reality.

The Roles of Teacher and Student

THE TEACHER AS A PERSON OF AUTHORITY From what has been said in preceding sections about differences in views about the nature of knowledge and differences in approaches to its acquisition, we would expect differences to be associated with these views about the roles of teachers and students in the teaching and learning process.

If we believe that the primary function of education is to transmit knowledge, it is clear that the teacher is the one who possesses knowledge and experience, while the child, relative to the teacher, lacks both. The teacher's job in this view is to present that knowledge to the student, and it is the student's job to understand what is as yet uncomprehended.

In this situation, the student is clearly dependent on the teacher for the knowledge that will provide him or her with an education. The idea of dependence implies social relations of power and authority, with the student occupying the subordinate status.

THE STUDENT AS AN AGENT OF KNOWLEDGE On the other hand, if we regard the student as being the most important agent in acquiring knowledge (as did Froebel and Dewey), the teacher's authority is correspondingly reduced. Further, if children develop in response to their own interests, needs, and spontaneous activities, then a permissive school atmosphere is indicated, one in which the line of authority between teacher and student is not so clearly drawn as in the traditional approach.

Basic Approaches to Educational Practice

Different philosophical positions regarding the nature and organization of knowledge, the nature of the learner, and the roles of teacher and student in the teaching and learning process have been related to two basically different views about what education should do for the individual, what it should

BOX 1.2 Characteristics of Teacher-Centered Instruction

Teacher-centered instruction means a teacher controls what is taught, when, and under what conditions within his or her classroom. Observable measures of teacher-centered instruction are

- Far more teacher talk than student talk during instruction.
- Most teacher questions call for reciting factual information.
- Most instruction occurs with whole group rather than in small groups or with individuals.

- Use of class time is determined by the teacher.
- Teachers often rely upon textbooks with lesser use of films, tapes, records, television, or other technology.
- Tests usually concentrate on factual recall of information.
- The classroom is usually arranged into rows of desks or chairs facing a blackboard with a teacher's desk nearby.

Source: Cuban, 1983, p. 160.

try to achieve, and how it should be achieved. In this section, we will consider these views.

The first approach is based in general (there are some exceptions) on the view that knowledge is objective and resides outside the individual. Further, there are different types of knowledge; of these, knowledge that is abstract and academic is regarded as superior to practical and concrete knowledge. Learning is a passive activity, and the teacher, since he or she is the possessor of knowledge, is a person of authority. On the basis of these views, the development of the individual is believed to be accomplished through becoming acquainted with the knowledge, beliefs, and values that have been built up over centuries of civilization. This view in one form or another has dominated most educational practice. Various terms have been used to describe it, such as "traditional," "classical," "content-centered," and "subject-centered." Styles of teaching to which this approach gives rise have been described as "direct," "closed," "didactic," "formal," "content-centered," "subject-centered," and "teacher-centered" (see Box 1.2).

The second approach in general (again, there are exceptions) emphasizes the importance of self-constructed knowledge that is based on experience. In this approach, knowledge is regarded as a pragmatic skill and artificial divisions between different types of knowledge are irrelevant in practice. Learning is an active activity and, since the individual is primarily the source of his or her own learning, the line of authority between teacher and learner is not clearly drawn. Supported by these views, the focus in teaching and learning is placed on the person who is learning, not on the precise specification of what has to be learned. Potential for development is seen to reside within the individual, and it is the task of the educator to create conditions within which that potential can be realized. Those conditions should include an environment in which the child's educational development can take place without interference. There are various versions of this approach. Terms used to describe them are "child-centered," "progressive," and "romantic;" the styles of teaching associated with them have been described as "indirect," "open," "exploratory," "informal," and "student-centered" (see Box 1.3).

We will now look in more detail at the two approaches and, in particular, at how they have been expressed at different periods in history.

BOX 1.3 Characteristics of Student-Centered Instruction

Student-centered instruction means students exercise a substantial degree of direction and responsibility for what is taught, for how it is learned, and for any movement within the classroom. Observable measures of student-centered instruction are

- Student talk on learning tasks is at least equal to, if not more than, teacher talk.
- Students ask questions as much as, if not more than, the teacher.
- Most instruction occurs either individually or in small (two to six students) or moderate-sized (seven to twelve) groups, rather than the whole class.
- Students help choose and organize the content to be learned.

- Teacher permits students to determine, partially or wholly, rules of behavior and penalties in the classroom and how they are enforced.
- Varied instructional materials are available in the classroom so that students can use them independently or in small groups, e.g., interest centers, teaching stations, activity centers, etc.
- Use of these materials is either scheduled by the teacher or determined by students for at least half of the academic time available.
- Classroom is usually arranged in a manner that permits students to work together or easily arrange work space; no dominant pattern exists.

Source: Cuban, 1983, p. 160.

Education Through the Transmission of Culture

The view that education is accomplished through the transmission of a society's culture to succeeding generations goes back a long way in history. It emphasizes the importance of passing on the knowledge that has been accumulated in past generations; indeed, such knowledge is regarded as the foundation of all learning. Curricula built on this idea came to be accepted as providing the basis of a broad education that would enable a person to adopt a broad view of problems and be adaptable in a variety of occupations. It was expected that the detailed and specific skills of an occupation would actually be acquired on the job. This view of education is found in Greek philosophy in pre-Christian times and has survived through the ages to the present day.

LIBERAL EDUCATION The ideal type of education for the Greeks was a liberal one. A liberal education was one that was considered appropriate for a "free" person, that is, a person that was politically free (not a slave) as well as free from the degrading necessity of doing physical work. The primary aim of such an education was to perfect the individual's intellectual powers, not to acquire vast amounts of knowledge. This was done through exercises in memorizing (to develop the memory) and in making logical judgments (to develop the power of judgment). In the course of education, the student would be exposed to formal studies (particularly of mathematics and philosophy) that would help lead to a knowledge of reality based on reason, as distinct from the "opinions" or "beliefs" which people hold about the world of appearances. The Socratic method, as set out in Plato's *Dialogues,* was designed to develop arts of knowledge through methods of enquiry and reasoning; it was not a method of transmitting information (Wingo, 1965).

It would seem that, over the span of history, people often lost sight of the basic aim of a liberal education to develop arts of knowledge. In practice, undue emphasis was often placed on the transmission of knowledge and information from teachers to students.

Over the past 2,000 years, there have been various strands and differences in emphasis in the traditional concept that education is based on the transmission of culture. These variations reflected differences in society in different periods of history and in the prominence given to religion, science, rationality, and the value of the individual. Up to the time of the Renaissance, religion and the supernatural occupied a central place in ideas about human nature, of the world, and of education. Education could contribute to salvation by making available to young people the accumulated knowledge of the culture; some of this had been revealed by God in the Bible and some had been deduced by human reason and was to be found for the most part in classical writings.

Saint Augustine (354–430) was an important bridge between ancient classical and Christian modes of thought. He was himself a product of a predominantly literary Roman education and so was in a position to become a key figure in the transition from classical pagan antiquity to the Christian Middle Ages. In his curriculum proposals, he maintained the Greek and Roman traditions, recommending seven "liberal arts" for study: three areas of "language" (grammar, rhetoric, and dialectic) and four of "science" (arithmetic, geometry, astronomy, and music). In the study of these subjects, the emphasis was very much on the abstract rather than on the practical.

These liberal arts, or variants of them, have proved to be remarkably resilient over time and have formed a central part of what has been called the liberal classical tradition of education that dominated Western education for many centuries. In medieval times, in the great universities of Paris, Bologna, Naples, Montpellier, Oxford, Cambridge, and elsewhere throughout Europe, the liberal arts achieved status as the most important field of knowledge, a status they have not entirely lost today. For example, instruction in most schools, particularly at the secondary level, is still organized around such disciplines.

In the seventeenth century, there was a gradual secularization of education under the influence of philosophers such as John Amos Comenius (1592–1670) and John Locke. This can be seen in the extension of the content of schooling to encompass the physical sciences, which were developing rapidly at the time. However, in most schools, religion remained an important consideration, partly because most schools were church schools. For example, the system of public education in New England in the seventeenth century was designed primarily to ensure that children would receive a proper religious education.

A recent categorization of modes of knowledge and experience is in many ways like Saint Augustine's and also reflects the Platonic view. It comprises seven groups: (1) formal logic and mathematics (which are concerned with relations of a general abstract kind); (2) the physical sciences (which are based on knowledge of the world of the senses); (3) awareness and understanding of our own and other people's minds (which includes such concepts as "believing," "intending," "wanting," and "hoping"); (4) moral judgment and awareness (which involve concepts such as "right," "wrong," "ought," and "duty"); (5) aesthetic experience; (6) religion; and (7) philosophical understanding (Hirst & Peters, 1970). Each of these modes reflects a certain way of looking at the world, involves the use of concepts of a particular kind, and has a distinctive way of testing the objectivity of its axioms. The purpose of education is to introduce students to these fundamentally different forms of objective experience and knowledge. Each student should learn enough about the different perspectives on the world embodied in these forms to be able to understand its character, to apply it in everyday life, and to be aware of further possibilities of study. This will prepare the student for "rational living" by providing the intellectual basis of rational action (Moore, 1982).

While many educators have maintained that the exposure of students to sections of the accumulated knowledge of our culture is an essential part of the educational process, there are important differences among advocates of this view. A brief discussion of three positions based on this view will serve to illustrate some of the differences. The three positions are essentialism, perennialism, and subject structuralism (Ornstein, 1982; Wingo, 1965).

Essentialism According to the essentialist position, the true purpose of education is the cultivation and training of the intellect (Bestor, 1955). Its proponents argue that all children need to learn those things that an adult needs to function intelligently as a productive member of society. The function of the public school is to give such a basic education to all children. This is best done through the rigorous application of the mind to the basic disciplines of knowledge, which have developed historically as systematic methods for solving problems. Such disciplines contain elements of our cultural heritage that are so important they cannot be neglected.

An elementary school student following the essentialist curriculum will receive instruction in reading, writing, spelling, and arithmetic, all taught as separate subjects. At the high school level, a student will take a common core of subject matter organized in terms of the traditional disciplines of English, mathematics, history, science, and foreign languages.

A recent example of an essentialist approach is the "back-to-basics" movement. This approach is based on the view that the supposed poor quality of American education has resulted in a "rising tide of mediocrity that threatens our very future as a Nation and a people" (National Commission on Excellence in Education, 1983, p. 5). The evidence for this view, it is claimed, is to be found in a variety of statistical sources, including the following: 23 million American adults are functionally illiterate; 13 percent of 17-year-olds are functionally illiterate; 25 percent of Navy recruits require remedial reading to understand written safety instructions. The proposed remedy is a return to an essentialist-type curriculum.

Perennialism For perennialists, as for essentialists, education is concerned with the development or cultivation of the intellect as a preparation for adult life (Hutchins, 1953). However, perennialism is more specific than essentialism in stating which fields of study best achieve this goal. They are the humanities and literature. To gain access to them, it is necessary for the student to know how to read, so perennialists regard reading (and writing) as part of the elementary curriculum.

The key concept in the perennialist curriculum is derived from Greek tradition and prescribes a core curriculum of liberal studies comprising "language" and "science" subjects. One proponent of perennialism (Hutchins, 1936) has categorized the liberal arts at the elementary and secondary school levels as rhetoric, grammar, dialectic, and mathematics. The sources for these areas of study are the "classics," or the great literary products of Western civilization that are regarded as embodying basic and unchanging truths.

While the essentialist view of education is one in which the teacher transfers the information of the core subjects into the minds of passive students, in the perennialist view the student must be active and should spend most of his or her time in reading, discussing, and analyzing the great books of literature. Hence teachers are regarded not as dispensers of knowledge but rather as guides, helping students to develop their intellectual powers. In this, perennialism views the self-activity of the learner as a key factor in learning.

Perennialism differs from essentialism in that it does not accept that the basic knowledge and skills needed for life change; they are immutable. Thus, the essentialist approach is more practical and pragmatic, more life-oriented, than perennialism. However, in practice, there is a good deal of agreement between the approaches regarding the core of subjects that students should be taught, except that the essentialists place more emphasis on practical subjects (such as science and foreign languages) than the perennialists, who place greater faith in the classics. Both approaches accept that students should be provided with opportunities to advance beyond a core curriculum, and both regard the authority of the teacher and discipline as being important.

Subject Structuralism Even if one accepts that curricula should be made up of existing knowledge, one is still faced with the problem of selection. Knowledge is expanding rapidly within subjects and, indeed, new specializations and subjects are continually being created, especially in the sciences. Given the constraints of time, it is becoming increasingly difficult to fit a reasonable representation of all the knowledge that exists into the school curriculum. Any attempt to select certain areas for inclusion is likely to be met with the objection that the selection is inadequate or biased.

To deal with this problem, attempts have been made to focus on the *structure* of subjects or disciplines rather than on their content. This seems an economic way of passing on basic information. Instead of learning a list of relatively independent facts and techniques, for each discipline the student would learn only the basic concepts, the rules or principles which govern their interrelationships, and the methods of inquiry used in the discipline.

During the 1950s and 1960s, considerable attention was paid to developing curricula based on the structure of disciplines, particularly in mathematics and science. The approach was seen as having several advantages. First, it presented the basic ideas of disciplines rather than a wide range of content, which made for a general economy in the construction of curricula. Second, the approach was based on the idea that knowledge is not fixed or permanent, and that curricula based on structure and principles are easier to revise and update than ones that have a large content component. Third, it was argued that the approach had pedagogical advantages. Understanding fundamentals makes a subject more comprehensible. That is, it is easier to remember general principles than detailed facts. Further, the application of learning to new situations is facilitated, since one is more likely to be able to apply a principle than a fact in a novel situation. For example, students who learned the basic concepts of commutation, distribution, and association, rather than a host of discrete number facts, are in a better position to be able to solve new problems involving the solution of equations in algebra than students whose knowledge is limited to isolated pieces of information (Bruner, 1965). However, critics argued that the structure of a discipline (such as mathematics or physics, as viewed by mathematicians or physicists) may not be in line with the discipline's pedagogic structure, that is, the way it has to be taught to pupils, particularly young children.

Education Through Personal Development

In contrast to the view that education is achieved through exposure to the accumulated knowledge of the culture is the view that children learn from their own experience. In the latter view, it is more important to know the world in which one lives than the world as interpreted by classical scholars. Rousseau is especially associated with this view. A similar view can be found in the writings of Comenius, who lived before Rousseau, and in the works of Pestalozzi and of Froebel, both of whom were clearly influenced by Rousseau's ideas.

ROUSSEAU'S VIEWS Rousseau set out his view of human nature and education in a book called *Émile; or An essay on education,* which was first published in France in 1762. He believed that children went through a series of stages, the sequence of which was determined by the laws of nature. If one does not interfere with that development and allows the child to progress in accord with its own true nature, all will be well; the individual will develop in a harmonious way to reach his or her potential for development. But, according to Rousseau, over the course of history people had interfered with nature. In his book, he set out to show how vice and error, though alien to the human constitution, had been introduced to it from outside and had corrupted it. People's nature, originally good, had been corrupted over time to such an extent that Rousseau regarded his contemporaries as living "in chains" (Grimsley, 1983).

Jean-Jacques Rousseau on the Education of Émile

Once more I say, my intention is not to furnish him with learning, but to teach him how to acquire it, when it may be of use to him; to show him how to set a just value on it; and, above all things, to inspire him with the love of truth (*Émile,* 1762).

In Rousseau's view, children should not be exposed to this accumulated corruption. On the contrary, harmful influences and obstacles should be removed from their environments. For example, in the very early years, the mother should avoid placing undue physical constraints on the child, allowing direct contact with the physical world. Later, the child should not be restrained in expressing feelings. Education involves responding to children's needs and allowing them to interact freely with the physical world.

While, as we saw, the cultural transmission view of education emphasized the objectivity of knowledge residing outside the individual, Rousseau believed in the primacy of knowledge based on direct personal concrete experience. He also believed in the education of the body and of the senses rather than in education based on learning abstractions contained in books. Even vocational education should be based on the direct observation of nature. Rousseau did not deny the importance of reason. It would have been difficult for him to have done so in an age dominated by Enlightenment intellectual activity. However, he did say that reason should be related to other, perhaps more fundamental, human characteristics. On balance, Rousseau's emphasis is on the affective rather than the rational aspects of development, and this marks a major break with earlier ideas about education.

DEWEY AND PROGRESSIVISM John Dewey's ideas about child-centered and progressive education owe much to Rousseau, although he was also influenced by a philosophical movement in the United States called pragmatism, with which the names Charles S. Peirce and William James are associated. Dewey believed that if we are faced with a problem, we should not start with speculation divorced from the real world. Neither should we seek to attain absolute knowledge of unchanging and eternal truths, as many philosophers had attempted to do in the past. Rather our approach should be to interact with the real world that is all around us, with the aim of attaining knowledge that is useful rather than eternal. Indeed, Dewey argued that something is "true" only insofar as it is found to be "useful." It follows from this that the idea that knowledge is something outside the individual waiting to be acquired in education has to be rejected. Instead, the important thing is to gain experience of the world.

The Nature of Progressive Education

Progressive education began as part of a vast humanitarian effort to apply the promise of American life—the ideal of government by, of, and for the people—to the puzzling new urban-industrial civilization that came into being during the latter half of the nineteenth century. The word *progressive* provides the clue to what it really was: the educational phase of American Progressivism writ large. In effect, progressive education began as Progressivism in education: a many-sided effort to use the schools to improve the lives of individuals (Cremin, 1964, p. viii).

Given these views, it is not surprising that Dewey reacted against the rigid curricula and rote learning which he found in schools toward the end of the nineteenth century and, in particular, against the notion that schools provided the opportunity of "learning how to think" through the traditional academic disciplines. In the 1920s, the effect of Dewey's thinking and of the progressive approach in general caused a shift in ways of thinking about the curriculum in the United States. This shift involved a move from an emphasis on subject matter to a consideration of the current psychological behavior, needs, and interests of the learner. Dewey did not reject the idea that traditional disciplines should be studied. He did argue, however, that the study of any discipline must, at the beginning, be based on materials which fall within the scope of ordinary life experience (Dewey, 1938). Despite the strong tradition in schools which accepted the preeminence of classical studies, Dewey rejected the view that the literary and classical knowledge (Latin, Greek, the classics, and so forth) taught in schools was superior to other kinds of knowledge. Any subject, including the sciences and trades, if properly taught, could contribute to personal growth.

The progressive approach also rejected a curriculum based on the likely needs of children when they would become adults, since children's needs develop and change. Indeed, Dewey believed that there can be no single curriculum that everybody should study, since there is no single set of abilities running through human nature. Neither should there be a dual system of education, with the future leaders of society following one curriculum and those destined for more menial positions following another. It was the business of the school to recognize the range of individual differences that exists among children and then to discover the interests and needs of each individual child and to teach everything that anyone is interested in. Only in this way could education promote the growth of intellectually developed human beings who would live life to the fullest.

Instead of regarding childhood merely as a preparation for adulthood, Dewey and the progressives regarded it as something of value in itself. And since Dewey considered childhood as consisting of a series of stages, education should take account of a child's level of development. Dewey expected that the findings of research in the behavioral and social sciences would provide teachers with the knowledge about children's development and learning strategies that they would need to guide the development of children.

For Dewey, children are agents of their own learning, active participants in the progress rather than passive recipients of knowledge. He considered experience to be the basis of all learning. Every individual, he noted, is engaged in continuous transactions with the natural and social world, the outcome of which is growth. It follows from this emphasis on experience and activity that knowledge is not something that is simply passed on to students by teachers and textbooks. Rather, it is something that is gained through an ongoing self-corrective process. Children, through experience and activity, learn what works and what does not work, and to know what works is the kind of knowledge needed in everyday life. In school, educational experiences should be made lifelike and should include lessons based on life experiences and field trips to help foster the development of students' problem-solving ability.

Dewey's interest in democracy and the problems of life in contemporary American society, which was becoming increasingly industrialized and urbanized, is reflected in his philosophy of education. He reacted against the isolation of traditional education from the world about it, and argued that the school should recognize its relationship to the larger society and reflect that society. Indeed, he saw the school as a miniature society with the same sorts of problems as exist outside it. Since Dewey was strongly committed to a democratic society, he argued that the school should pay particular attention to setting up its own structures so that students would not just learn about democracy but actually experience it. It was Dewey's hope that students would carry their experience of democracy in school out into their adult lives. This would help create a society that would be more truly democratic and in which all citizens would participate in decision making.

Many criticisms have been made of the progressive approach in education. First, it has been argued that it tends to be weak on aims and content. A major aim of progressive education is to develop problem-solving and life-adaptive skills, yet the precise specification of these skills is not easy. The main strength of progressivism is in its methodology; by contrast, the more traditional classical approach emphasizes aims and content to a greater extent. Second, if education is to meet the needs and interests of individual students, it is necessary to identify those needs and interests, again a difficult task. Third, it is argued that the progressive approach places too great an emphasis on different goals for different students. This differentiation of students and their course work becomes unmanageable. Dewey was opposed to sorting, tracking, and vocational education in the schools. However, the difficulties in trying to individualize education have often led to these strategies. Finally, it is said that the progressive approach does not pay sufficient attention to the cultural and intellectual heritage of our society.

In concluding our discussion of two major approaches to education (education through the transmission of culture and education through personal development), it is well to recall Dewey's (1938) point that we like to think in terms of extreme opposites and to formulate beliefs in terms of "either-ors." This helps us to focus our thinking and provides a framework for exploring further people's ideas about education. As you study these ideas in your reading, you will find that the philosophical positions we have described have been expressed in a variety of forms with many qualifications. You will also find that educational practice rarely totally reflects extreme positions. The fundamental issue, Dewey reminds us, is "not of new versus old education nor of progressive against traditional education but a question of what anything whatever must be to be worthy of the name *education*" (Dewey, 1938, p. 90). This brings us back to the fundamental questions about the nature of education that we raised at the beginning of this chapter.

Education and Society

Many philosophers, politicians, and writers have shown varying degrees of interest in how education and schooling fit into society. Some of these people, while recognizing that individuals may benefit from the education they receive, do not see that as its main purpose. For them the main purpose of education is to serve society's needs rather than the individual's.

Greek philosophers (such as Plato, Aristotle, and Socrates) thought that education that fostered rationality was the main method of reforming the state. Later, John Locke perceived the purpose of education to be to produce men who would advance the happiness of the community and thus contribute to the development of a good society. Pestalozzi, although he emphasized the individuality of children, also felt that education for all was important to bring about social reform. While Immanuel Kant believed in the need to develop fully the individual's faculties, he did not see that as the main purpose of education. Rather, the main purpose of education was to satisfy the needs of an emerging society that was industrially based, mobile, and pluralistic, and in general to promote the peaceful international state.

Education conceived as serving societal needs can be categorized under three headings: the promotion of national interests, the preparation of students to take their place in society, and the reconstruction of society.

Immanuel Kant (1724–1804) believed that the primary purpose of education was to promote social reform.

Education to Promote National Interests

Many nations perceive schooling as an important agency for promoting national identity and status. This was particularly so in the nineteenth century, which was a period of intense nationalism in Europe. The formation of countries such as Italy and Germany united people from different regions, sometimes speaking different languages and professing different religions. In this situation, the educational system seemed to be an appropriate place in which to promote national identity and solidarity. Schools used books that provided particular views of history, promoted patriotic music and song, emphasized national literature, and engaged in rituals of allegiance to national symbols, such as the flag.

America also faced problems relating to national identity in the nineteenth century, since many of its children were immigrants or the children of immigrants. The school was perceived as an important instrument in the transformation of a society composed of children who came from a variety of backgrounds, spoke different languages, and whose parents were, on the whole, poorly educated.

The nationalist influence on American schools was fueled by two world wars. Even after the wars, rivalry between countries continued to encourage nationalist feelings. These were evident in the mid-1950s when, with the launching of *Sputnik,* Russia moved ahead of the United States in the space race. When Americans looked critically at their schools, they found that many science curricula were out of date; the revision of curricula was seen as an important step in providing the nation with the scientific expertise that was needed to help reestablish America's international position. It was also found that many children from low socioeconomic backgrounds were doing poorly in school and were dropping out early. The question arose: Was a large amount of potential talent being lost to the nation? Again, the need to ensure that the potential and resources of all children would be developed was regarded as important to secure the status and prestige of the country. In this context, the role of education in developing the scientific capacity of the nation was seen as particularly important.

Views similar to those expressed at the time of *Sputnik* are again being expressed today. The current problem, according to a report of the National Commission on Excellence in Education (1983), *A nation at risk,* is that America's "once unchallenged preeminence in commerce, industry, science, and technological innovation is being overtaken by competitors throughout the world" (p. 5). The concern of the report is frankly nationalistic, the appeal emotive.

A Contemporary View of American Education

If an unfriendly foreign power had attempted to impose on America the mediocre educational performance that exists today, we might well have viewed it as an act of war. As it stands, we have allowed this to happen to ourselves. . . . We have, in effect, been committing an act of unthinking, unilateral educational disarmament (National Commission on Excellence in Education, 1983, p. 5).

Education to Prepare Students to Take Their Place in Society

Thomas Jefferson had observed that if a nation expects to be ignorant and free in a state of civilization, it expects what never was and never will be. According to Jefferson, the American public school was designed "to serve the general welfare of a democratic society, by assuming that the knowledge and understanding necessary to exercise the responsibilities of citizenship are not only made available but actively inculcated." The view that formal schooling is the way to improve the state and society as a whole was shared by Benjamin Rush, Noah Webster, Benjamin Franklin, and George Washington.

There are a number of implications of the belief that the preparation of students to take their place in society is a major purpose of education. First, students should have a good idea of how the society in which they live works; for example, they should know about the system of government, elections, the taxation system, and the distribution of authority and power in the society. Second, they should know the range of services provided by government agencies and their own rights and obligations as citizens. That these are still concerns of American education can be seen in the inclusion of questions about the functioning of democracy in the minimum-competency tests of some states. Third, as a preparation for life, students should acquire the basic skills needed to live and work in society. What precisely these skills are is not entirely clear. However, our society tends to regard basic language and math skills and attitudes toward work as important.

A number of recent reports on the American educational system have expressed concern about the economic crisis in the country and the failure of schools to prepare students adequately for work in the economy. The situation, according to the reports, is all the more serious because our society is changing rapidly and requires skills that the schools are not providing. The new society is seen as one in which the economy will be based on high technology, emphasizing information processing and computers. It is argued that to be able to meet the needs of this new society, students will have to spend more time studying mathematics and science and in mastering the English language (College Board, 1983; National Commission on Excellence in Education, 1983; Task Force on Education for Economic Growth, 1983; Twentieth Century Fund Task Force on Federal Elementary and Secondary Education Policy, 1983).

Although many people may agree that there is a need to raise general standards in American schools, there is less agreement about the precise skills that will be needed for work in America over the next 50 years. For example, while the use of high technology will increase, government statistical projections indicate that most new jobs in the coming decades will be in clerical and retail positions, rather than in engineering or computing (Stedman & Smith, 1983). However, projections are based on past trends and may not provide a valid basis for making predictions in a rapidly changing economy.

While it might be accepted today that it is not reasonable for schools to try to provide education and training for specific jobs, there is still a view that it is the function of the school to ensure that students are directed toward areas of education and training for which there is a need in society. The idea that the purpose of education is to provide an adequate supply of trained people for industry and generally to improve the efficiency of industrial society has obvious implications for what goes on in schools. It affects the kinds of things that are taught there; for example, if there is a shortage of engineers or technicians of some kind, then resources in schools will be directed toward the appropriate areas. Further, this approach attempts to identify and select those students who are most likely to be successful in the courses.

Education to Reconstruct Society

We have already seen that John Dewey ascribed great importance to considering the needs and interests of individual learners in planning an educational program. There was another aspect of Dewey's educational ideas that related to the role of education in reforming society. Dewey went beyond Thomas Jefferson's idea that schools should provide students with basic information and skills needed to function in a democratic society. While agreeing with Jefferson that individuals should be prepared for life in such a society, Dewey believed that through their experiences in a democratic school following progressive methods, young minds should be shaped in a way that would reform society, its democratic institutions, and its workplaces.

In this, Dewey reflected a general progressive view that was widespread in American society at the time, a view that was epitomized in Ralph Waldo Emerson's (1803–1882) belief in the perfectability of human life and institutions. According to this view, an unlimited increase in human knowledge, power, and happiness was possible, and this would lead to continuing reform and progress in society, making the world a better place to live in.

This belief did not originate in America in the nineteenth century. It goes back to at least the seventeenth century in Europe, when a number of philosophers, particularly the Englishman Francis Bacon (1561–1626) and Frenchmen René Descartes (1596–1650) and Blaise Pascal (1623–1662), laid the foundations of the development of scientific method and a rational approach to the solution of problems. Stressing that what people have to learn is more important than what they already know, these thinkers made clear that in dealing with the problems of the world, society was not confined to the philosophical and theological knowledge that had been handed down from preceding generations. Rather, the new methods of science and rational inquiry provided the means of acquiring new knowledge that could lead to the solution of problems that may have appeared insoluble to earlier generations.

At first, the focus was on the physical world in the study of physics and chemistry. Later it was suggested by such writers as Denis Diderot (1713–1784) and the Marquis de Condorcet (1743–1794), who were known as encyclopedists, that the spirit and methods of the physical sciences should be extended to the study of the organization of society and of human behavior. This extension, it was believed, would make progress possible in the social and moral spheres paralleling the progress that was being achieved in the physical sphere.

Dewey saw education as playing a key role in the progress and reform of society. So, too, did educationists who were influenced by the writings of the German revolutionary socialist Karl Marx (1818–1883). In socialist countries that have adopted Marxist views of the world, educational systems are carefully planned to achieve reform in society. For example, in the Soviet

Union, even kindergartens place a heavy emphasis on preparation for "collective" living. Experience in living closely with others is provided almost from birth so that the child will develop an awareness of the group or collective and its needs. Further, so that schooling at a later stage will contribute to economic production, curricula are given a heavy scientific and technical bias and attempts are made to match the curricula and the educational experiences of students to society's needs.

The politicizing of education is something that can affect every aspect of education if a strong central authority so decides. One might think that mathematics is a fairly universal and value-free subject and would be free of political overtones. While the major objective of presenting a mathematical problem to a student might be to test the student's ability to reason mathematically, the problem can also be used to convey a political stance. The example below illustrates this point. It shows a mathematical problem that appeared in a Chinese textbook at a time when relations with the United States were strained. The problem was meant to teach a lesson about the Chinese view that capitalism is decadent as much as it was meant to test a student's knowledge of fractions.

English philosopher Thomas Hobbes (1588–1679) thought that society needed a new foundation, based upon equality, to survive.

An Arithmetic Problem from a Chinese Textbook

In the United States of America, the number of half-starved people is twice the number of unemployed, and is five million less than the number of people who live in slums. As one-half the number of slum dwellers is eleven and a half million, what is the number of unemployed in the United States (cited in Swetz, 1978, p. 170)?

EQUALITY OF EDUCATIONAL OPPORTUNITY A striking example of the use of education to change society is found in the objective to promote equality of opportunity. Many educational systems throughout the world subscribe to this objective, and it has been a particularly dominant feature of American education. From an early stage, Americans placed great faith in education as the route to individual opportunity.

The principle of equal opportunity speaks to the questions: Who should be educated? and Should all receive the same education? The Greeks, as we saw, thought there should be two types of education: one for the select "talented" and future leaders of society and another less prestigious type for the majority of the population. History indicates that this pattern has prevailed in educational systems. Different sections of the population have received not only different types of education, but also different amounts. Despite America's strong commitment to equal opportunity, it was not until the beginning of the present century that a mass system of public secondary education was built, and not until the middle of the century that a mass system of public higher education emerged.

The concept of equality has its roots in the philosophy of natural rights (originating with Greek philosophers Plato, Aristotle, and the Stoics), which posited a divine order as the foundation of both nature and society; positive rights were a reflection of that order. The tradition of the exploration of a philosophy of natural right was of major concern in medieval scholasticism and was further developed by the Dutch jurist Hugo Grotius (1583–1645) and the English philosopher Thomas Hobbes (1588–1679), both of whom witnessed in the seventeenth century the collapse of the social, political, economic, and spiritual conditions that had prevailed in Europe for centuries. On a continent torn by war and strife, they saw the need to provide a new foundation (preferably a rational one) on which relationships between people and institutions could be based. In doing this, Hobbes set out in 1651 the basic egalitarian position.

Thomas Hobbes on the Equality of Man (1651)

Nature hath made man so equall, in the faculties of body, and mind; as that though bee found one man sometimes stronger in body, or of quicker mind than another; yet when all is reckoned together, the difference between man, and man, is not so considerable, as that one man can thereupon claim to himselfe any benefit, to which another may not pretend, as well as he (*Leviathan,* 1651).

Around the same time, Comenius was advocating what we might consider today to be a logical consequence of such an egalitarian position—universal opportunity for schooling in a system of public schools.

However, it is in eighteenth-century Enlightenment philosophy that we find what is generally acknowledged to be the foundation of contemporary positions regarding equality. The major model for Enlightenment thinkers was John Locke, who, in considering natural rights, said that the concepts of freedom and equality are fundamental in describing humanity's position in both nature and society. Locke went further than most of his predecessors in that he considered the relevance of educational influences in promoting freedom and equality, bearing in mind not only that people share a common nature but that they also exhibit a wide range of individual differences.

Locke gave much thought to the implications of natural rights for education. Since there is large variation among people, education should be adjusted to the faculties or personal qualifications of each individual. Individuals, for their part, should have the freedom to actualize their God-given endowments, each to a different degree and in varied combinations. Locke did not believe it was possible by means of education to change a person's natural endowments, but he did think it was possible to see to it that each individual received the necessary education for an optimal utilization of them (Sjöstrand, 1973).

Eighteenth-century Enlightenment philosopher John Locke (1632–1704) thought education should promote such natural rights as freedom and equality.

Locke had an enormous influence on developments in the latter half of the eighteenth century, which laid the foundation of present-day democracy. The two most important of these developments were the establishment of the United States of America and the French Revolution. Locke's influence in France is reflected in the thinking of Rousseau as well as in that of many theorists of the Revolution. American colonists Thomas Jefferson, John Adams, and Benjamin Franklin also relied on ideas from Locke's philosophy when they tried to justify their rebellion. Locke's influence is clear in the preamble to the American Declaration of Independence (1776).

Preamble to the American Declaration of Independence

We hold these Truths to be self-evident, that all Men are created equal, that they are endowed by their Creator with certain unalienable Rights, that among these are Life, Liberty, and the Pursuit of Happiness. . . .

DEFINITIONS OF EQUAL EDUCATIONAL OPPORTUNITY The meaning of the phrase "equal opportunity" has changed over time. Traditionally, it has been interpreted as Locke interpreted it, to mean that all children—irrespective of characteristics such as race, creed, social class, gender, financial resources, place of residence, or other irrelevant criteria—should have equal *access* to educational facilities. Social and occupational roles, and education to the extent that it contributes to obtaining such roles, should be left open to choice, individual effort, and competition (that is, they should be *achieved*). They should not be assigned on the basis of characteristics such as family, gender, or social class, over which an individual has no control (that is, they should not be *ascribed*). There should be no legal barrier to prevent a child from receiving any form of education. This conception of equity was instrumental in overturning the so-called separate-but-equal systems of education for blacks and whites. The public school's obligation is to remain available and free, thus providing an opportunity for students to learn. Furthermore, the school should provide similar facilities for all students: a uniform curriculum and similar resources (for example, per pupil expenditure, science facilities, teacher qualifications). Thus, the emphasis is on uniformity; all children should be treated in the same way (Coleman, 1968).

A step beyond access in defining equality of educational opportunity is to use *participation* as the criterion. Equality in this sense cannot be achieved if there is not an equal balance, in proportion to their numbers in the population, between boys and girls, among children from different races and social classes, and among children in different parts of a country at any given point in the educational system. Those fighting against race and gender discrimination in school assignments or programs use the participation principle in arguing for equity.

The expansion of educational facilities through the nineteenth century might be interpreted as having provided equal access to all students; however, even by the end of the century, only elementary schooling was available to the general population. Such education provided for the mass of students, while high school education was still mainly only for those likely to go on to third-level education. After the First World War (1914–1918), high school education, like elementary education, started to become a mass phenomenon. The idea was fast gaining ground that all students should have as much education as they wanted, and participation expanded rapidly.

A further definition of equality of opportunity uses *achievement* as the criterion. According to this view, not only should there be equality of access and participation, there should also be equality of outcome; that is, there should be equality of achievement between the genders, among children from different races and social classes, and among children in different parts of the country (Coleman, 1968; Coleman et al., 1966). This last definition is the most radical of all definitions of equality. Since the characteristics of students (including their readiness to learn) differ when they enter school, a definition of educational equality in terms of results or outcomes implies—in fact requires—not similar but different treatment for students at school. The ultimate aim is to make school achievement independent of students' backgrounds. This turns the initial concept of equal opportunity completely around. Rather than having equal access with the expectation of unequal results, this concept calls for unequal access to attain equal results. To achieve this may require positive discrimination in favor of certain groups of children.

Each of these different definitions has been stated or implied in debates and research about equality of educational opportunity and has also guided policy decisions; the usefulness of any of them, however, particularly in a policy context, remains a matter of doubt. Coleman (1975) concluded that neither a definition based on the criterion of equality of school input nor one based on equality of results of schooling is viable when taken at the extreme. Equality of input is unsatisfactory because it could be interpreted as providing minimal school resources for children; provided the same conditions applied to all children, little or no schooling would fit the input criterion. Further, Coleman argues that some children so manifestly require more resources than other children, if any kind of reasonable results are to be achieved, that a concept of equality based solely on the principle of uniformity is not acceptable.

Taking equality of output as the criterion for equal opportunity also causes practical problems. Coleman believes there is now sufficient empirical evidence to indicate that the influences on children from the environments outside school, particularly from the family, are so massive that equal output in schools simply cannot be achieved.

Because of these problems, Coleman regards the concept of equality of educational opportunity as "mistaken and misleading." He feels that we should be striving not for equality, but for a reduction in inequality. Such an aspiration would recognize the differences that exist among children when they come to school and the differences in environment outside the school which continue to influence children while they attend school. It would also recognize that the school's task is to help make up for some of the disadvantages from which children suffer in some environments.

CONCLUSION

In this chapter we considered philosophical views about education. We saw that education can be considered primarily either as a process to change individuals or as a process to change society. There are differences of opinion about the best way to achieve the aims of education. Your opinion about such things, whether it is explicitly acknowledged or not, will have implications for what you do in the classroom. For example, if you think that the aims of education are achieved primarily through learning about the great works of the past, then your role will primarily be that of telling students about these works and helping students gain access to them in their own reading. If, on the other hand, you regard the individual's needs and interests as paramount, you will become more of a facilitator than an instructor. The extent to which you will be able to express a particular point of view will of course be constrained by a number of factors—the ethos and philosophy of the school in which you teach, the grade level you teach, and the wishes and needs of your community, parents, and students.

It is important at this stage that you begin to formulate your own views about education and realize how these can affect what you do as a teacher. Your views will influence all your activities in the classroom—what you regard as important to teach, how you teach, how you organize your class, how you treat your students, and indeed how your students react to you and the school environment in which they find themselves, perhaps as involuntary and unwilling participants.

QUESTIONS AND ACTIVITIES

1. What, in your opinion, are the characteristics of an "educated" person?
2. Are your views about the nature of knowledge and the learner closer to those of Locke or to those of Rousseau? Why?
3. How do teachers' views on the nature of the learner influence how they teach and how they view discipline?
4. One perspective on the purpose of education is that schools should produce "good" citizens. Do you agree? What are the characteristics of a good citizen? Can they be taught?
5. Aristotle believed that "theoretical knowledge" is superior to "practical knowledge." Do you agree? Does American society reward people who acquire theoretical knowledge the same as or better than those who acquire practical knowledge?
6. You are a member of a school board that must cut 20 percent of its budget to comply with a town referendum. You can fire teachers; cut out the art, music, and physical education programs; or eliminate sports. What would you do, and how would you justify your decision philosophically?
7. You have taken your class on a field trip to a local courthouse to view a trial and meet various members of the court. While your students are outside eating their bag lunches, you overhear a passerby remark, "These kids ought to be in school; no wonder American education is going down the drain." If you had the opportunity to talk with this person, what would you say and how would you justify your trip?
8. Think back to your days in elementary and secondary schools. What was the predominant mode of teaching? What is the principal mode of teaching in your college? What mode of teaching would you like to follow? Why?
9. Which of the several views of equality discussed in the chapter do you hold? Why?

CHAPTER 2

Historical Foundations of Education

In this chapter we examine major developments in American education from colonial times to the present century.

- The need for a separate institution (the school) to support the home in its educational function emerged as society became more complex and industrialized.
- The Puritans recognized the need for basic education for all children to preserve religious, social, and political traditions.
- The Founding Fathers were committed to education too, but they saw its purpose differently from the Puritans. For the Founding Fathers, education was to contribute to the development of a new kind of society.
- In the nineteenth century, the common school was developed to provide elementary education for all.
- In the twentieth century, participation in secondary education expanded rapidly.
- As the educational system became larger and more urbanized, management techniques borrowed from industry were applied to the educational system, supporting practices such as consolidating schools and school districts, specifying goals for schools, testing students, and expanding specialized roles in the system.
- Equality of opportunity has been a consistent theme in American education, although it has been difficult to achieve.
- Quality of education has also been a consistent concern in American education.
- Education in America has been expected to deal with a variety of social and economic problems.

The American educational system is a product of history. It evolved over the last four centuries to meet what were perceived to be the needs of society at different times, and particularly the needs of children. Learning about its development will help you to understand better its role in contemporary society. If we are not to take our educational system and values completely for granted, an understanding of the past is crucial and will shape how we make choices today (Tyack, 1974).

In this chapter, we will provide an outline of developments in American education, beginning with the colonial period, continuing through the revolutionary period, and on to the nineteenth and twentieth centuries. First we will consider the recognition of the need for an institution separate from the family to support the family in its educational function.

The Need for an Institution Devoted to Education

Many of the early philosophers who wrote about education were speaking about formal methods of teaching even though they were not talking about schools as we know them today. When they wrote, mass education did not yet exist. There are examples of formal schools throughout history, yet it was not until the nineteenth century that some schooling for the entire population became a reality. Nevertheless, many philosophers from early times saw universal schooling as something desirable. Plato, for example, recommended a system of universal compulsory public education from birth to maturity. Much later, the reformers of the sixteenth century demanded universal public education, particularly religious education, a goal that was not achieved until 300 years later, and then not for religious but for secular education. Philosophers such as John Amos Comenius (1592–1670) and John Locke (1632–1704) also envisaged a kind of universal education, but they did not see the same kind of education as being suitable for all. They believed that a superior kind of education, preferably through a tutorial education at home, should be provided for the future leaders of society, while education for the poor should be limited to making them religious and self-supporting.

The circumstances in which people lived prior to the nineteenth century did not necessitate mass education. Of course, there is a need in any society for the young, if they are to survive, to assimilate some beliefs about the world in which they live, some attitudes toward it, and some skills to deal with day-to-day problems. However, in earlier preliterate, pretechnological cultures, the demands made on the young were not very great. Most learning was informal and took place around the home. The occupational skills that had to be learned were relatively simple and related to hunting, farming, fishing, housekeeping, and crafts. Boys learned the skills of their father, girls those of their mother. Prior to the invention of the printing press, there was little need to learn to read and write, as all important social transactions involved face-to-face oral communication (Postman, 1981). The line between infancy and adulthood was the point at which the child mastered the competence to speak and understand. In such a situation, there was no need for a separate person in the community to look after the training and enculturation of children, or for children to spend time in a formal school setting.

Even as societies developed, most adult skills could be learned at home. At the beginning of the nineteenth century, America was still a predominantly agricultural society (in 1820, only 7.2 percent of the population lived in urban areas), and this was reflected in attitudes toward the young and their education. In the farmer's family, boys were expected to contribute, at as young an age as possible, to caring for livestock and tilling the fields. Girls prepared the food, made clothes, and looked after younger children.

The clear distinction between childhood, adolescence, and adulthood, each with distinctive roles and responsibilities, is something that we may take for granted today. In America today, we do not expect 10-year-olds to work full-time to earn a living. However, as recently as the nineteenth century, 10-year-olds were working in factories, and even today, 10-year-olds in some non-Western societies can be found working all day on farms. Changes in society and in the family have had implications for the concept of childhood. Philip Ariès, in his book *Centuries of childhood* (1965), concluded, on the basis of a study of historical documents, that childhood as a distinct period in development emerged during the sixteenth and seventeenth centuries. During that period, the family became more intimate, more nuclear, and more protective, and in the process childhood became more distinctive. By the nineteenth century, childhood was characterized by a new degree of dependence, protection, segregation, and delayed responsibility. As the century passed, the number of children going to work at an early age decreased, and children were increasingly protected from the physical and moral dangers of life in a city. This was partly achieved by sending the children to school.

As societies became more developed and knowledge accumulated, a need arose for people to devote themselves full-time to the instruction of the young. The young could no longer learn what was required simply by observing and participating in the work of their elders. For example, after printing made the Bible readily available, many children were expected to learn how to read, a skill children could not readily acquire by observing or participating in the work of their elders. Beginning in the sixteenth century, some of the young (particularly in upper- or middle-class families) were separated from the rest of the community to be taught how to read (Postman, 1981). The newer learning required time and effort on the child's part.

The need for separate instruction became even more obvious during the Industrial Revolution in the eighteenth and nineteenth centuries, when work moved out of the home into factories and became more specialized and skilled. At the same time, the economy became more complex, and, beginning in the 1820s, large numbers of people moved from the countryside to work in centers of industry. With the development of factories and trade and the growth of occupational mobility outside the family environment, the family lost its importance as an economic production unit. The need for a special agency to deal with the preparation of children for such a society became obvious. Since the family could no longer provide the education and training that children needed to fill the new positions in industry, education and training became a community responsibility. Thus, the seeds of public tax-assisted systems of education were sown in Europe and in America during the nineteenth century as a response to the conditions created by industrialization and urbanization.

The Colonial Period

Even before the Industrial Revolution, America had shown a commitment to schooling. The growth of education in the colonial period was influenced in many ways by the traditions and values of the countries in Europe from which American immigrants had come. In Europe in the sixteenth century, education for most children was informal and was still a matter for the home. Formal education was limited. Private tutors were available for the education of children of aristocratic background; there were some Latin grammar schools for upper-class children, and some vernacular and craft schools to which access was also limited. A movement to provide widespread education so that everybody could read the Scriptures followed the invention of the printing press and the Protestant Reformation.

In America, too, religion was an important consideration in the Puritan ethos of seventeenth-century New England and was the motivating factor in establishing schools. (The first higher-education institution in the country, Harvard College, was founded in 1636, primarily to train clergymen.) Education had two major objectives in the Puritan plan to preserve religious, social, and political traditions. First, children should acquire reading skills so that they would be able to read the Bible and other religious texts. Second, since in the Puritan view children were born in original sin, they needed training and discipline (which the school would provide) to turn them into responsible, hardworking, law-abiding adults. It was in pursuit of these objectives that the Massachusetts Bay Laws of 1642 and 1647 were passed; they made education compulsory for all children and the local community responsible for maintaining schools.

The 1642 law decreed that all children should attain minimum educational standards (the ability to read and understand the principles of religion and the capital laws of the country). But the law did not require children to attend school. Since formal schooling was not generally available, it was envisaged that the required educational experiences (for learning to read, learning the catechism, and learning a trade) would be provided in the home by parents or by masters of young apprentices. If the home failed in its duty, then the child could be assigned to an apprenticeship by a court. By 1671 similar laws were found in all the New England colonies except Rhode Island.

Fear that the 1642 law would fail to secure literacy led to a new law in 1647 ("Ye Old Deluder Satan" Act). This law obliged towns of 50 or more households to establish and support by taxation schools in which, like schools in England on which they were modeled, children would be taught reading and arithmetic. An important aim of the schools was to instruct students in reading the Scriptures so that they would be able to thwart "Ye Old Deluder Satan" (see Box 2.1). At this time, the separation between private and public education, which later became an important and controversial feature of

It being one chief project of that old deluder Satan to keep men from the knowledge of the Scriptures, as in former times by keeping them in an unknown tongue, so in these latter times by persuading from the use of tongues, that so at least the true sense and meaning of the original might be clouded by false glosses of saint-seeming deceivers, that learning may not be buried in the grave of our fathers in the church and commonwealth, the Lord assisting our endeavors:

It is therefore ordered, that every township in this jurisdiction, after the Lord hath increased them to the number of fifty householders, shall then forthwith appoint one within their town to teach all such children as shall resort to him to write and read, whose wages shall be paid either by the parents or masters of such children, or by the inhabitants in general by way of supply, as the major part of those that order the prudentials of the town shall appoint. Provided, those that send their children be not oppressed by paying much more than they can have them taught for in other towns. And it is further ordered, that where any town shall increase to the number of 100 families or householders, they shall set up a grammar school, the master thereof being able to instruct youth so far as they may be fitted for the university. Provided, that if any town neglect the performance hereof above one year, that every such town shall pay five pounds to the next school till they shall perform this order.

American education, was not recognized. Education was provided by private groups, churches, and charitable organizations, as well as by local communities; generally, some payment by families was required for the service.

Basic education in reading, arithmetic, and religion was for the general population. For the children of well-off families, a further type of education was provided in what was called a Latin grammar school. The first such school in America, partly supported by public funds, was established in Boston in 1635. The school provided a college preparatory program, based mainly on the study of the classics, particularly Latin (Rippa, 1980). Other colonies followed the example of Massachusetts by setting up grammar schools.

Although educational provisions expanded considerably during the colonial era, not all children were actually receiving schooling by the time of the Revolution (Cohen, 1974). This was largely because the middle and southern colonies did not assume responsibility for education in the way the New England colonies did. Outside New England, the initiative to establish schools was left in the hands of the churches and of charitable organizations rather than the towns; in the mid-Atlantic states, for example, a tradition of parochial and private rather than state-supported schools developed.

The Revolutionary Period

While the roots of America's commitment to education are to be found in the colonial era, the reasons for supporting a mass-education movement were changing radically even as the colonial system of education was being set up. For the colonists, education was to be used to hand down and maintain their traditional culture, and especially their religion, in an environment in which it was feared that civilization might easily collapse. During the eighteenth century, ideas from Europe began to follow the colonists across the Atlantic. These ideas were to change not only the aims of mass education in America but also the whole nature of American society. They had to do with the equality of all individuals, the nature of knowledge and the way it is acquired, and the implications of ideas about these issues for change and progress in society.

New Ideas About the Role of Education

The ideas that came from Europe were associated with a movement known as the Enlightenment, which dominated eighteenth-century thinking. Many of the ideas proposed by prominent Enlightenment figures such as Voltaire and Diderot were the antithesis of what the original colonists had held dear. First, they emphasized the natural rights of all men. All men were regarded as equal whatever their background. Second, the kind of knowledge that was regarded as important was knowledge derived from an individual's own reasoning about the world, not knowledge based on Christian faith or tradition, or the Bible, or on convention, superstition, or prejudice. The new faith found encouragement in the developments in the natural sciences (mathematics, astronomy, physics) that were taking place at the time, and that were improving people's understanding and control of the world.

Faith in the ability of all people to develop their rational powers found support in John Locke's view that the mind is formed as a result of experience; that is, ideas are not present at birth in some form but grow out of individuals' interactions with the environment. If the environment could be controlled and if children could be provided with the best kinds of experience, it should be possible to develop fully the reasoning ability of all people. Such people, uncorrupted by religion, convention, or social structure, would then make rational decisions about their lives. These views assigned an important role to education, as is clear in the writings of Jean-Jacques Rousseau and Johann Pestalozzi.

All these beliefs add up to an optimistic view of the world and what can be done to improve it. They imply change and progress, ideas that we may take for granted today but that were fairly novel in the eighteenth century. They certainly did not form part of the colonists' dream.

Change and progress, however, were very much in the minds of the Founding Fathers, who were deeply influenced by Enlightenment thinking. For one thing, they rejected the idea of a hereditary aristocracy and decided in favor of democratic government, in which positions of power would be accessible to all. This raised two problems. First, how could they ensure that all citizens would be in a position to judge the issues of the day so that they could vote in an informed way? Second, in the absence of a hereditary form of government, how could they identify the most talented among the population who would become the future leaders in society? The Founding Fathers believed that the solution to both problems was to be found in education. Thus, schooling would support the political reforms associated with democracy.

While both the Founding Fathers and their Puritan ancestors had opted for mass education, there were major differences between their ideas about the purpose of education. The purpose of education for the Founding Fathers was not to maintain traditional ways and values, but to contribute to the production of new ones. Furthermore, education was to serve very practical purposes. It should be designed to meet the daily political, economic, and general vocational needs of people. There was never a great deal of enthusiasm for the European tradition that education was important for its own sake; indeed, some Americans thought that too much education might be bad, since it could put dangerous ideas in people's heads. Benjamin Franklin, for example, had established a school in Philadelphia in 1751 in which instruction was provided in a range of "practical" subjects (penmanship, arithmetic, bookkeeping, engineering) designed to prepare students for the world of work. (The school later lost sight of its purpose and became a classical grammar school.) Finally, schooling would also have a role to play in alleviating problems of poverty, crime, and inequality.

The Government's Role in Education

If education was deemed necessary for the well-being of the state, the question arose as to which level of government would provide for education—the federal government, the state, or the local district? The involvement of the state in education commenced around 1800 (earlier in New England), and growth in its involvement developed slowly, varying considerably from state to state. At first the state provided little more than encouragement for the private institutions involved in education. Thomas Jefferson tried to do more. In 1779, when he was governor of Virginia, he proposed a statewide system of public schools in that state, but the proposal was defeated by the legislature.

Later, the state granted land and financial support to communities and allowed local authorities to raise taxes for the support of schools. While the Articles of Confederation were still in force, two land ordinances for governance of the Northwest Territory (beyond the Alleghenies) in 1785 and 1787 set aside a parcel of land in each 6-mile-square township for a public school. These land grants were the first example of aid to education by the federal government. At a later stage, the states set minimum rates of taxation and tuition fees were prohibited. Finally, funds for schooling were made available from state and eventually from federal treasuries (Madsen, 1974).

The debate over the extent to which different levels of government should contribute to education is something that runs through the history of American education. This country is unique in the extent to which it assigns control of public schools to local interests. While social control of the schools is a highly prized value in America, in recent years there has been increasing concern that not all local communities can meet the financial demands of running an educational system. For some people, the answer to this problem is to be found in federal and state support for education. Suggestions about the role the federal government should play in the current economic and educational crisis and, in particular, about dealing with the problems of educationally disadvantaged children, appear in a report of the Twentieth Century Fund Task Force (1983), *Making the grade.*

The Nineteenth Century

In the late eighteenth and early nineteenth centuries, as immigrants flocked from Europe to the shores of America and American society became increasingly more diverse, concern arose about the rights of the ordinary citizen, who was in many cases poor and lacking in education. Pressure built up to establish "common schools" that would replace costly private schools and provide free, nonsectarian education, forming a solid basis for the well-being of a state founded on democratic principles.

The Common School Movement

A major figure in this movement was Horace Mann (1796–1859), who was secretary to the Massachusetts State Board of Education from its inception in 1837 until 1848 (see Box 2.2). Mann, aided by the decision of the board to take a more direct role in the supervision of schools, set out to reform the existing schools in the state and to establish a system of common schools that would put into practice the concept of education as a right for all citizens. By putting this principle into practice, the common school could serve as a training ground for citizenship in the American Republic, help to cure social and moral ills, and create a just and prosperous society (Binder, 1974). Although Mann saw the common school as a place where Christian ethical values would be inculcated, he did not think it should promote any single denominational religious doctrine. In practice, however, the common school was essentially Protestant in its approach. This did not create any great difficulty when America's population was largely Protestant and people could agree to Horace Mann's evangelical consensus for the schools: "to read the King James Bible without comment, letting it 'speak for itself'" (Tyack, 1974, p. 85). Large Catholic immigration, however, particularly in the second half of the nineteenth century, dented the homogeneity of America. When Catholics looked at the public school system, they saw it as a system which inculcated Protestant values and denigrated Catholic ones. This led them to develop their own school system.

Mann found some support for his work in political ideas associated with the Jacksonian Democrats, who were gaining support in the early nineteenth century. Jacksonian Democrats, like their predecessors, supported the idea of mass education. However, and in this they were unlike their predecessors, they did not think the function of the school was to select students of high ability for future leadership roles in society. Rather, they perceived the school's purpose as making all people equal by giving to all the same basic education.

Mann's task was not an easy one. In his travels through the state of Massachusetts, he found that school committees had little interest in what was going on in schools, that school buildings were inadequate, that teaching was poor and insensitive to the developmental levels of students, and that many children did not attend school regularly. To make matters worse, the public on the whole seemed apathetic about the schools.

BOX 2.2 Horace Mann (1796–1859)

Mann's youth was filled with the kinds of experiences that one might imagine are conducive to shaping a dedicated reformer. Fatherless from the age of 13, he assumed more than a boy's share of the toil required to scratch a living from the rocky soil of Franklin, Massachusetts. He obviously found scant comfort in the Calvinist preachings of his minister, the Rev. Nathaniel Emmons, who favored vivid descriptions of sinful man, a harsh God, and the fires of Hell. We know from Mann's recollections that these sermons brought him many nights of fitful dreams. In later years he abandoned the Calvinism of his childhood to embrace the more humane tenets of Unitarianism, but he never shook off the Puritan emphasis on the necessity for society to be governed by a strict moral code. The Unitarian in him that expressed itself in a deep faith in the essential goodness of man and the nearly limitless potential of human institutions always existed alongside an abiding Puritanism that led him, on various occasions, to angrily condemn such "vices" as profanity, drinking, smoking, and ballet dancing. Like his religious experience[,] Mann's personal school career was marked by contrasting shades of light and dark. Up to the age of 16 he attended the town school, but he was never able to be present for more than 8 to 10 weeks in any given year. And that institution offered a microcosm of the conditions in the schools of Massachusetts that Mann would later strive to correct. The curriculum was narrow, the teaching methods stultifying, and the teachers as cruel as they were ignorant. Yet the New England traditions of hard work and commitment to learning were evident in the Mann family, and he was encouraged to further his education. At 20 he began a six-month period of intensive study under the tutelage of an itinerant teacher named Barrett. This was sufficient to earn him entry to Brown University with sophomore standing. It was of no little significance that Mann achieved his first real success in life through an educational endeavor, assisted by an able, inspiring teacher.

Source: Binder, 1974, pp. 43–44.

Indeed, there was considerable opposition to the growth of public education, not just in Massachusetts but throughout the nation. Many people could see little need for educating children who, when they grew up, would work in factories or on farms. Private and independent schools saw common schools as a threat to their institutions' existence. The churches also saw public education as a threat to their schools, and many people believed that education was the function of the church, not that of the state. Common schools were perceived by some as a threat to their ethnic values, language, and religious beliefs. Finally, there was much opposition from people who would have to pay more taxes to support the public school system and who did not see education as a responsibility of the state (Gutek, 1986).

Despite these problems, the public school system grew throughout the century. Between 1830 and 1865, years known as "the age of the common school," many states had set up or were about to set up a system of universal tax-supported free common schooling. This does not mean that the development of the system was complete by 1865. Schooling was not uniform across the country; with significant exceptions, it was better in urban than in rural areas, and better in the industrial North than in the rural South. Further, public schooling was mostly at the elementary level. Secondary education still remained largely in private hands and was not available to the majority of students.

The curriculum in the common school varied somewhat, but on the whole emphasized "basic" education. From the beginning, elementary schools included reading as part of their curriculum. Computation, spelling, grammar, arithmetic, history, and geography, as well as "good behavior" and "manners and morals," were added later. Some schools required needlework for girls (Cubberley, 1934). High schools continued to emphasize a curriculum based on the classics and mathematics. Other subjects (such as history and modern languages) might be included, but it was not generally accepted that they had the same fundamental value in providing mental training as the classics and mathematics.

There were some attempts to change this narrow curriculum. Horace Mann and Francis Parker, for example, tried to introduce the ideas of European educationists, particularly those of Rousseau, Pestalozzi, Froebel, and Herbart. Francis W. Parker (1837–1902) developed what came to be known as the Quincy system, so called because the system was introduced in Quincy, Massachusetts, where Parker was superintendent of schools. Parker was appointed to do something about the standard of education in Quincy—about students who could not write a letter and who could read from their textbooks but not from other books. He abandoned the set curriculum and set out to interrelate school subjects to make them meaningful for the student. Thus, the child, rather than the subject matter of the curriculum, was placed at the center of Parker's educative effort.

Horace Mann (1796–1859) was one of America's first educational reformers. His greatest contribution was to put into practice the concept that education was a right for all citizens.

The main thrust of efforts such as those of Parker was to try to move schools away from the formalism that characterized their organization and teaching. In addition to extending the range of subjects covered, this involved moving away from the traditional book-centered method of teaching; paying more attention to the individual needs and interests of students; allowing children's own experiences to play a part in learning; recognizing the noncognitive characteristics of students by including subjects such as music, nature study, and drawing; and helping to prepare students for adult life by including agricultural and mechanical training.

The effect of these efforts at the national level does not seem to have been very great. Classrooms remained largely teacher-centered, and by the turn of the century critics were still commenting on the schools' emphasis on basics (reading, writing, arithmetic); on the sing-song drill, recitation, and rote repetition in classes; and on the omnipresence of textbooks. With classes of over 60 students, it is hardly surprising that teachers relied on drill and recitation (Cremin, 1964, 1965). Further, school buildings were run-down, poorly lighted, and overcrowded. These criticisms, propounded principally by Joseph Mayer Rice in a series of articles written in the 1890s, were not welcomed by the public.

Teaching in American Schools Around the Year 1900

Generally, classes were taught in a whole group. Teacher talk dominated verbal expression during class time (64 percent of the time, according to Stevens). Student movement in the classroom occurred only with the teacher's permission, e.g., going to the chalkboard. Classroom activities clustered around teacher lectures, questioning of students, and the class working on textbook assignments. Uniformity in behavior was sought and reflected in classroom after classroom with rows of desks facing the blackboard and teacher's desk (Cuban, 1983, p. 163).

Secondary Education

Early in the nineteenth century, the Latin grammar school began to decline in popularity. It had come to be regarded as an elitist institution, offering a type of education that was considered irrelevant to the needs of America. In its place, another type of secondary school called the academy, which had first appeared in the preceding century, became popular, replacing or absorbing Latin schools.

Academies varied a good deal. Some were private and run for profit; some were religious; and others were government sponsored, such as the military and naval academies at West Point and Annapolis. Programs offered by academies were broader and more practical than those offered in Latin schools; they included a curriculum in the English language for students who would end their education at the secondary level, as well as college preparatory programs (Sizer, 1964).

By the middle of the nineteenth century, the academy was the most popular type of secondary institution in the country; at the time, there were over 6,000 academies, serving over a quarter of a million students. The situation was about to change again, however, as another type of secondary school began to expand. This was the high school. The first public high school opened in Boston in 1821. Unlike Boston Latin, this school was completely supported by public funds. No tuition was charged, and the curriculum omitted the classical subjects and was designed to prepare students to become "merchants and mechanics." As the high school grew in popularity, the academy all but disappeared in the twentieth century.

Growth of the high school and of secondary education in general was slow. Although the Massachusetts legislature in 1827 mandated public high

TABLE 2.1 Percentage of Illiteracy[a] in the Population, 1870–1969

Year	Percent Illiterate	Year	Percent Illiterate
1870	20.0	1930	4.3
1880	17.0	1940	2.9
1890	13.3	1947	2.7
1900	10.7	1959	2.2
1910	7.7	1969	1.0
1920	6.0		

[a]Illiteracy is the inability to read or write a simple message either in English or in any other language.

Source: Eiden & Grant, 1979, p. 27.

schools throughout the state, districts were slow to follow the mandate. By the middle of the century, there were still only 300 high schools (and over 100 of those were in Massachusetts). At the same time, the growth of public-supported secondary education seemed inevitable. Elementary schools were flourishing throughout the country, preparing many children for more extended education. Further, the wealth that accompanied America's industrial growth made it feasible to raise taxes to support secondary education. However, it is not at all clear that the high school was an institution demanded by the masses. Rather, it seems to have been promoted by civic leaders in the interest of social unity, community prosperity, and individual opportunity (Katz, 1968).

A major impetus behind the development of public high schools came from a decision of the Supreme Court in Kalamazoo, Michigan, in 1874. The Court ruled against taxpayers who had brought suit to prevent the Kalamazoo Board of Education from levying a tax to support a high school and in favor of the community's right to tax residents for the support of high schools. The decision opened the way for other states to proceed with the establishment of high schools.

To achieve curriculum standardization, a Committee of Ten was set up by the National Education Association in 1892. The committee took the view that there should be a cutback in the variety of courses offered in high schools and recommended a liberal arts curriculum (English language and literature, mathematics, a second language, and science) in what was basically a college preparatory institution.

The acceptance of schooling by the American public in the latter half of the nineteenth century was remarkable. Elementary school enrollments increased from under 7 million students in 1880 to 16 million in 1900. In secondary schools (grades 9 to 12), enrollments over the same time period increased from 110,000 to just over 500,000 students. These figures were matched by a drop in the percentage of illiterates in the country (see Table 2.1).

While these figures show considerable expansion in enrollments, they also clearly indicate that relatively few students were going to secondary school up to 1900. Around that time, only 6.2 percent of 17-year-olds graduated from high school. Secondary education had developed at a much slower pace than elementary education. Arguments for free secondary education often paralleled arguments that had been used for free elementary schools. "And for many reformers the belief that education was a public necessity instead of a private luxury applied to the secondary schools as well as to elementary education" (Rippa, 1980, p. 131).

Despite these developments, the fact that so few students had the benefit of a secondary education by the year 1900 indicated that the American system of education at the time was what John Locke and the original Founding Fathers had advocated rather than what the Jacksonian Democrats had wanted. It was a dual system, providing differentiated educational opportunities appropriate to one's station in life. Essentially, there was a free system for the children of poorer people, designed to provide them with the basic skills required for work in an industrialized society, and a superior education (often provided in private and religious schools) for those who could afford it.

Education: Meeting the Aspirations of People?

The expansion of schooling in the nineteenth century took place at a time when there were major waves of immigration to the United States, at first mainly from northern Europe and later from southern and eastern Europe. During that century there were also major urbanization and industrialization movements. The growth of education can be seen as a response to a variety of political, social, economic, and cultural needs that these conditions gave rise to. Thus, common schools were used to promote social and cultural homogeneity in the country by imposing established values and the English language on a variety of ethnic and language groups. The schools were also seen as important agencies in preparing a literate and trained work force for expanding industries. The privileged classes expected that education would increase wealth, secure their prosperity, and prevent revolution. The less privileged (many of them immigrants), for their part, saw education as a vehicle of social mobility for their children, something that would break down class barriers and lead to equality (Gutek, 1986; Tyack, 1974).

How successful were the schools in meeting this variety of aspirations? On the one hand, it is argued that public schools, though they may not have succeeded in matching their promises, did provide enormous learning opportunities for Americans. On the other hand, some see schools as having been detrimental to the interests of the less privileged in society, to ethnic and racial minorities, and to females (Warren, 1978). The less privileged and females were poorly served to the extent that their participation and achievement in the education system did not match the participation and achievement of the more privileged classes, and particularly of male children from those classes. The members of ethnic and racial minorities (who, of course, also tended to be the less privileged members of society) not only did relatively poorly in school but also lost much of their cultural and linguistic traditions in the process of schooling.

The Twentieth Century

Through the later years of the nineteenth century and the early years of the twentieth century, expansion in the American educational system was enormous. Growth, which was at the elementary level in the last quarter of the nineteenth century, shifted to the high school level after 1900. By 1918, all states had passed compulsory attendance laws that required children to attend school until they either reached a certain age or completed a certain grade. At the same time, the functions of schools were broadening. Schools were taking on many of the functions which formerly had been handled by families, churches, or other community organizations. They were also turning their attention to vocational training at both elementary and high school levels (Graham, 1974).

From 1880 to 1930, enrollments in high schools approximately doubled every ten years. The half million students in 1900 had become almost 4 million by 1930. Ten years later (1940), it was over 6 million. By 1975, it was over 14 million. The percentage of 17-year-olds who graduated from high school increased from 6.2 in 1900 to 75 in 1977 (see Table 2.2).

Growth in student participation at high school level was greatly facilitated by the recommendations of the Commission on the Reorganization of Secondary Education. In 1918 the commission published its *Cardinal principles of secondary education* (U.S. Bureau of Education, 1918), which were in marked contrast to the

Moral education was considered one of the "basics" of eighteenth- and nineteenth-century elementary education.

recommendations of the Committee of Ten in 1892. Under the influence of progressive ideas, the *Cardinal principles* broadened the scope of the high school to make it comprehensive both in the students it served (with one institution accepting students of varying social, ethnic, and religious backgrounds) and in its curricular offerings. While the Committee of Ten had viewed the high school curriculum as basically a liberal arts college preparatory program of studies, the *Cardinal principles* suggested a wide range of curricular offerings for students.

Not only was there a vast expansion in the numbers attending school in this century, there were also movements designed to effect radical changes in the structure and practice of schools. Two major movements can be identified: progressivism and growth in educational administration on the one hand, and measures to ensure equality and quality in education on the other.

Progressivism

Progressivism had its roots in the experimental education of Francis Parker, Charles Judd, and H. C. Morrison, and further back in the educational ideas of Rousseau, Herbart, Pestalozzi, and Froebel. Its main exponent and popularizer was John Dewey. The movement, developed after the Civil War, had wide appeal among intellectuals at the turn of the century, and gathered momentum up to the First World War; after that it began to fragment and decline in influence.

Dewey provided a firm philosophical basis for his educational theories, but perhaps of greater importance in accounting for his influence was the fact that he had a high level of sensitivity to the problems facing America at the time, particularly those arising from industrialization. He also had a deep commitment to finding a solution to these problems. The most obvious place to look for a solution, he felt, was in education. It seemed to him that the school was the only institution that could take over the educational functions traditionally carried on by other institutions, particularly the family, the neighborhood, and the church.

TABLE 2.2 Percentage of 17-Year-Olds Who Graduated from High School, 1870–1977

School Year	Percent	School Year	Percent
1869–70	2.0	1929–30	29.0
1879–80	2.5	1939–40	50.8
1889–90	3.5	1949–50	59.0
1899–1900	6.2	1959–60	65.1
1909–10	8.8	1969–70	75.5
1919–20	16.8	1976–77	75.0

Source: Eiden & Grant, 1979, p. 23.

It is difficult to know exactly the extent of the impact of Dewey's views and of the progressive-education movement on educational practice in American schools. Certainly, progressive ideas were very helpful in easing the transition to mass secondary education. These ideas provided a rationale for the inclusion of vocational and other nonacademic studies in the curriculum of the high school, thus allowing the schools to retain an even higher proportion of the country's youth (Ravitch, 1983). As far as progressive practices in the classroom were concerned, however, the impact on most schools was not great (Cremin, 1964). According to a study of teaching in American schools from 1890 to 1980 (Cuban, 1984), most elementary teachers in the years 1920 to 1940 continued to practice teacher-centered instruction of large groups of seated children, allowing little student mobility in the classroom. Substantial minorities of teachers did, however, rearrange their classroom furniture, varying groupings of students for instruction, introducing project work, and allowing students to express themselves and move freely in the classroom.

The developments that did take place were accompanied by either criticism or opposition, or both. It was argued, particularly by essentialists, that progressivism did not pay adequate attention to the cultural and intellectual heritage of society. Critics also said that it placed too much emphasis on different goals for different students, leading to sorting, tracking, and differentiation of course work. Further, its emphasis on the teaching of specific "how-to" courses led to a neglect of traditional subjects (Adler, 1977; Hutchins, 1953). Progressivism eventually faded not just because of its critics, but because it seemed to lose its relevance and failed to adapt to changing conditions (Ravitch, 1983).

Though progressive education may have officially died in the mid-1950s, its influence is still found not only in American schools but in schools throughout the world. And the effects of that influence are still being debated.

A movement similar in some ways to the progressive movement, but more restricted, appeared in the 1960s and 1970s. It advocated informal education, open classrooms, and alternative schools. Features of this approach were learning centers, clustering of tables or desks so that students could work cooperatively, student mobility, and student-teaching planning of curricula. As with earlier reform proposals, the impact on the classroom work was not widespread. In general, instruction continued to be teacher-centered. There were some exceptions to this in elementary schools, fewer in high schools (Cuban, 1983).

Educational Administration

With the growth of the educational system and of population in cities, new approaches to the administration and management of education proliferated throughout this century. Early in the century, developments in science and in management theory invaded industry and in time were transferred to education. Frederick Taylor, who wrote a book called *The principles of scientific management* in 1911, was an influential figure in this movement. An engineer at a steel plant, Taylor sought to improve production by analyzing tasks performed by workers; his objective was to identify more efficient and cost-effective procedures for completing a task. Applied to the educational scene, scientific management led to attempts to specify the goals of education; to construct the curriculum according to measureable outcomes; to demonstrate the social or economic benefits of education; and to conduct widespread testing. It led to the grouping of students for administrative purposes, the consolidation of schools and school districts, the loss of local control, and the growth of centralized school boards (Callahan, 1962; Gumbert & Spring, 1974). It also led to changes in the role of the district superintendent from one in which his or her duties were primarily scholastic (from 1865 to 1910) to one in which they were primarily those of a business manager (from 1910 to 1930). The role of the school principal also changed from one in which clerical functions were important to one in which managerial functions dominated (Callahan, 1966). In the managerial approach, administrative issues were separated from educational ones; indeed, the latter tended to be ignored. New specialized roles, such as those of school counselor and psychologist, emerged.

The Great Depression led to an examination of the practice of education and its administration. It was hoped that education could help reconstruct a society ravaged by the depression. Under the influence of Dewey and the progressives, together with the findings of studies in social psychology that seemed to underline the importance of morale and the involvement of workers in decision making, school administration became more democratic in the 1930s and 1940s. However, the bureaucratic aspect of education was also growing, and from the 1950s onward, the characteristics of a bureaucracy became more pronounced in the education system. These characteristics included the strengthening of hierarchies, the growth of rules (including many new federal laws and regulations), and the increasing specialization of roles (Campbell & Newell, 1985).

In the 1960s, the idea of applying scientific management techniques to education received a new lease on life; techniques applied to the defense budget were extended to other areas, including education. Program budgeting was used and evaluation procedures were applied to federally funded social programs.

The application of concepts taken from industry, such as the scientific management model, to education raises several problems. First, there are difficulties in arriving at a definition of what the output or product of schools should be. Second, industrial models are based on the operation of a competitive market system, while public sector financing ensures that schools will be provided for even if costs are high. Third, as history has revealed, too great a concern with issues of management can lead to a situation in which there is little concern about what actually goes on in the classroom.

Equality and Quality in Education

Equality of opportunity and the quality of education have been persistent themes in the history of American education. During the revolutionary period, the Founding Fathers, under the influence of Englightenment thinkers, envisaged an egalitarian function for education. Concern with quality is evident throughout the nineteenth and twentieth centuries in the views of Horace Mann and the progressives. Both equality and quality are still important concerns of American education.

The question of equality of opportunity came to the fore in the 1950s and 1960s in the struggle against poverty and racial injustice. Major societal efforts to address the problems of inequality were centered in the educational sphere. It is not clear whether the choice of education as the principal domain in which to combat inequality was based on political or educational considerations. There were two factors which lent support to a policy of social and economic reform through education. First, schooling had traditionally been accepted as the vehicle through which cultural and linguistic barriers had been broken down in the past. Second, the policy suggested that change could be accomplished without a frontal assault on more politically sensitive areas such as housing and employment (Madaus, Airasian, & Kellaghan, 1980).

Attempts to ensure equality came from two major sources: legal action against segregation in schools and legislation to provide special educational facilities for children in disadvantaged areas. A landmark in legal action was the *Brown* v. *Board of Education* judgment in 1954. In this case, the Supreme Court overturned the separate-but-equal doctrine established in a case in 1896 *(Plessy* v. *Ferguson)*, ruling that racially segregated schools were "inherently unequal" and in violation of the Fourteenth Amendment.

Legislation to provide financial aid for the educationally disadvantaged was introduced in 1964 in the form of the Economic Opportunity Act. This legislation launched Head Start programs, which provided experiences for minority and poor preschoolers in order to remedy the educational deficiencies they commonly manifest when beginning school. The program was overwhelmingly popular, catering to over half a million preschoolers in 2,400 communities in its first year of operation in 1965. The Elementary and Secondary Education Act of 1965 followed, which was intended to stimulate innovation in schools and make the problems of the poor America's foremost educational priority. Since the 1960s, the federal government has continued to increase its involvement in education in pursuit of equality in schools.

In 1957, concern for quality in education arose following the launch of the Russian space satellite *Sputnik,* which put Russia ahead of the United States in the space race. Americans began to look critically at what was being taught in schools. Among other things, they found that many science curricula were out of date. They also noted the poor level of achievement and dropout rates of students from lower socioeconomic backgrounds. These observations gave rise to a number of questions. Were curricula in schools providing an adequate preparation for future scientists? And was a large amount of potential talent being lost to the nation?

In an attempt to provide a solution for perceived problems in schools, the National Defense Education Act was passed in 1958. The act set out to provide federal aid to help develop "the mental resources and technical skills" of American youth in areas considered important for national defense. Funding to improve instruction in mathematics, science, and foreign languages was made available.

Subsequent legislative measures allocated funding to education (for example, the Elementary and Secondary Education Act of 1965). Despite these reforms, debate about the quality of American education continues to the present time, fueled by information based on international comparisons of student achievement, declining test scores, and concern about America's competitive economic situation.

CONCLUSION

The history of American education in many ways is a history of remarkable achievement. Americans have shown a commitment to education that is equal to and in most cases surpasses that of any other nation in the world. It has achieved a very high participation rate at all levels—including higher education (college and graduate school), which we did not consider in this chapter.

As you proceed through this book, you will be presented with a picture of the system of education that evolved from the events described in this chapter. You will find that many of the issues that concerned our ancestors persist today—equality of opportunity, quality in education, the control of education, the nature of the curriculum, and the role of education in helping us deal with social and economic problems in society.

QUESTIONS AND ACTIVITIES

1. How old is the system of free public education in the community in which you grew up? When did it establish a high school?
2. Look at examples of past criticisms of our schools. For example, what did Rice say about the schools? What other critics from another age can you identify? Compare these earlier criticisms with those that you hear today.
3. List vestiges of the progressive movement that you experienced in your elementary and secondary schools.
4. Talk to a group of senior citizens about the style of teaching they experienced. Was it different from what you experienced?

CHAPTER 3

Social Science Foundations of Educational Policy and Practice

This chapter provides an overview of the place of the social sciences in education. The social sciences have added an important scientific dimension to the art and craft of teaching.

● The social sciences use systematic and controlled observation, experimentation, and case study techniques to study teaching, learning, and the organization of schools and classrooms.

● The physical, emotional, social, cognitive, and moral aspects of development in students are interrelated in complex ways and have to be understood and attended to by teachers.

● Much research on learning has been based on an associationist view and has concerned itself only with the overt behavior of individuals. This work has had a strong influence on many aspects of American education.

● Recent research on learning is sensitive to the complexity of human behavior and recognizes that the student's organizing processes and understanding play an important role in learning.

● Schools make much use of objective standardized tests.

● The classroom is a complex social system with informal as well as formal social structures.

● The environment outside the school, particularly the student's home, contributes substantially to the differences among students' school achievement.

There is a view that in order to teach, all that a teacher needs is a good knowledge of the subject matter. According to this view, in order to teach literature or classics, a teacher needs only to have studied these subjects to a reasonably advanced degree. Advanced knowledge of subject matter is considered less necessary at the elementary level, since much time goes to teaching the basics of reading, writing, and arithmetic. An alternative view holds that a teacher needs to have some knowledge about children and learning in addition to a command of subject matter. How else is a teacher to know how the content of material presented and the method of presentation should be varied for children who differ in age or in their rate of learning? And how is the teacher to assess the needs and interests of children and to decide how a classroom is best structured to respond to those needs and interests?

For answers to these questions, teachers must look to the social sciences, which have shown remarkable growth since the beginning of this century. In this chapter, we shall consider some of the contributions of the social sciences to educational practice. Since education has to do primarily with teaching and learning, it is not surprising that the main influence on the classroom has come from psychology. However, other disciplines, particularly sociology and economics, also have had an influence on what goes on in schools. For the most part, the influence of these subjects on classrooms has been indirect rather than direct, through their influence on general educational policy. Influence on policy can ultimately affect the resources that are made available to schools, expectations for schools in terms of their products and how those products fit into society, the adjustments required of schools in relation to their role as a social institution, and how that role relates to other institutions in society.

In later chapters, and in other courses you will take, you will have the opportunity of learning more about what the social sciences have to say that is relevant to education. This chapter will only introduce you to a selected number of topics and concepts. In it, we hope to be able to provide at least the flavor of the findings of the social sciences. Topics chosen for inclusion are ones that have received a lot of attention in American education: child development, including cognitive and moral development; learning; testing; the classroom as a social system; and home and school. The topics will be placed in a historical context. Other topics, such as individual differences and instruction, which could easily be included in this chapter on the basis of their importance in the social sciences, are treated in more detail in later chapters. Before considering the topics selected for this chapter, we will make some general comments about scientific inquiry in the social sciences and the use of its findings in classrooms.

Scientific Inquiry and Education

The eighteenth and nineteenth centuries were periods during which there were major developments in mathematics and in the physical sciences of chemistry, physics, and biology. In the light of these developments, it is not surprising that scientists moved from an investigation of the physical world to an investigation of people. Since the beginning of this century there has been an enormous increase in research about how people think, feel, and learn. There has also been a great deal of study of how people organize their society into institutions (such as schools) and the roles they play in those institutions. Much of the early work on these topics was largely theoretical or speculative and formed part of philosophy. Increasingly, however, the methods of the physical sciences have been applied to the study of human behavior. These methods have two major characteristics. First, they are *empirical;* that is, systematic and controlled observation and experimentation are the basis of any conclusions reached. Observation replaced speculation, which had been the basis of many philosophical conclusions. Second, they tend to be *positivist;* that is, they are based on the assumption that knowledge is limited to the "facts" that can be derived from empirical study.

The use of systematic and controlled observation can be seen in typical studies of teaching in which observers go into a number of classrooms to describe the behavior of teachers and students. The observers focus on actual overt behavior, rather than trying to make inferences about what students are thinking or feeling. In doing this, they use carefully prepared and detailed schedules to guide them in their observations and to record behavior. To measure student achievement, they use standardized objective tests. Having collected the data, they next examine it for relationships between teacher behaviors and student achievement. For example, do students in classes in which teaching is highly structured perform better on achievement tests than students in classes in which teaching is less structured? If such a relationship is found, can one conclude that style of teaching *causes* student achievement? Obviously not, since other factors could have been operating that affect achievement and that were not taken into account in the study. For example, it may be that teachers with a certain type of personality teach in a highly structured way and the personality characteristics of those teachers rather than their style of teaching affects student performance. Or it may be that the students receiving highly structured instruction shared some characteristic that the students receiving less structured instruction did not and that perhaps teachers adapted their teaching style to that characteristic. In this case, students' characteristics, rather than teaching style, might be the cause of achievement.

It is clear that observation and measurement, no matter how careful and accurate, will not provide unambiguous information about cause and effect. To eliminate the problem of ruling out the many possible alternative explanations of events, social scientists, like physical scientists, have turned to experimentation. Rather than observing what occurs spontaneously (as in the study of teaching just considered), the experimenter actually changes certain things and then observes the effects of these changes. For example, an experimenter might ask teachers in a number of classes to adopt a particular method for teaching reading and teachers in other classes to adopt a different method. Then, after a period of time sufficient to allow the two different methods to have an effect, the achievements of pupils in the two types of class would be measured and compared. This approach attempts to apply the experimental model of the physical sciences. However, it falls short of experimentation in the physical sciences in several basic respects. In particular, the social scientist cannot exercise the control of the physical scientist. In the example of teaching reading that we considered, it is not possible to ensure that all teachers will follow the method prescribed for them, or that other uncontrolled (and perhaps unknown) factors do not operate to affect student achievement. The complexity of human and social phenomena, as well as ethical considerations, means that experimentation cannot be carried out in the social sciences in the way that it can in the physical sciences.

Because of problems in applying the model of the physical sciences to the social sciences (as well as for other reasons), some investigators have adopted other approaches to research. These include case studies and methods taken from anthropology; in general, they are less rigid than the type of approaches we have been describing and are more sensitive to the cultural and social context in which studies are carried out. However, until recently, the vast majority of studies in the social sciences (including education) have tried to approximate the approaches of the physical sciences.

While the social sciences differ from philosophy in that they rely more on information obtained under conditions of controlled observation and experimentation, they are not free from underlying philosophical assumptions. For example, much empirical work in the social sciences is based on the assumption that the human being operates more or less on the principles of a machine—a highly sophisticated and wonderfully contrived machine, but a machine nonetheless. This view is found in the philosophical writings of Thomas Hobbes (1588–1679) and of Claude-Adrien Helvetius (1715–1771) and underlies the behaviorist movement in modern psychology, a movement that dominated American psychology for the first half of this century. It also colors many ideas in education—for example, ideas that the desirable ends of education can be stated in terms of behavioral objectives, that teaching is a matter of organizing desirable inputs (knowledge, skills, attitudes) for students, and that such teaching will shape or modify students' behavior in the direction of desired objectives—all ideas that are common in American education today. These ideas are explored in this chapter (when we consider learning and, in particular, behavior modification) and throughout the rest of this text (for example, in a discussion of representations of the school as an input-output system in studies of school effectiveness).

You will also come across less mechanistic views of human beings in this chapter and in the rest of this book. These views are in line with Friedrich Froebel's (1782–1852) organic view of human beings, in which each individual is regarded as a natural entity that is more than the sum of its parts. Further, unlike a machine, the human organism is capable of growth and development. Other philosophical positions that support this view come from Jean-Jacques Rousseau (1712–1778) and John Dewey (1859–1952). The same position is represented in Jean Piaget's (1896–1980) research on developmental psychology, some of which is described briefly later in this chapter, as well as in recent research that treats intelligence as an information-processing ability.

If you examine the relationships between variables found within educational research and also those found within the social sciences, you will find that they are typically weak. This does not mean that they may not be important. For example, while the relationship between a particular way of teaching and student achievement may appear quite weak, the achievement levels of several students might still be affected by it (Gage, 1985).

It is important that teachers realize that knowledge derived through scientific method holds only for a limited number of variables that have been observed under particular conditions. If new conditions are introduced, it is most likely that findings will change. You must assume that conditions not taken into account in research studies will operate in the particular classroom in which you find yourself; you must consider this when applying scientific knowledge.

Teaching can never be the mechanical application of rigorous laws or principles based on social science or anything else. While you may make use of rules, formulas, and algorithms, your teaching will also demand minute-to-minute choices, intuition, creativity, improvization, and expressiveness (Gage, 1978). In other words, teaching involves craftsmanship and artistry as well as the application of scientific knowledge. In this, it is similar to other occupations, such as medicine and engineering, that also require a combination of science, art, and craft.

Child Development

The belief that experience is the basis of all intelligence and education had a profound influence on the study of child development in the nineteenth century. An important figure in this context was the Swiss educator Johann Pestalozzi (1746–1827), who had been a disciple of Rousseau in Geneva and was strongly influenced by John Locke's (1632–1704) view that early learning must be based on sense experience. Pestalozzi paid close attention to child development, including that of his own son, and concluded that much of children's early learning results from direct contact with the objects in their environment—touching them, seeing them, and manipulating them. On the basis of these observations, he tried to devise graded teaching materials and methods that involved much practical activity (for example, the manipulation of materials and tasks involving hand-eye coordination) to develop the child's sensory and intellectual abilities.

It followed from Pestalozzi's work that teachers should know more than just the subject matter they taught; they should also learn to understand the development and characteristics of children—not only their intellectual characteristics, but also their physical, social, and emotional ones. Some American educators learned of Pestalozzi's work and were impressed by it. For example, at a time when American teachers depended heavily upon rote memorization and recitation, Horace Mann visited schools in Prussia in which Pestalozzi's approach was being used. When Mann came back to America, he suggested that Americans should adopt Pestalozzi's methods of teaching reading, writing, grammar, and arithmetic because he believed that the Prussian schoolmaster produced better results "in half the time" (Binder, 1974).

Pestalozzi's belief that educational practice demands greater scientific knowledge of children and how they develop was very much in tune with feelings about the importance of science in America toward the end of the nineteenth century. It was also in agreement with the ideas of the progressive movement in education that were developing at the same time; these ideas emphasized the importance of direct experience in learning and the need for educational practice to be informed by scientific knowledge.

The great pioneer of the study of child development in America was G. Stanley Hall (1844–1924), who collected an enormous amount of information about children. He believed that children go through a series of stages in development that are biologically determined, and that it is up to the school to adapt its procedures to these natural stages. It follows from this that the content of the curriculum should be determined on the basis of what is known about child development, as well as on the basis of what people think that students should know. Further, sensitivity to the developmental needs of children implies permissiveness and self-direction in child rearing and education. Hall's conclusions were interpreted as providing scientific evidence for what Rousseau had said, as well as for the contemporary position of John Dewey and the progressives.

Further support for the progressive position came from Arnold Gesell's (1880–1961) studies of infant and child development. His theory of maturation, like those of Rousseau and Hall, emphasized the internal control of development. Gesell's work suggested that there is a more or less consistent pattern in the development of all children during the first five years of life in sitting, standing, walking, grasping and handling objects, and talking. While environmental factors can support or modify such development, they cannot determine its nature or affect its rate. Such views were popularized in the Benjamin Spock's (1903–) writings about child rearing and became known to vast numbers of people throughout the world who used Spock's book as a guide to rearing children.

Since this early work on child development, psychologists have concerned themselves with all aspects of such development—physical, cognitive, emotional, affective, moral, and social. All these areas are relevant to education. For example, physical development, although almost entirely controlled by genetic factors, has psychological implications for the child. For example, a child who is abnormally small or abnormally large in comparison with his or her classmates may feel self-conscious about this, and the child's self-concept and relations with other students could be affected. Many students become acutely aware of their physical development during the adolescent period, when a sudden spurt in growth usually occurs. They may feel awkward, strange, and self-conscious, again leading to personal problems, and this may have repercussions on their work in school. This example of the interrelationship between physical and other aspects of development should serve as a reminder that while we might study different aspects of development in isolation from each other, in practice the child is a complex organism in which the various aspects interact.

Cognitive Development

Researchers have paid more attention to cognitive and intellectual development than to other aspects of development. The most influential description of cognitive development comes from Swiss psychologist Jean Piaget (Flavell, 1973). Piaget himself showed little interest in the educational implications of his work, but it has nonetheless been used as a basis for curriculum development, especially for young children. It has also been used in support of the importance of activity and the use of concrete materials in early childhood learning.

PIAGET'S STAGES OF DEVELOPMENT Piaget, like Hall and Gesell, describes development in terms of stages through which children pass in the course of their cognitive development. Each of his stages may be related to the approximate age of the child, although it is recognized that some children progress through the stages more rapidly than others. Piaget's five stages are as follows:

1. The sensorimotor stage (0–2 years) covers the first two years of life. Little thought occurs in the infant during this period. Most activity, as the title of the stage indicates, is sensory and motor (looking at objects, feeling objects, crawling). However, during the period, children are beginning to be able to represent in their minds objects and events that are not perceptually present. This marks the beginning of symbolic representation for children, a very important development.

2. The preconceptual stage (2–4 years) is a stage during which children relearn on a conceptual or representational level the lessons learned at the sensorimotor level. Language, which is a symbolic system of representing the world, develops rapidly during this period to replace the nonlinguistic thinking that is a feature of the sensorimotor period. While, according to Piaget, representation or thought occurs before language, and indeed language cannot develop in its absence, once children acquire language, they are freed from the domination of their immediate perceptions and their thoughts can range through time and space.

3. The intuitive stage (4–7 years) is a period during which children, through manipulation of the environment and interaction with people, correct intuitive impressions of reality. Children begin to think in terms of classes, numbers, and relationships, although their thoughts are still largely dominated by their perceptions.

4. The concrete operations stage (7–11 years) is a period during which

Jean Piaget (1896–1980) (at left, wearing beret) arrived at his theory of cognitive development by observing children's behavior.

children build a basic stock of concepts into an organized and coherent system that, according to Piaget, permits real reasoning. During this period, children develop the ability to manipulate these concepts and so their thinking is freed (though not entirely) from the dominance of their perceptions. The development of children to the stage where their reasoning is not overinfluenced by the appearance of things is illustrated in one of Piaget's best-known experiments, which involves showing children two glasses that differ in size and shape; one is tall and thin, the other short and squat. Water is poured from one into the other and the child is asked if there is more water in one than in the other. During the intuitive stage, children tend to say there is more water in the tall, thin glass. Their perception of quantity is influenced by the appearance of the amount of water. When the child reaches the concrete operations stage, he or she will recognize that while there may *appear* to be more water in the taller glass, the actual quantity remains the same.

5. *The formal operations stage* (11–15 years) is a period during which children's central cognitive processes become more autonomous, that is, less and less dependent on what they perceive. At this point they have at their cognitive disposal a full range of options, not simply those presented in the immediate environment. At this stage, children are able to deal with abstractions, form hypotheses, and solve problems systematically by going through all the possibilities (Piaget & Inhelder, 1969).

Piaget's description of development has been used to support a number of practices in education. It reinforces the idea that learning should be active rather than passive, since the child's role as an exploring, information-processing organism is crucial for development in Piaget's terms. This description also is used to support the position that learning should be matched to the child's interests and curiosity, since these factors can provide an indication of the child's level of development and the kinds of activities that will help that development to progress. The need to provide children with the opportunity to use concrete materials also finds support in Piaget's description of development, since continual interaction with the environment is necessary in order to reach the stage of formal operations, when such interaction becomes much less important. For when all is said and done, thinking for Piaget is a kind of doing, with foundations rooted in actions that have been internalized.

Barbara Inhelder, who collaborated closely with Piaget for many years, has suggested that the first two years of schooling might be devoted to "exercises in manipulating, classifying, and ordering objects in ways that highlight basic operations of logical addition, multiplication, inclusion, serial ordering, and the like" (see Bruner, 1965, p. 46), since these logical operations are the basis of the operations and concepts of mathematics and science.

MORAL THINKING AND REASONING Another important aspect of child development is moral thinking and reasoning. Laurence Kohlberg (1969), who was influenced by the work of Dewey and Piaget, describes development in terms of three levels, with two stages at each level:

- *Level I—Preconventional Morality*
Stage 1: Obedience and punishment orientation, during which the child is guided by considerations of punishment and obedience (to avoid punishment) in making moral judgments.
Stage 2: Naive instrumental hedonism orientation, during which the child is concerned with the selfish satisfaction of his or her own needs and conforms in behavior so as to obtain rewards.
- *Level II—Conventional Morality*
Stage 3: Conformity orientation, during which the child's judgments are influenced by his or her expectation of approval by others ("good boy"/ "good girl").
Stage 4: Authority orientation, during which the child relies on authority, rules, and the idea of "doing one's duty" in making a moral judgment.
- *Level III—Postconventional Morality*
Stage 5: Social contract orientation, during which the individual conforms in his or her judgments to standards or norms of rights and obligations that are generally accepted in the culture in which the individual lives.
Stage 6: Ethical principle orientation, during which an individual's judgments are guided by self-chosen ethical principles.

Kohlberg's stages do not cover the same age range as do Piaget's; nor are they so closely tied to chronological age. However, Piaget's and Kohlberg's stages are related, since, according to Kohlberg, advanced moral reasoning depends upon advanced logical reasoning. In other words, a person's stage of logical development puts a ceiling on the stage of moral reasoning that he or she can attain. Generally, children at the stage of concrete operations function mostly at the level of preconventional morality (stages 1 and 2). A person whose logical stage is only partially formal operational is limited to the level of conventional morality (stages 3 and 4). Children are capable of functioning at the level of postconventional morality at about 16 years of age, but many individuals never reach this stage. For example, while over 50 percent of late adolescents and adults are capable of full formal reasoning, only 10 percent display moral reasoning at the level of stages 5 and 6 (Kohlberg, 1975).

Kohlberg's work has been applied in the classroom in efforts to foster the moral development of students (Fenton, 1967). One approach that has been adopted is to have students discuss moral reasoning problems, or "moral dilemmas," that demand increasingly sophisticated types of moral reasoning. It is believed that when presented with problems requiring a level of development that is one stage higher than their present level, students exhibit a higher degree of moral reasoning.

One dilemma posed by Kohlberg raises the issue of stealing a drug to save a dying woman. The inventor of the drug is selling it for 10 times what it costs him to make it. The woman's husband cannot raise the money, and the seller refuses to lower the price or wait for payment. What should the husband do (Kohlberg, 1975, p. 671)?

Kohlberg's work has given rise to much debate among philosophers, psychologists, and educational practitioners. Among the questions debated are the following: Are the stages described by Kohlberg universal and independent of the contents of the judgments? Are the stages useful (1) in diagnosing a student's developmental level and (2) as a basis for devising instructional strategies? Through discussion of moral dilemmas, can you teach students how to make moral judgments and the values on which those judgments are made? Or does the development of the ability to make such judgments and the formation of values take place only if the student has other experiences, such as contact with adults who visibly and consistently exemplify those values in their behavior? Does it follow that if a child is capable of making a moral judgment at a level described by Kohlberg, that child will always behave in accordance with that judgment in a real-life situation? (The answer to the last question is no: an individual's behavior is influenced by factors other than the ability to make a moral judgment, such as self-interest, the perceived consequences of one's action, and one's feelings for other people.)

IMPLICATIONS OF STAGE THEORIES Both Piaget's and Kohlberg's descriptions of cognitive development are based on the idea that children go through a series of stages in their cognitive development. This idea has a number of implications. First, there are *qualitative differences* in children's modes of thinking or of solving the same problem at different ages. Second, these different modes of thought form an *invariant sequence* in individual development. Development may be speeded up or slowed down by environmental factors, but these factors cannot change the sequence in which stages appear. Third, each stage involves a *distinctive underlying thought organization*, which is applied in a diversity of situations. Fourth, cognitive stages are *hierarchical integrations;* that is, each stage builds on preceding stages and represents more complex thinking processes than earlier stages. Before reaching a particular stage, a child has to pass through the preceding ones. Finally, the modes of thought represented by stages follow the same *sequence* in all individuals (Kohlberg, 1969).

Learning

Since the child is the person at the center of the educational process, learning is the activity that is central to that process; most people would say that children go to school to learn. It is not surprising, then, that some of the earliest research in educational psychology relates to school learning.

Given the success of observational and experimental methods in the study of the natural sciences and the prospects of similar success in the study of psychology, it seemed reasonable to some educationists towards the end of the nineteenth century to attempt to apply the same methods to teaching and learning. One of the most influential of the early "experimentalists" in education was Joseph Mayer Rice (1857–1934), often regarded as the founder of educational research. Rice, like Horace Mann (1796–1859), contrasted teaching in Germany with that in America and concluded that teaching in American schools was mechanical, noncreative, and nonreflective. He singled out spelling drills for special attention and decided to investigate whether they were really beneficial. Between 1895 and 1897, he arranged for a large number of schools to administer objective tests of spelling to about 16,000 students. He also found out the number of minutes in the week devoted to the teaching of spelling. As Rice had expected, the students' scores on the test bore no relationship to the amount of time they had spent learning spelling in school. Rice concluded that the number of spelling drills could be reduced in schools without any loss in student achievement and that the time made available by this economy could be used for more intellectual activities.

Associationism and Structuralism

Much of the early research in learning was influenced by the tradition of associationism. According to the associationist approach, ideas form the elements of mental life and follow one another in a constant chain. It was believed that ideas are related to each other because they have occurred together in the past or because of their similarity or dissimilarity (Deese, 1958).

The work of Edward Lee Thorndike (1874–1949), a major figure in early twentieth-century educational psychology, typifies the associationist approach to learning. Thorndike planned a series of investigations in which he examined the transfer value of high school subjects (that is, that training in some tasks improves a student's ability to deal with other tasks). He gave an intelligence test to thousands of students before and after they had studied for a year. He then divided the students in his analysis according to the subjects that the students had studied during the course of the year. He was interested in determining whether students who had studied what were regarded as the more rigorous academic subjects—Latin, mathematics, and science—would show a larger gain on the intelligence test than students who had studied commercial and manual courses. The results of the study showed that the students who had followed the more demanding courses showed a slightly greater improvement on the intelligence test, but it was less than people who were convinced of the educational value of such study would have expected. Thorndike's study is open to many criticisms when judged by today's standards of research in education. However, at the time it was interpreted widely as casting serious doubt on the classical educational position regarding the value of formal discipline and the study of certain subjects. The evidence did not appear convincing that some studies are better for the mind than others and that they have a high "transfer" value.

These studies of learning provided support for some aspects of progressive views about education that were gaining ground in American education around the turn of the century. Not all research, however, could be interpreted as supporting such views. For example, on the basis of experimental studies (mostly with animals), Thorndike concluded that most learning can be explained by the direct "binding" of acts to situations. He believed that there was no need to suppose that ideas in the student's mind intervened between the acts and the situations. This may sound strange to the layperson, but in Thorndike's time psychologists were desperately attempting to establish the scientific respectability of their subject, and some thought that this could best be done by focusing on observable behavioral events and ignoring what happens in people's heads.

Thorndike's conclusions about learning had a profound effect on the teaching of arithmetic in schools. He advocated thorough practice and systematic drill of component skills before introducing more complex problems. However, he also recommended that practice and examples should deal as far as possible with relevant real-life situations so that the "bonds" or associations that were formed would not be insignificant or foolish.

Alternative approaches to the associationist approach in the study of learning, such as Gestalt and cognitive-field theories, assert that associationist learning theories oversimplify behavior. They point to the complexity of human thinking and to the importance of organizing processes and understanding in the human mind. Thus, for example, even in a relatively simple task such as learning a series of digits (for example, *58321654*), people will learn more efficiently if they group, or otherwise organize, the material to be learned (for example, *583 21 654* or *58 32 16 54*) (Katona, 1940).

Max Wertheimer (1880–1943) applied principles of field theory to classroom learning. Like Thorndike, he was interested in the transfer-of-training problem. However, he rejected the associationist view that transfer is best taught through emphasizing and drilling common elements. In experiments with teaching children the concept of the area of a rectangle, he divided a rectangle into 1-inch squares and showed the children that the area is equal to the number of squares in a row by the number of rows, that is, the multiplication of the base by the altitude. Once students had mastered this basic structural principle, he showed them an oblique parallelogram and asked them how to find the area, suggesting it be compared to a rectangle. Many students responded (as an associationist might expect) by saying, "I haven't learned that yet." Others, however, saw the middle portion of the parallelogram as a rectangle. They then were able to see that if the two ends were removed by a vertical cut, they formed a second rectangle. Once students had perceived this structural solution, they were able to apply the technique they had learned. From this kind of work, Wertheimer and others suggested that learning should involve structural understanding. Students should be taught to see into problems, to get a "whole view" of them rather than to follow rules or formulas blindly (Woodworth, 1963).

Jerome Bruner has also used the concept of structural understanding to develop what he calls *a theory of instruction.* The theory tries to outline (1) what is necessary in order to organize material that has to be learned and (2) the procedures to be followed in the learning process (Bruner, 1964, 1966).

Bruner's theory of instruction consists of four major elements:

1. *A theory of instruction should specify the experiences which most effectively implant in the individual a predisposition toward learning—learning in general or a particular type of learning. For example, what sorts of relationships toward people and things in the preschool environment will tend to make the child willing and able to learn when he enters school?*

2. *Second, a theory of instruction must specify the ways in which a body of knowledge should be structured so that it can be most readily grasped by the learner. Optimal structure refers to the set of propositions from which a larger body of knowledge can be generated, and it is characteristic that the formulation of such structure depends upon the state of advance in a particular field of knowledge. . . . Since the goodness of a structure depends upon its power for simplifying information, for generating new propositions, and for increasing the manipulability of a body of knowledge, structure must always be related to the status and gifts of the learner. Viewed in this way, the optimal structure of a body of knowledge is not absolute but relative. The major requirement is that no two sets of generating structures for the same field of knowledge be in contradiction.*

3. *Third, the theory of instruction should specify the most effective sequences in which to present the materials to be learned. Given, for example, that one wishes to teach the structure of modern physical theory, how does one proceed? Does one present concrete materials first in such a way as to elicit questions about recurrent regularities? Or, does one begin with a formalized mathematical notation that makes it simpler to represent regularities later encountered? What results are in fact produced by the use of each? . . .*

4. *Finally, a theory of instruction should specify the* nature and

pacing of rewards and punishments in the process of learning and teaching. Intuitively, it seems quite clear that as learning progresses there is a point at which it is better to shift away from extrinsic rewards, such as teacher's praise, toward the intrinsic rewards inherent in solving a complex problem for one's self. So, too, there is a point at which immediate reward for performance should be replaced by deferred reward. The shift rates from extrinsic to intrinsic and from immediate to deferred reward are poorly understood and obviously important. Is it the case, for example, that wherever learning involves the integration of a long sequence of acts, the earliest shift should be made from immediate to deferred reward and from extrinsic to intrinsic reward? (Brunner, 1964, pp. 307–308).

Bruner's work had a major impact on the curriculum reform in mathematics and science in the 1960s and early 1970s.

Experimental Studies of Learning

The tradition of studying school learning did not continue as a major feature of psychology following Thorndike's work. Although psychologists did not lose interest in the topic, they devoted most of their energies during the first half of this century to the study of learning in animals. This they did partly because of their preoccupation with the use of experimental procedures, which can obviously be used more readily with animals than with humans. But they also did it because they thought that their experimentation with animals would lead to the discovery of universal laws of learning that could be applied to all learning situations in all species.

Because of the nature of the experimental research on learning that dominated psychology for many years, the practical implications of the work for teaching and learning in the classroom were limited. E. R. Hilgard provided a number of statements derived from learning research that he felt had practical implications. These are listed in Box 3.2. All of them, you will note, are very general.

Behavior Modification

The limitations of experimental studies on learning (many of which have dealt with relatively simple learning tasks for animals) has meant that their application to the complex learning tasks of the classroom has been limited. However, the general view of learning that has emerged from such studies has had a considerable influence on how teachers go about their work. That influence is best illustrated, and is most specific, in the case of what has been called the behavior modification approach to teaching. American psychologist B. F. Skinner is particularly associated with this approach.

Teaching always involves moving students beyond behavior that is already in their repertoire. If, as a teacher, you follow Skinner's approach, you will have to establish goals that you wish to reach with students and then carry

BOX 3.2 General Principles of Learning

1. In deciding who should learn what, the age and ability of the individual are very important.
2. A motivated learner acquires what is to be learned more readily than one who is not motivated.
3. There is an optimum level of motivation. If it is too intense (especially pain, fear, anxiety), it may interfere with learning.
4. Reward is usually preferable to punishment in learning. Learning motivated by success is preferable to learning motivated by failure.
5. Learning under intrinsic motivation is preferable to learning under extrinsic motivation. Solving a problem can be a reward in itself.
6. Experience of success is important if the student is to go on learning; continual failure will make the student give up.
7. Individuals need practice in setting realistic goals for themselves. Goals should not be so easy that no effort is required or so difficult that the student is likely to fail.
8. An individual's personal experience (for example, in relation to authority) may hamper or enhance learning from a particular teacher.
9. Active participation by a learner is preferable to passive reception when learning (e.g., from a lecture or movie).
10. It is easier to learn materials and tasks if these are understood by the learner (i.e., are meaningful) than ones that are not understood by the learner.
11. Repetitive practice is required for learning certain skills (e.g., piano playing) and in the memorization of unrelated facts.
12. Knowledge of one's performance on a task (including the mistakes one made) aids learning.
13. The discovery of relationships and principles among tasks assists learning.
14. The spacing of the recall of material helps learning.

Source: Adapted from Hilgard, 1958, pp. 486–487.

out specific behavioral procedures designed to reach those goals. Having selected a final goal, you will have to decide on a sequence of subtasks that will move students toward that goal. This is done by applying the basic principles of reinforcement concerning reward and punishment.

Skinner provides guidance on the procedures. To induce students to exhibit one kind of behavior rather than another in a certain situation (for example, having students seat themselves for some classwork), you must manipulate stimulus conditions so that the behavior (for example, sitting down) occurs and then is *reinforced.* You will reinforce the behavior and thus make it more likely to occur again if you follow it by consequences that are rewarding (for example, by praising the students). People are also likely to repeat behavior that brings freedom from undesirable or painful situations. By the same token, people are likely to avoid behaving in a way that engenders behavior which has painful consequences or in a way that does not lead to any kind of reward.

Few teachers would accept Skinner's view, which he shared with Thorndike, that only what is observable and measurable is important in education. What about a student's thought processes, motivation, expectations, aspirations, feelings, application, and interest? Skinner does not attach importance to any of these concepts and proceeds solely on the basis of observable behavior and stimuli in the environment that can be manipulated. Most teachers, however, are so accustomed to terms that describe inner states and unobservable aspects of behavior that they are unlikely to be able to put all these things out of their own (unobservable) minds.

This does not mean that Skinner's views do not influence teachers' classroom behavior. Many teachers adopt a system of rewards for students that is compatible with a Skinnerian view of shaping behavior. Others adopt a Skinnerian approach to deal with limited aspects of classroom behavior, such as classroom management (O'Leary & O'Leary, 1977). Classroom management is going to be a concern to you as a teacher, especially in your early days in teaching. You may have to cope with disruptive behavior by one or two students who refuse to remain in their seats, who continue to talk without permission, who may be generally aggressive toward other students, and so on. The temptation in these situations is to limit your reactions to actions or statements of disapproval when students misbehave—to scold or reprimand them when they stand up or to restrain them from annoying other students. If you follow Skinner's principles, however, you will be much more likely to *ignore* unwanted behavior and to concentrate on rewarding students when they behave in the way you want. This is because scolding and reprimands are *reinforcers* if they are the only attention a student gets from a teacher. It is far better to approve appropriate behavior when it occurs and to ignore behavior that is inappropriate. However, as with everything else in teaching, you will have to constantly make judgments about the extent to which you follow or ignore general principles. There will be behavior on the part of some students that would be absolutely inappropriate for you to ignore or not reprimand.

Contemporary Studies of Learning

We noted that much research on learning has centered on animals or has dealt with relatively simple human processes, and that some psychologists have pointed out that these approaches do not pay sufficient attention to the complexity of tasks involved in learning in schools. However, some recent work has paid more attention to the learning of complex tasks such as those encountered in the classroom. For example, R. M. Gagné has drawn on the past research on learning to describe different types of learning, ranging from very simple unconscious reflex responses (conditioning) to complex situations in which an individual can combine principles already learned to produce new ones that can be applied to the solution of problems. Gagné has stressed the need to analyze learning tasks systematically in a hierarchical arrangement of components and sequences of operation within a task, so that the type of learning required can be identified and the best methods to teach the task specified (see Figure 3.1).

Gagné's approach to learning was influenced greatly by *training* in the military developed during World War II. In the 1970s he saw the applicability of training techniques to programmed instruction and computer-assisted instruction, which held out great promise at that time. This technological development, however, depended on breaking down learning tasks into discrete units such as those shown in Figure 3.1. Programmed learning and computer-assisted instruction never caught on in the schools, partly because the technol-

FIGURE 3.1 An Example of Breaking an Overall Objective into Component Behaviors

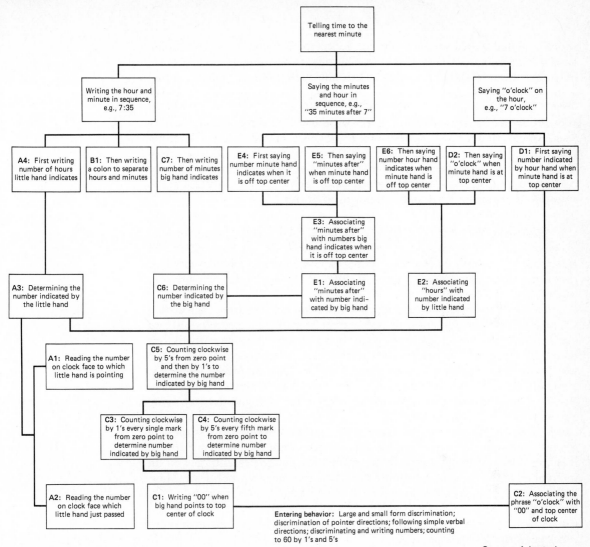

Entering behavior: Large and small form discrimination; discrimination of pointer directions; following simple verbal directions; discriminating and writing numbers; counting to 60 by 1's and 5's

Source: Adapted from Glaser & Reynolds, 1964, p. 64.

ogy was not powerful enough, but more important because teachers did not see it as helpful in dealing with classroom instruction and management (Cuban, 1986). Further, this training approach to learning is not equally applicable to all areas of the curriculum. It is most useful in dealing with educational objectives that involve skills. Skills (such as reading, telling time, and driving) that become refined, routinized, and predictable eventually may be performed subconsciously (MacDonald-Ross, 1973). However, there are many educational experiences that have nothing to do *directly* with skills—learning for the sake of learning is an example. In these situations, task analysis techniques are not particularly helpful.

Gagné's views of how students learn have influenced teaching in schools. He believed that the only really effective way to teach is to individualize instruction, which means that learning tasks must be tailored to the ways in which each individual student performs in school. His views had great influence on B. S. Bloom's thinking about modern learning, which we will discuss in later chapters. Gagné's approach to teaching skill subjects, such as reading and arithmetic, requires that the teacher should take account of two things. First, the teacher must consider the different skills of students, which may be affected by the backgrounds and cultures from which those students come. Second, the teacher must take account of the characteristics of the learning task with which the students must cope. Thus, the teacher must perform a high level of analysis of both the students' skills and the learning tasks to be performed. Much of Gagné's early work was directed toward developing the materials that teachers will need in performing this task.

RECENT TRENDS IN THE STUDY OF LEARNING The outcome of current efforts to explore effective teaching methods is presented in the *Handbook of research on teaching* (Wittrock, 1986), which has chapters that deal with teaching learning strategies to different types of students in different subjects and at different levels.

One major development has been the growing research on learning strategies. This development is an outgrowth of a shift from associationist and behavioristic theories of learning to theories that are more cognitively oriented. The way the teacher presents information is important, and so is the way the learner processes and structures that information. Much research is currently directed toward finding out more about these matters (Weinstein & Mayer, 1986).The cognitive approach to learning has changed the way many contemporary psychologists view the teaching-learning process. Rather than considering learning to be the passive recording of stimuli, this approach regards learning as an active process that occurs within the learner. Further, learning does not depend mainly on what the teacher presents but on an interaction between what is presented and how the learner processes it. Thus, both teaching strategies and learning strategies influence learning outcomes (Weinstein & Mayer, 1986). Weinstein and Mayer describe eight major categories of learning strategies that students employ, each influencing one or more types of learning outcomes:

1. *Rehearsal strategies for basic learning tasks—such as repeating the names of items in an ordered list. Common school tasks in this category include remembering the order of the planets from the sun and the order in which Shakespeare introduces the characters in the play* Hamlet.
2. *Rehearsal strategies for complex learning tasks—such as copying, underlining or shadowing the material presented in class. Common school tasks in this category include underlining the main events in a story, or copying portions of a lesson about the causes of World War I.*
3. *Elaboration strategies for basic learning tasks—such as forming a mental image or sentence relating the items in each pair for a paired-associate list of words. Common school tasks in this category include forming a phrase or sentence relating the name of a*

state or its major agricultural product, or forming a mental image of a scene described by a poem.

4. *Elaboration strategies for complex tasks—such as paraphrasing, summarizing, or describing how new information relates to existing knowledge. Common school tasks in this category include creating an analogy between the operation of a post office and the operation of a computer, or relating the information presented about the structure of complex molecules to the information presented about the structure of simple molecules.*

5. *Organizational strategies for basic learning tasks—such as grouping or ordering to-be-learned items from a list or a section of prose. Common school tasks in this category include organizing foreign vocabulary words into the categories for parts of speech, or creating a chronological listing of the events that led up to the Declaration of Independence.*

6. *Organizational strategies for complex tasks—such as outlining a passage or creating a hierarchy. Common school tasks in this category include outlining assigned chapters in the textbook, or creating a diagram to show the relationship among the stress forces in a structural design.*

7. *Comprehension monitoring strategies—such as checking for comprehension failures. Common school tasks in this category include using self-questioning to check understanding of the material presented in class and using the questions at the beginning of a section to guide one's reading behavior while studying a textbook.*

8. *Affective strategies—such as being alert and relaxed, to help overcome test anxiety. Common school tasks in this category include reducing external distractions by studying in a quiet place, or using thought stopping to prevent thoughts of doing poorly from directing attention away from the test and toward fears of failure (Weinstein & Mayer, 1986, pp. 316–317).*

One of your jobs as a teacher will be to help students develop these strategies. Each can be taught to learners who are at the appropriate level of maturity and readiness. As a teacher, you should try to stay abreast of research on learning and teaching; it provides new and valuable suggestions that should be helpful to you in teaching.

Testing

One of the major contributions of psychology to education has been the development of objective tests to measure a wide range of student characteristics. If teachers are to facilitate learning by attempting to match learning tasks to the knowledge and skills of students, they need some way of identifying that knowledge and those skills. Furthermore, teachers want to know if and when students have learned what is required of them. Both these tasks require some form of testing or assessment of the student's knowledge and skills.

Alfred Binet (1857–1911) was a pioneer in the testing movement (DuBois, 1970). French authorities asked him to develop an examination or test that could be used to identify students with learning difficulties and who were in need of special education. By 1905, Binet and his colleagues had put together a series of tests that could be administered to a child in about an hour and would, according to Binet, provide an index of the child's overall intelligence.

Binet's tests had to be administered on an individual basis; that is, only one person could be tested at a time. During World War I, "group tests" were developed by the United States Army to screen recruits for officer candidate schools and other jobs. These could be administered to a large number of inductees simultaneously and scored objectively by clerks. These were obviously important practical

French psychologist Alfred Binet developed one the first series of tests to measure intelligence.

considerations, given the large number of soldiers the army tested. The army tests involved the first large-scale use of multiple-choice items.

There was a boom in test development after World War I. Many tests were designed to measure a variety of traits, ranging from intelligence to special aptitudes (such as mechanical or spatial ability) to nonintellectual traits covering a variety of personality characteristics. While a variety of achievement tests in school subjects (such as spelling, arithmetic, handwriting, and language) had already been developed around the turn of the century, the success of the multiple-choice format developed during the war led to the adaptation of the older tests to that format. Thus, the variety of objective standardized tests of school achievement expanded greatly during the 1920s and 1930s.

Standardized objective tests were welcomed in schools because they were seen as having many advantages. They were considered to be particularly efficient for measuring knowledge of facts, they provided an extensive sampling of course content, scoring was easy and reliable, and the tests provided information that made it possible for teachers and administrators to compare a child's performance with that of groups outside the school (Anastasi, 1961; Cronbach, 1964).

Educators continue to make a great deal of use of standardized tests in schools. The available evidence indicates that teachers tend to like the tests and use them for a variety of purposes: to measure the educational growth of students, to help plan instruction for class groups and for individuals, to report to parents, to compare students with national peer groups, and to screen special-education students (Beck & Stetz, 1979). However, the use of tests has

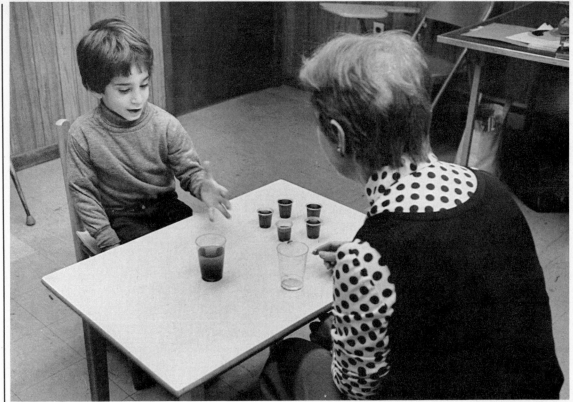

This child is being given a test to determine his stage of cognitive development.

not been without controversy (a topic discussed later in this text). Further, standardized tests are now being used by policy-makers to make important decisions about students, teachers, and schools.

The Classroom as a Social System

Most studies on learning conceptualize the learner as a lone individual working on his or her own to acquire new knowledge or skills. And, indeed, some classroom activity makes this possible. But there is another, more pervasive aspect to life in the classroom. Although learning might often depend on an individual's own efforts, the student is in the presence of other people. And once people are together, we have a social organization in which individuals interact among themselves. In this section, we will consider some aspects of research on the classroom as a social organization.

Life in the Classroom

Learning to live in a classroom involves, among other things, learning to live in a crowd. . . . Most of the things that are done in schools are done with others, or at least in the presence of others, and this fact has profound implications for determining the quality of a student's life (Jackson, 1968, p. 10).

Roles

A central concept in examining social organizations is that of *role* (Brown, 1965; Getzels & Thelen, 1960). All social systems have roles that consist of norms or rules about how members in a particular social category (for example, teacher, student) should behave. A role has certain privileges, obligations, responsibilities, and powers attached to it. A person is performing his or her role when he or she puts those obligations and responsibilities into practice.

A characteristic of roles is that they are complementary; that is, roles derive their meaning from other related roles. Thus the role of a teacher in a school can be defined only in relation to the role of a student, and vice versa.

The nature of the authority relationship between teachers and students has changed over time. At one time, it was accepted that teachers could use physical force to control students. Over time, however, the roles of teachers and of students have been gradually redefined as new conceptions of the proper treatment of children have developed (Lottie, 1975). Although society may allocate power and authority to teachers in the classroom, it no longer follows that students simply accept this situation or that the teacher's position is not vulnerable. Indeed, students very quickly devise their own means of coping with the classroom power structure, and this may give rise to problems of discipline for the teacher. For example, students may respond to unwanted teacher demands by interrupting classroom proceedings in more or less violent ways. Alternatively, they may simply withdraw psychologically from classroom proceedings.

Not all teachers or students implement their roles in the same way. Some of the differences that occur are due to the personalities of the role holders; each individual will stamp a role with the unique style of his or her own characteristic expressive behavior. Apart from this, there may be nonindividual factors arising from the ethos and value system of the school or of the teacher that lead to differences in the allocation of privilege, obligation, responsibility, and power to teachers and students. Whatever their reasons, some teachers may be autocratic in the way they control their classes, giving orders and using threats. Others may be more democratic, relying on the acceptance and approval of students. Again, teachers may differ in the amount of activity and expression they allow their students. How teachers express their roles affects "classroom climate."

Apart from the formal roles teachers and students play, every classroom also has its informal social structures in which teacher and students participate. Three major types of student status have been described: societal status (based on gender, social class, race, and ethnic group), achievement status (based on grades, recitation, and the ability group to which the student belongs), and sociometric status (based on the bonds of liking and attraction among students) (Cohen, 1972). A student's status in the classroom is determined by these characteristics. A student who comes from a upper-class background and receives high grades may be treated very differently, by both teachers and other students, from another student who comes from what is perceived to be a lower-class background and receives low grades.

Students may not accept the same basis for assigning status among themselves as teachers do. For example, students may confer greater status on the student who is good at athletics, the student who is popular, or even the student who is good at upsetting the teacher, while status in the teacher's eyes may depend more on good grades (Coleman, 1961).

Cooperative Learning

Much of the early research on learning did not take account of the social setting in the classroom. In recent years, however, research on cooperative learning methods has explored this topic (Johnson, Johnson, Holubec, & Roy, 1984; Slavin, 1983). Those involved in cooperative-learning studies have pointed out that American education is dominated by learning that is *competitive* (students working against each other to achieve a goal that only some students can attain) and *individualistic* (students working by themselves to accomplish learning goals that are unrelated to those of other students). As an alternative to this situation, they suggest cooperative learning, in which students work together to achieve common goals.

In a cooperative learning task, a group of students works together to solve a problem or to achieve some other goal. Each student has a part to play, so that the common goal can be reached only if all individuals in the group reach their individual goals. The teacher must take a number of decisions in setting up groups, concerning the size of the group (usually two to six students), which students are to be assigned to which group, arranging the room, choosing instructional materials that will promote interdependence, and assigning roles within a group (who will do what?) (Johnson, Johnson, Holubec, & Roy, 1984).

Cooperative learning has a number of advantages. It acknowledges the social nature of the classroom and encourages face-to-face interaction between students. It promotes interdependence among students, since they have to be concerned about the performance of all members of their group. Cooperative learning also provides the opportunity of developing the social skills, such as leadership, communication, and managing conflict, which are needed for collaborative work. It is hoped that these skills will be useful outside the school in work and family situations.

Those who advocate cooperative learning do not see it as being the only method to be used in the classroom. Effective teachers will choose different methods depending on the nature of learning tasks and other circumstances.

Home and School

One reason for the development of universal schooling was the need for an institution to perform some of the educational functions that, up to the time of the Industrial Revolution, had been carried out by other agencies. Leaders in the progressive movement around the turn of the century argued that there was a need for the school to extend its concern and activity to areas that had traditionally been the preserve of the community and the churches, since these agencies were no longer filling their traditional roles.

The evidence from psychology and sociology, however, has consistently (from the time Binet constructed his tests) indicated that the environment outside the school, and particularly the student's home, contributes substantially to the differences found among students in their performance on tests of mental ability, in their school achievements, and in their eventual economic accomplishments in adult life.

Children from middle socioeconomic backgrounds are, in general, better prepared for school than are children from lower socioeconomic backgrounds. The former are more likely to have acquired the kinds of skills and knowledge on which the school builds; they are also likely to be more interested in schoolwork and to have higher educational aspirations and expectations. For these reasons, the middle-class child settles into the school environment more readily, and this is reflected in school progress. The child from a lower socioeconomic background, on the other hand, is likely to find the school environment strange and schoolwork difficult. If this results in failure at an early stage, it may have serious implications for the student's entire school career, since the cognitive and affective foundations on which to build learning are not properly established.

In attempting to understand the relationship between home background and scholastic achievement, educators have considered the home from a number of different points of view. One set of studies took socioeconomic status (often based on a measure of parental occupation and/or educational level) as a variable that subsumes a variety of values, attitudes, and motives related to school performance. Families from different socioeconomic backgrounds tend to differ in a variety of ways—in their child-rearing practices, in their attitudes toward their children's education (particularly the value they place on it), and in the way they spend their leisure time.

However, you should not assume that all families within any social class are similar in their lifestyles. Obviously, there are considerable differences within social-class groups, and some researchers have argued that it is important, irrespective of social class, to try to identify the actual processes in the home that affect intellectual development.

Early work in this area was carried out at the University of Chicago in the 1960s. Researchers there identified a range of influences in the family that were found to be closely related to students' ability and school achievements. These included the goals and aspirations parents held for themselves and their children, the quality of the parents' language (richness and variety of vocabulary, fluency in expression), the provision of learning opportunities in the home, the number and use made of books, and, in general, the degree of structure and routine in the management of the home (Bloom, 1964, 1981, 1984).

Given the differences among children from different backgrounds, it is not surprising to find differences in the ways teachers react to children from different backgrounds. Indeed, many teachers try to adapt their teaching strategies to the different levels of children's needs, perhaps paying greater attention to children who seem poorly prepared for school than to ones who seem more comfortable in the school setting. There is evidence that teachers take social status into account in their evaluations of students and in planning classroom strategies for teaching them. However, this is sometimes done in a negative rather than in a positive way. For example, a number of studies indicate that children from higher-status backgrounds receive more positive reinforcement—more praise and reward—than children from lower-status backgrounds, who tend to attract more criticism and punishment. Teacher expectations also tend to be higher for middle- and high-status children than for low-status children (Brophy & Good, 1974).

These findings indicate that you should exercise caution in your evaluation and treatment of students from different socioeconomic backgrounds. There is a distinct danger that you may have preconceived ideas about the relationship between home background and how a child will perform in school. You must not assume that certain children are destined to failure.

This does not mean that all school failures should be laid at the door of the teacher. It is perhaps a hangover from the optimistic view of the progressives that the school should take on the responsibilities of all agents that contribute to the student's development. Current opinion is that the school cannot educate in isolation from other agencies, especially the home. Concrete expression of this philosophy is embodied in home intervention programs for young children from disadvantaged homes, which began in the 1960s, and more recently in the trend to develop work programs outside the school for adolescent students.

CONCLUSION

In this chapter, we provided examples of the kinds of specialized knowledge, based on theory and research, on which the practice of teaching can be based. This is not to claim that the theories of such disciplines as psychology and sociology are well developed, or that on the basis of those theories it is possible to form a well-developed theory of learning and instruction upon which the teacher can draw. Indeed, much of the kind of knowledge we have considered in this chapter is descriptive. However, developments over the past two decades are providing a sounder base of knowledge in the social sciences on which teachers can draw than existed in the past.

As a teacher, your major tasks will be to manage a classroom, to select and organize the material you will teach, and to instruct students. There are no simple rules of thumb for dealing with the variety of problems the teacher will meet (Gage, 1977). This is partly because teaching is a very complex process. It is also because teaching is a personal activity, and the sciences or theories on which it is based will always appear impersonal. In deciding what to do from one minute to the next in the classroom, you will have to rely on your own judgment and, in arriving at that judgment, you will have considerable autonomy (Lortie, 1975). Your judgments will be based on your perceived needs of students, the particular tasks to be accomplished, and the constraints under which these must be carried out. Your knowledge of the social sciences should help ensure that your judgments are informed ones.

QUESTIONS AND ACTIVITIES

1. Devise an experiment that you might use as a teacher to evaluate your effectiveness in teaching a course. What factors other than your teaching might affect your results?
2. Look again at Piaget's experiment. Try this experiment yourself with a 5-year-old and an 8-year-old. Can you think of other materials to use in an experiment on Piaget's stages?
3. Describe school experiences you have had as a student that you feel are examples of teachers using behavior modification.
4. Can you recall the most popular students when you were at high school? What were the characteristics of those students? Why do you think they were popular?
5. From your experience, what home factors do you think help or hinder a student in school?

PART TWO

The System

The organization and control of public education in America is unique in the Western world. The chief responsibility for education rests with the states. The states in turn traditionally have delegated authority for the day-to-day operation of the schools to thousands of local districts across the country. The federal government, through legislation and court decisions, also plays a large role in education.

Traditionally, local districts have had a great deal of control over educational policy and the curriculum, yet over the last two decades state and federal laws and regulations and court actions have eroded that control.

Other groups representing teachers and administrators, minority groups, those with disabilities (both physical and mental), businesses, churches, taxpayers, and commercial interests also exert a powerful influence on American education.

Further, our system of public education is only as good as the people who serve in it. Educational policy and the administration of public education are in the hands of a number of key people at the federal, state, and local levels. These key people have enormous influence over what our schools do and how they do it.

America's system of nonpublic education is also unique. Throughout our history, independent private schools (both religious and nonsectarian) have been an important segment of American education. Religious schools evolved from public schools, which were sectarian, into separate denominational schools. Schools affiliated with a particular religion offer parents a choice to educate their children in a tradition and value and belief system not available in the public schools.

The role of the state and federal courts is also significant in American education. The courts protect the constitutional rights of students, teachers, administrators, and parents. Court decisions in such matters as segregation, finance, the rights of nonpublic schools, the separation of church and state, school attendance, discipline, and collective bargaining have had a profound impact on our educational system.

It is important for persons considering education as a career, and for citizens in general, to understand the structure and control of American public and nonpublic education, who the key actors and organizations are, and the role of the courts in education. Information on these issues is presented in this section: Chapter 4 provides an introduction to the structure and control of public education; Chapter 5 covers key positions in public education; Chapter 6 treats nonpublic education; and Chapter 7 discusses the role the courts play in our educational system.

CHAPTER 4

The American System of Public Education

This chapter describes the complex series of relationships that control elementary and secondary education in America.

- Education is controlled by formal legal regulations but also subject to informal nongovernmental influences.
- Local districts still have considerable power over local schools, yet state and federal regulations have slowly undermined this power.
- The balance of control between the state and local districts varies from state to state.
- Numerous special-interest groups influence educational policy.
- Paying the bill for education is a complicated process and is the responsibility of all three levels of government (local, state, and federal).

Who controls American education? Who is ultimately responsible for providing education for our youth? How is our educational system financed? How are school systems organized? In this chapter, we will try to answer these basic questions about the system in which you may eventually teach. At times you may become confused, but this should not be a cause of worry; even our nation's education leaders and experts are sometimes confused by many of these issues. First, we will consider briefly the complexity of the American system of public education. Then we examine the roles of local government, state government, and federal government in the educational system. Following this, we shall briefly describe the role of key interest groups. Finally, we shall examine how elementary and secondary education is financed.

The Complexity of the American System of Public Education

Today, the organizational structure of education in the United States is so complex that attempting to understand it can easily lead to frustration. To a great extent the complexity is due to the fact that a number of agencies are trying to make schools simultaneously meet the needs of students, the community, and our nation. Picture three major groups with power over our schools: local, state, and federal governments. Sometimes these groups work together; sometimes they work separately. Sometimes they are in harmony; at other times they are embroiled in controversy. The three levels of government must abide by certain rules, both written and unwritten. The written or formal rules are laws and regulations. The unwritten rules are informal or indirect pressures emanating from vested-interest groups, individuals with strong personalities, and ingrained traditions of custom and prior practice. These formal and informal sources of control work interdependently to dictate how our schools are organized, managed, and financed. As Figure 4.1 illustrates, there are many people and institutions who want to influence what our schools do and how they do it. Politics plays a strong part in American education, and there is nothing wrong with that. It is a fact of American life.

At the formal level of control, the constitutions of both the federal and state governments are the basis for the legal rules governing education. Since education is not mentioned in the Constitution, it is a primary responsibility of states by virtue of the Tenth Amendment, which stipulates that all powers not enumerated in the Constitution are reserved to the states.

In their constitutions, state governments have appropriated responsibility for education. States have delegated some of the responsibility for implementing policy at the local level to local school districts. At the school district level, a board of education, either elected or appointed, directs the schools, formulates local policy, and ensures that state and federal regulations are met.

At the nongovernment level of control, many individuals and groups also affect educational policy. For example, a school principal can have a major impact on how a school is organized and run. Each teacher has a unique style, philosophical beliefs, educational preparation, cultural background, and personality that influence how he or she organizes a classroom. Vocal school board

FIGURE 4.1 Influences on the School 87

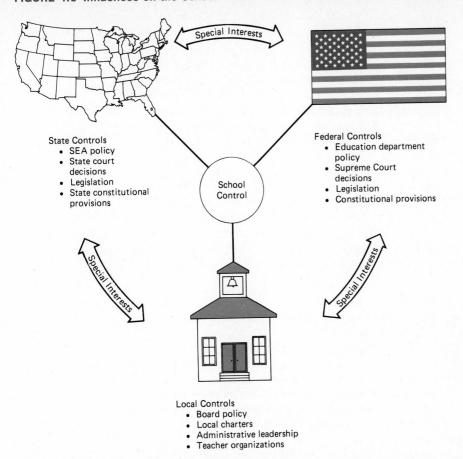

State Controls
- SEA policy
- State court decisions
- Legislation
- State constitutional provisions

Federal Controls
- Education department policy
- Supreme Court decisions
- Legislation
- Constitutional provisions

School Control

Special Interests

Local Controls
- Board policy
- Local charters
- Administrative leadership
- Teacher organizations

members, parents, special-interest advocates, and local citizens also have an impact on the schools.

People with similar views or interests may form groups or organizations that can affect educational policy. Examples of such organizations are the National Education Association (NEA) and the American Federation of Teachers (AFT) (both teachers' unions), the Education Commission of the States (ECS) (comprised of seven representatives from each of the 48 member states, generally including the governor, chief state school officer, legislative leaders, and individuals appointed by the governor), the National School Boards Association, and the American Association of School Administrators (composed mainly of principals and school superintendents). Other organizations made up of business people and industrial leaders also try to influence educational policy. Business people, for example, have an interest in ensuring that high school graduates possess the skills necessary to enter the work force.

The Local Government's Role in American Education

Americans have always fought to maintain as much local control of government as possible. Colonial America was an agrarian society, its citizens

were spread sparsely over large geographical areas, and communications between the nation's capital and the states took days or weeks. Consequently,
the concept of a centralized government was far removed from the lives of
most Americans. It simply was not practical. It is not surprising, therefore, that
the Founding Fathers left control of education to state governments. The
states, in turn, for similar reasons of size, transportation, and communication
did not assume responsibility for education. In practice, that meant delegating
control of schools to town or county governments. In New England, the towns
were given control over education, and in the South this power was vested in
county governments. As new states were admitted to the Union they adopted
either the southern or the New England model, depending on their needs and
history. Hawaii is a major exception, since it has no local school districts. There
the state is in direct control of education.

Today school district boundaries take many forms. Among the most
common are

1. Districts that are arranged on a county basis.
2. Small common-school districts, usually found in rural areas, many of
which have only elementary schools.
3. City school districts with boundaries that are the same or close to city
boundaries.
4. County districts within which cities are separate districts.
5. Independent districts that cross town or county boundaries or are
sections of towns or counties. These districts are formed by legislative
act. The majority of independent districts provide regional schools that
serve several small towns.
6. Town or township districts where the school district boundaries coin-
cide (Morphet, Johns, & Reiler, 1982, p. 241).

Some states adopt only one of these arrangements. Many others have
found that it makes more organizational and financial sense to use a combination of the approaches to school boundaries listed above.

Local Education Authorities

However local district boundaries are formed, the term *local education
authority (LEA)* is used to describe the local organization that runs schools.
Although an LEA is a quasi-corporation and a legal extension of the state
government, it has a great deal of autonomy in determining educational policy
for the schools within the district (Edwards, 1971).

Power delegated to LEAs varies from state to state, and even from
district to district within a state, depending upon city, town, and county
charters. One major difference among school districts is their ability to levy
taxes for education. Some LEAs have the power not only to develop the school
budget but also to assess taxes to pay for it. Others draw up the budget but
must present it to a town meeting, budget committee, or other elected body
for approval and funds. In some LEAs (particularly in the Midwest) the board
can pass a budget, but the voters must approve this if it involves an increase
in the tax or millage rate. When an LEA can assess taxes to pay for the budget,

it is said to have fiscal autonomy or fiscal independence; and when an LEA is dependent on another agency for its revenue, it is said to be fiscally dependent. An LEA with fiscal autonomy generally has more control over its schools and educational policy than one that is fiscally dependent.

School Boards

LEAs are governed by school boards or school committees. School boards vary in size, ranging from 3 to as many as 15 members. Members are elected in approximately 93 percent of the districts and appointed in the other 7 percent (Cameron, Underwood, & Fortune, 1988). Some boards have jurisdiction over districts that have both elementary and secondary schools. In other arrangements, the board has responsibility for only one type of school, for example, elementary, secondary, vocational, or technical.

While school boards differ in size, how they are formed, and their jurisdiction, they also share a number of crucial responsibilities. First, all boards work with a superintendent of schools whom they appoint or who is elected by voters in the district. The school superintendent is the executive officer of the board, and therefore is in charge of day-to-day operations of the school district. The board must work cooperatively with its superintendent if the schools are to function smoothly.

A second major responsibility common to all boards of education is the establishment of educational goals for the district. Goal statements are the "guiding lights" of the school district. The content of the statements should reflect the values of the community, the emphases that the district wants to stress in curriculum, an understanding of the characteristics of the learner, and an awareness of the needs of society. Content should also be in accordance with state and federal laws, regulations, and guidelines. Goals are much more general than statements of objectives, which generally describe the student outcomes sought. District goals not only unite the educators within the district in a common purpose, they also inform and guide decisions about the curriculum.

Establishing the goals of a district can be a difficult process, since most boards represent heterogeneous populations with various values, traditions, and expectations about education. Without a clear set of district expectations for the schools, educational policy and programs can become chaotic and disjointed. Therefore, goal statements and the setting of objectives to achieve goals are best developed cooperatively. Ideally, teachers, administrators, parents, students, community members, and school board members should have input into formation or revision of a school system's goals. Further, these different constituencies should work together to achieve the schools' mission.

Since each school district is unique, statements of specific goals and objectives will vary from district to district. The major focus of the statements, however, is similar. Box 4.1 outlines some selected goals of the Oyster River School District in Durham, New Hampshire. These goal statements are typical. Note the emphasis on communication skills, comprehension ability, analytic skills, and values important to the maintenance of democracy. In the case of the Oyster River system, examples of specific objectives related to the broader goals that students are to master by grades 5, 8, and 11 are included. These objectives make the general goal statements more concrete.

A third responsibility of school boards is to formulate and monitor the implementation of policies designed to achieve their goals. For example, a board might decide that a major goal of the system is to have all children reading at grade level by the end of elementary school. To ensure that this goal is achieved, the board will need to examine the reading curriculum and indicators of student progress, such as test scores, provide remedial support for students who need help in achieving the goal, and ensure that adequate financial and human resources are allocated.

A fourth responsibility of school boards is to develop the yearly budget and monitor expenditures. The budget can affect staff morale, program decisions, and taxpayer attitudes. The board's budget must reflect the dual—often contradictory—aims of assuring a quality education and keeping expenditures as low as possible.

Finally, school boards are responsible for hiring teachers and administrators, assessing their performance yearly, and, when necessary, terminating their employment. In hiring and releasing staff, school boards act on the recommendations of the superintendent. Staffing issues are complicated by contract negotiations with the various collective bargaining groups representing teachers, administrators, support staff, bus drivers, and maintainence workers. Collective bargaining agreements often dictate conditions of employment and of dismissal. For example, teachers with seniority may have to be given preference in filling some posts irrespective of how the principal feels.

School Administrative Structure

Although the LEA is subject to state and federal policy, it is the body that ultimately controls the way in which the school system is organized. It designs the administrative structure of the system on the basis of its own philosophy, financial considerations, and facilities. Sometimes one of these considerations outweighs the others. For example, during the early 1970s, declining student numbers forced many districts to close schools. While the district philosophy may have favored smaller, more personal neighborhood schools, the fiscal reality and empty classrooms swayed many school board members to close schools and transport the students to other schools in the district.

Basically, American public schools are organized on a system ranging from kindergarten (K) to grade 12. Some districts do not have kindergarten classes, but these are becoming rare as demands for kindergarten and pre-school education increase. Various combinations of grades are used to organize the schools. The K-through-8 system for elementary schools was for a long time the most popular model in American education, particularly in rural areas (see Figure 4.2). The K-through-6 elementary model is more common today and is usually part of a system that has a junior high school consisting of either grades 7 and 8 or grades 7 through 9. The third model has three components: K-through-4 or K-through-5 elementary schools, 5-through-8 or 6-through-8 middle schools, and 9-through-12 high schools. In all the models, the high school includes at least grades 10 through 12.

Elementary Schools

The majority of elementary schools are organized so that an individual teacher can instruct students in all the basic disciplines in the same class-room. Schools that use this approach are usually referred to as having self-contained classrooms. Most districts employ specialists to help teachers meet the varying needs of students. Such specialists include librarians, speech and hearing therapists, guidance counselors, social workers, reading consultants, school psychologists, and special-needs teachers. They may work out of a central office or, if the school is large enough, be located at the school. The next chapter discusses in more detail the roles of the principal and major support people.

Junior High and Middle Schools

At the junior high or middle school level, two basic organizational approaches are common. The two differ in structure and philosophical orientation. The junior high school structure is illustrated as model 2 in Figure 4.2 and includes grades 7 and 8 or 7, 8, and 9. In the junior high model, teachers are organized into different departments according to academic discipline (for

FIGURE 4.2 Typical Grade-Level Organization

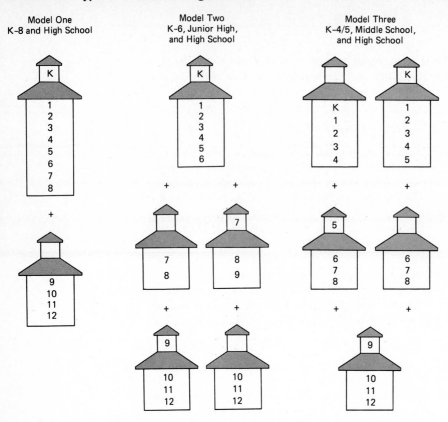

Model One
K-8 and High School

Model Two
K-6, Junior High,
and High School

Model Three
K-4/5, Middle School,
and High School

example, English, math, social studies). This approach is very similar to that used at the high school level. Students attend class for a set amount of time each day, then rotate to a different teacher's room. Extracurricular programs and interscholastic sports are "junior versions" of what students will encounter at the "senior" high school level. The philosophy behind this organizational structure is that the junior high school prepares students for high school by getting them accustomed to schedules, academic disciplines, and working with a variety of teachers on a daily basis.

The philosophy behind the organization of the middle school, on the other hand, is more student-centered than subject-centered. Its proponents feel that early adolescents (10- to 14-year-olds) have similar psychological, physical, and emotional needs; middle schools are organized to keep them together by grade in a 5-through-8, 6-through-8, or 7-through-8 organizational structure. Ninth graders are considered to be more advanced and can, therefore, be moved to the high school level. In addition to keeping students of similar needs together, the middle school often uses a different approach to staffing then does the traditional junior high school. Students are usually organized in groups of 80 to 120 and assigned an interdisciplinary team consisting of math, science, social studies, and English teachers. In some cases, foreign language or other specialized area teachers may be part of the team. The team cooperatively plans curricula and shares information about students. By using the interdisciplinary team-teaching approach, the students' curriculum may be less fragmented, teachers can share information about students, and students can develop a feeling of belonging to a group.

Middle schools are designed to help the early adolescent make the adjustment from the security of a self-contained classroom to the relatively more chaotic world of the secondary school. They try to help the early adolescent maintain a good sense of self throughout a period of rapid physical and emotional growth; learn to adjust to demands of studying more diverse subject areas in more depth than they were accustomed to in elementary school; and learn to become more independent and self-disciplined so that they may succeed at high school.

It is important to note that the junior high model can also focus on goals that are student-centered. Middle school advocates would argue that this task is more difficult because of the departmentalized structure and inclusion of grade 9 in the traditional junior high school. However, the influence of the building principal, support staff, and teachers can help to make the junior high school student-centered if administrators and staff believe in this orientation and work together to implement it. Likewise, simply implementing the team approach in the middle school does not guarantee the school will be student-centered.

High Schools

Since high schools have as their mission the preparation of students for the world of work and higher education, they offer a variety of courses, including college preparatory courses, vocational-technical, business, and general courses. Some high schools also offer apprenticeship and work-study programs. High schools have been the focal point of the educational reform movement of the 1980s. Consequently, high school standards regarding course offerings and graduation requirements have become more and more the concern of the state. In many cases, LEAs require their students to earn more credits or take more courses to graduate than does the state.

As in elementary, middle, and junior high schools, the person responsible for the administration of the high school is the principal. High schools are usually organized into departments by academic and vocational discipline. Each academic department usually has a chairperson who is responsible to the principal for the administration of the department. Specialists are also present to address the educational and psychological needs of students.

On average, it is one and a half times more expensive to educate a student in high school than in elementary school. Since it is difficult for smaller high schools to offer all the courses required by the state accreditation standards, many towns have petitioned the state to permit them to form regional high schools and so reduce the cost of secondary education borne by each town. This procedure avoids the need to duplicate expensive facilities such as science laboratories, business training equipment, and libraries. It also makes possible a wider variety of courses. Under a regional system, towns usually keep direct control of elementary schools, and secondary schools are under control of a regional board of education that is usually elected at large or appointed from the participating local boards.

The State Government's Role in American Education

A number of different models of state control of education have evolved since colonial days. States derive their power from three sources: state constitutional provisions, statutory law, and decisions of state courts. All state constitutions contain a section that acknowledges the state's responsibility to provide a free system of public education. Further, in each state the legislature enacts laws that deal with various aspects of education. State departments of education develop very specific sets of regulations dealing with how the laws are to be implemented. School districts must abide by these laws and regulations. Among the many statutory provisions enacted by legislatures are those covering graduation requirements, the number of days schools must be in session, school attendance, the age at which a student may leave school, teacher certification, and pupil transportation. Of course, states' statutes and regulations must not violate either the state constitutions or the federal Constitution.

The state education agency (SEA) is the specialized executive branch of government that implements constitutional and statutory law concerning education. The SEA also establishes educational policy and regulations. To understand the role played by state governments in education, you need to know the ways in which SEAs are structured, what they have in common across states, and how they differ from state to state.

SEAs usually consist of a board of education that establishes policy and a chief state school administrator and a staff of professionals working in the state department of education who implement policy. The way that state board members and the chief school administrator are selected affects the power they have in determining and implementing policy. Figure 4.3 shows four models used in 43 of the 50 states to organize their SEAs.

Model one shown in Figure 4.3 is the most common structure at the state level. The governor appoints the state board of education and, in turn, the board appoints the chief state school officer (CSSO). In model two, the electorate chooses the state board of education directly, and it in turn appoints the chief state school officer. In model three, the CSSO is elected by the people, and the governor appoints the state board of education. In model four, the state board of education and the CSSO are both appointed by the governor.

The seven states not included in Figure 4.3 have slightly different arrangements. In Florida, for example, the state board is composed of seven elected members of the governor's cabinet, one of whom is the CSSO. In New York and South Carolina, the legislature elects the state board of education; in Wisconsin the CSSO is elected on a nonpartisan ballot but there is no state board of education responsible for elementary and secondary education (Burnes, Palaich, McGuinness, & Flakus-Mosqueda, 1983).

In states where board members are appointed by the governor (models one and four), the governor can, through his or her appointments, influence educational policy. Boards elected by popular vote are more autonomous, accountable only to the electorate. In model four, where both the board and

FIGURE 4.3 State Education Governance Structures 95

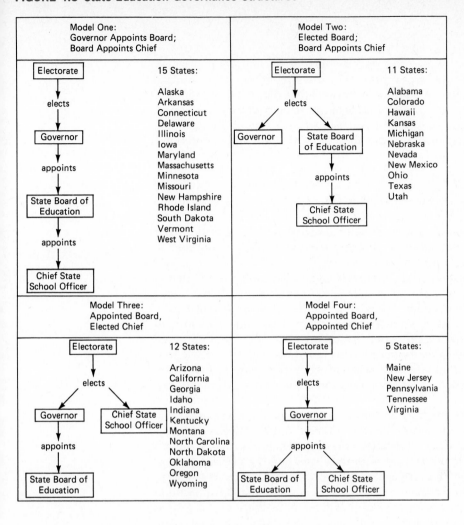

Model One:
Governor Appoints Board;
Board Appoints Chief

Electorate

↓ elects

Governor

↓ appoints

State Board of Education

↓ appoints

Chief State School Officer

15 States:

Alaska
Arkansas
Connecticut
Delaware
Illinois
Iowa
Maryland
Massachusetts
Minnesota
Missouri
New Hampshire
Rhode Island
South Dakota
Vermont
West Virginia

Model Two:
Elected Board;
Board Appoints Chief

Electorate

↓ elects

Governor   State Board of Education

↓ appoints

Chief State School Officer

11 States:

Alabama
Colorado
Hawaii
Kansas
Michigan
Nebraska
Nevada
New Mexico
Ohio
Texas
Utah

Model Three:
Appointed Board,
Elected Chief

Electorate

↓ elects

Governor   Chief State School Officer

↓ appoints

State Board of Education

12 States:

Arizona
California
Georgia
Idaho
Indiana
Kentucky
Montana
North Carolina
North Dakota
Oklahoma
Oregon
Wyoming

Model Four:
Appointed Board,
Appointed Chief

Electorate

↓ elects

Governor

↓ appoints

State Board of Education   Chief State School Officer

5 States:

Maine
New Jersey
Pennsylvania
Tennessee
Virginia

Source: Burnes, Palaich, McGinness, & Flakus-Mosqueda, 1983, pp. 17–19.

the CSSO are separately appointed by the governor, the governor can exert a great deal of influence in educational matters.

State Departments of Education

All states have a state department of education (SDE) comprised of professional educators and support staff to carry out the many responsibilities delegated to the state board and CSSO. State departments of education are run by the CSSO and are usually divided into sections that cover various aspects of education. For example, all state departments have divisions responsible for such areas as special education, professional certification, research, record keeping, and elementary and secondary curriculum and instruction.

When the legislature enacts a statute or the state board of education establishes a new policy, it is turned over to the SDE for implementation. The SDE in turn designs the rules and regulations that detail exactly how the statutes or policy will be implemented. The rules and regulations (called "regs") have the effect of law. The regs are extremely important because, depending on the way they are written, they can strengthen or weaken the provisions of the statutes. In addition to formulating regs, all SEAs monitor state and federally mandated programs, accredit schools, certify school personnel, approve educational facilities, oversee private or parochial education, and provide help and expertise in the areas of curriculum and instruction.

Changes in State Control

There is no question that states have gained influence in educational policy-making. A number of major reform reports since 1983 have contributed to the continued growth of state involvement in education. For example, between 1980 and 1985, 39 states have increased the number of credit hours required for a high school diploma.

Most states have adopted the *Carnegie unit* to determine the period of instructional time that is regarded as equivalent to one credit. The Carnegie unit was created by the Carnegie Foundation for the Advancement of Teaching in 1906. The unit was designed to standardize the time spent in high schools on different subject areas so that institutions of higher education would be better able to judge student qualifications for admission. A Carnegie unit is described as a course that meets 3 times per week for a minimum 40 minutes per meeting. This translates to at least 120 hours of class time during the year in the given subject.

States have different ways of enforcing the regulations they set. The most powerful and common sanction is to withhold funds until the district is in compliance. In some cases, the state will revoke the certification of schools in local districts that do not comply with state laws and regulations. A more radical punishment has been advocated in the National Governors Commission (1986) report *Time for results.* The governors suggested that minimum levels of student academic achievement should be set by the state. LEAs that do not meet these standards should be declared educationally bankrupt and placed in receivership, that is, taken over and run by the state until achievement reaches acceptable levels. Up to 1987 six states (Arkansas, Georgia, Kentucky, South Carolina, Texas, and New Jersey) have adopted bankruptcy/ receivership legislation. None of these states, however, has used student achievement as the sole criterion when declaring a school system bankrupt (Education Commission of the States, 1988).

The Federal Government's Role in American Education

Although education is not specifically mentioned in the federal Constitution, there has always been some degree of federal involvement in education. In addition to legislative action, the United States Supreme Court has mandated that changes be made in educational systems to comply with federal laws or with constitutional provisions arising from the Bill of Rights. The federal government became involved in education at a very early stage. The ordinances of 1785 and 1787 set aside areas within the Northwest Territory for educational purposes. During the nineteenth century, numerous acts were passed granting federal lands to states to help them provide for, and support, education. One of the more extensive of these land acts was the Morrill Act of 1862, which granted 30,000 acres of federal land to each state for every senator and representative from the state in Congress. The Morrill Act was important because it firmly established the notion that the federal government could become involved in education to provide for common defense and public welfare. Apart from these land acts, the federal government kept a very low profile in educational matters up to World War II. Since then, however, it has become a much more active participant in educational policy-making.

Major Federal Legislation

The first significant educational legislation passed by the federal government after World War II that directly affected public education was the National Defense Education Act (NDEA) in 1958. The motivation for passing the NDEA was the protection of the national interest. It was passed in the wake of the launching in 1957 by the Soviet Union of *Sputnik I,* the first satellite to be sent into space. The threat of Soviet technological superiority led the Congress to provide local districts with funds to improve instruction in math, science, foreign language, and other subjects critical to national defense interests. The NDEA also provided increased revenue to local and state agencies for providing better record keeping, improving multimedia instruction, developing testing programs, improving guidance and counseling programs, and establishing closer collaboration among colleges, local districts, and state education agencies.

Another theme in federal legislation has been the establishment and maintenance of educational equality for all students. This theme finds expression in two key pieces of legislation. The first was the Elementary and Secondary Education Act (ESEA) of 1965, an integral part of President Lyndon B. Johnson's "Great Society" legislative package. Its goal was the eradication of poverty and inequality by providing *compensatory* education for underprivileged children. The amount of revenue the federal government contributed to education rose from approximately $897 million in the 1963–1964 school year (before the passage of ESEA) to $2.8 billion in the 1967–1968 school year when the new law was in effect (National Center for Education Statistics, 1982). The largest program that was started under this act was Title I. Title I funds were used to establish and maintain programs for economically disadvantaged children in local schools. One of the major effects of the act has been that SEAs and LEAs have become more dependent on federal funds and have lost a degree of control over their schools and programs.

The second piece of federal legislation expressing the theme of educational equality is Public Law 94–142, the Education for All Handicapped Act of 1975. Until this act was passed it was common for districts to educate students with handicapping conditions separately from their peers. Under Public Law 94–142, however, students between the ages of 3 and 21 years who are evaluated as having handicapping conditions that could impair their educational performance must now be provided with an appropriate educational experience with their nondisabled peers. Public Law 94–142, in particular, has had a profound impact on curriculum design and implementation of special education, record keeping, physical facilities, and staffing. Under this law, control over the education of children with handicapping conditions has shifted from local to federal and state agencies.

President Reagan was elected in 1980 on a platform that included plans to reduce the involvement of the federal government in education. Many inside and outside the Reagan administration felt that the federal role had become too strong and bureaucratic. As a result, President Reagan attempted to return more power to state and local agencies by changing federal regulations and funding.

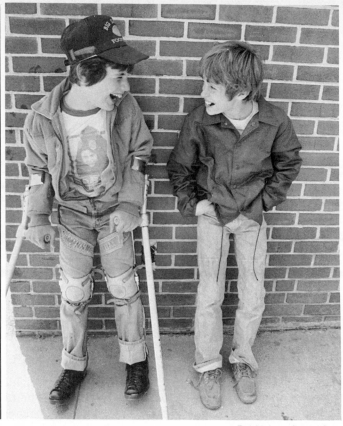

Public Law 94-142 guarantees that the civil rights of children with handicapping conditions are protected. This federal law mandates that disabled students must be provided with appropriate educational experiences with their nonhandicapped peers whenever possible.

Prior to the Reagan administration, all fiscal support to education from the federal government was designated exclusively for particular programs or categories, such as Title I. This practice is called *categorical aid.* A major complaint about this procedure focused on the amount of red tape involved in applying for, monitoring, and evaluating the numerous categorical grants available. Additional concerns were also raised about the narrowness of the categories and the lack of state and local involvement in determining where funds could best be spent. In an attempt to address such concerns, Congress passed the Education Consolidation and Improvement Act (ECIA) of 1981. This act repealed the old ESEA. Chapter 2 of the ECIA addressed complaints about the number of categorical aid programs. It consolidated 28 federal categorical aid programs into one large block grant. Under a *block grant* scheme the SEAs, in cooperation with LEAs, determine how a large block of money from the federal government will be spent. LEAs can choose to spend it on the old categorical programs or for entirely different purposes. However, the old Title I of the ESEA was retained as a categorical program to help disadvantaged students. It is now called Chapter 1 of the ECIA and accounts for the largest share of the federal budget for public education (23 percent) (National Association of Elementary School Principals, 1985).

Educators have had mixed feelings about the replacement of categorical aid by block grants. Most are happy with the reduction of red tape and the fact that they have more say in deciding where federal monies will be spent. Others, however, were upset when programs previously covered by categorical aid were terminated by SEAs or LEAs under the discretion given them under block grant funding.

The Education Department

The United States Department of Education (ED), a cabinet-level department, and the responsibility of the secretary for education, has been the agency responsible for regulating education at the federal level since 1979. Previously, educational matters were the responsibility of various other cabinet departments or agencies, the majority falling under the old Department of Health, Education and Welfare (HEW), now called the Department of Health and Human Services. When the new ED was formed, it assumed responsibility for educational programs previously under HEW, as well as programs that had been the responsibility of the Departments of Defense, Housing and Urban Development, Justice, and Labor, and the National Science Foundation. The ED is presently responsible for educational programs that are concerned with civil rights, elementary and secondary education, postsecondary education, educational research and development, vocational and adult education, and special education. Each of these areas is the responsibility of an undersecretary.

President Reagan's second secretary of education, William Bennett, has suggested that the proper function of this office is that of a "bully pulpit." Using his office as a bully pulpit, Bennett issued two major reports during his tenure. *First lessons: A report on elementary education in America,* preached his vision of what elementary education should accomplish (Bennett, 1986). His second report, *James Madison high school: A curriculum for American students,* contained his views on secondary education (Bennett, 1988). He made it clear in both reports that the recommendations were his, and not federal government mandates. Bennett politicized his office. Whether the next secretary of education continues to use that office as a bully pulpit remains to be seen.

The Role of External Nongovernmental Groups in American Education

Up to now we have considered the roles and organization of the three levels of government that formally control our schools. We now turn to other groups that influence the formation and implementation of educational policy. Government agencies and policymakers at all levels are influenced by powerful nongovernmental organizations. These special-interest groups can affect policy by lobbying individual legislators and legislative bodies, by distributing information to those in decision-making positions, by monitoring various programs, and through political endorsement. In addition to special-interest groups that lobby to influence legislators, there are commercial groups, such as textbook publishers, computer companies, software companies, and test publishers, who control the content and level of curriculum and instructional materials. In the following sections we shall introduce you to a few of the more important nongovernmental groups of both types and how they influence American schools.

Teacher Organizations

The two major teacher organizations are the National Education Association (NEA) and the American Federation of Teachers (AFT); the latter is affiliated with the AFL-CIO. Of the two, the NEA is the larger, representing nearly 2 million teachers; the AFT has approximately 450,000 members, mostly in large urban school districts. Both organizations have members in higher education and private schools, but the vast majority of members are elementary and secondary public school teachers. It is highly likely that if you become a teacher you will join one of these organizations.

Since both organizations have state and local affiliates, they exercise influence at each level of government. At the national level, they lobby for or against educational legislation that might benefit or damage public education and the working conditions of teachers. In 1976, the NEA endorsed Jimmy Carter for president in return for the promise to establish a cabinet-level position for education. In 1979, President Carter redeemed his promise when he signed into law the bill establishing the Department of Education.

Both the NEA and AFT gather statistics, conduct research, and mount public relations campaigns to influence the formation or implementation of educational policy that might affect their membership. State affiliates of the national organizations use the same approaches to influence decisions at the state level. Local affiliates of the NEA or AFT have one additional mechanism at their disposal for affecting policy, the power of collective bargaining. In addition to salary and benefit issues, most negotiated contracts have clauses that affect such things as class size, teacher evaluation procedures, due process, and grievance procedures. All in all, the combined efforts by local, state, and national teacher organizations have had a major impact on the control of American education.

Organizations of Educational Administrators

Several interest groups represent the viewpoints of the various types of school administrators. Among the largest organizations are the American Association of School Administrators (AASA), the National Association of Secondary School Principals (NASSP), and the National Association of Elementary School Principals (NAESP). While these groups do not have the numbers that the teacher organizations have, they too have been effective in lobbying for issues that they believe will enhance education in general and benefit their membership in particular. As in the case of teacher organizations, these groups have state and regional affiliates that distribute information, monitor legislation, and attempt to influence policy.

School Board Associations

School boards also have national and state organizations that are designed to influence decision making. The National School Boards Association

(NSBA) is an active organization that has developed into an effective lobbying group. The missions of the NSBA are to promote local control of education, influence federal legislation and court rulings in favor of local school boards, provide support services to local school boards, and act as an information clearinghouse for state and local school boards (Campbell, Cunningham, Nystrand, & Usdan, 1985). School board associations exert substantial influence on educational policy, particularly at the state and federal levels.

Parent Groups

Nearly every school district in the United States has a local Parent-Teacher Association (PTA) or Parent-Teacher-Student Organization. These organizations are designed to ensure that parents are aware of, and have some influence in, educational issues. The National Congress for Parents and Teachers, commonly called the National PTA, has been active in various issues related to education and children. For example, it has taken a leadership role in monitoring and lobbying for television programming for children. It has also successfully lobbied for such programs as school lunch subsidies for underprivileged children, school safety standards, and other health programs.

Private Associations

Two major private associations to which educational institutions voluntarily belong exert great influence over the training of teachers and of educational administrators. The National Council for the Accreditation of Teacher Education (NCATE) and the University Council on Educational Administration (UCEA) are bodies that accredit training programs for teachers and school administrators. They conduct evaluations of college and university programs for teacher preparation and have a very large influence on teacher training in this country. Programs accredited by the organizations in one state are recognized by numerous states for reciprocal certification of teachers and administrators.

Taxpayer Groups

A large special-interest group that is not directly involved in education but has a major interest in, and impact on, education is made up of taxpayer associations. State taxpayer groups helped pass legislation such as Proposition 13 in California and Proposition 2½ in Massachusetts. These tax limitation measures have severely curtailed local districts' ability to tax personal property to finance schools. Since property taxes are the principal basis for local revenues, taxpayer "revolts" have taken financial resources away from many LEAs, making them more dependent on state funds, thus increasing state control over education at the expense of the LEAs (Odden & Augenblick, 1981).

Advocate Groups for Children in General and Special Populations

Special-interest groups, such as the Children's Defense Fund and the National Coalition of Advocates for Students (an umbrella organization of a host of advocate groups interested in student rights), have been extremely successful in court litigation and legislation. The largest organization in the crusade for fair and equitable treatment of disabled children is the Council for Exceptional Children (CEC). Numerous other groups at the national and state level are active in lobbying for legislation and in monitoring the educational scene to enhance the education of children in general and those with disabilities in particular.

Advocate Groups for the Rights of Minorities and Women

Several organizations designed to protect the rights of minority group members and women have had a large impact on educational policy over the years. Among the groups that carefully examine educational practice and lobby for legislation in these areas are the National Association for the Advancement of Colored People (NAACP), the Congress on Racial Equality (CORE), the Chicano Education Project, the Puerto Rican Legal Defense Fund, the Maximum American Legal Defense Fund (MALDF), People United to Save Humanity (PUSH), the American Association of University Women (AAUW), the League of Women Voters, and the National Organization of Women (NOW). These are but a few of the organizations seeking better treatment for students.

Conservative Organizations

Several conservative groups representing diverse interests (some with religious affiliation) have organized to influence curricula, policy, and reading materials in public schools. These groups have been successful in influencing policy and practice. For example, they have succeeded in having magazines and textbooks removed from classrooms and school libraries. Some conservative groups are working on such issues as restoring prayer in schools and monitoring courses in sex and AIDS education.

Commercial Groups

Curriculum materials used by the teacher have a powerful influence on what is taught in the classroom. There are a variety of instructional materials available to the classroom teacher that are commercially developed. These include computer-assisted instruction, simulation games, films, videotape, and periodicals designed especially for school. Education researchers have found that despite availability of other resources, textbooks are the primary determinant of what is taught in the classroom. Studies have found that 75 percent of a student's classroom time is focused on textbook use (Farr & Tulley, 1985); consequently, the publishers that write and produce textbooks have a major impact on the classroom.

Textbooks have been a focal point of the educational reform debate. In response to charges that textbooks lack academic rigor, publishers have contended that their books respond to the demands of the marketplace. The marketplace is in part determined by textbook adoption committees at the state and local level. Currently, 22 states have statewide adoption committees to conduct reviews and make recommendations regarding which textbooks should be used at the local level. These statewide committees vary in the power they have to influence local decisions. Some simply publish a list of approved titles, and others actually pay for books if the local district adopts those they have approved. Many critics argue that textbooks are written to please the more powerful statewide selection committees (particularly those in California and Texas, which represent two of the largest potential markets for textbooks). It is difficult to determine whether publishers do write their textbooks to appeal directly to the adoption states, and because of this have "watered them down" to be more marketable. Few would disagree, however, that these adoption committees have an influence on the content and writing style of the books.

Financing Education

One of the most controversial issues in education is who should pay for it. And a lot has to be paid. Maintaining a system of free public education is very expensive. In the 1985 to 1986 school year, the cost of public elementary and secondary schools exceeded $160 billion in the United States. This figure represented approximately 4 percent of this country's gross national product (GNP). When all levels of public and private education are included, the total expenditure for 1985–1986 was approximately $266 billion, representing 6.7 percent of the GNP (Snyder, 1987, p. 24).

In the past, local districts paid the bulk of education expenses with money raised from local property taxes. However, as we saw, this situation has changed dramatically in the last 30 years with increased state and federal financial aid. From 1919 through 1970, more than half the cost of education was met by local government. In the 1979–1980 school year, for the first time in the history of the United States, the largest proportion of expenditure was borne by state governments. In the 1985–1986 school year, approximately 50 percent of per pupil expenditures were covered by state funds, 44 percent by local funds, and 6 percent by federal funds (Stern, 1987). Thus, today, state and local finances combined provide over 90 percent of all school funding. Let us examine these two major sources of funding in greater detail.

Local Funding

Local governments raise revenue for services primarily through local property tax. Education-related programs account for the largest portion of the local municipality's budget. Past and present dependence on local property taxes to fund schools has resulted in a great disparity between school districts in the amount of money they are able to raise for their schools.

Where real estate values are high and there is a considerable amount of wealth supporting these holdings, school districts are able to raise tax money fairly easily. Consequently, more money is readily available for schools. In districts that do not have valuable real estate or businesses, property taxes are a major burden for taxpayers. These poorer districts cannot raise as much money as more affluent communities. Often, such districts have to establish higher tax rates to raise less money than in wealthier towns.

Since 1970, numerous court cases and legislative actions have addressed the problem of the dependence of schools on property taxes and the inequalities to which that gives rise. The decisions in these cases, together with the taxpayer revolt movement and the demand for better education, have led to an increase in state expenditure. Further, the states have made several attempts to equalize the distribution of funding across districts. We will now consider state funding in general and equalized funding in particular.

State Funding

Although the funding of education by all the states has steadily increased over the last 30 years, there is still great variation among states in the amount they contribute to education. State contributions vary from a high of 89 percent in Hawaii to a low of 5 percent in New Hampshire (Snyder, 1987).

State governments use a variety of taxes to raise revenues for educational expenditure; these include income taxes, excise taxes, sales taxes, inheritance taxes, business taxes, and corporate taxes. Some states use monies raised in the state lottery. The money is apportioned to the LEAs in different ways. Among the more important are the following:

   1. Categorical Aid. Monies are earmarked for specific programs. Examples of such programs are special education, school physical plant improvement, transportation aid, and vocational education. The grants can also be used to fund innovative programs or practices through competitive grant procedures.

   2. School Bonds. School bonds provide long-term, low-interest loans to school systems that need to make major adjustments or improvements in their school system. Usually the loans are used for building new schools or repairing old ones.

   3. Direct Aid. This type of aid is given directly to local districts to help equalize educational opportunity for students across districts.

The Reform of Education Funding Through Equalization

Basically there are two objectives behind the movement to reform school finance. The first is equitable treatment for all students across the state regardless of the wealth of the community in which they live. The second is to ensure that taxpayers are treated equitably in accomplishing the first objective. These objectives came about following court challenges of the ways in which LEAs raised money for education. The first of these challenges was the 1970 California State Court case of *Serrano* v. *Priest* (commonly referred to as *Serrano One).* In this case, the court ruled that the California system of financing schools was unconstitutional under the state's equal protection clause, since the district's property wealth was the main factor in determining the quality of education. The court found that the richer districts could afford to offer a better education than poorer ones and that this violated the state's equal protection clause. Finance reforms in other states used the precedent established in the *Serrano* case to change the way education was financed.

In 1973, school finance reformers took their case to the United States Supreme Court. In *Rodriguez* v. *San Antonio Independent School District,* an attempt was made to show that the Texas plan for financing schools was in violation of the Fourteenth Amendment to the Constitution, the equal protection clause. The Supreme Court, in a closely divided (5 to 4) decision, ruled that Texas was not in violation of the Constitution, since education (though important) is not a "fundamental interest" protected by the Constitution. Two important results of the *Rodriguez* case were that first, the federal government did not become involved in school finance reform and, second, future litigation could not rely on the Fourteenth Amendment of the Constitution in seeking reform. Since the *Rodriguez* case, however, several state courts have found that their state financing of education was in violation of the state constitution. Among those were Connecticut, New Jersey, Washington, California, Arkansas, West Virginia, and Wyoming.

As a result of state court rulings, states use a number of ways to give direct aid to LEAs, designed to equalize both opportunity for students and equity for taxpayers. We will briefly consider a number of these approaches. (The formulas associated with these plans are very complex and and are not considered here.)

FULL STATE FUNDING. Full state funding means just what it says: The state government assumes all the costs of education. This provides equitable treatment throughout the state, since no geographical variation in school expenditure is permitted and all the funds are raised through statewide taxes. Among the disadvantages some see associated with full state funding are a loss of local control, the loss of "lighthouse" districts (districts where many innovative programs have started), and an increase in the educational bureaucracy of the state. Hawaii is the only state with full state funding.

MINIMUM FOUNDATION PLANS Minimum foundation plans guarantee school districts a fixed amount of money for education. The plans attempt to provide a foundation on which LEAs can build educational programs. First the state determines the amount of money it feels is needed per pupil to provide a minimum education program. Then the state determines each LEA's contribution to the program by setting a specific tax rate that the district must use when taxing property. The state then provides the difference between the amount of money the LEA can raise using the predetermined tax rate and the per pupil minimum foundation amount. A property-poor district will be able to raise very little using the specified tax rate and therefore will receive more aid per pupil than districts that are wealthier. Currently, this is the most popular approach used to equalize funding. Among the states using the approach are Alabama, New Hampshire, and Washington.

GUARANTEED TAX BASE The guaranteed tax base (GTB) plan uses statewide tax–based figures and the local districts' actual tax to determine the level the state contributes to the LEA. First the state establishes the LEA's tax base or wealth, and uses this to measure the LEA's effort in supporting education. Second, the state establishes a tax rate for education that it feels the LEA should be able to afford given its tax base. Third, the local district establishes its actual tax rate for education. Fourth, the state compares the tax rate set by the LEA with the rate it set for the district. The final amount of state aid per pupil is determined by taking the difference between the actual wealth of the district and the amount of taxes the district chooses to impose. When districts tax themselves in excess of what the state determines is reasonable based on their wealth, they are exerting more effort and are given more state aid. The difference between minimum foundation funding plans and the GTB approach is that more local effort yields more state support in the GTB plan. Thus, the plan encourages local districts to spend more on education. Among states utilizing a GTB system are Colorado, New Jersey, and Wisconsin.

PERCENTAGE EQUALIZING Percentage equalizing plans are designed so that all districts receive a percentage of their funding from the state. Both rich and poor districts receive funds according to need. Percentage equalization implies that the state will share in the financing of education by providing a fixed percentage of each school district's expenditures. The district can determine the size of its budget, no matter how large, and the state undertakes to provide a fixed percentage of it.

Much like other equalizing plans, the degree to which this plan yields equal treatment to all districts depends upon the percentage of support the state decides to assume. As states provide a larger percentage of funding, the equalizing effect of this plan improves. Pennsylvania, Vermont, and Rhode Island are among those states currently using this plan.

PUPIL WEIGHTING AND TRANSPORTATION Two other issues that concern equity in funding are (1) providing appropriate services for students with unique needs, and (2) allocating funds to districts that must bus students considerable distances.

In dealing with the issue of providing appropriate services for students with unique needs, many states have devised a pupil weighting system. To do this, state education agencies have identified specialized programs for students that cost more to provide than average programs. Students in these programs are counted separately from students in regular classroom situations. For example, a student placed in a regular classroom without special assistance would be counted as 1 student in the aid formula; a student requiring special-education support might be counted as the equivalent of 2 students; and a student requiring bilingual classes for part of the day might be counted as 1.5 students. The number of students calculated in the formula mirrors accurately the actual costs to LEAs that provide educational programs for special-needs students.

Transportation expenses provide another problem in funding. Since the cost of transporting students varies widely among districts, it is necessary to devise a method to ensure that no district loses a large share of its available resources in meeting this noninstructional expense. Many states have simply reimbursed local districts for either all or a large part of their transportation expenses. Because of this, state education agencies can focus on instruction-related expenditures when calculating their equalization formulas.

CONCLUSION

The system of school governance in the United States is based on a tradition of strong local control. Since the 1950s, local districts have had their influence eroded by court decisions and legislation at the state and federal levels. New federal controls have evolved to encourage educational improvements in areas vital to national interests in maintaining a strong defense system, contributing to the public welfare, and ensuring that individuals' constitutional rights are protected. States have exerted more influence in reaction to public criticism of education by mandating tougher standards for teacher certification, high school graduation, and school accreditations. Additional controls have evolved indirectly through regulations attached to all state appropriations.

Despite the loss of some control over their schools, local districts still maintain a powerful influence over what is taught. LEAs implement state and federal policy, set district priorities, design the curriculum, and determine who will be hired to administer the schools. Most important, LEAs hire and evaluate the performance of classroom teachers. Teachers are the most influential people in the whole issue of control. They implement policy as they interpret it, and in ways that they believe will best achieve the goals they set for their students and the goals set by the district. Simply put, they are the "bottom line."

The next chapter describes the roles of several key people at the state and local levels who are responsible for various aspects of education. Each plays an important part in helping to maintain and improve schools. The role of the most important player at any level, the classroom teacher, will be addressed in later chapters.

QUESTIONS AND ACTIVITIES

1. Present three reasons why the federal government should or should not play a more active role in education. What role do you think the federal government should play?
2. Many would argue that since education is too complex for laypeople to control, the current system of electing school boards should be abolished in favor of a board of professional educators. What is your reaction to this argument?
3. You have just been elected to a local board of education. What do you believe to be your most important responsibility? How would you make decisions?

4. What are some of the drawbacks of working in a state with a strong and influential state education agency? What are some advantages?

5. Investigate your state's method(s) of providing funding to local schools. What are the strengths and weaknesses of the method(s)?

6. For one week, track articles relating to governance of education in your local newspaper. What are the major issues relating to governance that arise?

7. Reexamine Box 4.1. What goals and competencies would you add to complete the list?

CHAPTER 5

Key Positions in the Educational System

This chapter describes in more detail a number of the key positions in the field of education at the state and local levels that were introduced in the last chapter. We describe the qualifications for these positions, what the people do who hold these positions, and who they are responsible to.

- State board members are responsible for developing and mandating policies to which all schools in the state must adhere.
- The chief state school officer is responsible for implementing board policy and monitoring compliance with it. He or she is the state board's executive officer.
- Local school board members are responsible for formulating policy and overseeing the schools in their communities.
- The superintendent of schools is the local board executive officer and is responsible for implementing state, local, and federal policy and for the fiscal management of the schools. If the district is large enough, he or she may have assistant superintendents to handle curriculum and instruction, finance and facilities, personnel, and pupil personnel services.
- The school principal is responsible for the daily management of the instructional leadership in the school. He or she may have department heads or assistant principals or housemasters.
- Key people at the state and local levels have a direct influence on the classroom teacher.
- Although role responsibilities differ, all key people are responsible for trying to meet the needs both of students and of society.
- Success in all the roles described in this chapter requires highly developed technical and human relations skills.

In Chapter 4 we saw something of the complexity of the American education system and of the interdependence of local, state, and federal policy and control. What we did not discuss in any detail was the role of individuals who hold key positions at the state and local levels. Just as important as, and perhaps more important than, institutional controls are the people who staff the system. Numerous positions have evolved at both state and local levels to develop and implement educational policy, provide specialized services for students, and attend to the day-to-day running of the schools. In this chapter we describe the key positions in the system, the qualifications of people who hold them, what they do, and who they report to. Knowledge about these positions is necessary to understand the system of American education. The people described in this chapter all exist to help teachers do their jobs better. As a future teacher, you need to know who the key people are, what they do, and how they can help you in your classroom.

The positions described in the chapter include the chief state school officer and state board of education members at the state level, and school board members, superintendent, assistant superintendent, business manager, principal, department chairperson, pupil personnel director, and guidance counselor at the local level. All these positions have roles associated with administration or policy-making, except that of the guidance counselor, who is a member of the support staff in the school. The role of the classroom teacher is described in detail in later chapters.

State School Board Members

As mentioned in a previous chapter, all states except Wisconsin have a state board that is responsible for establishing and monitoring educational policy. State boards of education evolved to provide lay control of education at the state level. They are responsible for formulating educational policy and monitoring the state department's implementation of it. In educational issues, state boards make rules that have the same weight as statutory law.

In practice, many state board policies are formulated by the chief state officer, the state department of education, or other interest groups and are submitted to the board of education for official adoption. Since most board members are not experts and do not have the time to develop policy from the "ground up," they often act as sounding boards and synthesizers of proposals made by different groups. An analogy can be made between the state board of education and the board of directors of a major company. While a board of directors is responsible for many decisions, many people within and outside the organization work to influence its opinion. Similarly, state board members listen to those who have expertise on a particular issue, take testimony from interested parties, and then make decisions based upon their personal philosophies, research, and the information and recommendations they receive from the state department staff.

State board members are usually elected or appointed because of their interest in education and their philosophical orientation. (See Box 5.1 for a job description of a state board of education member.) Members can vary in their

BOX 5.1 State Board of Education Member—Job Description

General qualifications:

1. An interest in educational policy
2. Political support

How appointed—state board members obtain their office by one of the following:

1. Appointed by governor
2. Popular election
3. Ex officio members of designated organizations
4. Elected by state legislative bodies
5. Elected by local boards of education

Compensation—one of the following:

1. No compensation
2. Reimbursement of expenses
3. Per diem payment (range: $18 to $136)
4. Salary (Wyoming: $10 day)

Report to—depending on state, one or more of the following:

1. Voters (directly)
2. Governor
3. Chief state school officer
4. Legislature

Source: U.S. Department of Education, 1983, pp. 1–20.

philosophical approaches from those who advocate that the state should be very active and assertive in educational policy to those who believe the state should maintain a more distant role. Consequently, the philosophical orientation of a board can change as new members assume their positions. It is also important to note that the power of board members varies depending upon whether they are appointed or elected.

Members of state boards of education work hard. One study indicates that the average member spends 10 to 15 hours a week working on education-related issues, despite the fact that only one of the 50 states pays its board members for their services. In terms of background factors, the majority of members (84 percent) are white, almost two-thirds are male, over 90 percent hold at least a bachelor's degree, and 88 percent are over 40 years of age (Wiley and Blaunstein, 1983).

To understand how a state board develops policy, consider the process that the New Hampshire Board of Education followed in revising the criteria for the accreditation of its secondary schools. Because of the concern with standards of high school education in the state, the board directed the commissioner of education to form a committee of education leaders within the state to review accreditation requirements. On the basis of testimony from various experts and standards in other states, the committee revised the New Hampshire standards. The committee's report was then submitted to the state board of education for adoption. The state board in turn reviewed the proposed changes in the requirements and held public hearings. As a result of this process, the board revised some of the new standards recommended by the committee. After fine-tuning, the board voted to accept the new accreditation criteria. Implementation and monitoring of the new state standards then became the responsibilities of the chief state school officer and the state department of education.

Although details may differ, most states follow a similar approach in adopting new policies. Written and oral testimony is taken from state department personnel, professional consultants, university professors, education practitioners, and laypeople. After studying the issues, considering recommendations of the chief state school officer, and making its own revisions, the state board votes to adopt or reject the policy.

Chief State School Officer

The most visible and potentially most influential education official within the state is the chief state school officer. States use different titles to describe this position, including commissioner, superintendent of public instruction, superintendent of schools, superintendent of education, director of education, and secretary of education. Since the names used to designate the post vary across states, the generic term "chief state school officer" (CSSO) is commonly used to describe the position.

As we learned in Chapter 4, the power and influence of the CSSO depends in part on whether he or she is elected or appointed, and upon his or her term of office. In the majority of states, the CSSO holds the position for a set number of years. Thus a new state board or governor cannot replace the CSSO until his or her term expires. In 16 states, however, the term of office of the CSSO is indeterminate and he or she serves at the pleasure of the state board of education or the governor. (See Box 5.2 for a job description of a chief state school officer.)

Although CSSOs in different states may have varying levels of influence and different working relationships with their state boards, all share similar responsibilities. Each plays a pivotal role in providing leadership on educational issues. All CSSOs initiate new policy or legislation, monitor existing policy, and act as chief administrators of the state department of education. (Since state board members can devote only part of their time to board business, they depend upon the advice of the CSSO for many of their decisions.)

Once a particular policy has been approved by the board or enacted by the legislature, working out the details of how it will be implemented is delegated to the CSSO. The process of developing the regulations (or "regs," as they are most often called), which spell out how the new policy will work, is complicated and time-consuming. It includes submitting proposed regulations for public hearings and for review by the state board. The content of the regulations can weaken or strengthen the original intent of the policy. In addition to supervising the writing of new regulations, a CSSO has the responsibility of monitoring the LEAs' compliance with existing state and federal policies. To this end, a major task of state departments of education is that of collecting and interpreting information from LEAs regarding their compliance with state and federal laws and regulations. The CSSO must be aware of how local districts are implementing policies and whether or not the policies are achieving the desired results.

The CSSO must depend on the state department of education staff to both develop regulations and monitor LEAs. Therefore, managing the state department staff is an important job of the CSSO. As the department leader, the CSSO is obliged to produce the best possible results for the taxpayers' dollars. This means that the CSSO must know how to motivate employees, manage information, establish budgets, and foster and maintain positive public relations.

These administrative and policy duties require a person with a clear vision of the goals of education and good managerial and human relations

Source: U.S. Department of Education, 1983, pp. 21–30.

skills. Since the CSSO must work with the state board of education, the governor, and the public, he or she must also possess excellent political skills.

The formal qualifications of the CSSO vary from state to state. Currently, 36 states have statutory or constitutional provisions regarding the training and experience required of the CSSO, and another 11 states have policies regarding requirements for the job. The most frequent requirement of those who wish to be *elected* to the position is that they are a certain age and citizens of the United States. For those who are *appointed,* many states require advanced degrees and experience in working in an education-related field. Some states have few formal requirements, and, particularly in states where the officer is elected, the CSSO may not be a professional educator but should have a legal, human service, or business background (U.S. Department of Education, 1983).

Do state board members and CSSOs, individuals far removed from the day-to-day operation of schools, make a difference in the classroom? The answer is yes. For example, state board members and the CSSO are responsible for accrediting the teacher preparation program you are now in or aspire to. They determine how much time students will spend in your class when you are a teacher. They determine what type of competency test your students will take to demonstrate mastery of the skills you are supposed to teach. They determine what you will have to do to stay certified to teach. In some states, they can choose your textbooks. They provide funds for instruction and support services and they can even determine the composition of your class through providing for mainstreaming for children with disabilities and by influencing how school districts assign pupils to schools.

Local School Board Members

In over 93 percent of districts, school board members are elected, and in the remaining districts they are appointed to represent the educational interests of the local community. Legally, they are responsible to the state for overseeing education in their local districts. (See Box 5.3 for a job description

Source: Cameron, Underwood, & Fortune, 1988; Campbell, Cunningham, Nystrand, & Usdan, 1985, p. 193.

of a local school board member.) The major responsibilities of local boards of education include: appointing the school superintendent, establishing goals for the district, monitoring all school activities that are designed to achieve the school goals, overseeing budgetary matters, hiring and evaluating staff, and maintaining a positive rapport with the community on educational issues. Since educational expenses account for the largest share of municipal budgets, school board members are very visible. More than a few school committee members have used this visibility to launch their political careers.

School board members are normally laypeople who have an interest in education. When elected board members were surveyed as to why they decided to run for the position, they identified the following reasons in order of priority: (1) to exercise civic duty; (2) to increase academic standards; (3) to improve education for their children; (4) to make local boards more accountable; and (5) to make schools more fiscally sound (Cameron, Underwood, & Fortune, 1988).

The majority of school board members are male, in their forties, earning $40,000 to $50,000 a year, and married, and most have one or two children in local public schools. Both minority groups and women are underrepresented on local boards. A study by the National School Boards Association (1988) found that nationally, only 3.6 percent of school committee members are black and even a smaller percentage (1.5 percent) are Hispanic. Unfortunately, these percentages have remained stable over the last decade. Given the demographic trends toward larger numbers of minorities in our schools, the paucity of minorities on local school boards is a growing problem if the views of minority parents are to be adequately represented. While females have not yet achieved parity with males, they have increased their membership from 25.9 percent in 1978 to 39 percent in 1988 (Cameron, Underwood, & Fortune, 1988).

Members of local boards generally reflect the range of philosophical beliefs and values found in the community—although underrepresentation by minority group members on some boards belies this general statement. A major source of tension on boards grows out of radically different value positions on fiscal matters. Since property taxes are a principal source of funds for education, school board budgets can be a major political issue each year. In many communities, debates between factions on the board advocating increased spending to improve schools and factions demanding budget cuts to minimize property taxes can become heated and intense. It is not surprising, then, that for six consecutive years (from 1983 to 1988) a national poll of school board members identified a lack of financial support as the biggest problem facing education in their districts. Other problems, in order of priority, were those of curriculum development, dealing with state mandates, facilities, and management/leadership issues (Cameron, Underwood, & Fortune 1988).

School boards usually conduct open meetings on a regular basis. When people outside the board want to present opinions or information to it, they formally request that their names and the issue they wish to address be placed on the agenda. This is usually done by submitting a written request in advance of the meeting. Rarely will the board allow people to speak without a formal request. When dealing with sensitive issues, such as personnel matters, the board meets in private session, called an executive or closed session. Some local boards are not permitted to hold executive sessions.

Each school board elects a chairperson to deal directly with the superintendent and to moderate meetings, setting their tone and keeping them on track. The chairperson can control meetings by his or her leadership style: the way he or she organizes agenda items, recognizes members and observers, interprets parliamentary procedure in determining whether motions or discussions are in order, and allows discussion and debate to develop. In theory, the chairperson should not use the position to influence other board members. In fact, before the chairperson speaks to an issue, he or she must relinquish the chair temporarily. In practice, however, the chairperson can influence votes through the political acumen and use of the power of the office. Consequently, the position of chairperson of the school board can be very powerful.

Box 5.4 is a hypothetical example of a typical school board agenda and illustrates the type of issues that board members have to deal with and the types of decisions they make. Notice the variety of actions the school board must consider in this single session: from approving a class trip to granting a costly transportation contract; from approving a school calendar to accepting building blueprints. The range of the agenda shown in Box 5.4 is one of the reasons the school committee must rely so heavily on its chief executive officer, the superintendent, and why this individual is so powerful.

Superintendent of Schools

The leader of the school district's daily operations is the superintendent of schools. In most cases, the superintendent is appointed by the school board. In some states (for example, Alabama and Tennessee), voters within the school district elect the superintendent. In both cases, the superintendent is the chief executive officer and advisor to the board. Most school districts have a full-time superintendent. Some rural districts share a superintendent, and others may have a principal fulfill a superintendent's responsibilities. However, given the growing importance and number of responsibilities of the superintendency, these exceptions are not as prevalent as they were in the past. (See Box 5.5 for a job description of a superintendent.)

A spirit of cooperation must exist between the superintendent and the

BOX 5.4 Board of Education Agenda—Deloville School District, Monday, January 11, 1988, 7:00 p.m., High School Library

I. Approval of 12/22/87 School Board Minutes
II. Committee Reports
   A. Building Committee
   B. Teacher Evaluation Committee
   C. Budget Committee
   D. Collective Bargaining Committee
   E. Athletic and Extracurricular Committee
III. Old Business
   A. Approval of transportation contract with V.C. Bus Co. Ms. Munson, Business Manager, and Mr. Condino, President of V.C. Bus. Co., will respond to questions about the contract.
   B. Sanction of the senior class trip to Washington, D.C. Peter Gailey, president of senior class, and Mr. Winn, senior class advisor, will speak to the issue.
   C. Review of revised blueprints for McCarthy Elementary School.
   D. Approval or denial of tenure for all eligible teachers. Superintendent Birrell will present an overview of personnel records and present recommendations and supporting evidence for denial or approval. Closed session.
IV. New Business
   A. Approval of Superintendent Birrell's recommended candidate for the high school English teaching vacancy.
   B. Approval of next year's school calendar.
   C. Discussion about requiring all seniors to pass a minimum competency test to graduate.
      1. Mr. Maxey, an alumnus; Ms. Smith, high school guidance counselor; Mr. Adams, private educational consultant; and Superintendent Birrell to speak on this issue.
      2. Presentation of Teacher of the Year Award to Mr. Thomas, high school history teacher.
V. Other Business

board if the goals of a district are to be achieved. The board is legally responsible for the operation of schools and programs. However, if a superintendent is to run the district, the board needs to delegate a certain degree of power to the superintendent. In return, the superintendent must assure the board that their intended policies are being implemented.

The superintendent is ultimately responsible for managing the funds within the district; maintaining a positive public image for the school system; acting as the educational leader for other administrators, teachers, and support personnel; establishing policies that facilitate the attainment of the district's goals; negotiating contracts with various employee groups; overseeing transportation; ensuring that the district's actions and policies are legal; and acting as a legislative liaison with state and federal lawmakers.

To successfully complete these tasks, a superintendent must be skilled in a number of areas. When superintendents were asked in a national survey to list what they thought were the most important ingredients needed for success, they identified general management skills, human relation skills, skills in data management and technology, a knowledge of the social and educational processes, the ability to resolve conflicts, political savvy, and research skills (Cunningham & Hentges, 1982).

The majority of superintendents are white males in their late forties. Only 3 percent come from minority backgrounds. Further, it is interesting to note that while a majority of teachers are female, only 4 percent of superin-

---

BOX 5.5 School Superintendent—Job Description

General qualifications:

1. State certification as a superintendent
2. Master's degree; doctorate in educational administration required by many districts
3. Strong leadership abilities
4. Experience in teaching and/or school administration
5. Alternatives to the above qualifications as the local school board and state certification officers find appropriate

How appointed:

By the local school board

Salary:

Salaries range from $33,000 to $125,000, with an average national salary of $64,580

Reports to:

School board

Source: Educational Research Service, Inc., 1987, p. vi.

tendents are women (Feistritzer, 1988). Women and minorities have made gains in other leadership positions in business and education over the past ten years, yet they have not made major gains in the office of superintendent.

Superintendents oversee numerous people within the district who help them run the school system. In most districts, an assistant superintendent or director will be in charge of such areas as the curriculum, personnel management, finance and purchasing, and pupil personnel. These managers, along with the superintendent and support staff, are generally referred to as the "central office" staff. In districts that do not employ assistants, the superintendent must perform all the duties we are about to describe under assistant superintendent categories.

Assistant Superintendent for Curriculum and Instruction

Curriculum and instruction (C&I) are critical areas for the local school district. The curriculum covers what will be taught, and instruction covers how it will be taught. The assistant superintendent in charge of C&I must formulate the curriculum for each grade level or subject area. Once the curriculum is set, textbooks geared to the curriculum must be adopted and purchased, other instructional materials designed or purchased, and teachers trained in their use. Once these tasks are accomplished, the assistant superintendent for C&I must continually evaluate the effectiveness of all the district's educational programs. Are goals and objectives of the curriculum being achieved? Are they being implemented in the most cost-effective manner? What changes, if any, need to occur? What new materials are available?

The assistant superintendent for C&I must be continually up to date on new developments in curriculum and instruction. He or she must know the current professional literature in crucial areas and attend professional meetings and talk to subject matter specialists. Further, he or she must have excellent human relation skills, since much of the work must be done through committees of teachers and department heads. Similarly, the director of C&I

BOX 5.6 Assistant Superintendent for Curriculum and Instruction—Job Description

General qualifications:

1. State certification for assistant superintendent/director of curriculum and instruction
2. Master's degree or doctorate in either educational administration or curriculum and instruction
3. Experience in teaching
4. Alternatives to the above qualifications as the local board and/or state certification officers find appropriate

How appointed:

By recommendation of the superintendent and approval by the school board

Salary:

Average salary is $48,810

Reports to:

Superintendent

Source: Educational Research Service, Inc., 1987, p. 15.

must keep abreast of changing values, attitudes, and needs within the community. This is accomplished by ongoing discussion with residents, reading the local news and, when necessary, conducting survey research. (See Box 5.6 for a description of an assistant superintendent for C&I.)

Assistant Superintendent for Personnel

The backbone of any organization is its employees. An assistant superintendent in charge of personnel—often called the director of personnel—must develop procedures for recruitment and hiring to identify and select the best candidates for a number of professional and nonprofessional positions. (See Box 5.7 for a job description of an assistant superintendent for personnel.) Personnel directors advertise positions in professional journals and in local and national newspapers. (*The New York Times* Sunday edition has many ads for positions for school districts nationwide, as does *Education Week.*) They also visit college campuses to recruit new teachers. In the mid- to late 1970s, the supply of teachers was considerably larger than the demand, and many qualified teachers were seeking jobs. This teacher glut was due in part to a declining student population that forced districts to reduce their staff (often called reduction in force, or RIF) and/or hire fewer new teachers and support people than in the past. More recently, in certain parts of the country (particularly the Sun Belt) teacher shortages have developed in mathematics, science, and other specialized areas, making recruitment more difficult. Future enrollment trends indicate that a shortage of teachers will continue. Therefore, the recruitment and retention of good teachers will increase in importance for the personnel manager.

Once hired, the new employee must be introduced to the school system. Initial training programs to familiarize new employees with procedures and expectations are usually conducted by the personnel manager. These training sessions are important if new employees are to feel comfortable and be productive during their first year in the school system.

The maintenance of employee records is also the responsibility of the personnel manager. Accurate records are necessary if benefits are to be paid, accountability and affirmative action standards met, and adherence to state and federal guidelines documented. The director of personnel must be knowl-

---

BOX 5.7 Assistant Superintendent for Personnel—Job Description

General qualifications:

1. State certification as personnel director
2. Experience in labor negotiations, human resource development, or related field
3. Master's degree or beyond in personnel management or related field
4. Alternatives to the above qualifications as the local board and/or state certification officers find appropriate

How appointed:

Recommended to the local board by the superintendent

Salary:

Average salary is $48,627

Reports to:

Person designated by the local school board or superintendent

---

Source: Educational Research Service, Inc., 1987, p. 15.

edgeable about a number of legal issues, record keeping, and automated data management systems, since most personnel files are now computerized.

The director of personnel must coordinate the staff evaluation program. Although the director may leave the actual assessment of personnel performance to other administrators (for example, the principal or department heads), it is his or her responsibility to ensure that the individual's rights are protected during the evaluation process, that documentation is accurate and complete, and that final decisions regarding retention, promotion, or termination of staff are justified and are arrived at fairly. The issue of teacher evaluation is extremely important and is covered in more detail in later chapters.

Practically all personnel in the education system work on a contractual basis. In most cases, these contracts are agreed upon by a process called collective bargaining. Collective bargaining involves the management team negotiating working conditions and salaries with the representatives of the employees' unions or professional associations. While the board officially assumes responsibility for the contract, the management team advises and sometimes sits on the board's side in developing the contracts. The personnel manager plays a key role in these negotiations and in advising the superintendent and board on the implications of competing salary and benefits packages (for example, health insurance, retirement, vacation) and the staffing and cost implications of proposals regarding working conditions (for example, limits on class size). He or she will often work closely with the assistant superintendent for finance (whose job is discussed below) in calculating costs and budget implications. Once the contract is agreed upon, the personnel manager must monitor its implementation and ensure that employees adhere to it. Collective bargaining as it relates to teachers will be discussed in more detail later.

Assistant Superintendent for Pupil Personnel Services

Being a student in our contemporary society is not always easy for some children and adolescents. Many of them must deal with stress caused by such

---

BOX 5.8 Assistant Superintendent for Pupil Personnel Services—Job Description

General qualifications:

1. State certification as pupil personnel director
2. Experience in guidance counseling, pupil support services, or special education
3. Master's degree or beyond in pupil personnel–related field
4. Alternatives to the above qualifications as determined by the local board and/or state certification officers

How appointed:

Recommended to the local school board by superintendent

Salary:

Average salary is $40,731

Reports to:

Person designated by the local school board or superintendent

---

Source: Educational Research Service, Inc., 1987, p. 15.

factors as family conflict, divorce, child abuse, alcoholism and drug abuse in the home, poverty, physical and mental disabilities, and poor health. The assistant superintendent for pupil services, commonly called the director of pupil personnel services, is in charge of programs designed to help children to cope with such disruptive factors. (See Box 5.8 for a description of an assistant superintendent for pupil personnel services.)

The director of pupil personnel must continually be alert to students in need of help. To do this, the director must ensure that pupil records are complete and that information on grades, test scores, assessments, and teacher judgments are up to date. The director must also ensure that records are kept confidential and used appropriately.

The planning, development, and supervision of testing programs to assess student progress also form an important component of the director's job. Numerous standardized tests are available to measure various aspects of student achievement, aptitude, and abilities. The director is responsible for ensuring that the tests selected are valid and are used correctly.

Special education and counseling services will be needed to address the noninstructional needs of certain students. The director of pupil services is responsible for the provision of services in both areas. With the implementation of Public Law 94-142 in the late 1970s, the requirements for specialized services have increased dramatically. Because of this important federal law, extensive guidelines and procedures must be adhered to in designing and implementing general programs for students with disabilities. The director must also oversee the cooperative development and monitoring of individual educational plans (IEP) for students covered under Public Law 94-142. State and federal procedures must be followed in regard to children with disabilities, and must be documented so that the state department of education has appropriate evidence of compliance.

The director of pupil services also supervises the system's psychologists and guidance counselors, ensuring that they deal with the emotional problems of students and provide them with proper career and academic guidance.

Source: Educational Research Service, Inc., 1987, p. 15.

(Guidance counselors serve many important roles within the school district and will be described later in this chapter.) The director must also make sure that the counselor carries out these functions in collaboration with teachers, principals, and other school personnel. Finally, the director must provide referrals when the school psychologist or counselor feels specialized help is necessary.

Assistant Superintendent for Finance and Budget

Education is the most expensive portion of any municipality's budget. Many school districts operate with budgets in excess of several million dollars. Districts receive state and federal money in addition to local funds. The budget director must monitor the receipt of local, state, and federal funds and keep track of how they are spent. Funds from different sources require different accounting procedures and analyses. These procedures are defined by the state or federal agency providing the funds and must be followed exactly. Once the funds are received, it is the business manager's job to translate all the district's programs into fiscal terms in order to build the overall budget for the district. (See Box 5.9 for a job description of an assistant superintendent for finance and budget.)

Developing a budget is but one aspect of the business manager's responsibility. Once the budget is developed, it must be presented to the board of education for review and approval. The business manager must work locally with the superintendent during this approval process. Since school board members are elected to oversee the district's expenditures, getting board approval is not always easy. Generally, when the budget is presented to the board, members examine it line by line and raise questions about various items. The budget may have to be revised several times before a final vote by the board. To see the budget through this process the business manager must be well prepared, be patient, and have excellent interpersonal skills.

In addition to his or her fiscal responsibilities, the business manager is

Source: Educational Research Service, Inc., 1987, p. 15.

often in charge of the maintenance of the system's physical plants and grounds. This requires the supervision of custodial staff, the negotiation of contracts for such things as repairs and heating oil, inspection of work completed, and the planning of future renovation and expansion. The role of business manager has grown in importance as expenditures for education have increased and the public has demanded greater returns for their tax dollar. Since fiscal responsibilities are so important, even some of the smallest school districts employ a business manager.

The Principal

The principal of a school is responsible for everything that goes on in the school building. He or she must provide leadership for the entire staff. Although overall policy about curriculum and instruction is set at the central office and board levels, the responsibility for implementation falls on the

A building principal must work closely with teachers in order to run an effective school.

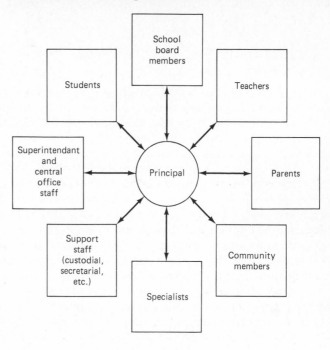

principal's shoulders. This places the principal in a highly visible middle-management position. To be successful, a principal must have organizational skills, be able to work with a wide range of people, and have a commitment to providing students with the best possible educational experience. (See Box 5.10 for a description of a principal's job.)

The principal is manager of a complex institution and is responsible for ordering supplies and materials, overseeing the maintenance of facilities, developing budgets, keeping accurate records, and completing reports as required by state and district policy. If the school is to run smoothly, the principal must also coordinate the work schedules of office staff, teachers, specialists, custodians, cafeteria workers, teacher aids, specialists, and those responsible for student transportation. These day-to-day responsibilities are often referred to as the *administrative* functions of the job. An effective principal must also function in an *instructional* capacity, working with the staff and students on matters more directly related to teaching and instruction.

Working with people who have a vested interest in the school is the most important and time-consuming part of the principal's job. Research has indicated that, on average, a principal spends about three-quarters of the day interacting with others (Morris, Crowson, Porter-Gehrie, & Hurwitz, 1984). Figure 5.1 illustrates some of the people who come in contact with the principal on a daily basis. These people often hold differing points of view and have different expectations for what schools should do. The successful principal must constructively manage conflict between groups, and not lose sight of what is best for students. The process of managing conflict, keeping the school working toward goal achievement, and evaluating and trying to help improve performance of employees are all part of what is often referred to as some of the *supervisory* responsibilities of the principal.

In large schools, the job of principal is simply too much for one person, and most systems appoint assistant or associate principals, housemasters, or administrative assistants to help the building principal meet the responsibilities of the post. Even with assistance, principals often spend long hours both at school working on instructional issues and after school attending meetings, extracurricular activities, athletic events, and community functions. Given the importance of the principal's responsibilities, it is not surprising to find that the reform reports we discuss later in this text all identify the building principal and classroom teachers as the key people in making schools more effective.

Department Chairperson

In larger schools, at both the high school and junior high or middle school levels, the curriculum requires that a person with expertise in a specific content area have responsibility for coordinating the activities of all the teachers within that discipline. The person assigned these duties at the school level is usually referred to as the department chairperson. The chairperson is responsible for a specific subject area and is accountable to the building principal and central office administrator in charge of curriculum and instruction. Many secondary schools have department chairpersons in charge of English, social studies, mathematics, foreign languages, and vocational education. (See Box 5.11 for a job description of a department chairperson.)

The department chairperson is first and foremost an expert in the discipline for which he or she is responsible. This ability is important in helping the building principal make informed decisions regarding curriculum matters and is necessary if the chairperson is to give technical assistance to the faculty in the department and work with the superintendent for C&I.

The department chairperson must also be aware of the content that must be covered in the various courses at all the grade levels within his or her field. This knowledge of content is important so that the appropriate material is covered in the proper sequence, necessary skills developed, and overlap between courses minimized. The chairperson also takes responsibility for helping teachers design new courses and, when necessary, revise or eliminate the current ones. Many school systems—generally under the supervision of the superintendent for C&I—involve teachers in the development and selection of curriculum and instructional materials. The department chairperson usually oversees this process in the school. Although final decisions about materials are usually made at the board and central office levels, recommendations from teachers and department chairpersons are usually the basis for their actions.

Since principals cannot be specialists in all areas of the curriculum, they must depend on department chairpersons to help in the evaluation of programs and staff. The process of evaluation requires skills that go beyond the knowledge of the content. To conduct evaluations, department chairpersons need training in how to observe teacher behavior and appraise their performance. Since the major purpose of any evaluation is to improve the teaching and learning experience, the final step of sharing the results of the evaluation with the teacher is most important. Criticism and commendation must be communicated in such a manner that it leads to personal and professional growth for teachers.

Because of the nature of the position, department chairpersons can sometimes be caught between the administration and faculty colleagues. They are directly responsible to the building principal for what goes on in their departments and the director of C&I. However, they are teachers themselves and are concerned with the interests of other teachers. Chairpersons must live with these dual roles and must resolve conflicts with the best interest of the student in mind.

Source: Educational Research Service, Inc., 1987, p. 15.

Guidance Counselors and Other Support Staff

Pressures resulting from trauma, parental conflict, demands for academic performance, and peer acceptance are among the many problems that can adversely affect students. In addition to assistance in handling such interpersonal stress, students need guidance in planning their future. To help students with these issues, school districts provide guidance counseling and other related support services. (See Box 5.12 for a job description of a guidance counselor.)

The first responsibility guidance personnel assume is that of promoting in students a healthy attitude toward life. The American School Counselors Association (ASCA) official statement of the counselor's role identifies the following functions that counselors should provide:

- *Structured developmental guidance experiences presented systematically through groups (including classrooms) to promote growth of psychological aspects of human development (e.g. ego, career, emotional, moral, and social development). Such interventions can logically become an integral part of such curriculum areas as social studies, language arts, health, or home economics. Individual or small group counseling is provided when the needs deserve more attention and privacy.*
- *Consultation with, and in-service training for, teachers to increase their communication skills, improve the quality of their interaction with all students, and make them more sensitive to the need for matching the curriculum to developmental needs of students.*
- *Consultation and life skills education for parents to assist them to understand developmental psychology, to improve family communication skills, and to develop strategies for encouraging learning in their children (American School Counselors Association, 1981).*

The ASCA role description also identifies specific factors that need to be addressed at each of the grade levels. Since students vary according to their developmental stages, different areas need attention during the elementary,

Source: Educational Research Service, Inc., 1987, p. 15.

middle or junior high school, and high school grade levels. The functions identified for elementary school counselors are as follows:

- *Provide in-service training to teachers to assist them with planning and implementing guidance interventions for young children (preschool to 3rd grade) in order to maximize developmental benefits (self-esteem, personal relationships, positive school attitude, sexfair choices, and so forth) in the hope of preventing serious problems or minimizing the size of such problems if and when they do occur.*
- *Provide consultations for teachers who need understanding and assistance with incorporating developmental concepts in teaching content as well as support for building a healthy classroom environment.*

Guidance counselors help students deal with problems ranging from family conflict to planning for future life.

- *Accommodate parents who need assistance with understanding normal child growth and development, improving family communication skills, or understanding their role in encouraging their child to learn.*
- *Cooperate with other school staff in the early identification, remediation, or referral of children with developmental deficiencies or handicaps.*
- *As children reach the upper elementary grades, effort is directed through the curriculum toward increasing student awareness of the relationship between school and work, especially the impact of educational choices on one's life style and career development (American School Counselors Association, 1981).*

At the middle or junior high school level, students are in transition from childhood to adolescence. This period can be extremely stressful for some students, teachers, and parents due to the many changes in the physical, cognitive, social, and emotional developmental processes within the adolescent. The ASCA indicates that the major functions of the counselor at this developmental level are to

- *Concentrate efforts (through group guidance, peer facilitators, and teacher in-service training) to smooth the transition for students from the more confining environment of the lower school to the middle or junior high school where students are expected to assume greater responsibility for their own learning and personal development.*
- *Identify, encourage, and support teachers (through in-service training, consultation, and co-teaching) who are interested in incorporating developmental units in such curriculum areas as English, social studies, health, and home economics.*
- *Organize and implement a career guidance program for students that includes an assessment of their career maturity and career-planning status; easy access to relevant career information; and assistance with processing data for personal use in schoolwork-related decision making (American School Counselors Association, 1981).*

High school counselors must focus on addressing the varying needs of adolescents and preparing them for life after high school. These counselors become very visible figures at this level, since most students seek their advice and counsel regarding career and educational decisions and the more intimate problems they face. The ASCA identifies the following functions as important for high school counselors:

- *Organize and implement through interested teachers guidance curricula interventions that focus upon important developmental concerns of adolescents (identity, career choice and planning, social relationships, and so forth).*

- *Organize and make available comprehensive information systems (print, computer-based, audiovisual) necessary for educational-vocational planning and decision making.*
- *Assist students with assessment of personal characteristics (e.g., competencies, interests, aptitudes, needs, career maturity) for personal use in such areas as course selection, post-high-school planning, and career choices.*
- *Provide remedial interventions or alternative programs for those students showing in-school adjustment problems, vocational immaturity, or general negative attitudes toward personal growth (American School Counselors Association, 1981).*

Since the issues addressed by counselors require specialized help at times, many schools employ school psychologists, social workers, speech and hearing therapists, and nurses as support personnel. These professionals are usually used on a referral basis.

The school psychologist conducts assessments of students referred to them, offers them suggestions for academic programs or how to modify their behavior, and acts as a consultant to teachers and counselors on a case-by-case basis. In certain situations, school psychologists provide therapy for students and parents if the child's school problems warrant the intervention.

Social workers work with families experiencing difficulties that are affecting their children's school life. Social workers coordinate and monitor services provided to students by various human service agencies outside the school system. These can include, but are not limited to, the juvenile court system, public welfare agencies, and foster-care homes.

CONCLUSION

In this chapter, we presented an overview of the various policy and administrative roles that are critical in the state and local educational systems. Obviously, we have not mentioned all the professional positions (for example, the athletic director, the reading specialist), nor did we deal with key nonprofessional positions (such as the custodian or clerks, without whom the system would grind to a halt). Although each state and district has unique titles and names for people fulfilling the functions discussed above, the tasks that have been outlined are relatively similar across states and districts. Different positions involve different responsibilities, yet all who play a role in the educational system have as their ultimate goal the provision of educational experiences that will meet individual student needs as well as the needs of society. The work they do should help the classroom teacher, who ultimately has the most direct influence on students, do a better job.

QUESTIONS AND ACTIVITIES

1. Arrange an interview with a person who is currently filling one of the roles described in this chapter. How do this person's perceptions of his or her role responsibilities differ from those outlined in the chapter?

2. Interview a teacher to determine how he or she thinks people filling the roles described in this chapter affect his or her classroom. In the teacher's opinion, who has the most impact?
3. Why do you feel there are so few minority and female superintendents? What could be done to change this?
4. What are the issues that your state board of education is currently considering? What impact might they have upon you as a future educator?
5. Attend a local board of education meeting. How much of the meeting is devoted to discussion, debate, and policy-making about substantive education issues? What other issues are addressed during the meeting?

CHAPTER 6

Alternatives to the Public Schools

Nonpublic (private) schools constitute a small but important part of American education, educating about 10 percent of all elementary and secondary school students.

● There are five types of nonpublic schools: Catholic schools, traditional church-related Protestant and Jewish schools, Christian fundamentalist schools, independent schools, and special schools for students with special needs.
● Nonpublic schools have a long and distinguished history of service dating back to the nineteenth century. Before that, there was little separation between private and public schools and the latter were not religiously neutral.
● The courts have played an important part in legitimizing nonpublic schools.
● Financial aid to nonpublic schools comes from both federal and state sources. This aid cannot help the schools directly but must have as its primary intent the provision of services to children.
● Nonpublic schools are characterized by decentralization and autonomy at the local school level.
● Nonpublic schools serve a variety of publics from upper-income to lower-income groups across the range of rural and ethnic groups.
● A key difference between the public and nonpublic sectors is that public schools are not free to choose whom they will educate and have to deal with serious problems with which nonpublic schools do not usually have to contend.
● Voucher plans have been proposed to aid nonpublic schools by providing parents with the money to choose a type of school.

Chapter 4 dealt with the structure of American public education, and Chapter 5 with the roles people play in the system. In this chapter, we turn to a small but important segment of American education outside the public sector known as nonpublic, or private, education. In the chapter, we will describe the current status of private education, its history and legal standing, government aid to private schools, how its schools are organized, and the public it serves. We will also look at significant questions raised by the existence of private schools. These questions deal with the roles of family choice, religious and personal values, and competition in education.

The Current State of Private Schooling

In recent decades, public schools in the United States have served approximately 90 percent of students. The other 10 percent attend private schools (Stern, 1987). Unlike public schools, which in their basic organization tend to be alike, private schools do not fit one description. In general, there are five types of private school:

1. Catholic schools, which include parish and regional schools
2. Traditional church-related schools, which include Lutheran, Episcopal, and Jewish schools
3. Fundamentalist schools, which include the new wave of Christian schools
4. Independent schools, which include the members of the National Association of Independent Schools
5. Special schools, which serve students with special needs in day or residential programs

These categories are not always mutually exclusive. For example, independent schools, sometimes referred to as high-tuition schools, include some Catholic and traditional church-related schools. The same overlap can be found in the category of special schools, which serve students with handicapping conditions or other special needs.

In 1980, Catholic schools represented one half of all private schools and enrolled close to two-thirds of all private school students, despite a 40 percent decline in Catholic school enrollment since 1966. Lutheran schools, the other large church-affiliated group, made up 7 percent of private schools and served 4 percent of all private school students. There were 300 Hebrew all-day schools in 1980, most of which were founded since 1940 (National Center for Education Statistics, 1982).

While Catholic school enrollment has declined, the fundamentalist Christian schools experienced dramatic growth in the 1970s and early 1980s. One association of fundamentalist schools based in Whittier, California, reported an increase from 500 schools and 63,111 students in 1976 to 1,482 schools serving 289,001 students in 1980 (*The New York Times,* April 13, 1983). The same *New York Times* article reported that from 1970 to 1980, the number of students in religious schools other than Catholic increased 47 percent in the Northeast, 49 percent in the Midwest, 99 percent in the West, and 314 percent in the Middle Atlantic and South, where in 1980, over half the total enrollment in fundamentalist Christian schools occurred. The member schools of the prestigious National Association of Independent Schools (NAIS) also increased their enrollment between 1965 (when it was 199,329) and 1975 (277,406).

More than one-half of all nonpublic schools in the United States are Catholic schools.

Despite these patterns of change in private school enrollment during a period of desegregation, busing, and a crisis of confidence in public schools, the general balance between public and private school enrollment has not changed noticeably for various sections of the population. Figure 6.1 shows that overall, enrollment in private schools relative to that in the public schools has remained relatively stable from 1970 to 1985. In fact, the proportion of private school students was the same in 1985 as it had been in 1970. In 1969, 16.9 percent of students in central city areas attended private schools; in 1979, the percentage was 16.3. In 1969, 12.2 percent of white students attended private schools; ten years later, 11 percent attended. During those ten years, however, the percentage of black students in private schools increased from 3.9 to 5.3 (Bell, 1983). These national statistics do not necessarily reflect significant changes that may have taken place in local areas where court-ordered busing and turbulent conditions in public schools have resulted in either an increase in private school enrollments or a leveling off of previously declining enrollments.

Historical Origins

The Era Before Public and Private Schools

The present pattern of American education for both public schools and private schools developed in the nineteenth century. Before that time, a clear

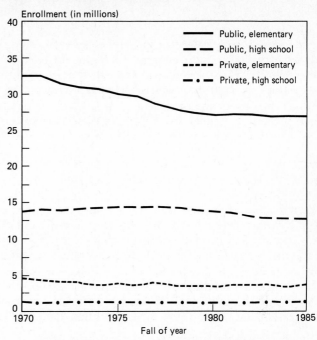

FIGURE 6.1 Public and Private School Enrollment by Grade Level: 1970–1985

Enrollment (in millions)

Public, elementary
Public, high school
Private, elementary
Private, high school

Fall of year

- Elementary school enrollment dropped during the 1970s in both public and private schools, but underwent little or no change in the first half of the 1980s.

- High school enrollment in public schools rose during the early and mid-1970s but then dropped.

- Private school enrollment at the high school level changed little from 1970 to 1985.

Source: Stern, 1987, p. 59.

distinction between private and public schools was not made (Bailyn, 1960). In the colonies, schools were seen as extensions of the family, the church, and the apprenticeship system—not as an arm of government. Civil authorities were asked to help with education only when other resources proved wanting. Schools were supported by legacies, by subscriptions from wealthy families, by rates or tuition, and by funds from the local treasury. Schools were established in all sorts of places—in worn-out tobacco fields ("old field schools"), in private homes, and in parish buildings, as well as in school buildings. In Massachusettes, there were "petty" and grammar schools, roughly corresponding to present-day elementary and secondary schools. The petty schools were often "dame" schools, that is, a household school conducted by a mother or a "maiden lady." Such schooling was neither free nor religiously neutral. (The preamble to the Massachusetts School Act used religious terms to warn of the "Old Deluder Satan" who kept men from the knowledge of Scriptures.)

Education in the Colonial Period

By the end of the colonial period, the school as an institution was firmly rooted in the American continent. But nothing resembling the modern concept of secular, free, compulsory universal education had as yet appeared. Even the impressive rhetoric of the Bay Colony's school laws envisioned a role for schooling quite different from that which developed in the twentieth century. The colonial schools were conceived to be supplemental to the informal education that the child received in the home, in church, on the farm, in the shop, in commerce, in village life, and by reading and self-study (Kraushaar, 1976, p. 15).

The major development in education immediately after the colonial period was the rise of the academies. While the rudiments of learning were provided for by an array of local or town schools, the need arose for precollege schools, which would be more comprehensive in curriculum than the classical grammar schools. These schools, usually called academies, were needed to provide college preparatory as well as terminal programs. The best academies overlapped and challenged the colleges; the poorest were only slightly above the level of the town school. In 1865, the national school census listed 6,185 academies, with an enrollment of 296,096 students.

Private Academies

In their heyday before the Civil War, private academies competed successfully with public schools. Academies served the middle class effectively in many areas and often received indirect public support, such as land grants, special funds drawing from state fees, and the proceeds of lotteries. Until the high school appeared, they were viewed as "public" institutions and a training ground for local leaders in the communities they served. Their demise is thought to be intimately connected with urbanization, since they were a rural institution (James, 1982, pp. 15–16).

The contribution of the academies included increased attention to instruction in the sciences, the introduction of pedagogy and courses in teacher education, and extended opportunities for the education of young women, either in coeducational or separate academies.

After the Civil War, the academies began a slow decline. In 1879, private academies and the preparatory departments of private colleges enrolled about 73 percent of all secondary students. As the public high school took hold, the number fell to 32 percent by 1890. By 1920, enrollment in private schools amounted to only 7 percent. The academies became mostly elite schools serving the well-to-do. They now serve fewer than 10 percent of private school students.

The Rise of Public and Church-Related Schools

After the Civil War, the distinction between public and private schools began to be clearly drawn. Along with the rise of the public schools, the main segment of present-day private education—church-related schools—began a period of rapid growth. For the most part, these schools were established as a response to the perceived religious posture of the public schools.

From their inception, public schools were officially neutral in their religious stance, yet they did reflect the social and religious values of local communities. Horace Mann and other early public school leaders had assumed that public schools would impart values that were religiously grounded, though free from any specific denominational allegiance. For over a century, religion in public schools was a "generalized" Protestantism based on the King James Bible, the Episcopal Book of Common Prayer, and moral counsels in the primer, some of them openly anti-Catholic. This generic brand of Protestantism incorporated into the life of the public schools contributed directly to the founding of Catholic schools and denominational Protestant schools (Kraushaar, 1976).

The rise of the Catholic schools in this country can be related directly to the large-scale immigration of Catholics in the nineteenth and early twentieth centuries. This influx of foreign-born Catholics prompted an often vitriolic and occasionally violent anti-Catholic campaign by Protestant and nativist groups. The campaign found its way into public school classrooms. One primer described the Pope as "the man of sin . . . worthy of thy utmost hatred" (Kraushaar, 1976, p. 15). The response of the Catholic community was to build its own schools. By 1860, 200 parochial schools were in operation. By 1870, there were 1,341 such schools. After years of debate, in 1884 the American bishops officially required every parish to maintain a parish school. By 1910, 5,186 parish elementary schools enrolled over 1.2 million students. This enrollment grew to 2 million in 1940. In a post–World War II boom, 2,000 elementary schools and 2.5 million students were added. By 1965 Catholic schools had reached an all-time enrollment peak of over 5.3 million elementary and secondary students. From then on, due to changes in the church and demographic shifts, Catholic school enrollment declined. By 1980, enrollments had fallen to 3.2 million, or roughly to their 1950 level.

The religious climate in public schools—especially as it affected Catholic students—changed dramatically in 1920 when Herbert Hoover defeated Al Smith, the Catholic governor of New York, for the presidency, and again in 1960 when John F. Kennedy, the Catholic senator from Massachusetts, became President. After World War II, as the public schools became more secularized, Catholic concern over their Protestant character lessened.

While the diminished religious stance of public schools made some Catholics comfortable with them, it made some evangelical Protestants uncomfortable. For years, the official stance of the fundamentalist denominations had been that public schools were sufficiently neutral and sufficiently religious to be suitable for their children, as long as the children were given adequate religious preparation in home and church. The 1963 United States Supreme Court decision *(Engle* v. *Vitale)* that outlawed official prayer and Bible reading in the public schools changed that stance. Many people of the fundamentalist faith decided to send their children to private schools. Christian fundamentalists claimed that compulsory schooling applied to their children amounted to an unconstitutional establishment of "secular humanism," which they regarded as a secular religious ideology (Arons, 1985). Furthermore, fundamentalists were disturbed by "drugs, sex, and rock" in public schools, the use of public monies to teach birth control, the life-styles of some teachers whom school boards were now powerless to remove, and the public schools' refusal to permit the teaching of creationism (Arons, 1985; Erickson, 1983).

The Legal Test of Private Schooling

The recourse that churches and other groups have taken in setting up their own schools has not gone unchallenged. In fact, private education has played a significant role in defining the legal status of all schooling in the United States. As Thomas James (1982) has pointed out, "Rights of private associations have been an edge against which the state has defined its role in schooling. On the other hand, state authority has been the edge against which private schools have asserted their identity" (p. 15).

The most important legal test of the legitimacy of private sectarian schools took place after World War I. By that time, public schooling had become the dominant pattern of schooling in America and some people felt it should be the only one. Reflecting this mood, the people of Oregon passed a referendum that required parents to send every "normal" child between the ages of 8 and 16 to a public school. This law was challenged in the courts and, in a 1925 decision *(Pierce* v. *Society of Sisters and Hill Military Academy),* the United States Supreme Court overturned the Oregon law and supported the claim of private schools for protection. The Court held that the law "unreasonably interferes with the liberty of parents and guardians to direct the upbringing of children under their control." The Court also asserted that "The child is not the mere creature of the state." While the state has a legitimate interest in compelling some form of schooling, the Court held that Oregon had gone too far in limiting the option to public schools. In the same judgment, the Court also affirmed the state's power "to regulate all schools, to inspect, supervise and examine them, their teachers and pupils; to require that all children of proper age attend some school, that teachers shall be of good moral character and patriotic disposition, that certain studies plainly essential to good citizenship must be taught, and that nothing be taught which is manifestly inimical to the public welfare."

A 1983 United States Supreme Court decision recognized the public contribution of private schools. In *Mueller* v. *Allen,* the Court upheld a Minnesota law that grants state income tax deductions for education expenses incurred by parents of students enrolled in public or private schools. The majority opinion affirmed that private or parochial schools, quite apart from their sectarian purpose, "have provided an educational alternative for millions of young Americans; they often afford wholesome competition with our public schools; and in some states they relieve substantially the tax burden incident to the operations of public schools." The state, moreover, has "a legitimate interest in facilitating education of the highest quality for all children within its boundaries, whatever school their parents have chosen for them." Thus, in 60 years, the highest court of the land has moved from acknowledging the right of private schools to exist to recognizing the positive contribution of these schools to American education.

Between these two decisions, courts have grappled with the limits of parent and state authority over education. In virtually every state, the enforcement of minimum standards for private schools comes through the vehicle of compulsory-attendance laws. Some states require attendance at schools with certified teachers, others at approved schools, and others at schools that provide only minimal evidence that schooling is taking place. States with strict teacher certification requirements are at times pressed into taking court and police actions in enforcing their laws. For example, recently Maine and Massachusetts have challenged the refusal of Christian fundamentalist schools to comply with teacher certification laws. In both instances, the federal courts ruled in favor of the Christian schools (*Braintree Baptist Temple, et al.* v. *Holbrook Public School et al.,* 1987; *Bangor Baptist et al.* v. *State of Maine,* 1985). Some states (for example, North Carolina) have chosen to deregulate private schooling entirely or in part. That is, they have exempted private schools from state attendance or teacher certification requirements.

Instruction in the home as a form of "private schooling" has been used to test the role of the state in education. Estimates of the number of children who receive schooling at home ranged from 10,000 to 100,000 in 1982. Such estimates are complicated by the practice of listing family groups taught by parents as "small schools." In 1982, laws in 38 states permitted home instruction in some form or another. Some educators have advocated schooling at home as a way of recapturing the rugged, pioneering spirit of America (Holt, 1981). Others see a future for home schooling through use of video and computer hookups.

Government Aid to Private Schools

Government assistance to private schools has come from both state and federal sources. In 1981, more than half of the states provided some form of aid for children in private schools (Duffy, 1981). The kinds of assistance provided included transportation (27 states), health services (26 states), vocational education (usually at a nearby public school) (23 states), aid for students with a handicapping condition (17 states), textbook loans (16 states), testing (14 states), guidance and counseling (9 states), loan of instructional materials (8 states), and remedial instruction (7 states).

Administrators have tried a number of approaches in seeking government aid to private schools. The courts have accepted only those methods that do not aid the schools directly, and that can be shown to have as their primary interest the provision of services to children, regardless of the type of schools they attend. The provision of state services to students in private schools increased between 1972 and 1982. Federal aid came chiefly from funds allocated under the Elementary and Secondary Education Act of 1965, which provided programs to aid disadvantaged students (Title I) and to augment school library resources (Title II). A 1982 survey showed that some 5 percent of nonpublic school students were served by Title I programs, usually at the nonpublic school they attended (Jung, 1982).

The Organization of Private Schools

The organization of private schools is characterized by decentralization and complete autonomy at the local school level. Even Catholic elementary schools that belong to a diocesan school "system" are only loosely directed at the diocesan level by their diocesan superintendent or director of schools. This autonomy is linked to the sources of funding for the schools, which, as a rule, are entirely local or school-based. With the exception of heavily endowed independent schools, the funds for private parochial schools come from tuition and local church, synagogue, or parish support. While such autonomy can have certain advantages for a school, particularly in terms of responding to local needs, it also means that the school may not have access to the support staff and services available in larger public school district organizations.

Differences in organization between private and public schools are reflected in the operating expenditures of schools. In a study comparing per pupil expenditures for different types of public and private schools, Sullivan (1983) found that Catholic schools spend less than public schools on instruction, administration, plant and equipment, and other services. This is, in part, accounted for by lower administration costs and teacher salaries, contributed services (that is, nuns, brothers, or priests teaching for a nominal salary), and higher student–teacher ratios. For example, Catholic private schools tend to have fewer instruction specialists (librarians, music and art teachers, and learning specialists) and to spend less than public schools on special-needs students.

While Catholic private schools are less expensive to run than public schools, other types of private school are more expensive. This is true of independent schools, which have much smaller classes and spend more than public schools for supplementry instructional personnel and for additional instructional and noninstructional services. The larger administrative costs of independent schools could reflect both their smaller enrollment and their added costs for admissions and recruitment.

The Public Served by Private Schools

Private schools differ from one another in the publics they serve. Independent private schools serve mostly upper-income families of business people and professionals. The majority of private schools, however, are church-related schools that serve families of skilled workers, professionals, and people in small businesses (Kraushaar, 1972).

Private and public schools are not, in fact, very dissimilar in the mix of students they serve. About 86 percent of high school students in private schools are non-Hispanic and white, compared with 76 percent in public schools. Hispanics were equally represented in both types of schools, constituting 6 percent of private school students and 7 percent of public school students. While blacks account for 14 percent of public school students, they account for 9 percent of students in the Catholic schools and 5 percent of students in the remaining private sector. Private high schools are not any more racially segregated than public high schools (Coleman, Hoffer, & Kilgore, 1982). However, how the growing number of minority school-age children will affect enrollment in nonpublic schools is difficult to discern at this stage.

Private schools do not function simply as alternatives to public schools. As a rule, they serve more particular needs of families. The reasons parents choose nonpublic schools vary with socioeconomic circumstances and with the type of school selected. In general, parents send students to independent schools for predominantly academic reasons—in particular, for the ability of these schools to prepare students for college (Baird, 1977). Similarly, inner-city parents tend to select nonpublic schools for academic reasons related to upward mobility, preparation for higher education, and classroom discipline and safety. Parents in middle-class suburban areas, however, tend to select private religious-affiliated schools chiefly for religious reasons (Gratiot, 1979; Kamin & Erickson, 1981). Parents who select comparatively new fundamentalist Christian schools do so predominantly for religious reasons linked to distrust of the public schools and rejection of some of the contemporary values of American society reflected in the public schools (Nevin & Bills, 1976; Turner, 1979).

A comparative study of inner-city public and Catholic school students attributed the relatively higher academic achievement of the students in the Catholic schools to their more supportive home environment (Levine, Lachowicz, Oxman, & Tangeman 1972). In another study in which Catholic and public high schools were compared, it was found that the families of nonpublic school students tended to be more motivated toward higher education and, in lower-middle-class families, toward social mobility through education (Morrison & Hodgkins, 1971). Several studies have confirmed the same pattern of higher educational aspirations among Hispanic students attending Catholic schools (Greeley, 1980; Lampe, 1973). Thus, a major difference between the publics served by public and private schools is the generally higher level of parent and student aspirations in the families served by private schools. The substantial influence that parents have on the achievement of their children—not only because of their own skills, knowledge, and capabilities, but by the motivation they provide—gives private schools a special advantage.

Choice of School

An important aspect of private schooling is that it allows family choice in the selection of a school. Such choice is not entirely absent from the public school system. Parents may choose to live in a neighborhood so that they can send their children to a particular school. Indeed, residential mobility in the interest of choosing a school seems to have increased over the years (Coleman, Hoffer, & Kilgore, 1982). However, choice is more obvious in the case of private schools.

There are a number of advantages that private schools are likely to have over public schools. First, parents who choose a school because it has particular characteristics are likely to be more supportive of the school than are parents who do not make that kind of choice. Second, the parents' attitudes toward the school and its mission are likely to be communicated to their children. Third, and this seems to apply only to religious schools, the relationship between the school and the parent community is likely to be strong and supportive of the school's values (Coleman, 1987). It is probably because of factors such as these that dropout rates before graduation are lower in private than in public schools (Coleman, Hoffer, & Kilgore, 1982) and that private schools in British Columbia were found to be superior to public schools on measures of student commitment, school effectiveness (assessed by parents), teacher commitment (as judged separately by teachers, parents, and students), social cohesion, school responsiveness to parents, sense of special mission, parental commitment, school justice, and student enthusiasm for work (Erickson, MacDonald, & Manley-Casimir, 1979). Following the partial public funding of private schools in British Columbia in 1978, there seems to have been a decline in these characteristics in private schools (Erickson & Nault, 1980; Erickson, 1981).

If parents are free to choose, so too are the private schools free to accept or reject students. That is not something the public school can do. "The central problem is that over the last 20 years, public schools have lost the authority to suspend or expel students and otherwise improve the disciplinary standards necessary for a productive school environment. Teachers in public schools have also lost the ability to impose academic demands like homework" (J. S. Coleman quoted in *New York Times,* April 26, 1981).

In the exercise of authority and discipline, it is a distinct advantage for a school to enjoy the support of students' families as well as to have the ability to suspend or expel unruly students. Because private schools have these advantages, they have higher student test scores and lower drop-out rates than public schools (see Coleman, Hoffer, & Kilgore, 1982; Coleman & Hoffer, 1987; Kane, 1987). However, public schools have the responsibility of educating *all* our students, the reluctant ones as well as the enthusiastic ones, and as long as this is so, they will have to deal with serious educational problems with which private schools generally do not have to contend.

Religion and Values in Education

Paul Hirst, an English philosopher of education, has commended the American public school as "a magnificent attempt at maintaining the strictest religious neutrality by the state while providing the best possible education for all" (1967, p. 33). Hirst argues that to be religiously neutral, the public school must confine itself to education that can be carried out within a framework of agreed-upon public values. It follows from this that public school teachers will be governed by "the objective concerns of the public world of reason," not by their own private beliefs and values. From this, Hirst concludes:

> *Precisely because the area of public values is not in general the
> total area of values for any individual, and because questions
> about the justification of values are frequently outside its
> competence, there are aspects of education which it (the public
> school) cannot appropriately undertake. That public schools
> necessarily have a limited scope is a simple point that needs much
> greater recognition than it normally gets (Hirst, 1967, p. 33).*

The problem in attempting to provide an education on the basis of agreed-upon public values has received the attention of a number of people. For example, Arons and Lawrence (1982) have considered the matter from a legal point of view and have argued that the present structure of education is inconsistent with the First Amendment and freedom of expression. They hold that it is neither sensible nor realistic to talk about value-neutral education as if it were attainable or desirable. Public education, according to Arons and Lawrence, is designed to inculcate "in rising generations those values and attitudes which support democratic institutions" (p. 235). This position is based on the assumption that educational and governmental decisions "are both the proper province of the political majority."

As Arons and Lawrence see it, the majority's control over what cultural and political values are taught in public schools is made tolerable only because parents have the right to choose a nonpublic school or the means to move into a different public school system. Because these safety valves protect the status quo, Arons and Lawrence contend that "majoritarian control of the transmission of personal belief, consensus, and world views through schooling is a problem whose magnitude is equaled only by our massive public refusal to discuss it" (ibid., p. 236).

Christian fundamentalists believe the public schools teach secular humanism, which in their view is not value-free but is a godless religion established by the public schools. However, the courts to date have not been persuaded by this view (Arons, 1985). A spokesperson for the fundamentalist Christian schools has described the dilemma seen by church educators in any effort to offer a curriculum that excludes religion: "Given that all the forms of knowledge are interrelated, religious knowledge must be logically interconnected with each of them. To attempt to separate religion from the rest of knowledge is to distort the structure of knowledge, and to do the latter is surely educationally subversive" (Thiessen, 1981, p. 63).

These views are shared by most educators in church-related schools. A Catholic position statement has echoed the same concerns. This statement noted that "an orthodoxy is expressed—inescapably so—even in a curriculum from which religious 'orthodoxies' are absent. . . . There is little guarantee that the public school can in actuality maintain a completely non-'value'-inculcating position" (NCWC Brief, 1981).

It is clear from these statements that private schools, especially church-related schools, have called attention to the role of religion and values in education. A consideration of these issues gives rise to a number of questions. How important are private beliefs and religious values in education? Can schools be religiously neutral? Can schools identify and adhere to publicly agreed-upon values? Are values for schools acceptable if they are simply those of the majority? These questions remain both important and unanswered.

Competition in Education

Private schools, by their very existence, raise issues regarding competition in the delivery of education. Because parents exercise choice in selecting a private school for their child and because private schools do not have the relatively assured revenue of public schools, some observers assume that private schools operate the way business firms operate in a competitive market. However, there are a number of ways in which private schools do not act like business firms. For example, since they are not oriented toward making profits, they are likely to start a waiting list rather than raise prices when demand exceeds supply (Garner & Hannaway, 1981).

The proponents of education voucher plans have argued that the benefits of market competition should be incorporated into education services. An educational voucher is a piece of paper that is redeemable for a designated sum of money that can be spent only on schooling. Two kinds of vouchers have been proposed: unrestricted and regulated. An "unrestricted" voucher could be used in any school, either alone or with additional funds paid by the individual or family. A "regulated" voucher could be used only in schools approved by the voucher agency and with no additions from family sources. Under either voucher plan, all schools, "public" and "private" alike, would be tuition-supported.

The proponents of the unrestricted-voucher plan see the concept as advancing the benefits of family choice and as eliminating the wastes and inefficiencies of the public monopoly in education (Friedman, 1973; West, 1981; Uzzell, 1985). Proponents of the regulated-voucher plan see their concept as both extending the benefits of family choice, now enjoyed by the affluent, to middle- and lower-income families and, at the same time, addressing the inequities of public school finance (Areen & Jencks, 1971; Coons & Sugarman, 1978). The voucher agency, according to the regulated plan, would regulate the use of the voucher in ways that would prevent racial or minority group segregation.

While the idea of the voucher plan can be traced back to John Stuart Mill (*On liberty,* 1859) and even earlier to Thomas Paine (*The rights of man,* 1792), it is a plan whose time has yet to come. A major reason for this is to be found in the opposition of public school interests. Despite this opposition, there has been a "voucher experiment" in Alum Rock, California, in which parents were allowed choices, although only *within* the public school system. The venture was funded by the Office of Economic Opportunity in an effort to increase the educational opportunities of lower-income families. Even this limited program, which delegated authority to the local school system and allowed only limited family choice, had some positive effects. For example, as a result of the program, one school redesigned its program and showed significant gains in student achievement.

In recent years, the public's attitude toward the voucher concept has varied. While in 1970, and again in 1981, only 43 percent of the general public favored the use of educational vouchers, by 1983 just over half (51 percent) had come to favor the voucher system. This marked the peak of support. By 1985, the percentages in favor had declined to the pre-1983 level of 45 percent; in a 1987 survey, 44 percent of the general public favored the use of vouchers (Gallup & Clark, 1987). Surprisingly, in 1987 parents of children attending nonpublic schools were no more favorably disposed toward vouchers than were other parents (see Table 6.1).

The provision of tax credits for students in private schools represents a more modest effort to give government recognition to, and encourage, competitive family choice in schooling. Like the voucher plan, the tax credit system has been regularly opposed by the public school interests, who insist

TABLE 6.1 The Public's Attitude Toward Educational Vouchers (1987)

	National Totals %	No Children in School %	Public School Parents %	Nonpublic School Parents %
Favor voucher system	44	42	49	49
Oppose voucher system	41	42	40	46
No opinion	15	10	11	5

Source: Gallup & Clark, 1987, p. 20.

that private education should be entirely private, although regulated in part by the state.

Some applaud and others oppose government actions that serve to increase competition and family choice in education. Those arguing in favor see a value in moving educational decision making close to the child and to those most responsible for, and interested in, the child. They see family choice as a means of resolving the value conflict between the "neutral" or majority-controlled values of the public schools and the "pluralism" of values that exists in our society. They also see increased choice as contributing to improved education, since it should have the effect of increasing the involvement of families and the accountability of schools to their immediate clients. They are heartened by the research on parent choice showing that intelligent and socially responsible choices tend to be made by middle- and upper-class parents, even though low-income families have tended not to be active choosers (Nault & Vchitelle, 1981). They see government action to extend family choice as providing to the less advantaged possibilities for choice now enjoyed by the more advantaged.

Others argue against increased family choice, since they see it as a threat to the social goods that have resulted from the growth and establishment of the nation's system of public schools. Further, it is feared that public schools, already faced with tax revolts, federal funding cuts, and a host of internal problems contributing to a crisis of confidence, would be further damaged by increased competition. Increased family choice might further encourage the flight of more motivated students, leaving the public schools as a "dumping ground" for the poor and educationally troubled. Opponents of government aid to support family choice also foresee increased social fragmentation and divisiveness and a diminished national consensus as a result of such choice. They question whether parents have the competence, the time, or the sense of social responsibility needed to make choices in the best interests of the child and the nation. They see public goods, such as racial integration and preparation for citizenship, as threatened by increased family choice. They also see public schools as an open and neutral marketplace of ideas and values that can offset or balance the more restricted views and beliefs of families and subcultures.

CONCLUSION

The issues raised in this chapter about private schooling concerning choice, values, and competition give rise to many fundamental policy questions. Among the more important are: Should the government encourage pluralism and competition in education? Should it provide direct or indirect financial support to nonpublic schools? What, if any, controls should states have over private schools? When are the rights of individual choice outweighed by the needs of the common good? These questions are not easily answered and will continue to be a source of debate.

As a future teacher, you should examine your philosophical beliefs and assess whether you will feel a greater sense of accomplishment in a private or a public school setting. It is important to help children learn but it is equally important to believe in the philosophical orientation of your school system.

QUESTIONS AND ACTIVITIES

1. Review the laws in your state that regulate private education. Explain why they are appropriate, too rigorous, or too lax in your opinion.
2. Interview a private school teacher and/or spend a day visiting a private school to get a better picture of what teaching is like in that setting. What are the advantages and disadvantages of teaching in private schools?
3. Should parents have the rights to teach children at home? What are the guidelines for home instruction in your state?
4. Investigate whether public funds are used to support private schools in your state or in a state where you plan to teach. Are they being used appropriately? Should private schools receive more funding and if so, for what purpose(s) and for what reason(s)?
5. What are the major arguments in favor of tuition tax credits?
6. What are the major advantages and disadvantages of using a voucher system in education?

CHAPTER 7

Legal Rights and Responsibilities of Teachers and Students

As a future teacher, you must have a basic understanding of school law, how it influences education, and how it protects your individual rights and those of your students. Being aware of the basic tenets of school law also lessens the chance that you will be involved in litigation arising from a teaching-related activity.

● State and federal courts strongly influence many important aspects of public and nonpublic education.
● Teachers and administrators must understand and respect the constitutional rights of individual students.
● School districts and teachers can set rules that limit individual rights if the rules can be shown to have an important and reasonable educational basis.
● As a teacher, you are responsible for taking precautions to prevent situations that could result in physical and/or emotional harm to students.

You are standing in the hallway monitoring students. Two students are standing next to an open locker and nervously glance your way. It is only your second week of student teaching but you have had behavior problems with these two on several occasions. You decide to see what they are up to and upon your approach they slam the locker shut. You ask them to open the locker and they refuse. You have a master key. What would you do?

It is the last week of school and the weather is very warm. You decide to take your second-grade class outdoors for storytelling time. Once outside you remember that you forgot your storybook. You direct the children to go outside and sit on the lawn while you return to get your book. During the three minutes it takes you to run inside, John pushes Laura into a puddle where she slips and breaks her leg. As Laura's teacher, are you liable for her accident?

What would you do in the first situation? Would you open the locker? If you did, would you be violating the student's right to be protected from searches? If you found incriminating material, would the student be suspended? In the second vignette, would you be liable? Would you have to pay damages?

Although you are preparing to be a teacher and not a lawyer, you live in a litigious society. Like all professionals, you need to know the law as it relates to your profession.

This chapter gives you a brief description of the legal issues that will most likely concern you as an elementary or secondary school teacher. This description should provide sufficient information to enable you to regulate your own conduct to comply with the law. Further, the information should also allow you to recognize when your own legal rights, or those of others, are being violated. However, you should remember that if you ever face a legal matter of serious magnitude, you should consult an attorney.

Legal Foundations

Unlike the situation in other nations, the system of public elementary and secondary education in the United States is heavily influenced by laws and court decisions. While some legal requirements regarding education in the United States—such as matters concerning accreditation, certification, and graduation requirements—have existed for many years and are shared with many Western nations, a great number of legal requirements have been established in the United States since the middle of the twentieth century. These more recent legal requirements involve, for the most part, protections of the civil rights and civil liberties of teachers and students and, to a lesser extent, requirements for schools and school districts participating in programs that receive federal financial aid.

To understand the laws governing education, you need to know something about the sources from which these laws derive. There are two such general sources. The first is that of elected or appointed governing bodies that formulate written statutes, rules, regulations, and policies. Legislatures, the Congress of the United States, state departments of education, and state and local boards of education all make laws concerning education. The second source of law is the judiciary, which imposes legal requirements on education through court decisions. Courts, in resolving disputes about education, interpret statutes, rules, regulations, policies, state constitutions, and the federal Constitution. Ultimately, of course, the provisions of the federal Constitution supercede any other legal authority and always prevail in the face of conflicting requirements.

Sources of Laws Governing Schools

FEDERAL LAWS The provision of educational services is not a function of the federal government, and the Constitution contains no explicit provisions about education. Under the terms of the Tenth Amendment to the Constitution, any governmental functions that are not specifically mentioned in the Constitution as being the responsibility of the federal government are left to the discretion of individual states. As the nation developed, it was for the most part up to each state to determine, through its legislature or a constitutional convention, whether or not it would provide for a system of public elementary and secondary education and, if it did, how the system should function. Each of the 50 states has made provisions for public education.

Although the Constitution does not specifically address the issue of public education, there are a number of constitutional requirements that directly affect the provision of elementary and secondary education. These requirements govern the manner in which federal, state, or local governments, or any public employees or officials deal with individuals or groups. Of particular importance in education are the constitutional requirements set forth, primarily in the Bill of Rights, that guarantee each citizen certain rights (listed in Box 7.1).

In addition to the civil rights and liberties guaranteed by the Constitution, the federal government has established a number of requirements for education. The power of the federal government to do this is generally based upon the General Welfare Clause of the Constitution. Under this clause, the federal government has the power to expend monies for the general welfare and, in doing so, to attach certain requirements to the receipt of federal money. As a result, Congress has, for example, exercised the power to require any state education agency or local school system that receives federal financial assistance to comply with federal laws prohibiting discrimination on the basis of race, ethnicity, language, gender, age, religion, or disability.

STATE LAWS Since the Constitution gives the states the power to control education, most laws concerning schools have been written by state legislatures. State laws specify the standards that teachers must meet to receive teaching certificates or the courses that students must take to receive high school diplomas. State laws regulate such matters as teacher hiring and discharge, transportation of students, curriculum and materials, and school attendance requirements. Box 7.2 describes the structure of the state and federal courts.

School Attendance and Programs

All 50 state legislatures have passed statutes requiring school attendance. In addition, all the states have laws that set forth requirements covering various aspects of educational programs such as the length of the school day and year and the number and types of courses needed to graduate.

Compulsory Attendance

Each of the 50 states requires school attendance, generally until students reach 16 years of age. The beginning age for compulsory attendance varies from state to state, often depending upon whether state law requires, or provides for, kindergarten programs. Some states are currently considering substantial changes in their laws regarding the ages of entry into and exit from school. These proposals are based on the premise that young people today are much more mature (physically, emotionally, and intellectually) than students in the past. Thus, they recommend a lowering of the ages for compulsory school attendance—from 6 to 16 years, as at present, to 4 to 14.

School attendance requirements apply to state-approved schools, both public and private. Many states even allow students to be taught at home, provided the educational program they receive meets state standards concerning the nature of the curriculum and instruction.

Curriculum

State legislatures and departments of education have the power to set requirements concerning curriculum and instruction for local school districts so long as those requirements do not violate federal statutes or constitutional guarantees. As a result, most states have established minimum course requirements for high school graduates. Some states also have requirements about the content of particular courses. Further, some states regulate the instructional materials and textbooks that local districts may purchase.

Many state requirements have provoked controversies in which people have argued that the requirements conflict with the U.S. Constitution. For example, parents have challenged curricular requirements and instructional content on the grounds that participation in certain educational programs violates religious rights. Individuals have also initiated court challenges because they feel that the state is trying to impose a particular religious belief through its requirement that certain materials be taught or that certain information, such as the theory of evolution, not be taught. In this context, there has been a great deal of controversy recently regarding state statutes that encourage or require the teaching of creationism in addition to or instead of evolution. Federal courts that have considered creationism requirements have rejected them, arguing that creationism is a religious belief rather than a bona fide scientific theory, and that it is unconstitutional for the government to impose a set of religious beliefs (McCarthy & Cameron, 1981; Valente, 1980; Yudof et al., 1982).

Teachers have raised constitutional challenges to some curricular requirements. Some of these challenges have focused on the extent to which individual teachers have the academic freedom to use certain books to which school administrators or parents object. These challenges have been based on the theory that teachers' freedom of expression, which is protected by the First Amendment to the Constitution, allows them to determine which materials they shall use in their classroom. Generally, courts have allowed school boards and administrators an overriding power in determining what materials may be used in classrooms, except when the teacher can demonstrate that the material is appropriate for the age and maturity of the students at issue, is educationally relevant, and is properly presented (McCarthy & Cameron, 1981; Valente, 1980; Yudof et al., 1982).

Extracurricular Activities

School-sponsored nonacademic activities, particularly athletic programs, are the source of numerous lawsuits. Some of these cases are based on charges that a school is engaged in unlawful discrimination because of sex or a handicapping condition. The results of lawsuits concerning participation in extracurricular activities have been more unpredictable than those associated with access to academic programs. This is because once a state mandates an academic program, all students must be afforded access to these programs if they are qualified to participate. If a court is willing to recognize that extracurricular activities are an integral part of a school's educational program, then the due process protections concerning student discipline (described later) would probably apply to attempts to exclude a student from any extracurricular activity. However, extracurricular activities are not always regarded as an integral part of a school's educational program to which all students must be given access. Often the rules for such activities are written not by a local school district or a state department of education, but by a voluntary state or regional athletic association. The courts generally uphold rules relating to codes of conduct for athletes and residency and academic requirements for participation in athletics either on grounds that the rules are made by private organizations over which the courts have little control or because the rule is a reasonable one for schools to employ to regulate student conduct (McCarthy & Cameron, 1981; Valente, 1980).

School Fees

Many schools make students pay fees for the use of textbooks; the rental of gym lockers, uniforms, or towels; the use of materials in art, shop, or home economics classes; and for participation in some extracurricular activity such as athletics. Low-income students and their families may be at a severe disadvantage because of such a fee requirement. In school systems that do not have funds to pay school fees for students who are unable to pay, successful legal challenges have been brought on behalf of the students on the basis that they were prevented from participating fully in school activities because of the fee requirement. Such challenges were based upon state statutes and constitutional provisions requiring the provision of free public education.

The best advice for dealing with the issue of school fees is to check state law or state court decisions regarding both fees and the right to free public education. If it is not stated therein that fees can be charged, the wisest approach is to avoid charging fees for any items that could be deemed to be part of, or fundamental to, the basic educational program, since most states guarantee the right to free public education for all students.

Testing and Achievement

The need to improve student achievement and the issue of accountability in education have received much attention from educators and the public in recent years. A decline in student performance on standardized achievement tests and assertions of increased rates of illiteracy have resulted in several new types of accountability laws being passed by state legislatures. Legal challenges have been raised in state and federal courts in attempts to set aside these laws.

The first attempt to challenge new accountability laws was a series of lawsuits filed in state courts. The suits were brought on behalf of students who, although they had completed 12 years of public schooling and in most cases had been awarded a high school diploma, still lacked basic scholastic skills. Some of the plaintiffs in these cases could not read, write, or perform basic math. In the lawsuits, termed "educational malpractice" cases, it was argued that school officials and teachers had been negligent in educating these students. The argument is similar to ones made in medical malpractice cases in which doctors have been found negligent in treating patients. In a medical malpractice case, a court or jury can find a doctor negligent if it can be proved that the doctor did not meet the standards of good professional practice commonly followed by doctors in dealing with certain types of patients. In the educational malpractice cases, courts and juries were asked to determine whether schools had been negligent by not meeting the standards of good professional practice commonly followed by educators. In every case, often after review by appellate courts, it was determined that there was no educational negligence or malpractice, mainly because there is no commonly defined and accepted standard of good professional practice for teaching basic skills (McCarthy & Cameron, 1981; Valente, 1980; Yudof et al., 1982).

Despite plaintiffs' total lack of success in winning educational malpractice cases, school officials and legislatures have become very concerned about the liability of schools when students fail to learn basic scholastic skills. This concern is heightened by increasing public pressure to improve the basic skills of all students. As a result, beginning in the mid-1970s, many state legislatures and some local districts passed new accountability requirements. One of these requirements is that standardized achievement tests of basic skills be administered at various points during students' school careers. The purpose of this is to gauge the progress of individual students as well as to measure the school's success in teaching basic skills. Some mandates have linked test results to student promotion, class placement, qualification to receive a high school diploma, and state aid to local schools.

The constitutionality of these testing schemes has been challenged in the courts. The challenges were based upon three sets of claims about the use of tests to make critical decisions about individual students: (1) that the test programs are unfair to students from minority backgrounds; (2) that the programs are unfair to students with disabilities; and (3) that the programs are unfair to all students when they do not have sufficient time to prepare or when the test measures skills that students have not actually been taught in school. Courts have ruled that schools have a general right to base the award of diplomas on test performance; however, schools may not use tests to deny diplomas if a court finds that the tests work to perpetuate the effects of past, unlawful race discrimination; if they discriminate against students with disabilities; and if students have not been afforded a fair opportunity to pass the test (McCarthy & Cameron, 1981; Valente, 1980; Yudof et al., 1982).

Student Records

While the Constitution does not specifically guarantee a right to privacy, the United States Supreme Court has determined that such a right can be implied under the Constitution. This right includes the rights of parents and students to confidential treatment of any personally identifiable information that schools may possess. In the past, there were many examples of situations in which educators disclosed information contained in school records to law-enforcement officials without parental consent. It was also not uncommon for educators to discuss embarrassing information about students with people who had no legitimate need to know the information. Now, federal statutes and regulations and, in some states, state laws contain specific provisions concerning the privacy of information in student records.

Under two federal statutes that apply to educational programs receiving federal financial assistance, parents have the right to inspect and review any of their children's educational records that are kept by schools. Under Public Law 94-142 (Education for All Handicapped Children Act of 1975)* and the Buckley amendment (Family Educational Rights and Privacy Act),† specific provisions are made that are designed both to maintain the privacy of student records and to afford parents access to those records. Of the two statutes, the Buckley amendment is the more important, since it applies to all students and to all school records directly related to a student. These include records maintained by any school or anyone working for the school. Public Law 94-142 provisions apply only to students in need of special education.

Parents have a right to see all records covered by the Buckley amendment. When a parent or a student over 18 years of age seeks to review school records, the records must be provided within 45 days. If the parent or age-eligible student wants copies of the records, these must be provided at a reasonable cost. If the parent or student believes that the records are inaccurate, misleading, or a violation of privacy or other rights, he or she may seek to have the school amend them. If the school chooses not to amend the records, the parent or student has the right to a hearing to resolve the matter. Parents and students also have the right to complain about a school's failure to comply with Buckley amendment requirements to a hearing by a review board of the United States Department of Education.

In addition to the right to inspect records and seek amendments to them, families have the right to exercise some control over access to records by others. Under the Buckley amendment, unless an educator within the school has a legitimate educational interest in seeing a student's records, access to the records is not allowed without the parent's prior explicit written consent to disclosure to that individual. In the same way, access to individuals outside the school requires prior written consent from the parent or, in the case of a student over 18 years of age, from the student.

Obviously, these federal laws and the laws of some states concerning privacy of student records mean that educators have to be very careful about how they generate and maintain records. Particular attention should be paid to ensuring that any information entered into student records is fair and

---

*This law can be found in Title 2 of the *United States Code,* Sections 1400 to 1432, available in the legal reference section of most public libraries. The law is further detailed in more specific regulations in Volume 34 of the *Code of Federal Regulations,* Part 300.

†This law can be found in Title 20, *United States Code,* Section 1232g. The regulations for the law can be found in Volume 34 of the *Code of Federal Regulations,* Part 99.

accurate. Teachers must also be very careful to maintain the confidentiality of information contained in records. This means nòt only refusing to disclose information without prior written consent unless another person in the school system has a legitimate educational interest in seeing the record, but also being discreet when discussing information about individual students with other educators.

School Discipline

Most education-related lawsuits involve complaints by parents and students about the discipline practices of schools. These lawsuits are usually based on allegations that (1) school rules were unfair, (2) the punishment administered was inappropriate given the nature of the student's misbehavior, (3) inappropriate procedures were followed in administering the discipline, or (4) disciplinary policies or practices discriminated against certain groups of students. For the most part, these challenges are based on provisions of the Constitution, although sometimes they are based on state statutes, since these may include specific provisions concerning school discipline. For example, Massachusetts has a statute that prohibits corporal punishment in the state's public schools.*

Due Process of Law

The most important constitutional protection concerning student discipline is the Due Process Clause in the Fifth and Fourteenth Amendments. The provisions of the two amendments are identical; one applies to the actions of the federal government, the other to activities of state and local governments. They require that no person shall "be deprived of life, liberty, or property, by the government, without due process of law." The definition of what it means for a person to have been afforded "due process" in a particular situation depends upon the nature of the situation and the potential harm that might result to the individual as a result of government action. The definition of "what process is due" in each situation is, therefore, very much dependent upon the individual interests at stake.

The basic components of due process of law are designed to ensure fundamental fairness in government's treatment of individuals. The most basic of the general requirements of the Due Process Clause as they relate to school discipline and other educational cases are set out in Box 7.3.

In most educational contexts, the requirements of the Due Process Clause may never come into play. As the language of the constitutional provision itself indicates, due process is required only when the government proposes to deprive a person of "life, liberty, or property." If one of these individual interests is not at stake, one cannot invoke the protections of due process. The definitions of these three interests are not, however, ordinary. "Liberty" means more than physical freedom; "property" refers to more than land and physical possessions. Liberty and property interests have come to have specific

*Annotated Laws of Massachusetts, Chapter 41, Section 376(a).

legal meanings defined by state and federal judges. In the case of schools, these terms have now been sufficiently well defined for us to be able to say that constitutionally protected interests are involved whenever a student is deprived of free public education (a form of "property" under the Constitution) or whenever a student's good name, reputation, honor, or integrity (all forms of "liberty" under the Constitution) may be harmed by what the school proposes to do.

The United States Supreme Court, in the case of *Goss* v. *Lopez*,* ruled that students have a "property interest" in public education, since each of the states has established a system of elementary and secondary schools that young people are compelled to attend. In the same case, the Court also stated that students, even though they may be minors, have a "liberty interest" in their good reputation. An infringement of either type of interest, according to the Court, triggers an entitlement to some level of due process unless the individual interest is *de minimus,* that is, of so little importance that it is not of value. Any discipline rule imposed by schools that deprives a student access to the standard educational program (expulsion or long-term suspension from school, for example) involves a denial of liberty and property interests and therefore triggers due process requirements.

In addition to the constitutionally protected interests in schooling recognized in the *Goss* case, the courts have recognized other interests related to education that are protected under the Due Process Clause. For example, the courts have recognized a property interest in reemployment for tenured teachers; a liberty interest in being free of stigmatization that may occur when a person is labeled as "handicapped"; a liberty interest in being free to enter into contracts, such as a contract for employment as a teacher; a liberty interest in the right of personal privacy, such as the privacy a person expects for his or her personal property; and a liberty interest in one's constitutional rights, such as the right to free speech or to free exercise of religious beliefs (McCarthy & Cameron, 1981; Valente, 1980; Yudof et al., 1982). The type and extent of the due process protections required will vary according to the extent of the deprivation of "property" or "liberty."

In addition to providing guidance on the types of situations in which due process protections will be imposed and the extent of those protections, the courts have defined two different types of due process requirements. The Due Process Clause has been interpreted to require both "substantive" and "procedural" protections for individuals. "Procedural due process" refers to

*419 U.S. 565 (1975); see McCarthy & Cameron, 1981, pp. 288–292; Valente, 1980, pp. 291–295; and Yudof et al., 1982, pp. 254–261.

requirements that the government follow proper procedures in order to minimize the chances of making erroneous decisions in dealing with people. "Substantive due process" refers to requirements that the results of governmental action be justifiable in terms of their outcome.

An example of how a court might conduct substantive and procedural due process analyses of a school problem will explain these concepts more fully. Some high schools have a rule that students may not participate in extracurricular athletics if they have been found consuming alcoholic beverages. A student might challenge this rule, arguing that it denies substantive due process of law, since it is not appropriate for a school to attempt to regulate the behavior of students when they are not at school or not involved in school activities, as when they consume alcohol at home. The school, of course, might argue that there is a justification for the rule on alcohol, namely that alcohol consumption by young people is illegal and dangerous and the schools should do what they can to prevent such behavior. A court would probably agree with the school and find that the rule does not deny substantive due process. But even if the rule on alcohol consumption is found to be justifiable, a claim may still be raised that the rule was not applied in a way that ensured a fair procedure for deciding whether students in fact violated the rule. The claim would imply that there had been a denial of procedural due process, and indeed this would be the case unless the school could prove that students had fair warning about the rule and were given a fair chance to prove whether or not they had violated it. If the school could not prove this, then a court could order the school to provide a fair hearing for the students or dismiss the disciplinary procedure for lack of fair prior warning of the rule.

Right to Notice of Rules

The first due process requirement in school discipline is that students be given reasonable notice of the standards of conduct to which they will be held. This requirement is based on the notion that fairness dictates that students be given an opportunity to regulate their conduct so that they can comply with the rules and that it is generally unfair to punish someone for doing something they may not have known was wrong.

Usually, the notice requirement means that school rules of conduct should be written and should be disseminated in writing, at least to older students. This means that rules should be written in such a way that all persons or students of ordinary intelligence would interpret the rule in the same way and would know how to adjust their conduct to comply with the rule. The enforcement of unwritten rules of conduct has been upheld by courts in situations in which it was found either that the student was clearly told about the rule or that the student should have actually known about it or realized that such a rule was probably in effect.

Legality of Student Rules of Conduct

Successful court challenges of rules for student conduct are possible when the school district does not have a justifiable and reasonable educational basis for the rule. Under the protections of substantive due process, for example, students have successfully challenged school rules prohibiting married students from participating in extracurricular activities or the standard school curriculum on the grounds that such rules are not reasonably related to the objectives of schools. In another case, two students used a substantive due process argument to prevent their school from excluding them after their mother had a fight with their building principal. The court ruled that it was a denial of substantive due process to punish a student for actions over which the student had no control (McCarthy & Cameron, 1981; Yudof et al., 1982).

School rules can also be challenged under a legal theory that the school has no power to make certain rules in the first place. In a Kentucky case, for example, a state court ruled that it was beyond a school's power to reduce class grades for unexcused absences resulting from disciplinary suspensions when the state statute authorizing suspensions did not include any provision for academic punishment of students who violated rules of discipline (McCarthy & Cameron, 1981; Valente, 1980; Yudof et al., 1982).

Legality of Forms of Punishment

Challenges to school discipline practices can arise from the nature of the punishment imposed on students. Controversies may arise when the punishment imposed seems to be beyond the power of school officials to impose. Other cases have involved assertions that the punishment violated the substantive due process guarantee; that is, that it was unfair, given the magnitude of the student's disciplinary violation. Students with special interests may present challenges to specific types of punishment. For example, handicapped students are entitled to protections designed to ensure that discipline be imposed in such a way that they are not punished for misbehavior that is a manifestation of their handicapping condition and that they continue to receive appropriate education.

The United States Supreme Court has scrutinized several forms of punishment for violations of school rules. In 1977, the Court considered a case in which the imposition of corporal punishment was challenged on the theory that it constitutes a form of "cruel and unusual punishment" in violation of the Eighth Amendment to the Constitution. The Supreme Court ruled, however, that the prohibition against cruel and unusual punishment applies only in situations in which persons have been accused of violations of the criminal law (McCarthy & Cameron, 1981; Valente, 1980; Yudof et al., 1982). It did not address another constitutional argument against corporal punishment: that it constitutes a denial of substantive due process when it is excessively violent. Subsequently, the United States Court of Appeals for the Fourth Circuit found that substantive due process might be denied in situations in which corporal punishment is administered if the punishment is too severe given the nature of the rule infraction.*

Some guidelines have emerged from court cases on corporal punish-

*Hall v. Tawney, 621 F.2d 607 (4th Cir. 1980).

ment. In considering these, you should remember that many education professionals feel that corporal punishment in the schools is inappropriate under any circumstances.* This aside, the individual educator should be aware of any state laws or school district or school policies concerning corporal punishment; if such punishment is allowed, the educator must know how it may be imposed. For example, some schools allow corporal punishment only for students whose parents have given prior written consent to such punishment. If corporal punishment is appropriate, some informal due process hearing, such as described in the following section, should be held prior to imposition of the punishment.

If corporal punishment is to be inflicted, it is probably wise to have a witness present. Caution would also suggest that if the punishment is being inflicted as a result of misbehavior consisting of direct confrontation with a school official, it should be carried out by someone other than the official involved in the incident; otherwise, the official might inflict excessive punishment. A major concern, of course, is the possibility that a student could be injured as a result of the infliction of corporal punishment. Such injuries could result in legal liability for the educators.

Searches of Students

Very often, in an effort to enforce school rules against drug, alcohol, or weapons possession or to find stolen articles, school officials may want to conduct searches of students' coat or gym lockers, purses or clothes, or even students themselves. The general rule under the Fourth Amendment to the Constitution is that all persons in this country have the right to be protected from searches of their bodies or of other places in which they expect privacy unless a judge provides a search warrant to law enforcement officials or unless exceptional circumstances exist. A recent United States Supreme Court case addressed the question of whether school officials who wanted to search students' purses or other private property would be required to obtain a search warrant prior to beginning the search. The Court decided that educators can conduct searches of students' purses or other places in which students would ordinarily expect privacy, on the condition that the search be reasonable considering the circumstances under which it is initiated. For example, a search of a student's handbag could be justified on the basis of information from a teacher that the student was seen putting something resembling marijuana into the purse. The search can involve only those places it was reasonable to examine given the original purpose, unless, during the search, additional evidence is found to indicate that the student has either broken the law or violated school rules.†

*The National Education Association, the largest teacher organization in the country, has an official position against corporal punishment. This policy, along with a discussion of studies concerning the use of corporal punishment, is contained in the report of their Task Force on Corporal Punishment (National Education Association, 1972). The American Psychological Association and the American Public Health Association have adopted similar policies.

†*New Jersey* v. *T.L.O.*, 53 *United States Law Week*, no. 27 (January 15, 1985).

BOX 7.4 Procedural Due Process Requirements

- Advance notification of the charges
- Sufficient advance warning of the impending hearing so that an adequate defense can be prepared
- Advance access to the evidence the school will present at the hearing
- The services of an impartial decision maker to conduct the hearing and decide the case (most courts have found that school board members are ordinarily sufficiently impartial)
- The right to counsel, or another representative, to present the arguments against imposition of penalty
- The right to an interpreter for a limited English–proficient or hearing-impaired person
- The right of the person to choose whether the disciplinary hearing should be open to the public or closed (although some state statutes may mandate a closed hearing)
- The right to confront and cross-examine the witnesses the school presents
- An opportunity to make a full presentation of his or her side of the case and to raise the issue of whether the particular penalty proposed is appropriate
- The right to have the hearing limited to the original charges about which the individual was notified
- The right to have any evidence excluded from use at the hearing if the evidence was obtained in violation of the Fourth Amendment to the Constitution, which prohibits unreasonable searches and seizures of persons or property
- The right to have some oral or written recording of the hearing
- The right to receive a written document from the impartial decision maker who conducted the hearing setting forth the determination on whether the rules infraction occurred and, if so, the nature of the penalty to be imposed

Procedural Due Process Protections in School Discipline

As indicated in the previous sections, if serious disciplinary action is contemplated, the utilization of some form of procedural due process protections is required. Clearly, courts will require procedural protections whenever a long (over ten days) disciplinary exclusion from any educational program is contemplated. The extent of the protections will vary according to the severity of the punishment contemplated. The more severe the potential punishment imposed on a student, the greater the extent of procedural protections required of school personnel. Procedural protections are most important when students face long-term suspension, that is, suspension for over ten school days or expulsion from school. The courts have ruled that certain protections, listed in Box 7.4 are essential in such situations.

A degree of procedural due process may even be appropriate in a teacher's own classroom when disciplinary action is considered that might exclude a child from receiving educational services or that might result in stigmatization. Such a situation would require the simplest form of due process procedures, which consist of a basic informal "hearing." In a hearing, a teacher (or other school official) who feels that a student may have violated a rule discusses the circumstances with that student. The discussion would focus on whether or not the student had infringed a rule and, if so, whether he or she has an explanation for the misbehavior.

First Amendment Guarantees in Education

The First Amendment to the United States Constitution provides some of the most fundamental guarantees of liberty in our society. It is designed to ensure that government does not unreasonably interfere with freedom of expression, freedom of association, freedom to practice religious beliefs, and that government does not impose an "official" religion. All these protections apply to both teachers and students.

First Amendment cases involving students generally occur when they face discipline for engaging in activity protected under the amendment (such as publishing or broadcasting allegedly subversive material on school property). First Amendment cases involving teachers or other school employees generally occur when these employees face some disciplinary action (such as dismissal or loss of pay) as a result of engaging in what they consider to be an activity protected under the amendment. Let us examine these situations in more detail.

Freedom of Expression

Freedom of expression is at the heart of the First Amendment. The amendment was expressly formulated to protect controversial points of view not shared by the majority. It was also designed to protect all forms of expression, from "pure speech," that is, talking or writing, to "symbolic speech," such as wearing a political button or symbolic armband. The content of expression can be limited only if it is defamatory or so provocative that it can be expected to result in a fight or other major disruption.

Courts have defined those situations in which limitations on the right to free expression can be imposed constitutionally. If necessary, schools can regulate the time, the manner, or the place in which speech occurs to prevent disruption of the school community. School rules restricting the free expression of students or employees must be very clear and specific so that all persons will understand their meaning. The rules must be applied uniformly so that only substantially disruptive speech or activity is limited and so that speech or activity is not curtailed merely because its content is unpopular or controversial. The rules must also be limited to activities that would actually threaten to disrupt the school community. For example, a school rule might be designed to keep libelous material from being published in the student newspaper, so as to preclude chances that the school could be sued for defamation. If such a rule exists, it should prohibit only the publication of items that could be legally defined as defamatory and not the publication of all controversial material.

Even when free speech can be limited, preference should be given to methods of limiting expression that do not restrain or curtail speech before it occurs. When forms of prior restraint have been allowed by courts, they have generally required that the restraints be accompanied by some procedural safeguards designed to ensure that individual interests under the First

Amendment were not violated. Thus, a school might adopt a rule requiring that all the items to be included in the school newspaper be submitted to a faculty advisor prior to publication. The rule might also allow that faculty member to refuse to publish any obscene or defamatory items. This would be an acceptable form of prior restraint if the rule defining "obscene" and "defamatory" materials is clear and if it provides a mechanism for procedural due process protections (such as the right to a hearing) for the authors and editors of material the advisor wishes to exclude. In a landmark decision (*Hazelwood School District* v. *Kuhlmeier,* 1987), the United States Supreme Court ruled that school administrators have wide authority to regulate student speech in school-sponsored publications. In the decision Justice White wrote, "[Schools] must be able to set high standards for the student speech that is disseminated under [their] auspices—standards that may be higher than those demanded by some newspaper publishers and theatrical producers in the 'real world'—and may refuse to disseminate student speech that does not meet those standards." This recent ruling strengthens the hand of school boards and school administrators in regulating student speech and conduct.

School administrators can limit the expression of free speech in school newspapers if they consider the material obscene or defamatory.

Freedom of Association and Assembly

The First Amendment provides that "Congress shall make no law . . . abridging . . . the right of the people to peaceably assemble." The same kinds of general provisions that govern freedom of expression also apply to attempts to regulate freedom of assembly. Therefore, the school must show a strong justification if it attempts to limit the rights of students to assemble on school grounds, and such justifications must demonstrate that the limitation is necessary if the school is to carry on its normal educational functions. No restrictions are allowable if they are based solely upon the school objecting to the reason or purpose for the assembly, unless the purpose is criminal. Schools can, however, through narrow and clearly written rules, restrict the time, the manner, or the place in which assemblies are conducted and can curtail asemblies that become violent or disruptive or that result in activities leading to the denial of access to school facilities.

A practical implication of court rulings on freedom of assembly is that if students or teachers wish to hold a rally (for example, to protest cutbacks in the school district budget), the school cannot prevent the rally from being held on school property, even though the rally might be embarrassing to school officials. The school can, however, require that the rally be held only during the lunch hour, that it be confined to a designated area, and that it end prior to the resumption of scheduled afternoon classes. If the participants in the rally violate any of these rules or if the rally in some other way creates a substantial disruption of the business of the school, then school officials can terminate it or discipline students or teachers who violate the rules governing the conduct of the rally.

Under the First Amendment, school officials can limit the right to free association only when they can prove that there is a compelling and legitimate governmental interest in doing so. Occasionally, school officials limit students' rights to free association by withholding the use of school facilities, meeting space, funds, or "official sanction" for a particular group's activity. Such limitations will be found to be unconstitutional denials of First Amendment rights unless school officials can present considerable justification for their action.

Religion and the Schools

In addition to the civil liberties just described, the First Amendment contains two clauses governing the relationship between governmental entities and religion that clearly affect education and the schools. The Free Exercise Clause prohibits governmental infringement upon the individual practice of religious beliefs. The Establishment Clause, which created the principle of separation of church and state, prohibits any actions by the government that would aid or advance any particular religion or that would have the effect of creating an official government-sanctioned religion. Both clauses apply to actions by federal, state, and local governments.

Separation of Church and State

The Establishment Clause has most frequently been involved in two types of cases: (1) those in which schools attempt to initiate school practices that have religious content and (2) those in which some state or federal aid program provides benefits to religious organizations.

Because the Establishment Clause is designed to prohibit any effort that might have the effect of creating an officially sanctioned religion, state laws requiring prayer in the public schools have been ruled illegal. This is valid even when such prayer is purportedly nonsectarian, since any form of prayer offends the beliefs of atheists and agnostics, who are also protected by the First Amendment.

While school prayer requirements have been invalidated under the Establishment Clause, other cases have been slightly more difficult for courts to resolve. For example, schools have been challenged when they installed Christmas trees or put on school-sponsored Christmas pageants or programs. These activities were allowed to continue when courts found that they were more secular than religious. Similarly, courts have upheld courses and instruction that teach about religion and religious beliefs, but they have invalidated attempts to inculcate particular religious views, such as the creationist view of the origins of the universe (McCarthy & Cameron, 1981; Valente, 1980).

Cases challenging government aid programs to sectarian schools have presented more difficult issues for courts to resolve, usually because of the complexity of such aid schemes. When government aid, either financial or programmatic, is made available to private religious schools, problems relating to the separation of church and state arise. Aid can be made available to private religious schools. However, such aid can be made available only if (1) the statute creating the aid program has only a secular legislative purpose, (2) the aid has a primary effect that neither advances nor inhibits religion, and (3) the aid can be administered in a way that minimizes government involvement with the religious institution. While the requirements of the Establishment Clause as interpreted by the courts may seem onerous to many, several aid schemes have in fact been validated. Among these are programs for providing bus transportation, textbooks, and special-education services for parochial school students.

Free Exercise of Religious Beliefs

The second clause in the First Amendment that addresses the issue of religion prohibits governmental interference with individuals' practice of their religious beliefs. Some of the challenges to school practices under the Free Exercise Clause have concerned student and parental objections to course requirements or to texts and instructional materials that they found offensive to their religious beliefs. Several other cases have raised objections to sex education requirements. These cases have generally resulted in a ruling in support of the student. Thus, a school may not require students to enroll in a course that conflicts with their bona fide religious beliefs (McCarthy & Cameron, 1981; Valente, 1980).

Judges assess claims presented under the Free Exercise Clause by weighing the very important individual First Amendment interests of those challenging a school rule against the importance of the interests the school seeks to further with the rule. In each such case, there will be a presumption operating in favor of protecting religious liberty.

Discriminatory Practices

In addition to the Due Process Clause, the other major provision affecting the operation of schools is the Equal Protection Clause of the Fourteenth Amendment. This clause requires that no governmental agency, official, or employee may deny any person "the equal protection of the laws." Many state constitutions contain a similar provision.

The Equal Protection Clause governs situations in which a governmental action has the effect of dividing individuals or groups of people into categories that are subject to different treatment. These sorting or classification processes occur frequently and in different contexts; most of them are legitimate under the Constitution. Students who misbehave are, for example, treated differently from those who do not. This is perceived as legitimate differential treatment. However, if the group of misbehaving students is further broken down into subcategories, some of whom are disciplined more severely than others, equal protection of the law may have been denied. For example, some schools tend to expel black students from school for misbehavior while using less serious punishment for white students who engage in the same misbehavior. To determine whether or not equal protection has been denied as the result of a school's actions, it is necessary to examine the goal of the school's action, the results of the action the school took, and whether, in light of those results, the school's actions were constitutionally justifiable.

The courts' methods of analysis in scrutinizing allegations of denial of equal protection provide greater understanding of the right. The depth to which a court will go to determine whether an action constitutes a denial of equal protection will depend upon the nature of the harm that results from the action. Courts have developed three very different kinds of "tests" that they use for determining whether a denial of equal protection has occurred. Which test a court will use depends upon the type of harm inflicted on the individual as a result of the school's actions.

The first kind of equal protection test is applied when school action has inflicted little harm. The court will require the government to demonstate that its action is rationally related to the furtherance of some legitimate governmental goal. Thus, in an equal protection challenge to an elementary school's use of ability grouping or tracking the school must demonstrate that the use of ability grouping is rationally related to a legitimate educational purpose. Presumably, this can be done through the presentation of research data indicating that students' educational achievement is enhanced (a legitimate school goal) through the use of ability grouping. If this evidence can be produced, the classification system will probably withstand scrutiny under the Equal Protection Clause.

Suppose, however, that the use of an ability-grouping scheme in the school results in a disproportionately large number of black students or students of a particular national origin or ethnic group (relative to the overall proportion of such a group in the school population) being placed in the lower track. If these students allege a denial of equal protection, the courts will scrutinize this claim using another kind of test. The school must prove that (1) its actions are essential to further some compellingly important governmental interest, (2) there is no reasonable alternative to achieve the goal that does not result in a disproportionate racial balance in the groups formed, (3) tracking is necessary to enhance the educational achievement of those affected, and (4) the grouping in fact works to enhance the achievement of black students, ultimately allowing them to be promoted to higher tracks with white students (McCarthy & Cameron, 1981; Valente, 1980; Yudof et al., 1982).

In *Plyler* v. *Doe,* the United States Supreme Court articulated a third test for courts to measure claims that equal protection has been denied. This case arose because of an attempt in Texas to make children of illegal aliens pay tuition to attend public schools. The Court said that, while education may not be a fundamental right, it is an extremely important public service. Because of its importance, the schools must do more than show that there is a fair relationship between the tuition requirement and a legitimate governmental purpose if they are to justify denying access to education. The test proposed by the Supreme Court was that the Texas schools should prove that the tuition requirement furthered a "substantial goal of the state." When the test was applied, the tuition requirement was invalidated on the grounds that it is important to educate all children in a state, regardless of how they arrived in the state.*

The Equal Protection Clause has been used as the basis for many challenges to school practices. It has also served as the source of several federal civil rights statutes prohibiting discriminatory actions by schools. These statutes, and their implementing regulations written by federal administrative agencies, prohibit discrimination on the basis of race or ethnicity, language, sex, age, or handicapping condition in programs benefiting from federal financial assistance.

Discrimination on the Basis of Race or Ethnicity

Perhaps the most well-known school law case is *Brown* v. *Board of Education,* decided by the United States Supreme Court in 1954. The decision established that racially segregated public schools deny black students their rights to equal protection of the law, since it was concluded that educational opportunities in racially isolated high schools attended by black students are inferior to those in schools attended by white students.† A year later, in a decision referred to as *Brown II,* the Supreme Court stated that separate schools for blacks should be speedily desegregated (McCarthy & Cameron, 1981; Valente, 1980; Yudof et al., 1982).

In the 20 years following the *Brown* decisions, hundreds of court cases have been filed to obtain judical assistance in desegregating all-black schools.

---

*457 U.S. 202 (1982).

†*Brown* v. *Board of Education of Topeka,* 349 U.S. 294 (1954).

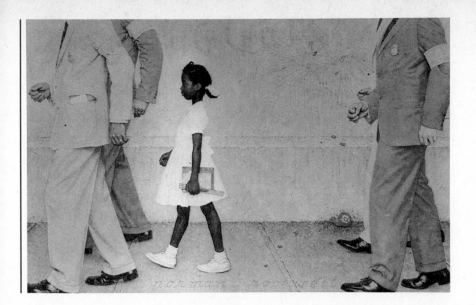

The Supreme Court ruled that racially segregated public schools denied black students their rights to equal protection under the law. This famous illustration by Norman Rockwell depicts a young black girl being escorted to a previously segregated school in the South.

These cases have resulted in some of the most controversial education law disputes in our nation because of the far-ranging political and social ramifications of court orders to desegregate.

In addition to the courts, the United States Congress has dealt with problems of discrimination by including principles prohibiting discrimination on the basis of race, color, or national origin in a statute, Title VI of the Civil Rights Act of 1964.* The act prohibits the denial of the benefits of any program or activity that receives federal financial assistance to students or teachers on the basis of race, color, or ethnicity. The statute has been widely used, usually in conjunction with the Equal Protection Clause, in cases involving school desegregation, although many of these were initiated under the Constitution alone before Title VI was passed. The provisions of Title VI have been used to invalidate school practices involving racial discrimination in student discipline, ability grouping, testing, and employment terminations.

Discrimination on the Basis of Sex

The United States Supreme Court has been unwilling to recognize that classification on the basis of sex is suspect and should require substantial justification by government agencies. Congress, however, began to incorporate into civil rights statutes provisions forbidding discrimination on the basis of sex. Title VII of the 1964 Civil Rights Act prohibits discrimination on the basis of sex in employment and hiring practices. Even more important is Title IX of the Education Amendments of 1972, a statute that specifically addresses sex discrimination in education programs that receive federal financial assistance.† Title IX bars schools from treating students or employees differently because of their sex except in the few instances when sex segregation is appropriate, such as in sex education classes or in physical education classes where contact sports (wrestling, for example) take place. Because of Title IX,

---

*Title 42, *United States Code,* Section 2000d.
†Title 20, *United States Code,* Section 1681.

Most school programs are now coeducational to prevent discrimination.

schools have increased extracurricular athletic opportunities for female students and have eliminated such requirements as those mandating that all girls take certain courses and all boys take other courses.

Education of Students with Handicapping Conditions

Educators have had to pay increasing attention in recent years to the legal aspects of educating students with handicapping conditions (both physical and mental). In addition to the constitutional protections for such students under the Equal Protection and Due Process clauses, two sets of detailed federal statutes and regulations govern the education of special-needs students. Further, each state has a set of laws and regulations that, for the most part, closely parallel the federal statutes' requirements.

For many years, many students with handicapping conditions were excluded from the benefits of a public education. In fact, most states in the past exempted such students from compulsory attendance requirements. By the early 1970s, courts began to recognize that the denial of special-education services to the handicapped constituted a denial of due process and equal protection. Once a state makes public education available to students, it must make equal educational opportunities available to all students (McCarthy & Cameron, 1981). As a result of these legal developments, and because of some states' failures to implement educational services for students with handicapping conditions, (*and* despite federal financial incentives), the United States Congress enacted two laws to redress the problem.*

The more important of the two statutes is the Education for All Handicapped Children Act of 1975 (Public Law 94-142). This statute established one of the nation's largest federal aid programs for education. However, as a condition for receipt of federal assistance, educational agencies are required to provide each student with a handicapping condition a program of free public education specifically tailored to meet the student's unique educational needs. Educational agencies also have to provide procedural due process safeguards in evaluating and placing students, allowing rights to administrative hearings and judicial appeal, and maintaining confidentiality of student records.

The second federal statute, Section 504 of the Rehabilitation Act of 1973, is a broad civil rights statute that prohibits discrimination against the handicapped by any program, educational or noneducational, that receives any federal financial assistance. The Rehabilitation Act is designed, among other things, to ensure accessibility to buildings and grounds; access to public education programs and services that are free and appropriate at the elementary, secondary, and postsecondary level; and procedural safeguards to allow parental participation in decision making about special education. This law also prohibits discrimination against school employees who are handicapped.

The two federal statutes, and their accompanying regulations, work together to provide considerable protections for students with handicapping conditions. Public Law 94-142 protects any young person who is mentally retarded, has a learning disability, is visually handicapped, has a serious emotional disturbance, or is orthopedically, hearing- or health-impaired. Section 504 of the Rehabilitation Act protects any student who has any physical or mental impairment that substantially limits one or more major life activities.

Right to Free Appropriate Public Education

Each student who is "exceptional" because of a handicapping condition is entitled, under Public Law 94-142 and Section 504 of the Rehabilitation Act, to an education that is appropriate to his or her unique needs and that is provided at public expense. "Free appropriate public education" (FAPE) consists of the provision, without charge, of regular or special education designed to meet each student's educational needs and of supported aids and services.

The entitlement to a free public education for students with handicapping conditions means that the parents of those students cannot be required to pay any of the costs for their children's education other than those fees (such as those for textbook rental, uniforms, supplies, and the like) that have to be

*The Education for All Handicapped Children Act (Public Law 94-142), Title 20, *United States Code,* Sections 1400–1432, and the Rehabilitation Act of 1973, Title 29, *United States Code,* Section 504.

paid by the parents of students who do not have handicapping conditions. If public agencies cannot provide appropriate services for a student, the school district or state must pay for private school placement. If a residential program is the only type of program that can meet a student's needs, the state or local school system must pay all education-related costs, as well as costs for non-medical care and room and board.*

A recent United States Supreme Court decision in a case involving a dispute over the meaning of the requirement that handicapped students be given an "appropriate education" provides some guidance for teachers who work with these students. According to the Court's decision in *Board of Education* v. *Rowley,* a student with a handicapping condition who is placed in a regular classroom on a full-time basis and receives supplementary aids and services is receiving an appropriate education if he or she is making average or above-average school progress compared with the progress of his or her classmates, is in a classroom with grade levels that approximate those used for students who are not receiving special education, and is being promoted successfully at the end of the school year.†

Related Services

The federal laws recognize that students with handicapping conditions may sometimes need to receive special supportive services if they are to benefit from special education. The laws, therefore, require the provision of "related services" if they are needed to allow the student to benefit from an education. These services might include special transportation, speech therapy, occupational or physical therapy, counseling, psychological intervention, nursing services, or special equipment. In a recent case, the United States Supreme Court ruled that under the federal special-education law requirement that related services be provided, the school must catheterize a student during the school day if catheterization is necessary to allow that student to stay in school and receive educational services.‡

Procedural Protections

To ensure fairness and accuracy in decision making about special education for individual students, the federal laws impose several procedural protections. Written prior notice must be given to the parents or guardians of a student whenever officials propose to initiate an evaluation or change the identification or placement of a student. To protect students who are wards of the state or whose parents or guardians are unknown or unavailable, Public Law 94-142 requires the appointment of a "surrogate parent" to protect the student's interests and to exercise the rights provided to parents and guard-

*See *Burlington School Committee* v. *Department of Education,* 53 *United States Law Week,* p. 4510 (April 30, 1985).

†*Board of Education* v. *Rowley,* 102 Supreme Court Reports, p. 3034 (1982).

‡*Irving Independent School District* v. *Tatro,* 52 *United States Law Week,* p. 5151 (June 26, 1984).

ians under the federal special-education statutes. The surrogate parent, however, cannot be an employee of any state, federal, or intermediate educational agency that is involved in the education or care of the student.

The procedural protections required by both Public Law 94-142 and the Section 504 regulations require safeguards for the confidentiality of student records and an opportunity for the parents, guardian, or surrogate parent to examine relevant records relating to the identification, evaluation, and placement of a student and the provision of a free appropriate public education.

The most significant procedural protections contained in federal special-education laws are those defining the right of parents and students to obtain hearings and court review of issues concerning identification, evaluation, placement, and the provision of services. Any complaint regarding any of these issues can be brought to an impartial administrative hearing officer, who can conduct a full hearing under provisions spelled out in state and federal law. If the family or school is dissatisfied with the outcome of the hearings, they can appeal to a state or federal court.

Employment of Teachers

While most state and federal laws and court cases involving schools have concerned the rights of students and parents, a growing number of laws and lawsuits concern your rights as a teacher. Understanding your rights requires an awareness of the legal provisions governing the certification, hiring, and employment of teachers. In addition, it is important to remember that the constitutional protections of the Equal Protection and Due Process clauses apply to teachers in their relationships to the schools in the same way those protections apply to students.

Certification

The laws of each state require that teachers in public schools be properly certified to teach. Certification is handled primarily by the states, not by local or federal agencies. Each state has established minimum qualifications for each of the teaching certificates it grants. Among the common requirements for certification is graduation from an accredited college or university teacher training program. Each state grants recognition for training in out-of-state institutions that have been accredited by an interstate accreditation agency. In addition to education and training requirements, state laws on teacher certification usually require that candidates demonstrate American citizenship and good moral character. Some states also require a loyalty oath or passing of a written examination.

Certification as a teacher means only that an individual is licensed and has met the minimum qualifications to teach. Local school districts have the authority to require qualifications above those required by the certification law. Local districts also have the power to request temporary waivers, or provisional certification, of teachers who are not properly certified in an area. These short-term arrangements need the approval of the state department of education, which usually requires that the teacher work to complete the additional training required for the permanent certification.

The same statutes that grant state departments of education the authority to award teaching certificates empower them to remove certification for proper cause. While local school districts may recommend the withdrawal of certification, only the state may actually revoke certification. Reasons for revocation may include proof of immorality, incompetency, or neglect of duty. An individual facing loss of a teaching certificate is entitled to the same type of full procedural due process protections that a student would receive if faced with a long-term disciplinary exclusion from school.

Contracts

Each state has detailed statutes governing the employment relationship between local school districts and their teachers. Permanent teachers must all be employed under a teaching contract, which is a written agreement between a local school board and an individual teacher. Only a board of education has the power to enter into a contract with a teacher; that power cannot be delegated, even to a principal or superintendent of schools.

Teaching contracts are like any other contracts for employment or other business relationships between parties. A contract is not valid unless there is a clear agreement between parties who are competent to enter into a contract, and it must be in the form mandated by law. To be competent to enter into a teaching contract, a teacher must, of course, be properly certified or have the requisite temporary certification or waiver. In addition to general contract law requirements, each state has a statute specifying how teacher contracts are to be formulated. A teaching contract should state the salary to be paid the teacher, the period of time covered by the contract (usually one year), and the duties and responsibilities to be performed by the teacher.

Collective Bargaining Agreements

In many school districts, a written contract, in addition to the one between an individual teacher and school board, governs the relationship between the school district and teachers. This contract is the written collective bargaining agreement between the school board and the teacher union or professional education organization representing the teachers in that district. Statutes in most states establish the rights of teachers to join together to bargain collectively with school boards over some of the general terms and conditions of employment of teachers in a school district. In school districts in which there is a collective bargaining agreement, the individual teacher is protected by the terms of both his or her individual teaching contract and the collective bargaining agreement. A court can resolve disputes over the meaning of the individual contract; disputes over the provisions of the collective bargaining agreement as they apply to the teacher can be resolved through the grievance process defined in the agreement or sometimes by a court.

Tenure

The terms of an individual teacher's contract usually include provisions relating to the circumstances under which a contract can be renewed following the initial one-year term. Each state's statutes contain provisions concerning the length of the contractual term and how long the teacher can expect to be employed.

Under most state statutes, teachers in their first three years of employment are probationary teachers who must be awarded a new contract each school year in order to continue in the same school district. If the district does not choose to renew a probationary teacher's contract at the end of a school year, it has the complete discretion to do so, and no reason for the failure to renew the contract need be given. However, once a teacher's contract is renewed for a period beyond the time of probation required in the state's statutes, the teacher acquires "tenure" or "continuing contract" status.

The acquisition of tenure status by a public elementary or secondary school teacher means that the teacher is entitled to continued employment by the school district until the teacher decides to terminate the teaching contract at the end of any school year, or the school district takes specific action, as specified by state law, to discharge or dismiss the teacher. The United States Supreme Court has recognized that the termination of a tenured teacher's contract by a school district requires full procedural protections, such as those described in the previous section on Procedural Due Process Protections in School Discipline.

Tort Liability

An area of growing concern to educators and school board members is the "tort liability" of school officials and school districts. A *tort* is a legal wrong committed by one person or agency that results in the injury of another. If a judge or jury find that a tort has been committed by school officials or employees, the court may order an award of monetary "damages" to compensate the victim for actual and projected financial losses resulting from the injury. These could include medical expenses, value of pain and suffering, and/or "punitive damages" designed to punish the party or parties for engaging in the behavior resulting in the injury and to discourage others from similar acts.

Negligence

Most school-related allegations of torts involve assertions that a school or its employees engaged in conduct that fell below the standard of appropriate behavior, or the "standard of care," that a reasonable person in that situation would have exercised. Negligence occurs when a person acts in a manner that fails to protect someone from harm or that results in harm, either physical or emotional. For example, teachers in woodworking classes should require that all their students wear safety glasses when working with an electric band saw.

A teacher who fails to ensure that all students working at the saw wear glasses is negligent. Other successful allegations of negligence have involved such issues as school districts' failure to adequately maintain school buses or school buildings and grounds; failure to maintain athletic equipment and properly supervise its use; or failure to adequately supervise classes of students either at school or while away on field trips.

Defenses Against Liability

Even in situations in which schools or their officials or employees have been negligent, damages may not always be awarded against them and ordered paid to an injured party. In any tort case, if the defendants can prove that the injured party somehow contributed to his or her own injury, then damages may be either reduced or eliminated entirely. When a student in woodworking class is injured by failing to wear safety glasses while using a saw, the teacher may be able to establish that, although he or she may have been negligent in failing to check that the student was actually wearing safety glasses, proper instructions and a warning to wear them had been given and the student was negligent in failing to wear the glasses provided.

Another defense against liability is that the injury was not directly the fault of the party charged with negligence but was instead the result of some intervening action by a third party. For example, the teacher might argue that his or her liability should be limited because of the fact that the injured student was not hurt by the saw but was instead indirectly injured by another student when that student stole the safety glasses.

Insurance

In actuality, most damage awards against schools, school officials, or school employees for negligence or other unlawful conduct are paid by insurance policies. Most school districts have purchased insurance coverage from private companies to cover legal claims and the costs of legal counsel to represent them in handling such claims. In addition, most professional educators and school officials belong to professional organizations, such as the National Education Association or the American Federation of Teachers, which, as part of their membership services funded through dues, provide automatic insurance coverage for members. If you do not join an association, it may be worth your while to investigate insurance options through other agencies.

CONCLUSION

At the conclusion of this chapter you may feel a bit frightened and overwhelmed by the number and seriousness of the legal issues that can affect teachers. There is no question that teachers need to be aware of school law in general, but they do not need to be lawyers. The following suggestions could minimize your chances of violating the law:

1. Take necessary safety precautions to reduce the chances of an accident occurring.

2. Do not leave younger students unsupervised.

3. Be fair and consistent when disciplining students.

4. Let students know your standards of discipline and the consequences of breaking rules.

5. Practice, and encourage students to practice, respect for basic human rights.

6. If incidents occur that might lead to litigation and you are unsure of what to do, consult your principal, teacher organization representative, and/or superintendent for advice.

7. If a questionable situation arises, keep written records of actions taken and copies of any written communication.

8. When in doubt, consult an attorney. Most state or local teacher organizations either have staff attorneys or will hire one if necessary.

Following these simple suggestions can help prevent litigation and enhance your chances of winning a case should problems arise.

QUESTIONS AND ACTIVITIES

1. Review the two scenes at the very beginning of the chapter. What were the major issues with legal implications? Would you agree with your original judgment on the basis of your reading of this chapter?

2. Contact your state department of education to secure a list of recent laws affecting education. What impact will these laws have upon local control of schools?

3. Obtain and examine discipline codes from several schools. Do the policies meet the requirements outlined in this chapter?

4. Write your representative in Congress and ask for the major pieces of federal legislation pending that directly affect education. What are the potential effects of these pending bills upon schools, teachers, and children?

5. What major arguments can you make to support or not support prayer in schools?

6. Read the procedures from several local districts regarding the education of handicapped students. How will these procedures affect you as a teacher?

7. Obtain a copy of a school district's collective bargaining agreement between teachers and the board of education. What parts of the contract will directly affect your teaching?

8. Should states set mandatory attendance laws for students between certain ages? If yes, what should the ages be? Why?

PART THREE

The Teacher

In this section we deal with various aspects of the career of teaching. For those who may wish to look beyond teaching to other occupations, either in education or outside it, we also describe occupations that make use of skills acquired in teacher preparation courses.

Chapter 8 considers professionalism, preservice training, professional growth, salary and security, and burnout. The chapter also suggests that you reflect on teaching as a career for yourself. Chapter 9 discusses career options outside the classroom that your teacher training will prepare you for. These range from occupations within traditional educational settings (for example, in early childhood education or in postsecondary education) to jobs in industry and business.

CHAPTER 8

The Career of Teaching

You are considering teaching as a career at an opportune time. A teacher shortage is developing, and efforts are under way to upgrade the professional status and salaries of teachers. Now is the time to seriously weigh your decision to be a teacher. This chapter offers you important information to help you make an informed decision.

- At present, teaching meets many but not all of the criteria of a profession. Steps are under way to upgrade the present status of teaching as a respected profession.
- The demand for teachers is growing dramatically. However, the serious shortage of minorities entering teaching is growing rapidly and is cause for serious concern.
- Teacher preservice training can be four or five years in length. The trend is toward requiring more liberal arts courses before teacher training may begin.
- Internship or practice teaching is an essential ingredient in your preparation.
- You will most likely have to pass some type of teacher certification test in order to teach. These tests at present are controversial.
- Professional development is a lifetime endeavor. School districts, professional associations, and yearly evaluations all play a central role in the continuing professional development of teachers.
- Teacher salaries are rising. Various kinds of incentive programs, including career ladders, are on the increase.
- Tenure and collective bargaining provide important protection for teachers. However, they have become increasingly controversial.
- Teacher burnout is a problem that teachers need to carefully guard against.
- There are a number of important questions you should seriously consider in deciding whether or not a teaching career is for you.
- The time to start thinking about finding a teaching job is now. Now is the time to begin to build your résumé, your academic reputation, and your experiential background.

Because you enrolled in this course, it is highly likely that you are seriously considering teaching as a career. The decision to become a teacher should be an informed one. This chapter examines some of the important facts you need to weigh in making your decision.

The chapter begins by asking if teaching is a profession. This is followed by a description of the demographics of teaching: numbers, composition, supply, and demand. The third section outlines preservice and certification requirements that you must complete in order to enter the profession. The fourth section considers professional growth (professional development, professional associations, and teacher evaluation). In the fifth section, we consider issues related to compensation and security: salaries, incentive programs, tenure, and collective bargaining. The sixth section deals with teacher burnout. In the seventh section, you are asked to reflect on your reasons for choosing teaching as a profession. The final section focuses on planning future job-hunting strategies so that, once you have made your decision and completed all the requirements to be a teacher, you are able to find a job. The strategies described in the final section can also help you when you apply to schools to do field practicums, which are part of most teacher preparation programs.

Teaching as a Profession

Is teaching a profession? Some would say that it is, others that it is not. The answer depends on what characteristics you believe an occupation should have before it can be called a profession, and on your assessment of whether or not teaching possesses those characteristics.

What constitutes a profession? Various characteristics have been proposed, although it is accepted that not all professions will display all the characteristics. Characteristics that have been proposed include the following:

1. The skills used in the occupation are based on a body or code of sophisticated and advanced knowledge.
2. There is an emphasis on intellectual rather than on craft, technical, or manual skills.
3. An extensive period of specialized education or training is required to enter the profession.
4. The practitioner accepts broad personal responsibility for judgments made and acts performed.
5. A broad range of autonomy is granted the individual practitioner.
6. A broad range of autonomy is given the occupational group in regulating itself and the work of the profession.
7. There is an emphasis on the service rendered rather than on economic gain.
8. The profession has a great deal of control over the training of those aspiring to join it.
9. To be admitted to the profession, an individual has to indicate that he or she possesses a certain level of knowledge, skill, and competence (Lieberman, 1956; Millerson, 1964).

Most laypeople would probably say that they regard teaching as a profession. However, teaching would not meet all the criteria set out above. In particular, teachers as a group do not regulate themselves or their work. They do not control training. Neither do they control entry to the profession, which is subject to state bureaucratic regulation. It can also be argued that the level of knowledge required in teaching is not sufficiently sophisticated or advanced (compared to such areas as medicine, law, or architecture) to warrant the title "professional."

In the past, it would probably have been true to say that teaching was partly a profession and partly a craft—professional in the service it rendered and in relationships between teachers and clients; a craft in the way in which pedagogical skills were exercised. Originally, training consisted of apprenticeship to a monitor or mentor teacher—an idea that is being revived at present (Carnegie Forum on Education and the Economy, 1986; Holmes Group Executive Board, 1986). Beginning in the late nineteenth century, formal teacher preparation courses were introduced; however, the skills that were taught in such courses were largely ones that had been developed over time by experienced teachers and that had little theoretical or real conceptual basis.

During the last quarter of a century, however, there has been enormous growth in the social sciences of psychology, sociology, economics, psychometrics, psycholinguistics, and social anthropology. Although there is yet a great deal to be learned, there is now a mass of data concerning child development, thinking, learning, and teaching that is of potential relevance to teaching. Teachers' adoption of the information that has accumulated in these areas could go a long way toward meeting the requirement that teaching, if it is to be regarded as a profession, should be based on a body of sophisticated and advanced knowledge.

Many suggestions and reforms to enhance the professional status of teachers have been made. Many states have lengthened teacher training, or are about to do so. The trend is toward requiring a bachelor's degree in the arts and sciences before intensive teacher training begins. Further, the establishment of a National Board for Professional Teaching Standards, which would be controlled by the teaching profession, has been proposed (Carnegie Forum on Education and the Economy, 1986). A reform report (Holmes Group Executive Board, 1986) and a number of bodies, such as the National Education Association and the American Federation of Teachers, have called for a national licensing board for teachers that is controlled by the profession. Salaries more competitive with other professions have been proposed. Further, career ladder proposals (discussed later in this chapter) that differentiate different levels of teachers from apprentice through master or mentor teacher are aimed at increasing the professionalization of teaching.

Teacher preparation and added incentives are not sufficient to allow the professionalism of teachers to develop fully. Indeed, there are certain aspects of schools that make it difficult for the teacher to act professionally. First, it has been argued that at the beginning of this century, the reorganization of schools to deal efficiently with expanding numbers resulted in schools that resembled industrial plants. In the process, schools became more hierarchical and governed by rules; administrators became managers with the responsibility of keeping the school plant functioning rationally and smoothly, and teachers became the workers in an institution that became increasingly bureaucratized (McNeil, 1988).

This factory metaphor had, and continues to have, a number of effects on the professionalism of teachers' work. While much of a teacher's work undoubtedly continued to derive its character from the exigencies of classroom events, administrative directives played an increasing role in the selection and purchase of books and materials, in the allocation of time, and in the inclusion of particular courses in the curriculum (Dreeben, 1973). Further, teaching became more mechanistic, ritualistic, and impersonal, "like the work of one who is punching a timeclock, with little commitment to or engagement with the task at hand" (McNeil, 1988). Finally, administrators frequently demeaned the authority of teachers in front of students "by subordinating instructional needs either to administrative efficiencies or to a preoccupation with order and control" (McNeil, 1988). As a result, teachers, especially those in large school systems, often feel dissatisfied because they have little voice in decisions that affect their classrooms and students (Lortie, 1986); decision making is one of the hallmarks of a profession.

Another difficulty arises from recent efforts by state and federal policymakers to legislate learning (Wise, 1979). Laws or regulations have been enacted that stifle teachers' discretionary power. For example, the minimum-competency testing of students has resulted in standardization of instruction in many schools. Many policies like these have conveyed this message to teachers: "We don't trust you; we have little confidence in your competence; we are going to scrutinize you carefully and, whenever possible, constrain your discretionary behavior with rules, prescriptions, systems, technology, and administration" (Sykes, 1983, p. 92).

A third factor that undermines professionalism in teaching is the fact that in many schools teachers work in isolation. "They work out of sight and hearing of one another, plan and prepare their lessons and materials alone, and struggle on their own to solve most of their instructional, curricular, and management problems" (Little, 1987, p. 491). In schools like these teachers are colleagues in name only, and have very few professional relationships. There are some schools—a minority—where serious collaboration between teachers takes place. Where collaboration has worked, teachers are enthusiastic. However, this type of professional collaborative relationship will "almost certainly require rethinking the present organization of human and material resources" (Little, 1987, p. 513).

Despite the institutional problems that tend to inhibit the practice of teaching as a profession, teaching does possess several of the characteristics of a profession that we outlined above. Look at these characteristics again. We feel that teaching certainly meets the criteria for a profession on characteristics 2, 3, 4, 7, and 9. It certainly does not meet them on 6 and 8, although, as we have seen, reform efforts are directed at changing this situation. As far as characteristic 5 is concerned, teachers have a lot of autonomy, but it is limited by the structure of the school and legislative action. The first criterion is perhaps the one that has been the subject of greatest debate. Whether or not teaching is regarded as a profession by this criterion will depend to some extent on the group that serves as your frame of reference. If your frame of reference is medicine or law, you might argue that teaching does not have a body of sophisticated and advanced knowledge. However, if your frame of reference is the ministry or accountancy, teaching is more likely to be regarded as a profession.

Progress on the road toward a situation in which teaching will improve its status as a profession will depend not only on the development of the social sciences to provide a basis for teaching but also "upon the degree to which we . . . are serious about educational reform and the degree to which efforts are made to improve not only the facilities and salaries available to teachers but the support they can count on from the community and from our universities" (Bruner, 1965, p. 89). Fortunately, you are considering a career in education at a time in which enormous effort is being made to upgrade the professional status of teaching and make the career more attractive.

The Demographics of Teaching

Classroom teaching is the single largest profession in the United States. Here are a few figures that illustrate the extent and the composition of the teaching profession (Snyder, 1987):

- There are almost 2½ million elementary and secondary school teachers employed in the public and private school sectors.
- Two-thirds of these teachers are female.
- Eighty-eight percent are white, 8 percent are black, and 3 percent are from other ethnic groups.
- About half of all teachers hold bachelor's degrees, and half of those have a master's degree or work beyond that level.
- The median age of teachers is 37 years.

You are considering teaching at a time of tremendous opportunity. First, the demand for teachers is rising dramatically as children of the baby boom generation begin to enter school. Second, teachers' salaries are being upgraded and incentive programs are being put in place. (We shall discuss salaries and incentives later in this chapter.) Let us first examine the demand for teachers in a little more detail.

Figure 8.1 presents the supply-and-demand curve for teachers and the enrollment trends in elementary and secondary schools between 1970 and 1992. The data are interesting. In 1970, the supply of teachers outstripped demand by about 80,000. Throughout the 1970s, the supply of teachers dropped dramatically in response to weak demand created by falling enrollment in elementary and secondary schools. However, at the end of the decade the supply of teachers still outstripped demand by 40,000. From 1982 through 1985, supply and demand were almost in balance. Starting in 1986, the demand for teachers began to rise faster than supply. Currently, school enrollments are rising, bringing about an increased demand for teachers; the numbers of teachers entering the profession is declining.

An important factor contributing to the decrease in the supply of teach-

FIGURE 8.1 Supply and Demand for Teachers, 1970–1992

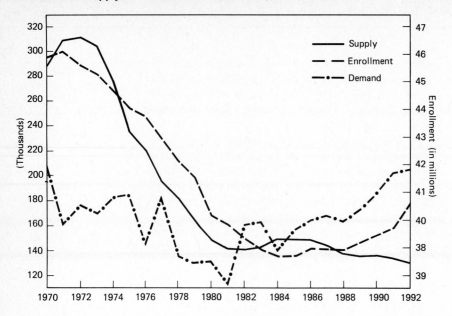

Source: Carnegie Forum on Education and the Economy, 1986.

ers has been the drop in the number of women entering teacher training. This decline is due to increased opportunities brought about by the women's movement in other more lucrative and prestigious careers previously all but closed to them. For example, over a 16-year period, women's interest in pursuing a career in business grew, while their interest in teaching declined. In 1968, 40 percent of women enrolled in college intended to teach, and by 1984 the percentage had dropped to 10; during that same interval, the percentage of women who intended to enter business rose from about 5 to over 20 (Carnegie Forum on Education and the Economy, 1986).

While there will be numerous teaching jobs available for the foreseeable future, there is a side to the teacher-supply-and-demand picture that is cause for serious concern. The pool of minority candidates for teaching is shrinking. From 1984 to 1985, as few as 2,533 Hispanics and 5,456 blacks earned degrees in education (*Education Week*, 1988; Graham, 1987).

This shortage of minorities qualified to teach is appearing at the same time that proportions of blacks, Hispanics, and Asians in the school-age population are rising. By the year 2000, one-third to 40 percent of all school children in the United States will be minorities. California already has a majority of minorities enrolled in the first three grades, and all but two of our 25 largest cities have had "minority majorities" in their schools (Carnegie Forum on Education and the Economy, 1986; Graham, 1987).

The supply of minority candidates for teaching is an inescapable function of the number of minorities that flow through the education pipeline in general. Of minority students who finish high school, about half enter college; of that half, a little less than half finish; of the half that finish college, about half enter graduate or professional schools. Finally, only about half of those who enter graduate or professional schools finish. Given that there are fewer minority students in the population to begin with, the dropout rate from secondary to college to graduate school means that the number of minorities available for teaching is insufficient to meet the demand. For example, only 100,000 bachelors of arts and sciences degrees across *all* disciplines were awarded to *all* minority students in the last year for which we have data (Carnegie Forum on Education and the Economy, 1986). However, only 14,209 blacks (to consider just one minority group) earned bachelor's degrees in education in 1976; by 1981 this figure had shrunk to 9,494; and by 1985, it had fallen to 5,456. Further, as mentioned above, only 2,533 Hispanics earned education degrees in 1985 (*Education Week*, 1988; Graham, 1987).

To help put these figures in perspective, consider the fact that minorities constitute close to 25 percent of the elementary and secondary student population and, as we saw, this percentage is growing rapidly. To obtain a rough equivalence in the number of *new* minority teachers, schools of education would have to produce 50,000 new teaching degree holders each year—one-half of *all* bachelor of arts and sciences degrees awarded minorities across all fields for the last year for which we have data (Carnegie Forum on Education and the Economy, 1986).

The demand for well-prepared minority teachers is acute. States have begun to realize that it is important for all students to have the benefit of minority teachers. Ways to identify, encourage, and support minorities to enter and, once in, to stay in teaching are becoming a top national priority.

Another area of concern in the demographics picture is the fact that those who major in education *on average* lag behind other college majors on rough measures of academic ability, such as combined SAT scores and type of high school program completed. Concern about the need to attract more students with higher academic abilities has been a focal point of many of the national reform reports. The reports emphasized the importance not only of recruiting but also of keeping those with higher academic ability in the profession. To accomplish these ends, recommendations are being made for incentives to attract more able students, such as low-interest loans or direct grants to those who stay in teaching after college, increasing starting salaries to the point where they would be more competitive with other occupations requiring similar degrees, and changing the opportunities for advancement within the profession. Recommendations to screen out weaker teachers include tightening entrance and graduation requirements for teacher education programs, extending the period of college training for teachers, instituting competency testing of teacher candidates, and strengthening teacher evaluation procedures. Many states have enacted legislation to implement these alternatives. We will look at some of these initiatives later in this chapter.

Preservice Training

The vast majority of teachers entering the profession have successfully completed a teacher training program at a college or university. Teacher training programs can vary quite a bit because of differences in resources and faculties and in the philosophical orientations of colleges. It is likely that teachers trained at different colleges will have quite different preservice course work and field experiences. The two most common approaches to teacher preparation are the traditional four-year program and the new five-year or extended program.

The Four-Year Program

The majority of teacher preparation programs follow the four-year plan, in which the prospective teacher completes requirements for certification and a bachelor's degree concurrently. The program of study is generally divided into four components. The first covers the general liberal arts courses required of all students for graduation. The second comprises course work in the academic discipline that the future teacher wishes to teach. (For example, someone who wants to be a history teacher would have to complete a number of credits in history and the related social sciences; someone majoring in elementary education might be required to take courses in science, mathematics, English, and social sciences.) The third component includes practical and theoretical course work in education. Courses might include philosophy of education, educational psychology, tests and measurements, curriculum design, child and adolescent development, educational sociology, educational technology, and general and special-methods courses. Field experiences form the final component. These are designed to relate concepts learned in course work to the classroom. The most important aspect of field experience is student teaching, which generally lasts an entire semester.

The Extended Format

Until recently, virtually all teacher preparation programs followed the four-year format. The catalyst for extending programs beyond the usual four years was the belief that more extensive training is needed. Proponents of extended teacher education programs argue that students need an extra year to build a stronger liberal arts base, to learn the skills necessary to be a classroom teacher, and to receive more extensive field experiences. Since the requirements of extended programs far exceed those necessary for a bachelor's degree, most award both bachelor's and master's degrees.

Two of the major education reform reports advocate extended programs for future teachers. Both the Holmes Group report *Tomorrow's teachers* (1986) and the report of the Carnegie Forum on Education and the Economy, *A nation prepared: Teachers for the 21st century* (1986), call for teachers to have a bachelor's degree in the arts and sciences as a prerequisite for the professional study of teaching. These reports see increased liberal arts education before teacher training as one of several key reforms needed for improving the teaching profession. As a result of these reports, many states are moving to change their teacher certification laws, and universities have begun to reorganize their teacher training curricula and have instituted, or are beginning to phase in, extended programs.

Perhaps the key component of extended teacher preparation programs is a full year of practice teaching, often referred to as an internship. The internship extends the traditional one semester of student teaching common in four-year programs. Another key feature of some extended programs is that the intern works under the direct supervision of a mentor teacher. The mentor teacher is an experienced, highly regarded master teacher who is given released time and additional compensation to work in the classroom with the intern. In some extended programs, some courses (for example, methods courses, and tests and measurements courses) are offered concurrently with the internship.

Practice Teaching

Practice teaching will allow you to apply the theory, methods, and skills learned in your course work; it will test your creative talents; it will help you decide if you enjoy working with students; and it will help you identify weaknesses that need improvement or extra study.

Two people will play a significant role in your practice teaching: your college supervisor and your cooperating classroom teacher. The latter will help you in the school, while the college supervisor will evaluate your teaching and act as a resource person.

Generally, the cooperating teacher has the strongest influence on the development of the student teacher's attitudes toward education and on his or her acquisition of practical teaching skills (Karmos and Jacko, 1977). The contextual factors of the school, including the students, community expectations, leadership, physical characteristics, and curricula, also influence the student teacher's attitudes and acquisition of skills (Copeland, 1977).

The college supervisor will influence your development during practice

This student teacher is viewing her teaching on videotape to identify areas where her instructional abilities can be improved.

teaching in a number of ways. As a resource person, he or she can provide suggestions for solving problems that you may encounter in the classroom. He or she will also act as an evaluator, providing critical feedback and positive reinforcement to you about your classroom performance. While cooperating teachers are role models, college supervisors are more likely to provide critical feedback during practice teaching (Zimpher, de Voss, & Nott, 1980). Recent proposals for mentor teachers would change the current situation and give the classroom teacher a much greater supervisory role (Carnegie Forum on Education and the Economy, 1986).

You will go through different phases as you progress through your period of practice teaching. The phases described by J. J. Caruso are fairly representative of what you can expect to feel as your practice teaching unfolds:

- *Phase 1* Anxiety/euphoria—a period of uneasiness and excitement about leaving the university campus for a classroom.
- *Phase 2* Confusion/clarity—you form ideas regarding your teaching yet have a limited view of teaching and your abilities.
- *Phase 3* Competence/inadequacy—your perception of your ability widens. You will feel adequate at times and inadequate at others.
- *Phase 4* Criticism/awareness—you develop more concern about individual pupil needs and professional issues.
- *Phase 5* More confidence/greater inadequacy—you might feel inadequate when not meeting high personal standards and at the same time seek more responsibility and autonomy.
- *Phase 6* Loss/relief—you show mixed feelings about having to leave the classroom, yet feel relieved that the experience was completed successfully (Caruso, 1977).

As you go through these phases (you might not experience all of them), it is important that a good relationship exist between you and your cooperating teacher and college supervisor. If you experience emotional stress, they should be able to provide emotional support, while at the same time continuing to help you examine new techniques and approaches.

During your practice teaching experience your cooperating teacher, university supervisor, and (in some situations) building administrators will examine your lesson plans, visit your class, review curriculum materials, and examine your performance in school-related activities outside of your classroom. They will most likely offer suggestions on how you may improve your performance as well as rate you on a number of teaching competencies.

Teacher Certification and Competency Testing

Before you can teach in a public school you must be certified by the state education department in the state in which you plan to teach. In most states, you will be eligible to apply for certification after successfully completing an approved teacher training program. The college program is designed to ensure coverage of course work and the acquisition of the teaching skills required for certification. In recent years, however, many states have made certification contingent upon passing a competency test. Currently, 44 states have competency tests that teachers must pass before obtaining certification. The majority of these states use the National Teachers Examination (NTE) administered by the Educational Testing Service; the others contract with test companies to develop their own tests.

There are five different types of assessment used for teacher certification. Various combinations of the five types are used across the 44 states (Haney, Madaus, & Kreitzer, 1987; Madaus & Pullin, 1987). The first four are paper-and-pencil tests, and the fifth is a direct assessment of classroom performance.

1. Tests of Basic Skills These tests are designed to assess basic reading, writing, and numerical skills. In 1988, 29 states required students to pass this kind of test before being allowed to major in education. A few years ago, two states, Texas and Arkansas, used this type of test to recertify their entire teaching corps.

2. Tests of General Knowledge These tests assess general knowledge in such areas as art, music, history, and scientific principles. The NTE is the only teacher test that currently includes this type of test in its battery.

3. Tests of Knowledge of Specific Content These tests examine prospective teachers' knowledge in the content area that they wish to teach. This type of test is also referred to as an area test.

4. Tests of Professional Knowledge and Skills Tests in this area are designed to assess professional knowledge across subjects such as philosophy of education, curriculum design, psychology of learning, classroom management, testing, and the structure and control of education.

5. Assessment of Teacher Performance The performance of teachers on the job is assessed by trained observers using a well-developed set of criteria. Currently, two states (Georgia and Oklahoma) offer temporary certification until an evaluation of a teacher's first-year performance is assessed by trained evaluators.

Before you take a teacher test you should obtain the 1984 *A Guide to the NTE core battery tests: Communication skills, general knowledge, professional knowledge* published by the Educational Testing Service in Princeton, New Jersey. It contains released versions of the NTE and will give you a good feel for the types of knowledge measured by the paper-and-pencil tests described above.

The competency testing of teachers is a controversial issue, stemming from the fact that little research exists to support the assumption that teachers who fail competency tests cannot be successful in the classroom (Haney, Madaus, & Kreitzer, 1987; Madaus & Pullin, 1987; Guyton & Farokhi, 1987). Passing the test, on the other hand, is no guarantee that a person will be a successful teacher. You might have the knowledge and skills measured by the test but fail to be successful because you lack the motivation, dedication, perseverance, courage, sensitivity, integrity, or a host of other attributes not measured by the test (Anrig, 1986).

However, the claim is made that those who fail generally *cannot* be successful because they lack the minimum knowledge and skills required. To date, the evidence contradicts this claim. Many teachers who failed teacher

"Mr. Bosworth, as teacher representative I must strongly protest your criteria for faculty competence."

Source: Phi Delta Kappan, 1980, p. 359.

certification tests have been judged by supervisors to be competent in the classroom. Put another way, there is little relationship between performance on the tests and direct evaluations of classroom performance. For example a recent study in Georgia of the relationship between the paper-and-pencil subject area teacher tests (type 3 test) and the teacher performance assessment indicator on which teachers were judged on 14 classroom competencies (type 6) found "no significant relationships between performance on a subject matter test and teaching behavior" (Guyton & Farokhi, 1987). This type of evidence is rejected by proponents of teacher testing on the grounds that ratings by supervisors are subjective and not reliable. Nonetheless, the burden of proof is on the test and, to date, it has not been possible to justify the tests in terms of actual performance in the classroom.

Despite basic questions about the validity of tests, it is apparent that state boards of education and state legislatures are convinced of the worth of testing prospective teachers and, in at least three states, even experienced teachers. They argue that other professions, such as law and medicine, require that applicants pass written examinations. Policymakers view teacher tests as a way of assuring the public that teachers have the knowledge necessary to teach. Recently, both the AFT and NEA have endorsed the concept of a national teachers' examination for entry-level teachers wishing to be certified. The Carnegie Forum on Education and the Economy (1986) called for the formation of a National Board for Professional Teaching. If the current trends continue, teacher tests will probably become a routine part of the certification process and a requirement that you will have to meet if you wish to teach in most states. However, it is hoped that the next generation of teacher tests will more accurately reflect teachers' knowledge and competence. Promising work on the development of a new generation of teacher tests is currently under way.

Professional Growth

An important outcome of formative teacher evaluation is the identification of areas that need improvement. Teachers, like all other professionals, need to stay abreast of new developments in their field. To help teachers in this task, school districts, professional associations, and universities offer in-service or professional development programs or courses. Professional associations also produce newsletters and journals that help teachers keep abreast of developments in the field. Also, yearly evaluations can help the teacher improve his or her teaching. Let us consider each of these avenues of improvement in turn.

Professional Development Programs

A common approach to in-service education is through courses at colleges and universities. Many colleges and universities offer courses during evenings and in the summer to make it possible for teachers to attend. Some school districts reimburse teachers for either all of, or part of, the tuition costs of such courses. In many districts, teachers receive a pay increment when they complete a certain number of credits, usually 30. Many states require teachers to take a certain number of graduate credit hours over a period of time to maintain certification.

A second approach to in-service training is through workshops. Workshops usually focus on a particular issue and involve participants in some type of "hands-on" activity. Workshops can be set up as "one-shot" programs or they can be arranged in an interrelated series. The one-shot workshops are appropriate for introducing concepts, demonstrating how to use specific materials, overviewing policy, or boosting morale. If the goals of the workshops are to examine an issue thoroughly or to seek a behavior change, then a series of coordinated workshops is more appropriate and effective.

The teacher center—a third approach to in-service education—is based upon the concept that teachers need to be involved in determining the nature of in-service programs. In the mid-1970s, the federal government provided funding to support the development and maintenance of teacher centers. This funding was stopped in the early 1980s. Teacher centers are now supported through state funds, private endowments, and local support. A teacher center is a place where teachers can plan in-service programs, participate in different professional activities, and share expertise. No two teacher centers are alike, since they reflect the uniqueness of the school districts they serve. The following six characteristics make the teacher center concept different from other in-service approaches:

1. Teachers decide on what they will study or work on.
2. Teachers develop many of the curriculum materials they will use in class in the center either by themselves or with others.
3. Teachers share ideas, materials, and expertise.
4. The teacher center brings teachers into formal contact with commu-

nity people, resources, and events. These contacts can enhance teachers'
learning and personal growth as well as enrich the curriculum.

5. The teacher center is a place where teachers can get help that addresses specific classroom problems.

6. The center offers teachers a continuous relationship with peers over
a period of time, not just a workshop series or a single course (Devaney,
1980).

A fourth approach to in-service education is that of action research, a
process that involves teachers collaborating with education researchers in
solving a specific problem identified by either the teacher or the district.
Together, the research team sharpens the focus of the problem, reviews
literature that relates to the problem, designs and conducts a study, and
finally disseminates the results. Action research programs not only address
problems identified by the school district, but also enhance the self-esteem
and sense of personal accomplishment of the teachers involved (Oja &
Ham, 1984).

Professional Associations

Teachers need to take the initiative if they want to continue to grow
professionally. One way to do this is to join and become active in professional
associations. Professional associations represent numerous special-interest
groups within the education profession. The number of different associations
represents the diversity and complexity of the education system.

Box 8.1 lists the names and addresses of some of the more prominent
national education organizations. You might want to investigate those organizations that look relevant to your career plans. Write and ask for information
about each organization in which you are interested. See if they have a student
membership. These associations publish professional journals and magazines
that are sent to members. You can find most of these journals in your library.
Start to read the prominent ones in your field on a regular basis. These organizations also sponsor state, national, and regional conferences. Some of them
act as lobbying groups to protect the special interests of their constituents. For
example, the Council for Exceptional Children was influential in organizing
support in Congress for the passage of the Education for All Handicapped
Children Act.

The National Education Association (NEA) and the American Federation of Teachers (AFT) are the two largest teacher organizations in the United
States. Together they represent 91 percent of classroom teachers in the country. The NEA is the larger of the two, with approximately 1.7 million members, while the AFT has approximately 600,000 members.

Both the AFT and NEA are interested in the professional development
of teachers. They publish journals, sponsor workshops, and actively promote
proeducation and prostudent legislation. They both work hard to improve the
status and working conditions of teachers. Because of this latter function, most
people consider these two organizations to be labor unions (Cresswell & Murphy, 1980). (We shall discuss the pros and cons of unionization under the topic

BOX 8.1 National Education Organizations

American Association for Gifted Children
15 Gramercy Park
New York, NY 10003
(212) 473–4266

American Association for Physics
  Teachers
Graduate Physics Building
SUNY (State University of New York)
Stony Brook NY 11794
(516) 246–6840

American Association of School
  Administrators
1801 North Moore Street
Arlington, VA 22209
(703) 528–0700

American Council on the Teaching of
  Foreign Languages
Two Park Avenue, Room 1814
New York, NY 10016
(212) 689–8021

American Federation of Teachers
11 Dupont Circle, NW
Washington, DC 20036
(202) 797–4400

American School Counselor Association
5203 Leesburg Pike
Falls Church, VA 22041
(703) 820–4700

Association for Experiential Education
P.O. Box 4625
Denver, CO 80204
(303) 837–8633

Association for Supervision and Curriculum
  Development
225 North Washington Street
Alexandria, VA 22314
(703) 549–9110

Council for Exceptional Children
1920 Association Drive
Reston, VA 22091
(703) 620–3360

International Council on Health, Physical
  Education and Recreation
1900 Association Drive
Reston VA 22091
(703) 476–3462

International Reading Association
800 Barksdale Road
P.O. Box 8139
Newark, DE 19711
(302) 731–1600

Music Teachers' National Association
2113 Carew Tower
Cincinnati, OH 45202
(513) 421–1420

National Art Education Association
1916 Association Drive
Reston, VA 22091
(703) 860–8000

National Association for Bilingual Education
1201 16th Street, NW
Washington, DC 20036
(202) 833–4271

National Association for Environmental
  Education
P.O. Box 400
Troy, OH 54373
(513) 698–6493

National Association for the Education of
  Young Children
1834 Connecticut Avenue, NW
Washington, DC 20009
(202) 232–8777

National Association of Biology Teachers,
  Inc.
11250 Roger Bacon Drive
Suite 19
Reston, VA 22090
(703) 471–1134

National Association of Independent
  Schools
18 Tremont Street
Boston, MA 02108
(617) 723–6900

National Business Education Association
1914 Association Drive
Reston, VA 22091
(703) 860–0213

National Congress of Parents and Teachers
700 North Rush Street
Chicago, IL 60611
(312) 787–0977

BOX 8.1 (*Continued*)

National Council for the Social Studies
3615 Wisconsin Avenue, NW
Washington, DC 20016
(202) 966–7840

National Council of Teachers of English
1111 Kenyon Road
Urbana, IL 61801
(217) 328–3870

National Council of Teachers of Mathematics
1906 Association Drive
Reston, VA 22091
(703) 620–9840

National Education Association
1201 16th Street, NW
Washington, DC 20036
(202) 833–4000

National Foundation for Gifted and
  Creative Children
395 Diamond Hill Road
Warwick, RI 02866
(401) 737–0180

National Middle School Association
25 Meadow Drive
Fairborn, OH 45324
(513) 878–2346

National Science Teachers' Association
1742 Connecticut Avenue, NW
Washington, DC 20009
(202) 328–5800

National Vocational Agricultural Teachers'
  Association
P.O. Box 15051
Alexandria, VA 22309
(no phone number given)

Outdoor Education Association
143 Fox Hill Road
Denville, NJ 07834
(201) 627–72124

Phi Delta Kappa
P.O. Box 789
Bloomington, IN 47402
(812) 339–1156

Women Educators
Educational Foundation Department
College of Education
University of New Mexico
Albuquerque, NM 87131
(505) 277–5967

of collective bargaining.) Although the AFT and NEA are united in their mission of improving working conditions, they are also rivals because they compete for membership and power.

The AFT and NEA have affiliates at the state and local levels. To join the National Education Association you must belong to the local and state affiliates (NEA, 1987). Although membership at the local level is not mandatory to join the national AFT, it is strongly encouraged, since the local affiliates also work to establish policy favorable to teachers. Local affiliates of both the NEA and AFT focus primarily on negotiating favorable contracts through collective bargaining. The state affiliates focus on state legislation and regulations and provide technical support to local affiliates. The national-level organization focuses on federal policy and education-related issues that affect the country as a whole. It also offers state affiliates technical and legal help.

Teacher Evaluation

Teacher evaluation programs have been designed to serve two purposes. The first is to provide a systematic assessment of teaching performance on which personnel decisions (for example, those relating to tenure, dismissal, promotion, or merit pay) can be made. This is called *summative evaluation.* The second is to improve the teaching and learning processes. This is called *formative evaluation.* Districts can adopt evaluation plans that stress either formative or summative evaluation or both.

Both the NEA and AFT have resolutions concerning the evaluation of teachers (see Box 8.2). Both emphasize formative rather than summative evaluation; that is, they ask for evaluation that helps to *improve* teacher performance rather than evaluation or judgments about good or bad teaching. Both the NEA and AFT have listed what they consider to be the essential elements of a good teacher evaluation. The NEA's list is shown in Box 8.3, and the AFT's in Box 8.4. Both lists stress formative evaluation and indicate that the process should be based on negotiated job descriptions, that the criteria be agreed on by all parties, that the results be communicated in writing, and that the report be subject to response and appeal. In evaluating these statements by the two largest professional organizations, you need to keep in mind that they, like any professional organization or union, must protect their weakest members and therefore are not apt to endorse summative evaluations of teacher performance. (For additional views on teacher evaluation see Millman, 1981.)

Districts conduct summative and formative evaluations of teachers in many different ways. If an evaluation program is to be successful, the district must first communicate clearly to teachers the *purpose* of the evaluation as well as the *process* and *procedure* to be used. Further, the evaluation process will be strengthened enormously if teachers participate in the development of the system. While conducting evaluation is a responsibility of the administrator, teacher involvement in the design and implementation of the evaluation process is often part of the collective bargaining agreement between the LEA and the teachers' organization.

There are five common techniques used to evaluate teachers:

1. Rating Scales Administrators rate teachers on an agreed set of clearly defined characteristics. These characteristics are usually those that the district feels, and/or research indicates, are qualities found in effective teachers. An example of such a rating scale is shown in Box 8.5. On this scale, the teacher is evaluated on performance in four major areas: professional qualities, human relations, personal qualities, and professional skills.

BOX 8.3 NEA's Twenty-two Essentials for Good Teacher Evaluation

On Purposes:

1. Major purpose is improvement of instruction
2. Clearly stated, committed to writing, and made public
3. Agreed on by those evaluated

On Criteria:

4. Related only to professional performance
5. Apply only to things in job description
6. Capable of clear and precise definition
7. Observable or otherwise clearly identifiable
8. Consistent with school goals and objectives

On Process:

9. Provides pre-observation conference
10. Observation time and length agreeable to teacher

11. Teacher's objectives agreed on by the evaluator
12. Samples of performance adequate in length and diversity
13. Evaluator knowledgeable of subject and properly trained
14. Context taken into consideration

On Follow-up:

15. Provides post-observation conference
16. Evaluation committed to writing
17. Both strengths and weaknesses described
18. Recommendations for improvement clear and specific
19. Opportunity for response
20. Appropriate levels of appeal
21. Time, materials, and human resources available for improvement
22. The total evaluation program regularly evaluated

Source: McKenna, 1982, p. 17.

2. Self-Evaluation The individual teacher is required to list his or her strengths and weaknesses. This assessment becomes the basis for developing a plan for improvement.

3. Setting Objectives The administrator and teacher sit down early in the school year and agree on aspects of the teacher's performance that will be assessed during the year. Once objectives and the areas to be evaluated are agreed upon, an evaluator observes the teacher in the classroom, keying on the agreed objectives and offering commendations or suggestions on how to improve.

4. Student Performance Evaluation Some districts use students' performance on standardized tests as a criterion in evaluating teachers. There are serious technical problems associated with this approach. It can also be quite unfair to teachers who have a preponderance of low-ability or problem students or students who had not been taught well in previous years.

5. Peer Evaluation This approach uses teachers to evaluate other teachers. Most peer evaluations are for formative purposes and the results are shared only among the teacher and peer evaluator.

Many districts incorporate one or more of these approaches into an overall evaluation plan. If teacher evaluation programs are to be effective, the evaluators must understand the teaching and learning processes. The evaluator must also remain as objective as possible so that teachers are treated fairly and equitably. Many districts have more than one person conducting evaluations to add different perspectives to the assessment and to increase the chances that the evaluation will be both fair and accurate.

Since 1985, 14 professional associations have been engaged in a project to develop standards to improve personnel evaluation in schools. A key purpose of the Standards for Evaluation of Education Personnel is to make present efforts at teacher evaluation fairer, equitable, and more accurate. The standards require that personnel evaluations be useful, feasible, ethical, and accurate. The following is an example of a standard:

> *The evaluation data about an educator should be interpreted in terms of clearly specified responsibilities, performance objectives, and qualifications so the judgments and decisions concerning such matters as selection, certification, counseling for improvement, promotion, and termination will be justified in terms of sound standards as well as high quality data (Stufflebeam, 1987, p. 61).*

Each standard is followed by an explanation of its concepts, a rationale, guidelines to facilitate implementation, common errors to be avoided, and one or more illustrative cases. You should become familiar with these standards, as they may well affect your career.

Salaries

One indicator of how society views a profession is the amount of money that people in the profession are paid. Although teachers' salaries have increased in recent years, it was not until the last few years that they kept pace with inflation. The average teacher salary from 1982 to 1983 was $20,531; this figure is the equivalent of $8,926 in 1972–1973 dollars. From 1972 to 1973,

BOX 8.5 Teacher Evaluation Appraisal Form

Teacher's Name _____   School _____

Administrative Evaluator _____   Date _____

Employment Status: _____ Probationary _____ Tenured _____ Other (Specify)

	Exceeds Expectations	*Meets Expectations*	*Needs Improvement*

I. Professional Qualities

A. Avails self of opportunities for professional improvement through self-study, workshops, and/or formal course work.   _____   _____   _____

B. Adheres to recognized ethical standards of the educational profession.   _____   _____   _____

C. Complies with rules and regulations of the school system.   _____   _____   _____

D. Participates in the process of change.   _____   _____   _____

E. Implements recommendations and requests made by supervisory and administrative staff which are in keeping with the philosophy of the system.   _____   _____   _____

II. Human Relationships

A. Makes an effort to develop the self-worth and dignity of students.   _____   _____   _____

B. Recognizes and provides for individual differences among students.   _____   _____   _____

C. Seeks opportunities to get to know students through school activities other than classroom instruction.   _____   _____   _____

D. Maintains cooperative and harmonious relationships with co-workers.   _____   _____   _____

BOX 8.5 (*Continued*)

	Exceeds Expectations	*Meets Expectations*	*Needs Improvement*
E. Maintains and encourages school-home cooperation by taking initiative in contacting parents when their help is indicated or when the child is to be commended.	____	____	____

III. Personal Qualities

A. Possesses health and stamina for effective job performance.	____	____	____
B. Exhibits self-confidence.	____	____	____
C. Demonstrates an interest and enjoyment in his/her work.	____	____	____
D. Maintains a neat appearance.	____	____	____
E. Speaks clearly, distinctly, and correctly.	____	____	____
F. Is tactful and courteous.	____	____	____
G. Is punctual in assuming responsibilities.	____	____	____
H. Is accurate in maintaining records and making reports.	____	____	____
I. Maintains self-control.	____	____	____
J. Takes proper care of equipment and materials.	____	____	____

IV. Professional Skills

A. Provides for physical, social, and emotional needs of children in planning their educational activities.	____	____	____
B. Effectively meets the objectives of the curriculum.	____	____	____
C. Has well-planned lessons.	____	____	____
D. Presents lessons in clear, logical manner.	____	____	____

BOX 8.5 (*Continued*)

	Exceeds Expectations	*Meets Expectations*	*Needs Improvement*
E. Involves students actively in the teaching-learning process.	_____	_____	_____
F. Relates educational activities to students' interests whenever possible.	_____	_____	_____
G. Gives clear, purposeful assignments.	_____	_____	_____
H. Assists students with extra help.	_____	_____	_____
I. Assists students in the development of effective study habits.	_____	_____	_____
J. Employs a variety of approaches in presenting materials to pupils.	_____	_____	_____
K. Provides opportunities for creativity.	_____	_____	_____
L. Creates a relaxed and friendly class atmosphere conducive to learning.	_____	_____	_____
M. Disciplines in a fair and positive manner, striving toward student self-control.	_____	_____	_____
N. Seeks and uses the advice and assistance of support staff when appropriate.	_____	_____	_____

Source: Adapted from the Newington, Connecticut, teacher appraisal form.

however, the average teacher's salary was $10,164. Thus, in real purchasing power, the average teacher's salary decreased 12.2 percent in a ten-year period (Feistritzer, 1983). During this same period, the personal income of all Americans increased by 17.8 percent in real dollar terms. Simply put, teachers lost ground in earnings while the average income of all other Americans increased substantially. Another way to consider teaching salaries is to compare them to other jobs. Figure 8.2 shows the average annual salaries for 12 selected occupations, including teaching; it dramatically shows that teachers' salaries rank below those of most occupations requiring a college degree. Further, teacher salaries are not much better than those of several occupations requiring only a high school diploma (Carnegie Forum on Education and the Economy, 1986). The reform reports have all recommended that teacher salaries be increased, and in a number of states this is happening.

Incentive Programs

As we mentioned earlier, teacher salaries have increased significantly in the last few years. While it is not likely that you will get rich, it is apparent

FIGURE 8.2 Average Annual Salaries for Selected Occupations, 1985   199

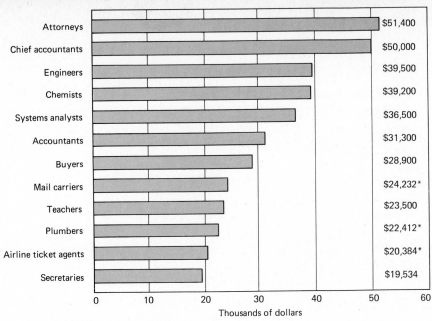

Attorneys	$51,400
Chief accountants	$50,000
Engineers	$39,500
Chemists	$39,200
Systems analysts	$36,500
Accountants	$31,300
Buyers	$28,900
Mail carriers	$24,232*
Teachers	$23,500
Plumbers	$22,412*
Airline ticket agents	$20,384*
Secretaries	$19,534

Thousands of dollars

*Based on average annual median weekly earnings.

Source: Carnegie Forum on Education and the Economy, 1986, p. 37.

that communities are willing to provide teachers with better salaries than they had in the past. One example of a community that has made a monumental effort to improve teachers' salaries is Rochester, New York, where the highest-paid teachers will make $70,000 a year. Teachers eligible for this salary must earn the rank of "master teacher."

The concept of having ranks within the teaching profession is known as the career ladder concept. Career ladder plans establish a series of ranks that teachers must earn through in-class evaluation of teaching, and in some cases by passing a written test. Each rank carries a different level of prestige, salary, and responsibility. The entry-level rank is usually referred to as the probationary, novice, or beginning teacher level. Depending on the plan, teachers can progress through several levels to the highest rank, which is master or head teacher. The master teacher is expected to have additional responsibilities such as being a mentor for a beginning teacher or helping to write curriculum.

The Carnegie Forum on Education and the Economy (1986) recommends a salary schedule, shown in Figure 8.3, for various steps on the Carnegie career ladder. Figure 8.3 also compares this salary schedule for the various teaching levels with the salaries paid to accountants with various levels of experience. As you can see, the salaries compare quite favorably, particularly when you consider that teachers do not work as many weeks during the year as do most accountants.

Performance based on merit pay is a second type of teacher incentive plan with which districts are experimenting. Pay-for-performance plans link teachers' salary increments to the quality of classroom instruction as judged by the teacher evaluation process. Merit pay is a highly controversial topic that evokes strong feelings on the part of teachers, who generally oppose the idea, and the public who support it.

Tenure

Tenure is a statutory provision that protects a teacher from dismissal for political, ideological, or other discriminatory reasons. Tenure laws guarantee that a teacher can be removed only for a specific professional reason and then only after due process procedures have been followed. Some tenure laws contain the phrase *continuing contract* instead of the word *tenure,* although both mean the same thing. Most states (the exceptions are Utah, Vermont, Mississippi, and South Carolina) have such laws. Thirty-nine states have tenure laws that cover all school districts in the state; in the remaining states, teachers in some districts are not covered by the law (Palker, 1980).

To dismiss a tenured teacher, the administration must prove that the teacher is incompetent, insubordinate,

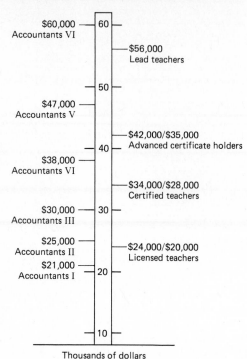

Thousands of dollars

Source: Carnegie Forum on Education and the Economy, 1986, p. 100.

or immoral, or has a disability that prevents him or her from teaching. Also, a teacher can be removed if the position he or she holds is eliminated and no equivalent position within the system exists for which the teacher is qualified. In some states, teachers may appeal termination decisions to state boards; in others they may appeal to the state court or to an arbitration hearing.

Traditionally, tenure has been a controversial issue. As in most controversies, proponents and opponents of tenure have apparently valid reasons for their positions. Supporters of tenure argue that it gives teachers security of employment during satisfactory service, protection against unwarranted dismissal, academic freedom in the classroom, permanent employment for the best-qualified personnel, staff stability and position satisfaction, freedom outside of the classroom commensurate with that of any other citizen, and liberty to encourage student freedom of inquiry and expression (Castetter, 1981).

Opponents of tenure register particular concern about the claim that tenure gives permanent employment for the best-qualified personnel. They contend that rather than ensuring that this happens, tenure provides a shelter for lazy, incompetent, or semiretired teachers. In short, they see tenure as protecting the weakest teachers. Opponents of tenure also argue that since tenure laws are designed to protect teachers, dismissal requires a great deal of time, effort, and record keeping on the part of administrators. With the many responsibilities administrators have, it is understandable that removing a tenured teacher is viewed as a difficult and time-consuming task. If taken to court, tenure arbitration can cost a great deal of money. In practice, many administrators avoid removal hearings or use them only as a last resort.

The tenure opposition also maintains that tenure laws are no longer needed. With the steady growth and power of teacher associations and unions, a new type of tenure—contract tenure—has developed. Contract tenure describes sections of collective bargaining agreements related directly to job security that very often go beyond statutory tenure guidelines, thus affording teachers greater job security.

Seniority clauses negotiated by unions are examples of contract guarantees exceeding statutory tenure protection. Under most statutory tenure laws, all tenured teachers are given the same job protection, regardless of the number of years they have been tenured. Thus, if budget cuts or declining enrollments dictate the elimination of tenured positions, all tenured teachers are equally at risk. However, in school systems that have a seniority clause in their collective bargaining agreement, tenured teachers with the least number of years of service are the first to go.

A major concern of those opposing tenure is that teachers lose the incentive to grow professionally after gaining tenure. To prevent this from happening, some school districts have developed evaluation programs for both tenured and nontenured teachers. Another approach is to require teachers to apply periodically to be recertified. To be recertified, they must show proof of professional development (for example, evidence that they have attended graduate or in-service courses or, in Georgia, that they have passed a written test related to their certification area).

Collective Bargaining

Collective bargaining allows employees to negotiate a contract as a unified group, represented by a union or association, rather than on an individual basis. Prior to 1961, government employees were denied this right. President Kennedy's issuance of Executive Order 10988 in 1961 gave them the right to bargain collectively.

In 1961, the AFT, a small organization at the time, successfully defeated the NEA in an election to represent the New York City teachers as their bargaining agent. In 1962, the AFT won a favorable contract that became the nation's first major collective bargaining agreement between a teachers' union and a school board (Cresswell & Murphy, 1980). The AFT success influenced the NEA to take a more active role in promoting collective bargaining as a means of improving the working conditions of teachers. Since 1961, both the AFT and NEA have become strong advocates of collective bargaining. Both worked to help pass legislation in 35 states that makes collective bargaining mandatory for school districts.

Collective bargaining has had an enormous impact on school districts throughout the country. Many teacher unions are now very strong and have won contracts that cover far more than salary and fringe benefits. For example, nearly all contracts contain clauses that limit the power of administrators to determine class size and to allocate duties outside of teaching. These agreements also cover such issues as the time spent in meetings after school and the amount and type of in-service education that the district will provide.

Collective bargaining causes heated debate among educators and the general public. Donald Cameron, executive director of the National Educa-

"Mr. Henshaw won't be here for the unit on the rise of unions in the 20th century. He's on strike."

Kappan, 1983, p. 92.

tional Association, contends that collective bargaining is the most important tool educators have in their efforts to promote educational excellence. He cites five reasons for this contention:

1. Collective bargaining increases communication because it guarantees that teachers' opinions will be considered.
2. Expectations for job requirements and performance are clarified through the bargaining process.
3. Contract provisions remove professional uncertainties and provide protection for the faculty to teach as they think best.
4. Collectively bargained compensation related to levels of educational attainment encourages excellence by encouraging and rewarding personal growth.
5. Collective agreements lead to a sense of community among faculty (Cameron, 1984).

Studies have found a number of desirable effects associated with unionization, including improved teacher morale, increased per pupil expenditures, and responsiveness to equity mandates (Sykes, 1983).

Those opposed to collective bargaining contend that forcing teachers to join an association, or not allowing them to negotiate a contract independently, is undemocratic (Staub, 1981). They also say that the collective bargaining process has not been as influential in securing increases in salaries and benefits for teachers as some contend (Wynn, 1981). More generally, they argue that the adversarial relationship encouraged by collective bargaining practices leads to a poor public image of education as a profession and has tilted teaching from a professional to a working-class orientation (Lieberman, 1981). To substantiate this later charge, observers point to

1) the formalization of a distinction between regular and extra duties, which has undercut teachers' traditional conception of their mission as holistic and narrowed their sense of responsibility;

Teacher strikes are extremely stressful for all those involved in the educational process.

2) the creation of a dual authority system within schools between line administrators and union representatives; 3) an emphasis on proceduralism at the expense of substantive engagement in the evaluation of teaching; and 4) a reduction of administrative flexibility in school staffing through contract provisions that govern such factors as class size and teacher transfers and layoffs (Sykes, 1983, p. 91).

The debate over collective bargaining and the influence of strong teacher unions stir deep emotions among many people. If teachers strike or take related job actions, feelings may intensify on both sides of the issue. Job actions by teachers are particularly stressful, since students are directly affected—they don't go to school. The choices of whether or not to join a union and/or support job actions, should labor problems develop, are ones that present ethical and moral dilemmas for many teachers. They are choices that you will have to make in your professional life.

Teacher Burnout

Despite recent improvements in teaching, the low status, poor pay, bad administrative practices in schools, and increased responsibilities can have a cumulative debilitating effect on teachers (Lortie, 1986). In some cases, teachers' attitudes about the profession change drastically. Teachers who develop negative feelings toward themselves, their students, and their profession have been described as experiencing teacher "burnout." Recent research on burnout has identified specific phases of it, the reasons that it occurs, and what effects it has on the individual and on others (Schwab & Iwanicki, 1982; Schwab, Jackson & Schuler, 1986).

The burnout syndrome has three phases. An initial phase involves a chronic feeling of emotional exhaustion and fatigue. Teachers find that their emotional energies are drained and that on a psychological level they have nothing more to give. The following comments from two teachers illustrate this first phase:

> *I feel emotionally drained and fatigued at the end of the day and end of the week. It's to the point where I go through the motions. I can't get up for the job anymore. (Elementary teacher with three years' experience).*

> *My excitement for the job has worn off. When I first started teaching I couldn't wait for the next day to work with my students. Lately I would rather stay in bed because I'm beat. (High school teacher with five years' experience) (Schwab, 1983, p. 22).*

In the second phase of burnout, the teacher develops negative, cynical, or depersonalized attitudes toward students. The teacher exhibits these attitudes by treating students as objects rather than as people. A teacher might use derogatory labels to describe students (for example, "Those students are all animals," or "What do you expect, they are a dumb class"). Another way in which teachers depersonalize students is by using academic or intellectual labels to describe them (for example, "I don't expect much from him, he's emotionally disturbed," "Why do I get all of those learning disabled kids?" or "Sit him next to the rest of the MR's"). Teachers can also display depersonalized attitudes toward students by psychologically and/or physically withdrawing from them. A common example of this behavior is when teachers continually ignore certain students when they raise their hands or seek assistance.

In the third phase of teacher burnout, the person loses a sense of accomplishment from the job. Teachers in this phase feel that they are not effective in their work and gain no sense of satisfaction from it. This is particularly disheartening for teachers, since the main reason most enter the profession is to help students. The following quotes from two teachers illustrate these feelings:

> *I feel no sense of appreciation for all that I do; I feel like I am wasting the best years of my life. (High school teacher with eight years' experience).*

> *I never have that great feeling of accomplishment. Teaching math at the seventh grade level does not offer much of a sense of triumph or feeling that you have done a great job, you really can't*

see or measure your results. Very frustrating. (46-year-old high school teacher) (Schwab, 1983, p. 22).

Burnout should be a concern of everyone involved with education because when it occurs in teachers, students are likely to suffer. Research among teachers and other helping professionals has shown that people who experience burnout have a higher incidence of family conflicts, are more often absent from work, are likely to want to leave the profession, and exert less effort on the job (Jackson & Maslach, 1982; Schwab, Jackson, & Schuler, 1986).

Job burnout can happen for a number of reasons. Teachers are more likely to burn out if

1. They work in schools that exhibit poor organizational practices (for example, if there is poor communication among faculty and administrators, ineffective leadership, ambiguous teacher evaluation procedures, inadequate reward structures, and insufficient curriculum resources).

2. They have unrealistic expectations about what they can accomplish in their teaching.

3. They have inadequate or improper training on how to handle classroom or student problems.

4. They lack effective social support networks that include colleagues, friends, or administrators who listen to problems, provide answers to technical questions, challenge the teacher intellectually, and provide emotional support.

5. They have chosen the profession for the wrong reasons (Schwab, Jackson, & Schuler, 1986).

Preventing Burnout

Burnout is a complex problem for which there are no easy solutions. However, you can lessen the chance of "burning out" if you keep some of the following points in mind:

1. Spend time in the school that you are planning to teach in before you take your first job. If the school climate does not appear positive, you might want to think twice about accepting the job.

2. Spend time during your practice teaching reflecting upon areas where you need additional training or course work. For example, if you are having problems adapting your classroom for exceptional learners, you might take another special-education course or consult with teachers who are strong in this area. By preparing yourself to deal with problems before you are working full-time, you will reduce the stress that will occur when you later face the problems in your classroom.

3. Be realistic about what you can accomplish in your first few years of teaching. While idealism is important for new teachers, if your expectations are unrealistic, failure to achieve them can lead to feelings of inadequacy.

4. Finally, it is important to choose the teaching profession for the right reasons. You should choose teaching because you have the personality and academic ability to do the job, coupled with the desire to teach and help students. If you are choosing teaching only because of its security, vacations, or short hours, you should think again.

Should I Teach?

The first step in choosing a career is to clarify your life goals. These will relate to both personal (social, spiritual, and family) and professional aspirations (financial autonomy, humanitarianism, power). Bear in mind that you may not spend all your life doing the same kind of work. It is normal and often healthy for people to make several career changes through their lifetime.

Research has shown that some of the reasons people give for entering teaching are a desire to contribute to the well-being of people, to share knowledge and interest in a particular subject area, to have variety in their daily work, to have more than average vacation time to explore personal or professional interests, to have security and stability, to continue to learn and grow in their profession, and to work with young people (Joseph & Green, 1986).

If, after reexamining your priorities, you find that your goals are not achievable in teaching, you may want to consider other options. A visit to your campus career-planning and placement office might be helpful in considering new possibilities or reconsidering old ones.

As well as considering your goals, you should take a realistic look at the profession. There are a number of questions you can ask yourself. Am I a person who enjoys working in a social environment? Do I have the patience needed to work with children? Can I work on many different tasks at the same time? Am I more interested in pursuing the scholarship aspect of my discipline than working with students? The only way you can answer these questions is to gain as much experience working with children as possible. Perhaps you will not be able to answer them until you have taught for a few years. If at that time your answers indicate that you should not be a teacher, remember that teaching does not have to be a lifelong profession. Many successful teachers remain in the field for only a brief time before taking up other challenges. The skills you will have developed and the enjoyment you will have gained from teaching will help you in whatever career you may eventually pursue.

Finding a Job

In this section, we will explore some ideas that you should consider as you progress through your professional training and that will help you when the time comes to begin your job search. There are probably two questions that will come to your mind when thinking about getting a job. The first is, "Will I find a teaching job when I begin to look?" The second is, "When should I begin to think about securing a job?" While no one can be guaranteed employment, the answer to the first question (given the supply-and-demand situation discussed above) most probably is *yes*. The answer to the second question is *now*.

As we saw, during the 1970s and early 1980s there were very few openings for new teachers, and many experienced teachers lost their jobs because of cuts and a declining student population. This process of eliminating teaching positions became known as "reduction in force," or "rifing." In many states, a large percentage of teachers were "rifed" by school districts. Not only were no new jobs available, but the rifed were competing with new graduates for the few available positions in other districts. Today, the outlook for those seeking teaching positions is brighter than it has been for many years (see Figure 8.1).

When the time comes to seek a teaching position, the process will be easier if you keep in mind some points that administrators consider when hiring new teachers:

1. Academic Preparation Most administrators who hire teachers are interested in the courses taken and the grades received by the job applicant. Your grades provide an indication of your skills as a learner. It is important, therefore, to maintain a good academic grade point average in your course work so that administrators will be convinced of your academic ability and commitment to learning.

2. Experiential Background A second area that administrators want to know about is how well you work with students in the age group you plan to teach, as well as with other adults. The more you are able to document that you have successfully worked with both children and adults, the more likely you are to be selected. You can gain experience in these areas through summer jobs, part-time work during college, volunteer work, participating in various organizations on campus, and taking courses that include field experience with children or young adults.

3. Successful Completion of the Practicum Part of Your Teacher Training Many administrators feel that the evaluations of a student teacher by the cooperating teacher and university supervisor are two of the most critical pieces of information available to help in the selection process. Those people responsible for hiring teachers are particularly interested in how well student teachers communicate with students, peers, administrators, and parents; how much responsibility they are willing to take on; and their ability to translate what they have learned in university courses into practice in the classroom.

4. Interview Process The interview is your chance to convince the school district that you are the person for the job. Keep in mind that the person interviewing you will be watching how well you handle stressful situations, how effectively you communicate, what your philosophical orientation is, and whether you care enough about the school to learn something about it prior to the interview (see Box 8.6).

As you progress through your professional preparation, gather information that might be helpful in the future. Keep a file with copies of letters you have received from employers complimenting your work, acknowledgments from volunteer organizations for your help, copies of other people's résumés to use as models for your own, videotapes or audiotapes of your teaching or directing of activities, newspaper articles that might have been written about activities you have participated in, and any other information that might be relevant. This file will not only help you to remember things when you make

BOX 8.6 Practical Suggestions for Interviewing

Pre-Interview

1. Make sure your application is complete and error free—if at all possible, type your application.
2. Make multiple copies of transcripts and letters of recommendation to include with each application.
3. Have multiple copies of a brief (one-page) resume available.
4. Have available (but do not submit until asked) a brief, typed statement including
   a. Your philosophy of education.
   b. Why you want to become a teacher.
   c. The biggest challenge in education today (as you see it).
5. Learn as much about the school or school district where you will be interviewed:
   a. Visit the school or district before the interview.
   b. Ask school secretaries for any information available in printed form.
   c. Scan the local newspapers for relevant information.
   d. Talk to teachers already employed (on an informal basis).
   e. Take a look at the most recent town report.

The Interview

1. Be prompt—the interviewer may not be, but you should be.
2. Bring duplicate copies of the items mentioned in the first section.
3. Dress properly—very important.
4. Be positive! Emphasize the good things about your previous academic or work experiences.
5. Stress your ability to be a cooperative and flexible person.
6. Be a good *listener* as well as a talker!
7. Ask questions that are aimed at the total school program as well as particulars about the position for which you are applying. You should be interested in things like
   a. The school's philosophy of education;
   b. Long- and short-range goals of the district and the school.
   c. Staff development master plan.
   Don't talk too much!

After the Interview

1. Critique the interview: Did I listen well? Did I ask pertinent questions? Did I set a date for a second interview? Did I leave the interview on a positive or upbeat manner?
2. Send a brief note of thanks.
3. Before you leave the building, thank the secretaries or anybody else who may have extended a small courtesy to you.

your permanent file, but also can be used to document your experiences when building your résumé.

Many professional services exist that can help you to locate a teaching job. The first one you should seek help from is your university or college placement office. Most colleges hire professional career counselors to help students in such areas as résumé writing, taking interviews, and developing strategies for conducting a job search.

A second resource you might use is a computer-based job bank. Many states and school districts have access to computer-based files of prospective teachers. Most of these collaboratives are nonprofit organizations but will charge a fee to add your file to their data base. Should you desire information about the availability of such services in your area, contact your state department of education.

A final resource to use is a professional placement agency. Professional placement agencies match teacher candidates with openings in various types of schools. Such agencies are used extensively by overseas and private schools. Private agencies usually charge a fee based on a percentage of the teacher's first-year salary. In some cases, the school hiring the teacher pays this fee. In most cases, however, the teacher seeking the position pays the fee. Before using such a service, be sure you are clear on who pays the fee, as it can be quite high.

Remember when the time comes for you to begin a job hunt that there are always openings for good teachers. If you have the skills, ability, training, and effective job-search strategies, the odds are in your favor for finding a teaching position that is right for you.

CONCLUSION

The career of teaching is again becoming an attractive choice as an occupation. The national reform reports and state legislation have resulted in better salary schedules and in incentive plans to improve the prestige of teaching. There will be an abundance of teaching jobs in the foreseeable future. Preservice training is being upgraded, new certification requirements are being put in place, and opportunities for professional growth are increasing.

Now is the time to give serious consideration to your motives for entering teaching. As you learn more about the career of teaching and especially as you obtain firsthand information in the classroom, your early choice may be reinforced or, alternatively, you may decide that teaching is not for you. Or you may decide that you would like to teach for a while and then move on to other things.

QUESTIONS AND ACTIVITIES

1. Do you feel teachers should be protected by tenure? Why? What about administrators?
2. Do you feel teachers should have the right to strike? Explain your answer.
3. What precautions could you take to prevent yourself from experiencing teacher burnout?
4. What is your reaction to the two quotes "Those who can, do; those who can't, teach," and "Those who can, teach, don't teach, or are frequently discouraged from doing so"?
5. What do you think would be the position of a principal, superintendent, school board member, and teacher about the positive and negative aspects of collective bargaining?
6. How do you feel about having to take a competency test before being able to teach? What type of teacher test is used in your state?
7. What aspects of teaching do you look forward to the most? The least?
8. Compare the NEA's and AFT's statements on teacher evaluation in Boxes 8.2 and 8.3. Where do they agree and/or disagree? Which statements do you feel best represent your viewpoints, and why?

CHAPTER 9

Careers in Education

Teaching is a wonderful career. The joy you will receive from watching your students learn can be immeasurable. For some, however, classroom teaching will lose its luster, and others will seek new challenges in other areas. Your preparation as a teacher can be a valuable asset in a number of nonteaching careers. Some alternative careers in business, including government and the arts, are educational in nature. You can also apply the skills you acquire in teacher preparation to jobs not directly related to education. This chapter explores alternative career options to teaching.

- It is normal and often healthy to change jobs during one's professional career.
- Teachers have marketable educational backgrounds, technical skills, and interpersonal communication abilities that are directly transferable to occupations outside of education.
- Experience as a classroom teacher is essential for most other careers in education itself.
- The key to being happy in your job is to choose one that complements your personal goals and abilities.

Q. *Is teaching necessarily something you do for an entire career?*
A. *No. A lot of college graduates are now seeing the possibility of spending three to five years in teaching and then going on to a varied career in education, or even a career in law, business, publishing, or some other field (Lawrence A. Cremin, cited in Fiske, 1984, p. C11).*

Today college graduates recognize that their college degree is but the first step in a lifelong career path. Your major in college does not necessarily mean you will spend your life working in that area. Several career changes are common for all college majors, and education majors are no exception. The quotation from Lawrence Cremin, an historian of education, aptly summarizes the opportunities open to education majors across a broad category of careers. Completion of undergraduate and graduate degrees in education can be the key that opens the door to a broad array of career alternatives in the education field itself, in fields related to education, and in fields that are traditionally not thought of as being related to education.

In this chapter, we shall consider roles and life patterns and how these can affect your career. We shall then outline career alternatives both in education and in noneducation settings. In both cases, examples of job-opening notices will be used to illustrate the qualifications employers seek, salary levels, and job expectations. The training and experience employers seek might, of course, change over time. If you are interested in exploring any of the career alternatives discussed in this chapter, you should check current qualification requirements. You can do this either at your campus career resource center, with someone you know who is employed in the job, or by writing or calling an employer.

The chapter should make you aware of the options you have in *addition* to classroom teaching. It should make you think about a variety of career choices open to you because of your education major. However, it is *not* intended to discourage you from a career of teaching if this is your ultimate choice. Quite the contrary! The demand for classroom teachers will exceed supply through 1992 according to forecasts. So job opportunities should not limit you if you wish to be a classroom teacher. However, the skills and knowledge you acquire in your education courses and later in school settings and your teaching experience will be valuable bases upon which to build other career interests and opportunities if you so wish. Your education major provides you with a broad foundation of transferable skills in organization, communication, problem solving, and human relations that are highly prized in any number of fields.

Today, we recognize that we have education, work, and family patterns, as well as life-styles that differ from those of our parents and grandparents. Today's life cycle is more fluid and dynamic than it was in the past. This means that you are likely to have more jobs and job changes than your parents did, and that you should think about careers and career paths rather than contemplating one job during your lifetime. A career is part of your lifelong development, which includes your college experiences (see Fredrickson, 1982, for further information about careers).

Ultimately a career comes down to a series of choices made over your lifetime with respect to the type of work you pursue and the particular jobs you hold. At different times in your life this series of choices can be both exciting and troubling. However, once you recognize that you will probably be making a series of choices related to your career, the process should become more challenging. You need to look beyond the first job you take after graduation. You should begin to think about the patterns of jobs and family life that give you options to make decisions and to choose among alternatives. Once you begin to think this way, you can then begin to identify the skills and experiences needed to attain your career goals.

One of the most important activities you can undertake while in college is an examination of the options open to you. In this chapter, you will have an opportunity to consider examples of career paths other than teaching. These alternative careers fall into two categories: those in traditional education settings and those in other settings, such as business, public service, government, and the arts. The chapter will also introduce you to available resources that will help you think about your career. Before we discuss alternative career paths, we need to consider briefly different roles and life patterns that can affect your career.

Roles and Life Patterns

Roles

The concept of *role* is a useful one in thinking about the career choices and decisions you will make. Roles are social positions that carry with them expectations for a certain type of performance (Otto, Call, & Spenner, 1981). Examples of roles include teacher, principal, friend, marriage partner, and parent. There are two aspects to any role. The first is the actual behaviors that people exhibit when they hold a particular role; the second is the expectations or normative beliefs associated with the role. These two aspects of roles—actual behaviors and normative beliefs or expectations—sometimes get confused and can result in stereotypes about individuals in particular roles.

Gender stereotyping often occurs because of confusion between performance and expectations relative to roles. For example, when young children are asked what they want to do when they grow up, they often respond with gender stereotypes of occupational roles. They will frequently say that boys can be doctors and police officers and that girls can be nurses and teachers. This same kind of gender stereotyping is found for the role of homemaker. For example, high school students tend to perceive women as being mainly responsible for cleaning house, mending, and washing clothes, while they tend to see men as mainly responsible for such household activities as repairing appliances (Tittle, 1981). However, as increasing numbers of women enter the work force, these normative beliefs or expectations about certain roles or jobs become less applicable. Today, it is more fruitful to think about an individual as a decision maker and negotiator who must adapt to multiple, often competing, role demands. This perspective is as applicable to men as it is to women.

Life Patterns

Your life pattern can be thought of as the sequence, timing, and age at which you undertake various roles. Variations in sequence and timing lead to different life patterns. For example, you can complete all your education at one time or return later to do graduate work. You can marry in your early twenties or delay marriage until your mid-twenties, thirties, or later, or never marry. You can start work briefly, become a parent, and return to work when your children are in school or grown. Each of these series of decisions leads to different "life patterns" for women and for some men. Traditionally, relatively few men have had life patterns that involve different timing and ordering of roles. Some women still have a choice between working and staying at home and raising their families. The trend, however, is for mothers to enter the work force. For example, current statistics show that 42 percent of the mothers of preschoolers are employed. The numbers of divorced women in the work force are higher: 60 percent with children under 3 years of age; 75 percent with children aged 3 to 5; and 87.4 percent with children aged 14 to 17.

The sequence in which roles are undertaken has a bearing on certain roles and life plans. For example, it is clear that while marriage and children have little effect on the long-term career attainment of men, early marriage and childbearing tend to depress or lower the long-term attainments, earnings, and status of women in the work force. There is a trend today for both marriage and childbearing to occur at somewhat later ages, if at all.

The "life span development" view of careers suggests that it is important to explore and anticipate the consequences of the plans you make (see Lunneborg and Wilson, 1982, for further activities and discussion of these ideas). If part of your life plan is to pursue a professional role other than teaching, you may want to consider the alternatives described in the sections that follow.

Career Alternatives in Traditional Educational Settings

There are many career paths open to you within formal educational settings in the public, private, state, and federal sectors. Specific jobs carry with them different requirements, for example, an undergraduate or graduate degree, teaching experience, permanent (or renewable) certification, special courses, or combinations of these requirements. Classroom teaching experience is usually a prerequisite for career alternatives within preschool, elementary, and secondary school settings. Such experience is not necessary (although it is often highly desirable) for many jobs in postsecondary education. Completion of graduate degrees, with the master's level generally a minimum, is often required for administrative or supervisory positions in the schools. A doctorate (Ph.D. or Ed.D.) is typically required for academic and major administrative positions in schools or colleges of education.

Careers in Day Care, Early Childhood, and Kindergarten Education

Since the 1960s, there has been increased emphasis on early childhood education not only because it was seen as developmentally and educationally important but also because there are increasing numbers of families in which both parents work. As a result, there are more schools and day-care centers for children under the age of 6 than ever before, and this trend is projected to continue. While state regulations governing private day-care vary widely, teachers with early childhood or "K–6" certificates will find opportunities as teachers, specialists, and directors in preschool programs.

There are employment opportunities within a number of different preschool settings. The federal government, through its Head Start program, is one of the largest employers of preschool personnel. Head Start provides educational programs for disadvantaged children aged 3 to 6. In the 1983 school year, approximately 75,000 paid employees and 1½ million volunteers worked in this program (NAESP, 1984). Examples of other options for preschool educators are given in Box 9.1.

There is a growing need in preschool education for teachers who have been trained in special education. Experts now agree that when intervention programs for handicapped children are begun early, they have a greater chance for success. Public Law 94-142 covers children from ages 3 to 21. Preschool programs in special education are run by nonprofit organizations, hospitals, school districts, and specially formed school district collaboratives.

There are also a growing number of private profit-making preschools, many of which were founded by former public school teachers. Such preschools often follow a particular approach to education (for example, Montessori or Froebel). If you want to work in such a setting, specialized training in certain specific approaches to education may be necessary. Eventually you might want to go into the preschool business for yourself. If you decide to do

---

BOX 9.1 Job Announcements for Preschool Positions

Administrative Director, Head Start Program Qualifications: BA early childhood education, NYS certification N–6, 2 years applicable experience. Also administrative experience in community-based program. Salary commensurate with experience.

Preschool Special Ed. Positions Brooklyn Catholic Guardian Society is expanding their preschool program for handicapped children in Queens. We have the following openings for highly skilled professionals;

experience is preferred: Classroom Teachers—MS in Special Ed.; Adaptive Phys. Ed. Teachers; Certified Speech Therapist; Social Worker, MSW; Occupational Therapist; Physical Therapist.

Special Educator Midtown university–affiliated hospital seeks individual with certification in area of early childhood special education or education of the deaf. Will work in pre-school program for deaf/blind children. Excellent salary and fringe benefits package.

this, you may want to take business as well as education courses while in college. No matter how good your education program is, it will not succeed if you cannot pay the rent!

Careers in Elementary and Secondary Schools

Think back to your precollege school days. How many different kinds of educators with specializations were present in your schools? There were probably many teaching specialists, including special-education teachers, teachers of the gifted and talented, and teachers of the physically disabled in your school. Box 9.2 shows a typical job announcement for teacher specialists in special education. Let's look at some other jobs you may or may not remember.

At the district level, there are a number of directorships or coordinator jobs. Box 9.3 illustrates the job announcements for two such district-level positions—coordinator of special education, and director of curriculum and instruction. Notice the qualifications, requirements, and expectations associated with each position.

In elementary schools, a supervisor may be responsible for curriculum development in such areas as reading, mathematics, or science. This position sometimes includes responsibilities for in-service teacher education or for developing special programs. A similar position in larger school districts may require a supervision certificate, based upon completion of graduate courses and supervised experiences, with advanced work in curriculum development.

At the secondary level, requirements for curriculum specialists and department chairpersons are more specific than at the elementary level. For example, the requirements for a public school social studies and science subject supervisor and for a private school English department chairperson are highlighted in the job announcement in Box 9.4. Although each advertisement is geared to a specific discipline, there are similarities in the requirements for the two positions. If you are interested in working in a foreign country, many international private schools offer exciting options, as you can see in the English department chairperson job announcement.

BOX 9.2 Job Announcement for Teacher Specialists in Special Education

New York City Public Schools: *Teachers and support staff needed now in Special Education. Positions available immediately for teachers:*

- Emotionally Handicapped
- Learning Disabled
- Neurologically Impaired

Minimum eligibility requirements for the above license areas: Baccalaureate degree and 12 semester hours in the professional study of education or possession of any New York City Special Education License plus a commitment to take 24 credits in Special Education at a rate of no less than six (6) special education credits for the next four (4) years.

BOX 9.3 Job Announcements for District Coordinator of Special Education and Director of Curriculum and Instruction

District Coordinator, Special Education

The Coordinator of Special Education will be directly responsible to the Assistant Superintendent, Pupil Personnel Services, for assisting in the planning, implementation, supervision, and evaluation of the District's Special Education Program. Credential: Must be eligible for a California credential authorizing the teaching of one or more areas of special education or a pupil services credential authorizing the person to provide psychological services. Eligible for a California supervisory or administrative credential. Master's degree required. Experience: Three years experience in school psychology or teaching special education. Supervisory or administrative experience desirable.

Director of Curriculum and Instruction

QUALIFICATIONS:

1. Education
   A. Licensed teacher, curriculum coordinator

   B. Administrative degree optional
2. Skills
   A. Functions effectively as an instructor
   B. Versed in staff development and clinical supervision
   C. Ability to develop planning in cooperation with administration, teachers, parents and students
3. Experience
   A. Successful, experienced as a teacher
   B. Background in curriculum and instruction
   C. Other alternatives to the above qualifications as the Board may find appropriate
4. Primary function
   A. To provide leadership in the development, delivery and coordination of the district's K–12 curriculum and instruction programs
5. Salary
   A. Negotiable

One of the first jobs that may have come to your mind is that of principal. Typical requirements for the job of an elementary school principal are shown in Box 9.5. In large school districts, a principal might anticipate moving into administration at the districtwide or citywide level. If you wish to follow such a career, you would do well to obtain a doctorate in education administration.

Box 9.6 shows a job announcement for a secondary school principal and an assistant principal. Note the qualifications required and how they differ from those required for the elementary school principal shown in Box 9.5.

Some principals seek advancement to the level of superintendent of schools. A superintendent's responsibilities are extensive; hence the requirements for the jobs described in Box 9.7 are demanding. A superintendent has the opportunity to move to the state department of education as chief state school officer; however, only 50 such jobs exist in the country. The superintendency may also lead to federal government jobs as secretary or deputy secretary of the Office of Education or to positions as deans of colleges of education if the individual has also earned a doctorate in education.

All the positions described so far start with classroom teaching experience and are "line" positions. That is, the people who hold the positions are

BOX 9.4 Job Announcements for Public High School Science Coordinator, Social Studies Department Head, and Private School English Department Chairperson

Coordinator of Secondary Science, $43,837–$50,312 Masters' degree; doctorate desirable; specialization in Science and course work in curriculum and supervision; 5 years outstanding secondary science teaching; Maryland supervisor certification; certification in at least two science subject areas (a life science and a physical science preferred); recent science curriculum and test development, science program implementation, and teacher training experiences; excellent planning, organization and communication skills; ability to supervise, organize, and lead curriculum development and in-service training; and assess program needs. Responsibilities include assessing program needs; planning and managing development and revision of curriculum and instruction materials; monitoring and evaluating implementation of instructional program in the schools and classroom.

Department Head in Social Studies, University High School, The Laboratory School of the University of Illinois Master's degree in social studies or social science discipline necessary, as well as four years high school teaching experience: training or experience in educational programming for academically able college-bound students. Administrative experience and experience in the development of curriculum materials emphasizing international and interdisciplinary content and use of educational technology also desirable. Salary negotiable, depending on background and experience.

English Department Chairperson Being Sought by Overseas School Robert College of Istanbul, the oldest American overseas school, is today the leading school in Turkey. With an enrollment of over 900 boys and girls (grades 6–12), admitted by a highly competitive national examination, the school sends a substantial number of graduates to the most selective American universities. Courses in English literature, science, mathematics and the humanities are taught in English. The remaining are taught in Turkish. The students and the program are equal in quality to those of the most demanding American independent schools. The school is a member of NAIS and is accredited by The New York State Association of Independent Schools.

The English department provides, in the early grades, a mastery of the English language which makes possible a sophisticated study of literature, including preparation for Advanced Placement Exams. In addition, all Humanities electives are under the purview of the English department. The School has a strong tradition in Drama, and a new theater is currently under construction. Also, there are plans for the expansion of an already strong library of 40,000 volumes.

The Head of the English Department is responsible for the entire program in its manifold aspects, including the direction of its twenty members. As the head of the school's largest, most diverse and most influential department, its chairperson would have a major impact on the school's academic programs, a program which is serving as a model for other Turkish schools.

Candidates for this position should have a strong academic background, significant and varied teaching experience with bright students, some administrative experience and/or aptitude, and the genuine desire to assume the responsibilities of academic administration in a stimulating but demanding bilingual and bicultural setting. Of particular interest is the ability to bring fresh ideas, direction and coherence to the department, in order to strengthen English language instruction, and to develop an upper level independent research program.

The principal is one of the most important administrators in a school system.

responsible for a certain area and are delegated a position on a line of authority that extends from superintendent down. Many who are in line positions hope to advance to the higher levels within the system. Others, as they develop their careers, hope to move on to larger districts that offer new or greater challenges.

Specialists who are not in line positions hold staff positions. Examples of staff specialists are counselors and guidance workers; school psychologists; clinical psychologists; and testing, evaluation, and research specialists. Counselor and school psychologist positions require a master's degree in counseling or school psychology that includes supervised counseling or clinical experi-

---

BOX 9.5 Job Announcement for Elementary School Principal

Elementary School Principal The School District of Oconee (near Clemson University) is seeking applicants for a principal of an elementary school (K–5, with an enrollment of 400). Applicants must have elementary teaching experience. Salary based on degree level and experience.

BOX 9.6 Job Announcements for Secondary School Principal and Assistant Principalships

Secondary School Principal The Pine Plains Central Schools, near Kingston and Poughkeepsie, seeks a superior principal for its 7–12 secondary school. Applicants must possess excellent qualifications and references. Prior secondary teaching is required and administrative experience at the secondary level will be a definite asset. Proof of certification and or elegibility as a principal in N.Y. state is required.

Junior and Senior High Assistant Principals Duluth Public Schools, 1985–1986 school

year. Minimum qualification: Secondary School Principal license. Desirable qualifications: Record of successful leadership and dependability in each previous job, knowledge and supportive of current staff development programs, familiar with the use and potential use of technology in secondary education, sensitive to the importance of coordinating special education with the mainstream program.

BOX 9.7 Job Announcements for Superintendent of Schools

Board of Education of Harford County Superintendent of Schools The Board of Education of Harford County is seeking applications for the position of superintendent of schools. Harford County is located northeast of Baltimore City and at the head of the Chesapeake Bay. The present population of the county is estimated at 180,000. The public-school system serves approximately 29,000 students in 42 schools and has a professional and supporting services staff of 3,000.

QUALIFICATIONS Candidates must meet or qualify for and obtain a valid Maryland Superintendent's Certificate. Additionally, beyond the certification requirements, an earned doctorate in education or a closely related field is desirable.

PROFESSIONAL EXPERIENCE The Board of Education seeks a candidate who has demonstrated leadership abilities in the

pursuit of educational excellence; possesses a sound instructionally-related philosophy; demonstrates successful experience as a classroom teacher; and serves as an aggressive advocate for public education.

SALARY RANGE $70,000 to $80,000

Superintendent of Schools, Boston Public Schools The Superintendent is expected to be an exemplary spokesperson for high quality education, school desegregation, and equal educational opportunity. Candidates must possess a demonstrated record of educational and fiscal leadership at a high level of educational administration. A record of success in relating constructively with students, parents, teachers, and community leaders is essential. A doctorate is preferred.

The current salary is $70,000 plus benefits. The initial appointment is intended to expire June 30, 1990.

---

ence. There is an increasing trend toward requiring a doctorate in counseling or school psychology and state licensure for clinical psychologists. Box 9.8 presents examples of job announcements for specialist staff positions in counseling and guiding and the qualifications required.

Most schools employ a range of specialists who teach and/or act as resource people for administrators and other teachers.

Testing, evaluation, and research specialists are very often employed by large city school systems and state departments of education. These specialists develop achievement tests, assess the effectiveness of curricula or educational programs (for example, how effective is a new reading program?), develop educational products (for example, a program to teach science on a microcomputer), or carry out research (for example, a study of the characteristics of effective schools). Entry-level qualifications for specialists in the research, testing, and evaluation fields are a master's degree (in education, psychology, sociology, or other related fields), and course work in statistics and computers is highly desirable. In practice, professionals in these specialities generally have doctoral degrees.

The staff specialists just described are not as likely as teachers to move

---

BOX 9.8 Job Announcement for Counselors and School Psychologist

Counselor/Group Instructor Institute for the developmentally disabled/mentally retarded has the above permanent position available for a Masters level Counselor/Group instructor to work with mentally retarded adults.

Psychologist School Certified Must have experience and knowledge in the area of drug/alcohol abuse. Psychologist will work with young people, parents, school and community organizations.

Guidance Counselor—Search Reopened Prestigious Westchester County School District seeks full-time high school guidance counselor, effective immediately. Permanent appointment. College counseling experience essential. NYS certification required. Full credit given for education and public school experience. Excellent salary, benefits, environment. Previous applicants need not apply.

into "line" career paths that lead to superintendency and chief state school officer positions. However, the positions held by these specialists have their own rewards and career paths that sometimes can lead to work at the state or federal level, to college or university teaching or research positions, or to an owner or partner position in an evaluation business or counseling practice.

A number of the jobs described above are available at the state department or federal level. For example, the Department of Defense runs a large school system. There are also a number of jobs available with professional education associations or organizations. Many organizations have staff specialists in many of the areas discussed above. A typical job announcement for a position with a state-level professional organization is shown in Box 9.9.

Careers in Postsecondary Education

How many different careers in education can you identify in the school in which you are now studying? The most obvious is probably that of college teacher, but there are a number of other very attractive jobs in higher education. There is a department or division chairperson for various special areas such as curriculum and teaching, educational foundations, reading, mathematics, counseling, and school administration. There are also positions that you can find listed in the college catalogue, such as director of student teaching or field experiences, associate deans for graduate or undergraduate education, dean of the school or college, director of admissions, and registrar to name but a few. The general categories of occupations or careers in higher education are those of professor (teacher), administrator, researcher, and support staff (admissions, registrar, financial aid, student affairs, and so on).

Careers in schools of education generally have as prerequisites undergraduate preparation as a teacher, several years of teaching in elementary or secondary schools, and additional study to attain at least a master's degree but more commonly a doctorate. The exception to this career pattern is the education researcher. In large colleges of education there may be some faculty who teach graduate students and conduct research. Their area of specialization may be in disciplines other than education such as sociology, psychology,

---

BOX 9.9 Job Announcement for a Position with a Professional Association

Director of Professional Development, Association of California School Administrators ACSA (statewide school management association). Manage, supervise, and coordinate all professional development activities of the association and its entities, which include academies, institutes, symposiums, workshops, conferences, and the annual convention and the staff/consultant assigned thereto. Five years' successful experience as a line administrator in a school position; minimum three years' successful experience in training and staff development; experience with budget development and budget monitoring. Earned doctorate degree desirable. Salary range $51,739 to $63,039 plus fringes.

history, or statistics. They apply their techniques of study to the field of education.

The qualifications for entry-level college of education teaching (instructor and assistant professor) and for a supervisor of student teachers are illustrated in the job announcement shown in Box 9.10. In the first announcement, the qualification that is unusual (when compared to those seen in previous boxes) is the one that requires the candidate to have skills necessary to conduct research. College and university faculty are often expected not only to teach but also to carry out and publish research that contributes to knowledge about educational processes, how children learn, and how teachers teach. (Throughout this book, you will find reference to research studies, most of which have been carried out by a college or university faculty member.) The career path for college faculty is from instructor to assistant professor, to associate professor (generally the tenure step), to professor. Advancement is generally based on successful teaching, research, and community service. In some colleges publication is an essential requirement; hence the phrase "publish or perish."

College and university administrators, such as deans, often have had experience as the chair of a department or as an associate dean, perhaps with responsibility for graduate studies or an undergraduate program. Occasion-

---

BOX 9.10 Job Announcements for Entry-Level College Teaching and Director of Field Experiences

Education: Instructor/Assistant Professor of Elementary Education. Tenure-track, nine-month appointment. Summer school teaching available. Earned doctorate (ABD considered) in curriculum and instruction with additional preparation in one or more of the following areas: social science education, mathematics education, and/or science education. Minimum of two years of appropriate teaching experience in an elementary or middle school. Demonstrated leadership skills in field-based programs. Responsibilities: supervise student teachers, teach methods courses in area of expertise, conduct personal research, and participate in university/community service. Salary is negotiable.

Education: Applications are being accepted for the position of Director, Office of Professional Laboratory Experience. The Director is responsible for arranging all field experience assignments associated with the University's teacher education program, including student teaching internship, practicum, and observation activities. The Director also provides leadership for campus and field-based supervisors, and works closely with the Director of Teacher Admissions and Certification. This 12-month, tenure-track position includes teaching particularly and supervision of student teaching, clinical supervision and effective education. Other responsibilities include participation in professional, campus, and community activities. Public school administrative experience with knowledge and background in teacher education is preferred. A demonstrated ability to communicate and work well with both university and public school educators is considered essential. An earned doctorate is required. Salary is competitive. Salary and rank will be commensurate with experience and qualifications.

ally, professors or deans of education will move to other administrative positions in a university, such as those of vice-president (for example, vice-president for student affairs, vice-president for development, academic vice-president) and even college or university president.

Other career paths for educators within a postsecondary institution include many specialist positions that we described earlier. For example, your college most likely has guidance counselors, career counselors, continuing-education specialists, and audiovisual specialists, to name but a few. There are also staff positions in such areas as financial aid, placement, development, admissions, registration, alumni, housing, and athletics.

Continuing education is a field of higher education that has expanded rapidly in the last decade. Many college graduates and adults take a wide variety of courses or workshops at colleges or universities that are outside the ordinary undergraduate or graduate programs. These continuing education programs can range from advanced training in highly specialized areas to personal enrichment topics such as stress management. There are many interesting careers open in continuing or adult education, including those of administrator, instructor, and counselor.

Community colleges offer particularly attractive career paths to former secondary school majors. High school teachers may move into community college teaching and administration, particularly after they have completed work at the master's level in their subject fields. Doctorates in the subject or field are not generally required to teach in a community college.

There are many others careers available in vocational/technical and private schools that focus on special groups of adult students, or that specialize in art, music, and foreign languages.

To get an idea of the wide variety of career alternatives in the education field at all levels, both private and public, consult *Careers in Education* (a special section in *The New York Times* Sunday edition). Another source is the section in the *Chronicle of Higher Education* entitled *Bulletin Board: Positions Available.* Both these publications will be in your library and are excellent sources to consult when you wish to explore alternative careers to teaching in educational settings.

Career Alternatives in Other Settings

There are a wide variety of other employment opportunities for those trained in education. These opportunities are to be found in business, in public service and government, in the arts, and within various special disciplines (law, medicine, nursing, and so on). In this section, these opportunities are described briefly.

The education of teachers involves a cluster of occupationally related courses that develop skills in human relations, problem solving, communication, and organization. These basic skills are applicable in a variety of settings. You can learn which organizations or industries employ people with these skills. After you read this section, you can begin to explore career alternatives in these "nontraditional" settings for educators. In the future, careers for teachers in such settings may become almost as common as those in the traditional settings we have described so far.

Business, Industry, and Other Professions

There are several ways in which you can classify the types of work you may be able to find in business and industry or in other professions. First, you can teach the subject you already know to a new clientele. Second, you can develop a new speciality, such as teaching salespersons or repair people who work for the company that employs you. Third, you can adapt your teaching skills to nonteaching careers. Excellent treatments of alternative careers in business and industry are to be found in a number of sources (Bestor, 1977; Zambrano & Entine, 1976; Kisiel, 1980; Goodman, 1982) that you should consult if you are interested in any of these alternative careers.

If you are an English teacher, you may be able to teach writing to the staff of a business or industry (for example, managers and sales personnel). Aerospace, banking, and engineering firms have ongoing classes in which employees are given training in the skills necessary to write basic reports. Language teachers and social studies teachers may find work with international firms that train their sales personnel in various foreign languages; they may also be able to offer courses in the history and social customs of other countries to employees who are being sent abroad (Zambrano & Entine, 1976). Another example of how a teaching career can be applied in a nontraditional setting—a law firm—is described in Box 9.11.

Some teachers have found work developing material for training programs for business. Business must continually train new salespeople, repair people, and other new staff. The qualifications for the positions of training developer and director of training are described in Box 9.12.

Teachers of literature, social studies, or humanities may change their

---

BOX 9.11 Job Announcement for Director of Continuing Legal Education

Director of Continuing Legal Education
A major NYC law firm with a substantial international practice and offices outside New York is seeking a creative person with undergraduate and graduate school teaching experience, preferably English, Linguistics, Communications, or Speech, for a position as Director of Continuing Legal Education. The Director will be expected to teach the firm's internal writing program and other pertinent subjects; to advise young attorneys in developing their writing skills; to edit reports, briefs and similar documents; to administer the firm's Continuing Legal Education Program; and to propose ways and means to enhance the professional growth of attorneys in both the domestic and foreign offices. While familiarity with the law or legal language is advantageous, a law degree is neither required nor particularly desired. A record of scholarly publications on advanced writing or related subjects as well as some experience in academic administration would be useful.

BOX 9.12 Job Announcement for Director of Training and Training Developers

National Director of Training Our Long Island–based internationally known health-related service organization seeks a National Director of Training to deliver training materials and techniques to our Trainers in the U.S.A. and Canada.

We offer a classroom program based upon leader/participant interaction and complemented by specific and sequenced materials. It is essential that the candidate for this position have experience training Trainers in either a corporate or educational setting. The ideal candidate will hold an advanced degree in education, be familiar with state-of-the-art delivery systems, and have demonstrated the ability to be a motivator.

The candidate selected for this position will have total responsibility for the function, including arranging and conducting regional and national workshops.

This position offers a highly competitive salary based on experience as well as an excellent benefits package.

Training Developers We are seeking qualified training development professionals to implement ongoing and new defense-related training initiatives. Prerequisites include Bachelor's degree in Education or Educational Psychology; Master's degree preferred. Experience with industry and military. Programs will be conducted in the Baltimore and Washington, D.C., area. U.S. citizenship required.

focus to teaching related skills of writing and communication. Similarly, math and science teachers often move into teaching or programming jobs with computer companies.

Two other examples of nontraditional areas for teachers are found in the health field and in publishing and writing (see Box 9.13). Many hospitals have established education programs for their patients (for example, young diabetics) and need educators to design, implement, and coordinate these programs. Sometimes these positions require a background in nursing or health education. Text publishers sometimes employ demonstration teachers to show how their textbook series, instructional materials, or audiovisual aids can be used. Major publishers need employees who have good communication skills and know the field of education. Many of these positions are quite broad in scope; others are more subject-specific. A number of such positions are illustrated in Box 9.13.

English teachers can find work with organizations that need technical, instruction, and owner manuals developed for their own employees or their customers. Many companies develop consumer information material. Banks need writers for policy and procedures manuals, newsletters, and advertisements. Other organizations that hire people with a background in writing are investment companies, foundations, professional associations, and research firms. Some teachers have become part of consultant groups that edit, write, draft, or develop grant proposals for companies or provide expertise in communications in such matters as consumer information, marketing, and public relations work. Of course, former teachers also write about education. John Holt and George Leonard, both former teachers, now write about educational issues with a lay audience in mind. Many education columns in newspapers are written by former teachers.

Other nonteaching careers in business and industry can be found in human resource or personnel departments. In many companies these departments are responsible for internal training programs for employees, recruiting, interviewing, and the evaluation and testing of new or potential employees. Persons trained in education might apply for entry-level positions in personnel work (for example, interviewing, conducting classes) and eventually advance to director of personnel. Once you are employed, you can take special classes to learn more about employment testing and employee relations laws. To develop a career in this area, an M.B.A. or other specialized work in personnel would be advantageous.

Some specialized companies that do education-related work employ former teachers. For example, there are several private testing companies that employ teachers much as book publishers do—as editors for subject matter tests and as sales personnel. Examples of such companies are the American College Testing Program, the Educational Testing Service, the California Test Bureau, and the Psychological Corporation. These and other companies also employ specialists with training (M.A. or Ph.D. level) in educational testing and evaluation (see Box 9.14).

Teachers also find alternative careers in such fields as consumer relations, public relations, public information services, and advertising. These fields are less related to education than some others we have discussed. Nonetheless, they all use many of the skills that teachers acquire as part of their training and experience. For example, utility companies need to educate the public about the efficient use of energy. Trade and professional associations want the public and influential policymakers to know their points of view on legislation and regulations. Advertisers want to be able to tell the public about their clients' products.

One of the fastest-growing fields is that of technology. Many teachers have found new careers in software development (the programs that the computer uses), training and development, and sales. Computer companies also must develop training and instructional manuals for those who purchase their microcomputers for home use. Many teacher education programs offer a number of courses in how to use microcomputers in instruction and classroom management. People with such education courses should have an excellent foundation to move into the computer field if they wish or to positions in business, industry, or higher education, training staff on the use of computers and various software packages.

Two other business-related career areas that use skills developed as part of teacher training are insurance, and retail and merchandising. Insurance companies hire public relations and writing specialists; some specialize in selling group policies to schools and colleges. Others offer financial and estate planning to school staff. These companies often prefer salespeople with education backgrounds. In the retail and merchandising field, teachers can find alternative careers as sales representatives. Finally, teachers might enter executive training programs offered by many large retailers and manufacturers.

If you can manage a double major while in college, still more career alternatives will be open to you. For example, chemistry or science teachers with majors in those disciplines may get jobs in private chemical or industrial research institutes or firms. Double majors in education and mathematics or accounting may find opportunities in bookkeeping departments, in survey firms, and in data-processing companies.

Public Service, Government, the Arts, and Media

Careers in public service that involve skills you will acquire as part of your training encompass a wide range of occupational titles: youth director, recreation worker, activity therapist, community relations specialist, rehabilitation educator, counselor, and agency field representative, to mention but a few. Specialists such as these may work for a variety of agencies that service particular populations such as the elderly, displaced homemakers, and disturbed adolescents. Many agencies focus on a particular function, such as family planning or housing needs. There are a wide variety of such agencies. The requirements for entry vary, but many require graduate training in social work.

There are also a number of nonprofit public service organizations that use people trained in education. These include the YWCA, the YMCA, the Red Cross, Scouts, church and synagogue groups, and private charities. Museums and libraries also have education-related career alternatives. Many museums now have educational programs.

There are a wide variety of federal agencies that employ college graduates. For many positions, a civil service examination is required as an initial step. The career center on your campus can help you find up-to-date information on such government jobs. Governmental career alternatives include positions in the Department of Education, Housing and Urban Development, Action/Peace Corps, U.S. Department of Agriculture, Food and Nutrition Service, Consumer Product Safety Commission, Internal Revenue Service, and Social Security Administration. The job titles that you may be interested in are very similar across all these agencies: personnel specialist, administrative assistant, public information specialist, educational specialist, caseworker or investigator, or project administrator. Lukowski and Piton (1980) offer excellent advice on how to get a government job.

At the state level there are corresponding opportunities for those at the federal level in many different types of agencies. In addition, the department of education or public instruction in many states operates regional technical assistance centers for local education authorities (LEAs). These regional centers have traditional positions open for curriculum, special-education, testing, research, and evaluation specialists. For many of these positions, both school experience and at least an M.A. or an M.Ed. degree are either desirable or required.

Another potential employer might be a nonprofit foundation. Many foundations employ people with education backgrounds. The type of person hired will vary with the programming efforts of the foundation.

The arts and media provide a number of career alternatives for educators. Positions in educational and commercial television offer opportunities to use education experiences to develop instructional programs. Positions in the arts and media include those of writer, investigative reporter, scriptwriter, and editor. Other careers in the arts involve giving private instruction in a wide variety of arts and crafts.

CONCLUSION

Your education major provides you with an excellent foundation on which to build a lifelong career path not only in teaching but also in numerous other areas. While it may not be possible at this stage to see too far down your eventual career path, you do have many decisions to make as you establish that part of your identity related to your life's work. The other parts of your identity are rooted in the relationships you establish with other people and in your sense of competence in fulfilling the various roles of worker, partner, and perhaps parent. The integration of these roles and the series of decisions you will need to make about how work and family fit together are important. Try to imagine different alternatives for yourself so that the choices you make are truly choices.

Give yourself as many alternatives as possible so you have choices along your career path. Work is central to the identity of both men and women, and a large portion of your life will be spent working, so as one young person put it, "It had better be work I like to do!"

QUESTIONS AND ACTIVITIES

1. Make a list of your personal and professional life goals. Do any of the careers discussed in this chapter match them?
2. For you, what advantages does teaching have over career alternatives outlined in this chapter? What disadvantages?
3. Interview a person who has left teaching for a different profession. Why did he or she leave? What skills did he or she develop as a teacher that are useful in the new profession?
4. Review job opportunities in your Sunday newspaper. How many require skills that teachers would have? What would those skills be?

PART FOUR

The Student

The student is at the center of the educational enterprise. Without students, there would be no such thing as education. If all students were exactly alike, the management of learning would probably be a much easier task. But they are not. Philosophers from the earliest days have remarked on differences between people, and social scientists have invested a lot of time and effort in identifying and quantifying the differences.

While no student is exactly like any other student, groups of students do share certain characteristics (for example, a group of students may speak a language other than English at home or a group may have a disability). Some of the groupings recognized in schools reflect groupings in the larger society that in turn reflect the different cultural traditions of sections of the American population. In school, the reasons for considering students as members of a group are both legal and organizational. From the legal point of view, legislators are interested in attempting to ensure that students who differ from the majority of students do not lose out in the educational system. Toward this end, the law may require that some students receive special services to help them deal with, for example, a difficulty in speaking English or one arising from a disability. From an organizational point of view, it may also be helpful to think of students in terms of their group membership so that services can be provided for them in an efficient manner. In Chapter 10, we outline some of the ways in which students fall into groups because of the variety of backgrounds from which they come and the particular characteristics they share with some but not all students. We also consider educational programs designed to serve the needs of different groups of students.

However convenient it may appear to categorize students into groups, when you find yourself in the classroom, you will be faced with a collection of unique individuals, each differing from all the other students in the classroom on a range of characteristics. These differences will have to be taken into account in teaching and managing students. In Chapter 11, we deal with the variability of students on a number of characteristics that have been the subject of many psychological studies. We also consider some strategies that have been developed to help the teacher cope with individual differences among students.

CHAPTER 10

Student Pluralism

While all good teachers view their students as individuals, sometimes for legal and other practical reasons it is necessary to discuss students in terms of their shared characteristics. This chapter discusses the characteristics of students who are disadvantaged, bicultural-bilingual, talented and gifted, and have handicapping conditions.

- Teachers, as far as is possible, should view their students as individuals and not as members of a particular group.
- Federal and state laws mandate specific programs or guidelines for educating students from disadvantaged backgrounds, students who are bicultural or bilingual, and students with disabilities. You need to be aware of the needs of each of these groups and of the programs set up to address their needs.
- You need to be aware of programs for talented and gifted students.
- You need to be aware of how gender stereotypes can affect the way teachers view and deal with students.
- Teachers hold different expectations for different groups of students. If teachers are not careful, these expectations can adversely affect individuals who are members of these groups.

Each student is different in some ways from all other students, and you as a teacher will have to take this into account when teaching. However, it is also obvious that you will not be able to deal with students as individuals all the time. Students do share some characteristics, and it is on the basis of these common attributes that some schools and teachers group their students. For example, students of similar age are usually grouped together to form classes. Students might come from a particular type of home; for example, all or most may come from high-income homes or they may come from low-income homes. Many of your students may use a language other than English when outside school and thus may need special consideration in school. A section of your students may be learning disabled or highly gifted and again need some kind of provision if they are to get the best out of schooling.

In general, it is probably better if you, as a teacher, do not think of students primarily in terms of their group membership (as being gifted, poor, or having handicapping conditions). However, group membership of students is recognized not only in the popular mind, but also in legal requirements; as a teacher, you must be aware of this fact. Group membership, for example, may form the basis of special facilities and programs in the school system. Thus, for example, special facilities that are not provided for the general population may be available for students legally classified as disadvantaged because of poor home circumstances or for students with a handicapping condition. You should be aware of these facilities and of the groups of students who qualify for them.

In this chapter, we will consider the way students are grouped because of the variety of backgrounds from which they come and the particular characteristics they share with some but not with all students. We shall consider students from disadvantaged backgrounds, bicultural and bilingual students, talented and gifted students, students, with handicapping conditions, and finally, students distinguished by gender. We shall also consider programs that have been developed for particular groups of students.

Students from Disadvantaged Backgrounds

In almost every classroom, you are likely to come across at least a few children who have great difficulty in acquiring one or more of the basic skills—reading, writing, spelling, or math. In some cases, the number of students may be large; a school in a poor neighborhood or the lowest class in a tracked system may contain many children with learning problems. The causes of learning problems are many, and it will not be possible for you to identify the precise reasons in the case of many of the students you will teach.

There is a high incidence of students with learning difficulties in areas of the country known as "disadvantaged." These are sections of cities with a heavy concentration of poor housing, a high proportion of unskilled and unemployed workers, and a high rate of educational failure. Various terms have been used to describe the areas, including "underprivileged," "lower socioeconomic," "socially disadvantaged," and "inner city" (Passow & Elliott, 1968; Reissman, 1962).

A child who comes from a disadvantaged background is likely to carry that disadvantage into school. There are a number of different frames of reference—economic, educational, cultural, and social—from which this disadvantage may be viewed. Some definitions of "disadvantaged" have tried to take these various aspects into account. According to one definition, a child may be regarded as disadvantaged if, because of sociocultural reasons, he or she comes into the school system with knowledge, skills, and attitudes that make adjustment difficult and impede learning (Passow, 1970). There are three aspects to this definition. The first refers to the *personal characteristics* of the student. The knowledge, skills, and attitudes the child brings to school are, by implication, different from those that most children bring. "Knowledge" here means such things as the store of the student's information and the range of his or her vocabulary. "Skills" may refer to perceptual ones (for example, the ability to analyze a geometric figure) or higher cognitive ones (for example, the ability to string sentences together, to listen to a story and repeat the main points in the given sequence). "Attitudes," too, can refer to a wide variety of things—attitudes toward knowledge, learning, books, or sitting down and staying quiet.

The second aspect of the definition points to the child's *background*. The child's knowledge, skills, and attitudes are the result of living in a particular kind of material and sociocultural environment. The disadvantaged home has been found to differ from the middle-class one in its material conditions (for example, space, amenities), in attitudes toward learning and education, in the way parents and children interact, and in the language used by adults. It is in adjusting to this kind of environment that the particular knowledge, skills, and attitudes of many disadvantaged children develop in the first place.

The third aspect of the definition refers to the *educational demands* made on the child in school. Since the child's skills, knowledge, and attitudes are often not in harmony with those demanded by the school, he or she tends to learn at a slower rate than, for example, the middle-class child. It has been argued that not only do underprivileged children start school with a disadvantage but, as they move through the grade levels, the academic gap between them and those from more enriched environments widens (Deutsch, 1963). The effect of all this is that many disadvantaged children are "unable to participate fully in that cultural heritage which the school transmits" and so "are deprived of part of their cultural inheritance" (Moss, 1973, p. 20).

Disadvantaged children are often concentrated in particular geographical areas and schools. If these areas and schools could be identified, then it might be possible to provide special assistance that would aid the educational development of the children. A number of states have developed approaches to identify disadvantaged children. For example, the California Advisory Committee on Compensatory Education used a combination of personal and environmental characteristics. According to the committee, children are regarded as disadvantaged, and so need additional assistance, if they are below average in school achievement as measured by standardized tests, in combination with one or more of the following problems: economic deprivation, social alienation caused by racial or ethnic discrimination, and geographic isolation. In the state of Michigan, scholastic achievement has also been used as a criterion for granting additional compensatory financial aid to schools. State funds for compensatory education were allocated on the basis of the number of students in elementary school (K through 6) who were found to be in need of "substantial improvement" in the basic skills of reading and/or arithmetic. Students with low scores on a statewide test qualified for assistance (Madaus & Elmore, 1973).

You should not conclude from what you have read that all children from disadvantaged backgrounds experience difficulties at school. Neither should you assume that the source of difficulties, when they do occur, lies exclusively in the deficiencies of the children themselves and of their backgrounds. For this reason, the very notion of compensation for disadvantaged children has been questioned (Sroufe, 1970). Unless it is assumed that children have some kind of deficit, compensation does not seem an appropriate procedure. However, with the abundant evidence that is available concerning the school failure of children from particular kinds of backgrounds, it seems reasonable to take some action to assist such children in adapting to school. This does not necessarily imply a "deficiency" in the students. As long as there are difficulties (not necessarily deficiencies), the teacher is not precluded from providing special means to help children function in two types of environment or subculture—their own and that of the school. In attempting this, the teacher must not assume that the onus of change must rest solely on the individual child. To help bring about desired changes in these children, it may be necessary for the school to change what it traditionally has done and to provide special programs and facilities.

Programs for the Disadvantaged

The need for the school to adapt to the needs of different groups of students becomes clear when we realize that some children come to school well prepared to partake in the activities of the school, while others, because they come from homes with different facilities, expectations, and values, are poorly prepared. In this situation, providing all children with the same educational treatment may make for unequal rather than equal opportunity. For real equality of opportunity, special treatment of students who come to school poorly prepared may be necessary (Passow, 1970). The idea that different sections of the community need to receive different treatment found political expression in the the Head Start, Title I, and Upward Bound programs, established as part of the "war on poverty" federal legislation of 1965. Federal funding is now provided for compensatory education programs for the disadvantaged under the terms of Chapter 1 of the Education Consolidation and Improvement Act of 1981.

Head Start, which has been, and continues to be, the most popular of the compensatory programs, began as an 8-week summer program in 1965. Later it became a full-year program. Since its inception, Head Start has served over 9 million children between the ages of 3 and 6. In 1984, 430,000 children (about one-fifth of those eligible) participated in Head Start programs. Practically all came from families with incomes below the poverty line. Nearly half (42 percent) were black, a third (33 percent) were white, a fifth (20 percent) were Hispanic, 4 percent were Native American, and 1 percent were Asian.

The results of early research studies on the effects of Head Start were not very encouraging (Kellaghan, 1977), yet there is some evidence from follow-up studies that children who have participated in the program have had fewer grade retentions and special-class placements, lower absenteeism, and better health during their school careers than students without Head Start experience (National Association of Elementary School Principals, 1985).

Many other programs and schemes have been set up to help schools cope with the problems of the disadvantaged. In fact, a major thrust of federal government policy in the 1960s and 1970s was the extension of educational assistance to disadvantaged populations. In the 1980s, the effective-schools movement has concentrated on identifying schools and treatments that are successful in reaching disadvantaged students. States such as Connecticut have statewide policies and programs to help students adapt to the instructional needs of poor minority disadvantaged students.

Bicultural and Bilingual Students

Most Americans come from different cultural and ethnic backgrounds. Even individuals whose families have been in the United States for many generations may still refer to themselves as German-American, Italian-American, Irish-American, Afro-American, or Spanish-American. However, most such individuals have moved a good distance from their ancestral roots and have been assimilated into mainstream American culture, which was once dominated by Anglo-Saxon values and traditions.

For many generations America was built on the "melting pot" idea that people from a variety of cultural and linguistic backgrounds should be fused into one American nation. Public school teachers used English, and immigrants were expected to learn that language. Often the parents of immigrant children used English to speak to their children, since that helped the children become assimilated into the dominant American culture and was beneficial economically. Thus schools, and in many cases parents, favored cultural and language uniformity rather than cultural pluralism. At the same time, the country remained in some respects a pluralistic society. This is evident when we consider the number of Americans who speak another language in addition to English. In 1975, nearly 28 million Americans (or 17 percent of the total population of the United States) claimed a language other than English as their mother tongue. The largest group claiming a non-English mother tongue were those of Spanish heritage (6.8 million). The next largest category were Italians (3.9 million) (Lewis, 1981). Apart from these, there may be up to a hundred language groups in the United States speaking various native American, European, and Asian languages.

We should not be surprised then to learn that many students in American schools live in a culture that differs from mainstream American culture and for whom English is a second language. Such students are said to be bicultural and bilingual. In 1982, the estimated number of 5- to 18-year-olds from homes where the primary language spoken was not English was about 4.5 million; this figure represented an 18 percent increase over the estimate for 1978 (3.8 million) (U.S. Department of Education, 1984).

Over the last two decades the melting-pot policy has changed. Groups that don't speak English have been demanding recognition of their languages and cultural values in this country generally and in the educational system in particular. Many benefits have been attributed to a policy of pluralism. First, it recognizes the worth of every individual, whatever his or her ethnic background. Second, it recognizes that differences among groups can contribute to the development of a richer, more varied society. Third, the maintenance of ethnic traditions can serve an important function for individuals, particularly in a society marked by rapid change; it can provide an anchor, a source of authority, for people caught up in that change.

Bilingual education classes use both the child's mother tongue and English as the means for instruction.

Education in cultural pluralism has a number of objectives. First, it strives to support cultural diversity (including language diversity) and individual uniqueness. Second, it encourages the development of minority ethnic cultures and simultaneously helps to incorporate them into mainstream American socioeconomic and political life. Third, it supports the exploration of alternative life-styles for students (American Association of Colleges of Teacher Education, 1972).

Since language is an important component of culture, bilingualism has been an important element in programs designed to foster biculturalism. Language keeps a student in touch with his or her cultural heritage; indeed, it is in many respects a reflection of that heritage. Thus biculturalism and bilingualism are inextricably interwoven. Ethnic minorities can better maintain a sense of identity and self-worth by retaining their native languages. A further reason for the development of bilingual programs was the fact that children from non-English-speaking backgrounds were at a disadvantage in school when they had to attend classes conducted solely in English. It was for this reason that the United States Supreme Court ruled in 1974 (Lau v. Nichols) that schools are obligated to make special arrangements for students who do not speak English.

Programs for Bicultural and Bilingual Students

The federal government passed the bilingual education acts (starting with Title VII of the Elementary and Secondary Education Act in 1965); these, along with other federal legislation and administrative regulations, court decisions, and state laws, have led to an increasing number of bilingual education programs in schools. This is true particularly at the kindergarten and early elementary levels. Such programs are directed toward children of "limited English proficiency" and thus cover not only children with limited English-speaking ability but also ones who have difficulty in reading and writing English. Programs funded under the bilingual education acts should use both English and the child's mother tongue as media of instruction; they should also include an appreciation of the cultural heritage of bilingual students (Gradisnik, 1980).

In many states, bilingual education is now mandatory, and in others there is legislation that authorizes the development of bilingual programs. In the early 1970s, the number of bilingual education programs increased from less than 30 to up to 500 (McLaughlin, 1978). However, a 1984 estimate showed that bilingual programs served only about 10 percent of the children who needed such services that year (about 234,000 students) (U.S. Department of Education, 1984).

There were several reasons for the development of bilingual programs. A major one was that it seemed that the melting-pot idea had not worked equally well for all ethnic groups, leaving the education system open to charges of discrimination. This position was taken up by the civil rights movement in the 1960s and 1970s, which argued not only for the need to maintain diversity and cultural pluralism in American society, but also for positive assistance from society in achieving this objective.

The development of bilingual programs has not been universally welcomed, for a number of reasons. The public education system was originally perceived to be a means of building a unified nation from the diverse linguistic and ethnic immigrants who came to its shores, and some people now fear that bilingual programs will result in a nation fragmented into different language groups. Other people think that the education offered in a second language might be inferior to that offered in English. Since the majority of children who participate in such programs come from economically disadvantaged homes, some people are afraid that the type of education these children receive may perpetuate their economic disadvantage rather than assist them in overcoming it.

Those who advocate bilingual education are conscious of a number of questions the concept raises. For example, what is the best kind of bilingual program for children? Is it best to place students in a *transitional* program in which they are introduced to schooling in their vernacular and then, when they have acquired adequate proficiency in English, move them to instruction in that language? Or should a bilingual program have as its objective the *maintenance* of the student's vernacular language and so continue to provide instruction in that language even after students have acquired enough proficiency in English to follow instruction in that language? Another question about bilingual education relates to its desirability. There may be cases in which education in the vernacular is the best approach, others in which education in the nonvernacular is best. To try to get the answers to these questions of desirability, it would be necessary to have some knowledge of the goals of the community in which the child lives as well as information about the demand for education in the community (Hartford, 1982).

Obviously, bilingual programs create practical difficulties for schools. What does one do in an area in which there are many minority group languages? How many additional teachers are required? Can enough teachers be found with knowledge of the languages and the desired cultural background? What about languages that few teachers may know? How should bilingual education teachers prepare for their work? The need for teacher training is obvious. For example, a recent survey found that only 21 percent of teachers who reported that they used a foreign language for instruction in their classroom said they had the foreign language skills and the basic academic preparation necessary to teach language arts or other subjects (U.S. Department of Education, 1984).

Bilingual education programs may take many forms, depending on the needs of students and the resources available to a school district. A description of different types of models for programs is presented in Box 10.1. These range from programs that involve a single teacher in a classroom to ones that involve cooperation between teachers and even between schools.

So far, research evidence on the effectiveness of bilingual education programs has been lacking. For example, a number of studies that sought such evidence failed to support the view that the programs result in gains in student achievement over and above what is expected in traditional classrooms. Neither did they find evidence that the programs positively affect students' attitudes toward school or diminished their alienation from school (Epstein, 1977).

Although the public school system may be far from having identified the most effective means of providing bilingual education instruction, its considerable investment in such programs will likely continue. These programs will remain as long as powerful political forces see their value and continue to be supported by legislation at the federal and state levels.

Talented and Gifted Students

There is a strong tradition in American education of emphasizing the development of the *whole* child. That is, the school should contribute not just to the intellectual development of its students but also to the students' wider personal, social, and emotional development. Some people have argued that, because of this emphasis, insufficient attention is paid to the development of the intellectual abilities of students, particularly in the case of those who are talented and gifted (Conant, 1959). This view was expressed forcibly in the

1950s when Russia moved ahead of the United States in the space race with the launching of *Sputnik*. Interest in the gifted faded in the 1960s, to be revived in the 1970s (Tannenbaum, 1983) and sustained in the 1980s as evidenced in the emphasis placed on the gifted in the recent national reports on education.

Talented and gifted students differ from average students on a number of dimensions that are relevant to instruction. Dunn (1984) lists the ways in which talented and gifted students differ from their peers. These are shown in Table 10.1. Teachers need to be aware of these differences so that they can not only identify talented and gifted students but also make their instruction more relevant to the needs of this special population.

In the following sections, we will consider the characteristics of gifted students and what the schools have been doing to foster their particular talents. The development of talent is important because it contributes to the personal fulfillment of individual students and ensures that the nation as a whole is well served by the particular talents some students have.

Characteristics of the Talented and Gifted

The terms *talented* and *gifted* specify neither the type of ability that talented and gifted people have nor the degree of superior ability requisite to be classified as "talented" or "gifted" (Getzels & Dillon, 1973). In their famous studies of 1,000 gifted children carried out earlier in this century, Terman and his associates preferred the word *genius* to *talented* and defined that term fairly narrowly; the definition was very influential in the area of giftedness up to the 1950s. For Terman, genius meant being in "the top one percent level in general intellectual ability, as measured by the Stanford-Binet Intelligence Scale or a comparable instrument" (Terman, 1925, p. 43). The drawback of a definition of talent in terms of "high IQ" is that it depends on a measure that includes few items requiring divergent reasoning or evaluation ability, two characteristics that are regarded as important in imaginative and creative work (Gallagher, 1975).

TABLE 10.1 Ways in Which Gifted/Talented Students (Grades 4–12) Differ from Their Peers

Grades	Findings
4, 5, 6	Gifted are independent, internally controlled.
	Gifted prefer independent study and discussions, but no lectures.
	Gifted are persistent, nonconforming, perceptually strong.
	Gifted prefer time to complete tasks, options, few/no lectures.
	Gifted prefer teaching games, independent study, peer teaching, programming.
	Gifted dislike recitations, lectures.
7, 8, 9	Gifted are persistent, self-perceptually strong.
	Gifted prefer learning alone, no lectures.
7–12	Gifted are highly motivated, perceptually strong.
9–12	Gifted are self-motivated, internally controlled, self-directed, task committed.
4–12	Gifted are self-motivated, persistent, perceptually strong, nonconforming.
	Gifted prefer options, formal design, no lectures, learning alone.
5–12	Gifted, highly gifted, and average students differ significantly in their learning styles and hemispheric arousal systems.
	Gifted prefer quiet, moderate temperatures, morning, and options.
	Highly gifted prefer sound when learning, cool temperatures, evening, and more options than the gifted. These revealed the highest levels of motivation and right-dominant processing/integration.

Source: Dunn, 1984, p. 6

Many writers would regard a definition of genius or giftedness that is confined to intellectual ability (even if divergent thinking were included) as altogether too narrow because it excludes those talented in a whole range of areas and activities—for example, art, music, psychosocial skills, leadership, and the performing arts (Bloom, 1985; Getzels & Dillon, 1973; Getzels & Jackson, 1962; Strang, 1958; Witty, 1958; Wolfle, 1969).

The definition of gifted and talented children provided by the United States Office of Education has been widely accepted in states and school districts (Marland, 1972). It recognizes six types of talent: three refer to intellectual behavior (conceived in broader terms than the kind of abilities required for high performance on an intelligence test–general intellectual ability, specific academic aptitude, and creative or productive thinking); one refers to social behavior (leadership ability); one to artistic behavior (visual and performing arts); and one to psychomotor behavior.

High ability in any one of these areas may not in itself be sufficient to ensure that a student will manifest "giftedness"; the student should also be able to bring creativity to bear on particular problem areas and should show task commitment when he or she becomes inspired by a particular topic, area of study, issue, event, or form of creative expression. Students are regarded as "gifted" to the extent that they possess, or are capable of developing, an interaction between above-average ability, creativity, and task commitment (Renzulli, Reis, & Smith, 1981). To identify such students requires more than information about their abilities, interests, and learning styles; it also requires "action information," that is, information obtained from observing students in a program designed to allow them to demonstrate their ability, creativity, and task commitment.

Given society's need for talent to produce ideas that enhance the moral, social, emotional, intellectual, physical, and aesthetic life of humanity, and given the individual's right to receive an education that will develop his or her potential to the full, Tannenbaum (1985) has proposed a decalogue of rights for gifted children (see Box 10.2). The decalogue stresses the need for early identification of talented children and the provision of educational experiences appropriate to their talents.

The identification of a potentially gifted child is not easy. This should be obvious given the variety of characteristics that society accepts as talents. There is the additional problem that some children may not show their talents at a very early age and so may be missed, whatever the identification procedures used.

The most frequent identification procedure is teacher observation and nomination. Next most frequent is performance on a standardized test (of school achievement or intelligence), followed by previously demonstrated accomplishments (including school grades) (Marland, 1972). A combination of approaches is preferable to reliance on a single one. While these procedures are likely to be reasonably successful in identifying conventional talents in students, such as those required by a physician, engineer, or business executive, they may miss more unusual kinds of talent, such as those of explorer or musical genius.

Programs for the Talented

A traditional method of dealing with talented students has been to accelerate them through grades. In this system, students may be admitted to school before the age of 6 or they may skip grades, or a group of students may be formed who will cover the course in less time than is normal. For example, students in a junior high school could complete grades 7 to 9 in two years instead of three, junior high school students could attend senior high classes for credit, or senior high school students could attend seminars for college credit (Gallagher, 1975).

The acceleration of talented students is no longer widely practiced. The most common means of dealing with talented students is the part-time special *"pull-out" class.* In this system, students are taken out of the regular classroom at different times and given special attention by a teacher trained in meeting the needs of gifted students. More than seven out of ten school districts use this system.

A common alternative to the pull-out class is *enrichment* provided in

> **BOX 10.2 A Decalogue of Rights for Gifted Children**
>
> 1. Children have the right to be identified as gifted at the earliest possible age.
> 2. Children have a right to be identified as gifted long before they are able to achieve renown.
> 3. Gifted children have a right to be regarded as precious human resources far out of proportion to their numbers.
> 4. Gifted children have a right to differentiated education that is uniquely appropriate to them.
> 5. Gifted children have the right to the kind of education that is the forerunner of education for all children.
> 6. Gifted children have the right to be educated by teachers who are specially qualified to teach them.
> 7. Gifted children have the right to a formal education that originates in their total environment (that includes resources beyond the school's staff, resources, and schedules).
> 8. Gifted children have a right to be nurtured in a school program (that is, in a long-term offering that is a major part of the school curriculum) rather than in fragmentary ad hoc school provisions.
> 9. Gifted children have a right to their own individualities.
> 10. Gifted children have a right to freedom and equality.

Source:
Tannenbaum, 1985,
pp. 146–150.

special projects and activities in the regular classroom. Almost two-thirds of school districts use this system. About a quarter of districts use a combination of pull-out and enrichment procedures (Richardson Foundation, 1985).

State or federal governments fund many special programs for talented children, and special curricula have been developed in a range of school subjects (Gallagher, 1975). In the case of mathematics, a basic educational objective is to improve students' understanding of abstract concepts and systems. A second objective is to help the student appreciate that mathematics is not a static subject in which everything is known, but rather a developing one that depends on the creative ideas of students and mathematicians.

Science also has received attention in programs for the gifted. In these programs there is less concern for the applications of science (for example, in television or airplane technology) than in understanding what scientists do and how they go about it. This means that students are given a lot of experience using experimental procedures to find out how the world works.

The approach in social studies programs for the gifted has been the same as in mathematics and science programs—to help students understand important concepts rather than providing them with a large number of unrelated facts. This involves introducing students to the fields of psychology, sociology, anthropology, and economics; areas that receive relatively little attention in normal social studies programs.

Despite such programs to help the gifted and talented, there is evidence that the needs of such students are not adequately met in American schools today (Richardson Foundation, 1985). First, many programs lack substance in terms of goals, curricula, and materials. Second, not enough time is available to students in special programs; usually, schools provide about three to five hours a week. Third, there is a need for more teachers who have had special training in dealing with the needs of the gifted. Fourth, the criteria for identifying gifted students are often too narrow (usually a score on a standardized test of ability or achievement is the main criterion). A variety of other more novel criteria are required if schools are to succeed in identifying all potentially talented students. These could include interviews with students and peer nominations. Finally, the numbers involved in special programs for the gifted is quite small. About 4 percent of students are regarded as gifted (about 1.6 million children); almost half of these receive no special education. Some states have no special provision at all for the gifted (Gallagher, Weiss, Oglesby, & Thomas, 1983). Even states that provide facilities for 4 or 5 percent of children may be missing many who are potentially gifted. As there is no obvious break between the gifted and the less gifted, there is no sure-fire method of identifying the gifted. If schools are to ensure that they do not overlook gifted students, they should allow a greater proportion of students to participate in special programs.

A number of approaches have been suggested to solve the problems of identification and of making programs available to more students. One such strategy is the pyramid approach, which would provide a wide base of enrichment activities in regular classrooms for a relatively large number of students, narrowing to more specialized programs (in special classes, special schools, and out-of-school locations) for more able students (Richardson Foundation, 1985). Another approach, the revolving door identification and programming model, stipulates that special programs be made available to a relatively large percentage of the student population (usually 15 to 25 percent) known as a "talent pool" for short periods of time (Renzulli, Reis, & Smith, 1981). Different levels of enrichment programs are then proposed for students: the first level is designed to capitalize on the existing interests in the talent pool and to promote new ones (type I enrichment); the next level is designed to develop a wide variety of thinking processes and research skills (type II enrichment); and eventually the most successful students in type I and type II programs go on to more creative work (type III enrichment).

It is hoped that the widening of selection criteria involved in these approaches will target all gifted students. It is also hoped that students' experience in programs for the gifted will enhance their creativity.

The identification of the potentially talented, or even their participation in special programs, can only be the beginning on the long road to the development of talent. For such development requires "a long process of development requiring enormous motivation, much support from family, the best teachers and role models possible, much time, and a singleness of purpose and dedication that is relatively rare in the United States" (Bloom, 1985, p. 538).

Students with Handicapping Conditions

Some students have characteristics that interfere with their ability to learn in school or function normally in society. These students are classified as "exceptional" when the condition they have is severe enough to interfere with their ability to learn in a traditional classroom setting. School districts spend a great deal of time, effort, and money to meet the needs of such students.

Public Law 94-142 is the most extensive federal law governing education for special learners. Under this law, students diagnosed as having problems with vision, hearing, communication, movement, perceptual-motor skills, social-emotional adjustment, or intelligence are eligible for special programs.

Types of Handicapping Conditions

The major types of exceptionality, as presented and defined in Public Law 94-142, are as follows:

- **Visually Handicapped** *"Visually handicapped" means a visual impairment which, even with correction, adversely affects a child's educational performance. The term includes both partially sighted and blind children.*
- **Deaf and Hard-of-Hearing** *"Deaf" means a hearing impairment which is so severe that the child is impaired in processing linguistic information through hearing, with or without amplification, which adversely affects educational performance. . . . "Hard of hearing" means a hearing impairment, whether permanent or fluctuating, which adversely affects a child's educational performance but which is not included under the definition of "deaf" in this section.*
- **Deaf-Blind** *"Deaf-blind" means concomitant hearing and visual impairment, the combination of which causes such severe communication and other developmental and educational problems that they cannot be accommodated in special education programs solely for deaf or blind children.*
- **Orthopedically and Other Health-Impaired Individuals** *"Orthopedically impaired" means a severe orthopedic impairment which adversely affects a child's educational performance. The term includes impairments caused by congenital anomaly (e.g., clubfoot, absence of some member, etc.), impairments caused by disease (e.g., poliomyelitis, bone tuberculosis, etc.), and impairments from other causes (e.g., cerebral palsy, amputations, and fractures or burns which cause contractures). . . . "Other health impaired" means limited strength, vitality, or alertness, due to chronic or acute health problems such as a heart condition, tuberculosis, rheumatic fever, nephritis, asthma, sickle cell anemia, hemophilia, epilepsy, lead poisoning, leukemia, or diabetes, which adversely affects a child's educational performance.*
- **Seriously Emotionally Disturbed** *"Seriously emotionally disturbed" . . . means a condition exhibiting one or more of the following characteristics over a long period of time and to a marked degree, which adversely affects educational performance:*
  - *(a.) An inability to learn which cannot be explained by intellectual, sensory, or health factors.*
  - *(b.) An inability to build or maintain satisfactory interpersonal relationships with peers and teachers.*
  - *(c.) Inappropriate types of behavior or feelings under normal circumstances.*

(d.) A general pervasive mood of unhappiness or depression.

(e.) A tendency to develop physical symptoms or fears associated with personal or school problems.

The term includes children who are schizophrenic or autistic. The term does not include children who are socially maladjusted, unless it is determined that they are seriously emotionally disturbed.

● ***Speech-Impaired*** *"Speech impairment" means a communication disorder, such as stuttering, impaired articulation, a language impairment, or a voice impairment, which adversely affects a child's educational performance.*

● ***Learning-Disabled*** *"Specific learning disability" means a disorder in one or more of the basic psychological processes involved in understanding or in using language, spoken or written, which may manifest itself in an imperfect ability to listen, think, speak, read, write, spell, or to do mathematical calculations. The term includes such conditions as perceptual handicaps, brain injury, minimal brain dysfunction, dyslexia, and developmental aphasia. The term does not include children who have learning problems which are primarily the result of visual, hearing, or motor handicaps, of mental retardation, or of environmental, cultural, or economic disadvantage.*

● ***Mentally retarded*** *"Mentally retarded" means significantly subaverage general intellectual functioning existing concurrently with deficits in adaptive behavior and manifested during the developmental period which adversely affects a student's educational performance."*

Programs for Students with Handicapping Conditions

To ensure that disabled students with handicapping conditions receive the programs and services appropriate to their educational needs, federal legislation passed in the 1970s, culminating in the Education for All Handicapped Children Act (EHA) (Public Law 94-142), requires that public schools provide these students with educational services. The number of students with handicapping conditions receiving special education under federal law rose from 9.1 percent of all students in 1978 (the first year in which the law was fully implemented) to 11 percent in 1984. The percentage of students in the learning-disabled category was the largest; it almost doubled (from 2.3 percent to 4.2 percent) between 1978 and 1984 (Stern, 1987).

Public Law 94-142 requires a full evaluation prior to the initial placement of a special-needs student. This evaluation cannot be conducted without written consent from a parent or guardian. Following placement, periodic reevaluation is required. This must take place at least once in every three years, and more frequently if the family or educators so recommend. Written consent for this evaluation is not required, but notice of an impending evaluation must be given to the family.

The individual student evaluations must be conducted by two or more

professionals who are skilled in assessment and programming. No decision about a student can be made on the basis of any single item of information, such as an intelligence test score or a single teacher's recommendation. Further, only validated and unbiased assessment techniques can be used; assessment instruments that are biased against racial or ethnic minorities or against people with handicapping conditions may not be used. If a student has only limited proficiency in the English language, this must be taken into account.

Under the federal law, a special team is responsible for designing a program for a student with a handicapping condition. The team usually consists of a school administrator, special educator, psychologist, classroom teacher, support personnel, and the student's parents. Under the terms of Public Law 94-142, the team must create an individualized education plan (IEP) that places the student in a learning environment appropriate to his or her needs and as close as possible to a regular classroom environment. The team, known in different states by different names—such as pupil placement team (PPT), staffing team, or core team—is responsible for determining the placement program and the services appropriate to a student's needs. A written document setting forth a detailed description of the program for the student is required. It should contain a description of each program element, as set out in Box 10.3. Each student's program must be reviewed and revised at least annually, with more frequent reviews if requested by either the school or the family.

The federal statutes require that all educational programs and services be provided in the "least restrictive environment" appropriate to meet a

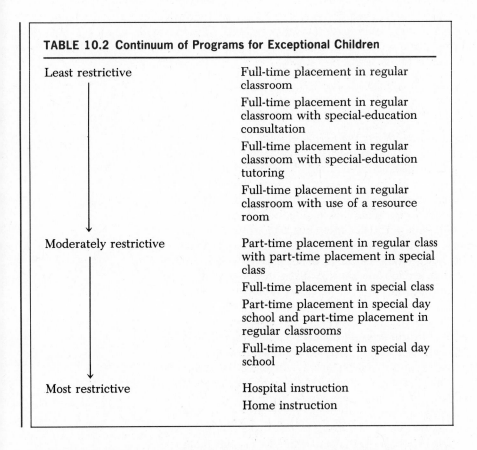

TABLE 10.2 Continuum of Programs for Exceptional Children

Least restrictive	Full-time placement in regular classroom
	Full-time placement in regular classroom with special-education consultation
	Full-time placement in regular classroom with special-education tutoring
	Full-time placement in regular classroom with use of a resource room
Moderately restrictive	Part-time placement in regular class with part-time placement in special class
	Full-time placement in special class
	Part-time placement in special day school and part-time placement in regular classrooms
	Full-time placement in special day school
Most restrictive	Hospital instruction
	Home instruction

Source: Hewett & Forness, 1984, pp. 55–58.

student's needs. Since the ultimate goal of special programs is to teach, train, and prepare students to enter the mainstream of society, it is important that the program be as close as possible to what other children experience. A regular class is generally considered to be the least restrictive environment in which a student can be placed. Institutionalization and home instruction are the most restrictive types of environments. The setting selected for a student can range from very restrictive placements to full-time mainstreamed placements in a regular classroom (see Table 10.2). Insofar as it is appropriate for the learner, the school will try to educate students with disabilities in the standard curriculum, among students who are not disabled, for both nonacademic and extracurricular programs.

School organizations offer different types of programs to exceptional learners. Programs will vary to meet the requirements of the IEPs. Normally, a school will have a resource room where students with minor disabilities receive extra help part of the day and spend the rest of the day mainstreamed in regular classrooms. Schools also usually have a self-contained room where students with more severe problems spend the whole day. When highly specialized, expensive programs are required for a few students, school districts pool resources to provide programs in one location. By sharing resources, districts can transport students to the program site, share the costs, and provide a better program than if they developed one independently. Teachers who serve on a pupil placement team will play a major role in deciding which setting is appropriate for exceptional learners.

Gender

It may seem strange to consider gender in a chapter on pluralism. All the other categories we considered are minority groups in our society and so can be regarded as in danger of being discriminated against, or at least neglected, in our schools. Obviously, since there are about equal numbers of boys and girls in our society, neither gender can be regarded as a minority. However, there is a danger, and there is plenty of evidence to support this, that society in general and schools in particular often react to a person simply as a male or as a female instead of considering the person as an individual.

To say that there are distinctions between males and females is to state the obvious. However, do those differences justify disparities in overall school grades (in favor of females), differences in mathematics achievement (in favor of males), or unequal pay for equal work (also in favor of males)?

Research on the subject of gender differences has not been conclusive. There is some evidence that in the areas of cognitive and intellectual skills, males tend to do better than females on tests of mathematical and visual-spatial abilities, while females tend to do better on tests of verbal ability. In the area of personality, males have been found to be more aggressive than females (Maccoby & Jacklin, 1974). These differences are not large. Further, while the mean score for girls and boys might differ for a particular attribute, there is always a very large overlap of the scores of the two genders (Hyde, 1981). Nevertheless, the differences are significant enough to suggest that the educational development and career prospects of girls are below those of boys.

Stereotypes about differences between males and females are widespread. Society does much to develop and perpetuate them. From an early age, boys and girls tend to be treated differently by parents and other adults. Even before birth, parents may have different expectations for boys and girls. As children get older, many of them are supplied with different kinds of toys—soft dolls to be cuddled by girls, blocks and metal to be built into bridges and houses by boys. In the past, gender stereotypes were reinforced in school

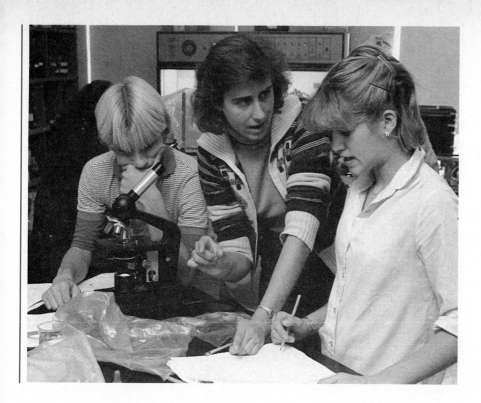

To help prevent
sex-role stereotyping,
teachers should treat
students as
individuals rather
than as members of
a particular gender.

textbooks by illustrations in which women were portrayed as home-based, passive, and unadventurous (cleaning the home and cooking), while men worked outside the home and from time to time came to the rescue of helpless females faced with the task of repairing an electrical appliance (U'Ren, 1971).

Many people perceive the role of girls and women as being passive, supportive, affectionate, dependent, submissive, maternal, gentle, and caring (denoting what has been called "expressive" competence), while the role of boys and men is perceived as being active, aggressive, competitive, ambitious, self-assertive, independent, supervisory, and dominant (denoting "instrumental" competence) (Broverman, Broverman, Clarkson, Rosenkrantz, & Vogel, 1970).

Such stereotypes are important because they can influence people's judgments, their expectations for behavior (their own and others'), and their actions. Indeed, how males and females *think* they differ may be as important as how they actually differ (Deaux, 1984). Since there is close agreement between men and women as to the characteristics that compose gender stereotypes, we can expect both men and women to conform to beliefs about what is "typical" masculine and feminine behavior. The effects of such conformity to gender stereotypes are to be seen all around us. Men tend to take up occupations that are in keeping with the male stereotype (for example, jobs as airline pilots, administrators), while women are more likely to be found in caring occupations (for example, jobs as teachers, nurses) and service occupations (for example, secretarial jobs) that might seem to demand the kind of characteristics associated with the female stereotype.

Part of the reason that gender differences exist in occupations can be attributed to the educational achievements of students. Both boys and girls tend to take courses in school that will prepare them for certain occupations. Mathematics provides a good example of this. At age 9, boys and girls exhibit no difference in performance on the National Assessment of Educational Progress (NAEP) mathematics test. By age 17, however, males perform better on the NAEP test and on other tests of mathematics. A variety of factors contribute to the creation of this gender difference. First, boys and girls differ in their participation in mathematics programs (for example, fewer girls take higher-level courses such as trigonometry). Second, there are differences in how boys and girls react to mathematics. Compared to boys, girls enjoy mathematics less, are less confident in their ability to do well, and are less likely to see mathematics as useful, particularly in their later careers. Third, in the mathematics class, girls are given fewer opportunities for answering questions, the level of questions they pose is less challenging, and they receive less individual help (Confrey, 1987).

Boys, too, may suffer in the educational process. Teachers often perceive them as being less well adjusted to the demands of schooling. Boys are regarded as being rougher, noisier, more immature, and more lacking in concentration (Hartley, 1978). Perhaps this is why teachers have more interactions with boys than with girls in the classroom. In general, boys appear to occupy a more salient position in the teacher's mind than do girls (Brophy & Good, 1970).

Part of a teacher's task is seen, by some teachers at any rate, to be that of making boys less rough and noisy, since roughness and noisiness are not considered to be conducive to learning. Given the fact that teachers wish to reduce the disruptive behavior of boys and make them conform to the demands of the classroom, it is not surprising that teachers direct more evaluative comments toward boys and are more critical of boys' behavior (Brophy & Good, 1970). There is also evidence that teachers assign higher grades to girls than to boys (Carter, 1952; McCandless, Roberts, & Starnes, 1972). In general, the stereotype in teachers' minds seems to be that girls are "better" students than boys.

Sex stereotypes are so deeply entrenched in the experience of all of us that it is difficult to avoid behaving in accordance with them. As a teacher, you should be sensitive to the dangers involved in such behavior—for example, in expecting boys to be rougher and noisier or, on the other hand, in expecting girls to do poorly in scientific, mathematical, or technical areas of study. Insofar as it is possible, you should react to students as individuals rather than as members of a particular gender. If your primary concern is to respond appropriately to each individual's particular abilities, interests, and needs, you will have gone a long way toward avoiding sex stereotyping.

CONCLUSION

We began this chapter by saying that the group membership of students is recognized by schools (when, for example, they place students of similar age in one class) as well as by the law when, for example, bilingual education has to be provided for students from non-English-speaking homes. We also began by saying that it is better if you, as a teacher, think of students primarily as individuals rather than as members of a particular group of students. In this concluding section we will consider some of the dangers that can arise if you make judgments about students on the basis of "inferential information" (that is, characteristics such as gender and ethnic group membership) rather than "direct information" obtained in face-to-face interactions with the student over a period of time in the classroom.

There is always the danger that when we judge people who are not members of our own group, certain biases will operate in those judgments. The majority of teachers are white, middle-class, and female. Are students who do not fit this categorization likely to be misjudged in some ways by these teachers?

The importance of this question becomes clear when we consider that teachers may form expectations concerning student achievement on the basis of their judgments. They may then proceed to treat students negatively or positively in accordance with those expectations; students who react to this treatment may end up conforming to what is expected of them, thus forging the final link in a chain of self-fulfilling prophecy.

Do teachers form different expectations for different groups of students? The answer would seem to be yes. On the basis of research studies, we can say that race and ethnic group membership can affect teachers' expectations (Jackson & Cosca, 1974), that teachers expect less of students from disadvantaged backgrounds than they do of students from more affluent backgrounds (Rist, 1970), and that teachers hold higher expectations for girls than for boys (Palardy, 1969). It does not follow, however, that all teachers base their judgments or treatment of students on such characteristics as the social or ethnic background of the student. Indeed, there is evidence that in their judgments teachers tend to minimize bias that might arise from such characteristics (McCandless, Roberts, & Starnes, 1972). If, as we have already suggested, you perceive students as individuals rather than as members of particular groups, you are less likely to be biased in your judgments and your treatment of your students.

QUESTIONS AND ACTIVITIES

1. Spend a day in a school doing one of the following activities:
   a. Shadow a student who is in a specialized program and answer the following questions: What are the goals of the program? How is the student treated by other students? By teachers? Does the program achieve its goals?
   b. Observe a regular classroom and answer the following questions: How does the teacher use grouping? What are the educational benefits and drawbacks to his or her approach?
   c. Review curriculum material used in the school. Are the materials biased toward or against any group(s) of students?
2. Interview a classroom teacher about his or her thoughts on specialized programming for certain students. What does he or she feel are the major

advantages and disadvantages of such programs for the teacher as well as the student?

3. A number of education critics claim that schools now offer an array of programs for specialized pockets of students at the expense of the 80 percent of students who fall in the "middle" or "average" group. What is your reaction to this contention?

4. In principle, do you agree with the advocates or critics of bilingual education? Why or why not?

5. What will you do as a classroom teacher to prevent sex-role stereotyping?

6. Do you agree with the Decalogue of Rights for Gifted Children in Box 10.2?

7. Do you believe schools should provide programs for gifted children? If so, which approach of those described do you think is most appropriate?

CHAPTER 11

Characteristics of Individual Students

This chapter focuses on individual differences between students. Education and social science researchers have spent the last century attempting to identify and measure characteristics of individuals. This chapter overviews some of the more important theories in this area and identifies the educational implications they present.

- Students in any classroom exhibit a wide range of variability on a variety of characteristics.
- Teachers should try to identify areas of student strength and weakness and respond to them in a way that will enhance the learning of each student.
- Some student characteristics are relatively difficult to alter. Because of this, the teacher will attempt to adapt instruction to them rather than attempt to change them.
- Modern approaches to the study of intelligence are directed toward identifying a variety of types.
- Modern studies of intelligence are aimed at identifying the processes involved in intelligent behavior.
- Tests that measure achievement in specific areas are more helpful in planning instruction than tests of general ability or achievement.
- Many strategies have been developed to help the teacher cope with individual differences among students.

As you begin this chapter, pause for a moment and picture in your mind some of your friends. You will readily agree that no two of them are entirely alike. Each is unique. A second fact you will readily accept is that despite this uniqueness, each of your friends is in some ways similar to your other friends. We would not call them all friends, or even people, if they did not share certain characteristics. Although it is not easy to say what the essential characteristics of friendship or being human are, there is a wide range of more or less superficial characteristics that people share to varying extents. We can use these characteristics simply to tell people apart. John is tall with curly blonde hair and blue eyes; Mary is medium-sized with straight black hair and hazel eyes.

We distinguish between people for a very important reason: to guide our responses to them. Initially we depend on the person's characteristics for simple recognition. If we recognize the person as a friend, we speak to him or her. If the person is not a friend, we may not speak. If we talk to both, we are not likely to speak in the same way to a stranger as we do to a friend. As we get to know people better, the physical characteristics (height, color of hair and eyes) we used to describe John and Mary become less important as a basis for our responses, while psychological traits (John is cold and distant, Mary is warm and friendly) become more important.

The students in your classroom will show just as much variability as your friends, if not more. Since you will have a professional responsibility to help each student to learn, your interest in the way your students are different from one another will not be the same as your interest in the way your friends are different. Physical characteristics are not likely to be of great importance (except in the case of very young children and children with handicapping conditions). You will have to look deeper and find variables that are relevant to the learning process. The first major task in this chapter will be to identify some of the characteristics that educators use to describe how students differ from one another. The characteristics we will consider are ability, cognitive styles, locus of control, learned helplessness, self-concept, and creativity.

Over the past decade, classrooms have become more diverse in the range of student characteristics represented in them. This is partly because there is a general policy, expressed in Public Law 94-142, to integrate students, including those with handicapping conditions, in a single classroom. The tendency to have mixed-ability classes rather than homogeneous classes, a practice that is supported by the research on effective schools, leads to a greater heterogeneity or range of student characteristics in classrooms.

Having identified the characteristics on which students differ and where students stand relative to each other on such characteristics, you will then be faced with the task of responding to those differences in a way that will enhance the learning of each student. This brings us to the second major task of this chapter: to consider some strategies that have been developed to deal with individual differences among students. These range from strategies in which differences are identified and are then more or less ignored by the teacher, and ones in which the problem of adaptation is left up to the student (grouping), to ones in which efforts are made to tailor specific learning tasks to the needs of the individual learner (individualized programs).

Historical Background of Individual Differences

Individual students undertake learning tasks in their own ways. We hardly need psychology to tell us that. However, it may not always be adequately recognized that such differences have implications for education. Plato (428–347 B.C.), in his *Republic*, suggested that tests be used to assess people's aptitudes; he made this suggestion because he claimed that people are different from each other in their natural endowments, and so one person will be suited for one occupation while another will be suited for a different occupation. In the days when classes were very large and much classroom activity consisted of repetitious recitation, it is unlikely that teachers considered their students as individuals.

In the nineteenth century, the study of individual differences received considerable support from developments in biology and psychology. For example, Sir Francis Galton (1822–1911) attempted to apply Charles Darwin's (1809–1882) evolutionary principles of variation, selection, and adaptation to the study of human individuals. Galton's main interest was in heredity and he published a number of influential books on the topic: *Hereditary genius* (1869), *English men of science* (1874), and *Natural inheritance* (1889). To study heredity and to describe the degree of resemblance among the characteristics of individuals, Galton felt there was a need to develop methods of measuring those characteristics. The instruments he developed tested rather simple processes such as sensory discrimination and motor capacities. He hoped, as some later investigators such as the American James McKeen Cattell

Physical differences are just one way that students of the same age and grade level may vary.

(1860–1944) also did, that from a measurement of sensory processes he would be able to obtain an estimate of an individual's intellectual level. However, it was left to French investigators, especially Alfred Binet (1857–1911), to develop tests that were designed to measure more complex functions, such as memory, imagination, attention, comprehension, suggestibility, and aesthetic appreciation. His work on more complex mental processes eventually led him to develop the first intelligence scale, designed to provide an index of the individual's overall level of intellectual functioning.

Dimensions of Individual Differences

Over a long period of studying individual differences, psychologists have described a large number of dimensions along which individuals differ from one another (Anastasi, 1958; Tyler, 1974, 1978). In this chapter, we can consider only a small number of these. We selected dimensions that are most related to learning: ability, cognitive styles, locus of control, learned helplessness, self-concept, and creativity. All these characteristics, by contrast with students' level of knowledge and cognitive skills, are relatively difficult to alter. Because of this, teachers attempt to adapt instruction to these ingrained characteristics (Gagné & Dick, 1983).

Ability

What do you mean when you say that somebody has a lot of "ability" or is "very intelligent"? In your mind, do the two things mean the same thing? Does one or do both of them mean that a student is doing very well at school and, if so, is he or she doing equally well in all areas of schoolwork? Or do you think that there are many kinds of "intelligence" and many kinds of "ability"? Do you think there are special abilities for different areas of schoolwork, so that the student who does well in English literature may not do so well in mathematics or music? And what about outside the school? Is the "good" student always good at solving the problems of everyday life?

At school, the term *ability* is often used in a general sense, particularly to indicate a student's overall readiness or competence to begin a course of study. Psychologists have used the word *intelligence* to describe this kind of ability. The word covers a whole range of abilities, among them the ability to learn; the ability to adapt to new situations; the ability to handle concepts, relationships, and abstract symbols; the ability to reason and to make judgments. However the terms *ability* and *intelligence* are defined, there is little doubt that teachers, as they begin each school year, are conscious of the fact that the students in their classes vary considerably in their knowledge and skills and in the facility with which they can acquire knowledge and skills. The capacity for learning is also known as *aptitude,* a term that is sometimes used instead of ability or intelligence.

The first intelligence test of the type we know today was developed at the beginning of the century by Alfred Binet and his co-workers in France. The test was designed as a general measure of intelligence and assessed a student's ability on a variety of different tasks, such as understanding vocabulary (defining the meaning of words), solving arithmetic problems, recalling facts from memory, and, for young children, manipulating objects manually. A student's score on the test depended on the number of items that he or she had answered correctly. In later versions of intelligence tests an individual's score was related to the average score of students of the same age to calculate an intelligence quotient (IQ) score.

It has been found that when a large group of students takes an intelligence test and a graph is drawn representing the number of students who obtain each score, the graph is found to approximate a bell-shaped curve. This curve is known as the normal or Gaussian distribution (named for the German mathematician, Karl Friedrich Gauss, who described the characteristics of the distribution) and is shown in Figure 11.1. You will note that the largest proportion of students score (see the X axis for the number of people) near to the average or arithmetic mean (see the Y axis for the mark or score on the test) and that there are fewer and fewer students under the curve as scores move away from the mean.

The idea that intelligence is really distributed among people in this way is disputed. Those who argue that it is say that many physical characteristics (such as height), which are determined by a large number of chance factors, are "normally" distributed. Therefore, they say intelligence must also be normally distributed. Against this, many argue that a normal distribution of results emerges because of the way in which items are selected for the test. If all the individual items included in a test are answered correctly by the vast majority of the students for whom the test is intended, obviously the scores will not give the kind of distribution described in Figure 11.1. Similarly, if all the items are too difficult for the vast majority of students, a "normal" distribution will not emerge either. To obtain the spread of scores represented in the distribution in Figure 11.1, it is necessary to include a lot of items in the test that will be answered correctly by about half the students taking the test.

FIGURE 11.1 The Normal Distribution of Intelligence: Spread of Marks Around the Mean

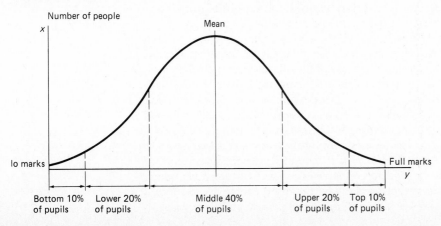

The concept that intelligence is normally distributed implies that intelligence is some kind of unitary entity that has an independent existence, which is then measured. However, just because we give something a name does not necessarily mean that the thing exists in any form other than in the name and in our idea of it. Gould describes this fallacy of reification, our tendency to convert abstract concepts into concrete entities, with regard to intelligence:

> We recognize the importance of mentality in our lives and wish to characterize it, in part so that we can make the divisions and distinctions among people that our cultural and political systems dictate. We therefore give the word "intelligence" to this wondrously complex and multifaceted set of human capabilities. This shorthand symbol is then reified and intelligence achieves its dubious status as a unitary thing (Gould, 1981, p. 24).

Our notions of intelligence and ability do have some basis in reality, however, insofar as they are inferred from certain kinds of behavior. Sometimes, the behavior may appear artificial, such as responding to questions on a standardized test; in other cases, it is more real, such as solving problems encountered in everyday life. In either case, intelligence is best regarded as a concept (sometimes called a construct), something in our own minds, which helps us make sense of certain aspects of people's behavior or describes observed differences in behavior between individuals.

ONE "INTELLIGENCE" OR MANY? A question that has concerned psychologists for a long time is: Is intelligence as measured by an intelligence test best regarded as a single ability or does the score one obtains on a test depend on the operation of several abilities? Researchers have examined the performance of individuals on a number of different tests. If people who score highly on one test also score highly on another test, it is inferred that both tests are tapping the same underlying ability. However, if performance on one test is not at all related to performance on another test (that is, students who have a high score on one test have a low score on another test), it is concluded that the tests are measuring different abilities. Psychologists have come up with answers that are to some extent a function of the range of tasks included in the tests, the way test scores are analyzed, and the nature of the individuals who take the tests (for example, their level of education).

In early studies of this issue, it was concluded that there was one general ability (called g) underlying performance on all types of intellectual tasks (Spearman, 1927). It was believed that this ability should be in evidence on a wide variety of tasks, for example, tests of vocabulary and reasoning with words as well as more practical tasks involving blocks and pictorial material.

Some investigators rejected the idea of general ability and considered intelligence to be made up of a number of abilities that are not related to each other in any systematic way. In one model of intelligence, 120 separate abilities were specified (Guilford, 1967). While accepting the differentiation of abilities, other investigators tried to conceptualize them in more economic terms. For example, while accepting the general-ability factor (g), they concluded that under this there were two other fairly general abilities: a verbal-numerical-educational one (called *v:ed*) and a practical-mechanical-spatial-physical one (called *k:m*). As their names imply, these two abilities split into further subabilities (Vernon, 1961). A somewhat similar distinction is made among crystallized abilities (mainly verbal-educational, evoked by familiar tasks and environments), fluid abilities (mainly analytic reasoning, evoked by novel tasks), and spatial-visualization abilities (Cattell, 1971; Snow & Lohman, 1984).

In recent years, some writers have tended to avoid using the term *intelligence,* partly because of its lack of clarity and partly because of its negative connotations. "Intelligence" conjures up the image, in many people's minds, of a fixed genetic characteristic or of an inherent mental trait, both of which are relatively unaffected by a person's environment and experiential background. This simplistic concept of intelligence can have negative implications when applied to someone with a low score on an intelligence test. A person with a "low I.Q." may carry this label through an entire school career, and indeed throughout life.

The idea that intelligence is a genetic trait forms the basis of the false belief that nothing can be done to improve a low-scoring individual's academic or career prospects (Block & Dworkin, 1976). Low scores on an intelligence test, especially in the case of minority racial and ethnic groups, cannot be taken as evidence of lack of "innate ability," since they may be due to differences in the language, culture, and educational opportunities.

In recent years, "intelligence" has been regarded in a very broad sense. For example, Gardner has described seven human intellectual competencies or intelligences that he regards as being relatively autonomous: linguistic intelligence, musical intelligence, logico-mathematical intelligence, spatial intelligence, bodily-kinesthetic intelligence, and two types of personal intelligence (see Box 11.1) (Gardner, 1983). These "intelligences" seem to be really broad clusters of talents rather than very specific abilities. It is clear that they range far beyond the abilities (largely verbal, logical, and mathematical) that are normally emphasized in schools and in traditional tests of intelligence. If we bear them in mind, we will perhaps be more sensitive to the total profile of an individual's abilities, and that might inspire us to make greater provision for them than is usually the case in educational goals and practice.

Another recent approach to the study of intelligence is to be found in the work of Robert Sternberg, which has focused on the dynamic processes involved in intelligent behavior rather than on intelligence as a static trait. He defines intelligence as "neural activity directed toward *purposive adaptation, and selection and shaping of, real world environments relevant to one's life*" (Sternberg, 1985, p. 45). He approaches intelligence from the point of view of reasoning and problem solving, since he argues that these are closely interrelated. To illustrate this interrelatedness he offers the following arithmetic word problem:

I planted a tree that was 8 in. tall. At the end of the first year it was 12 in. tall; at the end of the second year it was 18 in. tall; and at the end of the third year it was 27 in tall. How tall was it at the end of the fourth year? (Sternberg, 1982, p. 225).

Linguistic Intelligence

- Ability to use language to convince other individuals of a course of action
- Use of a language to store and recall information
- Use of a language to convey the meaning of concepts (orally or in writing)

Musical Intelligence

- Sensitivity to differences in sound
- Sensitivity to pitch (melody) and rhythm
- Affective/emotional sensitivity
- Sensitivity to proportions, special ratios, recurring patterns, and other detectable series (as in mathematics)

Logico-Mathematical Intelligence

- Ability to handle long chains of reasoning
- Ability to think abstractly

Spatial Intelligence

- Accurate perception of the visual world

- Ability to transform and modify perceptions
- Ability to recreate aspects of perceptual experience (even in the absence of relevant physical stimuli)

Bodily-Kinesthetic Intelligence

- Ability to use one's body in highly skilled ways for functional or expressive purposes
- Ability to manipulate objects with skill

Personal Intelligence 1

- Ability to examine and understand one's own life of feeling and emotion, and to use this in guiding one's behavior

Personal Intelligence 2

- Ability to notice and make distinctions among other individuals, in particular their moods, temperaments, motivations, and intentions

Source: Summarized from Gardner, 1983.

He goes on to point out that the question obviously involves problem solving, that it is labeled a "reasoning" problem on the intelligence test in which it appears, and that the test in which it appears is one of "intelligence."

In an attempt to describe intelligent behavior, Sternberg (1985) has proposed a triarchic theory. According to this theory, intelligence must be understood in its relationship to (1) the internal mental world of the individual, (2) the external environmental world of the individual, and (3) the individual's experience as it relates to these internal and external worlds (Sternberg, 1985).

The first part of his theory relates to the components of intelligent performance that deal with the internal world of the individual. The components are *(a)* metacomponents or executive processes used to plan, monitor, and evaluate problem solving; *(b)* performance components, or the nonexecutive processes used to carry out the instructions of metacomponents; and *(c)* knowledge-acquisition components that select, encode, and combine information to create new knowledge. These three knowledge-acquisition components are used to learn how to solve problems that are then controlled by the metacomponents and solved by the performance components. He offers the following example of how these three components operate:

Consider a problem of analogical reasoning: WASHINGTON: 1 : : LINCOLN: (a. 5, b. 10, c. 15, d. 20) [read as Washington: (is to) 1 : : (as) Lincoln: (is to) (5, 10, 15, 20)]. Metacomponents are used to judge the nature of the problem (that it is an analogy), to decide on the steps that are needed to solve the problem (e.g., understanding each of the terms of the analogy, inferring the relation between WASHINGTON and 1, applying this relation from

LINCOLN to each of the possible answers, and so on), to decide the order in which these steps should be executed, to monitor whether the steps one has chosen are really leading to a solution, and the like. Performance components are used to actually execute the steps in solving the problem. Knowledge-acquisition components were used at some time in the past to learn how to solve analogies of this sort. The three kinds of components are used interactively to figure out that the analogy deals with the faces of Presidents that appear on currency (Sternberg, 1986a, p. 278).

The second part of Sternberg's theory relates to the context in which intelligent behavior occurs and deals with the way in which individuals adapt or accommodate to shape and select their environment. The third part of the theory deals with experience and the operation of intelligence in a variety of tasks, particularly in dealing with novel tasks (insight) and situational demands.

These new approaches to intelligence (together with new approaches to the measurement of intelligence that are also being developed) have a number of characteristics (Sternberg, 1986b). First, they are based on a broader conception of intelligence than many earlier approaches, which seemed to focus primarily on school-related cognitive abilities. This is particularly obvious in Gardner's list of multiple intelligences (1983). Second, there is an increased emphasis on identifying and measuring the processes that underlie intelligent behavior. More than a single normative score is required if one is to decide, for example, whether a student's difficulties lie in the reasoning process or in a lack of relevant knowledge. Third, there is an increased emphasis on the practical side of intelligence, that is, on how people function in everyday life, not just on how they perform in school. Fourth, trying to measure learning potential, that is, to measure the latent potentialities of the student that are likely to respond to instruction, has become a priority. Fifth, since it is recognized that individuals may differ in their learning styles, tests are now being designed to accommodate and reflect not only abilities but also those stylistic variables. Finally, testing and learning are now more closely integrated than they have been in the past. Educational programs are sometimes geared toward the strengths and weaknesses that students reveal on intelligence tests.

ABILITY AND ACHIEVEMENT Ability or intelligence is frequently contrasted with achievement. The terms *ability* and *intelligence* are used to refer to more generalized aspects of thinking—techniques of analyzing, comprehending, and solving problems—that have developed as a result of an individual's experience, both in and out of school, and that can be applied to a variety of new situations (Ferguson, 1954). The term *achievement,* on the other hand, is used to refer to more specific knowledge, skills, and understanding that is regarded as the result of more specific curricular and learning experiences, such as those normally provided in a school.

The distinction between ability and achievement in practice, however, may not be as clearcut as these definitions might lead you to believe. There can be little doubt that some achievement occurs in nonformal settings, even perhaps in situations in which a person does not set out to learn anything at all. How much information or knowledge do children pick up watching television, reading, talking to friends, or observing their parents go about their everyday work around the home? And how much of children's experience within the school makes them more adaptive in dealing with new problem situations encountered both inside and outside the school?

Because it is not easy to distinguish between intelligence and achievement in practice, we should not be too surprised to learn that students' scores on intelligence tests, particularly tests with a high verbal content, are closely related to (correlated with) students' cognitive achievements following a significant chunk of formal instruction (for example, achievement in reading). This is particularly so when students' achievements are measured on standardized tests (Snow & Lohman, 1984). Intelligence test scores have also been found to be related to how far a student progresses in school. Thus, college graduates, on average, have been found to have higher scores than students who complete their education on graduating from high school, who in turn have higher scores than students who leave high school before graduating.

Over the past half century a number of different tests have been developed as broad measures of scholastic aptitude.

For reasons such as these, intelligence tests are often thought of as measures of "scholastic aptitude" and, over the past half century, scores on such tests have been used to make predictions about the performance of students in school. Further, decisions about placement, selection, and guidance of students have frequently been made on the basis of these predictions. Despite these practices, a teacher should be slow to attribute poor achievement to a lack of ability. There are many reasons why a student may be performing poorly at school. A child's poor eyesight may create problems in learning to read or in seeing the blackboard. The child may be poorly nourished and suffer from fatigue, or may come from a home where school learning is not valued and there is no opportunity, much less encouragement, for the child to study at home. Each of these situations requires a different approach on the part of the teacher.

As a classroom teacher, you will find that broad measures of ability or achievement will be of limited value in dealing with the learning problems of individual students. Your objectives in dealing with a student will be more specific than trying to help the student achieve the range of knowledge and skills covered by a standardized test of reading or arithmetic; such knowledge and skills represent the fruits not only of several years of formal instruction but also of the whole of a child's experience inside and outside of school. Your immediate concern as a teacher will be with much more discrete learning tasks, such as specific skills in mathematics (for example, addition or subtraction) or in reading (for example, learning phonics), or the skills involved in learning the content of a section of a book, or the material contained in a unit in a course. In teaching these tasks, educators may be helped by the newer approaches to the study of abilities that were described briefly above. Sternberg's view of intelligence as an information-processing ability has focused attention on ways to teach general problem-solving skills. Similarly, the study of students' aptitudes is providing insights into ways of matching types of instruction to different types of ability. For example, there is evidence that while more able students do quite well with instruction that is incomplete, less able students benefit from explicit, direct, well-structured instruction (Snow & Lohman, 1984).

Cognitive Styles

Researchers have identified several dimensions of individual difference in the performance of cognitive tasks that appear to reflect consistencies in manner or form of cognition. These dimensions are called cognitive styles and extend to a person's typical mode of perception, thinking, remembering, problem solving, and even areas of noncognitive behavior. The term *learning style* is sometimes used to describe a student's cognitive style in a learning task.

Styles differ from intellectual abilities or achievements in a number of ways (Messick & Associates, 1976; Witkin, Moore, Goodenough, & Cox, 1977). First, while abilities (traditionally, at any rate) refer to the content (or *what*) of cognition, styles refer primarily to the manner in which the behavior occurs (*how* we perceive, think, learn, and relate to others). They are essentially information-processing habits; that is, they are characteristic modes of operation that, although not completely independent of content, tend to function across a variety of content areas. Second, abilities refer to dimensions underlying a fairly limited area of behavior (for example, spatial abilities); styles, on the other hand, have a much wider and pervasive application, affecting a wide range of behaviors. Third, abilities usually are thought of in terms of a single continuum going from very little to a great deal of the same (for example, from "low" intelligence to "high" intelligence); cognitive styles are usually described in terms of two poles (for example, high risk taking versus cautious). Finally, abilities and styles are valued in different ways. It is generally regarded that it is better to have more of an ability than less of it, presumably because greater ability allows one to adapt better to the demands of a situation. In the case of cognitive style, however, each pole may have adaptive value under specific circumstances.

Since cognitive style represents a large domain of behaviors, it is not surprising that different investigators have focused on different aspects of it. We select four cognitive-style dimensions for discussion here (Messick & Associates, 1976).

FIELD DEPENDENCE AND FIELD INDEPENDENCE The field-dependent person reacts to the environment in a general, nonspecific way, while the field-independent person tries to analyze the environment and look for relationships within it. The field-dependent person also tends to be more sensitive to the human, social, and interpersonal aspects of the environment and is more skilled in social relations than is the field-independent person, who is more impersonal and less person-oriented (Witkin & Goodenough, 1981).

Whether a student's cognitive style is field-dependent or field-independent is not strongly related to the student's overall performance in more specialized areas of schoolwork. Field-dependent persons tend to be better at learning and remembering social material (things about people) than persons who are relatively field-independent. Field-independent people, on the other hand, perform better in the areas of science and mathematics. These differences may have implications for vocational choice. Relatively field-dependent persons are likely to favor careers with a "people" emphasis, that is, ones that involve interpersonal relations; the more field-independent person is more likely to become a physicist, a chemist, an engineer, or a dentist.

We should not be surprised to find that these two types of cognitive style favor different learning approaches. This has implications for the presentation of learning material and for the reward of learning behavior. Since field-dependent students do not tend to break down or analyze material to the same extent as field-independent students, they learn better when the material is presented to them in a well-organized and structured way. Field-independent students, on the other hand, tend to be able to impose their own organization and structure on material. Thus, they need less organization and structuring from the teacher when they are learning.

As a teacher, you should also bear in mind that field-dependent students are likely to be more sensitive to the reactions of other people in terms of their efforts to learn; field-independent students are more likely to have their own internal frames of reference to guide their behavior. While the field-independent student may get along quite well with his or her own self-defined goals and reinforcements (intrinsically motivated), the field-dependent student is more likely to require externally defined goals and reinforcements (extrinsic motivation).

REFLECTION AND IMPULSIVITY Students vary in the amount of time they take to reflect on an issue before coming up with the solution to a problem. A student who tends to give the first answer that comes to mind, often with little consideration of its adequacy, is known as "impulsive." A student who tends to think about various possible solutions, weighing the pros and cons of each, before actually deciding which one is correct is known as "reflective" (Kagan & Messer, 1975).

Some impulsive students will also be restless, easily distractible, emotionally uncontrolled, and aggressive. Others may give impulsive answers because of anxiety or nervousness. Over time, as you get to know your students, you will find out if a student's preferred cognitive style is reflective or impulsive, or whether his or her behavior in a particular situation can be explained by other factors.

RISK TAKING AND CAUTIOUSNESS Some individuals tend to take chances; others want to be sure before they act, avoiding situations in which there is a reasonable risk that they will not succeed (Kogan & Wallach, 1964). The avoidance of risk may reflect deeper tendencies of anxiety or defensiveness on the student's part, for example, a fear of a negative evaluation if he or she does not provide the right answer.

You may find examples of risk taking in children's performance on multiple-choice test items. The risk taker is more likely to guess the answer when not sure; the more cautious individual is more likely to skip the item. These approaches make a difference in the final test scores.

The relevance of risk taking obviously extends beyond the multiple-choice test. Most situations we encounter (particularly in learning) involve some uncertainty, which has to be handled one way or another. In such situations, students who are overcautious may invest too much energy in selectively scanning the environment in terms of its potential for success and failure and not attend adequately to the important features of the task at hand. This may interfere with their learning. Sometimes students are cautious because they are afraid of being negatively evaluated by the teacher or by other students. As a teacher, you should be sensitive to students' worries on this score when evaluating their work.

SENSORY MODE PREFERENCE We make primary use of three major sensory modes to obtain information from the world about us: kinesthetic (arising from touching, sensations of movement, and physical manipulation of objects), visual (arising from sight), and auditory (arising from hearing). People differ in their reliance on one or another of these modes, which may affect the way they represent reality. There is also a level beyond these that is highly abstract and symbolic and relies heavily on language (which may be written or spoken).

Our preference for a particular sensory mode can affect how we represent reality in our minds. Bruner has described three ways in which people translate experience into a model of the world: the enactive, the ikonic, and the symbolic. The *enactive* approach involves action. Much of a child's early learning is of this type and involves no imagery or words. Knowledge acquired later in life may also be of this kind: exactly how you learn to knit, ski, or ride a bicycle is very difficult to express in words. The *ikonic* approach depends on sensory organization; we "picture" things or organize our experiences on the basis of principles of perception. Finally, we represent things in words or language—the *symbolic* approach. Our use of symbols allows great flexibility and power in our thinking. Much of education is geared toward the development of symbolic modes of representation in the student.

Although teachers may aspire to have students attain high abstract levels of symbolic representation and manipulation, this aspiration must be modified by a number of considerations. Some students may need a hands-on physical approach to get them started on the path toward that goal. Other students may find aspects of ikonic representation helpful in their thinking and may need pictures, diagrams, or models to facilitate learning. Ikonic representation would be an important mode of thinking for an architect or a mechanic.

Some students, especially older ones, are quite comfortable with instruction that is verbal or written. In considering how material should be presented to students, the teacher should take into account not only students' individual preferences for different sensory modes but also the nature of the task to be learned. Some material is abstract, some can readily be illustrated, and some can be acted out.

Locus of Control

It is assumed that individuals differ in their beliefs regarding their ability to control their lives (Lefcourt, 1976). Students who believe that events in their lives are the result of their own behavior, personality, and efforts are said to have an expectancy of *internal control.* Students who see events as being determined by forces outside themselves are said to have an expectancy of *external control.* Those outside forces may consist of other people or they may be more vague, such as luck, chance, or fate (Levenson, 1981).

There is some evidence to support the view that children with an internal locus of control perform better in school than ones with an external locus. In a 1966 study conducted by James Coleman and his colleagues, students were asked if they agreed or disagreed with three statements: "Good luck is more important than hard work for success"; "Every time I try to get ahead, something or somebody stops me"; "People like me don't have much of a chance to be successful in life." People who agreed with the statements were regarded as having a sense of external locus of control; people who disagreed with the statements were regarded as having a sense of internal control. Children of minority groups (blacks, Puerto Ricans, Mexican-Americans) who exhibited a sense of internal control over the environment had considerably higher achievement than those who did not (Coleman et al., 1966). However, teachers must recognize that students in particular environments may be right in believing that, to a great extent, power over the environment lies outside themselves and is in the hands of other people. While this may be true, students can at least be taught which aspects of the environment they can control and which aspects they cannot.

Learned Helplessness

The idea of learned helplessness came from animal studies. In a typical study, two groups of animals were used. One group was constrained in a harness while being given electric shocks. The other group was similarly constrained but was not given any shocks. On a later task, it was possible for the two groups to avoid a shock by jumping over a low barrier. The group that had been constrained but not shocked in the first experiment quickly learned how to escape, while the other group that had been constrained and shocked tended to endure the pain without trying to escape. In the latter case it was concluded that the earlier experiencing of shock treatment and not being able to move had left them in a state of learned helplessness (Seligman, 1973).

Do human beings learn to be helpless just as the animals in these studies did? The answer would appear to be yes. In several studies, it has been found that individuals exposed to inescapable punishment had greater difficulty in learning subsequent tasks than individuals who had not been subjected to such punishment.

Feelings of learned helplessness have been found to be related to individuals' beliefs about their ability to control their lives (locus of control). Those who believe in an internal locus of control (ability and effort) are less likely to succumb to learned helplessness than are those who believe in an external locus (lack of ability, luck). However, individuals with an internal locus who are subjected to many situations in which they cannot control things will also develop the behavior associated with learned helplessness (Pittman & Pittman, 1979).

These findings have implications for learning in the classroom. If students have experienced a lot of failure and have learned to feel "helpless" in facing new tasks, they may not learn what the teacher had hoped they would learn. In this situation, the teacher can help a student by ensuring that learning tasks provide many successes and few failures. This involves a careful grading of the tasks that the student has to perform (Dweck, 1975).

Self-Concept

Students in your class may differ markedly in their self-concepts. Low self-concepts are thought to have a negative impact on the student's achievement in school. Head Start and other programs for disadvantaged students were designed to improve students' self-concepts in the hope that their cognitive achievement would also improve (Shavelson, Hubner, & Stanton, 1976). Thus self-concept is seen not only as a valuable educational outcome in its own right but also as a valuable vehicle to improve academic outcomes.

What do we mean when we talk of a person's self-concept? In broad terms, it is a person's perception of him- or herself formed through experiences with the environment, interactions with others, and attributions of his or her own behavior. It is both descriptive and evaluative (Marsh, Smith, & Barnes, 1983).

Does this perception apply in all situations in which the student finds himself or herself, or can a student's self-concept vary in different situations and activities? In other words, is self-concept a unitary trait or a multifaceted one? The answer would seem to be the latter. Shavelson, Hubner, & Stanton (1976) have broken the general construct "self-concept" into the hierarchical structures shown in Figure 11.2. For each of the blocks shown in the figure, a person has a perception of him- or herself relative to the items listed in the blocks. Thus Jim may have a negative perception of himself regarding mathematics, how he fits in with his peers, and his physical ability and appearance. His perception of himself may be positive in relation to English, history, his parents (significant others), and his personality and temperament. Locus of control and learned helplessness can be considered part of the nonacademic, emotional self-concept block shown in Figure 11.2. As you can see in the figure, the organization of self-concept is not only multifaceted but also hierarchical; that is, perceptions move from inferences about self in subareas (for example, personal history, peers, physical appearance) to broader areas (for

FIGURE 11.2 One Possible Representation of the Hierarchic Organization of Self-Concept

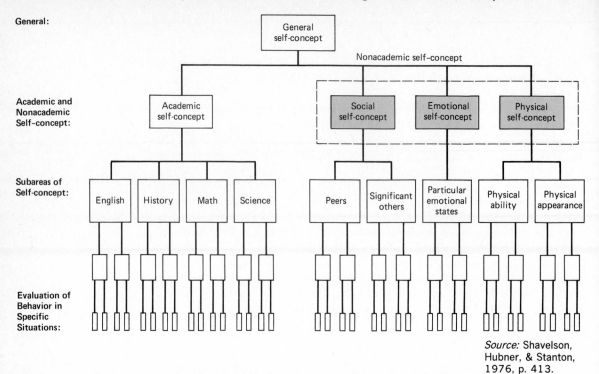

General:

Academic and
Nonacademic
Self-concept:

Subareas of
Self-concept:

Evaluation of
Behavior in
Specific
Situations:

Source: Shavelson,
Hubner, & Stanton,
1976, p. 413.

example, academic and nonacademic), and finally to overall self-concept. As the person becomes older, the self-concept becomes increasingly multifaceted (Marsh, Smith, & Barnes, 1983).

Because self-concept is multifaceted, you will need to be aware of possible differences on a number of different "self-concept" factors, both within an individual student as well as across students. While there are a number of questionnaires measuring self-concept that you might use to assess various aspects of it (Bloom, Madaus, & Hastings, 1981), ultimately you will need to rely on your own judgment as a teacher, based on daily observations about how a student sees him- or herself and how that might be affecting his or her performance in school. You will get a good idea of students' self-concepts as you talk to them and observe them, day in and day out, coping with academic tasks and social interactions in the class, schoolyard, and lunchroom. If you come to believe that a student has a negative self-concept in a particular area, you might try to provide him or her with situations that make success likely and then reward or praise the student when he or she does succeed. In other instances (for example, those relating to physical ability or appearance), you may talk with the student to help him or her become more comfortable about the characteristic in question. Self-concept can change rather quickly in the lower grades but is harder to alter as the student matures.

Creativity

When the word *creativity* is mentioned, different people are likely to think of different things. For some, creativity means originality of ideas and is exemplified in the work of a great philosopher, scientist, or inventor. Names such as Galileo, da Vinci, Newton, and Einstein come to mind in this context.

For others, an artist such as Picasso, or a person who uses language in an exceptional way, such as Shakespeare, is regarded as creative. Again, for others, a person is creative if he or she comes up with an unusual or unexpected solution to an everyday problem. Creativity in all these senses is obviously fairly rare.

The area of creativity received great attention from educators and psychologists in the 1950s and 1960s (Getzels & Jackson, 1962). At the time, many felt that American education had become too conventional and rigid, that this was having a stultifying effect on children, and that it was important to discover and encourage creative and innovative children. Psychologists set about developing techniques to measure creativity. A basic assumption in the development of such techniques was that creativity is not a rare and unusual ability to be found only in the work of recognized geniuses, but is spread through the whole population and is found in varying degrees in a great many people. While this might be so, researchers were far from agreement on what exactly constitutes creativity. Definitions emphasized any one of three aspects of creativity. Some were formulated in terms of a *product;* to be accepted as creative, the response or idea must be novel, unusual, and useful. Other definitions emphasized an underlying *process* in creativity; the process must be divergent, yet productive. A third type of definition was formulated in terms of a *subjective experience;* in these definitions, creativity is identified by such things as a flash or insight or a transcendent sensation, whether or not it results in anything tangible (Getzels, 1985).

Techniques that have been developed to measure creativity include interest and personality inventories, judgments of creative products, and, most frequently, tasks involving "divergent thinking" (Guilford, 1956; Torrance, 1974). Divergent-thinking tasks were developed on the assumption that such thinking is central to creative problem solving. In a typical task, people are encouraged to give a variety of answers to a common problem such as "List all the uses that you can for a brick." There is no one correct answer to that request. This differs from the approach in most tests of ability and achievement, which normally require "convergent" thinking; that is, the student's answer must "converge" to a single correct solution. For example, there is only one correct answer to the question: $3 + 5 = ?$ By contrast, in typical divergent-thinking tasks, a student is asked to write down as many uses as possible for an empty can, or to list unusual uses for a toy other than as a plaything, or to make objects or a design from 30 circles. Responses may be scored for quantity or fluency, flexibility, originality, and quality, as judged by the usefulness of the ideas.

Measures of creativity on paper-and-pencil tests of divergent thinking have not been consistently found to be related to measures of real-life creativity (Mansfield & Busse, 1981). Real-life creativity, it seems, is dependent on a variety of characteristics. For example, to be creative in the field of science, one needs to be autonomous and flexible, to be committed to one's work, and to have a need for professional recognition (Mansfield & Busse, 1981). Perhaps the characteristics vary for different areas of real-life creativity, such as technical creativity (for example, skill in making a violin), inventive creativity (for example, the invention of the telephone), or innovative creativity (for example, the formulation of alternatives to established ways of thinking about the world, as exemplified in the work of Galileo and Einstein) (Taylor, 1975).

Interest in the idea of creativity gave rise to attempts to develop programs that would increase creativity in students. Some of these are short-term approaches administered in one or two class periods; others are longer-term, extending over many lessons (Covington, Crutchfield, Davies, & Olton, 1974; Myers & Torrance, 1966). On a broader level, researchers have suggested a number of strategies that help develop creative problem-solving abilities in students:

1. Remove internal blocks to creativity by helping students feel secure in their relationships with others without worrying about the acceptability of their ideas or that their ideas will be ridiculed.
2. Create an awareness of the role of the subconscious by helping students appreciate that the subconscious keeps working on problems when they are no longer the focus of conscious attention.
3. Spend time considering a range of ideas that will provide a basis for alternative solutions to problems.
4. Accept that fantasy and flights of the imagination have an important role in development.
5. After fantasy and other forms of thinking, ideas should be reviewed critically.
6. Knowledge and information form the basis of new ideas.
7. Help children and parents understand the importance of creative thinking and the exercises that facilitate it (Parnes, Noller, & Biondi, 1977).

Coping with Individual Differences

How is the teacher to deal with the wide range of individual differences on many dimensions that are to be found in any classroom? Teachers and schools have always been faced with the problem that students cannot be categorized neatly into groups. Attempts to deal with this problem have varied over time, from allowing students who could not adapt to the system to fail and drop out to attempts to adapt the system and instructional methods to the needs of every student (Cronbach, 1967; Gagné & Dick, 1983; Glaser, 1977; Walberg, 1975). We will consider two approaches. In the first, students are grouped on the basis of some characteristic they share. In the second, an attempt is made to match instructional treatment to the characteristics of each individual student.

Selection and Grouping

At one time, there was a common curriculum in which educational goals and instructional models were the same for all students. In this system, it was up to the individual student to adapt to the instructional approach and to achieve the educational goals. Students who had difficulty in doing this dropped out early. This is really a process of *selection* and was common up to the beginning of this century, when few students (those who were "fit" for education and could adapt to the system) stayed beyond elementary schooling.

Another form of selection is to group students of similar characteristics together, either in a class of their own or within a class according to ability or achievement. This implies that different educational goals and curricula are being set for different *groups* of students. Students with a high level of ability and/or achievement are placed in one group, those with lower levels placed in other groups. This practice is often called homogenous grouping; at the high school level it is called tracking. Tracking is usually based on expectations about students' future careers. Those who are likely to go to college are assigned to an academic track, others to a vocational track.

The acceleration or rapid promotion through grades or the repetition of a grade are other popular approaches to dealing with individual differences. Yet another way of handling such differences is to allow "branching" for remedial work for some students. In this system, a remedial teacher takes students for part of the day or part of the school year on the assumption that with the extra help given in the remedial class, the student will be able to catch up with other students and return full-time to the regular class.

While grouping, acceleration, and enrichment have been features of American education for over a hundred years and thus probably have some merit, none of the approaches comes to terms with individualizing instruction for each student. Usually, these practices result in different curricula for different groups of students, but not in different instructional approaches. However, if we accept that every individual is unique, ideally we would require a separate program of instruction for every student. This would allow students

Teachers often group students who share similar characteristics within their classrooms for instructional purposes.

to work individually (at least some of the time), use the methods and materials most appropriate to their needs, and complete assignments at their own pace.

Individualized Programs

Individualized instruction is difficult to manage. It increases the complexity of events with which teachers have to deal—the multi-dimensionality, simultaneity, and immediacy of things happening in the classroom (Doyle & Carter, 1987). However, there have been several attempts to build programs that would allow students to work individually with appropriate materials at their own pace. Most such programs have involved allowing for individual differences in the time taken to learn tasks rather than in the way material has been presented. Early examples of this approach were the Winnetka Plan, the Dalton Laboratory Plan, and the Morrison Plan (Whipple, 1925). These approaches divided schoolwork into units, provided appropriate materials for each unit, allowed students as much time as they required to complete a unit of work, and made use of diagnostic and achievement tests. The teacher provided help and guidance to students.

Obviously, the sheer task of preparing adequate materials for students was a major problem for teachers in these systems. That problem seemed to be partly resolved in the 1950s with the introduction of programmed instruction (Skinner, 1954). In a typical programmed-learning sequence, as designed by B. F. Skinner, a student is presented with one item at a time. The student reads a statement that has one or more words missing and completes it by adding or selecting a word. The correct answer is then revealed. If the student is correct, he or she moves on to the next item. If incorrect, he or she is directed to other material. The approach was seen to have a number of advantages. First, each student is continuously active; second, the student proceeds at his or her own pace; third, the student receives a lot of immediate and positive reinforcement for correct responses; and fourth, the teacher has complete information on each student's progress. The potential of programmed instruction was never realized, however, and soon died out. This was due in part to the inadequate technology of the time. Today, with the availability of the microcomputer, interest in programmed instruction has returned.

Although contemporary programs of individual instruction do not follow Skinner's principles in detail, many of them are influenced by those principles. Examples of such programs are the Individually Prescribed Instruction (IPI) materials, the Program for Learning in Accordance with Needs (PLAN), and Individually Guided Education (IGE). These programs begin with testing to identify the student's achievements and needs. On the basis of this, appropriate instructional objectives are identified and learning materials are assigned to the student for individual work. On completion of a unit of instruction, a student is again tested to see whether he or she has mastered the material. Students who have achieved mastery move on to the next level; those who do not have to practice on alternative materials. The implementation of these approaches may require considerable alteration in the organization of the class and the school as well as the employment of additional personnel (for

FIGURE 11.3 Bloom's Mastery Learning Model
275

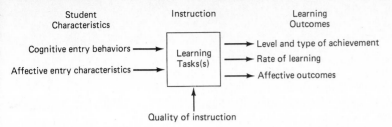

Source: Bloom,
1976, p. 18.

example, teacher aides) and the acquisition of equipment (for example, computers).

An approach that is more readily implemented in the normal school is Benjamin Bloom's approach to mastery learning (see Figure 11.3) (Block & Burns, 1976; Bloom, 1976). This approach is very flexible, can be used individually or with groups, and does not require any particular materials or resources. It is really a general approach to teaching, of which there are many versions.

Bloom's mastery learning model was developed to counter the traditional belief of teachers that about a third of their students will adequately learn what they have to teach, a further third will fail to or just "get by," and the final third will learn a good deal of what they have to, but not enough to be regarded as "good students." This set of expectations is transmitted to students through the schools' grading procedures and through methods and materials of instruction. The system creates "a self-fulfilling prophecy" so that the final sorting of students through the grading process becomes approximately equivalent to the original expectations (Bloom, Madaus, & Hastings, 1981).

Bloom (1976) has illustrated the consequences when students proceed through courses without having adequately mastered the basic skills and knowledge required for the course. Suppose that a learning unit has three learning tasks (see Figure 11.4). If task 1 is taught without paying much attention to students' levels of achievement before the task is taught, at the end of the period of instruction you are likely to find that the distribution of postassessment test scores follows the curve shown opposite task 1 in Figure

FIGURE 11.4 Theoretical Achievement Distributions Where Inadequate Learning Is Not Corrected at the End of Each Learning Task

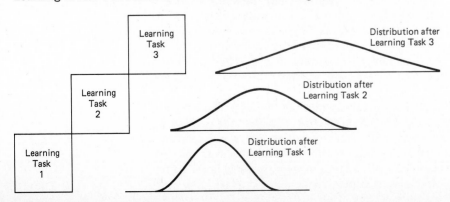

Source: Bloom,
1976, p. 35.

11.4. This distribution, you will note, is very similar to the "normal" distribution (shown in Figure 11.1). If teachers do not attend to learning problems at this stage and all students proceed to task 2, the distribution of scores widens when students are tested at the end of task 2. Student difficulties become even more obvious on later learning tasks, as is illustrated by the distribution of students' test scores on task 3. The effect of all this is that the distribution of achievement on a sequence of learning tasks becomes more and more varied when inadequate learning by some students is not corrected before all go on to more difficult tasks. A major purpose of instruction should be to reduce rather than increase differences between students in achievement. This can be accomplished only by ensuring that every student "masters" each section of a course before going on to the next.

Bloom (1981) argues that this traditional set of expectations held by teachers is simply incorrect. He believes that *most students* (as high as 90 percent) *can master what the schools have to teach.* Under this assumption, the principal task of instruction is to find the means to enable students to master the subject under consideration.

In mastery learning, an aptitude to learn is defined in terms of the amount of time required by the learner to attain mastery of a learning task rather than in terms of some innate ability to learn. The faster the student can learn something, the higher is his or her aptitude. Implicit in this formulation of aptitude is the notion that given *enough time* and *proper instruction,* all students can attain mastery of the learning task (Bloom, Madaus, & Hastings, 1981). Thus, the amount of time and quality of instruction are key ingredients in a mastery learning model.

CONCLUSION

In this chapter, we considered some of the various student characteristics that are relevant to education. Teachers who believe that these characteristics are ingrained try to adapt instructional procedures to them rather than try to change them. However, research is providing new insight into some student characteristics and how they relate to learning that may change this. One important development in this area, which we touched on in our discussion of intelligence, involves a shift from the study of intelligence as a static characteristic to a study of the processes that students engage in when being "intelligent" (Pintrich, Cross, Kozma, & McKeachie, 1986). Greater understanding of such processes may lead not only to the design of more appropriate teaching and learning strategies but also to the development of procedures that will improve students' information-processing capabilities.

You may find it helpful to bear in mind a number of points when dealing with individual differences among students on the characteristics considered in this chapter, as well as any other characteristics that affect learning. Unfortunately, there are no simple rules of thumb for dealing with individual differences in the classroom. There are, however, some general guidelines which may help you (Good & Stipek, 1983):

1. Bear in mind that student characteristics vary among students. Thus, one student may have greater overall ability and field-dependence, and another may also be very field-dependent but lack general ability.

2. As a consequence of our first statement, it is probably better not to focus on comparisons between different students, but to attend to how each student's traits interact with each other. This involves looking at each students' unique profile of characteristics. Rather than looking at how an individual stands relative to his or her peers on a particular characteristic (for example, ability or cognitive style), you should consider how these characteristics come together and interact *within* the individual to form a unique constellation (Bem & Funder, 1978).

3. An implication of individual differences is that some learning situations suit some students, while other situations are more suitable for other students. For example, some students may do well in a formal situation in which rules are clear and teachers are aloof, and others may prefer a more informal situation in which teachers and students work closely together. This implies that a student may do better in one type of school or classroom than in another. In practice, however, such a choice is not usually available. The school or classroom has to accommodate all types of teachers and students. As a result, we have to think not in terms of how successful students will be in predetermined situations but how situations and institutions can be adapted to meet individual needs.

4. Although we spoke of characteristics as if they were traits that manifested themselves the same way in all situations, the fact is that people do not always react to situations as we might expect them to. If we are to understand an individual's reactions, we have to take into account not only the characteristics of the individual but also characteristics of the situation to which the individual is responding (Bem & Allen, 1974). Thus, for example, a student may be interested, motivated, or anxious in one situation but not in another, depending on the nature of a learning task.

5. In every classroom, there is a unique combination of student characteristics. Thus, strategies that are successful with one class may not be successful with another.

6. You should begin the year with a program with which you feel comfortable. As the year goes on and you become familiar with your students' individual differences, you can make changes in the classroom to address these differences.

7. It is easier to adjust to such differences if your approach is varied and flexible. That is, it should involve some "lecturing," some discussion, some group work, and some individual work.

8. You should also allow students some flexibility and choice in activities. This provides an opportunity for the teacher to observe students' preferences over a range of activities.

9. Finally, you will find tests that measure achievement in specific areas more useful than those that measure general ability or achievement (such as reading or mathematics) in planning instructional programs for individual students.

QUESTIONS AND ACTIVITIES

1. Spend a day in a special needs classroom and a regular classroom. Which focuses more on the individual needs of students? What did you learn about individualizing for instruction from both of them?
2. Reflect on the courses you have taken during your college career. How many were designed to meet your individual needs? What could your professors have done to make them more individualized?
3. How would you define intelligence?
4. Should schools use intelligence tests to group students for instruction?
5. Which of the four cognitive styles discussed best describes yours? How do you think your style might influence your teaching?
6. What adjustments must a classroom teacher make in his or her classroom to account for the individual differences described in this chapter?
7. What characteristics described in this chapter should teachers accept in a student? Which should they try to change?
8. What activities or programs might teachers incorporate into their classrooms that will improve students' self-concepts?

PART FIVE

Teaching and Instruction

You are embarking on a program of preparation to teach. In the following five chapters, we will try to help you anticipate what you can expect your work as a teacher to involve. We explore various aspects of the context in which teaching takes place and of the actual process of teaching. Our exploration will be governed by a number of key considerations. First, there are important moral dimensions to the work of the teacher. Second, teaching is influenced by events beyond the walls of the classroom, in particular by the expectations that people have for what schools should try to accomplish. Third, teaching is an extremely complex activity and involves much more than merely the delivery of instruction. Fourth, the social aspects of classrooms have important implications for teaching. Fifth, a teacher's work begins before he or she enters the classroom and does not end when he or she leaves it; preparation for class and a review of students' work (evaluation) form an important part of the teacher's work. Finally, in the classroom and in the school generally, there are certain principles and guidelines that, if followed, should make instruction more effective.

There are two types of knowledge that we will explore in the following chapters, and they are the same two types you will need to draw on when teaching (Jackson, 1986). First, there is the knowledge that relies on common sense. The absence of such knowledge would be a real handicap in teaching (as it would in any other profession). There is a second kind of knowledge based on research that can help the teacher. Up to the early 1970s, there was relatively little such knowledge available to guide teachers in their day-to-day work in the classroom. That situation is changing. For example, in this section you will see how the many years of research on the relationship between teacher behavior and student achievement are beginning to pay off and how findings related to the effectiveness of a variety of classroom and teaching practices are being put into practice (Richardson-Koehler, 1987; Wittrock, 1986).

While we might distinguish between common-sense and research-based knowledge, in practice the distinction will usually not be clear to you when you are making decisions as a teacher. The two types of knowledge will be fused in your mind, each influencing the other. When you find yourself in the complex setting of the classroom, a place "filled with language and motion and people" (Doyle & Carter, 1987, p. 189), you will have to combine information from a variety of sources in making your decisions. Given the complexity and uncertainty of the environment in which you operate, your decisions will be "reasonable" rather than "rational" (Berliner, 1983; Borko & Niles, 1987).

CHAPTER 12

The Moral and Social Contexts of Teaching

This chapter deals with moral and social dimensions of teaching and the educational goals of society and teachers.

- Teaching is a moral undertaking. There are moral and ethical relationships between teachers and students and in grading and punishing students. Teachers need to be explicitly aware of the moral dimensions of teaching.
- There are certain basic rules of conduct and social norms that all teachers are expected to instill in their pupils. These rules constitute the school's hidden curriculum. Without these rules teaching would be chaotic.
- There are societal and parental expectations that teachers will cover the prescribed curriculum and give students the necessary skills to function in society.
- Teachers report that their most important goal is student involvement.
- There are always positive and negative unintended outcomes associated with teaching. You need to be particularly aware of possible negative unintended outcomes.
- Teaching is a complex art; it involves more than instruction and is ultimately a creative performance.
- The classroom is a busy, complex social system, characterized by the immediacy and unpredictability of events.
- Each class is unique, and teachers build up a store of hidden knowledge about each class and the individuals in it. This hidden knowledge helps the teacher deal with classroom complexity.

In this chapter, we begin our exploration of teaching by considering its moral aspects. In doing this, we will first encounter important issues concerning responsibility, authority, discipline and, in particular, the relationship of power and trust between teacher and students. Next we will examine the goals that society and the school expect teachers to achieve and the goals that teachers themselves report as most important to them. Of course, the best laid plans of mice and men oft go astray, and this is true for teaching. Therefore, we will also consider unintended or unanticipated outcomes of teaching that are a direct or indirect result of what or how you teach. Finally, we will consider the social context in which most teaching takes place—the busy, crowded, unpredictable classroom.

The Moral Dimension of Teaching

Whatever else teaching is, it is a moral undertaking. Your actions and your overall goals in teaching clearly fall in the moral domain. Further, the ways in which you go about working toward those goals are subject to moral evaluation. Teaching is a moral undertaking precisely because teachers are trying to change their pupils for the better—to equip them with knowledge and skills, to shape their development so that ultimately they will become better adults and better citizens.

Almost 2,000 years ago, the Roman rhetorician Quintilian wrote about teachers. His words are ones that anyone preparing to teach should savor and reflect upon (see Box 12.1). They outline not only the characteristics that you as a teacher should have, the tactics you may employ in teaching, and your relationship with students, but also, and most important, they describe your role as a model of imitation for your charges. While Quintilian's observations are ancient, they are applicable today and speak to the universality of the moral aspects of the teaching art and act. Down through the centuries, those characteristics have been, are now, and always will be true of teachers. Interviews with teachers about the satisfactions they receive from teaching reveal that this moral dimension is inherent in what they are trying to accomplish.

The quotation below illustrates the desire teachers have to help each pupil become a better overall person, a better-functioning adult. The last sentence goes even further; the teacher assumes partial responsibility not only for any success his or her pupils eventually have but also implicitly for any future failing of character.

Teachers on the Moral Dimension of Teaching

I think when you're helping young people, and—I don't know, it's rather hard to answer—you're teaching them something new all the time, you're helping them to develop. . . . I like to think that whatever these kids become, I have put my licks in somewhere along the line (Jackson, 1968, pp. 134, 141).

BOX 12.1 Quintilian's View of Teaching

Let him [the teacher] therefore adopt a parental attitude to his pupils, and regard himself as the representative of those who have committed their children to his charge. Let him be free from vice himself and refuse to tolerate it in others. Let him be strict but not austere, genial but not too familiar: for austerity will make him unpopular, while familiarity breeds contempt. Let his discourse continually turn on what is good and honorable; the more he admonishes, the less he will have to punish. He must control his temper without, however, shutting his eyes to faults requiring correction: his instruction must be free from affectation, his industry great, his demands on his class continuous, but not extravagant. He must be ready to answer questions and to put them unasked to those who sit silent. In praising the recitations of his pupils he must be neither grudging nor over-generous: the former quality will give them a distaste for work, while the latter will produce a complacent self-satisfaction. In correcting faults he must avoid sarcasm and above all abuse: for teachers whose rebukes seem to imply positive dislike discourage industry. He should declaim daily himself, and, what is more, without stint, that his class may take his utterances home with them. For however many models for imitation he may give them from the authors they are reading, it will still be found that fuller nourishment is provided by the living voice, as we call it, more especially when it proceeds from the teacher himself, who if his pupils are rightly instructed, should be the object of their affection and respect. And it is scarcely possible to say how much more readily we imitate those whom we like.

Source: Cited in C. M. Fuess & E. S. Basford (Eds.), *Unseen harvests: A treasury of teaching* (1947).

The Ethical and Moral Relationship Between Teacher and Pupil

Teaching is a moral enterprise in another sense as well. There is an ethical or moral relationship that exists between teacher and pupil. As a teacher you will stand in a position of power relative to your pupils. You will have the power to compel students to do certain things and to forbid them to do other things; the power to reward and punish, ridicule or praise, recognize or ignore; the power to make the student feel secure or insecure, to experience success or failure. You must always remember that the pupil is relatively defenseless in this moral relationship: "The teacher, clearly through no fault of her own, is the agent of vulnerability, and she transmits the sense of vulnerability to the child through two weapons thrust into her hands, sometimes against her will—discipline and the power to fail the child" (Henry, 1971, p. 11).

The way a teacher exercises this power is subject to moral or ethical scrutiny (Hawkins, 1973). As a teacher you are morally constrained not to abuse your power; you are under a moral obligation to be just, reasonable, and honorable in your dealings with each and every one of your pupils. Pupils recognize and appreciate these qualities in their teachers. They do not respect the teacher who gives high grades easily, who lets pupils off easily, who changes punishments, or who grades at the pupils' suggestion (Waller, 1967). "Tough, but fair" is a complimentary way children describe some teachers.

The Moral Dimension of Grading and Punishment

The moral relationship between you and your pupils has particular implications when you assign grades or punish offenses. Schoolwork of generally similar quality should receive similar grades. Marking work that is equal with different grades or giving unequal work the same grade represents unfair grading. Marks for effort are one device a teacher has to reward pupils "whose achievements do not quite measure up to standard but who have improved or worked hard, or worked up to their 'academic' potential. On the other hand, low marks for effort can be used to admonish a pupil whose work is more or less satisfactory but could be considerably better" (Dreeben, 1968, p. 234).

As another example of how this moral obligation of fairness impinges on the teacher, consider the case of pupils complaining that a test was unfair, that it contained questions not covered in class, trick questions, or ambiguous questions. Here, generally speaking, they are not focusing primarily on technical shortcomings of the questions but are implicitly accusing the teacher of accidentally or deliberately misusing his or her evaluative power.

Likewise, in punishing offenses a similar moral principle holds: The punishment should fit the crime, and similar forms of misbehavior should be treated alike. This moral necessity to act fairly in making formal evaluations or in administering punishment is one of the reasons teachers often tend to keep a distance between themselves and their pupils. Anytime one must act in the role of judge in relation to another, a certain amount of social distance is necessary for objectivity.

Norms of Universality and Specificity

Fairness in grading and in administering punishment helps students to internalize the important norms of *universalism* and *specificity* (Dreeben, 1967, 1968). That is, individuals should be treated similarly because they are members of a common group, for example, "third graders in Mrs. Smith's room" *(universality)*, rather than as special cases, "Mrs. Smith's boy Joe" *(specificity)*. However, certain pupils often are treated differently from others precisely because they are "Mrs. Smith's boy." In small towns, for example, teachers may give the sons or daughters of prominent citizens a certain edge (Waller, 1967). Likewise, the child of complaining parents might be treated differently from the child whose parents are silent ("the squeaky wheel gets the grease"). If and when this happens, the teacher walks a very thin line indeed; if he or she is perceived as playing favorites, his or her reputation can be seriously compromised in the eyes of the entire class.

Teachers' evaluations of students are in turn evaluated both by individuals and the class as a whole in terms of the moral concepts of fairness and reasonableness. Teachers evaluate students so often and so spontaneously that they do not always have time to reflect on their fairness or justice. Similarly, pupils do not explicitly and coldly judge each of a teacher's evaluations but, over the course of weeks and months, a shared belief emerges about the overall fairness of a teacher's actions. Pupils recognize when a teacher "picks on" an individual or when he or she unfairly favors a "pet."

Of course, most teachers don't deliberately violate the moral relationship they have with their pupils. However, teachers can unwittingly misuse their power as they react to ordinary incidents that are bound to occur in the classroom. Like any human being, a teacher can unconsciously favor or dislike a given individual because of personal appearance, speech, behavior, or manners. That some pupils are simply more or less likeable than others is an inescapable fact. When you begin teaching, you will need to constantly remind yourself of this reality and adjust your actions and reactions accordingly so that you are seen to be, *and in fact are,* fair-minded toward all pupils.

Treating Students Fairly

The most wholesome teachers, however, find it difficult to avoid picking favorites on the basis of personal attractiveness. In every class certain faces stand out; a class itself appears as a constellation of a few outstanding faces against a background of mediocrity, and it is to be expected that this selection of faces which are highlights should be made in part on an esthetic basis. The selectivity, however, is not wholly in terms of abstract beauty, for it is also based upon intelligence and responsiveness, and it is possible for any alert and reasonably intelligent student to conduct himself with reference to the teacher in such a manner as to make his face one of the accustomed resting places for the teacher's gaze. The teacher looks at him rather than the others because he registers as significant personality, which the others fail to do (Waller, 1967, p. 147).

Expectations for Teachers

Societal Expectations for Teachers

Society expects certain things of its schools. Briefly, it expects schools—through the teachers—to socialize pupils and help instill in them the dominant values of the society.

Sometimes the values of a society are directly integrated into the school curriculum. More often, however, values are transmitted indirectly and are implied by teachers. Most teachers have internalized the dominant values of their society and reflect them, or in some cases contradict them, in their behavior. When the latter happens, teachers can quickly find themselves in conflict with the community.

Society also expects the schools to equip pupils with those basic language and math skills it feels are necessary for success in the adult world. The importance that the public places on basic language and math skills explains why there is a periodic furor in the media over reports that reading levels have slipped or that standards have fallen, and it explains the present emphasis in our schools on basics and competency testing. Society expects the verbal-conceptual aspect of schooling to be the teacher's central concern.

Institutional Expectations for Teachers

The school as an institution not only reflects large societal expectations but also directly imposes its expectations on teachers and determines what they should try to accomplish in the classroom. The school focuses on two main outcomes, one moral, the other cognitive.

THE MORAL DIMENSION OF INSTITUTIONAL EXPECTATIONS There are certain basic behaviors that all teachers are expected to try to instill in their pupils. The rules of conduct and social norms that teachers are obliged to make students conform to, and as far as possible internalize and accept, constitute the *hidden curriculum* of the school. This hidden curriculum is the embodiment of the moral values that schools want teachers to instill. A great deal of teacher effort, particularly in the early years, is directed toward the transmission of these values (Dreeben, 1967, 1968). Of course, the exact content of the "hidden curriculum" will differ. For example, some schools will be very strict and regimented, others more relaxed and permissive.

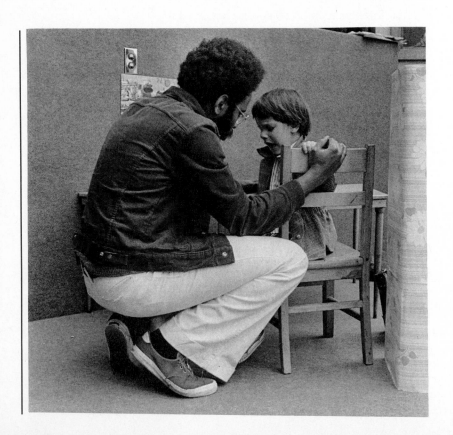

Teachers are expected to help students develop proper social and ethical behaviors as well as to assist them in cognitive development.

As a teacher, you can actually plan how you will handle aspects of the hidden curriculum. Some rules can be explicitly communicated (for example, no running on the stairs); in these cases, you have leeway to plan what you will say to the class and how to enforce the rule and to decide on the sanctions to be meted out for violations. You may have time to reflect on how to handle a troublesome student. You may even be able to drill pupils in how to behave in certain circumstances (for example, during fire drills, when lining up for recess). However, much of the hidden curriculum is transmitted spontaneously and implicitly in the interactive teaching situation. Your reaction to concrete situations; your gestures and expressions; the tone of voice you use in evaluating students; your use of praise or ridicule in different situations; your choice of who gets to collect the erasers, lead the line, or empty the basket; who you send to the office—all these reactions, together with interactions with students, subtly but inexorably convey impressions to pupils about "the rules of the game." These more indirect cues tell a student what is important and what is not; what is tolerated and what is taboo; how far one can push without going too far; how liked or disliked one is in the teacher's eyes. These are the values that are primarily "caught" rather than taught and consequently tend to be unplanned rather than planned.

The Need for Rules, Regulations and Rituals There are, of course, good reasons why schools insist on certain rules, regulations, and rituals. Classrooms are crowded, active places. Anywhere from 15 to 30 youngsters (sometimes more), bursting with energy and enthusiasm, are placed in close physical proximity to one another for anywhere from four to six hours a day. In the very early grades this is the first group experience for many children, and behavior and expectations acceptable at home are often no longer appropriate (Dreeben, 1967). Faced with this conglomerate of active children or adolescents, you are expected to cover a range of content and skill areas during the course of the day. Because of these academic pressures, concepts of time, decorum, and routine are essential if a semblance of order is to be maintained.

Reasons for Rules

Every teacher knows that in school, certainly up to the freshman year in college, there is a strain towards disorder, not toward homeostasis (equilibrium), in classrooms. When one studies the actual situation, whether in the family or in a classroom, one perceives that the concept of homeostatis is not applicable to social situations and that we must take Cannon literally when he observes that what has to be explained about the body is its stability in the presence of enormous strains towards instability (Henry, 1971, pp. 39–40).

Good teachers start off a new year, usually on the very first day, by establishing academic expectations and the rules and routines under which their classes will operate. Some expectations and rules are directly stated (if you are absent, bring a note the next day; your books must be covered by

Wednesday; bring a ballpoint pen and notebooks by Tuesday; *you* are to do your own homework—no copying; if you are late for school, go see the principal). Many rules are indirectly but nonetheless clearly communicated when the teacher responds to a pupil's behavior (there will be no gum chewing in this room, Mary; sit up straight, Martha; put that comb away, Eileen; George, please raise your hand before you speak; turn around and be quiet, Sarah; stop that daydreaming, Joseph, *wake up*).

Imposing Rules and Regulations Sometimes there is no need to verbalize a rule for students to infer that something is taboo. A teacher's growing impatience, tone of voice, facial expression, or gesture may get the message across more clearly than any direct command (First & Mezzell, 1980). These cues may be used very early in the year and are often followed by some direct sanction when they are ignored until pupils learn their meaning and consequences. The chief benefit of punishing a particular pupil is that the punishment serves to define the situation clearly, not only for the offender but also for the rest of the class. The teacher asserts his or her dominance, and the class can see that the offending behavior has gone too far (Waller, 1967). Box 12.2 lists 14 tactics that teachers regularly use to either establish or impose their rules and regulations—their authority over the pupils—to meet institutional expectations for order in the classroom (Henry, 1971).

Different teachers, of course, will employ different techniques of exercising authority. Some will be relaxed, others strict; some gentle, some quite harsh; some primarily verbal, some nonverbal. Likewise, teachers will pick and choose from these techniques when dealing with different pupils in different circumstances. Your effectiveness will depend to a large degree on knowing how your pupils react to different methods of control. For example, the tactic of ridicule can be devastating to one child and beneficial to another. However, the use of ridicule puts you on a very slippery slope and in general is to be avoided. Keep in mind the moral dimension of teaching when you assert your authority or apply a particular tactic.

Rules of conduct are very important in the daily functioning of the classroom. Generally, it is permissible to make mistakes in academic matters, but a pupil will not lightly transgress the rules that govern classroom behavior. In fact, research has shown that children are scolded or punished for violation of rules much more frequently than they are for academic mistakes (Jackson, 1968). Thus, the moral components of classroom behavior are a central focus in a teacher's informal interactive evaluation of pupils.

Teachers differ not only in their techniques of control, but also in their reasons for exerting control, as well as in their ability to control students (Cohen, 1972; First & Mezzell, 1980). Unfortunately for some teachers (for example, for ones working in schools in disadvantaged urban areas), control is a more important goal than substantive learning—"it's such a tough class that all I do is keep the lid on." This attitude runs counter to a primary characteristic of successful urban schools—an expectation that all pupils will learn.

Some teachers, even in the most privileged schools, are not able to establish rules and routines, and students quickly pass this information on. In

BOX 12.2 Tactics Teachers Use to Establish Rules and Impose Regulations

1. *Appealing to sense of propriety:* "It is not polite to shout your answer."
2. *Direct reprimand:* "You should not have behaved like that, Michael."
3. *Impersonal reprimand:* "Some of you are holding us up."
4. *Ridicule:* "You are acting like a baby, Stephen."
5. *Exhortation:* "How can I teach you if you keep making so much noise, Pat?"
6. *Command:* "Sit down and be quiet!"
7. *Instilling guilt:* "Nice people don't use that kind of language, Carol."
8. *Cessation of activity:* "Since you cannot listen, class, turn to page 28 and do the first 20 examples."
9. *Group sanction:* "If the guilty party does not own up, I will keep the whole class after school."
10. *Threat:* "I will send you to the office if you throw another paper airplane in this class."
11. *Putting the child on his or her honor:* "When I step outside the room, you are on your honor to act as you do when I am here."
12. *Promise of reward:* "Now, if you all quiet down and listen, I will read you a story later on."
13. *Awakening fear:* "You remember what happened the last time I sent a note home to your parents."
14. *Exclusion:* "Go stand in the hall."

Source: Adapted from Henry, 1971.

the case of new teachers, students will recognize and play on this weakness. In such teachers' classrooms noise and confusion are high and chaos and bedlam lurk just below the surface. For other teachers, order can be deceptively "educational" in character when they impose a lot of written work or busy work to maintain classroom control. Of course, most teachers strike the right balance between control and the cognitive goal of teaching the prescribed skills and content.

The Effects of Establishing and Maintaining Rules Classroom rules and regulations are meant to do more than merely ensure that instruction and study are not interrupted. In the early grades, rules and routines are used to initiate students into the mores and social rules of the school system. Teachers in later grades are expected to maintain and enforce these rules and, in turn, they expect that similar standards of conduct have been established and habituated in the lower grades. Thus, primary teachers are constrained by colleagues' expectations that they will devote considerable time to the process of socializing children in the rules of the school.

THE COGNITIVE DIMENSION OF INSTITUTIONAL EXPECTATIONS School authorities, as well as parents, expect that a teacher will cover the formal prescribed curricula for a given grade. It is taken for granted that when you teach, you work to develop certain skills in your pupils and that you "cover" the expected content areas. After all, this is what you are being paid for, or so the sentiment runs. Although, as we have seen, teaching involves much more than content coverage and general instruction, society in general (and parents in particular) also expects that teachers in the early grades attempt to convey basic skills, and teachers at higher grade levels are expected to cover certain content areas to prepare adolescents for further education or future vocations.

Colleagues exert indirect pressure on their peers to cover the syllabus

Teachers are expected to cover the formal prescribed curriculum for the grade level they are teaching.

or course of study. Much of what you will eventually do as a teacher will be behind the closed door of your classroom and will be hidden from your colleagues. This is particularly true in schools where there is no team teaching or integration of curricular areas (Bernstein, 1971). Other than from gossip in the teachers' room, or if your room is particularly noisy and disturbs your neighbor, much of what you will do during the year will be unknown to your colleagues. However, you will soon realize that your class will pass on, more or less intact, to a new teacher who expects that the majority of your class will have more or less mastered a set of mutually recognized skills and have been exposed to a mutually recognized body of content.

Not all your pupils will be "up to standard" at the end of the year. Some, because of lack of "ability," a "poor" home background, emotional problems, or learning disabilities, will not measure up. All teachers have their share of "problem" pupils. Nonetheless, your colleagues do expect that, on average, your pupils will have been properly prepared when they receive them the following September. Most teachers spend a good part of the first few weeks of the school year testing their pupils to determine their levels of knowledge and skill. Teachers also spend time in the first few weeks having pupils practice last year's skills to remove the accumulated "rust" of summer before moving on, and they expect to find some evidence of work accomplished when the rust is removed.

Thus, an elementary school teacher is not "free" to decide to neglect curricular areas that colleagues assume will be taught; his or her professional reputation will quickly become tarnished. If, on top of this, the teacher's class is unruly, any vestige of professional reputation will vanish.

Teacher Goals

We have considered the goals that society and the school have for teachers, but what do teachers themselves view as their goals when teaching? When we compare teachers' goals and those of the general public, we find that they are not always in agreement (see Table 12.1). While there is fairly high agreement between the two groups in objectives relating to cognitive achievements (developing students' abilities to think creatively, objectively, and analytically and to use mathematics in everyday problems), there is considerable disagreement relating to many moral, vocational, and academic objectives. For example, while almost two-thirds of the general public give a high rating to the objective of developing standards of what is "right and wrong," only a third of public school teachers do. Again, close to half the general public rates helping students get good and/or high-paying jobs as a high teaching priority, yet only 6 percent of teachers do (Gallup, 1985a, 1985b).

STUDENT INVOLVEMENT In fact, when teachers are allowed to specify what goals they think are important (rather than rate goals chosen by a pollster), they are likely to mention ones related to motivating and involving students in a specific instructional experience and maintaining their attention during the lesson. The teachers' goal seems to be that of student involvement, rather than student learning per se or more long-term objectives. Further, teachers report that they gauge how well they are doing in the classroom not on the basis of formal evaluation results but on the basis of students' expressions, posture, and other cues, which indicate attention or inattention, interest or boredom, involvement or noninvolvement (Jackson, 1968).

Given the goal of pupil involvement, it should not be surprising that much of a teacher's activity is directed toward arousing pupils' interest initially and then maintaining their attention and interest as the lesson progresses. John Dewey equates attention with the relevance of the lesson itself. He described inattention or mind-wandering as "nothing but the unsuppressible imagination cut loose from concern with what is done" (Dewey, 1916, p. 236).

The way subject matter is presented affects curiosity, which, in turn, sustains interest. This suggests two contrasting techniques that teachers can use to foster student involvement (Waller, 1967). The first can be likened to the approach of a newspaper reporter, who tells the gist of the story in the first few sentences and then fills in this summary with increasing details. The second approach can be compared to the novelist who operates on a principle of suspense; incident after incident is given, each complete but adding to the suspense while details are filled in as the plot progresses. "Each of these techniques sustains interest and avoids ennui; ennui arises only when the mind is confronted with too many facts of the same order, or when it is compelled to attend too long to the same thing" (Waller, 1967, p. 15). Yet interest can be sustained beyond the intellectual level. Part of the art of sustaining attention is through the manipulation of the interactions and responses of the class itself.

The goals of arousing interest and sustaining attention seem reasonable, and in fact they are. However, in attempting to achieve these goals, the equally valued goal of class control can be put in jeopardy. Particularly in the early grades, when pupils are still very spontaneous and uninhibited, there is the danger of arousing a level of pupil interest that gets out of control. The

TABLE 12.1 The Importance of Selected Education Goals as Seen by Public School Teachers and the General Public (1984)

	Highest Rating	
	All Teachers %	U.S. Public %
To help develop good work habits, the ability to organize one's thoughts, the ability to concentrate	56	48
To develop the ability to think—creatively, objectively, analytically	56	51
To develop the ability to speak and write correctly	55	68
To develop the ability to use mathematics for everyday problems	53	54
To encourage the desire to continue learning throughout one's life	51	41
To encourage respect for law and order, for obeying the rules of society	46	52
To develop the ability to live in a complex and changing world	41	51
To prepare those who plan to attend college for college	36	46
To develop skills needed to get jobs for those not planning to attend college	34	54
To develop standards of what is "right" and "wrong"	33	64
To develop the desire to excel	32	51
To develop an understanding of democracy and to promote participation in the political process	31	33
To develop the ability to get along with different kinds of people	31	42
To develop respect for and understanding of other races, religions, nations, and cultures	30	39
To develop the ability to deal with adult responsibilities and problems, i.e., sex, marriage, parenting, personal finances, alcohol and drug abuse	28	46
To help students make realistic plans for what they will do after high school graduation	27	52
To develop an understanding about different kinds of jobs and careers, including their requirements and rewards	20	56
To gain knowledge and understanding of science and scientific facts	17	45
To gain knowledge of the important facts of history, geography, etc.	15	42
To develop an appreciation for and participation in the arts, music, literature, theater, etc.	14	35
To help students overcome personal problems	13	45
To develop the ability to understand and use computers	12	43
To promote physical development through sports programs	8	20
To help students get good/high-paying jobs	6	46
To develop an appreciation of the "good" things in life	6	32

Source: Gallup, 1985b, p. 327.

Motivating students to learn is one of the most important yet most difficult tasks facing a teacher.

dilemma of the necessity to maintain interest and control at the same time has been described as follows:

> *A dialectic opposition between mobilizing children's attitudes to a pitch of excitement and attempting to control them. This dialectical contradiction is witnessed in much of classroom management at levels above the nursery school and is a constant hazard in elementary school, where on the one hand an effort is made to relieve boredom by excitement, while on the other the children may be penalized for responding in the desired direction (of excitement) (Henry, 1971, pp. 29–30).*

A teacher can easily find that he or she is so successful in arousing involvement that the class becomes chaotic. Control is lost and, in order to regain it, the teacher ends up punishing or scolding the children for doing what he or she wanted them to do.

Student involvement and attention are not only sought after and constantly monitored but also are both formally and informally evaluated by teachers. A formal grade for "effort" on a report card certainly includes a large attention-participation component. Throughout the day, the teacher frequently admonishes pupils to "get down to work," "pay attention," "wake up," "try harder," and "keep your eyes on the book." Such admonitions come from informal evaluations that indicate that attention is flagging and are designed to keep the students alert and paying attention to the lesson.

Aside from simple whispering or talking, misconduct during instruction can be of two types. The first is called *side involvement*, which is carried on privately by pupils and involves actions such as playing with a pencil or ruler, writing on the desk, or doodling. The second type of misconduct is called *main involvement* and is a more direct escape from the lesson. It involves such things as daydreaming, staring out a window, transfixion on a spot on the floor, and even sleeping (Stebbins, 1975). Teachers dislike side involvement because it signals a slipping away from the lesson; they dislike main involvement because the student is no longer with the lesson at all. Both are signals to the teacher that he or she is not getting through. In effect, the pupil is telling the teacher that he or she is not interested in what the teacher has to say.

To avoid teacher displeasure, some pupils will feign attention, going through the motions to try to appear attentive and interested. Teachers in turn become adept at recognizing pseudoattention. In both instances, there is an implicit but clear recognition that attention, interest, and involvement in the lesson are expected. Habitual student inattention generates teacher hostility, and a vicious circle may be set up.

Some of the emphasis on attention is due to the teacher's belief that children must be present both *physically* and *mentally* to profit from instructional experiences. But the importance teachers place on student attention and effort is also related to the teacher's ego involvement in the lesson. Teachers are interested in the stylistic qualities of their own performance as much as in whether specific instructional goals are reached (Jackson, 1968). Thus, a pupil's inattention—staring into space, yawning, loud shuffling, doodling, passing notes, or shifting in the seat—may not only convey that Johnny isn't involved but may also be read by the teacher as a comment on the quality of his or her performance. The teacher, after all, is performing before an audience (in some cases a very tough audience), and if he or she is ignored, it can be seen as an affront (Waller, 1967).

Unintended Outcomes of Teaching

The intent of a teacher in any given lesson may be student involvement and attention and/or it may be that the pupils master a given piece of content or acquire a specific skill. Whatever the goal of the teacher, unanticipated outcomes result from the interaction between teacher and class. Some unintended outcomes might be regarded as positive or beneficial; others might be characterized as harmful, destructive, or negative. For example, a heavy emphasis on drilling the arithmetic facts may achieve the intended goal of mathematical proficiency but may also have the unintended result that children come to dislike arithmetic or are not good at problem solving.

Unintended Consequences

The teacher not only gives instruction in a subject matter but also does many other things—like being sweet or sarcastic, telling the child to stand up straight and take his hands out of his pockets, or giving a pat on the back. Thus the child may not only "learn science", but at the same time also learn to hate the sarcastic teacher or to love the benign one, to loathe standing up straight, to enjoy being patted on the back, etc., etc. (Henry, 1971, p. 169).

Henry (1971) describes the mechanisms through which unintended outcomes come about. The teacher's actions tend to elicit culturally determined and more or less standardized responses from students. For some students, the complimentary response is natural, while for others the action of giving it may cause pupils to react to the teacher's actions inwardly in an covertly antithetical way. Thus, in a spelling competition, the complimentary response—the one expected by the teacher and conditioned by the majority culture—is for the child to compete. For some children, such a response is more or less natural—a product of their home and cultural experiences. For other children in the spelling bee, competing may cause anxiety and tendencies to withdraw. Because of strong teacher and peer pressure to participate, these pupils may compete; yet they may also learn to dislike spelling, the teacher or, if it happens often enough, even school in general.

Henry also points out that in any instructional situation there are, in addition to complimentary and antithetical attitudes, attitudes that are *indeterminate.* The attitudinal response is one not easily predictable from mere knowledge of the learning situation, either by the teacher or an observer. Indeterminate attitudinal responses, in other words, are those responses to events as they unfold in the interactive setting. The spelling competition may engender any number of indeterminate responses. For example, it may give rise to anxiety and feelings of depreciation on the part of the pupil picked last for a team, feelings of self-depreciation and/or hostility when students snicker at an error, and anxieties and feelings of self-confidence or self-depreciation to random commands and evaluations by the teacher as the "game" progresses. Statements such as "stand up straight," "stop the fooling," "very good," "who can spell that word for Joe?" can give rise to indeterminate attitudinal responses, since the student's reaction to these situations cannot be foreseen in advance; they develop as the instructional situation unfolds.

Henry describes a final type of pupil response that can produce unintended outcomes as *pseudocomplimentary.* Pupils give this type of response on the basis of what they perceive the teacher wants, but they give it without conviction. In this situation, the unintended outcome is docility or conformity. Henry sums up how unintended outcomes are learned as follows:

What a child learns (i.e., what responses are reinforced) is a result of the teacher's actions and intentions and of the child's own tendencies to respond. Out of the interplay between these grow complimentary, pseudo-complimentary, antithetical and indeterminate responses on the part of the child. At any given time, any of the last three may be unintended by the teacher (Henry, 1971, p. 173).

When you teach, you should be conscious of how your formal and informal evaluations of students and the techniques you use to motivate and control student responses can contribute to these "unintended outcomes."

The Social Context of Teaching

Teaching as Performance

Teaching involves careful planning and preparation. However, teaching ultimately is a creative performance and it is the teacher's personal style and performance before the class that stamps it as unique. It is a performance that must begin with the bell and stop approximately when the bell rings again. All teachers are to some degree artists. All artists engage in a dialectic between the conventions or rules of their art on the one hand and individual personal interpretation and style on the other. Teachers are no exception. An example from music may help make the meaning of this dialectic clearer. A. L. Lloyd, a famous collector of folk music, explains the Arabic term *maqam* as follows:

> [*A maqam*] *is but a tune pattern, a melody formula, based on one or other modal scale and having certain stereotyped, more or less obligatory moments and passages, but otherwise allowing great freedom of treatment. In short, the maqam is a kind of skeleton or, better, scaffolding of melody which the musician, observing certain rules, is able to fill in for himself according to his fantasy and the mood of the moment. For westerners, the clearest, most familiar example of the maqam principle is provided by the Blues, always the same yet always different, a well-known, well-worn frame apt for any extemporization, baffling to strangers, and listened to by fans not simply as a tune but as a traditional exercise at once achingly familiar and arrestingly fresh. The Blues is an extreme example, but in some measure all folk tunes in the natural state, unfixed by print or other control, nourished by constant variation, having no single "authentic" form but somewhat altering from singer to singer and even from verse to verse, are made on the maqam principle, with its balance of constraint with freedom, fixed model with fluid treatment, communal taste with individual fantasy, traditional constancy with novel creative moments, sameness with difference* (Lloyd, 1967, p. 63).

Teaching, like the blues, has its obligatory "moments and passages," its well-established skeletal frame around which you are free to extemporize and create, as long as you observe certain rules. Your creativity, backed up by careful preparation, will unfold during the complexity of interactive teaching.

A performance would not make much sense without an audience. Further, while the performance can often be rehearsed, it must be adapted to the audience. In teaching, the class is the audience. Social interactions among the audience can heighten the impact of the teacher's presentation. The importance of audience reaction in sustaining interest can perhaps be better understood if you compare your reactions when seeing a thriller like *Halloween* in a packed theater to seeing it in a drive-in movie theater or in your own living room on television. Very often in the latter cases the impact of the film is not as great because you did not get the feeling of tension transmitted by an audience. Similarly, watching a lecturer on TV or a class on videotape does not have the same impact as being part of a "live" audience. An audience contributes an intangible something to a teacher's total presentation. There is a social compulsion to listen when in an audience (Waller, 1967). If this audience chemistry is successfully tapped, the interest and attention of individuals can be greatly heightened. Similarly, the class as an audience can have a beneficial effect on the teacher, who, in the course of questioning, lecturing, and demonstrating, keeps eye contact with the class to see if the point is understood and if students are still involved.

The Complexity of Teaching Activity

Relatively little is known in a systematic way about the details of classroom life. It is only in recent years that attempts have been made to describe what actually goes on within the classroom (Doyle, 1986; Shavelson, Webb, & Burstein, 1986; Hawkins, 1973). Investigators now frequently get involved in extended observations of classrooms to learn about and describe what happens when a teacher closes the classroom door and engages a class of active youngsters for five or six hours a day, five days a week, forty weeks of the year.

This line of research is still in its infancy, and we still do not understand differences among classrooms and teachers at the same grade level, let alone differences between the quantity and quality of teacher-student interactions as students move up the educational ladder. However, research has revealed that important similarities exist across classrooms. All are characterized by features of group settings, regardless of the particular teacher or students who inhabit them. Four major characteristics of classroom environments have been described: (1) multidimensionality and simultaneity of events, (2) immediacy and unpredictability of events, (3) publicness of events, and (4) shared history. These characteristics create pressures and demands to which teachers and students must respond (Doyle, 1986; Doyle & Carter, 1987).

MULTIDIMENSIONALITY AND SIMULTANEITY OF EVENTS The fact that there are a great many events and tasks in the classroom becomes obvious when we consider that it is made up of many individuals, each with his or her own personality, interests, and levels of achievement. Each student can contribute (and often does) to the action at any one time. Not only does each student represent a dimension of the classroom, but students also interact with each other and with the teacher to create a whole new series of dimensions to which the teacher must be responsive. Add to this scenario the fact that in a classroom a variety of goals are being pursued, often at the same time, relating to the cognitive, personal, and social development of all students. Prolonged observation in classrooms shows that during the course of a five- to six-hour day, an elementary school teacher may engage in as many as 1,000 interpersonal interchanges or episodes, each lasting only a few seconds, rarely more than a minute (Jackson, 1968). Even in classrooms with the least amount of activity, change of one sort or another occurred on an average of once every 18 seconds. The number of episodes in each lesson—involving a change of one sort or another—ranged between 157 and 138, and over the course of the school day between 4,500 and 1,200 separate episodes occurred (Adams & Biddle, 1970).

It is clear that the complexity of the classroom arises in part from the fact that teaching involves much more than instructing students on the prescribed curriculum. In fact, the instructional activities of lecturing, demonstrating, questioning, reading, and explaining constitute only a portion, albeit a central portion, of the daily activities of the teacher. Cohen reminds us that even the seemingly direct act of instruction is not as straightforward as it seems:

> *It is most unwise to use a simple unidirectional causal model to characterize the classroom; for example, teachers affect students through what they say, how they question, how they explain, and through the use of curriculum materials. Studies of the classroom as a complex system suggest that cause and effect can run in several directions. Students have effects on the teacher, who in turn affects the learning of the student. Students have effects on each other; the informal social structure produces differential treatment of students by the teacher. Furthermore, the effects which students have on the teacher and on other students tend to build up over time (Cohen, 1972, p. 444).*

IMMEDIACY AND UNPREDICTABILITY OF EVENTS In the crowded and busy places that are classrooms, the pace of events is steady, rapid, unrehearsed, and unpredictable. When you become a teacher you will quickly discover that you simply cannot predict with any accuracy what will happen next in most lessons. For this reason planning can take you only so far. Many things unrelated to a lesson can happen that will upset your preplanned activities. A novel thought injected by a student can change the course of the lesson. Questions from students can also dictate the direction of a class.

Interruptions in your planned approach come from outside sources as well as from events related to instruction: a call on the public address system, a knock on the door, muffled giggles signaling something is afoot, a fire drill, a pupil reading a comic book surreptitiously, or restlessness before recess.

Examples of Students' Questions That Affect Teaching

But there are, to be sure, foolish questions. Every teacher has heard them, and it is folly to argue otherwise. There are questions which reveal a failure to prepare the daily lesson, questions intended to divert the teacher's attention or to kill time, questions reflecting a total and irremediable failure to comprehend subject matter, questions intended to impress the teacher, questions intended to amuse the class, questions intended to trip up the teacher, questions intended to show up the teacher, questions asked merely because the person asking them wants to say something (Waller, 1967, p. 287).

PUBLICNESS OF EVENTS Classrooms are public places in the sense that all a teacher's (and students') actions and interactions can be observed by others. Anything a teacher or student does is likely to affect more than the person the action might have been intended to affect. Because the class is a public place, what happens to one or several members can affect the total ecology of the system. The whole is vastly greater than the sum of its parts.

SHARED HISTORY While all classrooms share certain characteristics, no class is quite the same as any other class. Because class groups meet regularly over long periods of time, experiences accumulate, people get to know each other, relationships develop, routines and norms are established, and the class takes on a personality of its own (see Box 12.3).

The fact that each classroom has its own peculiar history and "personality" means that teachers and students on the high school level must adjust to four or five different configurations or social systems as the teacher changes with each class and/or as the mix of students comprising the class changes from one period to the next. For the elementary school teacher, generally there is one class, one configuration, one set of attitudinal responses. However, at the end of the year, the slate is wiped clean and the following September the teacher must again begin to adjust to and become part of the new class—a different and distinct organism.

Dealing with Classroom Complexity

The immediacy, volume, and rapidity of classroom cues and events seldom give the teacher time to reflect on which course of action to follow or its likely consequences. Instead, minute by minute, the teacher is compelled to act spontaneously and intuitively. However, the seemingly snap reactions of the teacher are guided by a framework of subtle but meticulously nurtured rules and expectations against which student behavior is evaluated, and by an accretion of a large store of idiosyncratic knowledge about individual students and classes. This is what Jackson (1968) has called the teacher's *hidden knowledge*. A framework of rules and expectations, along with a store of idiosyncratic knowledge about each student, evolves imperceptibly over the year.

THE TEACHER'S HIDDEN KNOWLEDGE The ability to cope with events in the classroom, to establish and maintain rules and expectations, and to build up a store of hidden knowledge varies widely from teacher to teacher. The elementary school teacher's hidden knowledge of a class of 15 to 25 students is probably more extensive and deeper than that of a secondary school teacher who may be responsible for upward of 200 students.

The importance of hidden knowledge can be most easily illustrated by considering the substitute teacher. Substituting for a few days in midyear can be an extremely difficult task, precisely because the substitute does not have a store of hidden knowledge about individual students (Jackson, 1968). The substitute finds it hard to sense or feel what motives or emotions are embedded in, or concealed by, a student's behavior. The substitute lacks the insight that comes only from daily intimate contact and the many nonverbal and verbal contextual impressions built up over an extended period that permit

For let no one be deceived, the important things that happen in the schools result from the interaction of personalities. Children and teachers are not disembodied intelligence, not instructing machines and learning machines, but whole human beings tied together in a complex range of social interconnections. The school is a social world because human beings live in it.

A class, as a crowd, develops a definite personality, and that personality can very easily be observed from where the teacher stands for a class is never a sea of faces, after the first day. It is a pattern, a structure of highlights and shadows, a configuration with shifting points of tension, a changing equilibrium of ease and unease, of beauty and loveliness. The maintenance of discipline depends upon the emergence in the teacher's mind of configurations enabling him to keep the whole class in view without sacrificing any of its parts.

Source: Waller, 1967, pp. 1, 162.

the regular teacher to, as it were, "read the pupil's mind." A pupil not only *gives* information in countless classroom encounters but also *gives it off* through facial expressions, body language, tone of voice, general conduct, motivation, humor, trustworthiness, truthfulness, interaction with peers, leadership qualities, and other personal characteristics.

The teacher's hidden knowledge derives from a variety of sources. Students are one of the more influential sources. Peer evaluations about who is the tattletale, the gossip, the class Casanova, athlete, grind, teacher's pet, cheat, or brown nose are evident to the teacher. Isolated instances and subtle cues are stored away until imperceptibly a mosaic takes shape in the teacher's mind that eventually evolves and informs future actions and reactions to student behavior.

A substitute simply is not privy to this type of information. Further, the teacher's hidden knowledge is not something that can be communicated in a lesson plan that might be left in the desk for the substitute. Students very quickly realize the disadvantage under which substitutes work and begin almost immediately to play on their blind spots. In self-defense, the substitute often is forced to resort to written assignments, busywork, novelty, or threats to leave a note for the regular teacher about misbehavior in order to manage the class.

Although the teacher may pass on some of this hidden knowledge to a teacher for the following year, much of it cannot be articulated or made explicit. As a result, each September a teacher must begin from the beginning, building up a new store of "hidden knowledge" about the new class (Jackson, 1968). Even in rural schools where a teacher may stay with a class for several years, his or her hidden knowledge is far from static but grows, evolves, and changes imperceptibly as new students arrive, old ones leave, and individuals mature or change in ways that subtly change the chemistry of the classroom.

A teacher's "hidden knowledge" can color his or her informal evaluations of students, particularly those evaluations concerned with general classroom deportment. Teachers often use this hidden knowledge to explain misconduct as well as to guide their reaction or lack of reaction to an incident. A teacher's personal knowledge of a pupil is most likely to be activated when the pupil is "above average" or "below average," is a chronic behavior problem, or has special psychological or physical problems (Stebbins, 1975). Thus when a bright, motivated boy misbehaves, the teacher may interpret the infraction as an indication of boredom; when a poorly motivated low achiever misbehaves, the teacher may see the act as disrespectful or threatening good order. Sometimes misbehavior is attributed to the student's personality or to the influence of the student's home and neighborhood (Stebbins, 1975). Occasionally, teachers will explain or interpret misbehavior in terms of their past experience with siblings or other relatives ("Of course he's trouble; so were his two brothers").

This personalized knowledge about pupils' aptitudes, attainment motivations, personalities, and family backgrounds can *unfairly bias* as well as *properly guide* informal evaluations of students. As a teacher, you must keep in mind the moral relationship that exists between you and your pupils, and you must be aware of subtle, unavoidable ways in which your hidden knowledge of students can affect your evaluations and how your students perceive these informal evaluations.

THE USE OF VERBAL AND NONVERBAL CUES There are literally thousands of fleeting verbal and nonverbal cues and actions by students that bombard the teacher's senses during the day. The experienced teacher can ignore or filter out many of these cues and events. However, many cues require some form of immediate response, often without interrupting the flow of instruction. For example, you have probably had a teacher who could throw an icy stare at a yawning, giggling, or whispering student to bring that student in line without interrupting the ongoing lesson.

The successful teacher must be adept at comprehending nonverbal as well as verbal communications. Box 12.4 lists nonverbal signals that are applicable in the classroom setting and to which teachers need to be attentive in managing the class. Nonverbal cues signal attitudes and feelings and often complement verbal communication. Some students can manipulate nonverbal cues to their advantage by smiling and nodding at the teacher at the appropriate time, thereby reinforcing the teacher. When this happens, some teachers may zero in on the student because he or she is registering nonverbal feedback that others are not (Waller, 1967).

Teachers can be influenced by nonverbal factors in their perceptions and treatment of students. Research has found this to be so in the use of space and distance. For example, teachers perceived students sitting toward the front of the classroom to be more attentive than students at the rear of the room. They also interacted more frequently with those near them. Gestures, facial expressions, and eye gaze also affect teachers' responses. For example, students who smiled often were ranked higher on "teachability" than students who did not. The general attractiveness of students (appearance, grooming, dress) and such factors as voice tone and errors in speech are other aspects of nonverbal factors that have been found to affect teachers' perceptions of students. Thus, students portrayed as attractive and with good voice quality were judged to be more intelligent, enthusiastic, and academically successful than students who did not have these qualities (Woolfolk & Brooks, 1983).

Verbal cues, of course, are also very important. The teacher can commu-

1. *Bodily contact:* Contact signals friendship and intimacy.
2. *Bodily proximity:* Changes in proximity are used to begin and end encounters; people sit or stand closer to those they like.
3. *Bodily orientation:* Co-operating pairs sit side-by-side; competing or hostile pairs sit facing; those in discussion or conversation prefer 90 degrees.
4. *Gestures:* General emotional arousal, as well as specific emotions (e.g., fist-clenching for aggression), are communicated through gestures. They can also be used to complete the meaning of verbal utterances in various ways, and to replace speech.
5. *Facial expressions:* These communicate emotions and attitudes toward others, though they are hard to interpret since they are heavily controlled. They also provide immediate feedback by showing disbelief, surprise, pleasure, displeasure, etc.
6. *Eye movements:* These give feedback about another's reactions, help to synchronize speech, and signal degree of interest in the other person.
7. *Emotional tone of speech:* This is a more reliable indicator of emotions than facial expression, since it is not so well controlled for most people.

Source: Adapted from Argyle, 1972, 1975.

nicate much to the student, and the student to the teacher, through myriad verbal cues. Clarke has identified 43 speech acts, shown in Box 12.5, that act as cues or signals that influence other people. Since both you and your students will use all these speech acts during the course of the year, you must become adept at both recognizing and using them.

The teacher needs verbal and nonverbal feedback from the class to adjust presentation as it unfolds. As Waller writes, "One does not explain to empty air: one explains to people . . . and one watches the audience narrowly to observe the effect. There is an interplay of gestures which keeps the process moving; the crowd makes the orator" (Waller, 1967, p. 364).

Here again you can see the immediacy of the teaching situation and the necessity to "play it by ear" to a large extent. The teacher's ability to read cues from the class is to an important degree dependent on eye contact. If you continually look away from the class—out of the window, at a space at the back of the room, or down at your notes—you cannot hope to receive or process those vital audience cues that tell you how successful you are in making a point. Not all students communicate cues to the teachers, or if they do, teachers seem to focus on five or six key students for that nod or smile or the frown or puzzled look. Teachers often hold these key students in higher regard than they do other members of the class (Waller, 1967; Stebbins, 1975).

The teacher must have some facility as an actor and improvisor, not only to control the mood of the class but also to signal to it when that mood has changed and a new situation has evolved; when, for example, he or she is kidding or serious, when the children can laugh and talk, or when silence is necessary.

READING THE CLASS A good teacher "reads" the looks and behavior of pupils. He or she instinctively feels when something is amiss, that attention is waning or is being diverted by some competing event. For example, con-

> **BOX 12.5 Speech Acts**

Accept	Challenge	Joke	Promise
Accuse	Cheer	Justify	Question
Advise	Command	Laugh	Refuse
Agree	Complain	Minimize	Reject
Answer	Comply	Offend	Request
Apologize	Confess	Offer	Sympathize
Assert	Continue	Pacify	Terminate
Attend	Defer	Pardon	Thank
Bid farewell	Deny	Permit	Threaten
Blame	Fulfill	Praise	Warn
Boast	Greet	Prohibit	

Source: D. D. Clarke, quoted in Argyle, Furnham, & Graham, 1981, p. 194.

sider the following account by an anonymous teacher describing the change that came over a class as an apple core was surreptitiously being passed from seat to seat:

> *A slight slackening in attention. Something in the air. Movement of body and mind betokening a drop in concentration. Looking at them, all seemed to be clear. Heads down to the books. Silence. The vacant stare of the student half-listening to the teacher's monologue and half-calculating how much time would be needed to get his homework done that night. The idle fiddling with the compass. The scratching of various parts of the anatomy. The writing of names on textbooks and the making of railways on the desks with pencils. But all was not right. The over-determined attention to the books of those who did not normally indulge themselves thus. The angry glances at certain others by those who wanted to get on with their work. The crumbling self-control of those whose low laughter threshold always lets the cat out of the bag (Frank, 1975, p. 3).*

Even a decision about who to call on is not always straightforward but is often determined by the flow of events in the class. A student is called on to read but has lost his or her place; do you point out the correct place or call on the next student? From which of the many raised hands should you pick, or should you ignore them all and call on someone who has not volunteered? Answers to previous questions often indicate whether a student should be called on or ignored.

Your power to decide who to call on can be an effective device to keep the class attentive. Students will be quick to detect any patterns in who you call and often will adjust their attention and behavior accordingly. Nor have students' attempts at evading teacher questions escaped the attention of humorists. For example, Ephron offers the following tongue-in-cheek advice on how to act if you do not want to be called on:

> • *Make yourself invisible. Align head and shoulders with those of a student directly between the teacher and you. If the teacher moves, adjust alignment.*

● *Make yourself inconspicuous. To accomplish this, assume a casual pose. Concentrate on fitting the top of the pen into the bottom; perhaps even hum to yourself. Or engage in nonchalant play with a pencil: Hold it upright, point against paper, and slide fingers from eraser to tip. Turn pencil over; slide from tip to eraser. Turn and slide. Turn and slide.*
● *If the teacher calls on you anyway, do not respond immediately in the hope that a kid with the answer will just yell it out. If no one rescues you and the question calls for a yes or no response, pick one. Otherwise, give a joke answer. The class will laugh. The teacher will say that it won't be so funny when you get your report card (Ephron, 1978, p. 37).*

Beating the System

She also knows the teacher's strategy of asking questions of students who seem confused, or not paying attention. She therefore feels safe waving her hand in the air, as if she were bursting to tell the answer, whether she really knows it or not. When someone else answers correctly, she nods her head in emphatic agreement. Sometimes she even adds a comment, though her expression and tone of voice show that she feels this is risky. It is also interesting to note that she does not raise her hand unless there are at least half a dozen other hands up. Sometimes she gets called on. The question arose the other day, "What is half of forty-eight?" Her hand was up; in the tiniest whisper she said, "twenty-four." I asked her to repeat it again, because many couldn't hear her. Her face showing tension, she said, very loudly, "I said that one-half of forty-eight is . . . and then, very softly, "twenty-four." Of course, this is a strategy that often pays off. A teacher who asks a question is tuned to the right answer, since it will tell him that his teaching is good and that he can go to the next topic (Holt, 1964, pp. 12–13).

As a teacher, you must react to unpredictable events, to the continuous flow of cues—visual, auditory, olfactory, bodily, and verbal—and adjust and readjust to the flow of the lesson while it is in progress. Frowns, the light in the eyes, clock watching, the conspiratorial whisper, the guilty look, the smile, the blank stare, the puzzled expressions must be judiciously ignored or dealt with. And all this in the twinkling of an eye. Because of the rapidity with which events occur, you will have to judge very quickly what is right, how far you can go, when to back off. You will have to feel within yourself which is the right course to follow. You will have to use your sixth sense and learn to trust your feelings and hunches. But remember, even the most expert teacher is fallible, sometimes misreads cues and overreacts, sometimes misses what perhaps should not have been missed. We all get tired, irritable, and grouchy; we all have bad days as well as good ones.

CONCLUSION

In this chapter, we considered the complexity of the classroom as a social system and the teacher's essential part in its ecology. Our brief description of the complexity of teaching was itself a simplification of reality. In attempting to describe complexity we inevitably break down the total process into bits in order to deal with them. To do this, however, is to oversimplify teaching, which is much more than the sum of any parts we may use to describe it.

You may dismiss our emphasis on the complexity of the classroom as obvious—a truism. However, this truism and, more important, its implications, are often lost sight of or not fully appreciated, either by the general public or by educators. Teachers themselves, when asked to talk about what they do, seldom advert to many of the important details of classroom life recorded by a skilled and patient observer (Jackson, 1968). However obvious the complexity of the social system that is the classroom, it still needs to be fully appreciated if you are to understand the true nature of teaching and be successful as a teacher.

Try to become aware of what you are doing, of your vast store of hidden knowledge and, above all, of your moral obligations as you try to achieve the teaching goals you have set for yourself as well as those that society and the school expect of you.

QUESTIONS AND ACTIVITIES

1. What do you feel are the major moral and ethical issues you will face as a teacher?
2. For the following questions reflect back upon your elementary and secondary school experiences.
   a. What do you think your community expected from the schools you attended? Why?
   b. What were the major focuses of the hidden curriculum in your school?
   c. List some of the rituals at your school that contributed to the hidden curriculum.
   d. Where did your school experience fail to meet your expectations now that you are able to reflect on them?
   e. What experiences can you recall that involved a teacher's abuse of power?
   f. How many of Quintilian's descriptions (see Box 12.1) have you experienced? Which stand out most graphically in your mind? Why?
   g. What unintended outcomes associated with teaching have you experienced?
   h. Give an example of a piece of hidden knowledge that one of your teachers might have had about a class you were in.
3. What has the hidden curriculum of your college or university attempted to achieve?

4. What values do you hold at this point in your education regarding grading?
5. List the reasons you are planning to teach. How many of them reflect your mores and values? Might any of these conflict with ones held by a school you might work in? If so, what will you do?
6. Have a principal identify two or three teachers with a good reputation for discipline. Observe and interview these teachers. What do these teachers depend upon for maintaining control?
7. Ask several teachers what they feel their most important teaching goals are.

CHAPTER 13

Preparing for Class

A teacher must spend a considerable amount of time outside the classroom preparing to teach. The planning activities of teachers are directed at making the time students spend in their classrooms as productive as possible. This chapter introduces you to the planning functions of teachers.

● Preactive teaching ranges from simple housekeeping and record keeping through preparation of the classroom to daily lesson planning. Preactive teaching is reflective, deliberate, rational, orderly, and premeditated.
● You should plan the physical environment of your room so that it is safe, orderly, manageable, and visually and intellectually stimulating.
● You should plan the psychological environment of your classroom so that students feel accepted, confident, and secure.
● Routine and rules must be firmly established during the first weeks of school.
● Grouping for instruction is a problem that all teachers must face. You need to be familiar with different kinds of grouping and the problems associated with this practice.
● As the director of learning experiences in your classroom, you will need to develop both long-range and daily lesson plans that address the objectives of the school district's curriculum and the individual needs of your students.
● The teaching-learning process is very complex and dynamic. Therefore, the flexibility to depart from your plan as the need arises is essential.

Your work as a teacher does not begin when you enter the classroom; neither does it end when class ends. The phrase *preactive teaching* was coined in 1968 by Philip Jackson to describe the many professional activities that teachers perform that do not directly involve interaction with students. *Preactive* teaching encompasses the activities that you will engage in when students are not present. It involves planning and thinking about what you will do in the classroom. In contrast, *interactive* teaching deals with what you do after you close your classroom door, take that lonely seat, and look into those shining morning faces. A third aspect of teaching might be called *postactive.* In this phase, you review the effectiveness of your teaching and the learning level of your students. It might involve grading homework or scoring tests. In a sense, some postactive teaching is preactive insofar as it determines what you will do in later classes.

The importance of the preactive phase of teaching is underlined by research findings indicating that one of the strongest correlates of student achievement is the student's "opportunity to learn," that is, the extent to which he or she is exposed to curricular material and actually spends time learning it. How much time is available for academic activities depends, of course, on the teacher having organized "the classroom as an efficient learning environment where academic activities run smoothly, transitions are brief and orderly, and little time is spent getting organized or dealing with inattention or resistance" (Brophy & Good, 1986, p. 360). So that as much time as possible in the school day is available for curriculum-related activities, it is important that before going into class you give time and thought to the physical environment of the classroom and to planning the structure and content of lessons. This kind of preparation is important not only to ensure that things flow smoothly in class and that classroom order is maintained so that students can learn, but also to provide an atmosphere in which students can feel comfortable and develop positive attitudes toward themselves and toward learning.

In this chapter, we shall first outline some of the main characteristics of preactive teaching. Next, we shall consider the planning required to prepare the classroom for teaching. We shall see that planning involves preparing the physical environment as well as the psychological environment of the classroom. It also involves making sure that the classroom is an intellectually stimulating place and a safe place for students. Planning is also required to group students for instruction and to follow the curriculum. Having considered these issues, we will review in the final sections of the chapter some of the major concepts in lesson planning. Some aspects of planning will be done at the school district and individual school levels; you will be responsible for other aspects in your own teaching.

Preactive Teaching

Some preactive activities involve simple housekeeping or record-keeping chores, for example, ordering supplies, arranging displays for the bulletin board, decorating the room for different seasons or events, arranging classroom furniture, and writing assignments on the blackboard. Other preactive tasks involve attempts to anticipate or resolve learning or discipline problems. Here, you may simply reflect on how best to handle a problem child or evaluate how your tactics with a problem child have been working. On the other hand, you may engage in more direct tasks such as talking to the principal or guidance counselor, writing to a parent, or holding a parent conference.

The various activities subsumed under preactive teaching are premeditated, rational, deliberative, and orderly. In your preactive teaching you will have time to reflect on events, consider tactics, and weigh alternatives. However, the realities of the classroom situation mean that much of what you

Planning your lessons in advance is an important aspect of preactive teaching.

do during interactive teaching, in contrast to what you do during preactive teaching, will be spontaneous, reasonable rather than rational, and often unplanned and unpredictable. The events that unfold during instruction dictate how the lesson *actually* proceeds, who is called on and when, what material needs to be repeated and what needs to be discarded. Some of this interaction will be directly related to the progress of the lesson itself (for example, which students raise their hands and which apparently are lost); other interactions will be unrelated to the lesson but affect the flow of instruction (for example, interruptions, discipline problems). Therefore, you cannot be a slave to your plan, no matter how carefully thought out it may have been. You must be flexible.

Perhaps the greatest amount of your preactive teaching time will be devoted to lesson planning, an important part of teaching. Many schools require teachers to fill out plan books and make them available for perusal by the principal or other supervisors. During your teacher training, a substantial amount of time in methods courses will center around building lesson plans for different types of units. A lesson-plan book contains the evidence of your planning. It is important documentation of the learning activities that have occurred in your classroom and is the record of your students' formal schooling.

Planning the Physical Environment of the Classroom

Good classrooms do not just happen. They are products of careful planning based on a knowledge of the cognitive and maturity level of each student who refers to it as "my room." The classroom environment exerts a powerful influence upon the quality and quantity of learning that takes place within its walls. If your classroom is to be a dynamic and fertile environment (not static and sterile), it should be visually attractive, it should be physically comfortable, and it should lend itself to a practical and functional arrangement of furniture.

The Visually Attractive Classroom

Classrooms can be visually exciting places, despite the usual routine school decor. Although you may be able to do little about some characteristics of your classroom (color, location, shape), you can still create an attractive environment.

While classrooms were never meant to resemble antiseptic, sterile hospital rooms, neither were they designed to be disorganized closets. If your desk overflows with student papers, books, and assorted memorabilia, your students will soon learn that messy desks and work areas are the rule, not the exception. Therefore, a major component of an attractive, functional classroom is neatness.

What can you do with all the items you use for teaching? A small bookcase or table next to your desk can hold class textbooks and the occasional overflow of assignments. Papers that students turn in for correction can be placed in trays or boxes located on the top of a file cabinet rather than on your desk. If you are an elementary teacher, label the trays or boxes by subject area, minimizing the chance of misfiled papers. Assign a student to collect the papers you need to take home each evening for correction and to place them in a special folder. This technique will go a long way toward eliminating a major source of visual disorder.

Even at the best of times, your students' desks will overflow with the "tools of the trade"—crayons, pencils, markers, notebooks, binders, and the like. In the elementary grades, add to this assortment the normal number of textbooks needed daily and you have a collection that no desk can handle. If your students have lockers, have them store items not in use there. However, if no convenient place has been provided for each student's supplies, then create one. Assign each student a section of space in a classroom bookcase. Textbooks not in immediate use can be stored neatly along with other items. As long as neatness is the rule, your students will appreciate the extra storage space.

The Physically Comfortable Classroom

The amount of light and its source are two important factors in creating a physically comfortable classroom. Do you remember how tired your eyes were the last time you engaged in a long bout of studying under a high-intensity lamp? If that light was the only source of illumination in the room, your eyes were strained even more. Why? Intense light directly focused on the surface you are studying produces a glare that continually forces your eyes to adjust and readjust, which is quite tiring. A similar situation can occur in your classroom. As a teacher, you will need to ensure that the students have balanced lighting. Before the school year begins, spend a day in your classroom and note when the natural light produces a glare on classroom surfaces, particularly the chalkboard. In this way, you will know when drapes or shades need to be pulled, and you can also arrange seats accordingly. Performing the same check with artificial lighting is also wise. Proper lighting in the classroom will aid in the learning process.

Your classroom should be neither too hot nor too cold. Although you may have a personal preference, students work best in classrooms where the temperature is between 68 and 70 degrees. If your classroom is self-contained (the students are there for all subjects), ensure that fresh air circulates; this will provide an ample supply of oxygen and will prevent the classroom atmosphere from becoming stale.

The source of heat in your classroom is important. Many primary grade students sit on the floor during group activities. If the room is heated through the floor, this arrangement may not be possible. Classrooms that are heated by water or steam use large radiators often located on one side of the classroom. Since the metal pipes and radiators are hot, care should be taken that students will not easily come in contact with them. In areas of the country where air conditioning is a necessity, check that students are not seated too close to the units.

Classroom Furniture

Depending upon your preference, the arrangement of your classroom furniture will change frequently or will remain relatively stable. In either case, you should not arrange seats so that students will directly face windows. Ideally, natural lighting should come over their left shoulders, or from behind.

Your classroom seating arrangement depends upon the type of desks you have, the age level of your students, and your personal preference or teaching style. Individual desks or units (desk and chair) can be arranged in a formal manner, or they can be grouped to provide a greater flexibility in arrangement. A worktable arrangement is less flexible but allows more informal activities in the classroom. Figure 13.1 provides an illustration of formal, informal, workable (or cluster), and circular desk arrangements.

If your students are difficult to control, a formal seating arrangement will help. A specific seat restricts student movement while permitting you to monitor quickly each pupil's physical and psychological presence. Seat assignments can also be used to strengthen order. For example, you can change the seating arrangement in order to break up a clique that has developed. Be sure to separate students who are disruptive.

Seating arrangements may have serious implications for instruction as well. Research findings indicate that such arrangements can become associated with teacher-student communication and student participation (Adams & Biddle, 1970). Students seated in what has come to be called the action zone, or "T-zone," figure more prominently in communication exchanges with teachers (Cohen, 1972). The T-zone includes students sitting along the front row and down the center aisle directly facing the teacher's

FIGURE 13.1 Desk Arrangements

A. Formal Desk Arrangement

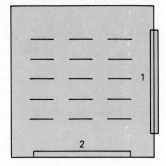

B. Informal Desk Arrangement

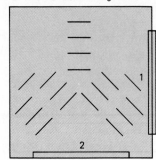

C. Cluster Desk Arangement

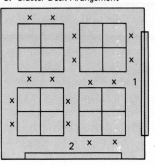

D. Circular Desk Arrangement

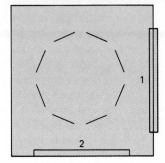

1 = Windows   2 = Chalkboard

desk or where the teacher stands when instructing. Greater participation from students in the T-zone has been attributed to the level of eye contact associated with seats in this area (Somers, 1969). Other research findings indicate that on-task behavior is more frequent among students seated in circles than among those seated in clusters, who in turn engage in more on-task behavior than students seated in rows (Rosenfield, Lambert, & Black, 1985). Teachers in the primary grades have been found to have a tendency to assign students with higher ability or of higher social status seats closer to them (Brophy & Good, 1970; Rist, 1970).

If you have a worktable or teaching aids such as an overhead projector, a television, a filmstrip projector, or a record player in the classroom, choose convenient locations for them. If the machinery is rarely used, storing it in a closet would be fine, but if you use a particular piece of equipment often, determine the most accessible spot to place it. Are the bookcases in your classroom built in, or are they movable? Can your room be sectioned off to provide a private work and storage space for students?

Planning the Psychological Environment of the Classroom

A Feeling of Acceptance

One of your most important jobs as a teacher will be to accept each student for what he or she is. Under normal circumstances your students will challenge you and try your patience. If each student in your care understands that while you may disapprove of a particular action he or she may perform, you do not disapprove of him or her as a person, the student will understand that "the teacher likes me" and will feel accepted and valued.

One of the qualities that will earn you the label of an "accepting teacher" is that of fairness. The normal interactions that occur in day-to-day relationships are magnified in the classroom. If you are fair, your classroom will be a healthy environment for your students. A fair teacher is one who treats each student in a consistent manner. Actions that rate disapproval on one occasion should provoke disapproval whenever they occur. The same standard of fairness should apply to *all* students—those who can melt your heart with a glance as well as those who harden that organ no matter what they do. A wise teacher never ignores the accusation "You're not fair." Fairness is one of the most important moral attributes of a successful teacher.

A Feeling of Confidence

Students differ in their readiness to learn, in their ability to learn, and in their level of achievement. To provide for these differences in the classroom, the teacher needs to create a climate of confidence. Confidence has reciprocal aspects. Success in academic activities builds students' confidence in their ability to succeed. To build confidence, the student must make honest progress and be rewarded for it. As a teacher, you will build students' confidence by adapting instruction to provide for success at all levels of ability. When asking questions, plan a few that your less able students can answer. In team competitions (such as a math race), group students so that challenging teams have the same levels of competence. Discover the areas in which each of your students is most knowledgeable and call upon those individuals to share their expertise. Your students will take greater pride in their schoolwork when you allow them to choose the papers they want you to display. In this way, each student's achievement will become a real and recognized success rather than a charitable handout.

Praise is often considered important for building students' confidence. Unfortunately, teachers (and other adults) frequently make the mistake of misusing it. They praise too often, not enough, or do not clearly communicate to the students what actions they are encouraging through praise. If praise is to build your students' self-esteem, it must mean something to them. Table 13.1 outlines characteristics of effective and ineffective praise.

A Feeling of Stability

Stability, one of the most powerful factors in creating the proper emotional tone in your classroom, refers to the daily routine that students follow and the consistency with which the classroom is run. During the first week of school you must establish the order and routine of your classroom.

Stability is a function of confidence and acceptance and is based upon the relationship you will develop with your students. A teacher who exhibits mercurial moods creates an unstable atmosphere; a teacher who remains even-tempered promotes a calm classroom. The classroom routine provides the underlying security needed for learning and academic achievement.

THE IMPORTANCE OF THE FIRST WEEKS The importance of the first weeks cannot be stressed enough. First impressions are lasting. Researchers from the Institute for Research on Teaching at Michigan State University have identified three phases of preparation for the new school year: the "Get ready" phase, the "Get set" phase, and the "Go" phase (Clark & Elmore, 1979). During the "Get ready" phase, which takes place the week before

TABLE 13.1 Effective and Ineffective Praise

Effective Praise	Ineffective Praise
1. Is delivered contingently.	1. Is delivered randomly or unsystematically.
2. Specifies the particulars of the accomplishment.	2. Is restricted to global positive reactions.
3. Shows spontaneity, variety, and other signs of credibility; suggests clear attention to the student's accomplishment.	3. Shows a bland uniformity that suggests a conditioned response made with minimal attention.
4. Rewards attainment of specified performance criteria (which can include effort criteria, however).	4. Rewards mere participation, without consideration of performance processes or outcomes.
5. Provides information to students about their competence or the value of their accomplishments.	5. Provides no information at all or gives students little information about their status.
6. Orients students toward better appreciation of their own task-related behavior and thinking about problem solving.	6. Orients students toward comparing themselves with others and thinking about competing.
7. Uses students' own prior accomplishments as the context for describing present accomplishments.	7. Uses the accomplishments of peers as the context for describing students' present accomplishments.
8. Is given in recognition of noteworthy effort or success at difficult (for this student) tasks.	8. Is given without regard to the effort expended or the meaning of the accomplishment.
9. Attributes success to effort and ability, implying that similar success can be expected in the future.	9. Attributes success to ability alone or to external factors such as luck or (easy) task difficulty.
10. Fosters endogenous attributions (students believe that they expend effort on the task because they enjoy the task and/or want to develop task-relevant skills).	10. Fosters exogenous attributions (students believe that they expend effort on the task for external reasons—to please the teacher, win a competition or reward, etc.).
11. Focuses students' attention on their own task-relevant behavior.	11. Focuses students' attention on the teacher as an external authority figure who is manipulating them.
12. Fosters appreciation of, and desirable attributions about, task-relevant behavior after the process is completed.	12. Intrudes into the ongoing process, distracting attention from task-relevant behavior.

Source: Brophy, 1981, pp. 5–32.

students arrive, the teacher plans how to organize the physical classroom environment so that the first days of school will be smooth and enjoyable for the new students.

During the "Get set" phase, which takes place during the first and second weeks of school, teachers test students to help them decide which students should work at which levels of the curriculum. Thus the main activities are diagnosis and placement. Teachers also set the classroom behavior structure during the "Get set" phase. The teachers are concerned with first impressions, establishing order, and clarifying the rules under which the class will operate. In the third, or "Go," phase, which continues for about two weeks after the "Get set" phase, the teacher debugs the systems of management and instruction before embarking on the rest of the year. During this time the teacher develops workable daily and weekly schedules and adjusts student groupings.

Many of the discipline problems that teachers face throughout the school year have their roots in the first week of school. Plan some of your best and most interesting activities for those crucial days. Establish your reputation as an interesting and well-prepared teacher. Learning students' names early is a valuable asset in classroom management.

SETTING RULES Students learn the extent to which rules are enforced very early in the year by testing, either deliberately or inadvertently, the teacher's limits and reactions in a host of situations. Once the pattern of rules is normalized and internalized, it is very difficult for the teacher to make dramatic shifts. Thus, very early on, the teacher starts to impose rules and expectations on students. Box 13.1 presents examples of classroom rules. A general rule statement covers a wide range of situations and uses terms that are not directly observable. General rules communicate basic expectations. Operational rules give observable specifics that concretize or make explicit aspects of the general rule (Purdom & Fardig, 1985). Conditions for movement within the building and within the rooms and general housekeeping rules are also spelled out at an early stage.

Classroom rules should be clearly explained. This requires that you spell out such mundane procedures as

1. Where on the paper students will write their names (across the top of the page, left-hand corner, right-hand corner)
2. Where and how students will hang their coats and retrieve them
3. How textbooks will be distributed
4. How and where worksheets will be collected
5. How you will deal with absences and tardiness
6. The procedure to be followed when entering and leaving the classroom

Some rules can create problems if you are not careful, if you rigidly apply them without exception or without considering extenuating circumstances, or if the implications of the rule are not carefully considered. Box 13.2 gives examples of rules that can cause trouble. Before stating a rule, think it through. If you find a rule unworkable, drop it.

BOX 13.1 Examples of Typical Classroom Rules

General Rule
Create a classroom setting in which you and other students can work and learn.

OPERATIONAL RULES

- Use a very low voice when speaking to others.
- Talk only to people close by.
- Move about the room only when it is related to your work; move quietly.
- Raise your hand when you need help; wait patiently.
- Take turns using materials and equipment.

General Rule
Maintain effective work habits.

OPERATIONAL RULES

- Be in your seat and prepared to work when class begins.
- Bring calculator and appropriate books to class.
- Begin work promptly.
- Keep working until all your work is finished.

General Rule
Submit homework when due and in acceptable form.

OPERATIONAL RULES

- Make written work neat and legible.
- Use correct English grammar, usage, punctuation, and spelling.
- Check your homework for accuracy.
- Type all homework assignments.

General Rule
Use effective expression and active listening skills during lessons and class discussions.

OPERATIONAL RULES

- Clear unneeded materials from your desktop.

- Raise your hand and get permission before speaking.
- Use standard English when speaking.
- Look at the person who is talking.
- Comment and ask questions about what the speaker is saying.
- Challenge and criticize ideas, not people.

General Rule
Keep the classroom clean and orderly.

OPERATIONAL RULES

- Return materials and equipment to their proper places.
- Clean the work area immediately after your work is completed.
- Replace instructional materials neatly in the resource center.
- Put your personal belongings in the proper place.
- Dispose of litter found in the classroom.
- Keep books, furniture, and walls clean.

General Rule
Treat each other with courtesy and respect.

OPERATIONAL RULES

- Keep your hands and feet to yourself.
- Ask permission before borrowing others' belongings.
- Speak politely; say "Please," "Thank you," and "Excuse me."
- Offer to share materials and equipment.
- Ask others to join in class activities.
- Ask others to express their ideas.
- Compliment others for their accomplishments.
- Make sure the preceding student has finished with the equipment before using it yourself.
- Wait until the teacher dismisses the class before leaving the room.

Source: Purdom & Fardig, 1985, pp. 9–10.

BOX 13.2 Examples of Classroom Rules That May Create Problems

- *RULE: Assignments are never accepted late.*

  If this were actually enforced, students who have acceptable reasons or valid excuses would not be able to submit their work late.

- *RULE: Directions will only be given one time.*

  Sometimes an extraneous noise or an interruption makes it necessary to repeat directions. Sometimes the teacher's explanation is confusing and needs restating.

- *RULE: Homework assignments must be submitted at the end of each class session.*

  Students might be tempted to complete homework assignments during the class session.

- *RULE: There will be total silence and absolutely no moving about the room unless the teacher gives permission.*

  This requires the teacher to continually decide who can get out of his or her seat and who can speak to others. With 20 or 30 students needing to use the restroom, get supplies, work with others, etc., the teacher will be swamped with requests and will spend an inordinate amount of time enforcing this one rule.

- *RULE: All work must be checked by the teacher before students can begin another activity.*

  Such a rule can create long waiting times for some students while the teacher is checking others' papers or lab work.

- *RULE: All term papers and reports must be submitted in official school report covers or school notebooks.*

  This kind of rule may well be seen by students as unnecessary and could be considered a whim of the teacher. It may cost students extra money or create trouble and therefore be resented or violated.

- *RULE: Only those doing the best classwork will be allowed to read magazines in the resource area.*

  There will likely be constant disagreement as to who does the "best work." Students will see this as unfair, and some will feel permanently disqualified because they work at slower rates.

Source: Purdom & Fardig, 1985, p. 11.

While some rules are stated explicitly, more often students infer the rules from the way a teacher responds to some student-initiated action or request: "You cannot sharpen your pencil during arithmetic"; "The library books in the back of the room can be used only if your exercises are all done"; "You go to the toilet at recess time"; "When I give permission to go to the toilet, I expect you to return immediately"; "Line up for recess now"; "Pick up those scraps off the floor."

The list of rules is long but, as the first few days pass, rules, regulations, and limits are both explicitly and implicitly set. Eventually they begin to operate invisibly, by force of habit; after a few weeks a word, a look, or a gesture by the teacher can bring the rules immediately into play.

CLASSROOM DISCIPLINE Classroom discipline is a major concern of veteran and beginning teachers alike. Establishing a routine for handling discipline with which you and your students feel comfortable is essential if learning is to proceed in the classroom. Misbehavior is not the result of a single moment, nor is it a personal affront to the teacher. Poor behavior often grows out of a pupil's restlessness during "dead spots" in a lesson. Poor teaching techniques or methods are often a cause of student misbehavior. Preventing discipline problems involves following a few simple rules:

1. Begin lessons immediately.
2. Be prepared; have materials that you need where you need them.
3. Have a few rules and keep them faithfully. (A preponderance of rules serves no purpose except confusion.)
4. Provide creative problems and worthwhile activities for students to do if they complete their regular lessons ahead of time.
5. Be aware of the individual differences among students and provide varied activities in your lessons.
6. Call out names *after* a question, not before.
7. If some type of punishment must be given for poor behavior, ensure that the punishment fits the crime.

A Feeling of Security

Feeling secure means knowing that you belong—that you fit in and always have a place. Security and stability are two sides of the same coin. Both depend upon establishing a routine within your classroom that you and your students can live with. For a student in the elementary grades (K through 8), a secure atmosphere involves having his or her own desk—a place that will always be there. For the student at any level, security involves knowing that the teacher will be there and will provide for instruction. Classrooms that have an unusually high number of substitute teachers usually have little security.

Being a teacher involves creating an atmosphere that allows for acceptance, develops confidence, and provides stability and security. Once the physical comfort and proper emotional climate of the classroom have been created, you can concentrate on developing the intellectual atmosphere of your classroom.

Making the Classroom an Intellectually Stimulating Environment

The classroom is an environment in which learning is supposed to take place. Since information comes through the senses, every facet of your classroom can foster learning. Three things in particular can help to make your classroom an intellectually stimulating place: learning centers, "touch and look" tables, and bulletin boards.

Learning Centers

A learning center is a place where students can take advantage of teacher-constructed learning activities. These learning activities are self-explanatory and are set up to let students experience them on their own. Most learning centers are designed around a display that extends the knowledge presented in a specific subject area. Any activity that does not need direct input or explanation by the teacher can be presented in such a center. The learning center is not necessarily confined to elementary school activities. Many interesting units in secondary school science, in social studies, and in literature can be designed for a learning center as challenging extensions of a semester's work.

Be wary of placing activities in the learning center that are little more than busywork for students and that you never correct. If you do not evaluate work and provide feedback, students will soon get the message that the learning center activities are unimportant and ignore them.

"Touch and Look" Tables

"Touch and look" tables differ from learning centers in that worksheets are not required. Although the tables provide learning experiences, the students are not required to do any written work. "Touch" tables contain items you want the students to handle, and "look" tables are just that—set up for looking only. You can use "touch" tables in the classroom for science experiments (make sure they are safe, and use no dangerous chemicals), a rock collection, supplementary books and artifacts for social studies, and glasses filled with different levels of water for experimentation with musical sounds. A "look" table could contain an active anthill or an aquarium.

"Touch and look" tables can provide an interesting introduction to a new unit in a particular content area. If the table is assembled four or five days before the unit is begun, students will have had the opportunity to become familiar with the items and will be interested in learning more about them.

Bulletin Boards

Much of what we learn is presented visually. Used properly, a bulletin board is a powerful aid for visual learning because it can be used to display pictures and terms that relate to a specific topic under study.

The bulletin board provides an excellent display area for colors and color words, as well as for sets depicting number concepts. If you are teaching in grades K to 3, one of your bulletin boards should be devoted to the alphabet. Colorful illustrations that depict activities to which your students can relate are excellent motivators for lessons in oral expression and creative writing. For students learning to read, flash cards and lettering need to be clear, horizontally aligned, and placed from left to right. Color contrast in lettering adds to legibility.

If you are teaching students in grade 4, 5, or 6, you will need a bulletin board for the cursive alphabet. If students are having a problem with letter formation, they can easily refer to the display. Since science and social studies are major subjects at this level, another board may be devoted to these areas. Pictures, vocabulary, and pertinent items can be arranged and pinned on the cork. You can also use a board for displaying students' work.

Bulletin boards also have a place in grades 7 through 12. Since teachers usually concentrate in a particular academic area at these grade levels, displays can center around important concepts in those areas. For example, if you require your students to learn definitions and formulas, they may be displayed on the bulletin board.

Your students might appreciate a bulletin board for news and/or events. You can use the board to post the many notices that form an integral part of life in junior and senior high schools.

Whatever the grade level, the following considerations are important to keep in mind when designing bulletin boards:

1. Construction paper fades very quickly in sunlight. To maintain the color, cover the paper with colored chalk or paint before putting it on the bulletin board. If possible, purchase fadeproof paper, which maintains its color for a long time.

2. Fluorescent colors are visually intrusive. Use them sparingly or tone them down with a darker shade of paper.

3. The larger and thicker the lettering, the easier it is to read.

4. Many good commercially made bulletin board materials are available.

Planning a Safe Classroom

Part of your job as a teacher will be to provide a safe environment for your students. That means you must be able to take charge in any situation and to remain calm. It also means that you must prepare your students to react calmly in an emergency. Most schools have established policies for dealing with emergencies. Before the school year begins, become familiar with your school's procedures for dealing with emergency situations such as fires or tornadoes. Here we will consider briefly some points relating to medical safety and general classroom safety.

Medical Safety

Assuring the medical safety of your students involves three major problem areas: medication, medical problems, and injury. Although you may never be faced with life-threatening situations, a basic knowledge of first aid is important. You should know if any of your students are on regular medication, such as insulin or Ritalin. Check each student's permanent record card to determine pertinent medical information. Student health records are filed in the school office or in the school clinic and are usually available to teachers upon request. If required information is not listed on the health card, ask parents to alert you to any possible medical problems that might occur.

At times during the school year your students may be taking prescribed medication. With primary grade students you may have to administer that medication. Do so only upon the *written request* of the parent or guardian, and then only if a school nurse is unavailable and the district policy allows you to do so. Keep and file the note and follow the directions scrupulously. Under no circumstances should you give a student any nonprescription drug (such as aspirin), even if the child assures you that it will be all right. If your school has a policy concerning the use of medication in school, be sure that every student knows the policy.

Another problem area in medical safety concerns allergic reactions. Although a plethora of allergens exist in the environment (dust, chocolate, plants, animals), few are life-threatening. Consider the possibility of allergies before you decide to bring an animal (such as a mouse or hamster) into your classroom. Consider also the peer pressure allergic students may encounter if a class pet must be removed because of their allergies. It is also helpful if you know which students are allergic to insect bites and which students can experience respiratory distress or asthma attacks brought on by allergies, stress, or anxiety.

Injuries are common in the school environment. Use your common sense in treating minor injuries. Most physical injuries require only simple medical attention. However, should a major problem arise, follow three simple rules (unless you have documented medical training). First, do not move the student. Second, attend to immediate dangers (for example, by applying pressure to stop bleeding), but give no medication or liquid. Third, never leave the injured student alone; send another student to the principal's office for help.

General Safety Guidelines for the Teacher

A safe classroom will be your responsibility when you become a teacher. In creating the physical arrangement of the class, ask yourself the following questions: Are scissors or other sharp objects easily accessible to students? What rules should I establish concerning the use of potentially dangerous materials? Are there any sharp edges on tables or bookcases that could cause injury? Have I placed any dangerous items on the "touch and look" tables? Is the general arrangement of my class conducive to safety? What procedures have I established to ensure student safety? May students wander? Are there specific rules for classroom movement? When and how many students leave their places? What rules will govern behavior when I am not in the classroom? Answering such questions will enable you to create a safe environment for your students.

Grouping for Instruction

The problem of finding an appropriate method of grouping children is one that all schools, especially larger ones, must face. It seems reasonable to assume that a teacher's effectiveness will partly depend on how the school is organized, that is, how children and teachers are allocated to classes. Educational practice has long been based on this belief. However, precise patterns of organization vary from school to school. In fact, one author has listed 32 ways of grouping children that he regards as "historically interesting and educationally promising" (Shane, 1960).

Vertical and Horizontal Grouping

School organization may be considered as vertical or as horizontal. Vertical organization refers to how children progress from the time they start school to the point at which they leave. In most school systems children progressively pass through a number of "grades" or "standards." Horizontal organization, on the other hand, refers to the division and grouping of pupils at any given point in the course of their vertical progression through the school. Horizontal class groups are often based on a consideration of the characteristics of children (for example, children with the same level of ability are sometimes grouped together). Other considerations that may be taken into account in horizontal organization are the curriculum and the qualifications of the teachers. The curriculum is the main consideration when, for example, children are assigned to classes on the basis of the subjects they take. This system is more likely to operate in high school than in elementary school. The qualifications of the teacher are the main consideration when different teachers are responsible for handling particular areas of study. Some methods of organization (for example, team teaching) combine considerations of children, curriculum, and teacher qualifications (Goodlad & Rehage, 1962).

Ability grouping, or tracking, is a common way of allocating students of a particular age or grade to classes on the basis of their abilities or achievements. Students are grouped together on the assumption that the more limited the range of ability or achievement of students in a class, the easier it will be to teach them and the better students will learn, since all should be able to proceed at more or less the same pace.

Problems with Ability Grouping

While the rationale appears attractive, there are several problems that arise when tracking is put into practice. The first relates to the criteria used in forming classes. A group may be fairly homogeneous with respect to one variable (for example, reading readiness) but be heterogeneous in other respects (for example, in social development). The use of one criterion may result in reducing the range of variability on one particular variable, but students may still remain diverse on other variables.

Second, the idea of total homogeneity is completely counter to what we know about human variability. The best you can hope to do by grouping is to reduce the amount of variation in a class. For example, in one study in which children were assigned to three groups on the basis of a composite achievement test score, it was estimated that the average variation on a number of other student characteristics within tracked classes was only 26 percent less than that in untracked classes (Borg, 1966). Since tracking seems to imply homogeneity, there is a danger that teachers may not appreciate the range of diversity that remains in the most perfectly graded system.

Third, decisions about a student's future career may be made too early. Once students are placed in an ability track, they tend to remain there throughout the year or even longer. This means that students whose rate of learning changes over time (for example, late bloomers) will be at a disadvantage and may find their course options limited at a later date.

Recent research on tracking has produced some negative findings. In considering the evidence, however, you need to remember that tracks can be set up in many different ways and in many different contexts (in elementary and in high schools, in schools in which most students come from a similar socioeconomic background, and in schools in which the backgrounds of students are very mixed) (Rosenbaum, 1984). Because this recent research takes little account of such differences, it is uncertain that the conclusions reached are valid for all schools that practice grouping. Bearing this in mind, we will summarize the main points that have emerged from research on tracking (Good & Marshall, 1984; Good & Stipeck, 1983; Hallinan, 1984; Mergendoller & Marchman, 1987; Persell, 1977; Rosenbaum, 1984; Slavin, 1987):

1. Teachers in low-ability classes can easily err by holding expectations that are too low for students and this may affect the way they treat students.

2. Teachers in such classes tend to provide less appropriate instruction and resource materials; they tend to pace instruction too slowly, to ignore or underemphasize the substantive aspects of tasks, and to provide instructional materials that are less interesting and less challenging.

3. Less task-related verbal interaction occurs between teachers and students in low-ability classes.

4. More time is spent "off task" for administrative and disciplinary reasons in low-ability classes.

5. Teachers spend less time in preparing lessons for such classes.

6. There is no consistent evidence that ability grouping does what it is designed to do—enhance academic achievement. It may in fact help students in the highest ability groups, but it can have adverse effects on the achievement level of students in average and particularly in low-ability groups.

7. Grouping can also have adverse effects on the self-esteem of students in the low-ability group.

8. While high-track students tend to have high social status in the school, low-track students tend to have low status and may attract the label of "slow learners."

Curriculum Planning

As a teacher you will be responsible for guiding the learning experiences of your students. The social dynamics of teaching combine with your individual orientation to make each classroom a unique social system. Although uniqueness allows you to be creative, it can cause problems if students in different classrooms do not share common levels of knowledge, content, and skill development. Students need to share such experiences so that they are adequately prepared for the next grade level and eventually for life when they leave school. Schools attempt to deal with this problem by developing a general plan to guide student learning. This plan and the programs designed to achieve the plan are referred to as the curriculum.

The Role of Planning in the Instructional Process

The curriculum of a school district articulates what the district wants students to learn, what skills they have to master, and what values, attitudes, and habits they should acquire. Ideally, the curriculum should be the result of the combined efforts of school personnel (principal and teachers), the district administration, and the district's governing board, which consult with parents and other members of the community. It should be set out in documents that describe what teachers are expected to teach and what students are expected to learn (National Association of Elementary School Principals, 1984).

Whatever curriculum orientation a school adopts, the learning activities that are developed to achieve the goals of the curriculum must be organized so that they relate to and complement each other. A school curriculum should identify what it wants students to learn (curriculum ends) and how activities will be organized to achieve what they want students to learn (curriculum means). An important issue for schools in determining curriculum means is to decide how students will be grouped in the school. Finally, a school has to try to determine the extent to which learning has taken place (evaluation).

CURRICULUM ENDS The first step in organizing the curriculum is to determine what students should know or be able to do when they have completed their educational experience. These outcomes are usually stated as the goals or objectives of the curriculum. Ideally, these goals should be set after considering the nature of the subject matter, the needs of the learner, the needs of society at large, the values and mores of the community, and the resources that are available to achieve the desired results (Tyler, 1949). It is also important to identify common curriculum elements that weave the curriculum areas together. Some of the common elements in the curriculum are concepts (for example, culture, growth, evaluation), generalizations (for example, scientific and cultural), skills (for example, reading and math) and values (for example, interests, attitudes, and values) (McNeill, 1977). The goals of the curriculum and its common elements provide the school with a sense of purpose, cohesion, and direction.

CURRICULUM MEANS Once the desired curriculum goals have been established, the means by which the goals will be attained can be addressed. In organizing appropriate learning activities and plans, two kinds of relationships, vertical and horizontal, need consideration. *Vertical organization* refers to how learning experiences build upon each other to achieve the desired results. *Horizontal organization* refers to how learning activities that occur concurrently relate to each other (Tyler, 1949).

Two concerns need attention in the vertical organization of the curriculum: continuity and sequence. Continuity refers to the reinforcement of common curriculum elements throughout the curriculum. For example, if reading for pleasure is a common theme throughout the curriculum, then students at various grade levels should have the opportunity to be involved in learning activities that reinforce such reading.

Curriculum sequence refers to the process of building and expanding upon elements in the curriculum. While continuity is concerned with reiterating certain curriculum elements, sequence focuses on ensuring that each new learning experience uses previous knowledge as the basis for the elaboration and progressive development of more complex skills, attitudes, or conceptualizations. For example, sequencing involves ensuring that the grade 2 reading program builds on what has been learned in grade 1. Again, the development of public speaking skills as part of the English curriculum might involve show-and-tell exercises in grade 4, oral presentation with note cards in grade 5, and a small-scale debate on a particular topic in grade 6.

The horizontal organization of learning experiences involves the integration of concurrent learning experiences. Whereas continuity and sequence are concerned with reinforcing and building upon previous knowledge, integration is concerned with relating different learning experiences that happen at the same time. For example, in grade 7, lessons in social studies topics might be integrated with essay writing in language arts.

CURRICULUM EVALUATION The third issue that must be addressed in organizing the curriculum is how to assess the extent to which students have achieved curriculum goals and objectives. Evaluation is needed throughout the curriculum to determine where adjustments are needed in instruction and whether students are adequately prepared to advance to the next unit or to a higher grade level.

Planning at the Classroom Level

As a teacher, you will be guided by the school district's curriculum guides and courses of study in selecting objectives and activities for your class. The plans you draw up for these activities should reflect the overall objectives of the school as well as the needs and abilities of the students in your particular class. Planning will be necessary at five levels:

1. Think about what you want students to achieve by the end of the year so they are ready to progress to the next grade level.
2. Break down the yearly plan into work for each term.
3. Plan units that focus on particular concepts, skills, and content.
4. Make weekly plans to help you prepare in advance for activities that might affect daily planning.
5. Construct daily lesson plans. These are the most specific of all your plans.

Table 13.2 gives more detail on planning at each of these five levels.

In thinking about planning, you need to distinguish between decisions that may affect you and your classroom but that you have little or no part in making, and decisions that you can make. Table 13.3 lists examples of both

TABLE 13.2 Planning Required at Various Levels of the Curriculum

	Planning Goals	Information Sources	Form of the Plan	Criteria for Judging Planning Effectiveness
Yearly planning	1. Establishing general content (fairly general and framed by district curriculum objectives). 2. Establishing basic curriculum sequence. 3. Ordering and reserving materials.	1. Students (general information about numbers and returning students). 2. Resource availability. 3. Curriculum guidelines (district objectives). 4. Experience with specific curriculum and materials.	1. General outline listing content and possible ideas in each subject area (spiral notebook used for each subject).	1. Comprehensiveness of plans. 2. Fit with own goals and district objectives.
Term planning	1. Detailing of content to be covered in next three months. 2. Establishing a weekly schedule for term that conforms to goals and emphases for the term.	1. Direct contact with students. 2. Time constraints set by school schedule. 3. Availability of aides.	1. Elaboration of outlines constructed for yearly planning. 2. A weekly schedule outline specifying activities and times.	1. Outlines— comprehensiveness, completeness, and specificity of elaborations. 2. Schedule— comprehensiveness, fit with goals for term, balance.
Unit planning	1. Developing a sequence of well-organized learning experiences. 2. Presenting comprehensive, integrated and meaningful content at an appropriate level.	1. Student abilities, interests, etc. 2. Materials, length of lessons, set-up time, demand, format. 3. District objectives. 4. Facilities available for activities.	1. Activity and content lists or outlines. 2. Sequenced activity lists. 3. Notes in plan book.	1. Organization, sequence balance, and flow of outlines. 2. Fit with yearly and term goals. 3. Fit with anticipated student interest and involvement.
Weekly planning	1. Laying out the week's activities within the framework of the weekly schedule. 2. Adjusting schedule for interruptions and special needs. 3. Maintaining continuity and regularity of activities.	1. Student performance in preceding days and weeks. 2. Scheduled school interruptions (e.g., assemblies, holidays). 3. Continued availability of materials, aides, and other resources.	1. Activity names and times entered into a plan book. 2. Day divided into four instructional blocks punctuated by A.M. recess, lunch, and P.M. recess.	1. Completeness of plans. 2. Degree to which weekly schedule has been followed. 3. Flexibility of plans to provide for special time constraints or interruptions. 4. Fit with goals.

TABLE 13.2 (*Continued*)

	Planning Goals	Information Sources	Form of the Plan	Criteria for Judging Planning Effectiveness
Daily planning	1. Setting up and arranging classroom for next day. 2. Specifying activity components not yet decided upon. 3. Adjusting daily schedule to allow for last-minute interruptions. 4. Preparing students for what to expect in the lesson.	1. Clarity of instructions in materials to be used. 2. Set-up time for activities. 3. Assessment of class "disposition" at start of day. 4. Continued interest, involvement, and enthusiasm.	1. Schedule for day written on the chalkboard and discussed with students. 2. Preparation and arrangement of materials and facilities in the room.	1. Completion of last-minute preparations and decisions about content, materials, etc. 2. Involvement, enthusiasm, and interest communicated by students.

Source: Adapted from Yinger, 1978, p. 21.

TABLE 13.3 Decisions Over Which Teachers Have Little Control and Those Over Which They Do Have Control

Little Control	Control
1. How many and which students should be in the class.	1. How the classroom space and furniture is arranged.
2. Which students should leave the class because they are not profiting from instruction.	2. How students should be grouped for instruction.
3. What extra instructional help students will get.	3. Who should talk, and under which circumstances.
4. How long the school day or class period should be.	4. To what degree and under what circumstances students should participate in classroom activities.
5. Whether teachers should have planning time in the daily schedule, and if so when.	5. Which tasks are most appropriate to get students to learn what is expected.
6. Which texts will be used for each subject.	6. Which instructional tools (textbooks, television, film, photographs, radio, etc.) are most productive in reaching classroom goals?
7. Which grades or subjects each teacher will teach.	
8. What the format and content of the report card should be.	
9. Which standardized tests will be given.	
10. Which subjects the teacher will teach.	

Source: Adapted from Cuban, 1984, p. 252.

kinds of decisions. In your planning, concentrate on those things over which you have direct control but be aware of how decisions over which you have little or no control can affect what you plan to do. For example, you might be fond of a particular classroom activity, but the size and nature of the classroom may preclude it.

The Context of Lesson Planning

Lesson planning will be a major concern for you as a beginning teacher. Before beginning, you must consider three important factors: the type of subject you are teaching, the scheduling of the subject, and the grouping you need for instruction.

Type of Subject Matter

All subjects are not taught in the same way. This diversity results from the structure of the various subject areas themselves. Different mental and physical skills are required to learn different subjects, and these skills can operate differently depending on whether students are learning content area subjects, skill subjects, fine arts subjects, or psychomotor skill subjects.

Content area subjects rely heavily upon reading and include the sciences, social studies, and some aspects of language (for example, literature).

These subjects present global knowledge, show cause and effect, and require the student to form generalizations about topics. Debate, speculation, and hypothesizing are popular strategies used in teaching most content area subjects, which rely heavily on prerequisite knowledge and skills such as reading and mathematics.

Skill subjects, on the other hand, require the student to know specific aspects or building blocks of a subject. Reading, mathematics, spelling, and grammar are skill subjects and depend heavily upon the mastery of prerequisite skills. For example, you would not teach the multiplication or division of fractions before students had mastered the multiplication and division of whole numbers. There is no room for ambivalence or opinion in a skill subject—answers are precise and unique; for example, 5 plus 2 equals 7, not 5, 6, or 8.

Fine arts subjects, such as music and crafts, require a blend of knowledge and psychomotor skills. Aesthetic growth is a major goal in the fine arts, along with acquiring a knowledge of the principles of art and music and of the skills necessary to create art and music. Two students might attain varying degrees of proficiency in their ability to create art and music, despite having the same amount of knowledge about the subject. Individual ability and creativity are important variables to consider when teaching in the fine arts areas.

Physical education and handwriting are the two subjects that are usually classified as psychomotor skill subjects. Success in both these areas depends heavily upon the student's motor coordination and physical skill; both also include a knowledge component. You cannot write or print an *a* unless you know what an *a* is; neither can you play field hockey unless you know the rules of the game. As in fine arts, there are great variations among individual students in their psychomotor abilities.

Scheduling

Scheduling is an important factor in lesson planning. What time of the day the lesson takes place and how long it lasts will determine what you plan for. The teacher's responsibility in scheduling varies depending upon grade level and school policy. In most elementary schools, the teacher is responsible for scheduling lessons specific to the grade level, while generally the school administration schedules special areas of the curriculum—physical education, art, library, and music. You will need to coordinate your teaching schedule around this master schedule. If your school has no "special" teachers, you may have to schedule all the subjects on your own. The principal creates high school schedules in advance. They must incorporate any required minimum standards set by the state for graduation.

Elementary-level schedules seldom if ever take into consideration the amount of time spent in transition between lessons. If your students have mathematics from 9:30 to 10:15 and gym from 10:15 to 11:30, some time must be lost from both subjects. Within the classroom itself, time can be lost when changing subjects. Time is a precious commodity in the classroom and can be used wisely and well or squandered. It is possible to lose as much as 30 minutes a day in transition time between lessons, adding up to two and a half hours

TABLE 13.4 Housekeeping Routines

Situation	Routine
Daily schedule	"You will find the schedule on the chalkboard. Notice that today you will refine your outline and begin writing the introduction to your short story."
Daily assignment	"Every day your math group's assignment will be listed on the right corner of this board." (Teacher points to the chalkboard.) "You are to do the problems in the order in which they are listed."
Beginning class	"When you enter the room, I expect you to go to your desk. You may talk quietly until the bell rings. If you need to sharpen your pencils or return materials, that is the appropriate time. Every day you will spend the first five minutes of class time on an independent activity. It will vary from day to day. It may be a challenge activity, a quiz, a reading task, or thought questions to prepare for a review session. You will find the directions for this assignment on the small board. I expect you to begin promptly when the bell rings."
Collecting papers/ distributing papers	"The last person in each row will collect papers for his/her row and place them in the correct section in this file box. I will grade the papers and return them to the file box. The following day your papers will be in your folders."
Accessibility of books, kits, other materials	"The books and kits you will need are along this shelf. Notice that there are labels taped to the shelf indicating the names of the books. After you use the books and other materials, return them to the correct spot for the next class."
Moving to books or other materials	"I will call one table of students at a time to get art materials. Table One will go first. In picking up your materials, begin nearest the window and move toward the front of the room."
Requesting teacher's help	"If you need my help during your classwork, list your name on the board. I will move around the room helping each person following the order of the list. If you are unable to do the work until I reach you, do one of your other pages, or read silently for those few minutes."
Checking papers	"After you finish a page of math, check your paper at the checking station. No more than two students should be using the teacher's guide at any one time. Return to your desk and correct any problems you missed. Place your corrected paper in your work folder. The folder will be collected at the end of class."

TABLE 13.4 (*Continued*)

Situation	Routine
Homework	"When the first bell rings, check your homework with the answers on the board. At the top of your paper, indicate the number of problems you did correctly. Place your paper in the tray as you leave the room at the end of class."
Purchasing lunch tickets	"Remember to buy your tickets before school. If you need to borrow a ticket, get a white slip from the file box."
Extra activities	"When you have completed and corrected your papers, place them in your folder. We will collect the folders at the end of the period. Then choose one of this week's extra activities listed on the chart. If you go to one of the learning centers, observe the rules for that center."
Restroom procedures	"During independent activities, one person may use the restroom at a time. Sign your name on the board by the door."
Water fountain	Fountain in room: "During independent activities, one person at a time may get a drink." Secondary: "You will need to get your drinks of water between classes."
Pencil sharpener	"Sharpen your pencils before the first bell rings. During independent activities, one person at a time may use the pencil sharpener."
Wastepaper basket	"Do not make a trip to the wastebasket for one piece of paper. Place your paper in the wastebasket as you leave the room."
Cleanup procedure	"It's almost time for you to stop your projects for today. . . ." A few minutes later: "Stop your work. Place your work in your packets. Section leaders collect packets from groups. Those students who are assigned clean-up tasks this week, clean your area." (Teacher points to chart containing jobs and students' names.)
Dismissal	"The bell signals us that class time is over. The teacher will give you permission to leave."
Beginning laboratory	"When you enter the lab, notice which light is on in the display board at the front of the room. If the green light is on you may go right to work in the lab, continuing where you left off the day before. If the yellow light is on, prepare for a laboratory demonstration. A red light indicates you should be seated in the classroom area, ready for a related theory lesson or quiz."

Source: Geyer, Slyck, Thigpen, & Wilson, 1985, pp. 25–27.

a week, or 90 hours a year! Using transitional activities between lessons will also minimize misbehavior problems. Another area where precious time can be lost is in general "housekeeping." Teachers who use time wisely provide their students with clear instructions regarding the daily schedule, the daily assignment, collecting papers, sharpening pencils, checking papers, handing in homework, and using the restroom. Table 13.4 (pages 330–331) presents common housekeeping situations and suggestions on how a teacher might handle each situation to maximize the use of time.

Although the secondary school schedule allows for the time lost in changing classes, additional time is often lost in "settling down." High school students are skilled in using time to their own advantage. Teachers may begin the class by writing a challenging problem on the board and requiring the answer before the period is over; this helps students to settle down immediately.

Time allotments for particular subjects are usually specified in terms of a weekly total of minutes per subject. Art and physical education are not taught daily because of the structure of the subjects themselves. Depending upon school policies, music may also fall into this category. In the primary grades, social studies and science are secondary subjects, which means that they are taught only two or three days a week.

Reading and mathematics present a difficult challenge for many elementary school students. If you are able to schedule these subjects early in the day, the students generally will be able to concentrate better and may learn the concepts more easily. Remember, the more difficult the concept to be learned, the greater the need for physical and mental "freshness."

Within-Class Grouping

In light of the research evidence we considered relating to the homogeneous grouping (or tracking) of students in the school, such a method of organization would not seem to have many advantages. This appears to be particularly true at the elementary level. On the other hand, at the high school level, and particularly in the upper grades, some system of grouping is necessary to allow students to follow different curricular options. Whether a school tracks will be a matter of school policy, and as an individual teacher, you may not be able to influence that policy. Within your own classroom, however, you will be able to decide whether you are going to teach your class as a unit or break it into groups for instruction. While the practice of within-class grouping is not very common in schools generally (Doyle & Carter, 1987), it is common in the early elementary grades, particularly for teaching reading and to a lesser extent for teaching mathematics.

The basic rationale for such grouping is similar to the rationale for tracking: by having students of similar levels of achievement or ability working together, the teacher should be in a better position to adapt to individual differences. It is also sometimes argued that such grouping can be a force to motivate children "to move up." However, if you decide to break your class into groups, you should bear the following points in mind:

1. You should aim to reduce the range of achievement in each group in the specific skills being taught, not in general ability or overall achievement.

2. Student placements should be reassessed frequently and students should be moved to another group if their achievement warrants it.

3. Your level and pace of instruction for each group should be adapted to the level of readiness and learning rates of pupils.

4. You should keep the number of groups in your class small so that you will be able to give enough attention to each group (Slavin, 1987).

Although teaching a small group may help you to meet the specific instructional needs of your students, within-class grouping can present problems. It requires you to divide your attention between the group and the rest of the class. In this situation, there is likely to be a lot of student talk and low engagement in tasks among the students who are not receiving your immediate attention (Doyle & Carter, 1987). An important aspect of your role as a teacher involves planning stimulating activities for the children who are not part of the group receiving instruction. Your professional courses will give you many ideas on how to handle this situation. Suffice it to say here that a steady supply of busywork in the form of worksheets is not the answer.

Small groups lend themselves to discussion-type lessons in the intermediate and advanced grades. As long as the students are sufficiently knowledgeable about the subject, they will be able to participate in discussions profitably. If you group students carefully (buddies are not good discussion partners) and set good discussion standards—such as keeping to the topic, letting everyone have a turn speaking, and speaking softly—group discussions will be valuable experiences for your students. An appointed or elected leader should be made responsible for controlling the flow of the discussion and for reminding group members of the above discussion standards.

Music is another area where grouping will occur. You will need to group students according to their voices, basing the groups on the students' natural range of tones. These groups will be assigned special seating areas in the class to promote listening and singing skills. Teachers often group students to work on projects in art or in other content areas. Before you use the grouping strategy extensively, consider the following three points:

1. Project groups composed of more than three students often degenerate into one worker and three or four socializers.

2. Grouping students requires that a teacher have good control of students and be able to attend to what is going on in all the groups.

3. Group work requires that students have good independent work and study skills. Students in the early elementary grades are not well equipped to work in project groups but do well in art and discussion groupings.

Research indicates that many of the disadvantages associated with tracking in the school can also apply to within-class grouping (Brophy & Good, 1970; Hiebert, 1983). There is evidence, for example, that teachers interact differently with groups of high- and low-ability pupils within the same classroom. Students of high ability are provided with more reinforcement and are encouraged to participate in classroom activities. The teacher spends more time "on-task" with high-ability groups, allowing fewer interruptions; gives them more time to answer questions; and asks questions that are more analytic and demanding. In some studies teachers spent more time with high-ability students and worked with them at times when children would presumably be more alert, such as in the early part of the morning. Further, when teachers treat pupils in different groups in different ways, pupils become aware of their teachers' perceptions of them and are influenced by these perceptions (Weinstein, 1986). In fact, even quite young children recognize the "grading" inherent in membership in, for example, the "robin" and "bluebird" reading groups.

If you feel you need to group on the basis of achievement or ability, you should be aware of the implicit "grading" messages you may convey to students. Negative perceptions should be minimized by making groups flexible and temporary. Thus, a student may belong to one group for reading and another for mathematics. If you need to have small groups to accomplish some task, consider bases other than achievement or ability for grouping.

Whether you group or not, there is always a danger that you will direct your teaching and explanations to some students more than to others and that your questions will also be directed toward those same favored students. It is important to make a special effort to ensure that you attend to all students and to their progress. Benjamin Bloom has suggested a number of points to help you do this:

1. Try to find something positive and encouraging in each student's response.
2. Find ways of engaging all students actively in the learning process.
3. Get feedback from a representative group of students on how they are learning, not from the same set of students all the time.
4. Find ways of supplying additional clarification and illustrations for students who need additional help (Bloom, 1984).

CONCLUSION

Planning for your classroom and for teaching will help to make your room as conducive to learning as possible. The climate or mood you create through your planning should serve to enhance student learning and social interactions; its absence will lead to needless chaos and conditions that make learning difficult.

While lesson planning is an essential part of teaching, too great a reliance on plans may have the unfortunate side effects of narrowing the concept of teaching in two ways. First, it can give the impression that teaching is primarily a scientific, orderly, deliberate process, and that the teacher is first and foremost a rational decision maker, some sort of behavioral engineer. Second, too much reliance on lesson planning can easily lead to equating teaching with instruction. In fact, instruction is only one facet of teaching.

Students' attitudes, feelings, self-concepts, and motivation to learn can all be influenced by what the teacher does in subtle and often unconscious ways. To be insensitive to these factors is to miss important components of the teaching-learning process.

These considerations should not be taken to imply that preactive planning is useless. Quite the contrary. Your planning will underpin and guide your spontaneous and seemingly intuitive reactions to classroom events. Proper planning will permit you to successfully "play it by ear" in front of a very tough audience—your class.

QUESTIONS AND ACTIVITIES

1. To answer the following questions, reflect back upon your elementary and secondary school experiences.
   a. Describe a visually attractive classroom and one that you felt was not. What were the key ingredients that distinguished these two classrooms?
   b. Describe a physically comfortable classroom and one that you felt was not. What were the key ingredients that distinguished these two classrooms?
   c. What arrangement of furniture did you find most appealing during your elementary grades? During your high school years? Why? How much control did your teachers have over how the classroom furniture was arranged? Explain.
   d. Give an example of how one of your teachers used furniture arrangement to help him or her with control. How successful was this technique in your opinion?
   e. Describe a classroom in which you felt particularly accepted and one where you did not. What were the classroom experiences?
   f. Describe a classroom in which you felt particularly confident and one where you did not. What were the key ingredients that distinguished these two classroom experiences?
   g. Describe a stable and an unstable classroom. What were the key ingredients that distinguished these two classroom experiences?
   h. Describe a secure classroom and one in which you felt insecure. What were the key ingredients that distinguished these two classroom experiences?
   i. Describe a learning center that you experienced. Why does it stand out in your mind?
   j. Did you ever experience a classroom that was not safe? If so, describe the characteristics that made it so.
   k. Describe how vertical and horizontal grouping was handled in your elementary school; in your high school.
2. If you are observing in an elementary or secondary school, keep track of the extent to which the teacher interacts with students in the T-zone as opposed to those sitting outside it. When is the teacher effective in his or her use of praise? When is he or she ineffective?

3. How would you design your ideal classroom?
4. What rules for your classroom would you establish at the beginning of the year? Justify each rule.
5. What personal touches do you plan to use to make your classroom a comfortable place?
6. If you are observing in a classroom, ask the teacher or principal for the *school system's curriculum guide.* What are the system's curriculum ends for the grade level or subject area you are observing? What are the curriculum means? Are continuity and sequence mentioned? If so, in what way? How is evaluation handled?

CHAPTER 14

Classroom Instruction

This chapter treats topics related to the development of a proper learning environment and the planning and delivery of effective instruction.

- There are key ingredients that must be considered when structuring lessons.
- Research on effective teaching has identified a number of factors that contribute to effective instruction and improved learning.
- Motivation is a key element in successful instruction.
- Instructional clarity has an extremely powerful effect on student achievement.
- There are at least seven different types of lessons that focus on different aspects of learning. The type of lesson is dependent on the topic and on students' state of knowledge, skills, and personal preferences and style.

Although teaching is a much broader activity than instruction, the latter will occupy a central position in your work. Much of what you do by way of preparation for class will be to ensure that your classroom is organized as an efficient learning environment. Research has shown that when classroom activities run smoothly, time is not lost in dealing with discipline and nonlearning activities. When most of your time is allocated to achieving academic objectives, lessons are paced, and teaching presentations are clear, you will have the optimal conditions for learning.

In order to create an effective learning environment in the classroom, you must perform a variety of tasks. You will have to decide what the objectives of your lesson will be, how you will set about achieving those objectives, how you will arouse your students' interest in what you plan to do, and how you will assess whether or not your work has been successful. You must choose materials and consider how to present the lesson in ways that will maximally involve every student. Questions to consider in deciding on presentations are: How do I involve "problem" students? How will I use the blackboard or audiovisual aids? How will I channel discussion? How will I group students? What homework will I assign? How will I reinforce correct responses? You must also try to anticipate student errors and consider ways of correcting them constructively. All these activities need to be informed by a familiarity with the subject matter or skills you are going to teach as well as by a knowledge of all your students individually and of the "chemistry" of the class as a whole.

In this chapter, we will deal with a number of topics that should help you in the delivery of instruction. The topics are lesson structure and practice, mastery learning, motivation, and types of lessons.

Lesson Structure and Practice

Teachers follow no single lesson structure. However, there are certain ingredients in most lessons that you should consider in preparing your class and in teaching. Some educators have incorporated these ingredients into lesson designs, and they have listed the steps they regard as necessary to ensure that learning occurs (Berliner, 1979, 1983; Bloom, 1976; Borko & Niles, 1987; Brophy, 1986; Brophy & Good, 1986; Doyle & Carter, 1987; Gagné & Dick, 1983; Hunter, 1979; Pintrich, Cross, Kozma, & McKeachie, 1986; Rosenshine & Stevens, 1986; Shulman, 1986). We present 12 considerations based on this work that you should attend to in preparing lessons and in your actual teaching.

Preparing for Class

There are a number of points that you should bear in mind before class begins. First, you should be aware of, and sensitive to, the cognitive and affective characteristics of your students. General ability and accumulated effects of prior learning are the two variables that are most powerfully related to school achievement. Second, have high performance expectations for your students. Third, believe in your own ability to be effective and have confidence in the belief that your teaching can affect student learning. Fourth, organize your classroom as an efficient, task-oriented learning environment. This means, among other things, that the physical environment of your classroom should be well prepared, that your lesson plan has also been well prepared and that it is geared to the needs of your class, and that you have established clear rules and procedures for the classroom (preferably at the beginning of the year).

Capturing Students' Attention and Interest

Begin class in a way that will capture your students' attention and interests and prepare them for the kind of learning that is going to take place. You want to give students a reason for beginning the lesson. You may do this by reciting a poem, showing them a picture, having a brief discussion, or simply asking some questions. Once students' attention has been aroused, you must maintain it. Motivating students throughout a lesson is an important teaching skill.

Review earlier work to ensure that students have the prerequisite skills needed to learn the new concepts or skills you are about to teach. You may want to review and check the previous day's work, asking questions about it, and reteaching if necessary. "Today, we are going to begin division with two-digit divisors. Try this example with a one-digit divisor to show that you are ready to tackle a new skill."

Reviewing earlier work also helps students to use what they already know. "Class, I know that last year you learned about compound predicates. Take a minute to think about the definition of a compound predicate and then I'll call on some of you to give your thoughts."

Finally, it is helpful to give your students a clear definition and overview of what has to be learned. Tell students the objectives of the lesson and/or describe the lesson's contents. You might provide what have been called "advance organizers," which cover general concepts, propositions, and rules that will be dealt with in the lesson and provide a structure for the knowledge that will be covered (Ausubel, 1960; Luiten, Ames, & Ackerson, 1980).

Defining Objectives

The objectives of your lesson arise out of the subject matter or skills you have chosen to cover; they are an essential part of your plan (written or unwritten). However, you have to think of more than the content or skill area you want to present to your class. By the end of the class period, what would you like your students to be able to do, think about, or feel relative to the content area? You must have an explicit idea of how you want students to be changed as a result of your planned instruction.

Some educators say that the teacher should state objectives in terms of observable student behavior (Tyler, 1949). For some kinds of skills and content, this can be a reasonable and helpful approach, particularly in the selection of materials and learning experiences. However, not all the objectives of education can be readily observed in student behavior, and in such cases you will have to be content with more general and intangible objectives. Nonetheless, it is always good to have some objectives in mind, even if they are not stated in terms of observable student behavior.

Because of their importance in instruction, the topic of objectives has received a lot of attention. In one classification, three categories of objectives have been described (Bloom, Engelhart, Furst, Hill, & Krathwohl, 1956):

1. *Cognitive objectives* concentrate on intellectual and informational outcomes. (For example, the student will recite the preamble to the Constitution correctly.)
2. *Affective objectives* stress attitudes and values. (For example, the student will appreciate the music of the *Nutcracker* suite.)
3. *Psychomotor objectives* deal with the development of physical and motor skills. (For example, the student will do a somersault correctly two out of three times.)

Each objective—whether cognitive, affective, or psychomotor—has two components: a *content* component, which refers to the concept or skill to be learned, and a *behavioral* component, which describes an observable student behavior. Writing an objective in behavioral terms enables the teacher to specify the "point-at-able" behaviors that indicate learning has taken place. For example, "to understand" or "to know about" are very vague terms. How does a teacher know that a student "understands" a concept? Where possible, it is better to specify an appropriate action verb, an observable action that the student will perform or a product that he or she will produce that permits you to say, "Yes, the student does understand."

The objectives of a lesson spell out the specific changes in student behavior you wish to bring about. The processes that effect this behavioral change occur within the cognitive, affective, or psychomotor domain. On a difficulty continuum, the cognitive, affective, and psychomotor processes range from the simple to the complex. The cognitive processes are (1) knowledge, (2) comprehension, (3) application, (4) analysis, (5) synthesis, and (6) evaluation. The affective processes are (1) receiving, (2) responding, (3) valuing, (4) organizing, and (5) characterizing by value system. Psychomotor processes include (1) perception, (2) set, (3) guided response, (4) mechanism, and (5) complex overt response. (Consult Bloom et al, 1956, and Krathwohl, Bloom, & Masia, 1964, for a further description of each of these taxonomic levels.) Table 14.1 lists specific terms, actions, or verbs that may help you to define "point-at-able" behaviors in the cognitive and affective domains.

A simple strategy for writing objectives is to identify the content or skills you want the pupil to acquire and to describe the behavior that indicates the concept has been learned (see Table 14.2).

You may have in your objectives one umbrella statement that includes a series of subordinate objectives or a list of two or three very specific objectives that involve only a single skill. The students must be aware of exactly what is expected of them in the lesson. "Class, by the end of the day you will be able to identify prepositions and their antecedents" is an umbrella objective and specifies the major skill students will be expected to perform. "You

TABLE 14.1 Terms to Use in Determining Components in the Cognitive and Affective Domains

COGNITIVE PROCESSES
(Simple) ←──→ (Complex)

1.0 Knowledge	2.0 Comprehension	3.0 Application	4.0 Analysis	5.0 Synthesis	6.0 Evaluation
Count	Associate	Apply	Analyze	Arrange	Appraise
Define	Classify	Calculate	Detect	Combine	Assess
Draw	Compare	Classify	Explain	Construct	Critique
Identify	Compute	Complete	Group	Create	Determine
Indicate	Contrast	Construct	Infer	Design	Evaluate
List	Describe	Demonstrate	Order	Develop	Grade
Name	Differentiate	Employ	Relate	Formulate	Judge
Point	Discuss	Examine	Separate	Generalize	Measure
Quote	Distinguish	Illustrate	Summarize	Integrate	Rank
Read	Estimate	Practice	Transform	Organize	Recommend
Recite	Extrapolate	Relate		Plan	Select
Recall	Interpret	Solve		Prepare	Test
Recognize	Interpolate	Use		Prescribe	
Record	Predict	Utilize		Produce	
Repeat	Translate			Propose	
State				Specify	
Tabulate					
Trace					
Write					

AFFECTIVE PROCESSES
(Simple) ←──→ (Complex)

1.0 Receiving	2.0 Responding	3.0 Valuing	4.0 Organizing	5.0 Characterizing by Value System
Appreciate	Accept responsibility for	Actively participate	Classify	Change behavior
Be alert to	Acquaint self with	Assume responsibility for	Develop a plan for	Develop code of behavior or philosophy of life
Be conscious of	Be willing to comply with	Be committed to	Form judgments as to responsibility	Judge problems or issues
Be sensitive to	Enjoy	Be convinced of	Systematize	Revise judgments
Perceive	Find pleasure in	Believe in the importance of	Weigh alternatives	Show mature attitude
Show awareness of	Obey	Desire to develop		
Tolerate		Be devoted to idea, ideals		
		Have faith in		
		Rely upon		
		Subscribe to		

TABLE 14.2 Writing Objectives

Content or Skills	Behavior or Action	Objective
Correct spelling of 15 words	Write	The student will write the correct spelling for 15 words.
Causes of the Civil War	Recite	The student will recite four causes of the Civil War.
The water cycle	Draw a picture	The student will draw a picture that explains the water cycle.
The multiplication tables from 2 to 9	Write the answers to 10 problems correctly in five minutes	The student will write the answers to 10 multiplication problems correctly in five minutes.

will write the letter *a* correctly three times" identifies a simple skill that the student is expected to be able to perform.

Choosing the Type of Lesson

Having decided the objectives of your lesson, there are several instructional strategies you can use in presenting the lesson. We will describe seven main types of lessons later in this chapter (each type has different steps, which are described in Boxes 14.2 through 14.8). The type you select will depend on the nature of the particular topic you wish to teach, the students' state of knowledge and skills relating to that topic, as well as your personal preferences and style.

Choosing Materials

Once the objectives of your lesson are clear, the selection of materials to be used in the lesson needs careful consideration. The material selected is one of the chief means you will have for arousing and maintaining student interest and involvement. Because different lessons require different materials, you should list the items you are going to need and make sure they are prepared and available for the lesson.

Choosing Procedure

The *procedure* of your lesson flows directly from your objectives. What do you have to do to ensure that learning takes place? The procedures you use are the "recipe" of your lesson, the steps you will use to achieve your objectives.

In deciding on procedure, you have to take into account the information needed by the students to reach the objectives and the means by which success will be established. *Information* refers to the content of the lesson (what will be learned). How you convey that content to students (the means) will depend on the type of lesson you deem appropriate, and on your general teaching style. One approach is for the teacher to supply all or most of the required information to the students (this is called the *behavior control model*). Another approach is to have students and teacher explore different sources of information together (this is called the *discovery learning model*). In yet another approach, students are asked to search out for themselves which source of input is most appropriate for their purposes (this is called the *rational model*). The last model requires the least teacher direction and input.

Focusing on Academic Activities

Most time during the class period should be allocated to instruction and learning activities. These activities should run smoothly, and time should not be lost in dealing with discipline and other nonlearning activities. To achieve and maintain these conditions, you will have to continuously monitor what is going on in the classroom, including seat work. Of course, it is not sufficient to provide time only for academic activities; students must be actually engaged and involved in school tasks during this time. "Time on-task" is a necessary condition for learning. How you organize your classroom can affect student engagement.

Research shows that in elementary schools, the amount of students' time on-task is higher when students are being taught by teachers than when they are working on their own (Brophy & Good, 1986). Student engagement was found to be higher in teacher-led small groups than when the whole class was taught as a unit; it was lowest when pupils were making long presentations of their work (Gump, 1969).

Providing Instructional Clarity

Ensuring instructional clarity is another important activity in teaching. Your presentation throughout the class period should be clear, well structured, and well sequenced. Instructional clarity involves three teacher behaviors:

1. Giving correct and appropriate information
2. Giving clear and precise directions
3. Asking clear and appropriate questions

These behaviors can have a powerful positive effect on student achievement (Land, 1985; Rosenshine & Furst, 1973). How do you ensure that instructional clarity is evident in your lessons? You must know your subject matter and be able to present it in the proper sequence and free of inaccuracy. Besides the importance of correct information to student learning, your credibility as a teacher is on the line during every lesson and is a good reason for careful preparation of your material.

Good delivery of information is as important as the ring of authority. Teaching is one of the professions in which the message given is often obscured by the instrument piping the tune.

Modeling

You can ensure that your students are learning correctly by modeling or demonstrating (both visually and verbally) the critical elements involved (students themselves can be effective models or demonstrators). For example, when multiplication of three-digit numbers is being presented for the first time (or the fifth time, as the case may be!), the teacher should present each step and explain the reason for what is being done. In this way, students should learn the process and be able to repeat it with any given three-digit example. It is important in new learning that the model be teacher-controlled to ensure proper initial learning. It is easier to teach a new skill or concept than to reteach an incorrectly learned one.

Providing Guided Practice

Guided practice is an activity in which students attempt to demonstrate the behaviors or produce the products that are the objectives of your lesson. It is an opportunity to appraise performance and offer guidance to students. Not unexpectedly, errors will occur during guided practice. On the basis of your objectives, you will make instant decisions about remediation or acceleration. For example, let's suppose that you have just taught your students to diagram sentences. They have ten sentences to do before the lesson is complete. Even though your students are working individually, you need to walk around and check that each student is practicing the skill correctly. Tomorrow will be too late to find out that there was a common problem.

Providing Independent Practice

Students should have the opportunity of independently practicing the skills they are required to learn. Before allowing students do this, make sure that there are no serious errors in their understanding or performance. If students are having trouble in guided practice, they should not proceed to independent practice. At the primary level (grades 1 through 3), independent practice often occurs as seat work, when the teacher is busy with another mathematics or reading group. At the intermediate, middle, and secondary levels, independent practice may be assigned as homework. Independent practice with basic skills should continue until students achieve a high rate of success (90 to 100 percent correct).

Some skills need to be practiced until they become automatic. This is because the human attention span is limited. In the case of reading, for example, students who cannot automatically decode letters will focus their energy and attention on decoding when it will be needed for higher-order reading activities (for example, comprehension). Obviously, a student who has not automated decoding skills will have difficulty with higher-order skills.

Independent practice provides an opportunity for the teacher to individualize and provide special help for slower students and more challenging

Guided practice allows students to demonstrate the behaviors you are attempting to teach. It provides an opportunity for appraising performance and offering guidance.

activities for gifted students. Generally speaking, however, independent practice is successful because it is preceded by careful, guided practice.

Evaluation

During the lesson, check that students understand the task and that they are acquiring the essential information, content, or skills needed to attain an objective. Evaluation is an integral part of every lesson and flows directly from the objectives you set for the lesson. There are many procedures for obtaining information necessary for evaluation. You can ask a question of the entire class: "How many of you think this is an interrogative sentence"? Or you can call on one student: "Tell us which of these sentences is declarative." You can also check for understanding by eliciting private responses from students; a written quiz or a "walk-about," during which you ask individual students questions, will serve this purpose. Sometimes, you will use more formal and extended methods of evaluation, such as a paper-and-pencil test.

Checking for understanding will provide you with feedback about where students are in relation to an objective, whether remediation is needed, whether the lesson is moving too slowly and the students are bored, or whether a vital component of the process has been missed. In particular, it is important that you should be able to reorganize and deal with student difficulty or failure. In the light of the information yielded by your evaluation, you in turn will provide feedback to students by identifying correct and incorrect responses. This identification should not include personal criticism

Students must have time for independent practice of new skills

of the student. On the basis of your evaluation, you may have to change your approach and lesson plan.

Concluding the Lesson

At the conclusion of a lesson, summarize by reviewing the main ideas, concepts, or facts that you have covered. (Similar summaries at a number of points throughout the lesson can also be helpful.) The summary should help students to better organize their learning. It is also helpful to assess students' understanding and performance at the end of a lesson.

Weekly and monthly reviews serve to enhance retention and the transfer of knowledge and skills to other situations.

Questioning

Questioning is a critical part of teaching and can be used for a variety of purposes. Teachers can use oral questioning to

1. Introduce a lesson, relate the new lesson to what was learned before, and provide a context for the lesson.
2. Clarify points within the lesson, and bring up points omitted or given insufficient attention.
3. Check students, expand their thinking, and develop new insights into the subject.
4. Reinforce what an individual student or the group has learned.
5. Summarize or review the lesson, as a check both on the students' comprehension and on the teacher's instruction.
6. Help students solve problems by going through a series of questions leading to a solution (Silverman & Shearer, 1985).

You need to consider several issues in posing oral questions to students. First, you must consider whether students understand what you are asking and whether they have sufficient time to respond. Many teachers feel anxious when silence follows a request for a student's response to a question. The lack of student response could in part be due to a lack of clarity in the question or because the student needs time to think of the response.

A second issue you need to consider in questioning is whom to ask and when. Shy students who do not volunteer to respond need to be encouraged to speak in public and to develop their communication skills. Boisterous students who blurt out answers off the top of their heads need to be coached about thinking their responses through. You must also avoid repeatedly calling on the same students because you know they will respond in the proper manner; this may boost your ego, but it may also create a false impression that all students are "getting the answer."

A third issue teachers must consider is whether questions and answers should be oral or written or some combination of both. You can ask a more complex question in written form than you can orally. Often students can give more complete answers in writing than they can orally. Because most of the give and take of daily classroom interaction involves oral questions and oral answers, these questions must be clear and concise.

A fourth concern in framing questions deals with types of answers teachers want from students. Questions should often be posed that tap more than simple recall of facts. There is a danger that questions will not extend the student beyond simply recalling information. Thus, you will have to give thought to questions that will stimulate students to think critically. If you use Bloom et al.'s taxonomic levels, you will have seven levels of cognitive ability that you need to consider when questioning students.

Mastery Learning

Like other individualized approaches to learning, mastery learning operates on a number of basic principles (Torshen, 1977):

1. A course or subject content is broken into a sequence of smaller learning units.

2. Specific *objectives* are stated for each unit; these are the outcomes or goals that students are expected to reach as a result of the program. They should be stated in terms of specific concepts, knowledge, and skills that the student must learn.

3. The teacher administers a test (oral, written, or performance-based) geared to the objectives of the unit, and determines the level of performance all students will be expected to achieve on it *(minimum pass levels).*

4. Students are assessed before the unit begins to determine their starting point, that is, their present level of skills and knowledge *(preassessment).*

5. A course of *instruction* is designed to help the student proceed from his or her initial status (as determined in the preassessment) to mastery of the objectives (as specified in the minimum pass levels).

6. Diagnostic or formative assessment is carried out during the instructional program to see how well the program is working for each student. The information derived from this assessment is used to pace each student's learning and, if necessary, to modify the instruction.

7. The information derived from the assessment leads to *prescription:* what to do. If a student needs further instruction, the prescription is *remediation,* which might involve different textbooks, workbooks, audiovisual materials, or individual or small-group tutoring. The prescription of *relocation* arises when it is clear that the student is not able to cope with the instruction that is being given. This might involve specifying a more appropriate objective or moving to another topic. *Enrichment* is prescribed for a student who is performing successfully and who, it is judged, would benefit from additional learning activities at about the same level of difficulty as the main instructional tasks. In dealing with learning difficulties, it is often useful to have small groups of students meet to review their test results and to help one another overcome difficulties identified in the tests. This practice can lead to a kind of "peer tutoring," which can be very beneficial to students.

8. The final step in the mastery learning sequence is *postassessment,* which measures the degree to which each student has reached the outcomes specified in the objectives. Students who fail to master crucial concepts, skills, or knowledge may reject some of the instructional program or may be provided with an alternative experience designed to achieve the same objectives (see Figure 14.1; also see Figure 11.3 on page 275).

A key objective of the mastery approach is to match instruction to the achievements of students and to ensure, through routine diagnostic assessment, that they are not overwhelmed. If a student does not have the prerequisite concepts, skills, and knowledge to comprehend an instructional sequence, it is unlikely that he or she will meet the objectives of the learning unit and more advanced learning tasks will present ever-increasing problems.

FIGURE 14.1 Components of the Mastery Structure

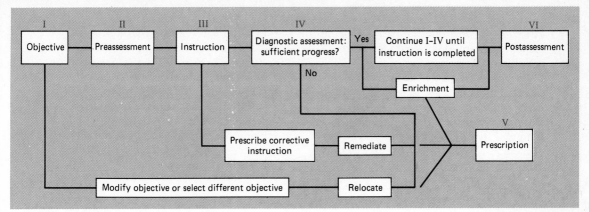

Source: Torshen,
1977, p. 45.

Motivation

How are you going to motivate students to do what is expected of them in a lesson, to become excited about the topic being presented, to really want to learn? Here we will consider six strategies that should keep students motivated.

1. Level of Concern You should try to keep the anxiety level of students at a moderate level. This might involve raising the level of concern from apathy—"Write this down because it will be on the test next week"—or lowering it from a level of high anxiety—"Don't worry about your spelling; this is just a first draft."

2. Positive Tone A positive, pleasant tone is generally a more powerful motivator for students than a negative one. While each can motivate, and each may be necessary on some occasions as a motivational tool, the upbeat approach has a more lasting positive effect. A statement such as "Let's all work on this together so we can show the rest of the school what a great group you are" is based on positive motivation; as opposed to a statement like "You will need to really buckle down and do a better job than that."

3. Interest By using examples and materials that have personal meaning for students or are novel or vivid, you can capture the students' interest. An example of a personal appeal is: "You visited the state legislature yesterday. What things impressed you the most?" Novelty would be introduced if you arrived in a costume out of Dickens to teach *David Copperfield.* Slides, pictures, and colored chalk add vividness to your lesson.

4. Reward for Learning Students frequently are motivated because they expect an *extrinsic* or tangible reward (for example, points for reading a book, or good grades). We hope students will be motivated to learn simply because it pleases them. When this happens, we say that motivation is *intrinsic* (for example, a student decides to pursue a topic independently at the library.)

5. Success So that students will be successful, you should set tasks at an appropriate level of difficulty. For example, if students are able to correctly complete nine out of ten math problems involving a particular concept, they will be "successful" and will be ready to move on to the next concept.

6. *Knowledge of Results* Students are better motivated to continue to learn when they are told how well they are doing in specific and immediate terms: "Your opening sentence was especially good because you selected words that describe your interest" or "You need to use more descriptive words in your explanation."

Types of Lessons

Since you will be learning more about lesson planning in your professional courses, this section will deal only with general descriptions of the basic types of lessons and their structure. A sample lesson of each type is presented with each description. Categorizing lessons by type aids in establishing a focus and in determining the procedure of the lesson. Lessons may be categorized as (1) developmental, (2) discussion, (3) practice, (4) review, (5) directed study, (6) independent study, and (7) evaluation.

Developmental Lessons

A developmental lesson is used to present new material to students. In this kind of lesson, the teacher explains new concepts and imparts new information. Box 14.1 shows six behaviors to consider when introducing a new concept. Vocabulary development is an important part of the lesson. Although students can have an input into this kind of lesson, the teacher is the prime presenter. A lecture, an experiment, a film, or a filmstrip can be a part of the lesson. Because it is used in every subject area, the developmental lesson is an essential strategy that you will use in your teaching career. An example of a developmental lesson is given in Box 14.2.

Discussion Lessons

A discussion lesson is one you will use in content subjects. It is useful in reinforcing learning through the sharing of ideas (see Box 14.3). Discussion

BOX 14.2 The Developmental Lesson

Subject: Variables: What They Are and How to Use Them

Type: Development

Objectives: Through this lesson the student will
1. Use a letter as a placeholder in simple number sentences.
2. Write a variable expression for a given word in a sentence.
3. Evaluate a simple expression involving a variable.

Procedure:

A. Approach:
1. Show an empty box to the students.
2. What could we put into this box? (Brief discussion.)

B. Presentation:
1. We can call this box a "variable." A variable is a holder for the value you put into it. (Using marbles or noodles, or any item, show various values in the variable.)
2. Any letter can signify the variable. We use a variable as an unknown value in a word sentence.
3. Three more than another number is twenty:

$$x + 3 = 20$$

Seven and another number is 4:

$$7 + a = 4$$

(Use various examples until the students can give back their own sentences and open equations.)

4. If we know the value of the variable, we can solve an open equation:

$$3x + 4 =$$

What is the answer if

$$x = 2 ?$$
$$x = 1 ?$$
$$x = -1 ?$$
$$x = 10 ?$$

(Use as many examples as the students need to master the concept. Use various letters.)

C. Check-up (to identify those students who have not understood the concept). Use a transparency.
1. Define a variable.
2. Write an equation for this number sentence:

    A certain number minus 4 is 30.

3. Evaluate these variable equations using the following values:

$$a = 2, x = 4, y = 3, b = 0.$$

a) $2a + x =$ _____
b) $(y + a) - b + (x + y) =$ _____
c) $x =$ _____
d) $3b + 4 =$ _____

Materials:
1. A small box with a cover
2. Marbles or small items for variables
3. Transparency for the check-up
4. Overhead projector

---

lessons require a substantial amount of student knowledge and good control on the part of the teacher. They can take the form of full-group discussions, in which the entire class participates, or small-group discussions of three to five students. Or you may use student presenters in either round-table or panel discussions. Remember to set clear standards for speaking and listening in a discussion.

Practice Lessons

A practice lesson, as the name implies, involves practice. It usually follows a developmental lesson in which the skill to be practiced has already been

BOX 14.3 The Discussion Lesson

Subject: Contributions of the
               Immigrants

Type: Discussion

Objectives: Through this lesson the
               students will
               1. Follow good discussion
                  standards.
               2. Share information about the
                  contributions of the
                  immigrants.
               3. Contribute pertinent
                  information to the
                  discussion.

Procedure:
A. Approach: Play the song "Coming to
   America" by Neil Diamond.
B. Presentation:
   1. Set discussion standards.
   2. Appoint group leaders.
   3. Divide into small groups for
      discussion.
   4. Hand out list of initiating questions.
   5. Summary of the discussion to the full
      class by group leaders.
   6. Evaluation of standards.
C. Conclusion: Class forms an acrostic for
   the word AMERICA.

explained and taught. Its purposes are to strengthen the learning outcomes
that have already been established (see Box 14.4) and to facilitate the application of skills and concepts learned (in other words, to give the student the
ability to use the new knowledge correctly). Skill areas such as math, grammar,
physical education, and handwriting require practice lessons. A practice lesson is *specific* if it concentrates on only one concept or skill (for example, the
correct use of the words *to, too,* and *two*). A practice lesson is *mixed* if it
combines many skills in the same lesson (such as the addition, subtraction,
multiplication, and division of fractions). Although many practice lessons are
based on worksheets, some activities do not require them.

BOX 14.4 The Practice Lesson

Subject: Using an Encyclopedia, Atlas,
               and Almanac

Type: Practice

Objectives: Through this lesson the
               students will
               1. Acquire greater ability in
                  the use of an index and a
                  table of contents.
               2. Use reference books to find
                  needed information.
               3. Find the answers to a list of
                  questions.

Procedure:
A. Approach: Discuss the importance of
   resource materials.

B. Presentation:
   1. Set standards for the activity.
   2. Distribute the list of questions to the
      students, i.e.:

   What movie won the Oscar for best
   picture in 1964?

   What is the latitude and longitude of
   Paris, France?

   What is the chemical formula for
   table salt?

   3. Students work from resource books.
   4. Correct the questions orally.
   5. Evaluate standards.
C. Conclusion: Students use an
   encyclopedia to answer a question of
   fact.

Review Lessons

Wise teachers use a review lesson before they formally evaluate students' knowledge of a subject area. In a review lesson, the concepts to be tested are presented in the form of a game or high-interest activity. The natural challenge and competition generated by these activities motivate the students to review large amounts of material effectively (see Box 14.5).

Directed-Study Lessons

The directed-study lesson allows students to learn by reading specific material in a content area (see Box 14.6). Questions can then be presented in the form of a worksheet or they may be given orally by the teacher; again, students may choose their own questions by drawing them from a "jackpot" or "fishbowl."

Independent-Study Lessons

An independent-study lesson provides students with practice in doing research on their own (see Box 14.7). Such a lesson may also include new areas in which students will need to develop and apply their critical and logical thinking skills.

Evaluation Lessons

An evaluation lesson is an entire lesson period devoted to testing, assessing, or measuring the mastery level of students' learning (see Box 14.8). Both informal and formal evaluation are essential parts of the learning process (these two types of evaluation are discussed in detail in later chapters);

BOX 14.5 The Review Lesson

Subject: Switzerland

Type: Review

Objectives: Through this lesson the students will
1. Identify names and terms dealing with Switzerland.
2. Locate designated places on a map of Switzerland.
3. Reinforce learned information about this European country.

Procedure:
A. Approach: Let's take a trip today to a lovely European country—Switzerland.
B. Presentation:
   1. Set standards for review.
   2. Present activities:
      a. Fill in places on the map.
      b. Complete the acrostic.
      c. Answer the questions from the "Q-Box."
   3. Evaluate standards.
C. Conclusion: Summarize in one sentence all you know about Switzerland.

you need to know what progress your students have made in a particular subject area and what additional learning is required to meet your objectives for students. Evaluation lessons are part of every subject area of the curriculum.

The next chapter tells you how to construct a classroom test to use during an evaluation lesson.

BOX 14.6 The Directed-Study Lesson

Subject: The digestive system (pp. 71–82)

Type: Directed study

Objectives: Through this lesson the students will
1. Explain the process of digestion.
2. List the organs of the digestive system and describe the function of each organ.
3. Listen carefully to questions presented orally.
4. Read the correct answer for each question.

Procedure:
A. Approach: Why does the body need food? (Brief discussion.)
B. Presentation:
   1. Read the assigned pages.
   2. Set standards for the activity.
   3. Teacher gives questions.
   4. First student to find the correct answer raises hand, gives page, and reads the correct answer.
   5. Evaluate standards.
C. Written evaluation: List the organs of the digestive system and the function of each.

BOX 14.7 The Independent-Study Lesson

Subject: Contributions of the Immigrants (pp. 210–228)

Type: Independent study

Objectives: Through this lesson the pupils will
1. Organize ideas to support the statement "The immigrants brought great contributions to their new homeland."
2. Increase their ability to take notes in outline form.
3. Collect information to support their beliefs about the immigrants.

Procedure:
A. Approach: Discuss the following scenario:

   You are a space traveler who has just landed on the planet Xetron in the Beta galaxy. How would you feel?

B. Presentation:
   1. Set standards for independent study.
   2. Read text pages silently.
   3. Take notes in outline form.
   4. Evaluate standards.
C. Conclusion: In 25 words or less, explain how you feel about America.

BOX 14.8 The Evaluation Lesson

Subject:	Unit 12—Spelling
Type:	Evaluation
Objective:	Through this lesson the students will spell at least 80% of the dictated words correctly.

Procedure:

A. Approach: Today is the day that you get to flex your spelling muscles and measure your progress over the last week. Ready?

B. Presentation:
1. Students set up spelling papers.
2. Teacher dictates words; students write them.
3. Exchange spelling papers.
4. Correct the test.
5. Teacher collects corrected tests for "final check."

C. Conclusion: Teacher discusses words commonly misspelled on the papers.

CONCLUSION

In this chapter, we provided a framework for your tasks as an instructor. We described a general structure for lessons, ranging from arousing students' attention and interest to lesson conclusion. We stressed the need to specify objectives, to chose appropriate learning activities (which must be organized and sequenced), and to evaluate. Experienced teachers often seem to pay relatively little attention to objectives and evaluation, stressing instead the importance of subject matter content and the selection of appropriate activities. This may be because objectives are usually implied in materials and curriculum guides, while experience allows them to use subtle means for deciding who is learning satisfactorily and who is not (Borko & Niles, 1987). While many skills will become more or less automatic to you as you gain experience, we suggest that in your early days teaching you pay attention to all the steps we have outlined.

In later sections in the chapter we considered the topics of motivation and instructional clarity and suggested ways in which you might deal with these issues in your lessons. Finally, we outlined seven different types of lessons and the occasions on which you might choose one rather than another.

Our recommendations should be used as guides to practice, not as simple prescriptions to be followed in detail. Teaching and learning—the procedures, skills, and strategies involved—and the contexts in which they take place are too complex to allow for simple presumptions (Pintrich, Cross, Kozma, & McKeachie, 1986). However, the framework outlined in this chapter provides you with general schemata to help you to interact effectively with the unique students in your unique classroom.

QUESTIONS AND ACTIVITIES

1. Choose a topic that you would like to teach to a class. Design a *developmental* lesson plan for a grade level of your choosing that incorporates the following:

     a. Behavioral objectives
     b. Materials
     c. Procedure
     d. Evaluation
     e. Conclusion

2. Review the list of personal strengths you constructed for Chapter 8, "The Career of Teaching." What personal strengths can you utilize to help develop strategies to motivate students? What strategies would you like to try?

3. Besides testing, what other ways can a teacher evaluate student performance?

4. Design a discussion lesson plan on a topic you are interested in. Write several questions that tap different levels of Bloom et al.'s taxonomy for the lesson and identify which level(s) the questions address.

5. While observing a classroom, list the ten elements of lesson structure that you see as they unfold. For the elements you didn't observe directly, ask the teacher if they are in his or her lesson plan.

6. For the following questions, reflect back on your elementary and secondary school experiences.
     a. Describe the techniques a teacher used that you felt were particularly effective in motivating his or her class. Do they agree with the categories described in this chapter under motivation? Why or why not?
     b. Describe a teacher who you felt was particularly successful in ensuring instructional clarity. Did he or she use the techniques described in the chapter? How? If not, what techniques did he or she employ?

CHAPTER 15

Teacher Evaluation of Students

This chapter considers the formal and informal aspects of student evaluation by teachers. Teacher expectations for students are discussed, and an outline of how to construct a classroom test is prescribed.

- Formal evaluations tend to be objective and center on what the student gives for an answer. Informal evaluation is an integral part of teaching and, as such, is more subjective, focusing on what the student "gives off": clues from the student's expression and behavior.
- Grading—a form of reward or punishment—is a motivator which socializes students into the reward structure of the school.
- Formal evaluations are generally private, with the exception of classroom questioning. Informal evaluations are very public. Your public evaluative statements should be carefully considered.
- Classroom evaluation is carried out to diagnose student weaknesses, improve learning while it is in progress, and grade students.
- Teachers cannot avoid forming expectations for students. However, you should be aware of the potentially powerful effect your expectations can have on your behavior and the subsequent behavior of students.
- The construction of a classroom test involves careful thought, planning, and preparation. There are steps you can follow that will help you build better classroom tests.
- Record keeping is an important administrative function of all teachers, a function that must be carried out with care and dispatch.

A large part of the teacher's work involves the formal evaluation of students' work. Evaluation activities include, among other tasks, checking students' homework and recording completed homework in a mark book. Planning for a quiz or test will include a review of the material to be covered and the writing of suitable questions. The questions will generally need to be typed and duplicated or written on the board before class begins. Once administered, the test must be corrected and graded, which often involves writing extensive comments on the paper. Finally, marks must be entered into the mark book. Essays, book reports, and projects must be read and commented on. Several times a year you will have to prepare report cards. The routine clerical work involved in this can be done only after all students' work across a range of subject areas has been evaluated and graded and their noncognitive characteristics (such as effort, conduct, and citizenship) appraised. Make no mistake—formal evaluation will engage a large portion of your time.

In this chapter we will consider the formal and informal aspects of teacher evaluation. Since evaluation is sometimes public and at other times private, we will consider these aspects also. Following this, we will discuss three functions of classroom evaluation: diagnostic, formative, and summative. An interesting aspect of student evaluation that has received a lot of attention in recent years concerns teachers' expectations for students. Expectations and how the expectancy process operates in the classroom are considered in another section of the chapter. This is followed by an outline of the steps to be taken in the construction of a classroom test. Finally, we shall consider what you have to do to keep proper records.

Formal and Informal Evaluation

Formal evaluations take many forms including written tests, exams, oral recitations, homework, and term or book reports. Formal evaluations usually result in the assignment of a letter grade or percentage mark to the product or the performance of the student being evaluated. Generally, formal evaluations tend to be objective; that is, for the most part, or at least consciously, teachers evaluate only what the student actually does—what he or she "gives" for an answer. In informal evaluations, on the other hand, teachers evaluate what the student "gives off," such as attitudes, dispositional attributes, facial expressions, and body language.

Informal evaluations are much more subjective and generally take place during interactive teaching; they are spontaneous, unplanned, and inferential. This type of assessment is endemic to the teaching situation; teachers are continually evaluating student cues. Informal evaluation does not result in grades; rather, the results are embedded in how the teacher reacts to the student: "That's very good, Claire," or "Bill, sit down, you're not prepared today."

Grading as Reward or Sanction

Formal evaluations by the teacher—tests, quizzes, daily questioning—are directed not only at assessing what and how well students are learning but also at motivating them to work hard on the prescribed curriculum. In addition to establishing and enforcing rules of conduct and school routine, teachers at the primary level are expected to impress upon students that grades and marks are rewards and sanctions for academic achievement (Dreeben, 1967), thus laying the foundations for grades and marks to take on the overtones of reward or punishment. Teachers in the upper grades assume that students have been socialized to view grades as a form of reward and punishment, and lean heavily on this incentive to motivate students.

In the early years of schooling, and to some extent in later ones, grades or marks need not take the form of a letter (for example, A, B, C, D, or F) or of a percentage (for example, 92, 63, or 75). A star, the comment "very good" penciled on a paper, hanging a paper on the blackboard, or merely putting a check on a paper are all used by teachers to reward good work. Verbal comments to the student in front of the class, the poor work sent home to be signed, the extra work, or the tearing up of a paper are also forms of informal grading and sanctioning and may have a powerful effect on the student's motivation and attitude toward schoolwork.

Reacting to Students

When a teacher is spoken to by a pupil, or receives a piece of writing, he may reply to it, or comment on it, or assess it; and his habitual choice amongst these three will influence his pupils' future uses of language; no one readily embarks upon personal reminiscence when he expects to receive in reply a cool assessment of his delivery. But the teacher's influence is still more persuasive; a snub or bored acceptance, or an interested or enthusiastic reply all have immediate as well as long-term effects. When a criticism is made it can vary both in intensity and in the degree to which it is publicly made (Barnes, 1973, p. 62).

Another aspect of establishing a reward system of marks and grades is that it encourages student to learn to work independently. "Children and pupils are early socialized into the concept of knowledge as private property. They are encouraged to work as isolated individuals with their arms round their work" (Bernstein, 1971, p. 213). Students learn that others expect independent work of them and that the work should reach a certain standard. Students also learn that they must be self-reliant, that they must accept personal responsibility for their work, and that there are situations when they can legitimately expect help from others (Dreeben, 1968).

Learning the Game

The eagerness with which young students raise their hands when the teacher asks a question symbolizes the educated person's desire to display his knowledge in a socially approved manner. The child with his hand up (even when he has only raised it to please the teacher) has begun to understand the social pleasure that can come from knowing, and the social discomfort that may accompany ignorance (Jackson, 1969, p. 144).

Students are quick to realize that grading is a form of reward and punishment. Further, they learn that top grades are a relatively scarce commodity and that every student is in competition with other students for positive feedback. Some students thrive on this competition; some shrink from it; some pay no attention to it, since good grades come easy for them; others become resigned to losing; and still others see marks as irrelevant and follow a different drummer entirely. Often, in later grades, the sanctioning power of marks is mediated by the peer subculture. In some schools, and in some classes within a school, high achievement status is valued; in others, in which there is peer pressure against "grinds," high grades have little value.

Public and Private Evaluation

There are interesting differences between formal and informal teacher evaluations. Formal evaluations are generally private, and informal evaluations tend to be much more public. In general, formal evaluations are designed to obtain samples of students' unassisted work—what they can do without the aid of parents or peers. The results of these formal evaluations are generally returned to the individual and not made public. There are, however, notable exceptions to this rule. For example, very good test papers are sometimes publicly displayed on a bulletin board; conversely, students who fail a test may be publicly told to bring it home and have it signed by their parents. Achievement levels become common knowledge when students compare their grades. However, most teachers treat student grades and test results as confidential.

Informal evaluations, on the other hand, are powerful and take on overtones of reward or punishment precisely because the classroom is a public place. While students are often expected to work alone among a crowd, to look on knowledge and skills as private possessions, they are forced by the very nature of classroom interaction to reveal at least some of what they know and do not know. Further, students are to some extent also forced to reveal—although they might try to hide it—how they feel about certain issues.

Through teachers' questions and students' recitations, students are put on the spot publicly. They must answer, and the answer is immediately judged by both the teacher and other students (Moumoto, Gregory, & Butler, 1973). Thus, the extent and correctness of the pupil's knowledge is publicly evaluated daily by the teacher and openly communicated to the class (Barnes, 1973). In fact, sometimes the teacher will ask the class to correct a student's performance.

> ### *Informal Evaluation*
>
> Sometimes the class as a whole is invited to participate in the evaluation of a student's work, as when the teacher asks, "Who can correct Billy?" or "How many believe that Shirley read the poem with a bit of expression?" At other times the evaluation occurs without any urging from the teacher, as when an egregious error elicits laughter or an outstanding performance wins spontaneous praise (Jackson, 1968, p. 20).

Class participation can heighten a student's anxiety since his or her performance is subject to teacher and peer criticism (Henry, 1957). This poses a dilemma for some students. One way to reduce anxiety is to seek the teacher's approval by conforming to classroom rules and answering the teacher's questions. In doing this, of course, the student is leaving himself or herself open to evaluation by teachers and by peers. The alternative can be equally anxiety-producing. Not to participate, cooperate, pay attention, or abide by classroom rules may generate a teacher and/or peer response that is equally threatening to the student. Thus, the student is open to criticism if he or she does not participate actively, but is also open to negative evaluation of his or her performance if he or she does participate.

In the primary years, grades and informal evaluations are slowly but inextricably linked to a sense of self-worth and self-respect for some students. Jules Henry looked at the ways in which teachers evaluated pupil prose and poetry and noted that the student's self-esteem was often intensely caught up in what he or she had produced. Because of this ego involvement, teacher and/or peer criticism or praise was often very telling (Henry, 1957).

When you become a teacher you will have a moral obligation to be aware of the possible consequences of your public evaluative statements. Such statements are unavoidable products of the classroom situation, and you should be conscious of what they may be communicating to a student and his or her peers. Evaluation information should be communicated constructively to students; otherwise, you run the risk of damaging the image some students have of their work and of their academic potential.

The Functions of Classroom Evaluation

There are three main types of classroom evaluation: diagnostic, formative, and summative (Bloom, Madaus, & Hastings, 1981). All three can take a variety of forms, ranging from informal teacher impressions to more formal tests and examinations.

Diagnostic Evaluation

You can expect considerable variation among your students on a whole range of learning characteristics—in what they have already learned (at home and at school), in their interest in further learning, and in their learning styles. You must take this variation into account when you are planning your instructional program. Diagnostic evaluation is carried out to help you do this.

Individual
conferencing is one
way to conduct
diagnostic evaluation
in your classroom.

More specifically, the purpose of diagnostic evaluation is to obtain information on the strengths, special talents, deficiencies, or special problems of your students. It may be carried out before you begin instruction or while instruction is underway. Evaluation carried out prior to instruction attempts to establish the extent to which students are "ready" for your program, that is, the extent to which they possess behaviors or skills judged to be necessary to study a course or unit. On the basis of this information, you can decide the most appropriate starting place in the instructional sequence for each individual student. For example, if you find that a student has already mastered the objectives you have planned for a course, the student can be advised to elect another course, or, if this is not possible (as it might not be in an elementary school), you can provide an enrichment program of more advanced work for the student. If, on the other hand, students lack the competencies or knowledge needed to start a course, you will have to help them acquire these.

Diagnostic evaluation carried out while instruction is under way is designed to determine the underlying causes of learning deficiencies that occur during a program or course. The causes for such deficiencies may lie in the fact that goals, instructional methods, or materials are inappropriate for the student. If difficulties persist and these causes can be ruled out, you will then need to investigate the possible role of physical, emotional, cultural, or environmental causes. The assistance of a psychologist or counselor can be helpful at this stage.

Formative Evaluation

Errors in learning can occur at any stage of a course or program. It is important that such errors be detected when they occur or soon afterward. If they pass unnoticed by the teacher, they can have long-term and serious effects, since a student who misses out on some important knowledge or skill will most likely have difficulty in later learning tasks.

The purpose of formative evaluation is to determine the degree of mastery of a given learning task and to identify the parts of a task that have not been learned. It is carried out at frequent intervals during a course or program and deals with only a section or portion of the course or program, not with the whole. However, it deals with those sections in a detailed and exhaustive fashion. For example, while a general evaluation at the end of a course (summative evaluation) might have as its major purpose to determine the degree to which a student can translate word problems into quantitative expressions in order to solve them, formative evaluation would seek to determine at an earlier stage what precise type of errors a student made in problem solving and whether, for example, a deficiency in solving word problems was due to vocabulary inadequacies or to an inability to deal with specific mathematical operations.

Formative evaluation does not stop when student deficiencies or problems are identified. The purpose of formative evaluation is to provide teachers and students with feedback on what each student has learned and still needs to learn. It is important to provide this feedback as soon as possible after the errors or difficulties occur, so that later learning is not impeded by the student's failure to master certain skills or acquire certain knowledge.

On the basis of evaluation that identifies problems or errors, the teacher prescribes corrective procedures to help the student to learn important points he or she has missed. This can be done in a number of different ways, depending on the students' problems and the resources that are available to the teacher. They include additional instructional time, supplementary materials, students helping each other, and assistance from an aide or tutor.

Summative Evaluation

Summative evaluation is used at the end of a course, program, or term. Because it is carried out when instruction and learning are complete, it is very often too late for the teacher to take any action relating to a student's poor performance. The information derived from summative evaluation can be used for a variety of purposes: for grading, certification, general evaluation of progress, and reporting to parents and administrators. Note that the information derived from summative evaluation often benefits an external audience or decision maker, while the information from formative evaluation is solely for the use of teachers and students.

Teachers' Expectations

The role of teachers' expectations for student achievement and how these can affect student behavior and achievement levels has received a lot of attention in studies that have tried to explain why some students perform poorly in school. Thinking about teachers' expectations was influenced by the work of Robert Merton, who used the theorem of William Isaac Thomas and Dorothy Thomas (1932): "If men define situations as real, they are real in their consequences" (Thomas & Thomas, 1932, p. 572). Merton points out that it is a normal feature of life for people to ascribe meanings to situations. These ascribed meanings, in addition to "objective" features of a situation, affect the subsequent behavior of an individual. It seems obvious that a great deal of behavior is, in fact, governed by beliefs or expectations of what will follow if we take one line of action rather than another. However, Merton makes the point that even when the initial perception of a situation is false, that perception can still influence future events. That is, a false perception can evoke behavior that in time can have the effect of making it come true. This is known as a self-fulfilling prophecy. An example of a self-fulfilling prophecy is the case in which customers lose confidence in their bank because they think it has gone broke; afraid of losing their money, they withdraw it from the bank, with the result that the bank, though financially sound, is left without money and so collapses.

In the 1960s, a book by Rosenthal and Jacobson entitled *Pygmalion in the classroom* captured the attention and fancy of many, spreading the "faith" about the power of the self-fulfilling prophecy. The book described a study that attempted to test the proposition that teachers' expectations can influence the intellectual ability and achievements of their students. Rosenthal and Jacobson concluded that they found evidence to support this hypothesis. Students who had been described to teachers as "late bloomers" (though they were in fact no different from other students) tended to do better on tests of ability and achievement after a period of time in which teachers "expected" them to do well. This was called the "Pygmalion effect" for the Greek mythological character Pygmalion who fell in love with an ivory statue he had made; Aphrodite granted life to the statue and Pygmalion married it. Although critiques of Rosenthal and Jacobson's study showed it to be seriously flawed (Thorndike, 1968; Snow, 1969), they did not undermine its widespread appeal; many studies of teacher expectations were carried out to determine whether, in fact, teacher's expectations affect students' achievements and, if they do, how the expectancy mechanism operates.

The Expectation Mechanism

On the basis of research on teachers' expectations, four basic steps in the expectancy process have been posited (Brophy & Good, 1974; Good & Brophy, 1973; Kellaghan, Madaus, & Airasian, 1982). First, the teacher *expects* specific behavior and achievement from individual students. Second, these expectations affect the behavior of teachers toward their students. Third, the student "reads" the teacher's behavior. Fourth, if teacher "treatment" is consistent and the student accepts it, it will shape the student's behavior and achievement. The result is that high-expectation students will be led toward high achievement and low-expectation students toward low achievement.

THE FORMATION OF TEACHER EXPECTATIONS When you begin to teach, you will form opinions of each of your students. Myriad verbal and nonverbal cues will contribute to these expectations. For example, you will form expectations about students' achievements on the basis of your formal and informal evaluations of students' knowledge, reasoning, language proficiency, and performance on standardized tests.

Although most research studies of teacher expectations have focused on expectations for cognitive performance, teachers also form expectations for the noncognitive behavior of their students. These relate to the "moral" or deportment dimension of behavior and involve several components. As a teacher, you will informally evaluate each student for cooperativeness, attentiveness, ability to get along with others, neatness, and general decorum. You will also assess each student on traits such as leadership, popularity, cheerfulness, self-confidence, curiosity, and comfort in school. While we can neatly characterize expectations and behavior as being cognitive or moral in nature, your ultimate expectation for a student will be based on a fusion of these two dimensions. Both influence each other in the ultimate formulation of expectations.

Expectations apparently are formed quickly. Consider the evaluations made by three first-grade teachers, shown in Box 15.1. While these provide insight about what influences teachers' expectations, they are of particular interest in that they were made *after only three days of school, before* teachers had seen the academic records of the students. Given that teachers form judgments about students at an early point in the school year, we can ask what cues or stimuli they use in forming their expectations.

There are two main sources of information about students that influence teacher expectations: firsthand information obtained in face-to-face interactions with the student and secondhand information obtained from other sources (Rist, 1977). It should be pointed out that the teacher's evaluation of both types of information is complex and, to a large degree, idiosyncratic; that is, different teachers will weigh cues in different ways, depending on their background, experience, and personality. Ray Rist, for example, has argued that the characteristics of the "ideal" or "success" prototype are rooted in the teacher's own social or subcultural background. Further, the more the subculture or background of the teacher is congruent with that of the child, the more likely the teacher is to have a high expectation for the child.

Teachers' perceptions are influenced by firsthand information gained through the give-and-take of the classroom. Teachers are constantly evaluating their students in every class, during every lesson. The cues they use are often fleeting—a student's momentary facial expression, tone of voice, shift in posture, or hand-raising. At other times they are less transient—a student's response to a question or written work. Philip Jackson has called these face-to-face cues the "language of the classroom" (Jackson, 1968).

Firsthand information, while important in and of itself, is often interpreted in the light of other evaluations of the student made on the basis of Rist's secondhand sources. These sources are numerous, but the literature indicates that prior information about the student's family, gender, socioeconomic status, and race are of particular importance.

TEACHERS' TREATMENT OF STUDENTS VARIES ACCORDING TO EXPECTATION If teachers form expectations about their students, the question arises: How are these expectations communicated to students? Teachers tend to interact differently with high- and low-expectancy students. Differential treatment of students can be overt or it can be very subtle. Re-

Mary: Very, very babyish. She sits and daydreams, looks at other children and does anything she can to entertain herself. Anything except settle down and do her work. . . . This child I think will be a problem all year.

Nancy: Comes from a family in which all the other children have had many, many problems all during their school lives. . . . She will be one of the best of this particular family but she will be a slow learner.

Pete: All the other children in his family have excelled. . . . But I'm afraid Pete may possibly be a disappointment because I don't think he's going to excel. I think he's going to be a good student.

Robert: Robert is very slow, tries to a certain extent. I'm afraid he's going to have to work real hard to get out of the first grade.

Jean: Tall, pretty little girl. Well behaved, seems to have such lovely manners. Very interested. I had her little cousin, who was one of my favorite pupils, so I'm expecting Jean to do real well this year.

Source: Brophy & Good, 1974, pp. 25–26.

searchers have identified 12 of the more common ways in which teachers treat high- and low-expectation students (see Box 15.2). Further, teacher expectations about an individual student are communicated not only to that student, but, because they are public, to all the other students in the class. The other students in turn can amplify teacher expectations in their language and behavior toward individual students (Rist, 1970).

It is very important to note that not all teachers treat low-achieving students in self-defeating ways (Good & Brophy, 1977). Further, treating high- and low-expectation students in different ways is not necessarily inappropriate or damaging. Some teachers spend considerable time and effort in providing low-expectation students with positive encouragement and experiences. The issue is not only whether high- and low-expectation students are treated differently but whether "the teacher's behaviors toward students [are] based on informed educational judgments about individual students, or . . . [are] grounded in certain biases regarding race, sex, cleanliness, student demeanor, quality of English usage or participation in class" (Eaker, 1984, p. 4).

STUDENTS READ THE TEACHER'S EXPECTATIONS If a self-fulfilling prophecy is to come true, the student must conform to the teacher's expectations. But do students, in fact, accept and conform to the expectations communicated to them by teachers? How any individual student will react to teacher expectations is personal and idiosyncratic. Some students will accept teachers' evaluations, others will reject them. Acceptance or rejection will depend on a student's age, personality, background, values, and family expectations, as well as past experience with other teachers. A student who, for whatever reason, accepts a teacher's evaluation is more likely to be affected by that evaluation than one who rejects it.

STUDENTS CONFORM TO TEACHERS' EXPECTATIONS If a teacher's expectations are strong and consistent and if the student accepts them as valid, then, over time, the student's behavior will move in line with those expectations (Madaus, Airasian, & Kellaghan, 1980). According to this line of reasoning, the acceptance of high expectations by the student leads to the student working hard and doing well at schoolwork. Acceptance of low expectations, on the other hand, may mean that the student loses interest in school and does not work hard. These attitudes and behavior will ultimately be reflected in the student's school achievements. In these circumstances, teacher expectations become a reality.

Dealing with Expectations

Thomas Good and Jere Brophy offer some excellent advice to teachers to help them deal with their expectations for students. First, you have to accept that as a teacher you cannot avoid forming expectations for students. This invariably will involve low expectations for some students. Further, you should not think that simply having high expectations for all students will create a self-fulfilling situation that will raise the achievement level of an entire class. Nor should you treat all students in the same way. To do that would be to deny the existence of individual differences among students and the need to adjust to those differences in teaching. But you should be aware of how you are treating students, particularly ones for whom you do not have high expectations. The following are ten questions that Good and Brophy suggest you ask yourself about low-expectancy students:

1. *Do you praise or encourage low-expectancy students when they initiate comments?*
2. *Do you stay with low-expectancy students in failure situations?*
3. *Do you stay with lows in success situations?*
4. *Do you avoid calling on lows in public situations?*
5. *How often do lows have positive success experiences in public situations?*
6. *Do you needlessly criticize lows for wrong answers or failing to respond?*
7. *Do you place lows in "low groups" and treat them as group members rather than as individuals?*

8. *Do you ignore the minor inappropriate behavior of lows, or do mild violations of rules bring on strong reprimands?*
9. *How often do lows get to select a study topic?*
10. *How frequently do lows have a chance to evaluate their own words and to make responsible (important) decisions? (Good & Brophy, 1977, p. 393).*

In short, treat all students as individuals worthy of your consideration, kindness, and respect.

Constructing a Classroom Test

One of your principal responsibilities when you evaluate students' achievements will be to construct paper-and-pencil tests. In Chapter 19, we will discuss the concept of what a test is and issues of test validity and test reliability. These concepts apply to your own classroom tests as well as to professionally made standardized tests (you may want to read those sections before proceeding). In this section we shall outline some considerations you should be aware of when selecting and writing test questions.

Using the following seven steps can be beneficial when constructing classroom tests.

1. Develop a table of specifications for the test. A table of specifications is simply a two-dimensional grid; the student behaviors you wish to measure are listed on one axis, the content areas to be covered in the test on the other. Table 15.1 provides an example of a table of specifications for objectives in early language development. The check marks in the cells indicate the objectives for which you want to write items. The cells without check marks are empty because you do not have that combination of behavior and content as an objective of your instruction.

2. Write or select test items for the cells in the matrix. There are two basic types of item that can be used to measure a particular objective: supply items, where the student writes an answer as in an essay test, and selection items, where the student picks an answer from competing alternatives. The choice of the item type will be governed by the nature of the objective to be measured. Table 15.2 presents a comparison of essay and objective-type questions. The method that permits the student to exhibit the desired behavior most directly is preferable. You need to keep in mind, of course, that many objectives cannot be measured by paper-and-pencil questions at all—speaking skills, pronunciation in a foreign language, the correct use of laboratory techniques, the repair of a carburetor, the use of a microcomputer (Bloom, Madaus, & Hastings, 1981).

Once you decide on the kind of item you want, you must then write the item in a clear, unambiguous way. The item should make the problem that is to be solved or the question to be answered clear to the student. This is not always as easy as it sounds. Rules for writing different types of items can be found in any test and measurement book (Bloom,

TABLE 15.1 Table of Specifications for Preschool Education: Objectives in Early Language Development

Content	Cognitive									Affective
	A	B	C	D	E	F	G	H	I	J
1. Sounds	✓							✓	✓	✓
2. Words	✓						✓	✓	✓	✓
3. Grammar	✓						✓	✓	✓	✓
4. Objects		✓		✓						✓
5. Events			✓	✓						✓
6. Ideas				✓						
7. Reality discussion					✓					✓
8. Fantasy dramatic play					✓					✓
9. Thought						✓				

Source: Cazden, 1971, p. 348.

Madaus, & Hastings, 1981) and are too detailed to present here. Table 15.3 (pages 373–376) presents a checklist to help you judge the quality of different kinds of items—multiple-choice, matching, true-false, completion, and essay questions.

3. Choose items that test the various cells by sampling in some rational way. Once you have prepared a specification table, you can decide on the emphasis or weight you wish to give to each cell. You can do this on one of several bases. For example, you could decide on the basis of the time you spent covering the objective in your classroom or of your opinion of its importance. Whatever criterion you use, try to assign a *rough* weight in terms of a percentage to each cell. This will then give you an idea of how many questions you should write for each cell. If the percentage of a particular cell is 20 percent and you plan a 50-question test, then you want to construct roughly ten questions to measure the objective with that cell.

4. Arrange the chosen items systematically. In some cases, you may arrange the questions by subgroups representing types of behavior or content. Within the content or behavior grouping you would then do well to arrange the items from easy to difficult. You should group together items of a common type; don't mix true-false, multiple-choice, and matching items. Another consideration in arranging questions is ease of scoring.

Researchers offer the following guidelines on assembling items on the test:

- *Make sure that test items are spaced so that they can be read, answered, and scored with the least amount of difficulty. Double-space between items.*
- *Make sure all items have generous borders.*
- *Multiple-choice items should have alternatives listed vertically beneath the stem (i.e., question).*
- *Do not split an item onto two separate pages.*

TABLE 15.2 A Comparison of Essay Items and Objective Items

Essay	Objective
ABILITIES MEASURED	
Requires the student to express himself in his own words using information from his own background and knowledge.	Requires the student to select correct answers from given options, or to supply answer limited to one word or phrase.
Can tap high levels of reasoning such as required in inference, organization of ideas, comparison and contrast.	Can also tap high levels of reasoning such as required in inference, organization of ideas, comparison and contrast.
Does not measure purely factual information efficiently.	Measures knowledge of facts efficiently.
SCOPE	
Covers only a limited field of knowledge in any one test.	Covers a broad field of knowledge in one test.
Essay questions take so long to answer that relatively few can be answered in a given period of time. Also, the student who is especially fluent can often avoid discussing points of which he is unsure.	Since objective questions may be answered quickly, one test may contain many questions. A broad coverage helps provide reliable measurement.
INCENTIVE TO PUPILS	
Encourages pupils to learn how to organize their own ideas and express them effectively.	Encourages pupils to build up a broad background of knowledge and abilities.
EASE OF PREPARATION	
Requires writing only a few questions for a test. Tasks must be clearly defined, general enough to offer some leeway, specific enough to set limits.	Requires writing many questions for a test. Wording must avoid ambiguities and "give-aways." Distractors should embody most likely misconceptions.
SCORING	
Usually very time-consuming to score.	Can be scored quickly.
Permits teachers to comment directly on the reasoning processes of individual pupils. However, an answer may be scored differently by different teachers or by the same teacher at different times.	Answer generally scored only right or wrong, but scoring is very accurate and consistent.

Source: Educational Testing Service, 1973, p. 5.

- *With interpretation exercises, place the introduction on a single page with all related items on a single facing page.*
- *If no answer sheet is used, the space for answering should be down the right-hand side of the page.*
- *The most convenient method of response is circling the correct answer.*
- *Items should be numbered consecutively throughout the test.*
- *Tests reproduced by processes available to school systems should be duplicated on one side of the sheet only.*
- *If a separate answer sheet is used, test booklets can be reused. They should be numbered so that a check can be made for complete sets of materials after test administration (Hambleton, Eignor, & Swaminathan, 1978, p. 42).*

5. Design an objective-scoring scheme to furnish the kind of information you want. You must know at the outset what you will accept as a correct answer. This is particularly true for supply-type questions. You must decide how you will handle poor handwriting and grammatical or spelling errors. For example, you can give separate marks for the objective and another for grammar and spelling errors not related to the objective.

In reading essay questions, remove or cover the student's name

TABLE 15.3 A Summary Checklist for Item Writing

	Yes	No
1. Have I used items measuring important parts of the curriculum?	✓	
2. Have I avoided using items that are presented in an ambiguous fashion?	✓	
3. Have I followed standard rules of punctuation and grammar in constructing items?	✓	
4. Have I constructed only items that have a right or a clearly best answer?	✓	
5. Have I kept the level of reading difficulty appropriate to the group being tested?	✓	
6. Have I constructed test items from statements taken verbatim from instructional materials (for example, textbooks)?		✓
7. If any items are based on an opinion or authority, have I stated whose opinion or what authority?	✓	
8. Do items offer clues for answering other items in the text?		✓
9. Do students learn things from items that help them answer other items in the test?		✓
10. Do any of the items contain irrelevant cues?		✓
11. Have I made any items overly difficult by requiring unnecessarily exact or difficult operations?		✓
12. Do any of my items have words such as "always," "never," "none," or "all" in them?		✓
13. Have I included any "trick" items in the test?		✓
14. Have I checked the items with other teachers or item writers to try and eliminate ambiguity, technical errors, and other errors in item writing?	✓	
15. Do any of the items try to test more than a single idea?		✓
16. Have I restricted the number of item formats in the test?	✓	
17. Were the most "valid" item formats used in the test?	✓	
18. Have I grouped items presented in the same format together?	✓	
19. Do the correct answers follow essentially a random pattern?	✓	

Multiple-Choice Items

	Yes	No
1. Is each item designed to measure an important objective?	✓	
2. Does the item stem clearly define the problem?	✓	
3. Have I included as		

TABLE 15.3 (*Continued*)

	Yes	No
much of the item in the stem as possible?	✓	
4. Have I put any irrelevant material in the item stem?		✓
5. Have I included any grammatical cues in the item stem?		✓
6. Have I kept to a minimum the number of negatively stated item stems?	✓	
7. If the negative is used in an item stem, have I clearly emphasized it?	✓	
8. Is there one correct or clearly best answer?	✓	
9. Have I avoided the use of answers such as "all of the above" and "none of the above"?	✓	
10. Have I made sure that all answers are grammatically consistent with the item stem and parallel in form?	✓	
11. Have I avoided stating the correct answer in more detail?	✓	
12. Have I made sure that all distractors represent plausible alternatives to examinees who do *not* possess the skill measured by the test item?	✓	
13. Have I avoided including two answers that mean the same, such that both can be rejected?	✓	

	Yes	No
14. Have I avoided the use of modifiers like "sometimes" and "usually" in the alternatives?	✓	
15. Have I made sure to use important-sounding words in the distractors as well as the correct answer?	✓	
16. Are all answers of the same length and complexity?	✓	
17. Have I made the answers as homogeneous as possible?	✓	
18. Have I varied the length of the correct answer, thereby eliminating length as a potential clue?	✓	
19. Have I listed answers on separate lines, beneath each other?	✓	
20. Have I used letters in front of the answers?	✓	
21. Have I used new material for the students in formulating problems to measure understanding or ability to apply principles?	✓	

Matching Items

	Yes	No
1. Are the entries in the two sets homogeneous in content?	✓	
2. Are there more answers than premises?	✓	

TABLE 15.3 (*Continued*)

	Yes	No
3. Is each answer a plausible alternative for each premise?	✓	
4. Is the set too long (greater than 8–10 premises)?		✓
5. Are the entries in the sets arranged in some logical order?	✓	
6. Have I indicated whether an answer can be used more than once?	✓	
7. Do my directions specify the basis on which the match is to be made?	✓	
8. Have I made sure that the matching exercise is on one page?	✓	
9. Have I used headings for the premise and answer choices?	✓	
10. Have I made sure that the information couldn't be better obtained using another format, such as multiple-choice?	✓	

True-False Items

	Yes	No
1. Would another item format be more appropriate?		✓
2. Is the item definitely true or false?	✓	
3. Does each item contain a single important idea?	✓	
4. Is the item short?	✓	
5. Is simple language used?	✓	
6. Have I made sure that		

	Yes	No
one part of the item isn't true while another part of the item is false?	✓	
7. Does an insignificant word or phrase influence the truth or falsity of an item?		✓
8. Have I avoided using negative statements?	✓	
9. Have I avoided using vague words such as "seldom" and "frequently"?	✓	
10. Have I avoided use of words that give clues to the correct answer, for example, "always," "never," "usually," and "may"?	✓	
11. Have I made sure my true statements are no longer than my false statements?	✓	
12. Are there approximately an equal number of true and false statements in the test?	✓	

Completion Items

	Yes	No
1. Would another item format be more appropriate?		✓
2. Is the item written so that a single brief answer is possible?	✓	
3. Have I omitted unimportant words?	✓	
4. Have I left too many blanks?		✓
5. Are the blanks near the end of the item?	✓	

TABLE 15.3 (*Continued*)

	Yes	No		Yes	No
6. Have I avoided the use of specific determiners, such as "a" and "an," and singular and plural verbs?	✓		for answering questions?	✓	
			5. Are students aware of the time limits?	✓	
7. Have I made sure the length of my answer blank is equal from question to question?	✓		6. Do students know the points for each question in the test?	✓	
8. If the problem requires a numerical answer, have I indicated the units I want the answer stated in?	✓		7. Have I used new or interesting material in my essay questions?	✓	
9. If the problem requires a written answer, do students know how spelling errors will be scored?	✓		8. Have I tried to start the questions with words or phrases such as "Compare," "Contrast," "Give the reason for," "Give original examples of," "Explain how," "Predict what would happen if," "Criticize"?	✓	
10. Is each problem written so clearly that there is a single correct answer?	✓		9. Have I written a set of directions for the essays?	✓	
Essay Items			10. If several essays are used, have I used a range of complexity and difficulty in the questions?	✓	
1. Are essay questions only being used to measure higher-order objectives?	✓				
2. Are the questions closely matched to the objectives they were written to measure?	✓		11. Have I prepared an "ideal" answer to each essay question *before* administering the test?	✓	
3. Does each question present a clear task to the student?	✓		12. Have I allowed the students a choice of questions only in those instances when students aren't going to be compared?	✓	
4. Is there sufficient time					

Source: Adapted from Hambleton & Eignor, 1978, pp 61–66.

before reading to help lessen bias in evaluating answers. Read all the responses to one question, then shuffle the pile and read answers to the next question, rather than reading each individual essay test completely. Remember, grades are different from marks, and you need to consider how to convert the number of correctly answered test items into a grade.
6. Develop unambiguous directions for the examinees. Each type of question (multiple choice, matching, true-false) needs a clear set of directions on how to proceed. You should tell the student how much time is

available for the test and, in the case of essay questions, the form and length of the expected answer. You should also tell the examinee how you intend to score the test.

7. Inspect the final product.

The following checklist can help you construct and evaluate your test:

Item format

- *Are the items in the test numbered?*
- *Is each item complete on a page?*
- *Does the reference material for an item appear on the same page as the item or on a facing page?*
- *Are the item responses arranged to achieve both legibility and economy of space?*

Scoring arrangement

- *Has consideration been given to the practicability of a separate answer sheet?*
- *Are answers to be indicated by symbols rather than underlining or copying?*
- *Are answer spaces placed in a vertical column for easy scoring?*
- *If answer spaces are placed at the right of the page, is each answer space clearly associated with its corresponding item?*
- *Are the answer symbols to be used by the students free from possible ambiguity due to careless handwriting or deliberate heding?*
- *Are the answer symbols to be used by the students free from confusion with the substance or content of the responses?*

Distribution of correct responses

- *Are correct answers distributed so that the same answer does not appear for a long series of consecutive questions?*
- *Are correct answers distributed to avoid an excessive proportion of items in the test with the same answer?*
- *Is patterning of answers in a fixed, repeating sequence avoided?*

Grouping and arrangement of items

- *Are items of the same type requiring the same directions grouped together in the test?*
- *When juxtaposition of items of markedly dissimilar content is likely to cause confusion, are items grouped by content within each item-type grouping?*
- *Are items generally arranged from easy to more difficult within the test as a whole and within each major subdivision of the test?*

Directions for answering questions

- *Are simple, clear, and specific directions given for each different item type in the test?*
- *Are directions clearly set off from the rest of the test by appropriate spacing or type style?*

- *Is effective use made of sample questions and answers to help clarify directions for unusual item types?*

Correction for chance

- *If deductions are to be made for wrong answers, are students so informed?*
- *If no deductions are to be made for wrong answers, are students advised to answer every question according to their best judgment?*

Printing and duplicating

- *Is the test free from annoying and confusing typographical errors?*
- *Is the legibility of the test satisfactory from the viewpoint of type size, adequacy of spacing, and clarity of printing? (Adapted from Neill, 1978, pp. 80–81.)*

Record Keeping

It is two weeks before your college graduation. You stop at the registrar's office to collect your transcript of credits. Expecting to gaze with adoration at all those lovely grades, you unfold the paper and discover two grades are missing . . . two sophomore grades are missing! Somehow, in the last month, you have been reduced to a senior, six credits shy of graduation.

Farfetched? Not really! Poor record keeping can be the bane of a teacher's existence. Whether they like it or not, teachers are expected to keep up-to-date records of their students' progress in the form of *permanent records, attendance records, subject grades,* and *report cards.* They should also keep a *lesson-plan book,* a record of classroom learning activities.

Permanent Records

A permanent record is the official school record of students who were, or are being, educated in the system. Although these records take various forms across districts, they all contain the same basic information: name, address, parents' or guardians' names, birth date, semester or yearly grade averages, and the name of the student's teacher for that year. At the beginning of the school year, you need to update the information on each student's card and enter the new grade and your name on the permanent record card. Remember to fill in the grade averages at the end of the term. By law, permanent records are confidential.

Attendance Records

Attendance records are essential, especially if the school system in which you teach has a promotion policy contingent upon attendance. In many states, they are also legal documents. Resist the temptation to take attendance "later"; do it at the beginning of the day. Once you have learned your students' names, a simple scan of the classroom will supplant calling the roll. In a special folder, keep all notes from parents that explain absences. If a strict attendance policy is in operation, these notes may become important documents when it comes to retaining students.

Grades

Grading has two aspects: the assignment of grades and the recording of grades. Try to be as objective and as fair as possible in assigning grades. Some subject areas—math, spelling, reading—present few problems because of their structure. Tests measuring progress in these areas usually ask for specific, nonnegotiable answers. Essays, compositions, reports, and projects, however, require a more subjective evaluation. If you set standards before the activity, and the students are aware of what constitutes an A, B, or C, your grading will be much easier and more objective. More than one grade may be given for an assignment. Since spelling and handwriting are an integral part of written communication, you could assign several grades to a paper. For example, a history essay might be graded: History B+, Spelling A—, Handwriting C.

One of the most important records in your classroom will be your students' grades. In a self-contained classroom, the teacher is responsible for keeping records of all student grades. In a departmentalized classroom, although you will record the grades of the students you teach, you will not have a running record of all your homeroom students' grades. Whatever your class structure, the following hints may prove helpful:

1. If your school has a grading policy, adhere to it strictly. Let students know how percentage grades and letter grades are equated.

2. If you choose to grade on a point system, determine the total number of points needed and post your standards.

3. At the top of your grading record, note the assignment. For example, "p. 189 on a math grade sheet," or "Unit 12 on a spelling page" will alert you to what grades are missing for a particular student.

4. Record grades daily. (Nothing is more depressing than a mountain of papers to be graded over the weekend.)

A grade book or not? That is the question. Personal preference will dictate your choice of record, but you may wish to use an alternative strategy for departmentalized classes. If you mimeograph a grid that contains the names of your students by class period, you will eliminate the need to rewrite lists each time a set of grades needs to be distributed. No matter what type of recording structure you use, keep careful records. These will be invaluable when report cards are due.

Report Cards

Report cards are student progress reports that teachers are normally required to complete four or more times a year. In many cases, teachers are required to complete additional midterm assessments of student progress to

Keeping parents and guardians informed of student progress is an important responsibility of teaching.

let parents and students know where students stand halfway through the term. Although no standard form exists, most secondary schools use a letter grade/percentage report form and elementary schools tend to take a more varied approach.

The secondary school report card usually consists of a straightforward listing of courses with space for recording grades, percentages, and comments, a record of absences and tardiness, and a place for parents to acknowledge that they reviewed the document.

In elementary schools, report cards vary from school to school and from grade level to grade level. Often, instead of giving students grades such as A, B, C, D, and F, descriptive terms such as C (commendable), S (satisfactory), N (needs improvement), and U (unsatisfactory) are used. Further, there is often room for the teacher's written comments, which help personalize the report. An alternative approach to reporting student progress at the elementary level is the checklist report. A checklist format is much more definitive in what skills are assessed. It usually has a space for a grade, what group the student is working in, and a space for teacher comments.

Regardless of the form used, teachers need to keep a number of things in mind when completing report cards. Among the most important are:

1. Grades represent important information. They should be assigned because students earned or deserved them.
2. They should be assigned in accordance with school policy (for example, 90 to 100 equals an A in all classes within the school).
3. Keep accurate records of all correspondence concerning student grades and work habits.

4. Be careful when writing messages to or corresponding with parents. Poor grammar or misspellings can cast serious doubt on your professional competence.

Keeping parents and guardians informed of student progress is an important responsibility of teachers. Teachers infrequently provide feedback when students have done something positive or commendable. A phone call or letter informing parents about such things can help motivate students as much as, if not more than, correspondence that takes place when problems arise. When you get your own classroom, set a goal for yourself of recognizing the good work or behavior of at least two students each week. You will be encouraged by the results of your efforts.

CONCLUSION

In this chapter, we covered a number of topics relating to classroom evaluation. A consideration of these topics should serve to underline the complexity and pervasiveness of classroom evaluation. In one sense, a teacher is continually evaluating a class and modifying his or her approach in the light of feedback received. At the other end of the continuum are more formal evaluations in the form of tests. The uses to which evaluation information are put are also varied. Whatever kind of evaluation you engage in while teaching and for whatever purposes you use evaluation information, beware of its possible negative impact on students, particularly when it is public. Good evaluation practice should promote student learning, not place limits on student achievement.

QUESTIONS AND ACTIVITIES

1. Review a school's curriculum for a particular area (for example, language arts, K through 6 math, or high school biology). How is the curriculum sequenced? Compare it with other curricula at the same grade level. How well do the two integrate?
2. Conduct a brainstorming session to come up with a list of activities to introduce one of the following lessons; subject and verb identification, ecological systems, the concept of freedom and responsibility, socialism, energy conservation, racism, sexism, or the circulatory system.
3. Design a series of model lessons that
   a. Stresses different types of objectives (cognitive, affective, psychomotor).
   b. Exemplifies each of the seven types of lessons.
   c. Has a self-developed test that follows the guidelines outlined in the chapter.
4. Which of the report cards described in the text do you feel are most appropriate for the grade level at which you plan to teach? Why do you

feel that way? Can you think of any other method of reporting progress that may be more beneficial to students and parents?

5. Select a concept or topic that interests you. Develop a series of questions that would address each of the seven levels of cognitive ability.

6. Interview two or three teachers for whom you have developed respect. What are their opinions on the various aspects of the expectancy mechanism discussed in this chapter?

CHAPTER 16

The Effective School

All of us have experienced the fact that some students are more motivated to learn in some classrooms than they are in other classrooms. This chapter takes a step beyond the classroom and looks at what makes some schools more effective than others.

• Contrary to what many researchers thought in the 1960s and 1970s, recent research has shown that schools do make a difference in how much students learn.

• When considering the term *effective school,* ask what does the term *effective* really mean.

• Effective schools share common characteristics. These include high academic expectation, administrative leadership, and carefully targeted instruction.

Schools have always received their share of criticism. Before the mid-1960s, people, on occasion, had doubted the effectiveness of particular schools, types of schools, or school practices. It was said that schools were inefficient, that curricula were out of date, and that teachers were inadequately prepared. These criticisms, however, did not undermine the widespread belief that essentially there was nothing that the schools, given new curricula, better facilities, or improved teachers could not set right. The challenge of these criticisms was not directed at the institution of schooling itself or its goals but rather to specific practices or characteristics of schools.

In the second half of the 1960s, the nature of the criticism changed radically. For the first time the effectiveness of the whole enterprise of schooling was seriously challenged. Social scientists began to raise disturbing questions and reach pessimistic conclusions about the belief many people had always taken for granted—that schools are effective, and that they make a difference to the development of students.

By the late 1970s, a strong reaction to these pessimistic and negative conclusions began to emerge. A mounting body of research evidence confirmed many educators' intuitive beliefs that schools do make a difference and that some are more effective than others. Furthermore, researchers attempted to identify the characteristics that distinguish effective schools, and it was argued that this information could serve as a basis for improving schools that were not doing a good job. The effective-schools movement was born.

The purpose of this chapter is to introduce you to the educational, social, political, and philosophical issues surrounding the school effectiveness debate that began in the mid-1960s, clarify what is meant by the term *effective school*, and finally, describe the important characteristics that have been found to be associated with "effective schools."

The School Effectiveness Debate

During the 1960s, the struggle against poverty, social injustice, and unequal opportunity in our society became intense. At the time, it was widely believed that one of the main causes of social and economic inequality in American life was inequality in education. Further, it was widely believed that eliminating educational inequality would reduce inequality in society. The hope of social and economic reform through reducing educational inequality was appealing to federal policymakers, since it did not involve direct action in more politically sensitive areas such as housing and employment. In other words, many people believed that through the provision of better educational programs, the life of the "have-nots" could be improved without having to redistribute wealth, which would disturb the lives of the "haves" (Madaus, Airasian, & Kellaghan, 1980).

The need to document, and then remedy, unequal educational opportunities, particularly as they related to poor and minority children, led to a major nationwide study of school effectiveness that was destined to become one of the most famous studies in the history of American education. It was called the Coleman Report, and it led directly to the debate and controversy over whether or not schools were effective (Coleman et al., 1966).

The Coleman Report

The Civil Rights Act of 1964, a cornerstone of President Johnson's historic War on Poverty, required that the commissioner of education conduct a nationwide survey and report to the president and to the Congress on the "lack of availability of equality of educational opportunity for individuals by reason of race, color or national origin in public educational institutions" (Section 402, Civil Rights Act of 1964).

There were two widespread beliefs about schooling when James Coleman began his now famous survey. First it was believed that traditional resources (commonly called *input variables*) such as per pupil expenditures, teacher experience, number of books in the library, class size, and many other similar variables were strongly related to pupil achievement. Second, there was a strong belief that there were large inequalities among American schools relative to these important resources—in particular, that there were large disparities in the quality of schools attended by black and white children (Mosteller & Moynihan, 1972). While Coleman did find, ten years after the famous *Brown* decision, that racial separation still characterized the vast majority of American schools, he also surprised people by concluding that both these beliefs about schooling were wrong. His findings led him to conclude that the physical facilities, curricula, teacher characteristics, and other input variables were much more similar in black and white schools than most Americans believed. The bigger surprise, however, was his conclusion that when home-background variables were taken into account, school characteristics and resources appeared to make little difference to students' measured level of achievement. This was the crucial finding in the report. The quality of schools assessed in terms of access to materials and facilities (the measures most commonly used by education reformers and school administrators) bore virtually no relationship to students' measured achievement.

Conclusions of the Coleman Report

Schools bring little influence to bear on a child's achievement that is independent of his background and general social context; . . . this very lack of an independent effect means that the inequalities imposed on children by their home, neighborhood and peer environment are carried along to become the inequalities with which they confront adult life at the end of school. For equality of educational opportunity must imply a strong effect of schools that is independent of the child's immediate social environment, and that strong independent effect is not present in American schools (Coleman et al., 1966, p. 325).

Thus, according to the Coleman Report, it was not the quality of the school but the students' home backgrounds *prior to entering school* that mattered most in terms of students' achievement. Many people interpreted this to mean that "schools make no difference; families make the difference" (Hodgson, 1973, p. 35).

Head Start and Title I Evaluations

The concept that "schools make no difference" was further strengthened by pessimistic but consistent findings of various evaluations of Head Start and Title I programs during the 1960s and 1970s. The evaluations concluded that federally funded programs designed to narrow the achievement gap between advantaged and disadvantaged pupils appeared to have very little effect on students' achievements. These studies certainly did not provide much reassurance that enhancing the school environment of disadvantaged children by means of extra expenditures, smaller class size, additional staff, enrichment activities, or extra resources would result in either substantial or permanent achievement gains (Madaus, Airasian, & Kellaghan, 1980).

The Rise of the Effective-School Movement

While the Coleman Report and the negative evaluations of Head Start and Title I programs lead many critics to conclude that schools were not very effective, another group of equally vocal critics were blaming the schools for the ills of society in general and, in particular, for falling academic standards, declining test scores, and graduating pupils who lacked the basic skills necessary to survive in society. One such critic put it this way: "With skills down, standards down, and grades up, the American educational system perpetuates a hoax on its students and on their parents" (Copperman, 1980, p. 16). Thus, schools and educators were caught in a crossfire of accusations; on the one hand that they were not making a difference in students' academic lives, and on the other that they were responsible for students' academic shortcomings (Rutter, 1983).

While many in education reeled from this double-barreled attack, a small group of researchers and educators began to proclaim good news: they were finding compelling evidence that "schools can and do make a difference," some schools are instructionally effective for poor and minority children, and certain characteristics of schools are important in affecting scholastic achievement (Klitgaard & Hall, 1975; Brimer, Madaus, Chapman, Kellaghan, & Wood, 1978; Brookhover, Beady, Flood, Schweitzer, & Wisenbaker, 1979; Madaus, Kellaghan, Rakow, & King, 1979; Rutter, Maughan, Mortimore, Ouston, & Smith, 1979; Edmonds, 1979; Madaus, Airasian, & Kellaghan, 1980; Austin, 1981). A pioneer in the effective-schools movement summed up the optimistic outlook generated by this newer line of research: "We can whenever, and wherever we choose, successfully teach all children whose schooling is of interest to us. We already know more than we need, in order to do this. Whether we do it must finally depend on how we feel about the fact that we haven't so far" (Edmonds, 1979, p. 52). The effective-schools

> **BOX 16.1 Towards Effective Schools**
>
> Schools can and do make a difference in the achievement of children. Despite public skepticism that prevails concerning the quality of public education, we are now at a significant turning point. We can identify schools in urban areas where poor children are performing at grade level. Furthermore, we know the characteristics that differentiate these schools from their less-productive counterparts. In Connecticut we have specific methods for helping any school carry out an introspective self-analysis to determine the extent to which the school displays those characteristics that have been shown to be coincident with substantive achievement by students. We can help schools also to develop action plans which focus on improving student achievement and can assist the principals and faculties of these schools to locate affordable resources and people in the state to help them implement their action plans. A number of schools have been involved in this process for about a year and the testimony of the principals and faculty members of these schools provides initial evidence that our combined efforts are beginning to make an impact. We also state unequivocally that the same characteristics that will help urban schools function will help suburban schools flourish.
>
> *Source:* Gauthier, 1983, p. 1.

movement is based on three assumptions. First, some schools are unusually effective in teaching, and among these are schools that are effective in teaching poor and minority children the basic skills. Second, successful schools have common characteristics that can be identified and that distinguish them from less successful schools. And third, these characteristics provide a basis for improving less effective schools (Bickel, 1983).

Many states and local school districts have designed school improvement programs around these three assumptions (Edmonds, 1982). In fact by 1985, there were nearly 40 effective-schools programs in operation in 1,750 school districts and 7,500 schools throughout the country (Miles & Kaufman, 1985). The Connecticut State Department of Education is typical in this regard. It issued a document entitled "Instructionally Effective Schools" that was designed to help school districts become more effective. The optimism and the philosophy of the Connecticut program is made explicit in the opening paragraph of the document, shown in Box 16.1.

The new wave of studies does not refute Coleman et al.'s findings that home background outweighs traditional static input variables such as teacher-pupil ratio, teacher salaries, and number of books in the library in its effect on student achievement. (We shall return to this point presently.) Instead, the new studies have looked at other school characteristics and resources and found that their presence is strongly related to school effectiveness (Purkey & Smith, 1983).

Effective Schools: What Do We Mean?

What does it mean when a school is labeled "effective"? Effective at doing what? Different analytical techniques and different outcome measures have been used to identify and then study "effective" schools. It is necessary to consider such differences if we are to understand what is meant when someone says one school is more effective than others. In this section we shall consider three problems associated with the identification of effective schools. First, we shall consider the difference between the *absolute* effects of schooling and the *relative* effects of particular school resources and programs. Second, we shall examine the techniques used to identify effective schools. Third, we shall consider the limitations of the outcome (criterion) measures used to characterize effective schools.

Absolute and Relative Effects of Schooling

On the basis of the Coleman Report, some people claimed that schools do not affect a student's scholastic achievement. This blanket generalization goes far beyond saying that certain types of schools may do little but that other types may do a lot, or that schools with more of a particular resource or facility may help pupils develop cognitive abilities to a greater extent than schools with less of that resource or facility. The judgment made in the report's conclusion concerning the effects of schooling was absolute—*schools make no difference.* Implicitly, a comparison was set up between schooling and no schooling and the conclusion was reached that going to school does little to foster students' cognitive abilities.

Studies such as the Coleman survey were not designed to answer the question: Does schooling make a difference to student achievement? To determine this, it would be necessary to compare the achievement level of a group of children that had gone to school with a comparable group that had not. All that school-effectiveness studies have done is look at the *relative* effectiveness of particular school resources, characteristics, and programs in improving pupils' achievement. Thus, they sought answers to questions such as: Does greater teacher experience, per pupil expenditure, or smaller class size relate to higher pupil achievement? Do newer textbooks or more remedial programs contribute to achievement? In putting the questions this way the investigators seek evidence about the *relative* or *differential* impact of *different quantities* of a given school resource or characteristic on pupil achievement levels, rather than evidence about the absolute effectiveness of schooling.

Since most children go to school nowadays, it is difficult to obtain evidence on the absolute effects of schooling. However, we do know from history that the expansion of education in Western countries in the nineteenth century, and in developing countries in this century, was paralleled by tremendous increases in literacy in the population. Further, there are a few recent cases in which children were deprived of schooling because schools were closed or simply not available, either because of war or attempts to avoid racial integration; in such cases, the cognitive performance of the children has been found to be retarded. For example, the public schools in Prince Edward County, Virginia, were closed from 1959 to 1963 to avoid integration. As a result, the majority of black children received no formal education during those years. Compared to children who attended school in an adjacent county, the intelligence test scores of nonattenders were depressed by 15 to 30 points (Green, Hoffman, Morse, Hayes, & Morgan, 1964). Similar conclusions were reached in studies of migrant children who had extremely poor school attendance records (Gordon, 1923). Taken together, this evidence points to an absolute school effect. School attendance, as opposed to nonschool attendance, does benefit students' cognitive development (Madaus, Airasian, & Kellaghan, 1980).

How Do Researchers Identify Effective Schools?

There are two principal ways in which effective schools have been identified and studied to determine the characteristics that typify them. The first method relies on expert judgment. The second matches sets of schools on the basis of home background characteristics, compares standardized test scores among these groups, and then isolates characteristics of effective schools.

THE EXPERT-JUDGMENT METHOD In the expert-judgment method, knowledgeable persons are asked to nominate an exemplary school on the basis of their firsthand experience. It is left to the expert to apply his or her own criteria of what it means to be "exemplary." Nominated schools are contacted to see if they are willing to open themselves to scrutiny for three or four days by an investigator who will observe, interview people, and gather material to paint a portrait of the school. This visitation technique is known as the "case study" approach. The portrait that results provides a composite of characteristics of the exemplary school (Graudbard, 1981).

The expert-judgment or case study method is sometimes criticized as being too subjective, for two reasons. First, school nominations depend on the criteria of excellence in the minds of different experts who have different ideas about what makes a school exemplary. Second, the school portrait reflects the intellectual, social, and moral preferences of the person who visits the school to study it. The visitor is analogous to an artist, and no two artists would produce an identical portrait of the same school.

While the danger of subjectivity is real, it is not a fatal flaw. The portraits reflect an experience and perspective that are important. "The 'perspectives' of those who know schools well—having daily familiarity with them and their students and teacher populations—have a unique authority" (Graudbard, 1981, p. vii). And while it is true that different individuals will draw different portraits of a school, the agreement among independent visitors concerning the important characteristics of exemplary schools is impressive. Further, a comparison of the profiles of such schools reveals a common core of characteristics related to student achievement (Good & Brophy, 1986).

THE OUTLIER METHOD The second method of identifying effective schools is called the "contrasting groups" or "outlier" method. This method entails matching urban elementary schools serving poor and minority children on the home-background characteristics of the pupils, factors over which schools have no control. All the schools in the matched group have roughly the same number of poor and disadvantaged children, children from differing socioeconomic backgrounds, boys and girls, and blacks and whites. This approach tends to rule out or "control" for the influence that background characteristics have on achievement. Once home-background factors have been neutralized in this way, it is possible to attribute any differences in school achievement to school factors.

Once they have matched the schools, experts compare the students in each school on the basis of their average scores on a standardized test of achievement. The aim is to identify a set of schools that have much higher than average reading test scores and a second group in which students score much below average. The "positive" outlier schools (those with high reading scores) are labeled "exemplary" or "effective"; the "negative" outlier schools (those with low reading scores) are called "ineffective." The outlier schools identified are then visited and studied in depth to determine the characteristics, resources, and programs that are present in the "effective" schools but which are not present in the "ineffective" ones (Brookhover et al., 1979; Austin, 1981).

Like the first method of identification (the expert-judgment or case study technique), there are several problems associated with the outlier or contrasting groups approach. First, the same outlier schools may not emerge when slightly different background measures are used to equate the schools. Second, some experts argue that the positive outlier schools—the highly effective ones—should be compared to average schools rather than to unusually poor schools. The reason behind this suggestion is that the differences between the characteristics of effective schools and average schools might be quite different from the differences in characteristics that exist between effective and ineffective schools. If, in fact, this is true, then it might be harder for the ineffective schools to immediately adopt the characteristics of the highly effective schools than for them to try, as a first step, to develop the characteristics of average schools (Purkey & Smith, 1982). A third problem is that the kinds of schools used in such studies have been almost exclusively elementary and urban and attended by low-income and minority pupils. The characteristics that differentiate these kinds of positive and negative outlier schools may not be the same characteristics associated with effective secondary schools or with nonurban elementary schools.

The Measurement of School Outcomes

The two techniques of identifying exemplary schools that we have described above ultimately depend on the indicators of effectiveness, called criterion measures. We need to pay attention to these measures and ask what the "effective" schools are doing or accomplishing that the "ineffective" schools either do not do at all or do not do as well.

In Connecticut, an effective school has been defined as one "that brings children from low-income families to the minimum basic skills mastery level which now describes the minimally successful performance for middle-income children" (Gauthier, 1983, p. 2). Because this definition is so precise, it is very restrictive, referring only to the performance of low-income children relative to that of high-income children on paper-and-pencil tests of basic skills (reading, arithmetic, and writing).

A problem arises when people lose sight of the limited nature of the performance measured in studies of school effectiveness and start talking about effectiveness as if it were a generic term covering all aspects of the school. The outcomes of schooling are multiple and extremely complex. Some schools may foster certain outcomes and neglect others. Take a simple example, such as the admittedly important goal of fostering basic reading skills. Many argue that a good index of effectiveness in reaching this goal is the performance on a standardized multiple-choice reading test. However, many people also believe that reading is not merely a utilitarian skill but the door to a world of enjoyment. Using the scores on a multiple-choice reading test will not give you any idea of how effective schools have been in motivating children to read for the sheer pleasure of it.

Despite the complexity and broad range of outcomes that most schools encourage in their quest to develop students on many levels, studies of school effectiveness have not, for the most part, concerned themselves with a broad range of outcome measures. Instead, they have relied almost exclusively on student performance on standardized norm-reference achievement tests of reading and arithmetic to identify successful schools. However, other outcomes—performance in other curricular areas as well as social, attitudinal, and affective factors—are also very important. Broader outcomes that the effective-schools movement has tended to neglect are classroom behavior, attitudes toward learning, continuation in education, and ultimately, employment (Rutter, 1983; Glickman, 1987).

These considerations should serve to remind us that it is important not to overgeneralize the adjective "effective" when describing a school. We should be aware of the limited and specific nature of the particular outcome measures used to characterize schools. It is very likely that if outcome measures other than standardized achievement tests were used, a different set of "effective" and "ineffective" schools and a different list of school characteristics that differentiate the two types of schools would be identified. Keeping this reservation in mind, let us now consider those school characteristics that have been found to be associated with effectiveness.

The Characteristics of Effective Schools

The Coleman Report (Coleman et al., 1966) and other studies of school effectiveness concluded that students' home backgrounds have a greater effect on their achievement levels in school than do traditional indexes of school resources, such as per pupil expenditure, teacher experience, number of books in the school library, age of the school building, presence of science laboratories, and class size. This conclusion was very discouraging, since these traditional resources would have been relatively easy for policymakers to manipulate if they had been found to be strongly related to achievement. For example, if per pupil expenditure had turned out to be an important factor, then policymakers could have simply increased the amount of money to schools with low per pupil expenditures. Similarly, if number of library books had been found to be related to achievement, it would have been a simple matter for legislators to increase the number of books in schools with few library holdings.

On reflection, it is unlikely that a gross index, such as per pupil expenditure, could ever have been of much use to the policymaker. Per pupil expenditure includes a variety of factors, such as salaries for teachers, administrators, supervisors, clerks, librarians, institutional aides, and janitors as well as expenditures for physical plant, heating, books, and equipment. How the money is actually used to deliver instruction varies from district to district as well as from school to school. Gross expenditure does not indicate how funds are actually distributed. Gross indexes such as per pupil expenditures do not capture the important variable of how the money is spent—on school buildings, on library facilities, or on teacher salaries. How the money is actually spent can make a difference in pupil achievement.

Dissatisfaction with variables such as per pupil expenditure, resources, and facilities led researchers to look more closely at school characteristics that capture the *activity* or *processes* that go on in schools. A new generation of researchers worked on the assumption that how people organize and use facilities is likely to be more important in improving student achievement than the mere presence of the resources and facilities. This line of reasoning does not deny that there may be interactions between facilities and staff. Physical facilities may set limits on the types of interactions that can occur. However, given the availability of a library or laboratory, *how* and *by whom* such facilities are used is of prime importance.

Concentrating on what actually goes on in schools has led researchers to identify a number of characteristics that consistently relate to pupils' cognitive achievement. These characteristics are not easily manipulated by simple changes in policy. Nonetheless, schools can be changed, generally with difficulty, but often for very little money, to resemble schools found to be effective (Purkey & Smith, 1983). No single characteristic that differentiates effective schools from less effective ones is crucial in and of itself. Rather, the characteristics form an ensemble of reinforcing factors and activities. In the complex environment that is the school, "nothing works all the time. Almost anything that makes sense will work more often than not, if it is implemented with enough self-critical optimism and zest. Some changes work more often than others, but hardly anything works for everybody. Nothing works by itself, and everything takes a long time" (MacKenzie, 1983, p. 13).

What school-related characteristics differentiate effective schools from less effective schools? How do they work together? Different reviewers come up with slightly different lists. Box 16.2 contains a synthesis of the major characteristics found to be associated with effective schools. These are clustered into three dimensions (leadership, efficacy, and efficiency), which are further divided into "core elements" (for example, positive climate and overall atmosphere) and "facilitating elements" (for example, shared consensus and values on goals). Core elements are more frequently found in the research literature on school effectiveness than are facilitating ones. The facilitating elements are specific conditions that make it easier to implement the core characteristics (MacKenzie, 1983). We shall use the three dimensions of leadership, efficacy, and efficiency shown in Box 16.2 to organize our discussion of the characteristics of effective schools. Rather than consider each of the characteristics separately, we shall discuss them in related clusters.

BOX 16.2 Dimensions of Effective Schooling

Leadership Dimensions

CORE ELEMENTS

Principal exercising leadership in academic and instructional areas.

Positive climate and overall atmosphere and professional collegiality among staff.

Shared purposefulness over the important goals and objectives of the school.

Goal-focused activities by teachers.

In-service staff training for effective teaching.

Regular and consistent communication with parents about the school's expectations and their child's progress.

Emphasis on regular school attendance.

FACILITATING ELEMENTS

Shared consensus on values and goals.

Long-range planning and coordination.

Stability and continuity of key staff.

District-level support for school improvement.

Efficacy Dimensions

CORE ELEMENTS

High and positive academic expectations with a constant press for excellence conveyed to all students.

Clearly defined homework policy.

Visible rewards for academic excellence and growth.

Cooperative activity and group interaction in the classroom.

Total staff involvement with school improvement.

Autonomy and flexibility to implement adaptive practices.

Appropriate levels of difficulty for learning tasks.

Teacher empathy, rapport, and personal interaction with students.

FACILITATING ELEMENTS

Emphasis on homework and study.

Positive accountability; acceptance of responsibility for learning outcomes.

Strategies to avoid nonpromotion of students.

Deemphasis of strict ability grouping; interaction with more accomplished peers.

Efficiency Dimensions

CORE ELEMENTS

Effective use of instructional time; amount and intensity of engagement in school learning.

Orderly and disciplined school and classroom environments.

Continuous diagnosis, evaluation, and feedback.

Well-structured classroom activities.

Instruction guided by content coverage.

Schoolwide emphasis on basic and higher-order skills.

FACILITATING ELEMENTS

Opportunities for individualized work.

Number and variety of opportunities to learn.

Frequent assessment of student progress on a routine basis.

Precise and informative report card with emphasis on acquisition of basic math and language skills. Reading, mathematics, language instruction beginning in kindergarten.

Emphasis on test-taking skills and motivation to do well on tests.

Direct instruction as the main pedagogical approach.

Source: Synthesis from MacKenzie, 1983; McCormack-Larkin & Kritek, 1982.

Leadership

THE PRINCIPAL The leadership in a school generally, although not exclusively, rests with the building principal. The principal has the power to initiate, stimulate, sustain, and alter expectations for student and teacher performance. (Little, 1982). There is a growing body of evidence that one of the key characteristics of effective schools, one not present in less effective ones, is a building principal who is an instructional leader rather than merely a manager or administrator (Austin, 1981; Edmonds, 1982).

Principals of effective schools actively exploit the authority and resources of their position; they have an evangelistic vision of excellence that they actively pursue; they seize initiatives for improvement; they are proactive in working with teachers; they are the key resource persons for teachers in helping them decide on and implement instructional strategies. They are knowledgeable about instruction, but they do more than talk about, encourage, and endorse innovations; they provide specific demonstrations and assistance in implementing new techniques. They are visible in the halls, washrooms, stairwells, schoolyard, and classrooms and spend more time outside their offices than in them. They often take over a class to demonstrate a new technique or method for a teacher who is having difficulty with a particular aspect of the curriculum (Little, 1982).

As instructional leaders, the principals of effective schools take care to see that discipline and good order are maintained in and out of the classroom. They take the leadership in developing, in conjunction with their staff, firm, fair, and consistent policies and rules governing behavior and discipline. They then stand behind these policies and behind the efforts of teachers to enforce them. Further, they work to limit intrusions in the classroom by providing teachers with adequate materials and support for special projects and by relieving teachers of burdensome levels of paperwork (Little, 1982).

Perhaps the most important characteristic associated with the principal of an effective school is that he or she sets the tone or the climate of the school. This positive tone or climate is characterized by order and discipline and by a belief and expectation that all children can learn and can be taught effectively.

SHARED PURPOSEFULNESS "Shared purposefulness," which has been consistently shown to be an important characteristic of effective schools, means that there is a match between parents', students', teachers', and administrators' notions of the important ends of education. Further, all parties work together toward achieving those ends in a purposeful, organized way (Smith, 1976). In short, the school has a clear mission that is understood and pursued by all. Joan Lipsitz, who has done case studies of exemplary schools, describes shared purposefulness this way:

> *Excellent schools have a distinct history and a sense of community. What is not unique, and therefore of import, are things all schools can control: positive attitudes about students; high expectations for students, staff, and parents; energy; organization ingenuity; a coherent philosophy of how young adolescents grow and learn that pervades every aspect of school life. In addition, all these schools share a positive criterion: joy. Each rates high in laughter, vitality, interest and smiles (Lipsitz, 1982).*

Effective schools are characterized by a belief that the school's mission can be achieved. For example, Ronald Edmonds found that in less effective schools, the teachers and principals attributed student reading problems to factors outside the school, particularly related to the pupils' home conditions. The staff of these schools felt that, because of poor home conditions, they could have little impact on the students' reading levels. They expected children to fail. Staffs of effective schools, on the other hand, felt that students had the ability to succeed and that teachers could help improve the achievement levels of children despite their disadvantaged home conditions (Edmonds, 1982).

GOAL-FOCUSED ACTIVITIES Effective schools are ones in which activities are directed, structured, and focused toward accomplishing the goals of the school. Marshall Smith calls this characteristic "closeness." Closeness means that if the purpose of the school is to teach reading, then the principal, teachers, and pupils should concentrate on the reading process rather than on more indirect approaches, such as attempting to change the child's self-concept and thereby effect a change in reading (Smith, 1976). Again, the results of European studies support the notion that successful schools work toward the attainment of fairly well-defined objectives as communicated in school syllabi and through teachers, pupils, and parents (Brimer et al., 1978; Madaus et al., 1979; Rutter et al., 1979). The more successful preschool programs for the disadvantaged have also been identified as ones having clearly stated cognitive goals, combined with structured attempts to achieve those goals (Kellaghan, 1977).

The Connecticut State Department of Education describes the relationship between a clear mission for schools and the important characteristic of goal-focused activities this way:

> *Effective schools make a conscious decision to become effective*
> *schools and that is their mission. A collegial decision and*
> *commitment is made to assure minimum mastery of basic school*
> *skills for all pupils. Pupil acquisition of basic school skills takes*
> *precedence over all other school activities, and when necessary,*
> *school energy and resources are diverted from other activities to*
> *achieve that end (Gauthier, 1983, p. 6).*

This statement of policy illustrates a very real danger inherent in certain aspects of the effective-schools movement: a focusing and narrowing of the curriculum to achieve improvement in a limited number of basic skills (Porter, 1983).

An exclusive emphasis on basic skills—to the extent of diverting energy and resources from other areas—generally results in improvement in scores on basic skills tests. In 1911 a chief inspector of schools wrote about the use of external state examinations in Great Britain, warning about the dangers of an overreliance on test scores as the sole measure of effectiveness:

> *Whenever the outward standard of reality (examination results)*
> *has established itself at the expense of the inward, the ease with*
> *which worth (or what passes for such) can be measured is ever*
> *tending to become in itself the chief, if not sole, measure of worth.*
> *And in proportion, as we tend to value the results of education for*

their measurableness, so we tend to undervalue and at last ignore
those results which are too intrinsically valuable to be measured
(Holmes, 1911, p. 128).

Holmes's point is well taken. Other skills and other areas of the curriculum
may suffer as a result of an overconcentration on measurable skills. Further,
students who easily acquire basic skills may be penalized when resources, and
the energy and emphasis of the staff, are focused primarily on helping slower
students acquire those skills. Once again, keep in mind that a school can be
"effective" in one regard but ineffective or less effective in terms of other very
desirable outcomes. So (we are reminded again) when someone says a school
is effective, we must ask ourselves, "Effective in terms of what?"

   STAFF DEVELOPMENT Important elements of the leadership associated with effective schools are those of staff selection, development, and
continuity. Successful schools are characterized by principals who recruit their
own staff rather than having staff assigned to them by a central office (Austin,
1981). Often collective bargaining agreements give teachers with seniority the
right to select the school in which they wish to teach and to "bump" teachers
with less seniority. The research evidence from the effective-schools movement would indicate that such a practice is detrimental to the development of a
shared consensus about the values and goals of the school and of policies for
behavior and discipline. Further, if the principal cannot recruit his or her own
teachers, it is more difficult to maintain staff stability and continuity and to
engage in collegial long-range planning and coordination.
   Effective schools are characterized by staff development programs designed to meet the needs that have been identified by teachers themselves
rather than ones identified by a central office. Further, the principals in such
schools often use portions of faculty meetings and lunch hours to talk with the
staff about new ideas (Little, 1982). An important aspect of staff development
is that the principal announces to the staff his or her expectations for improvement and then works continuously with them to scrutinize, evaluate, improve,
and judge their performance. Principals of effective schools reward teachers
for their efforts at school improvement through encouragement, public praise,
released time, and provision of additional materials and assistance. They sometimes cover classes so a teacher can observe a colleague or attend a workshop
(Little, 1982).
   Staff recruitment and development at the building level cannot take
place in the absence of district-level policies that permit such practices. A final
key element in the leadership dimension of effective schools, then, is a school
committee and superintendent who support efforts at school improvement.

Efficacy

   The effective-schools movement proclaims the good news "that poor
and minority children *can* and *will* learn if adults believe in them" (Brandt,
1982, p. 3). We have already seen that a key element of effective schools is a
climate that emphasizes academic excellence (Box 16.2). Study after study has
shown that effective schools are characterized by a commitment on the part

TABLE 16.1 School Policies and Classroom Practices that Convey Academic Press

School Policy Areas	Classroom Practices Areas
Policies on school function and structure 　School purpose 　Student grouping 　Protection of instructional time 　Orderly environment	Establishing an academically demanding climate Conducting an orderly, well-managed classroom
Policies on student progress 　Homework 　Grading 　Monitoring progress 　Remediation 　Reporting progress 　Retention/promotion	Implementing instructional practices that promote student achievement Providing opportunities for student responsibility and leadership

Source: Murphy, Weil, Hallinger, & Mitman, 1983, p. 24.

of teachers to academic values which, in turn, are clearly transmitted to students. Teachers expect pupils to achieve and they continually convey this expectation to them. Table 16.1 is a list of school policies and practices that help convey to students the academic emphasis, or "press." The word *press* is used to describe the prevailing emphasis of the school. A school press can be academic, social, or athletic. Figure 16.1 shows a working model of how a positive academic press is created in a school. A positive press is a direct outgrowth of the positive climate of a school, which is associated with leadership. This in turn is translated into staff responsibilities resulting in school policies and classroom practices that communicate to students the expectation of academic excellence.

Students experience the impact of this press in three ways: academic norms, self-concept of academic ability, and a sense of academic efficacy. Academic norms involve an emphasis on grades, the amount of time devoted to study and homework, and the overall centrality of academic work as opposed to nonacademic work. Self-concept refers to a belief on the part of students that they are capable of high academic work. The final aspect, academic efficacy, is the students' belief that they have control over their academic destiny, that hard work is more important than luck, and that their

FIGURE 16.1 A Working Model of How Academic Press Is Created in Schools

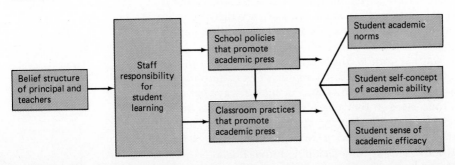

Source: Murphy, Weil, Hallinger, & Mitman, 1983.

In effective schools, homework is regularly assigned and expected to be done on time.

efforts can make a difference in school. Let us examine some of the mechanisms that convey a school's academic press to students.

EMPHASIS ON HOMEWORK AND STUDY In effective schools, homework is regularly assigned and is expected to be done on time. Assignments are corrected promptly and returned to students so that they can learn from any mistakes they may have made. Homework is never used as a punitive device or as busywork. The functions of the homework assignment are to allow students to practice the skills and objectives that are the focus of the lesson and to let teachers identify problem areas so that they can go over the lesson again or modify their approach for those that need it.

VISIBLE REWARDS FOR ACADEMIC SUCCESS All academic work is embedded in a classroom-accountability system set up by the teacher to which students quickly adapt. Students are fast in learning the formal and informal ingredients of the teacher's systems of rewards, grading, and marking. In effective schools, teachers and principals publicly recognize that success at academic tasks as an essential ingredient in building up a press for academic excellence. Displaying exemplary student work on corridor bulletin boards is one such public acknowledgment. Frequent, detailed report cards to parents is another visible reward mechanism. Students are made aware that their homework, classroom participation, and test scores are directly related to the report card, which in turn becomes an important motivating device in establishing academic press or climate for a school (Doyle, 1983).

However, if the reward system is consciously used to foster a press for academic excellence, teachers must avoid discouraging slower students. To do this, the instructional process must be structured in such a way that all students can succeed and thus share in the rewards for academic success. This requires that the material be presented at the appropriate level of difficulty for each student. (We shall discuss the need to structure instruction so that all students can succeed when we treat the efficiency dimensions.)

DE-EMPHASIS ON STRICT ABILITY GROUPING Effective elementary schools are characterized by classrooms in which pupils of *mixed ability* are grouped together. Studies of effective schools have shown that test scores are higher, on the average, in such classes. It is the pupils of below-average ability that benefit most from this arrangement; it would appear that they perform better in heterogeneous classes by interacting with pupils of higher ability. This suggests that, at the elementary level at least, a range of ability within a class may be an essential component for optimal learning (Cuttance, 1980a and 1980b). Sometimes grouping within a classroom may be necessary so that instruction on a *specific* skill or objective can be geared to the individual needs of students. When such groups are formed in effective schools the same students are not always found in the bottom group, and the groups are dissolved once the objective or skill has been mastered (Rutter, 1983; Rutter et al., 1979).

High schools, unlike elementary schools, are organized around curricular tracks and, therefore, grouping is hard to avoid. Not all students can benefit from, or want to pursue, a college preparatory physics course. However, in effective high schools, steps are taken to minimize the negative, stigmatizing effect of tracking. First, pupils are grouped separately for each subject. A student may be in a high track for English and in a lower track for math. Second, the quality of teaching does not differ from one track to another; the weakest or least-experienced teachers are not automatically allocated to the lowest tracks. Finally, students in the lower tracks have equal opportunities for success in the nonacademic aspects of school life.

Efficiency

Box 16.2 outlines six core elements and six facilitating elements that work in concert to produce higher pupil achievement. These 12 elements are congruent with Benjamin Bloom's model of schooling called "mastery learning" (described in Chapters 11 and 14). The last four core elements under efficiency in Box 16.2—continuous diagnosis, evaluation and feedback, well-structured classroom activities, instruction guided by content coverage, and schoolwide exphasis on basic and higher order skills—are treated in detail in Chapter 14 and will not be discussed further here. The first two core elements in Box 16.2—effective use of time and orderly and disciplined environments—are discussed in this section.

EFFECTIVE USE OF TIME Effective schools differ from less effective ones in the amount of instructional time available and in the way in which this time is used. Actual learning or working time, or "time on-task," is a necessary condition for learning (Pintrich, Cross, Kozma, & McKeachie, 1986). Time on-task is the amount of time that a student *actually spends* studying a particular subject or engaging in a learning activity (AASA, 1982; Wiley & Harneschfeger, 1974). The total amount of time available in the school year is roughly the same for all schools. Effective schools, however, use more of their time on learning tasks than do less effective ones. The National Commission on Excellence in Education recognized the importance of time in improving the quality of education when it recommended that "significantly more time be devoted to learning the new basics. This will require more effective use of the existing school day, a longer school day, or a lengthened school year" (NCEE, 1983, p. 29). The commission based this recommendation on the fact that children in other industrialized countries spend more of their lives in school than do American children.

In a similar vein, the Task Force on Education for Economic Growth, in their report on the state of our nations' schools, recommended that

> *every state should* increase both the duration and the intensity of academic learning time *in the schools. . . . Using the existing school year and the existing school day to the fullest must be emphasized first. But the states and local school systems should also consider lengthening the school year and the school day and extending teachers' contracts (TFEEG, 1983, p. 38).*

In our country, the typical school year is 180 six-hour days. Elsewhere, it is not uncommon for the school year to consist of 220 eight-hour days. A book about school effectiveness has as its title *15,000 hours;* the title refers to the amount of time a child in England spends in school from kindergarten through high school (Rutter et al., 1979). American children spend only 12,000 hours in school—3,000 fewer hours than their English counterparts. Nonetheless, increased time does not mean increased quality. Especially important is the way in which available time is used. Effective schools are successful in squeezing from the total amount of allocated time the greatest amount of time on task.

The length of the school year, school day, and class periods, as well as transitional time spent passing from class to class, time out for recess and lunch, and time needed for administrative chores (such as taking attendance and making announcements), determines the amount of available time on-task. This available time provides the upper bound on the time a student can spend on learning (AASA, 1982).

Studies of elementary school classrooms show that allocated time can be divided into three components. The first consists of academic activities. This includes time devoted to reading, mathematics, science, and social studies and takes up about 60 percent of the school day. The second component, "nonacademic" activities, which includes music, art, story time, and sharing, accounts for about 23 percent of allocated time. The last component, "noninstructional" activities, which includes taking attendance, making announcements, transitions, waiting between activities, and passing out supplies, accounts for about 17 percent of allocated time (Rosenshine, 1980).

Not all of the 60 percent of allocated time associated with academic activities is spent on learning activities, however. Actual time on-task can be affected, positively or negatively, by a number of classroom factors (see Box 16.3). For example, time on-task is reduced by student social interactions, tardiness, absence, misbehavior, or daydreaming. In effective schools, teachers organize their classes so as to reduce such interruptions. It is important that teachers strive to gain and maintain student cooperation, establish and enforce rules, and set up procedures for routine administrative necessities so that all the time available for teaching is used efficiently (refer back to Table 13.4

BOX 16.3 Classroom Factors That Affect Learning Time

Students

PERSONAL BEHAVIOR

Misbehavior
Absenteeism
Tardiness

PSYCHOLOGICAL TRAITS

Aptitude
Ability
Prior knowledge
Motivation

Teachers

PERSONAL BEHAVIOR

Managerial skills
Preparation
Organizational
Ability to implement strategies

TEACHING STRATEGIES

Seat work
Individual instruction
Groupings
Whole class/direct instruction
Mastery learning
Peer group tutoring

Special Cases

Pull-outs
Interruptions

Source: American Association of School Administrators, 1982.

on pages 330–331 for suggestions on how to reduce time spent on routine administrative or housekeeping chores) (Doyle, 1983).

In the typical class, seat work, which includes assignment completion, silent reading, homework checking, or test taking, consumes between 60 and 70 percent of available class time (Doyle, 1983). Unless seat work is carefully planned, it can reduce the time pupils actually spend on-task. For example, students who finish seat work quickly have time to waste. Conversely, students who do not understand what the seat work requires of them are lost. For seat work to run smoothly, a teacher cannot sit at his or her desk and correct homework or complete other paperwork. Instead, the teacher needs to circulate, looking for students in need of help, answering questions, giving positive reinforcement and encouragement, and having additional work ready for faster students (AASA, 1982).

Too much individualized attention given to one or two students greatly reduces the time on-task available to other students. When the class period is 50 minutes long and there are 25 students in the room, simple arithmetic shows that the teacher can devote only two minutes of attention to each student. However, a teacher's time is never equally distributed. If the teacher spends more time with the brightest students, or with the slowest, or with the most disruptive, then the time on-task for the class as a whole suffers (AASA, 1982).

ORDERLY AND DISCIPLINED ENVIRONMENT One of the hallmarks of an effective school is that of firm but not oppressive discipline (Edmonds, 1982). Effective schools are orderly, are relatively quiet, and have a pleasant atmosphere. While sanctions and punishment are necessary to enforce rules of discipline, excessive use of punishment may aggravate behavior and attendance problems (Rutter, 1983). Disruption and misbehavior not only reduce time on-task but generally wreak havoc on a learning environment. It is impossible for a teacher to be effective in a disorderly, disorganized, noisy atmosphere.

In effective schools, the establishment and maintenance of good discipline begins with the principal, who, working with the teachers, sets school policy and clear and consistent rules governing such matters as respecting and obeying adults, coming to school on time, smoking, fighting, and vandalism. These rules are communicated clearly to pupils and enforced uniformly across all classrooms. Most important, the principal reinforces the authority of the teachers in disciplinary matters.

The appearance of the building is an important element in maintaining discipline, which deteriorates with institutional neglect. Effective schools are clean; broken furniture and windows are promptly repaired and graffiti are quickly removed.

Some exemplary schools actively involve older students in the formulation of rules of conduct. Bringing students into the governance of the school helps develop a sense of community and ownership (Lipsitz, 1981). The following is an example of how establishing discipline and dealing with discipline problems can be handled a mutual responsibility; the scene is Ketcham High School in New York City.

The appearance of the classroom is an important element in maintaining discipline.

Developing a Discipline Code for a School

In the past year and a half, our school has worked on a new Discipline Code, which was developed by a committee made up of parents, teachers, students, and administrators. After the code was created, workshops were presented to parents during an evening meeting, and an entire day of school was spent teaching the code to the students. Members of the committee worked with groups of 25 students, answering questions and explaining rules and regulations in the code. A workshop was also provided for the teaching staff and school monitors. We now have a Review Committee of teachers, students, administrators, and parents who updated the code to make sure it is being properly implemented (Lasley & Wayson, 1982, p. 29).

TABLE 16.2 Sample Lists of Causes and Symptoms of Discipline Problems

Symptoms	Causes	Activities
Extensive vandalism of property	Lack of student involvement	Written rules and definite consequences
Disrespect for people	Lack of rules on attendance, discipline	Staff cooperation
Falling test scores	Lax follow-up for disruptive behavior	Consistent enforcement of rules and regulations
Student disinterest in school	Staff not working together	Better supervision in all areas; strict enforcement of hall passes
Lack of school spirit		
Lack of participation in school activities	Extensive exceptions made	
	Wishy-washy leadership	Support of staff by administration
	Limited activities in community	Communication and meetings with parents
	Staff concerned with self-preservation	Student handbook
	Parent apathy and disinterest	News articles on school policies and practices

Source: Lasley & Wayson, 1982, p. 29.

In Table 16.2, we present a list of symptoms and causes of discipline problems in schools. There is also a list of activities to reduce such problems. An examination of these activities shows the importance of strong leadership and the development of a sense of community within the school. Discipline problems are minimal when a majority of the students want to participate in the learning process and are convinced that they can succeed; discipline problems increase when students act out of fear of punishment.

CONCLUSION

The good news from recent research on school effectiveness contradicts the earlier pessimistic interpretations of the Coleman report. Schools do make a difference, and some schools are more effective than others. People are now saying that children, regardless of their home background, can learn and will learn if the school staff believes that they can and acts on that belief. Researchers have begun to isolate the characteristics that differentiate effective schools from those that are less effective; these characteristics, taken together rather than singly, suggest strategies for change that should help to improve schools in need of improvement.

The characteristics of effective schools when considered as a whole suggest an overall climate and an organizational setup, at both the school and the classroom levels, that focus on making it easier for teachers to teach and for pupils to profit from that teaching. Effective schools are blessed with strong leadership and have firm but not oppressive rules for behavior. These schools exude a businesslike atmosphere and make maximum use of the time available for learning. At the classroom level, lessons are structured and geared to the achievement level of pupils. Ample cues and reinforcement are provided. Teachers operate systematic mechanisms for monitoring and feedback. Perhaps most important of all, the effective school and classroom are characterized by the expectation that all students can and will succeed.

As you progress in your professional careers, you will need to keep abreast of developments concerning school and teaching effectiveness. It is one of the most important areas of current research in education. There is great promise in this work. It is often said that if you want to understand something, try to change it. Research on effective schools is based on the idea that if you want to change something, try to understand it.

QUESTIONS AND ACTIVITIES

1. Reflect back on the elementary, junior high or middle school, and high school you attended. What characteristics of effective schools did they model? Which ones didn't they model?
2. Think back over your years as a student and identify your favorite teacher. List the attributes of that teacher and compare them to the characteristics of effective teachers identified in this chapter. What qualities are shared? Which differ?
3. As a future teacher, would you prefer to teach a class with students of mixed or similar abilities? Why?
4. What major points from the effective-schools research do you plan to stress in your classroom? Why?
5. How do you plan to establish a classroom climate that includes effective discipline? Explain.
6. Critics of mixed ability grouping of students contend those students at the top of the class are held back by the slower students. What are your opinions regarding this view?
7. What role do you think state education authorities (SEAs) should play in ensuring that schools in the state use practices associated with the effective-schools literature? What should the role of local education agencies (LEAs) be? The federal government?
8. In what ways might working in an "effective school" reduce stress for classroom teachers?
9. What characteristics do effective principals have in common with effective leaders in other professions (for example, business or politics)?
10. What might school administrators do to encourage a consensus of "shared purposefulness" in schools?
11. Do you feel the school day or school year should be lengthened? Why? Why not?

PART SIX

Current Issues

The last decade has witnessed several important developments in education that not only affect your current preparation, but also have profound implications for your future career in teaching. This final section explores these developments, the issues they raise for teachers, and their implications for practice.

Chapter 17 describes the emerging place of the computer in the classroom: the nature of the new technologies, how the computer can help in instruction, what technology is currently available, and what you can anticipate in the future. Computers will never replace the teacher, but for the first time in the history of education there is a technology that can substantially assist the teacher in instruction, particularly in skill areas. The computer also can help in preparing attractive instructional material and in incorporating graphic material into the instructional process that has heretofore been limited by the constraints of the typewriter. Many of your students will already be familiar with computers.

Chapter 18 introduces you to the concept of accountability. As a teacher, you will be evaluated and held accountable for your work to an extent unknown by past generations of teachers. The reasons for the growing demand for accountability are discussed and mechanisms such as testing, vouchers, performance contracting, and teacher incentive programs are described. The chapter explores how much an individual is accountable for, to whom people are accountable, and when they are accountable. Accountability can be a contentious issue. It is one that you will have to deal with both in your preparation to become a teacher and once you are in the job.

Chapter 19 describes the growing role of standardized testing in education. Standardized testing affects countless students every year and tests are fast becoming a principal indicator of educational equality. Basic concepts about testing are explained and the benefits and dangers associated with the testing movement are discussed.

The final chapter takes you through an analysis of the many reform reports that have altered the landscape of public education. These reports will have an impact on many aspects of your career. They have brought about changes in teacher preparation, teacher certification, teacher salaries, elementary and secondary school curricula, and a host of other areas. You must understand the political nature of these reports, why they were written, and how they might affect your career.

A problem with the four chapters in this section is that they all deal with areas that are developing rapidly. Although the chapters provide background and vital information, it will be up to you to keep abreast of developments in these areas.

CHAPTER 17

Computers in Education

Computers are fast becoming an important part of the education scene. Computer literacy for students is becoming a requirement. Teachers and administrators can use this powerful technology to aid them in certain aspects of their work. Computers will never replace good teachers, but good teachers will increasingly use them to facilitate aspects of their job.

● The main components of the computer are input, memory, processing, and output. Specialized languages let you tell the machine what to do. Some of these languages are nontechnical and designed to let teachers develop instructional units.

● Computers can be used as a tool to help teachers and administrators with records, accounts, planning, testing, and material preparation. The computer can be used to tutor pupils or it can function as a tutee: in the former case the computer tells the student what to do and is powerful for drill and practice; in the latter case the student tells the computer what to do (that is, students and teachers can program the machine).

● Computers can be a source of trouble; introducing computers into schools can be problematic.

● You do not need to be an expert or a programmer to use computers in your classroom. Commercially developed software programs are available for instructional use in all curriculum areas and at all grade levels. However, you must be able to intelligently evaluate and use software.

The "computer revolution" is upon us. Computers, increasingly power-ful yet decreasingly expensive, are transforming many parts of society—busi-ness, government, leisure time, and particularly education. This revolution brings with it a new and seemingly foreign language. To "boot" a computer, for example, does not mean to kick it. And "byte" is not the favorite meal of a vampire who can't spell. These are words from the new language of comput-ing.

The purpose of this chapter is to introduce you to the world and lan-guage of computers in general and to the uses of computers in education in particular. First, we will describe what a computer is and how it works. Sec-ond, we will describe four roles of computers in education: the computer as a tool, the computer as tutor, the computer as tutee, the computer as trouble. Finally, we will look at the probable future of computers in education.

Although new, the computer field is already very large and is growing at a stupendous rate. For example, "If the aircraft industry had evolved as spectacularly as the computer industry over the last 25 years, a Boeing 767 would cost $500 today and it would circle the globe in 20 minutes on five gallons of fuel" (Toong & Gupta, 1982, p. 87).

This chapter focuses mainly on the personal or microcomputer, which is the type of computer that is having the greatest impact on education. Undoubtedly, you will be taking courses in educational technology in which you will develop many of the skills described in this chapter.

Computer Basics

A computer is really nothing more than a machine that receives, stores, manipulates, and communicates information. The main components of a com-puter can be described in terms of four functions: *input, memory* or *storage, processing,* and *output.* Before describing these functions you first need to know a little about the language that computers understand and use.

The Language of Computers

There are two different types of computers—analog and digital. This is a general distinction, something like the distinction between flora and fauna in the world of biology. Both types use amounts of electricity, but in quite different ways. Analog computers use variable electrical voltage to represent numbers or information. Digital computers use on/off electrical signals for the same purpose.

Because voltage can be used to control the speed of electric motors, analog computers are particularly useful in manufacturing, where they are used to control machines such as variable-speed drills. Digital computers are the ones used in education. They represent numbers or information in the form of numbers or digits, but the digits are not the familiar 0 to 9 of the common base 10 number system with which you are familiar. Rather, they are the 0 and 1 of the binary number system you may have studied in junior high or high school. Binary numbers are used for digital computing because they can be represented simply as on/off electrical signals. Hence, the binary number system has become the "machine language" of digital computers. In binary language, information is coded as strings of 0s and 1s. Since this language is not easy to read, codes have been developed to translate groups of 0s and 1s into numbers and letters with which we are familiar and comfortable. For example, the letter *D* in machine language is represented by the binary code 1100 0100. There are standard codes for representing letters and numbers in machine language; the most common is ASCII (pronounced ASKEY), which stands for American Standard Code for Information Interchange.

Computer programs can be written using these binary codes but, since that can be very difficult, most computers have built into them something called an *operating system* to make programming easier. An operating system is something like a housekeeper. It helps communication between the machine and various special computer programs (software) that can be used to do thousands of different jobs. In a moment we will describe the various jobs computers can do to help in teaching and learning. First, however, let us briefly talk about the equipment that performs the four computer functions of input (receiving), memory (storing), processing, and output (communicating information).

INPUT Before you can get a computer to do anything, you have to tell it precisely what to do; that is, you have to input information. A variety of input devices allow the computer to receive information. The most obvious is the keyboard. Most computer keyboards resemble a regular typewriter keyboard, but computer keyboards are different in some important ways. For example, most computer keyboards have a variety of special keys, often called function keys, not found on any typewriter. Perhaps the most common is the control key, which is something like a super "shift" key that allows a variety of special symbols, called control symbols, to be received by the computer.

Other common computer input devices are tape cassettes and disk drives. These allow precoded information, recorded on the tape or disk in magnetic form, to be electronically read into the computer. Many early home computers used tape cassette recorders to input information but, generally, disk drives are preferable because they are faster and more accurate than tape cassettes in handling data.

The disks used in disk drives look like small phonograph records. Because they are flexible, they are sometimes called floppy disks, and because they are small they are sometimes called diskettes. Disks always come in a square or rectangular protective envelope or plastic case. The most common sizes of floppy disks are 5¼ inches and 3½ inches. The latter are encased in hard plastic and are very durable, they are often called shirt protect disks. The trend is toward the smaller 3½-inch disk, but schools that use older machines will still use the 5¼-inch variety. Although a disk looks small and simple, it can actually hold a lot of information—at present, the equivalent of as many as 500 typewritten pages of text.

In addition to the keyboard and disk drives, a number of other input devices are available for most microcomputers. These include "joysticks" or game controllers for playing video games, electronic scratch pads (which allow you to input information by simply touching different places on the pad), and electronic "mice," which allow the input of information at the press of a button, scanners that can read text or graphic material directly into the computer, video cameras, and video disks.

MEMORY There is one other very important way of getting information into a microcomputer, and that is to build it in when the computer is manufactured. This brings us to the memory, or storage, function of computers. Putting aside the possibility of external storage (that is, information stored outside the computer itself on disk or on tape), there are basically two types of storage available inside a microcomputer, called random-access memory (RAM) and read-only memory (ROM). Both kinds of memory reside inside microcomputers on what look like small pieces of plastic; actually, they are integrated circuits (ICs) containing a network of infinitesimally small electronic circuits.

ROM, as the name implies, can only be accessed when the computer is used. It is permanently in the machine and cannot be written over or erased. RAM, on the other hand, is a bit like a blank memory bank. When the computer is used, information can be read into RAM and retrieved from it at any point. Unlike ROM, every time the computer is turned off, whatever is in RAM is erased.

Microcomputers are often advertised as having 48K, 64K, 128K, 512K, or 1 meg of RAM. Since "K" stands for one thousand, an advertisement for a 64K RAM machine means that it has roughly 64,000 bytes of RAM. A byte is the amount of space needed to store a character in memory. The more ROM and RAM a machine has, the more powerful it is.

PROCESSING After information is put into a computer (input) and recorded in memory, the machine can process it. For example, if you wish to solve the simple division problem "11 divided by 37" using the computer, you would input the numbers "11" and "37" and the instruction to divide, usually symbolized on computers by the backslash (/). These items of data would be sent to the "brain" of the computer, that is, its central processing unit (CPU). It is the processing unit that actually operates on the data to give the answer: "11/37 = .2973." But first a computer program translates the problem to an intermediate computer language understood by the machine (often called assembler language) and sends the problem to the operating system, which in turn translates it to machine (binary) language and sends it to the CPU, where the operation is performed in binary mathematics. Then the process is reversed (CPU to operating system to program) so the answer can be seen on the monitor or printed on paper.

Fortunately, all this happens with tremendous speed. A microcomputer's CPU can usually divide one number by another in 500 microseconds or less, that is, within 500 millionths of a second. Indeed, in the last few years, as the circuitry of microcomputers has improved, the speed of processing is measured not in microseconds but in *nanoseconds*, that is, billionths of a second. Hence, the "brains" of microcomputers can carry out literally millions of arithmetic or logical operations in a second.

How does a computer operate at such speeds? If you open one up and hunt for the CPU, you very likely will be disappointed. You will find nothing more than a small piece of plastic, usually colored black and looking rather like a domino. This piece of plastic is called a chip and is an integrated circuit (IC). It is what has really powered the computer revolution.

Before the 1950s, electronic computers used vacuum tubes as switching

The invention of the silicon chip helped make computers practical for large-scale use in classrooms by making them smaller and more affordable.

devices. The transistor did away with vacuum tubes in a variety of electronic devices (for example, the radio). The transistor made possible the development of the second generation of computers, which were smaller, more powerful, and more reliable. The third generation of computers came in the 1960s; the most famous of these was the IBM 360 mainframe computer. Thousands of these machines were sold in the 1960s. What set the 360 apart from its ancestors, in addition to its commercial success, was its use of integrated circuits, which, as the name implies, integrated in one unit the functions previously housed in several different electronic devices, such as transistors, diodes, and resistors.

The next major development in the world of hardware was the introduction of microcomputers (micros) in the 1970s. These microcomputers were small and cheap enough to be purchased and used not only by large organizations for research or commercial purposes but by individuals for their own use. Micros became possible because of "large-scale integration" (LSI). With LSI, manufacturers could fit thousands of electronic circuits on a single IC chip, smaller than a fingernail, to make up a complete CPU.

OUTPUT If computers have been miniaturized so successfully, you might well ask, why do they still cost hundreds or thousands of dollars and take up considerably more space than a fingernail? The answer is that the main factors in limiting the size and cost of small computers are the devices that allow you to get data into and out of the computer. Recall some of the input devices already have discussed. Take the keyboard, for example. In principle, we could make keyboards shrink to the size of a matchbook. The obvious problem with doing this is that we can't shrink people's fingers to similar proportions.

The other end of the process—output—imposes limits on size and raises the cost also. The most common output device is a monitor, which looks like a television set. In fact, relatively cheap home computers often use the television as an output device. More expensive microcomputers usually come with their own monitor or screen, either built in or as a separate unit. Since the heart of such video screens is a cathode-ray tube, these devices are sometimes called CRTs. Four types of monitor are commonly used: black and white (just like a black-and-white television screen), color (for use with graphics or video games), green, and amber (the last two are often used to reduce eyestrain).

The second most common type of output device is the printer, which outputs data onto paper. The three most common types of printer are dot matrix, letter-quality, and laser printers. Dot-matrix printers use printing heads that can form rectangles or matrixes of dots. Letters and numbers are formed from different patterns of dots (see Figure 17.1). Letter-quality printers are more like typewriters. They use wheels or thimbles that have physical representations of letters and numbers. Output is produced when a "hammer" selectively strikes portions of the print wheel or thimble to produce letters on paper. Letter-quality printers generally produce print that looks better than dot-matrix print, but they are more expensive and slower. In fact, you can easily spend more on a letter-quality printer than on some microcomputers. The laser printer operates on a principle similar to a standard photocopier but, unlike a photocopier, which uses reflected light to place an image on the paper, the laser printer uses a laser to "burn" a character onto the paper. Laser printers produce very high quality characters and are fast and quiet. They are used primarily in business and are relatively expensive. However, the costs are already beginning to drop; in the near future the laser printer will probably replace both dot-matrix and letter-quality printers.

There are several other ways to output data. For example, tape cassettes and disks can receive output, but only for use at a later time. There are, however, several other forms of output that communicate directly to the user. Most microcomputers, for example, have at least a small speaker allowing voice or music output. Also, there are special devices that translate output into tactile form. Automatic Braille devices, for example, allow blind people to "read" output in the form of Braille characters they can feel with their fingers.

The proliferation of powerful, yet increasingly cheaper, microcomputers and associated technologies has opened the way for huge changes in modern society—changes in the way business is conducted, in the way things are manufactured and sold, in the ways medicine is practiced, in our leisure time, and, of course, in the world of education. Before we focus on the uses of computers in education, it is important to point out that, even if there were not a single computer in any school, the computer revolution would still profoundly affect education in several ways: through students' experience with home computers and video games and through the changing requirements for computer skills in many jobs. But computers are, in fact, rapidly going to school. Parents, business people, and government officials are demanding that computers be introduced into schools. Computer literacy has been added to the list of basic skills that many people feel our schools should impart to all students.

In the school setting, the computer plays three major roles, also known as the three *T*s: *tutor, tool,* and *tutee* (Taylor, 1980). A fourth *T* can be added: a *T* for *trouble.* Let us consider each of these four *T*s in more detail.

FIGURE 17.1 How Dot-Matrix and Letter-Quality Printers Work

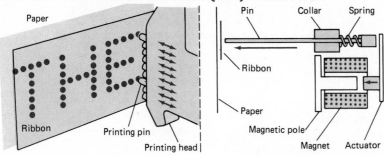

The dot-matrix printer is relatively inexpensive, fast (up to 200 characters per second), and flexible: it can generate compressed, expanded, or bold characters, or even graphic images, depending on the commands it receives from the computer. The printing head is a vertical array of pins that are fired selectively as the head is swept across the paper to press an inked ribbon against the paper and thereby form a pattern of dots (*left*). Here each capital letter is a subset of a matrix seven dots high and five dots wide; two more pins are available to form the descenders of lowercase letters such as *p*. The pins are fired by individual solenoids (*right*). The mechanism illustrated here is that of a dot-matrix printer made by Epson America, Inc.

(a)

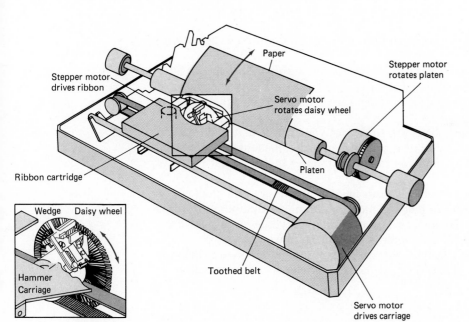

The daisy-wheel printer produces "letter quality" copy at a rate of from 20 to 55 characters per second. This is a schematic representation of a Qume Corporation printer. The printing wheel has a plastic hub around which are arrayed 96 (in some models 130) radial spokes; a letter, number, or other symbol is molded into the end of each spoke. In response to signals from the computer the wheel is rotated either clockwise or counterclockwise to bring the proper symbol into position and is stopped; the hammer strikes (with an energy proportionate to the area of the symbol: much harder, say, for a *W* than for a comma), driving the sliding wedge against the end of the radial arm to press the inked ribbon against the paper; the carriage and ribbon advance as the wheel is spun to bring the next symbol into position.

(b)

Source: Toong & Gupta, 1982, pp. 102–103.

The Computer as a Tool

Traditionally, computers in schools have been used for word processing, financial management, and record keeping.

Word Processing

If you have never seen a word processor, the name may lead you to think of something that chops up, sterilizes, and cans words. This image is not altogether off the mark, but word processing can probably be better described as electronic typing and printing. The idea is that a letter or report can be typed into a computer and revised and edited as many times as you feel necessary.

There are dozens of word-processing programs on the market today. They range in price from twenty dollars to thousands of dollars. Whatever they cost and whatever machines they run on, they tend to have several basic features in common:

- When you type on a word processor, the words show up on a monitor screen.
- Special keys on the keyboard allow you to back up and erase or write over mistakes.
- Special functions may be implemented (either by striking special function keys or combinations of keys) to allow you to do things like rearranging words, lines, sentences or paragraphs, and adding information to the text at any point.
- Word processors allow you to format your words or text in various ways (for instance, by adjusting the size of pages, the length of lines, and the size of print), before you tell the computer to print what you have written.
- More advanced word processors have utility programs that allow you to integrate graphic or pictorial material, count the number of words in the text, check the spelling against a dictionary stored on disk, use a thesaurus, or even check some aspects of grammar.
- There are specialized word-processing programs designed to help you construct overheads and other material for classroom presentation.

Electronic Spreadsheets

When used with an electronic spreadsheet, the computer can become a tool to manage financial information and school budgets. Electronic spreadsheets are software programs that present the user with a large grid of rows that are numbered (1, 2, 3, and so on) and columns that are lettered (A, B, C, and so on). Each column letter and row number identifies a cell in the spreadsheet. Cell A1, for instance, would be the cell in the upper left-hand corner of the spreadsheet.

When you use an electronic spreadsheet, you usually start by labeling the rows and columns. For example, each column might be used for the year and month within a school budget, and rows might be labeled with different budget items. Thus, column N might be used for school expenditures in the month of January 1990, cell N6 to record professional salary expenses for that month, and cell N7 for all other salary expenses for the month. Cell N8 might be defined as the sum of cells N6 and N7, that is, total salary expenses for January of 1990. Electronic spreadsheets are powerful because once one

Computers can be a useful tool to help teachers with such tasks as lesson planning, record keeping and word processing.

cell value is defined in terms of other cell values (in our simple case, N8 = N7 + N6), any change in one of the original cell values (say, N7) automatically changes the total (in cell N8). This is a very simple example, but you can probably begin to imagine how elaborate budget programs might be laid out on an electronic spreadsheet, with many cell values defined as functions of other cell values.

A school principal or superintendent can lay out an entire school budget on such a spreadsheet. In a matter of seconds, an administrator could see how the "bottom line" would be affected if, for example, teacher salaries were raised by 5 percent or 10 percent or fuel-oil prices were to increase by various amounts. Because spreadsheets can be used to explore the impact of many such hypothetical budgeting situations, they are sometimes called "what-if" devices.

Teachers can use spreadsheets to keep class records. The columns contain students and the rows various pieces of information relating to, for example, attendance, grades, and marks for quizzes, chapter tests, and homework.

Data Base Management Programs

Schools must keep many kinds of records: records of students' names, addresses, classes, grades, attendance, and so on. Data base management software programs are used to store lists (records) of information, manipulate them in various ways, and retrieve or print different records or combinations of records. Data base management system (DBMS) programs come in many different forms. One of the simplest such programs is used for storing lists of names and telephone numbers; you could type a person's name and automatically his or her telephone number would appear. DBMS programs can also be designed to store test questions coded by objectives, retrieve selected items, and print a test. These kinds of programs are often called item-bank programs. Other DBMS programs are designed specifically for teachers to keep grades and other records (spreadsheets used for this purpose work on a different principle).

Simpler DBMS programs are dedicated to a particular purpose, like grading or item banking. This is all they can do; they cannot be modified. More complex all-purpose DBMS programs are now available; they allow the user to design a data base to suit a particular purpose. A school principal, for example, might develop a data base consisting of information on teachers. Each teacher might have a single record containing information such as address, home phone, birth date, and room number. For example, if the school principal wants to send birthday cards to teachers, the data base retrieves the names and addresses of all teachers having birthdays in any particular month. The uses of DBMS programs in schools are virtually infinite.

DBMS, word-processing, and spreadsheet programs have been widely used as tools by education administrators. They also use computers as tools to schedule classes and print report cards. These "tool" programs are also used for instructional purposes; that is, teachers use them to help students develop the necessary computer skills. Some schools, for example, now teach word processing instead of typing. Accounting and business classes teach the use of electronic spreadsheets and DBMS programs.

In addition, many teachers are excited about the possibilities of improving student writing by having students use word processors, on which students can easily respond to a teacher's critique and repeatedly revise an essay or report. For example, Cornell University has developed a program called PROSE. Students type their writing assignments using a standard word-processing program, then pass their disks in to the instructor. The instructor uses PROSE to enter comments about the student's work directly on disk. Some of the comments for problems with mispelling, split infinitives, punctuation, and so forth, are "canned"; all the instructor does is type a number that corresponds to the type of error. The instructor types other comments about style, usage, organization, word choice, and so forth directly onto the disk, the equivalent of writing comments on a pupil's paper. The disk is then returned to the students, who use their copy of PROSE to revise the writing exercise. PROSE will not let the student proceed past an instructor's comment until it has been addressed. While PROSE can be used only on a particular type of machine—the Apple Macintosh—similar programs will soon be available for other computers.

The Computer as Tutor

The computer can be used as a tutor to help teach students. Literally thousands of tutorial programs are available for microcomputers. There are several different ways of classifying this large domain of educational software. Here, we will discuss only four types: drill and practice, tutorial, simulation, and educational games.

Drill and Practice

There is software designed to give students drills and practice in a variety of skills. The computer presents the student with a problem, the student types an answer, and the computer checks it and then provides feedback on whether or not it is correct. The kinds of problems suitable for this kind of use obviously are ones that can be presented in a small amount of space and have answers that are clearly right or wrong. At the elementary school level, dozens of programs have been created to drill children on arithmetic skills. The computer monitor might, for example, show the following instructions and problems:

WHAT IS THE ANSWER TO THE FOLLOWING MULTIPLICATION PROBLEM?
$7 \times 6 = ?$
PLEASE TYPE IN THE NUMBER YOU THINK IS CORRECT

The student then would type in his or her answer. If the student answers "42", the computer might respond with something like "GOOD, THAT'S THE RIGHT ANSWER. WOULD YOU LIKE ANOTHER PROBLEM?" However, if the student answered with anything other than the correct answer, the computer might respond in several different ways. If the answer was only a digit off in the tens place, the computer program might be designed to respond with encouraging feedback such as, "YOUR ANSWER IS CLOSE, BUT NOT QUITE RIGHT. PLEASE TRY AGAIN." If the student mistakenly typed letters instead of numbers, the program might point this out with a response such as, "YOUR ANSWER MUST BE IN NUMBERS. PLEASE TYPE AN ANSWER USING ONLY NUMBERS."

These simple examples of drill and practice programs in arithmetic suggest some of the useful features of such programs. First, they give the student immediate feedback. The student does not have to wait for the teacher to check the answers. Second, the computer does not become impatient or tired; it will repeatedly give the student appropriate prompts without

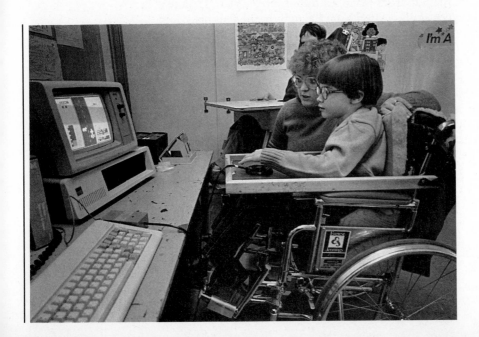

Thousands of computer software programs have been developed to help students learn.

losing its cool, and can present as many problems as the students want to try. Third, it allows students to progress at their own pace.

There are a number of other common types of drill and practice programs. Most deal with material such as arithmetic skills, solutions to algebra or geometry problems, spelling, and factual material in science, geography, and history.

Although drill-and-practice software programs span a fairly wide range of subject material, they are limited in several ways. First, they can get boring rather quickly. Second, since they tend to deal only with the right and wrong answers to factual material, they can cover only a small aspect of learning. There is more to education than facts or arithmetic skills. Third, there are some drill and practice programs on the market that were hurriedly developed and contain factual errors.

There is one additional drill-and-practice program worth mentioning, because it is designed to give the teacher diagnostic feedback on the type of errors students make on basic arithmetic operations. Called BUGGY, it analyzes specific answers to detect a specific "bug" or defect in the child's procedure (Brown & Burton, 1978). Consider the following addition problems (Barr & Feigenbaum, 1982) and their answers:

A	B	C	D	E
41	328	989	66	216
+ 9	+917	+ 52	+887	+13
50	1345	1041	1053	229

Notice that A, C, and E are correct; B and D, while correct in the units and tens place, are wrong in the hundreds place. In this example, BUGGY determines that the student successfully carried from the units to the tens place and then continued to carry the same digit from the tens to the hundreds place.

Teachers do not often recognize the kinds of errors that BUGGY is programmed to detect. Consequently, they may conclude that the child needs more drill and practice with basic number facts or is simply careless. While BUGGY is only available for use on large computers—to which most schools do not have access—it represents the type of program that eventually will be available for use with microcomputers. A program that could both inform the teacher that a child is having difficulty with a certain skill or operation and also suggest reasons for the difficulty would be invaluable.

Tutorial

A second type of educational software can be labeled tutorial. Tutorial software programs are designed to teach you how to do something within a fairly limited domain of knowledge or skills. Probably the most common types of tutorial software are those that teach you how to use a particular kind of hardware or software. There are, for example, literally dozens of tutorial programs to teach you how to use each of the most common types of microcomputer. In recent years, several new companies have sprung up that simply develop and sell software tutorials to teach people how to use other kinds of software!

Most tutorials are organized into lessons, analogous to the chapters of a textbook. When you first use a tutorial, you are usually presented with a menu of different lessons from which to choose. The tutorial program then presents you with instructional material pertinent to the particular lesson you chose. At this point, tutorials diverge into several different types called straight-feed, feed-and-refeed, feed-and-regurgitate, and feed-and-ferment tutorials.

Straight-feed tutorials simply present the user with information to be learned. The computer presents a screen of information; after you have read it, without necessarily digesting it, you simply go on to the next screen of information.

Feed-and-refeed tutorials allow you some flexibility. After you are "fed" one or two screens of information, you are offered the possibility of backing up to review the material previously presented. In effect, the tutorial allows you to review information previously presented if you are unsure of it.

Feed-and-regurgitate tutorials go one step further. After one lesson or a small set of lessons, they ask you a question or set of questions on the material presented. In other words, you are asked to "regurgitate" the material presented. If you cannot correctly answer the questions or perform a task after one or two tries, the program may encourage you to try again, give you a hint, or automatically recycle to refeed you one or more lessons.

Feed-and-ferment tutorials go still one step further. They may encompass all the features just described—that is, lessons are presented, with opportunities to back up and review, and you are asked to answer specific questions on material presented. In addition, feed-and-ferment tutorials periodically require you to combine various specific pieces of information or skills to solve a problem or answer a question. Thus, the program requires you to integrate several previously learned concepts to solve a more general problem.

Simulation

Simulation software presents you with a situation about which you must make decisions. The software has a built-in model from which it predicts what will happen on the basis of decisions you make. One example of a simple piece of simulation software is a program called Lemonade Stand. In this simulation, you are asked to pretend that you are running a lemonade stand. You are presented with information about business conditions for a particular day (for example, the weather, since presumably lemonade sales will be better when it is hot) and how much it will cost to make up each gallon of lemonade. You are then asked to make some business decisions on how much lemonade to prepare for the day and what price to charge. After this, the computer runs a model of the business day using your input and you are informed how much profit you made or how much you lost. You obviously will suffer a loss if you try to sell the lemonade for less than it costs to produce or if you charge so much that no one will buy.

Lemonade Stand is designed to teach you something about running a small business; for example, that pricing decisions must take into consideration business conditions. Other simulations may take you through very different and much more complex situations such as dissecting a frog; running a country; exploring a historical event from the point of view of various participants; or flying and landing a plane.

Educational Games

Game software takes advantage of certain features of the computer to translate the learning of various skills into electronic games. Typically, such educational games employ computer graphics, fast action, and some sort of competition in an effort to make learning more fun. For example, you might score points for how fast or accurately you apply a particular skill.

One popular educational game is called Master Type which helps teach typing skills. You type letters or words randomly presented in the four corners of the monitor before projectiles sent out from the words or letters destroy your "spaceship" which appears in the center of the screen. The only way you can achieve a high score in this game is by becoming a faster and more accurate typist.

This is just one example of an educational computer game. Other software programs use the electronic-game format to teach things such as mathematics skills, vocabulary, motor skills, and various kinds of reasoning or logic.

The Computer as Tutee

When using the computer as tool and as tutor, you are in a somewhat passive role. You use the computer as a tool to do work *for* you or you use it to learn a restricted domain of knowledge or skills *already defined* by the program. When you use the computer as tutee, you reverse the roles of teacher and learner. Instead of the computer being the "teacher" and the user the learner, you "teach" the computer to do whatever it is that you want done. You do this by learning how to program the computer.

There are dozens of computer-programming languages now available for use on microcomputers. A computer-programming language is essentially a set of instructions you use to make a computer do an infinite variety of tasks. In the 1940s and 1950s, someone who wanted to program a computer had to write instructions in a language that the computer could directly understand, namely "machine language." Machine language is difficult to use because it typically deals with extended sets of binary code, that is, extended strings of ones and zeros. From the 1950s to the 1970s, a variety of "higher-level" programming languages were invented; they translate the users instructions into machine language which the computer "understands." The first widely used high-level computer languages were FORTRAN (which stands for *Formula Tran*slation), introduced in 1957, and COBOL (*Co*mmon *B*usiness-*O*riented *L*anguage), introduced in 1960.

Over the last 30 years, literally hundreds of high-level computer-pro-gramming languages have been invented. At present there are three that are widely used in education: BASIC, Pascal, and LOGO. BASIC (*B*eginner's *A*ll-purpose *S*ymbolic *I*nstruction *C*ode) was developed in the 1960s at Dart-mouth College, for use by college students. By the early 1980s, BASIC had become the most widely used high-level computer-programming language in education. Its main advantage is that it is very easy to learn. With less than an hour of instruction you can begin to write simple computer programs in BASIC. The main criticism of BASIC is that, at least in its simpler versions, it does not have the power to allow structured programming, that is, program-ming that allows use of special control structures to solve a variety of more complex programming problems.

This criticism of BASIC led to a growing use of Pascal. This programming language is named after the seventeenth-century French mathematician Pas-cal, who invented one of the first calculating machines. The Pascal language became popular in the 1970s as a vehicle for teaching structured program-ming at the college level. In 1982, the College Board Entrance Examination instituted an advanced-placement examination in computer science for high school students going on to college. The examination used Pascal rather than BASIC as the programming language. This gave Pascal a tremendous boost at the high school level.

While BASIC and Pascal are the two languages most generally used on microcomputers, another language called LOGO has aroused even more in-terest in education circles. LOGO was developed at the Massachusetts Insti-tute of Technology by Professor Seymour Papert and his colleagues as a lan-guage to help introduce children to computer programming. Development of LOGO was actually begun before the advent of microcomputers. Originally, it was developed using a mechanical device, similar to a robot, that moved around the floor. Since it resembled a shell, it came to be called a "turtle" and the name has stuck. On microcomputers, the small pointer that the user moves around a computer screen is still called a turtle, and LOGO itself is often called "turtle language."

Communicating with the LOGO turtle can be exciting for both chil-dren and teachers. It is controlled through a variety of commands; that is, instructions that direct or command the machine to do certain things. Once a series of LOGO commands have been defined as a procedure, you do not have to repeat the individual commands again. You can simply use the pro-cedure to go on to do bigger and better things. This is the aspect of LOGO that has excited many educators. It has the potential to allow children to start with some very simple commands and build on them to explore much more complex problems that they themselves have defined. Thus, LOGO not only introduces children to programming, but also (and potentially more important) creates an environment in which students can engage in reactive and exploratory problem solving. LOGO offers a vehicle for doing what many education theorists have long advocated, namely, allowing children to learn by working on their own problems, trying out solutions, and correcting mistakes in their own creations (in computer lingo, "debugging" their programs). By doing this repeatedly, children (or adult programmers) can become more skilled and practiced in reasoning and problem solving. The hope is that users will apply these skills in other contexts (Upchurch & Lockhead, 1987).

The Computer as Trouble

Although the future of computers in the field of education seems rosy, there have been innumerable problems in introducing and using microcomputers effectively in schools. The computer has been a source of trouble in schools, most frequently in the areas of money, equity, teacher preparation, and quality of software.

Money

The money problem is a simple one. Even though the price of computing power has dropped sharply over the last quarter century, small computers still are fairly expensive when compared with what schools usually spend on educational materials such as textbooks. In 1988, a microcomputer, including a monitor and at least one disk drive, cost $900 or more, and this did not include the costs of a printer, software, and maintenance of the equipment. Repairs and maintenance are not inconsiderable expenses. However, those who argue for the benefits of investing in educational computing maintain that spending even $2,000 on one computer per student would actually be a relatively small increase in what we now invest in the public education of our children (Papert, 1980). At present, school districts nationwide spend around $2,000 per year per pupil. Ignoring the issue of inflation for the moment, this implies that over the 13-year (K through 12) public school career, the nation spends an average of about $26,000 for the education of each student. From this perspective, a one-time investment of $2,000 to equip each student with a computer would result in only an 8 percent increase in educational expenditures. Of course, computer technology changes so fast that over a 13-year period the hardware and software would have to be updated rather frequently. Nevertheless, the investment over a 13-year period would still be relatively small in relation to overall expenditure.

The problem, however, is that recently school budgets have been squeezed to the limit. The federal government's investment in education has lessened in recent years and many state governments have placed limits on education budgets. There have been tax "revolts" that have placed a limit on how much money school districts can raise through property tax. Teachers' unions continue to seek salary increases for their members. Necessary programs for special populations limit availability of education dollars for new initiatives. So the problem remains: How can school boards pay for the introduction of computers into classrooms in sufficient numbers to allow students easy access to this most promising educational technology?

Equity

Naturally, of course, the money problem is not equally severe in all school districts. Surveys have shown that students in more affluent districts have greater access to computers than students in poorer districts. This has led to concern over the question of equitable access to computers. How can we assure that students, rich and poor alike, have access to computers within their schools?

There are two additional equity issues. First, disadvantaged students generally have less nonclassroom computer experience and computer knowledge. One study found that when disadvantaged students took computer courses in school, initial differences in nonclassroom computer experience (i.e., use of home computers) and computer knowledge between them and their middle-class peers widened. Further, by the end of the course they held less positive attitudes about computers (Chambers & Clarke, 1987). Thus, computer availability outside school raises equity issues about their use in school. A second issue is that of gender. There is evidence that compared with girls, boys have more exposure to computers; this is due in part to higher male enrollment in programming courses. Further, compared with females, males have more positive attitudes toward computers; compared with males, females have stronger feelings for the need for more equity in computer use (Chen, 1986; Becker & Sterling, 1987; Smith, 1987). The significance of these findings in terms of school policy is not yet clear. Until we know the full extent to which computer skills will be necessary in the adult world, it is difficult to justify a policy that would require all students, regardless of predispositions or interests, to take specific training in computers or programming (Becker & Sterling, 1987). However, the equity concerns of females cannot be overlooked or dismissed.

Teacher Preparation

The equity issue may be viewed as simply the flip side of the money problem. But even tougher than the problem of money or equity is that of teacher preparation. As of 1979, around 90 percent of the nation's elementary- and secondary-level teachers had been teaching for three years or more (Dearman & Plisko, 1979). This means that the majority of today's teachers graduated from college before microcomputers were even *invented.* Your generation of teachers is the first to have been college-trained in the use of computers in education. Thus, while the problem of teacher training will be taken care of in the long run, any school system that is currently using computers must provide special in-service training for teachers. Training costs money and is another drain on financial resources.

Quality of Software

Even if money, equity, and teacher preparation problems can be solved, a fourth general problem troubling the future of educational computing remains: the poor quality of many software packages. Currently, there are literally thousands of software programs available for the different makes of microcomputers now found in schools (for example, Apple, Radio Shack–Tandy, IBM, Commodore, and Atari). Yet, according to many observers, much of this software is not of a very high quality, at least from an educational point of view.

There are four main problems with regard to the quality of available software. First, much of the software is not very well documented and many manuals are poorly written; when teachers have questions about how a program works or what to do if they encounter a "bug," the answers are often unclear. Second, many software programs are not particularly easy to use; that is, they are not "user-friendly."

Third, computer programs have yet to be successfully integrated into the regular course of classroom instruction. Many educational games and drill and practice programs keep children busy and stimulated, and some programs help students learn particular skills (such as touch-typing, basic math, and spelling). But much work remains to be done on integrating software programs and microcomputers into the broader functions of schooling, such as teaching students how to reason, to communicate, and to contribute to society as mature and responsible adults.

The final problem applies to both software and hardware. Many computers are not compatible with others and, therefore, the software developed for one machine might not run on another. It is as if you had a Bruce Springsteen tape that you could play only on a Sony tapedeck. This incompatability is a serious problem, since once a school commits itself to a particular brand of computer it is locked into software designed for it.

The Future of Computers in Education

We have reviewed briefly some of the basics of computers, discussed some of the positive roles that microcomputers can play in the world of education (as tutor, tool, and tutee), and identified some of the most common problems encountered when computers are used in schools. Let us now consider the future of computers in the field of education.

Predicting the future—even with a computer—is not an easy job, although people ranging from palm readers to presidents regularly try. Nevertheless, in thinking about the future of computers in schools, several points are worth noting. First, computers were not the first technological tools that held out the promise of transforming the field of education. Nearly a century ago, it was hoped that science laboratories in which students could conduct experiments on their own would help to make education a more satisfying and productive experience. In the 1950s, so-called teaching machines were touted as promising more effective and efficient means of teaching and learning. These were devices that methodically presented content material in small increments, asking the student to answer simple questions about the material before proceeding to the next item. In the 1960s, much hope was pinned on the potential of educational television. Each of these earlier educational technologies has surely contributed to the improvement of education in the twentieth century, but it also seems that, in terms of their impact on education, the grand hopes held for them were not borne out.

Lawrence Cuban argues that these previous educational technologies did not live up to their advanced billing because they were not as simple, versatile, or efficient as textbooks and chalkboards in coping with the problems that arise from the complicated, busy, fast-moving realities of classroom instruction. Shaped by the "crucible of experience and the culture of teaching," teacher repertories are both resilient and efficient (Cuban, 1986, p. 109). Cuban believes that teachers

"Let's see, you've got your calculator, word processor, personal computer, VTR disc, electric typewriter, cassette recorder, and spare batteries. Have a good day at school."

Source: Phi Delta Kappan, 1983, p. 636.

evaluate new technologies on the basis of a "practicality ethic"; they ask themselves, "Will this new technology help me to cope with the problems I must face because of the way schools and classrooms are structured and because of the dynamic social context of the classrooms?" Teachers will assess school computers by invoking this same "practicality ethic." If teachers do not see the computer as helping them cope with problems arising from the classroom context, this newest technology will not have the influence its proponents are claiming. The jury is still out.

A second point worth considering is that the future development of computer use in schools depends on the kind and degree of support that schools receive. Many groups and observers have called for the widespread introduction of computers in educational institutions. But how well and how fast this can be done primarily depends on cost effectiveness and on the availability of money, training for educators, and educational software of high quality.

Third, how the use of computers develops in schools will be affected greatly by developments in the computer industry itself. At the moment, there is great ferment in the computer industry in the United States, Europe, and Japan. New computer companies seem to be started nearly every week, while older ones regularly go out of business. Educational use of computers in schools is a very small proportion of the computer market. In 1985, sales of small computers for education-related purposes amounted to only a tenth of sales for business and home use. Therefore, what happens with computers in schools is likely to be affected by developments in the business and home, where the market is potentially larger and more lucrative.

Fourth, the future of computers in schools may be affected by evidence regarding their effectiveness in promoting learning. At the moment, there is some encouraging evidence that computerized instruction can indeed promote learning (Kulik, Kulik, & Cohen, 1979). Most of this research is, however, based on the use of large computers in educational institutions in the 1970s.

Since microcomputers weren't widely introduced into schools until the early 1980s, we do not yet have much in the way of concrete evidence on their educational effectiveness.

A final but fundamental factor that will affect the future of computers in education is philosophical. All educational practice is influenced by an underlying view of the nature of the learner. The computer in education is no exception. Will those developing computer software have an implicit view of the human learner as a relatively passive person whose behavior is uniform and predictable and to whom information and knowledge is to be imparted? With such a view, software would be designed to present students with information or ideas that they would associate with or relate to other ideas. Drill and practice programs certainly adopt this view of the learner.

Can computer software incorporate a view of the human learner as an active, problem-solving free agent, transforming perceptions and experience into knowledge, a being who can radically alter his or her pattern of behavior? LOGO already incorporates features of this view of the learner. Some believe that programming in a computer language like LOGO encourages the development of higher-level thinking skills in students. Teaching the syntax and semantics of the computer language as an end in itself will not accomplish this goal (Upchurch & Lockhead, 1987). Will computer software become traditionally content- or subject-centered, direct, formal, and didactic? Or will it be child-centered, romantic, indirect-open, exploratory, and informal? Of course, it could become both depending on the situation. Unfortunately, the former seems more likely than the latter, but only time will tell.

In sum, we do not yet know the future of computers in education. But it is certainly safe to say that computers will play a more prominent role in the schools of the twenty-first century—schools in which you will be teaching—than they have played in the past. How prominent that role will be reamins to be seen. It should be an exciting story, of which you will be part.

CONCLUSION

Computers are a new and potentially valuable resource for classroom teachers. The impact they have made in some classrooms over the past few years has been substantial, and all signs indicate this will continue as computers drop in price and as better-designed software is developed. Research has just begun on the effect of languages such as LOGO and of other software designed to improve the problem-solving abilities of children. As with any new development, much of what will be learned will be through trial and error.

The future of the computer industry in general, and of computers in the field of education in particular, is one that will influence your teaching career. Try to remain knowledgeable about new developments. As a future teacher, you do not have be a computer wizard or a programmer, no more than your teachers had to be textbook writers. Instead, you need to familiarize yourself with the microcomputer so that you may use it to complement your teaching. If there are elective courses in computers available in your college, try to fit one in. However, remember that first and foremost you are a teacher, not a technician. Nonetheless, the computer offers your generation of teachers a powerful new tool. Use it wisely and well.

QUESTIONS AND ACTIVITIES

1. Visit a classroom where the teacher and students use computers on a regular basis.
   a. How does the teacher integrate the microcomputer with the rest of the curriculum?
   b. How do students respond to using the computer?
   c. What role does the teacher think the computer will play in the future of education?
2. Go to the library and review back issues of various microcomputer magazines. Generate a list of software packages available for use in your future classroom.
3. What place do you think computers will have in classrooms ten years from now? Twenty years from now?
4. How can a microcomputer make a teacher's job easier? How can it make it more difficult?
5. Of the various uses for microcomputers in the classroom, which do you feel will have the greatest impact upon students?
6. What effect might computers have on equality of educational opportunity if only the wealthy school districts are able to place them in every classroom? Why?

CHAPTER 18

Accountability

This chapter explores the rise of the accountability movement in education. Unfortunately, it is much easier to agree that people should be accountable for what happens in schools than to design fair and reliable ways to do it.

● Teachers, students, parents, policymakers, and the public must all share responsibility for accountability in schooling.

● As a future teacher, you need to carefully examine accountability programs to determine who is held accountable for what purpose and how and when accountability will be carried out.

Once you begin your professional life as a teacher, one issue you can be assured of encountering again and again is that of accountability. People generally accept that they are responsible or accountable for many of their actions, and many, of course, believe that accountability extends to the here-after. Therefore, that the concept should extend to education, which at its core is a moral enterprise, should not come as a surprise.

There are many forms of accountability that you will encounter as a teacher. These may range from something as simple as a request from a parent for more information about a child's performance in your class to something as elaborate as a merit pay scheme that could affect your salary. As a teacher, you will hold your students accountable for their homework when you assign them grades; occasionally, you might try to hold a parent accountable for a child's failure to do homework; or you might hold an administrator account-able for not providing you with material necessary to do your job properly. You might even find yourself in a school system that uses student test scores to hold you directly accountable for their level of achievement. The profes-sional organization to which you will belong, whether it be an affiliate of the National Education Association (NEA) or the American Federation of Teach-ers (AFT), issues position statements on various accountability schemes, such as performance contracting, merit pay, educational vouchers, and tuition tax credits. As a professional, you need to know how to evaluate such statements, and to do this properly you will need to keep abreast of the pros and cons of the issues as they develop.

In this chapter we shall first examine the reasons why demands for accountability have grown during the 1970s and 1980s. Second, we shall consider four major expectations behind the rise of accountability in educa-tion. Third, we shall examine four questions: Who is accountable? For what are they accountable? To whom are they accountable? When are they ac-countable? Fourth, we shall analyze what accountability programs attempt to accomplish. Finally, we shall describe various schemes for implementing ac-countability programs.

Reasons for Demands for Accountability

Accountability in education is sometimes thought to be a recent develop-ment that began in the early 1960s when President Kennedy brought the scientific management techniques of the business world into government, including the Department of Health, Education and Welfare. In reality, there are many examples of accountability procedures in the history of education. One of the earliest recorded efforts took place in 1444 in Treviso, Italy. The town fathers entered into a contract with the schoolmaster whereby his salary depended in part on the degree to which pupils achieved certain skills (Ariès, 1960/1965) (see Box 18.1).

In the United States, the first clear example of legal accountability is to be found in the Massachusetts Bay Law of 1642 for the training of children and servants in the home. According to this law, parents were held accountable, under penalty of a fine, for ensuring that their children had "the ability to read and understand the principles of religion and the capital laws of the country." Later, when the foundations of the school system had been laid down, the target of accountability shifted from the parent to the teacher.

The pressure for accountability has become quite strong in recent years. There are a number of reasons for this pressure. The public holds two very basic expectations for our schools. The first is that children will benefit from schooling, and the second is that children will not be harmed by schooling (Mizell, 1981). These twin expectations are, of course, flip sides of the same coin. Starting in the late 1950s and continuing with the Great Society programs of the 1960s, there was a massive effort to reduce educational inequality in America by reallocating school resources, eliminating segregated schools, and bringing more and better education to previously neglected groups of students. These efforts were an attempt on the part of the government to ensure that children who were previously ill-served by the system would benefit from school and would not be harmed by the schools. This effort was largely successful.

Ironically, this very success gave rise to criticism of our schools. Many special-interest groups previously excluded from any voice or power in the system were allowed—in fact, encouraged—to participate actively in the formulation of educational policy. These groups represented the poor, different racial and ethnic minorities, various bilingual and bicultural groups, and women, to name a few. As they became active in the system, they began to argue that too many of the children they represented were still not benefiting from school and that too many were harmed by their experiences in school. Along with the criticism by special-interest groups, a broader-based feeling for greater accountability began to emerge across the country. Politicians, educators, and the general public argued that in meeting the goals of providing equality of educational opportunity for all, standards in schools had been diluted and excellence in education had suffered. These criticisms put the schools under pressure to become more accountable for what they were accomplishing.

A very diverse collection of political types marched together under the banner of accountability. The issue appealed to fiscal conservatives who believed it would result in better management and reduce costs. Community organizers liked the notion because they felt it would lead to direct political control and promote change beneficial to their constituencies. Bureaucrats and academics jumped on the bandwagon because they believed that clear goals and ways of reaching them were important (Murphy & Cohen, 1974).

Extract from President Nixon's Education Message to Congress in 1970

School administrators and schoolteachers alike are responsible for their performance, and it is in their interest as well as in the interests of their pupils that they be held accountable.

Let us briefly consider the criticisms of the public schools that generated this pressure for educational accountability.

Pressure from Concerned Special-Interest Groups

As evidence mounted in the early 1960s that the country had succeeded in providing equal facilities, staff, and resources to most groups, advocacy groups began to point to gross inequalities in the educational achievement levels of different groups. For example, data from the Coleman study showed that minority students—with the exception of Oriental Americans—scored lower than majority (white) students on standardized tests of verbal and nonverbal ability and of achievement in reading, mathematics, and general information (Coleman et al., 1966). These groups also pointed to results from minimum-competency testing programs that showed that, after 11 years in school, inordinate numbers of minority students had failed tests of basic skills. For example, in the 1979–1980 school year, 53 percent of minority students in Florida failed that state's competency test; in North Carolina, 70 percent of black students failed the test the first time it was administered. Such results are by no means unique to those states. In Colorado, Chicano children were three and a half times more likely to end up in special-education classes than were Anglo children and three times more likely to be retained in a grade; their dropout rate was twice that of Anglo students, and they were further behind at every grade level than were Anglos (Cisneros & Rosser, 1981).

Many minority group advocates pointed to this kind of data to support their argument that not only are some children not benefiting from school but also, by not acquiring basic skills during their time in school, those children are being harmed. As a consequence, advocacy groups were often in the forefront of efforts designed to hold the schools accountable.

General Criticism of Schools

In addition to various special-interest groups, the general public lost confidence in public education. This decline was part of a much larger and deeper erosion of confidence in all public institutions (Weiler, 1982). Erosion of confidence was partly an outgrowth of the rise of the consumer movement during the 1960s. In the 1970s and early 1980s the press, TV, and other media focused on the apparent shortcomings of American education. And, despite the fact that public opinion surveys show that education is listed as third among institutions in which people have the greatest amount of confidence (surpassed only by medicine and science), and the one on which they would be most prepared to spend federal money, criticism of education has been far greater than that directed against any of our other public institutions (Hodgkinson, 1982; Atkins, 1979).

It was perhaps in the final report of the National Commission on Excellence in Education, entitled *A nation at risk: The imperative for educational reform,* that criticism of the public schools reached its zenith. The commission, which had been appointed by the secretary of education to examine the American educational system and to recommend reforms, summarized much of the recent criticism of schools in its opening comments (see Box 18.2). Let us briefly examine some of the causes of the loss of confidence in, and dissatisfaction with, our schools that these sentiments express.

Declining Achievement

A number of studies have been interpreted as indicating that student achievement levels have declined through the 1970s. Some people claim that the evidence from these studies points to a number of specific problems. First, student achievement, as measured by standardized tests and by the Scholastic Aptitude Test (SAT), has been steadily declining (more recently, however, this decline has stopped and scores are rising slightly). Second, too many high school graduates lack the basic skills necessary to fill out job applications or to successfully hold entry-level positions in business, industry, or the military. Third, instead of striving for excellence, schools are emphasizing minimums in such programs as minimum-competency testing; these minimums quickly become maximums. Fourth, despite the fact that we spend more money on education than any other advanced nation, the measured achievement in our schools trails that of other industrialized nations. Fifth, "higher-order" cognitive skills such as comprehension, application, and analysis are declining. Sixth, achievement in science is declining. Finally, curricula and textbooks have been homogenized and diluted.

Is the academic performance of our students as poor as these conclusions would seem to indicate? There are definitely weak spots, particularly with higher-order skills at the secondary school level; yet there is also evidence that our schools are doing a fine job. Test scores at the elementary level are going up, and the top 20 percent of our high school students compare quite well with students in other industrial countries in every area of the curriculum. Declines and weak spots may

"*A word with you, Mr. Sanderson.*"

Source: Phi Delta Kappan, 1981, p. 425

be due in large part to nonschool factors (Stedman & Smith, 1983). Despite this, critics *perceive* the evidence to be negative and use it to demand an improvement in standards. Such improvement, they believe, will be achieved when schools are held accountable for poor performance.

Dissatisfaction with Teachers

Public confidence in teachers has eroded not only because of the declining student achievement levels noted above, but also because of other factors. When disturbing numbers of teachers failed simple tests of reading, writing, and arithmetic, the public was informed. When teachers write poorly and spell words incorrectly in notes sent home to parents, and when placards carried by teachers walking picket lines display such incompetence, the public notices. By 1987, 39 states had initiated testing programs for teacher certification that cover not only pedagogical knowledge but also basic skills.

Greater teacher militancy in collective bargaining for wages and working conditions and numerous teacher strikes on the first day of school have soured many former supporters of teachers. Despite the fact that many people recognize that teachers have been historically underpaid, this increased militancy, when combined with negative reports about student achievement levels, has led to demands that teachers be held more accountable than ever before.

Concerns over Rising Costs and Lack of Efficiency

Concerns about the increasing costs of education are also behind calls for greater accountability. During the 1970s and early 1980s, enrollment in public schools dropped dramatically; at the same time, costs rose faster than inflation. Many citizens began to wonder what kind of education they were getting for their tax dollars at a time when they were reading about test score declines, functional illiteracy, delinquency, and the like. Was their hard-earned money being used efficiently by the schools? When the matter was put to a vote, citizens began to vote their pocketbooks rather than acceding to requests for increased expenditures. The general public and policymakers are now more willing to spend on education, but only when they can expect increased expenditures to produce better student performance and a lower dropout rate.

Expectations for Accountability Programs

In general, there seem to be four major expectations behind the rise of educational accountability: efficiency, monitoring, control, and punishment.

Efficiency

The first expectation underlying demands for accountability is that it will cut costs and increase efficiency and productivity. To be able to this, we need to know how much money is put into education and how that money is spent (for example, for building, supplies, salaries, and the like), and we also need to have some measure of the quality and quantity of what the system produces (educational *outputs*). Only then can we relate our expenditure to what we get for our money and decide whether or not we are getting good value (Duncan, 1971). This concept of accountability is based on the assumption that the educational enterprise is analogous to that of business or industry. Critics of this mentality have pointed out that schools do not operate in the same way as factories. For example, in the factory, spray-paint nozzles apply paint to automobiles. The nozzle is active, the automobile passive. In the classroom, however, both teacher and student are active, and subject matter and skills cannot be applied like paint (Campbell, 1971). A fundamental difference between the educational and industrial systems is that in education the major "inputs" and "outputs" are human beings and, consequently, the process is comprised of human interactions rather than mechanical processes (Quintero, 1981).

Monitoring

People also expect that accountability will permit them to *monitor* the working of schools to see if they comply with general or specific policies. In this view, accountability is a means of finding out if the educational system in general, or one school in particular, is successful in, for example, increasing participation and achievement levels of students from rural or disadvantaged backgrounds. Or an accountability program could be used to determine if schools do what most people expect them to: to teach all children to read, write, add, subtract, multiply, and divide.

The monitoring function of accountability is often seen as simply providing information about the school to concerned parties without describing how the information can be used to make judgments and decisions about individuals, or without setting up formal procedures to act on the information. For example, Robert Stake defines accountability as having good records and making action open to view: "Strictly speaking, an accountable school is one that (1) discloses its activities, (2) makes good on staff promises, (3) assigns staff responsibility for each area of public concern, and (4) monitors its teaching and learning" (Stake, 1973, p. 1). Stake goes on to describe two types of information that a school should make available: a yearly public report by a visiting team of citizens and standardized test measures of basic skills and professional observation.

While such a nonthreatening information scheme might lessen educators' fears concerning accountability and might increase public knowledge of what is occurring in the school, critics have argued that it has little value if it is not used to evaluate and to hold individuals within the school accountable (McDonald, 1973). The information by itself does not provide a mechanism for making the schools more responsive (Levin, 1974). For example, in the 1960s the mere provision of information concerning the relatively poor school performance of disadvantaged or low-income children did not substantially alter their plight.

Control

A third motive behind demands for accountability is that of control. Frustration, brought on by the realization that monitoring information about the system is not enough, has led to the design of accountability programs aimed at controlling the educational process itself. Faced with what appears to be mounting evidence of poor or declining achievement levels, legislators and school boards naturally want to do something to correct any deficiencies in the system. However, they soon realize that it is impossible to mandate how teachers must teach or to install a particular instructional system. Faced with this reality, policymakers do the next best thing: they mandate an accountability program. Examples of such programs are the minimum-competency testing programs that were mandated in many states in an effort to improve the basic skills of students. Student achievement levels were specified and if they were not reached, sanctions were prescribed (for example, students who failed the test could not graduate from high school). In this situation, the test becomes an administrative device used to implement a policy of improving basic skills. Test information is no longer used merely to *inform* policy (as it may be when the purpose of an accountability program is to monitor schools) but to *regulate* the educational process.

Programs based on performance incentives for teachers are another form of control through accountability. For example, increments in a teacher's pay schedule are sometimes linked to some form of accountability measure, such as pupil test scores. Evaluating teachers, and sometimes administrators, on the basis of student progress is a form of product accountability and is often linked to efforts to control the system. This approach to accountability ignores the fact that there are a large number of factors over which teachers have little or no control that are strongly related to student performance on achievement tests. These factors include the student's home background, native language, aptitude, attendance, and age. At least one system (in St. Louis, Missouri) told teachers that beginning in 1983 they would be rated unsatisfactory and lose their jobs unless their students reached specified levels on standardized tests. That scheme, at the time of this writing, is being challenged in federal court (Shanber, 1986).

When considering accountability as a control mechanism, you need to distinguish between the mechanism or program that is *internal* to a particular school system and the one that is *external* (that is, run by the state or federal government) to the system. Opponents of external accountability systems believe that the best form of accountability is internal, that is, controlled by local school boards and sensitive to local issues and information needs. It is argued that internal accountability programs give various groups or individuals interested in the system the ability to ask more pertinent questions about the system's goals or performance, get answers to these questions, make informed judgments on the basis of the information received, and, when necessary, engage in oversight and corrective action (Schwartz & Garet, 1981). All this is done at the local level.

One problem with the concept of internal accountability is that many systems simply have refused to implement them. A second problem is that internal accountability programs often are controlled by the very people who should be held accountable—administrators and school board members. Further, it is argued that such systems are accountable to a limited number of groups within the community. In this situation, the school board may be perceived as giving priority to the welfare of children from a particular segment of the community (Mizell, 1981). It is clear that an internal system of accountability can work only if there is a substantial degree of trust among all parties in the system—teachers, administrators, parents, pupils, school board members, and the general public. When trust does not exist, particularly on the part of citizens' groups, demands for external accountability systems arise. However, when such external systems are mandated at the state level, they affect all districts—even those that may have successfully run their own accountability programs.

Punishment

Some people regard increased accountability in the field of education as a punitive measure. In this view, accountability programs are seen as mechanisms to weed out incompetent staff or to punish lazy or recalcitrant students. This punitive dimension is what generates the most fear on the part of teachers toward many accountability programs. We saw in the last section that many programs associate sanctions, such as the denial of a diploma or loss of accreditation, with poor test performance. Test scores and their associated sanctions become sticks either to threaten people into toeing the line or, failing that, to punish people for their poor performance.

Basic Questions About Accountability

In this section we shall examine basic questions about accountability: Who are accountable? What are they accountable for? How are they accountable? To whom are they accountable? When are they accountable? There often are no simple answers to these questions and, in fact, the questions give rise to further questions.

Who Are Accountable?

It is not unusual to read or hear statements calling for schools or school systems to become accountable. However, only a moment's reflection should reveal that it is impossible to hold the "system" as such accountable. Strictly speaking, accountability must have as its reference point individuals who run the system (for example, teachers, administrators, paraprofessionals, and school support staff), individuals who control or govern the system (school board members or legislators), or individuals directly served by the system (students or parents).

We said in the introduction to this chapter that, in principle, most people *accept* the concept of accountability. However, very few people, whatever their role in the system, really *like* to be held accountable. Accountability ultimately involves an evaluation and judgment about a person's actions, and people generally do not like to be judged or evaluated, especially if the evaluation is likely to be negative. Further, many people do not like the idea of having to formally judge or evaluate another person. But whether individuals want accountability or not, and whether they fear it or not, matters little; it is a reality.

TEACHERS Historically, many accountability programs focused immediately and primarily on the teacher. If students were not learning, as reflected in poor test performance, the teacher was held accountable. While this point of view may be understandable, it does not take into account the fact that there are many factors that affect student learning over which the teacher has no control. And teachers naturally do not want systems of accountability in which they might be blamed, or even punished, for results over which they have no control. However, teacher evaluation techniques, when used for summative evaluation (for such issues as tenure, promotion, dismissal, or salary decisions), obviously hold teachers accountable for their performance.

Perhaps the most common form of accountability (and it is one that you will encounter very early in your teaching career) occurs when a parent comes to you with concern about a child's homework, or about discipline, or about your teaching methods. Sometimes parent complaints are based on unreliable or biased information supplied by their children. One teacher chose to address this problem by sending notes home to the parents of all the children in the class, promising that she would not believe what their children told her about what went on at home if parents would disregard what their children told them happened at school.

"You must remember, Miss Jenkins, that their little minds are thirsty for knowledge. If they don't find fractions fascinating, you have failed as a teacher."

Source: Phi Delta Kappan, 1982, p. 567.

Parental criticism, of course, is sometimes deserved. Parents do have the right and obligation to question teachers about their child's progress, and teachers need to be accountable to parents. It is easy, however, for a teacher to become discouraged over such questioning. As you begin to teach and to manage a classroom of students, you will need to develop your own philosophy toward, and methods of dealing with, efforts by parents of individual students to hold you accountable for their offspring's lack of progress.

STUDENTS Many people feel that students cannot be regarded as entirely passive agents, that learning is largely under their own control and therefore they are accountable for their performance. Others, of course, disagree with this view. They point out that we know home-background factors can negatively affect a student's ability to profit from instruction. They ask whether it is fair to deny a diploma to the student who fails a minimum-competency test after being promoted from grade to grade for 11 years, often receiving B and C grades. In such cases, many ask if it is the system that has failed the student.

Both sides in this argument are correct to a certain extent; it is clearly *not* an "either-or" situation. Responsibility for learning is a shared one, not only between teacher and student but between them and other parties as well. Certainly the age of the student, his or her home background and past educational history, and the instruction he or she received all need to be taken into account in determining student accountability. After considering these factors, you may well decide that many students, particularly at the secondary level, are to a great extent responsible for their performance in school. You will have to decide in individual cases the degree to which the student is accountable for his or her scholastic performance as well as the extent to which other parties, or other factors, might lessen that accountability. You must also be able to analyze the fairness of programs that try to focus accountability primarily on the student.

SCHOOL ADMINISTRATORS If teachers and students are accountable, then clearly school administrators, whose job it is to facilitate the instructional and learning processes, must also be regarded as accountable. Too often teachers and students find themselves in the glare of the spotlight while principals and superintendents remain in the shadows. But if one of the principal's primary jobs is to supervise teaching, then he or she must be held accountable when a poor teacher remains in the school year after year. Similarly, if one of the superintendent's primary jobs is to be responsible for the supervision of principals, then he or she must be accountable when a school has, for example, a bad academic record.

Teachers are sometimes castigated for promoting children on the basis of seat time rather than on the basis of achievement. Most teachers know who the weak students are; if they do not, they should be held accountable. In promoting weak students, they often are merely following an explicit or implicit administrative policy of social promotion. Teachers cannot be expected to retain children if, when parents complain, they do not receive the backing of either their building principal or the superintendent of schools.

Administrators, whatever their rank, should not be exempt from scrutiny. They are paid to supervise, or be responsible for, the actions of those whom they administer. Accountability should work down from the top as well as up from the bottom.

PARENTS Parents, too, must take their place in the accountability network. They have the obligation to see to it that their children are educated. It would seem the parents' legal responsibility is fulfilled when the child is sent to school. But don't parents also have a moral obligation to share major responsibility with teachers for their children's progress? Shouldn't they see to it that their children do homework? Encourage them to study and work hard at school? Support the school when discipline problems emerge? Most people would answer yes to each of these questions, and most parents, because they want the best for their children, accept these responsibilities.

Unfortunately, some parents may not fully accept their obligations in the matter of schooling. They are happy to send their children to school and leave the rest to the teacher. If you happen to be the teacher, you will have to come to terms with this lack of parental involvement. Presumably, you will do your best to establish communication with parents and diplomatically point out to them their responsibilities in the educational process. Unfortunately, establishing communication may not be easy. Too often, the parents of students most in need of help are the very ones who are most unavailable or unwilling to communicate with the teacher.

LOCAL SCHOOL BOARDS Whether they are elected or appointed, school board members must formulate policies and ensure that those policies are implemented. They are also accountable for the expenditure of taxpayers' money. Finally, they must evaluate the superintendent's efforts to carry out his or her responsibilities.

In most school districts, any member of the school board can be voted out of office if the voters feel that he or she has not measured up to their expectations. The ballot box is a direct and powerful form of accountability,

I WENT TO THE BOARD OF EDUCATION TO COMPLAIN THAT AFTER TWELVE YEARS, I WAS PRACTICALLY ILLITERATE.

THEY TOLD ME TO PUT IT IN WRITING.

THAVES 3-26

Source: Color Sundays, 1979

one that many advocacy groups have come to appreciate. As a consequence, such groups work hard to register their constituency, to get them to vote in school board elections, and to run candidates sympathetic to the needs of their constituents. When board members are appointed, the public official who makes the appointments can be held accountable by voters.

STATE AND FEDERAL LEGISLATORS An increasing amount of state and federal funding is needed to provide many of the services the public has come to demand from schools. Legislators, therefore, must see to it that there are sufficient funds available to local districts to implement programs, and they must work for the passage of legislation that corrects deficiencies and injustices in the system.

Unfortunately, legislators can mandate new programs that local districts must implement without providing those districts with the increased funding needed for implementation. For example, the state legislature in Massachusetts passed a bill requiring the local districts to provide a whole range of new and costly services for students with handicapping conditions. Few would argue that these services were not needed. However, the local districts had to find additional monies from property taxes to fund the services. One might ask, "If a legislature mandates programs, is it not responsible to see to it that the programs are adequately funded?"

THE GENERAL PUBLIC Ultimately, it is the public who provides the major financial support for the public education system. If the system is failing in some way because of lack of resources, is the public accountable? Further, is not the public accountable for voting in school board elections, mayoral elections, and state and national elections?

How Much Is an Individual Accountable For?

The educational system has been described as an hourglass (see Figure 18.1); few people would disagree that accountability is shared by all the groups within the hourglass as well as by an important group not specifically included in it—parents. To determine the degree of accountability of any individual in any of the groups, however, is a particularly difficult, if not impossible, task.

FIGURE 18.1 Hourglass Model of a School System

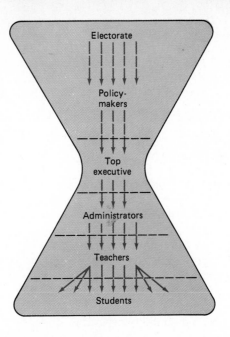

In practice, when specific accountability programs are implemented, they generally fall on individuals from only one of the groups (for example, teachers or students).

We are faced with a practical dilemma here. It simply is not fair to hold someone solely accountable for an outcome if one does not have control over *all* the factors that can affect the outcome. This can be stated as a general principle:

> *Each participant in the educational process should be held responsible only for those educational outcomes that he can affect by his actions or decisions and only to the extent that he can affect them (Barro, 1970, p. 199).*

Source: Dyer, 1973, p. 15.

While this principle certainly sounds reasonable on first reading, it is virtually impossible to disentangle the impact that various people or various factors can have on any given outcome. Take a simple example: arithmetic achievement in a third-grade class. How much of this achievement, or lack of it, can be attributed to the third-grade teacher? How much can be attributed to the first- and second-grade teachers? How much to the principal, to the reading specialist? How much to the influence of the parents and home conditions? How much to the school board? How much to the individual pupil?

It is our inability to disentangle the contribution of different individuals or factors to any given outcome measure that leads to simplistic solutions of placing the accountability burden solely on one group. This practice, of course, breeds resentment and fear of accountability. People will accept accountability only when they see it as fair and as involving all parties who participate in the process of education.

To Whom Are People Accountable?

Teachers are regarded as being responsible to students, parents, colleagues, the school principal, and the official hierarchy. Students are responsible to their parents, their teachers, and ultimately to themselves. Parents are responsible to their children, their children's teachers, and to the legal system for their child's attendance.

Within the school system, administrators (principals, assistant superintendents) are responsible to the top executive (the superintendent), who, in turn, is responsible to the policymakers (the school board), whose members, in turn, are responsible to the general public (see Figure 18.1). Ultimate responsibility rests with the general public.

Despite this broad range of responsibility, specific accountability programs focus on a narrow set of relationships, generally those at the bottom of the hourglass shown in Figure 18.1. The general public, policymakers, and the superintendent need to be drawn more closely into the circle of accountability.

When Are People Accountable?

This question, like the last one, is one that has received relatively little consideration. For example, there have been criticisms of minimum-competency testing (MCT) programs that focus on the basic skills at grade 11 and that hold the student's diploma at ransom. Some people feel that this form of accountability comes much too late in the student's educational career. For this reason, many MCT programs have been introduced in the elementary years; earlier identification makes it easier to correct deficiencies, and students who have not acquired the basic skills cannot benefit from a high school program.

Outside of external accountability programs, students are held accountable at report card time (generally every eight or ten weeks). Teachers are held accountable yearly when salary incentive programs tie teacher pay to measures of teacher performance. In some situations, teachers may be held accountable on a daily basis by the principal or periodically by parents who might question them about their child's progress. Principals are evaluated periodically by the superintendent, who, in turn, is scrutinized by the school board annually at budget time or when citizens complain about aspects of the system. And, as we saw, many board members, mayors, and legislators face the ultimate test of accountability, the ballot box, every year or every two years.

Accountability Mechanisms

Accountability can take many forms. In this section, we shall briefly consider some of the more common contexts in which accountability operates.

Accountability to Parents

Parents have a number of accountability mechanisms available to them. The most obvious is the traditional parent-teacher conference, which, if not satisfactory, can be extended to include the principal, the superintendent, and ultimately the school board. In some districts, the parents can join or request a hearing from a formal citizen advisory council, mandated by state law or by various programs legislated by the federal government. Public Law 94-142 gives parents of children with handicapping conditions an additional accountability mechanism.

As we mentioned earlier, school board elections, or school bond or tax referenda, are forms of accountability open to all citizens. If all other efforts fail to obtain a benefit or to prevent a child from being harmed, parents can seek the services of a lay advocate provided through community organizations and legal-aid groups, or they can hire their own lawyer (Mizell, 1981). All these accountability mechanisms unfortunately do not work equally well for all parents. Most people assume that parents are interested, informed, fairly articulate, confident, and persistent; this, of course, is not always the case.

Minimum-Competency Testing

Minimum-competency testing (MCT) is a generic term applied to a wide range of different accountability programs. By 1987, some sort of MCT program had been enacted in 39 states. Some programs are controlled exclusively by the state (for example, Florida and New York), some share control between the state and local districts (for example, Oregon and California), and some are exclusively local (for example, New York City and Washington, D.C.). Some programs simply test students and report the results to the public (for example, in Kansas), some test students to identify those in need of remediation (for example, in New Jersey and Massachusetts). Some have used test results to appropriate funds to low-scoring districts (for example, in New Jersey and Michigan), while some have used the results to make decisions about the accreditation of schools or school districts (for example, in New Jersey), or whether a district should be placed in receivership. Twenty-five states or cities use the results to make decisions about graduation from high school (for example, New Jersey, Florida, New York, and California) or decisions about promotion from grade to grade at the elementary level (for example, New York City, Washington, D.C., and Boston). The uses of MCT for graduation and promotion decisions have been the most controversial.

Educational Vouchers

Educational vouchers are an attempt to foster competition among schools. Instead of requiring that each child attend the public school in his or her neighborhood, an educational voucher provided for each child by the state or federal government would mean that parents would have public funding to send their children to the school of their choice, be it public or private. If parents were not happy with a school, for whatever reason, they could withdraw their children and redeem their vouchers at other schools. Such a scheme, it is argued, would make schools and the personnel who operate them more accountable. Various educational-voucher plans receive periodic attention and political support.

In addition to the educational vouchers discussed in Chapter 6 there are two variants that are specifically designed to increase accountability, called "vouchers for literacy" or "second-chance education." Simply put, each family would have the option of sending a child to a private school of their choice at the taxpayer's expense but only if the child had failed a minimum-competency test in the public schools for three years in a row (Lerner, 1981). This plan combines minimum-competency testing and the education voucher in a single accountability system.

The second variant of the educational-voucher system is the "educational coupon," which is analogous to food stamps. Parents could purchase these coupons. The lower the family income, the less the coupons would cost, but everyone would have to pay something. The coupons could then be used to purchase additional tutoring at a private or public school that wished to provide such a supplementary service at a price (Garms, 1983). Here again, the idea behind the proposal is to introduce competition into public education. Parents use the coupons as an accountability device by spending them where they get the best value.

Performance Contracting

Another attempt to introduce accountability into the system, which periodically comes in and out of fashion, is performance contracting. A performance contract, as the name implies, is an attempt to link payment for a service to some measurable aspect of the performance of that service. A performance contract differs from a fixed contract in that the latter involves a fixed fee for a product or service and does not vary with the amount or quality of the service or product supplied. For example, the school board contracts with teachers to teach so many days a year for a certain agreed-upon salary.

During the late 1960s there were several attempts, funded by the federal government, to hire private firms to teach students on the basis of "performance contracts for results." A formal legal agreement, or contract, was reached between a private firm and the school board whereby the firm would work with the district's teachers to raise student achievement. Once the program was operating successfully, it, along with all equipment and materials, would be turned over to a school system. This aspect of performance contracting introduced a new word to the educational lexicon—"turnkey." The firm was paid on a sliding scale depending on the number of pupils whose achievement levels improved over the course of the contract. Improvement was measured by the differences between the scores on a standardized test at the beginning of the effort and at the end. In some programs, the dropout rate was also used to measure success. In such schemes, the test became a very important part of the process.

Performance-contracting programs are perceived to have a number of advantages:

1. They can bring about change in the education system.
2. They place increased emphasis on accountability for student learning on school administrators and on the firms with which they contract.
3. They bring new views and new techniques from private industry into the present closed bureaucratic system of public education.

A number of disadvantages of performance-contracting programs have also been pointed out:

1. The programs are complex and costly to manage.
2. They are narrowly focused on test results in the basic skill areas.
3. The selection, administration, and security of the tests used in the programs become important.

4. There are insurmountable problems associated with measuring "gains" or "growth" in students' scholastic achievement.

5. The status of teachers is threatened by the programs.

6. The whole approach is based on an incorrect, narrow, technological factory-model view of education.

Merit Pay Programs

A final form of accountability that is very popular in some circles, and very controversial in others, involves paying "outstanding" teachers more money than that paid to "ordinary" teachers. Proposals to reward certain teachers in this way are generally called merit pay plans. In general, teachers and the public hold opposite views on merit pay. Teachers are against such plans by a 2-to-1 margin, while the public supports the concept by a 2-to-1 margin (Gallup, 1985a, 1985b).

The incentives associated with merit pay programs can take different forms. A salary increase for outstanding performance is an obvious one. "Teacher of the year" awards, accompanied by a great deal of publicity, is another form. Other forms are paid sabbaticals, during which teachers can renew themselves, and small grants to teachers that they can use as they wish to improve their instructional programs. Finally, some school systems pay teachers more if they are willing to go to "difficult" inner-city schools.

Proponents claim that teacher incentive programs have certain advantages:

1. They will attract talented people to education who otherwise would not consider a teaching career.

By Oliphant

2. The provision of merit salary increments will motivate teachers to do a better job.

3. Merit programs will help retain the best teachers in the system, who otherwise might seek financial rewards by going into school administration or leave teaching altogether.

4. Merit programs should have the effect of improving the performance of the less capable teacher and driving out the incompetent ones.

5. Even if these advantages did not materialize, it is the right thing, as a matter of justice, to reward excellence.

6. Since the public is interested in how its money is spent, merit programs will make them more willing to support high salaries.

7. Merit or bonus incentive schemes are used in industry with good results; if they work there, why shouldn't they work in education?

There are, however, difficulties associated with merit-pay plans:

1. We do not know how much money would have to be added to a teacher's salary before incentives would attract people from other occupations to teaching. Would someone be willing to embark on a teaching career at the minimum salary in the hope that he or she *eventually* might qualify for merit pay?

2. There is no equitable mechanism available to link incentives to teacher performance. Critics ask what criteria will be used to determine who is and who is not an "outstanding teacher." Most programs use a principal's or superintendent's judgments about teaching performance as the criterion. Teachers' groups view such judgments as subjective and arbitrary. For example, teachers who are critical of administrators or who are late in complying with bureaucratic requirements for paperwork might be punished under the system. On the other hand, teachers who support management might be rewarded. Thus, using the subjective judgments of administrators is seen as opening the way to fostering politics, patronage, discontent, and unrest in the system rather than as rewarding outstanding teaching.

3. Merit pay schemes set up competition and negative attitudes among teachers, thus hurting morale and working relationships.

4. Industry usually awards merit or bonus monies on the basis of quantity, not quality. Anyhow, teachers are not like salespeople or pieceworkers who need a bonus or commission to motivate them to work hard. Poor teachers will not get better by offering them more money; what they need is more help (Educational Research Service, 1979).

You can expect that merit pay plans will be proposed during your professional career. You will need to weigh the pros and cons of such programs carefully so you can anticipate their effects.

CONCLUSION

Accountability is a concept that most people accept in principle, but one that is often difficult to implement. As we saw, all parties to the education process must share responsibility for what happens in schools. Administrators, parents, school board members, state and federal legislators, and the general public are all accountable for some aspect of education. However, it is difficult to determine the degree to which any person is accountable.

During your professional life you will encounter various kinds of accountability programs. You must be able to analyze the hidden assumptions behind programs and answer the question: Who benefits and who is hurt by such programs? For any program that is proposed, you should also try to identify who is accountable, to whom are they accountable, when are they accountable, for what are they accountable, and how will this something be measured? As a professional, you need to be able to articulate your views and philosophy on accountability in general and on a wide range of programs that continually gain support and then wane. Like death and taxes, accountability is something teachers can count on. They must therefore learn to live with the concept while at the same time recognizing pitfalls associated with specific programs.

QUESTIONS AND ACTIVITIES

1. Do you agree with merit pay plans for teachers? Why?
2. What forms of accountability do you think school systems should implement? Why?
3. What arguments can be made for and against paying teachers on how well students do on criterion-referenced tests that measure a set of behavioral objectives at the beginning of the year and evaluate them at the end?
4. Do you agree or disagree with the quote from the National Commission on Excellence in Education in Box 18.2? Why?
5. What means of accountability do other occupations use? Are any of these appropriate for education? Why or why not?
6. Interview a teacher, administrator, school board member, and parent. What are their views on accountability? How do they differ? How are they the same?

CHAPTER 19

The Role of Testing in Education

Standardized testing is fast becoming an increasingly important but controversial aspect of American education. You need to understand what a test is, and to be able to ask the critical question, "Does the test do what it purports to do?" Further, it is important that you be familiar with the strengths and weaknesses and the uses and abuses of standardized tests so you can use or react to them intelligently.

● A test is a small sample of student behavior from which you make inferences back to the larger domain represented by the test or to a different domain not measured by it.

● There are many different kinds of standardized tests that can be distinguished by what they measure, the type of questions they use, and whether scores are interpreted in terms of a norm group or some absolute performance criterion.

● Standardized tests can be used in schools for many useful purposes, and can also be misused for a variety of reasons.

● Standardized tests have been the subject of criticism involving the nature of the test, their use in school, and their effects on people in schools. In some cases, the criticism is well founded; in others, the criticisms flow out of ideological or political positions.

● Standardized test results are now used routinely to inform public policy and mechanisms to implement policy.

Think back for a moment on your school days. How many tests have you taken since you enrolled in kindergarten? It is a difficult number to estimate, but it is safe to say it is large. Here's an easier question. How many different *kinds* of tests have you taken over that same period? The most common and most frequent were, of course, written and oral teacher-constructed tests. Some teachers may have given you daily or very frequent quizzes. You certainly took longer tests weekly, bimonthly, just before the close of a marking period, or upon completion of a chapter in a textbook. Your grades on these teacher-made tests were a very important factor—but not the only one—in determining the grades you received on your many report cards.

Over the years and through the grades, in addition to these ubiquitous tests created by teachers, you also took numerous commercially prepared standardized achievement, aptitude, and ability tests. Can you ever forget those tests, with their separate answer sheets and the required number 2 pencils? It is easier to put a number on how many of these kinds of tests you took. It is estimated that in the United States, students take between 6 and 12 such commercially prepared test batteries between their kindergarten and twelfth school years (Houts, 1975). Any child who falls outside the norm in school performance, is a nonnative speaker of English, who has a handicapping condition, is learning-disabled, or is economically disadvantaged will probably have taken many additional test batteries on his or her journey through the grades (Wigdor & Garner, 1982).

A *test battery* is a collection of separate tests covering different content areas. A typical test battery might include separate tests of reading, arithmetic, social science, science, and study skills. More than 75 percent of all school districts nationwide regularly use these commercially developed test batteries for their annual school testing programs (National School Boards Association, 1977).

Commercial testing is a highly competitive, multimillion-dollar industry. Over twenty years ago it was estimated that more than 100 million commercially produced ability tests were administered annually (Goslin, 1963). The Association of American Publishers estimated that sales of tests grew from $26.5 million in 1972 to $52 million by 1978. In 1977, test sales were $44.9 million, or one-tenth of 1 percent of the total school instructional budget nationally (Wigdor & Garner, 1982).

In addition to the commercially prepared standardized tests you had to take as part of your school district's annual testing program, it is very likely that in certain grades you took tests required by the state. In some states students have to pass a state test in order to graduate from high school. At last count, 48 of the 50 states required some sort of elementary and secondary school testing (Pipho & Hadley, 1984).

As you can see, testing plays an important part in American education. This chapter deals with the role and function of commercially prepared standardized tests and of state-mandated tests in our schools. Most of you will eventually take a full course devoted to testing, providing you with skills in preparing your own classroom tests and in interpreting and using commercial

FIGURE 19.1 Universe or Domain of a Test with a Sample of Questions

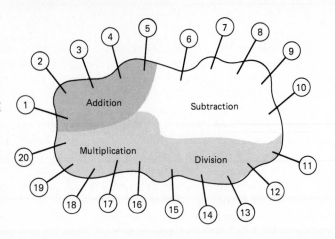

tests. This chapter will only introduce you to testing and to the place of standardized testing in the schools. First, we shall clarify what a test is. Second, we shall describe the different kinds of standardized tests and their various uses and misuses in schools, with particular emphasis on achievement tests. Third, we shall discuss the controversies that have been associated with standardized testing. Finally, we shall describe how states use tests either to inform educational policymakers or as administrative devices to implement policy.

What Is a Test?

You should be quite familiar with tests; after all, you have taken a lot of them over the years. How would you describe what a test is to a visitor from outer space? What would you say to your new acquaintance if it asked you, "What are these things called tests that your Earth children take so often?" Here is how we might answer your new friend's deceptively simple question.

The first and most basic concept behind a test is that it is a *sample* of questions—sometimes called items—from some universe or content domain that we are interested in. A *content domain* is a clearly defined body of knowledge, skills, and/or abilities. It is defined in a very precise and specific way so that you can decide whether or not a particular piece of knowledge or particular skills or tasks are part of the domain.

Figure 19.1 illustrates the concept of sampling from a domain. Let us assume that the amorphous closed area shown in the figure is the content domain of fourth-grade arithmetic problems. This particular content domain could be divided into four sections representing the basic operations of addition, subtraction, multiplication, and division. In the figure, these *subdomains* (or *facets* of the domain, as they are sometimes called) are numbered 1 to 4. Not all domains can be divided into subdomains or facets in this way.

Theoretically, there are a very large number of questions that you could ask a student about a given content domain. In terms of our example, there are a great many more addition, subtraction, multiplication, and division questions about the domain than could reasonably be asked of a student on a 40-minute test. One way to reduce the large number of potential questions associated with a domain is to define it more precisely. For example, we might limit the addition facet of our arithmetic domain to tasks involving three or fewer digits, with no carrying. While this more precise domain definition reduces the number of potential addition questions, there are an enormous number that we still could conceivably ask.

Since you cannot test the student on the entire range of possible ques-

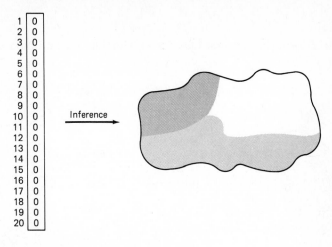

tions related to a domain, the way around the problem is to draw a sample of questions to represent the important aspects. In Figure 19.1, the small circles that lie outside the domain with the lines running back into it represent a sample of arithmetic questions drawn from each of the domain's four facets. This sample of questions is packaged together to make the test.

There is a second basic concept we must explain to our inquisitive alien, and it is closely related to the sampling concept of a test. We are more interested in the student's performance in terms of the domain than we are in his or her performance on the particular small sample of questions that make up the test itself. Figure 19.2 illustrates this second basic concept that underlies a test. The sample of 20 questions, now called a test, is represented by the 20 circles enclosed in the rectangles on the right. Based on the student's performance on the test (that is, the small sample of 20 questions) we make an *inference* about the student's mastery of the entire domain. This inference is represented by the broad arrow in the middle of the diagram.

The correctness of this inference is the central most important concept in testing. It goes by the technical name of test validity. *Test validity* refers to the degree to which a particular inference description or decision made from a person's test score is appropriate or meaningful. There is no such thing as a generically valid test, nor is a test valid in the abstract. In other words, it is incorrect to broadly and simply assert, "This is a valid test" without any further clarification. Instead, when someone talks about test validity, you must ask the question, "Valid for what?" The answer must always be in terms of the correctness of particular inferences, decisions, or descriptions that are made on the basis of a person's test score.

In an achievement test, it is important to show that the sample of questions (the test) adequately represents the content, skills, or behaviors of the domain. This concept is technically called the *content validity* of the test. In addition, all tests involve inferences concerning the degree to which an examinee possesses certain constructs or traits. A *construct* or *trait* is a "theoretical idea developed to explain and to organize some aspect of existing knowledge" (APA, Joint Committee on Test Standards, 1985, p. 29); examples of such constructs are intelligence, motivation, musical aptitude, mathematics problem-solving ability, reading comprehension ability, and spatial ability. We have tests that purport to measure these, and many other constructs as well. On the basis of such tests, inferences are made about the degree to which a person possesses the construct or trait in question. The correctness of this type of inference is called *construct validity*.

There is another type of inference often made on the basis of a person's performance on a test. It is illustrated in Figure 19.3. Here the test, as usual,

FIGURE 19.3 Using a Test to Make an Inference About a Different Domain

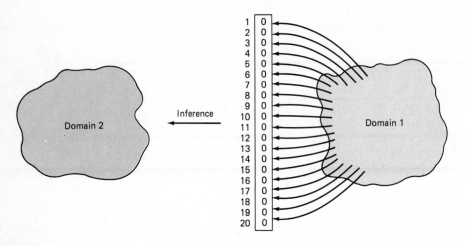

is a sample of questions drawn from a domain, but it is used to make an inference about how a student might perform on another, quite different domain. For example, the SAT and ACT, one of which you probably took to get into college, represent samples of questions from the domains of verbal and quantitative skills. The scores on these tests, however, are used to predict how well a student might perform on the domain of academic tasks required in college. It is this second *criterion domain* that gives the correctness of this type of inference its name: *criterion-related validity.*

There is another technical but very basic and easy-to-understand concept associated with standardized tests that your alien friend needs to grasp. It is called *test reliability* and refers to the degree to which a test score, and hence, the inferences made from it, are consistent, dependable, and free from measurement error.

Reliability speaks to the issue of the trustworthiness of the test. If you had a bathroom scale that gave you very different readings when you stepped on it twice in one morning, you would not trust the weight you saw, or the scale itself. The scale would not be reliable. It is the same with a test. We expect, within a narrow band, that a person will get a similar— not necessarily identical—score if he or she takes the test again, after a short interval. No test is completely free of error (and when you look at any test result you should always remember that), but a reliable test minimizes measurement error.

A test can be reliable but not valid. It can consistently give you the same score—give or take a few points—but the inference made from the score could, nonetheless, be incorrect. For example, a vocabulary test designed for twelfth graders, given to first graders, would give you consistent results; the first graders would get very few questions right. However, the inference you make about, for example, the extent of their vocabularies would be incorrect. There is a wide variation in vocabulary among first graders that would not be revealed by the twelfth-grade test. On the other hand, a test that permits valid inferences must be reliable.

Our alien should now understand that a test is a sample of questions, or tasks from a domain, that is used to make inferences about a student's performance on that domain, or on a different "criterion" domain of interest. The test's validity refers to the correctness of the inference made from the test score. The reliability of the test refers to the consistency and dependability of the scores. It should be clear to your alien friend that the two key questions one should always ask about any test before using it are "Can I trust the score?" and "Are the inferences I make from the scores correct?"

Different Kinds of Standardized Tests and Their Uses in the School

In this section we shall focus on cognitive tests that are used in elementary and secondary schools. There are also tests that measure affective traits such as personality, motivation, attitude, interest, self-concept, and anxiety. While such affective instruments are sometimes used in elementary and secondary schools, they are used much less frequently than cognitive tests. When they are used, it is generally in a specialized setting, such as in guidance or counseling situations, or for program evaluation. Because of their comparatively limited and specialized use, we shall not discuss affective tests in this chapter.

Cognitive tests can be distinguished according to the type of questions used. They can also be separated into ability tests, aptitude tests, and achievement tests. Achievement tests, in turn, can be either norm-referenced or criterion-referenced. Let us explore these different categories.

Type of Questions Used

Cognitive tests can be divided into ones that ask supply-type questions and those that use selection or objective-type questions. As the name implies, a *supply-type question* requires that a student produce an answer. The essay question, a short-answer question, a fill-in-the-blank question, and a straight computation question are all examples of supply-type items. Teachers prefer supply questions, either the essay or short-answer type, when they create their own tests. Examples of supply-type items are shown in Box 19.1.

Individually administered standardized ability tests such as the Stanford-Binet Intelligence Scale or the Wechsler Pre-School and Primary Scale of Intelligence are commercially developed tests that use supply-type questions. The student is asked to define a word orally, or to recite from memory a string of numbers. However, most commercially produced tests at the elementary and secondary school levels use selection questions almost exclusively.

The *selection question* requires that students select a correct answer, the best answer, the answer that best fits, or the answer that is most nearly correct, from a given list. Because selection items eliminate subjective human judgments that necessarily enter into the scoring of most supply-type answers, they are called *objective items.* Tests that use selection items are generally called *objective tests.* The most common type of objective items are ones with which you are quite familiar—multiple-choice and true-false questions. Box 19.2 presents examples of selection-type questions.

Students use a separate answer sheet to record their responses to selection questions. This permits optical-scanning machines to score the sheets quickly and accurately. Commercial test publishers make the bulk of their money not from the sale of the test booklets, which can be used over and over, but from the scale of separate answer sheets and from their machine-scoring services. Thus, there is an economic reason why most commercially available standardized tests use objective questions rather than the supply questions. Related to this economic factor is administrative convenience; selection answers eliminate the costly and time-consuming hand scoring necessary with supply answers.

Objective tests have many advantages. They are particularly efficient in measuring knowledge of facts; they provide an extensive sampling of course content (that is, you can ask many more objective questions in a 40-minute period than you can essay questions); scoring is easy and reliable; and, as we shall see, they provide information that makes it possible to compare a child's performance with that of some *norm group* outside the school.

It is important to remember, however, that there are many important school outcomes that cannot be measured by an objective test. An obvious example is writing. If you want to measure or judge a students' writing skills, then students must supply you with samples of their actual writing. As obvious as this may appear, there are, nonetheless, multiple-choice objective tests that purport to measure writing (Madaus & Rippey, 1966). Don't be misled by test names. Ask yourself whether the test name really reflects what is measured by the test questions.

Ability Tests

There is a group of cognitive tests that are designed to measure a more or less general ability (or a very small number of such abilities) that is "assumed to underlie, or condition performance across, a considerable range of tasks primarily intellectual in character" (Lennon, 1978, p. 1). Such tests were, until recently, commonly called *intelligence tests.* However, the use of the adjective *intelligence* to modify the noun *test* has fallen into disfavor. *Ability* is now the preferred adjective, since it is regarded as a more neutral descriptor of what this class of tests actually are meant to measure. The term *ability* does include skills that can be influenced by both experience and education. Thus, currently, the preferred label for this first category of cognitive tests is that of *scholastic* or *academic ability tests.*

Scholastic ability tests have a long history dating back to the work of Alfred Binet, who first developed a test to identify children who could not profit from regular instruction. Binet's test, which had to be individually administered by someone specially trained, was the forerunner of today's individually administered intelligence tests such as the Stanford-Binet Intelligence Scale (a direct linear descendant) and the Wechsler intelligence scales.

Intelligence tests that could be administered simultaneously to large groups of examinees were first developed by Arthur Otis for the United States Army in World War I. These were called the Army Alpha and Army Beta tests. The former was used to screen recruits for Officers' Candidate School, the latter to screen recruits who were illiterate. Both tests could be administered to large groups and scored objectively by clerks. After the war these *group intelligence tests,* as they were then called, evolved into the present commercially available tests presently used in many schools, such as the Otis-Lennon School Ability Test, the California Test of Mental Maturity, and the Thorndike-Hagen Cognitive Abilities Test.

From Binet's time, ability tests have measured about a dozen skills: vocabulary, general information, analogical reasoning, series or sequence manipulation, perceptual acuity, spatial abilities, quantitative skills, classification, and syllogistical reasoning (Lennon, 1978). Ability tests that are used in the elementary and secondary schools typically are heavily weighted toward four of these areas: vocabulary, general information, quantitative skills, and analogical reasoning. A moment's reflection reveals that all four of these traits depend heavily on a student's home background *and* what they learn in schools.

It is almost impossible to distinguish many ability test questions from achievement test questions. For example, both may contain identical-looking vocabulary questions. When a series of objective test questions, half drawn from ability tests, the other half drawn from achievement tests, were presented to individuals who were challenged to categorize the items by the type of test they came from, most of them failed (Cooley & Lohnes, 1976, Schwartz, 1977). An objective vocabulary question looks the same whether it is part of an ability test or part of an achievement test.

What do the ability tests used in our schools actually measure? The evidence now indicates that they are good measures of the skills needed to do school work. Students who do well on ability tests generally do well in school, and on the average tend to stay in school longer. However, the evidence also suggests that such tests do *not* do a particularly good job of predicting success in life after school (Bane & Jencks, 1976).

Aptitude Tests

A second category of cognitive test used in the schools is called the aptitude test. An *aptitude test* is designed to estimate future performance on tasks that do not bear an obvious similarity to the tasks measured by the test itself. Aptitude tests are also used to assess an individual's readiness to learn a skill or to develop a proficiency in some given area if a particular type of education or training is made available to them (APA, Joint Committee on Test Standards, 1985). As a class, aptitude tests overlap both the ability test category and the achievement test category.

Originally, aptitude tests were designed to measure special abilities, or aptitudes, not measured by tests of global intelligence. While ability or intelligence tests were originally designed to measure heterogeneous traits and to yield one global score (or two at the most) such as an overall I.Q. score (or verbal and quantitative I.Q. scores), multiple aptitude batteries were designed to give separate scores on a number of quite distinct and homogeneous traits. Aptitude tests do not measure—as some people assume from the name—an "innate capacity" that is independent of learning. Aptitude tests, like ability tests, measure *developed* or *learned* abilities.

As we saw, aptitude tests are generally used in schools to predict future performance, estimate whether an individual will profit from particular types of training, or estimate a person's probable achievement level in a new situation. It is this predictive use that distinguishes them from achievement tests, which are used to assess what a person can do at the present time in a given subject field (Anastasia, 1982). However, achievement tests can be transformed into aptitude tests when the results are used to predict subsequent learning. For example, the best predictor of a student's aptitude in a French II course is his or her achievement test score in French I.

There are special aptitude tests designed to measure psychomotor skills, mechanical aptitude, clerical aptitude, and artistic aptitude. These tests are most often used in schools for vocational or occupational career counseling or placement.

Standardized Achievement Tests

The most widely used standardized tests in our schools are achievement tests. These tests are designed to measure the extent to which a student commands a certain body of knowledge about subject matter or possesses certain basic skills, such as reading or arithmetic computation.

There are two types of standardized achievement tests currently in use in our schools: norm-referenced tests and criterion-referenced tests. This distinction has little to do with test format; the two kinds of tests look very much alike. Further, it is impossible to tell a criterion-referenced test question from a norm-referenced one. The principal difference lies in how the scores derived from each test are interpreted. Let us consider each type of score in turn.

NORM-REFERENCED TESTS Each year, school systems routinely administer commercially available norm-referenced achievement batteries, either early in the fall or in late spring. Tests are called *norm-referenced* when they permit a teacher to compare a student's test performance with that of a normative group. A *normative group* or *norm group* is a group of individuals carefully selected to represent students in a particular grade in school or students of a particular age group. Most publishers provide national norms, and some provide regional and state norms, and others go so far as to provide norms based on certain school characteristics (for example, public, private or parochial; urban, suburban, or rural; size of school district). Further, when publishers score the tests for larger school systems, district, school, and even classroom norms can be provided.

The idea of a norm may become more clear when we consider the following situation. A boy comes home to his father and tells him he received a 38 on an English test. What is the father likely to say? The first thing he will probably ask him is, "Thirty-eight out of what?" As it happens, there were 100 questions. Some fathers might jump to the conclusion that 38 correct answers out of 100 is a very poor score; after all, it is only 38 percent correct. But not this father. He wants to know more. And in his next question, he tries to find out something about how the other students in the class did. He wants to know the boy's standing in relation to the rest of the class. His score was the tenth highest in a class of 40, and the highest mark in the class was 58. And the average mark? The boy didn't know that, but he did know that his friend who came in 20th out of 40 had a mark of 33. The father now knows that the median score—the halfway or middle point in the distribution of test scores—was 33. The father also knows that his son (in tenth place) did better than 30, or 75 percent, of the other students. He also knows something about the distribution of the scores. This certainly is more meaningful than knowing only that his son got a mark of 38, or even 38 out of 100. What norms try to do is to relate a student's *raw score* (the pure number of correct answers) to information about the performance of other students and provide you with the answer in a simple figure. Norms transform the raw score into what is called a *derived score* to make it more meaningful in terms of the student's performance in relation to the norm or comparison group.

The three most common derived scores associated with norm-referenced tests are percentiles, grade equivalents, and standard scores. A *percentile rank* shows, as a percent, the proportion of the norm group that received either the same raw score or a lower score. Suppose a student, Mary Carter, answers 28 questions correctly on a reading test. The teacher goes to the norm table and finds 28 and discovers that the corresponding percentile rank is 87. Mary's percentile rank (87th percentile) means that she received a *raw score* (number correct) that was as high as, or higher than, 87 percent of the norm group. It follows that 13 percent of the norm group scored higher than Mary.

The particular norm group table that the teacher used to look up Mary's raw score of 28 makes a big difference. It is entirely possible for a raw score of 28 to be at the 87th percentile on the national norm table and at the 55th percentile on the local district norm table, particularly if the district is relatively affluent or suburban. Thus, it is essential that a teacher be clear on the characteristics of the norm group to which he or she compares a student's performance.

The percentile is the derived score least open to misinterpretation. However, one caution is in order: A percentile rank should *not* be misread as the percentage of "correct" answers. Mary's 87th percentile does not mean she answered 87 percent of the items correctly, or that her score is equivalent to a B+ grade in the traditional grading system used by teachers. It is, rather, her relative position in the distribution of scores of the norm group.

Figure 19.4 illustrates the concept of a person's relative standing in a distribution of scores in terms of a foot race. There are 100 runners competing in the race. Their raw scores (shown in the top scale on the vertical axis) are the number of feet they have run in ten seconds. The runners are distributed in terms of their scores in something approaching a "normal" or bell-shaped curve (compare this with Figure 11.1 on page 259). On such a curve, most students bunch near the middle of the scale (around the average score); the rest spread out toward each extreme. The number of people behind a runner at a given point shown on the bottom portion of the vertical axis corresponds to a percentile rank. In Figure 19.4, a raw score of 220 feet run in ten seconds corresponds to the 50th percentile, since 50 people are behind that point in the distribution and 50 people are beyond it (Patton, 1975). This example is easy to follow, since everyone can directly relate to the physical concepts of speed and distance. In a standardized test, the raw score of distance run in the given period would be replaced by a raw score, that is, the number of questions answered correctly. The concept of number of questions answered correctly does not have the intrinsic meaning that distance has; therefore, a person's relative position in the score distribution becomes more important in describing his or her performance.

A *grade-equivalent (GE) score* is perhaps the most widely derived score used in schools. Unfortunately, it is also probably the most widely misinterpreted score. GEs are derived scores based on the average performance of

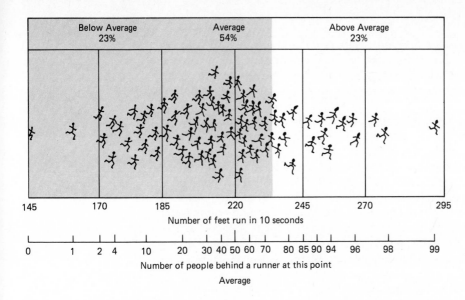

Number of feet run in 10 seconds

Number of people behind a runner at this point

Average

Source: Patton, 1975, p. 20.

students in a series of grades on a test designed for a particular grade. Thus, a test designed to be used with fourth graders would be given not only to them but also to the second and third graders, as well as to the fifth and sixth graders. The average performance of second-, third-, fourth-, fifth-, and sixth-grade pupils on this *fourth-grade test* would be assigned grade equivalents of 2.0, 3.0, 4.0, 5.0, and 6.0, respectively. Grade equivalents expressed in school months between grade levels are then interpolated (for example, 3.8 stands for third grade, eighth month of the school year).

Suppose Mary, a fourth grader, has a raw score of 34 on our fourth-grade arithmetic test. The norm table indicates that this raw score is equivalent to a GE score of 5.6. This means that Mary's performance on a test measuring *fourth-grade material* is equal to the performance of a student in the sixth month of fifth grade on the same *fourth-grade material*. It does *not* mean that Mary can do fifth-grade arithmetic, which is the most common misinterpretation associated with GE scores.

Beyond elementary school, GEs have little meaning. Clearly, a GE of 10.6 on a sixth-grade arithmetic test does not mean the student can do algebra or geometry.

Norm-referenced tests are constructed to attain the dual aims of representative norms and commercial feasibility. In selecting content for standardized achievement tests, it has become common practice to review the 10 or 12 most widely used textbooks or curriculum guides in a particular subject to obtain a preliminary list of topics or objectives to be tested. The relative weighting, in terms of number of questions given to these topics, is also determined. Often, the median number of pages devoted to a particular topic in the textbooks surveyed is used as a rough indication of the topic's importance. Sometimes, a review of popular textbooks is supplemented by a review of the course syllabi used by a number of large city school systems. After a tentative list of topics has been derived, teachers and authorities in the subject area are asked to review the list for adequacy and completeness. This review can result in additions or deletions of topics and objectives. It is on the basis of one or more such refinements that experts make the final specification of topics and skills.

The content topics are more easily delineated in certain school subjects and at certain grade levels. For example, for a secondary-level English literature course, in which teachers are allowed a fair amount of discretion in selecting topics and books and poems to be read, the determination of common content nationwide is far from straightforward. When this happens, publishers cannot identify enough common topics to build a test that can be marketed nationally. As one would expect, there are very few commercial standardized tests in English literature; this is true of many subjects at the secondary level, where greater specialization is accompanied by more diversity in content coverage across school systems (Bloom, Hastings, & Madaus, 1971).

Because they include only the most common curricular content and objectives nationally, standardized norm-referenced achievement tests often inadequately reflect the specific content and objectives of particular school programs. Thus, for some districts that deviate from the national norm in terms of textbooks used or content covered, a particular standardized achievement test may not be a good measure of achievement levels in that district (Madaus, Airasian, & Kellaghan, 1980). However, these norm-referenced tests do permit educators to compare student performance norms on subject matter and objectives most commonly found throughout the country.

American schools use norm-referenced standardized tests to a great extent. Available evidence indicates that educators tend to like such tests and use them to measure the educational growth of students, to detect systemwide general strengths or weaknesses, to help plan instruction for class groups and for individuals, to report to parents, to compare students with national and state peer groups, and to screen special-education students (Beck & Stetz, 1979).

CRITERION-REFERENCED TESTS As we saw, norm-referenced tests compare a student's performance with that of a norm group. However, they do not tell you what a student can do or cannot do, or what objectives the student has mastered or failed to master. A *criterion-referenced test*, sometimes called a *domain-referenced test* or an *objective-referenced test*, gives scores that describe an examinee's status with respect to a clearly defined behavior and content domain.

In increasing numbers, publishers are marketing criterion-referenced achievement tests (CRTs) in reading and arithmetic. These tests are geared to a set of carefully defined behavioral objectives. Each objective is measured by 3, 4, 5, or more questions. The *mastery criterion*, sometimes called a *cut score*, for an objective is set at a fixed number of questions answered correctly (for example, 3 out of 3; 4 out of 5). If a student attains the criterion score (for example, 4 out of 5 items answered correctly), he or she is said to have "mastered" the particular objective. No reference is made to the performance of other students. The inference is absolute, not relative; the student has, or has not, mastered the skill or content of the objective. It is possible, however, to add a norm-referenced interpretation to a criterion-referenced interpretation if the publisher also provides in the test manual the percentage of students nationwide who reached the criterion score. The upper scale at the bottom of Figure 19.4 is criterion-referenced in terms of how far a person can run in ten seconds; the lower scale is norm-referenced in terms of percentiles (the number of people behind a runner).

One criterion-referenced test, called the Degrees of Reading Power, (DRP), provides scores that are concretely referenced to the difficulty level of various reading materials. The DRP gives three criterion-referenced scores. First, it yields an *independent-level score,* which represents the difficulty level of materials a student can read and understand without any help. Second, it yields an *instructional-level, score,* which indicates the difficulty level of materials a student can read and understand with help from the teacher, classroom discussions, dictionaries, and other instructional aids. Third, it yields a *frustration-level score,* which identifies the difficulty level of materials a student would find hard or frustrating to read. If a student's independent-level score was 58, this would indicate an ability to handle material in teen magazines without help. If the instructional-level score was 65, this would indicate an ability to read and understand consumer news in adult general-interest magazines with help. A frustration-level score of 70 means that the student probably could not handle business news found in those same kinds of general-interest periodicals. This type of criterion-referenced scoring gives a teacher concrete information on which to base his or her selection of reading materials.

Commercially available criterion-referenced tests offer teachers a wealth of achievement information that helps them decide the proper academic placement of students and whether or not students have the necessary prerequisite skills to benefit from planned instruction.

How Tests Are Used in Schools

Results from commercial standardized tests, both norm-referenced and criterion-referenced, can be used for many purposes and by many different people. Tests can be used for classroom purposes, for supervisory and administrative purposes within a school system, or for use related to policy or legislation outside the individual school system (Gardner, 1982). The first two categories will be described in the next two sections, and the third category will be explored when we consider the role of tests in educational policy in the final section of this chapter.

Users of test results include teachers, students, parents, school administrators, state education officials, state and national policymakers, members of the media, and the general public. Table 19.1 lists legitimate uses and the various users of test information.

TABLE 19.1 Legitimate Uses and Users of Test Information

Results About . . .	May Be Used by the . . .	To Help . . .
The individual student	• Student • Student's parents • Student's teacher • Student's counselor	• Evaluate individual progress • Make decisions about teaching • Make predictions about future work
A single class	• Students in class • Teacher of class • Building administrator	• Evaluate class progress • Improve programs
Students in school	• Students in school • Teachers in school • Building administrators • District administrators	• Evaluate programs • Identify needs
A school district	• Teachers in district • Administrators in district • Public of district • State administrators	• Evaluate programs • Identify needs
All the schools in a state	• District administrators • State administrators • Federal officials • General public	• Identify needs • Assess progress
All the schools or students in the nation	• State administrators • Federal officials • General public	• Identify needs • Assess progress

Source: National Council of Teachers of English, 1975.

Classroom Uses

Teachers use criterion-referenced and norm-referenced standardized tests in the classroom for the following purposes:

1. Identifying the level and range of ability, or mastery, among students on certain objectives or on certain skills
2. Identifying areas of instruction needing greater emphasis
3. Identifying discrepancies between scholastic aptitude and achievement
4. Identifying readiness for learning
5. Diagnosing learning errors and planning remedial instruction
6. Sectioning groups of pupils for short periods of remedial instruction (Gronlund, 1981)

In addition to these six applications, another can be grouped within the classroom category: guidance counselors, parents, and students use test results in career, vocational, and educational planning.

Supervisory and Administrative Uses

Supervisors and administrators use criterion-referenced and norm-refe-renced test results for the following purposes:

 1. Identifying strengths and weaknesses of programs
 2. Comparing the performance of a district against national norms
 3. Informing the public about how the schools are doing
 4. Identifying areas where groups of students are not doing well
 5. Designing new instructional or remedial programs
 6. Identifying students with special needs

The Misuse of Test Results

Test results are often misused in a number of different ways (Madaus, 1988):

 1. By accepting a test title as an indication of what the test actually measures
 2. By ignoring the error of measurement in test scores
 3. By using a single test score to make important decisions
 4. By misunderstanding test scores and/or report forms
 5. By incorrectly using descriptions obtained from tests to explain per-formance

Accepting a Test Title as an Indication of What the Test Actually Measures

Some people take the test name at face value, believing that the test measures what its name implies. We have already talked about the mispercep-tions that surround the use of the term *intelligence* to describe a test. A similar misuse would arise if a non-English-speaking student were given a test printed in English and labeled a "verbal aptitude" test in order to discover his or her verbal aptitude. Even the title *achievement test* can sometimes be misleading. Achievement tests are usually administered to determine what a student has learned, or achieved, as a result of instruction. However, an achievement test that measures material never covered in class is not a valid index of school learning. Students must draw heavily on their out-of-school experiences when they attempt to answer questions on material not covered in class. In this situation, the so-called achievement test may really be a measure of the stu-dent's home background and socioeconomic status (Madaus, Airasian, & Kel-laghan, 1980).

Ignoring the Error of Measurement in Test Scores

In our earlier discussion of test reliability, we learned that every test, no matter how well constructed, contains some measurement error. It is wrong, therefore, to take a single test score as a student's "true level" of ability. For example, taking a single score of 120 on a scholastic ability test and placing all students at or above this score in an accelerated group and those below this score in another group is a misuse of that score. Students with scores of 122 are probably not different, in terms of their "true ability," from students with scores of 118.

Because of the measurement error associated with every test, a score on any standardized test should be thought of as a range rather than as a single point on the score distribution. For example, the "true score" of a person who receives a 120 on an ability test would fall, 68 times out of 100, somewhere in the range of 115 to 125; 95 times out of 100 the person's "true score" would fall between 110 and 130. The "true score" of a person who scores 117 on the same test would be, 68 times out of 100, between 112 and 122. Note that in these two examples, the "true score" ranges overlap. Therefore, to think of the two students who scored 120 and 117 as essentially different—to put one of them in an accelerated group and not the other solely on the basis of their test scores—would be a misuse of those test scores.

Using a Single Test Score to Make Important Decisions

While this misuse is closely related to the concept of measurement error just discussed, it has another, different dimension to it. A test is a limited sample of behavior. There are many extenuating factors that need to be considered when interpreting a test score. Further, while a student may not be able to exhibit the desired behavior on a paper-and-pencil multiple-choice test, he or she may be able to show it in other more direct ways (for example, picking up a book, reading a passage aloud, and telling someone what it means). The rule is that one should use all the data available when making a decision about a student, not just a single score on a single test.

Today, there is a trend toward using a single test score by itself to make crucial decisions about students, such as whether they should be promoted from grade to grade or whether they should graduate from high school. Many people feel that this is a misuse of a test; that the test should be only *one* piece of information, along with other data, that teachers and administrators use to make these important certification decisions. According to this point of view, decisions should be made by professionals on the basis of all the available information to them. They should not be made automatically on the basis of a single test score without any teacher input (Madaus, 1985).

Misunderstanding Test Scores and/or Report Forms

Many people—teachers, administrators, parents, students, those employed by the media, and the general public—simply misinterpret test scores. We saw how percentile ranks and grade equivalents can be misinterpreted. It is not uncommon for a teacher to misinterpret a student's GE of 6.6 on a fourth-grade test as indicating that the student can do sixth-grade work. Another common misinterpretation is to argue that a school district's test results are poor because the scores of one half of the students fall below the 50th percentile in terms of the district's norms. However, because of the way in which percentiles are calculated, one half of the group *has to be* above and one half *has to be* below the 50th percentile—at least when the norm is derived for the first time. Moreover, such an interpretation says nothing about the absolute performance of the students and about how the scores compare to national or state norms. It is very important, therefore, that you understand the meaning of any test score you use, how to interpret it properly, and how to explain it to laypeople.

Incorrectly Using Decriptions Obtained from Tests to Explain Performance

Many people confuse information provided by a test with possible interpretations about what caused the performance described by the test score. A test score gives no information as to why the individual achieved a particular score. For example, a common reason given to explain a low score on an ability test is that the person "lacks intelligence." Since psychologists and others define *intelligence* as what an intelligence, or ability, test measures, the argument becomes circular when educators maintain that a person is intelligent *because* he or she scored high on an intelligence test.

An achievement test can identify a student who performed poorly on, let us say, arithmetic problem solving, but it gives no information about the underlying cause of the poor performance. In fact, the cause of low performance can differ from student to student. One student could perform poorly because of reading difficulties; another, who reads well, might not have command of the fundamental arithmetic operations; still another, who both reads well and knows his or her arithmetic operations, might have done poorly because he or she was upset or preoccupied on the day of the test. Always remember that test scores are descriptive, not explanatory.

Criticisms of Standardized Tests

Since the 1920s, when commercial standardized tests became popular, they have from time to time been the object of severe criticism. Indeed, the controversy over the use of standardized tests in our schools is one of the longest-running battles in American education. In a recent commentary on standardized testing in America, it was claimed that the "misapplication and misinterpretation of test results can injure individual students and erode curriculum and instruction . . . create social and intellectual segregation, foster elitism, fashion a punishment/reward syndrome, reduce learning to rote and regurgitative modes, deprecate, stigmatize, exclude" (Cooper & Leiter, 1980, p. 35).

Box 19.3 shows a list of common criticisms often leveled against standardized testing. In this section, we shall examine these criticisms. In general, they fit into three categories: those related to (1) the nature of the tests, (2) the

BOX 19.3 Typical Criticism of Standardized Tests

Examples of criticisms related to characteristics intrinsic to the tests include the following:

- Standardized achievement tests take for granted that everybody places equal value on the skills being tested.
- Standardized achievement tests assume a homogeneous culture and/or a common set of curriculum objectives.
- Standardized achievement tests are biased in favor of white, middle-class children.
- Standardized achievement tests are constructed on the assumption that about half the pupils tested will be below average.
- Standardized achievement tests are impersonal, ambiguous, imprecise, undemocratic, and irrelevant.
- Standardized achievement tests measure only a small portion of what teachers and schools try to do.
- Standardized achievement tests are not valid measures of school-specific achievement.

Examples of criticisms related to characteristics not intrinsic to the tests include the following:

- Standardized achievement tests are not diagnostic.
- Standardized achievement tests do not measure the goals of new, innovative, or "different" instructional interventions.
- Standardized achievement tests do not measure creativity, interest, initiative, or values.
- Standardized achievement tests do not assess an individual's learning; rather they compare students' achievement.

Examples of criticisms related to the effects of the tests include the following:

- Standardized achievement tests "label" pupils.
- Standardized achievement tests "mislabel" pupils.
- Standardized achievement tests dominate school curricula and foster teaching for the test.
- Standardized achievement tests foster competition in the classroom.
- Standardized achievement tests arouse fear and satisfy greed.

Source: Airasian, 1979, pp. 6–7.

use of tests in educational settings, and (3) the effects of testing on participants in the educational process (Kellaghan, Madaus, & Airasian, 1982).

Criticisms of the Nature of Standardized Tests

Critics claim that test publishers build tests on the dual assumptions that all students share a common culture and have equal opportunity to learn a common curriculum taught by the schools. These assumptions have been seriously challenged. Critics argue that not all students share the middle-class culture that is most common in the schools and go on to point out that if tests reflect only the dominant culture's knowledge, language, and behavior, they will not be valid or reliable measures when given to students from minority cultures. This problem with the nature of standardized tests is sometimes referred to as *test bias.*

The fact that certain groups of students score poorly on tests does not necessarily indicate test bias. For example, if a minority student does poorly on an English verbal ability test, it may very well indicate that the student has poor vocabulary and verbal skills in English and needs remedial help, not that the test is biased (Gardner, 1982). However, if the same type of test were to be used to classify a minority pupil as educably mentally retarded, and as a result the student were placed in a special-education class, then the test could be considered biased. There have been two important court decisions that have ruled that ability tests are biased against minority students when they are used for tracking or for placement in special-education classes [*Larry P. v. Riles,* 495 F. Supp. 926 (W.D. Calif. 1979); *Hobson* v. *Hansen,* 269 F. Supp. 401 (D. Wash, DC 1967)].

Another criticism of the nature of objective standardized achievement tests is that they do not permit the evaluation of many important student characteristics such as the ability to learn, the ability to make informed judgments, creativity, or imagination. While this charge is certainly true, standardized achievement tests have never claimed to measure those traits.

The Use of Tests in Educational Settings

Critics point out that administrative procedures in giving tests can vary from place to place because of teacher errors in following directions and in timing the test. If this happens, the administration does not follow the standardized procedure upon which norms are based and therefore any normative comparisons made will not be valid. Further, as we saw above, there can be mistakes in interpreting and using test results that adversely affect judgments or decisions about students.

The Effects of Testing on Participants in the Educational Process

It is generally assumed that standardized achievement and ability tests are used to select and classify students. These functions have been criticized on the grounds that they lead to rigid tracking and grouping. Further, such practices can lead to pejorative "labeling" of students who score below average on tests. For example, since disproportionate numbers of poor and minority children score lower than majority students on such tests, labeling encourages and perpetuates distinctions on the basis of race and social class. Furthermore, some students are clearly mislabeled when, for example, they are classified as mentally retarded because they had difficulty with a test that was not in their primary language.

Critics also claim that standardized testing programs pressure teachers into teaching for the test, leading to a narrowing of the curriculum to focus on test items. Testing is seen as perpetuating a standard, limited curriculum, and discouraging diverse and innovative programs. At the student level, standardized testing has been accused of dampening creativity and encouraging conformity and intellectual dishonesty. Critics also point out that standardized testing takes time away from instruction; they argue that slow learners are neglected because teachers concentrate on better students whose scores are easier to raise. Finally, critics contend that, some students, particularly minority students, may accomplish less because teachers expect less of them, thus setting in motion a self-fulfilling prophecy.

Critics also claim that standardized tests have negative psychological effects on students. A frequent accusation in this regard is that such tests are potentially damaging to a student's self-concept; this will most likely happen when action, such as a referral to a remedial class, is taken on the basis of a test score.

An Evaluation of Criticisms of Tests

The criticisms discussed above cover a wide range of supposed defects and negative consequences of testing. In some cases, the criticisms point to real weaknesses in the test; in others, to the misuse of test results. Evaluating the claims of test critics depends very much on how you frame the questions. You can ask a series of negative questions: To what extent does testing lead to social stratification, to labeling students, to self-fulfilling prophecies, to competitiveness, or to weak self-concepts? Or you may ask a set of questions with a different focus, such as, To what extent do tests reflect injustices rather than create them? How many of the negative consequences attributed to testing would occur if testing never took place?

Another way to put test criticisms into perspective is in terms of a series of questions about the positive effects of tests, such as, Does standardized-test information provide teachers and counselors with information that is helpful in their teaching and student guidance? Does test information contribute to the improvement of a student's learning and to the enhancement of his or her self-concept? Are teachers who do not have access to test results at a disadvantage in their work compared with those who have access? Are students likely to be at a disadvantage when their teachers do not have the kind of information that can be derived from standardized testing (Kellaghan, Madaus, & Airasian, 1982)?

Comparing the answers to all three sets of questions permits a person to make a more reasonable assessment of the positive and negative effects associated with test use. This is a crude type of *cost-benefit analysis.* You decide, on the basis of your answers to such questions, whether or not the good features outweigh the bad.

Much of the debate about the positive and negative effects of testing has been confined to statements deduced from ideological or political positions. Those who reject the use of standardized tests often base their opinions on a mixture of intuitive feelings about effects and a strong egalitarian philosophy of education. Those who vigorously accept and advocate the use of standardized tests very often also argue from an entrenched value position that sees "scientific" or "objective" measurement as superior to "subjective judgments." Some proponents of standardized tests argue their case from an elitist philosophy of education or from the perspective of people who make money from the sale of tests.

Value positions aside, what is the empirical or research evidence on the effects of standardized testing? A large-scale study that centered on teachers' use of standardized-test information found that teachers tended to use test results to support, rather than to challenge, existing school and teacher practices. In most cases, test information was found to confirm previous teacher evaluations of student ability and achievement. It was the exception, rather than the rule, for a teacher to be confronted with test information that might lead to a change in the way the teacher viewed a student. Teachers did not see test results as leading to labeling or neglect of students, nor did test results seem to affect their conscious organizational or evaluation practices. The study concluded that teachers easily assimilated standardized-test information into the operating evaluative system of the classroom. There was no support for the position that standardized-test information, when under the control of the teacher, differed in kind in its effects from any other evaluative procedure available to teachers (Kellaghan, Madaus, & Airasian, 1982).

In the study just described, the standardized-test information was made available *only* to the classroom teachers for their personal use. What happens when standardized-test results are used by persons other than the classroom teacher? First, there is little doubt that test results can provide important independent information to parents and the public about our schools, information that these groups now demand and to which they are entitled. However, the impact of any testing program appears to be a direct function of the rewards or sanctions attached to the results. If there are not important rewards or sanctions linked to test performance, then the use of the test results will be relatively slight. On the other hand, it is axiomatic that when important rewards such as funding, teacher evaluation, and student promotion or graduation depend (in whole or in part) on standardized achievement test results, the impact of the testing on students, teachers, and the curriculum is substantial.

When achievement test scores are linked to important consequences, those scores begin to control and to restrict what is taught, how it is taught, what is learned, and how it is learned. Areas not tested no longer receive much emphasis. Teachers begin to teach to the kinds of questions asked on the tests. Students are drilled on past test questions for weeks or even months before the examination. If the reward or sanction is directed at the student rather than the teacher, students will be placed under considerable pressure and spend considerable time cramming for the tests and worrying about them (Madaus, 1983, 1985, 1988; Madaus & Greaney, 1985; Smith 1986).

The practice of making rewards or sanctions contingent on the results of standardized tests is not a common one in local school districts. However, at the state level, test results are often used to influence policy decisions.

The Use of Tests in Setting Education Policy

There are two principal ways in which policymakers use test results: (1) to inform them, and (2) as administrative mechanisms to implement the policy itself. Let us briefly consider each of these uses.

The Use of Test Results to Inform Policy-Making

In the early 1960s, state and federal policymakers began to use test results to *inform* themselves about the condition of education. Test scores or test results were used to buttress political arguments for certain kinds of legislation or reform proposals. For example, advocates for minority groups began to point to the large discrepancies between the test scores of white middle-class students and their constituents to lobby successfully for compensatory funds for programs to reduce these disparities. Recently, various national commissions and study groups used test results to argue that our educational system is in need of drastic reform.

Test scores are often used for informational or lobbying functions. However, until the late 1960s and early 1970s there were no immediate or automatic decisions made about individuals, schools, or districts on the basis of test scores, and rewards or sanctions were not linked directly to test results.

The Use of Tests as Administrative Mechanisms in Policy-Making

In the early 1970s, policymakers began to use test results not only for informational or lobbying purposes but also to make certain things happen. One of the first instances of this new use of test results by policymakers was that of *performance contracting.*

At about the same time, policymakers in a number of states linked the allocation of compensatory funding to school districts directly to *low* test performance. The procedure, called *test-based funding*, awarded a fixed amount of money to a school district for every student falling below a certain percentile rank on a standardized achievement test (usually the 20th or 25th percentile). These programs were criticized for creating a *negative incentive*—money was available only for low-scoring pupils; if student performance improved, the district would lose money.

More recently, legislation has been proposed at the federal level to provide school districts with money for high test performance. A positive financial incentive for doing well on a test elevates the importance of that in the school district. When this happens, the negative effects on curriculum and teaching described above can easily ensue.

In both kinds of test-based funding (that is, positive and negative incentive programs), the test becomes the administrative mechanism for awarding compensatory funds. Policymakers began to use test scores as an award criterion because their exclusive use of a socioeconomic index to award funds resulted in the neglect of those districts where low-scoring students were educationally, but not economically, disadvantaged.

Twenty-five states have enacted legislation requiring students to pass a minimum-competency test (MCT) for graduation; some states require that students pass a test for promotion (Stern, 1987). *Minimum-competency tests* are designed to measure a student's command of basic skills at about a seventh- or eighth-grade level. Table 19.2 presents a list of positive and negative claims about MCTs, the validity of which await empirical confirmation. For political reasons, states are reluctant to evaluate the impact of MCT programs or to ask potentially damaging questions about such programs. However, it is safe to say, based on experiences in other countries, that if a test is linked to graduation, then it will influence the curriculum, what is taught, how it is

TABLE 19.2 Potential Positive and Negative Effects Associated with Minimum Competency Testing Programs Used to Make Graduation and Promotion Decisions

Area of Impact	Potential Positive Effects	Potential Negative Effects
Mastery of the basic skills	By systematically isolating student deficits in fundamental skills and then remedying them, more students will master basic skills as reflected by their performance on competency tests.	Focus on the "test" as a guide for instruction will result in students learning to take the test. The development of competence in the basic skills is not assured.
Attitudes toward self and school	Many students will acquire more positive self-concepts and more positive attitudes toward school as a result of becoming proficient in basic skills.	Minimum-competency testing labels children as "failures," which hinders their further educational progress and subsequent employment. Failing an MCT has a serious negative effect on children's self-concept, and increases their anxiety.
		De-emphasizes a broad range of educational outcomes; the minimums embodied in these all-important tests become the maximum.
		Inordinate amounts of time are devoted to teaching for the test, to the detriment of other subjects.
		Raising or inflating test scores and not the improvement of competencies becomes the object of the exercise.
Teacher effectiveness	Clearly defined competencies permit teachers to enhance their instructional effectiveness by (a) providing students with more time on-task, that is, practice relevant to the competencies, and (b) acquiring more positive expectations which will enhance teachers' perceived sense of efficacy.	The test narrows teaching to drilling and cramming for the test. MCTs stifle teacher creativity.
Curriculum coverage	Increased efficiency in promoting the MCT program's target competencies will result in more available time for other instruction and thus lead to expanded curriculum coverage. Teachers of higher courses will no longer be forced to teach basic skills. They will be able to turn their efforts and resources to higher-level course content.	Focusing on minimum-competency test scores deflects attention and resources from the broader aims of schooling, including development of specialized talents and vocational preparation. Typically, this includes reduced investment of time, personnel, and money in the higher academic areas such as music, art, physical education, and vocational education, which are not covered on minimum-competency tests. Subjects not tested are seen as less important.
School effectiveness	Improved pupil performance. The test-based evidence of improved student attainments will reassure an incredulous public regarding the schools' educational effectiveness.	The public will be misled by apparent gains from one year to the next on MCTs that are often simply the result of making the tests, rather than being attributable to sound teaching and effective learning of the real skill required.

BOX 19.4 What Citizens Should Look For: Developing and Evaluating Minimum Competency Programs

1. *A minimum competency test must have curricular or instructional validity.* This means the test must be designed so it only measures what the school is actually teaching the students. Otherwise the students will be penalized for the school's failure to each specific competency. There is always the danger a competency test might be designed to test what policymakers (legislators, state or local school board members) think students should know, while in fact the instructional program does not emphasize the skills which are tested. Inherent in any minimum competency program should be a guarantee by the State, the school district, and school that the students will be taught those skills necessary to pass the competency test.

2. *A minimum competency testing program should not penalize those students who have been in school for a number of years prior to the imposition of the minimum competency program.* In other words, if a minimum competency test is administered for the first time when a student is in the tenth grade, it must be understood that the student is taking the test without the benefit of adequate preparation resulting from the school system's new emphasis on the skills to be tested. Thus, to be fair to the students who are currently in the upper grade levels, the competency program should probably be phased in beginning at the elementary level.

3. *The minimum competency program must use multi-cultural tests.* This means that the tests must assess those "competencies" which the various racial, ethnic, and language groups agree are important for children to attain. It is likely that the best way to reach such a consensus is through a careful and

deliberate process of community education and discussion about the minimum competency program and what it should include. Before a competency test is purchased from a publisher or is developed at the state or local level it should be carefully reviewed by legitimate and knowledgeable representatives of various racial, ethnic, and language groups to assure that the test measures only those skills which the groups agree are necessary for success in adult life.

4. *The minimum competency program must not penalize those students who were formerly enrolled in schools offering inferior educational programs.* Many state and federal courts have issued decisions declaring that students received unequal educational opportunities when they had to attend racially segregated schools, or poor schools which were denied adequate financial resources because of a state's school finance system. In many places there are students currently enrolled in schools who began their educational careers in such segregated or economically deprived schools. Many of these students still have not received the assistance they need to overcome the basic skill weaknesses resulting from attending segregated or underfinanced schools. Therefore, any minimum competency program now imposed should take account of this fact. Special provisions, such as a "grandfather clause," should be made so they do not suffer penalties for a condition for which the State is responsible.

5. *Any laws or policies which are enacted for the purpose of establishing a minimum competency program should include provisions which will allow*

BOX 19.4 *(Continued)*

exemption procedures to be established for handicapped and non-English-speaking students. Minimum competency programs which require students to repeat a grade, to be enrolled in a special program, or not to receive a regular high school diploma if they do not meet the minimum requirements should not apply to students who, by virtue of their handicap or language barrier, cannot perform on an equal basis with other students. The tests may have to be administered in a different way, other kinds of competencies may have to be tested, diplomas indicating the specific competencies achieved may have to be developed, or tests assessing different levels of competencies may have to be developed, but the special situation of handicapped and language minority students must be taken into account.

6. *A minimum competency program must set forth a specific process for consultation with and involvement of parents.* This process should include a sophisticated reporting system which communicates to parents what specific competencies the school is teaching and what competencies the child has mastered. It should also provide for a systematic process of parent-administrator-teacher-student conferences. Such communication between parents and schools should be mandated to take place before mandated minimum competency tests are administered. The conference should be designed so that both the parents and

the school personnel commit themselves to specific actions which will aid the student in correcting weaknesses identified during regular classroom experiences.

7. *Minimum competency programs should not be used to deny promotion or graduation based solely on a student's performance on a single test.* If a student's competencies are to be used as a major criterion for promotion or graduation then the student's competencies in a broad range of areas must be examined. These might include competencies demonstrated in extracurricular activities, vocational classes, working in a part-time job in the community or in summer employment, etc.

8. *Teachers must be trained to properly administer and interpret minimum competency tests.* In the past, the abuse of tests has often occurred because teachers were not adequately prepared to administer them or to interpret their results. Any minimum competency program must mandate that all school personnel directly involved in administering and interpreting minimum competency tests receive in-service training before minimum competency tests are used. Such mandates must also clearly indicate which agency or officials are responsible for providing the training, and for periodically assessing the quality of the training. Some processes for determining how effectively the school personnel are using the test must also be established.

Source: Southeastern Public Education Program, 1978.

taught, what is learned, and how it is learned. Box 19.4 presents a list of important questions to ask when evaluating a minimum-competency program.

Recently, several national reform proposals have called for maximum-competency achievement tests to be administered at major transition points in a student's educational career and have suggested that these tests be used to certify student credentials. A *maximum-competency achievement test* is one designed to measure achievement in a specific subject at a level appropriate for the grade in which it is used. In the case of both minimum- and maximum-competency tests, policymakers see the test as an administrative mechanism to restore standards, make diplomas meaningful, or eliminate social promotion.

Policy makers in 44 states have also passed legislation requiring testing for teacher certification. Some states are considering linking teacher and administrator merit pay to their students' test performance (Haney, Madaus, & Kreitzer 1987). Again, the test is being used as a mechanism for allocating rewards, which policymakers feel will result in positive changes in the delivery of educational services.

In all these examples, policymakers are linking rewards or sanctions to test performance, thus making the tests an integral part of educational policy itself. Policymakers tend to view tests as a readily available, well-developed, relatively cheap, and administratively simple technology. By linking rewards or sanctions to test results, they can sidestep the issue of having to deal directly with curriculum and instructional processes and still effect change in those processes. There are tremendous social pressures on administrators and teachers to see to it that their students acquit themselves well on such tests. Furthermore, to the extent that administrators, teachers, and school systems are held directly accountable for student performance on these policy-related tests, the areas tapped by these measures will be emphasized in teaching. In fact, teachers may be doing themselves and their students a disservice by emphasizing new or unexamined objectives or competencies. The threat of losing funds or certification, or some other sanction, bullies the instructional delivery system into preparing students to take these tests, and so the material covered in the tests becomes the de facto curriculum.

The use of tests as an administrative mechanism in educational policy has the potential to transform our educational system. First, for the most part, such tests are *external tests,* not controlled by local education authorities. External tests that are linked with important sanctions shift control over the curriculum and instruction from the local district to the state agency that controls the tests. This shift in power away from the local education agencies (LEAs) to state education authorities (SEAs) could, in the long run, represent a profound shift in the structure of American education. Second, these tests, when used independently and automatically to make a decision about a student, can cannibalize teacher judgments. Promotions or graduation decisions made solely on the basis of a test score take these important decisions out of the hands of the professionals who know students best because of their daily interaction with them. Finally, these tests will control curriculum and teaching, narrowing to a focus on knowledge measured by the test (Madaus, 1988).

This use of tests to make policy decisions is essentially different from the use of tests in traditional local district standardized testing programs. Policy-related testing will have a stronger impact on what you do as a teacher than will the results of traditional school-based testing programs. While testing for policy purposes is primarily used by SEAs, it is also true that increasing numbers of LEAs are beginning to link important rewards or sanctions to results from their traditional testing programs (for example, for merit pay, promotion, or graduation decisions). Policy-related testing is expanding rapidly and is something that you will need to keep abreast of throughout your teaching career.

CONCLUSION

Standardized testing plays an important and expanding role in American education. As a future teacher, therefore, you need to understand thoroughly the uses and abuses of such testing. To take advantage of the benefits of standardized tests you will need additional training in testing and in the use and proper interpretation of test results. Testing can be a powerful tool that can aid a teacher in his or her instruction. It can also help teachers and students build on strengths and overcome identified deficits. It can also help inform policymakers and the public about the state of education. However, there are negative aspects to testing that you must also be aware of and guard against.

QUESTIONS AND ACTIVITIES

1. Marie is a third-grade student who obtained a grade-equivalent score of 6.4 on a standardized reading test in your class. Marie's mother insists that since her daughter's score indicates she is reading on more than a sixth-grade level, she should take reading with the sixth-grade class. What is your response?
2. Do you feel students should have to pass a minimum-competency test to receive a high school diploma? Why or why not? If your response is yes, who should set the standards: The local education agency? The state education authority? The United States Department of Education?
3. Now that you have read Chapter 19, how would you respond to our space visitor's question, "Do you think schools should use standardized tests on our planet?"
4. Interview a principal and a teacher about their views on standardized testing. What are their views on the usefulness of the tests, the cost versus benefit of the tests, the abuses of testing, and the role they think tests will play in the schools of the future?
5. What are the major differences between norm-referenced tests and criterion-referenced tests?
6. Kay is a sixth-grade student whose raw score on a standardized math achievement test was 52. She is at the 90th percentile for her local district norm score and at the 75th percentile for the national norm. Her grade equivalent score is 8.7. How would you answer a letter of inquiry from a parent who requested that you explain these scores?
7. Vincent had a combined verbal and quantitative score on his SATs that varied from 1050 his first time, to 990 his second time, and to 1080 his third. How might one explain his variation in test performance?

CHAPTER 20

The Reform Reports

Education is currently in the grip of an important reform movement that began in 1983. A number of reports by various prestigious bodies have set forth a reform agenda for American education. This chapter examines these reform reports.

● The reports were a response to a growing disillusionment with various aspects of our educational system.

● Most of the reports have an important political dimension that is important to understand.

● The reports share a number of common beliefs and themes including: Educational reform is necessary if the United States is to regain the competitive and economic edge in the world; there needs to be a more rigorous approach to learning at all levels; and academic excellence and equality are inseparable from equity.

● The reports contain recommendations concerning the curriculum, testing, teaching as a profession, teacher training, certifications and remuneration, and school management and organization.

● These reports will eventually affect you in your teaching career. Therefore, you need to keep abreast of reform reports, and in the state in which you plan to teach, of legislation aimed at reform.

1983 came to be known in American education as the Year of the Reports. Beginning in April, when the National Commission on Excellence in Education released its seminal report *A nation at risk,* it seemed as if each succeeding month for the next two years saw the publication of yet another report, book, or proposal prescribing remedies to cure the perceived ills of American education.

Such was the climate for change wrought by these national reports that within 18 months:

- There were more than 280 state commissions or task forces formed across all 50 states to recommend to legislators, state boards of education, boards of regents, and governors the states' responses to the calls for the reform of elementary and secondary education.
- Twenty-seven states had approved measures to extend instructional time.
- Nineteen states had passed legislation for differential, merit pay, and/or career ladder compensation for teachers; seven other states had such legislation pending.
- Thirty-three states had implemented new student-testing programs for promotion and/or graduation; four other states had proposals pending.
- Forty-five states had increased certification requirements for teachers and/or administrators, including requirements for longer periods of student teaching, additional course work or in-service training, and new standards for teacher education programs.
- More demanding requirements for high school graduation had been established in 41 states, and three other states were in the process of raising requirements.
- Computer-literacy requirements for teachers and students had been enacted in more than half the states.
- Thirty-nine states had adopted teacher competency tests (Bell, 1984; Education Commission of the States, 1983; Buchner, 1984; Pipho, 1984; Walton, 1983).

Not all of these actions were in response to the national reports. A number of changes were well under way before their release. Nonetheless, it is true that the impact of the national reports gave additional impetus to state efforts and created a climate for change that helped to justify state-level reform proposals.

The immediate effect of the reports was to shape the education you are currently receiving. Schools of education began to modify their curricula and training as a result of the state and national reports. You will again see the effects of the reports on your entrance to the profession when you attempt to meet the new certification requirements growing out of reform recommendations. The reports will also influence your salary and working conditions for years to come as states implement new career ladders and salary schedules. Finally, recommendations regarding changes in the curriculum will affect what you teach throughout your career.

In describing their long-term impact, one observer compared the implementation of the recommendations in these reports to the implementation of the project that put the first person on the moon. Just as it took a decade for the moon project to be fully realized, it will take five to ten years for most mandated reforms to completely transform the schools (Boyer, 1984).

Since the recommendations of these national and state reform commissions will profoundly affect your teaching career, a thorough familiarity with them is essential as you prepare to become a teacher. This chapter introduces you to the reform proposals arising from the reports. It does not summarize each report, since excellent comparative summaries and critiques are available elsewhere (Education Commission of the States, 1983; Forbes, 1984; Stedman & Smith, 1983).

Because of the number and diversity of the state reports, this chapter will treat only the national reports. However, it is the states that have constitutional responsibility for providing education, and it is at the state level that most reform legislation or regulations will be implemented. Therefore, you need to identify and study any reform reports and resulting legislation in the state in which you plan to teach.

We begin the chapter with a brief sketch of the background to the reports. Then we provide a short profile of the reports, which is followed by a discussion of their political dimensions. While the reports differ individually in their diagnosis of what is wrong with American education and in their prescription for a cure, there are common themes that cut across them; these are discussed next. Finally, we discuss major findings and recommendations contained in the reports for the curriculum and testing, teachers, school management, and school and community relationships.

The Background to the Reports

There was a growing disillusionment with many public institutions in the late 1970s. Benjamin DeMott captured this general air of disenchantment when he wrote: "Before the 1960s, pundits say, the economy and foreign policy made sense; afterwards, chaos. Before the 60s, education was looking up; afterwards, schools collapsed. Before the 60s family was a value; afterwards, the family became a time-study problem. So it went with everything American in the aftermath of the killer decade, according to consensus—finished, ruined, to hell in a handbasket" (DeMott, 1984, p. 1).

As indicated in this passage, one aspect of the general air of disenchantment was the perception, which crystallized into a belief, that our schools were in serious trouble. Critics cited declines in levels of student achievement, dissatisfaction with teachers, concern over rising costs, and lack of efficiency as symptoms of the malaise they perceived to be endemic in our schools. If this perception was correct, clearly something had to be done. The formation of task forces, study groups, and commissions was the professional and political response at both the state and national levels. They were charged with documenting the problems and offering recommendations to alleviate them.

A Profile of the Reports

A profile of 16 reform reports is presented in Table 20.1. It provides information on the sponsoring organization, the chairperson(s), the makeup of each group, the data or evidence used, the time frame of the study, and the date of release.

One very important difference between the reports is the type of evidence or data base they utilized to arrive at their findings and recommendations. Six of the reports *(Action for excellence, America's competitive challenge, Making the grade, A nation at risk, Educating Americans for the 21st century,* and *Time for results)* used existing data as the basis for their descriptions of American education. They collected no new data or evidence. Their recommendations were based on expert opinion, commissioned papers, or existing studies.

Tomorrow's teachers, the report of the Holmes Group, is unique in that it was written by a consortium of deans of schools of education. It is a reflective essay on past mistakes and future directions for teacher education without citing any research evidence to substantiate its conclusions.

James Madison High School is also a reflective essay. William Bennett, in his role of secretary of education, describes models of curriculum excellence from seven school districts and then offers his ideas of a four-year curriculum plan for high schools.

The Paideia Proposal also stands by itself. Its author, Mortimer Adler, did not resort to empirical data at all but instead relied on a tight philosophical or rational-deductive analysis to arrive at a description of what the ideal school curriculum should look like.

The remaining reports, *(Academic preparation for college, A place called school, High school, A study of high schools, The good high school, A nation prepared,* and *First lessons)* all collected new data, primarily through questionnaires and actual observations in schools. These studies are much more objective in their description of our schools and more qualified in the recommendations they propose than are the other reports. However, as we shall see, there is great agreement across all the reports in terms of basic assumptions and many of the recommendations.

Another important point about the reports is that they are heavily oriented toward secondary education. As their names indicate, five reports *(Academic preparation for college, High school, A study of high schools, The good high school,* and *James Madison High School)* deal exclusively with the reform of secondary schools. *The Paideia Proposal* and *A place called school* treat both elementary and secondary education, and *First lessons* is the only report that deals exclusively with the elementary school.

The reason for the emphasis on secondary education is not hard to discern. Much criticism had been directed at secondary schools. There was the much broadcast SAT score decline; there were widespread complaints from employers and the military that high school graduates lacked basic skills forcing them to spend millions of dollars on remedial education and training;

TABLE 20.1 Profile of Reports

Title	Sponsor/Author	Chair(s)	Representation of Task Force Members	Data Bases Utilized	Time Frame of Study	Date of Release
Academic preparation for college: What students need to know and be able to do	Education Equality Project—The College Board	Not identified	200 high school and college teachers as members of various college board committees and councils	Data collected from 1,400 people through questionnaires and meetings; also judgments and recommendations	3 years	May 1983
Action for excellence: A comprehensive plan to improve our nation's schools	Task Force on Education for Economic Growth, Education Commission of the States	Governor James Hunt, Jr.	41 members, governors, legislators, CEOs, state and local school board members, and labor	Task force concensus on problems and recommendations	1 year	May 1983
America's competitive challenge: The need for a national response	Business–Higher Education Forum	R. Anderson; David S. Saxon	16 members: business and higher education	Past surveys and contemporary expertise	1 year	April 1983
Educating Americans for the 21st century: A report to the American people and the National Science Board	National Science Board's Commission on Pre-College Education in Mathematics, Science, and Technology	Cecily Canman Selby; William T. Coleman	Members of commission and 14 additional members from the public and private sectors	Review of special programs and activities from federal, state, and local governments and school districts; institutes of higher education; professional societies and associations; business and industry; other informal education programs, museums, and science academies.	1.5 years	September 1983
The good high school: Portraits of character and culture	Sara L. Lightfoot	Not applicable	Author and 3 research assistants	Field studies of 6 private and public high schools	3 years	1983
High school: A report on secondary education in America	The Carnegie Foundation for the Advancement of Teaching	Ernest L. Boyer	National panel of principals, superintendents, university administrators, parents, school board members, and citizen representatives; team of 25 educators acting as observers	Past research and field studies of 15 public high schools	2 years	1983

TABLE 20.1 (*Continued*)

Title	Sponsor/Author	Chair(s)	Representation of Task Force Members	Data Bases Utilized	Time Frame of Study	Date of Release
Making the grade	Twentieth Century Fund Task Force on Federal Elementary and Secondary Education Policy	Robert Wood	11 members: state departments, local school level and higher education	Background paper by Paul E. Peterson utilizing existing data	1.5 years	May 1983
A nation at risk: The imperative for educational reform	The National Commission on Excellence in Education—U.S. Department of Education	David P. Gardner	18 members: governor, legislators, state boards, local school level, higher education, and professional associations	Commissioned papers; public oral and written comment; existing analyses; and descriptions of notable programs	1.5 years	April 1983
The Paideia Proposal: An educational manifesto	Mortimer J. Adler on behalf of the Paideia Group	Mortimer J. Adler	22 members: national-, state-, and local-level educators	Primarily philosophical	1 year	September 1982
A place called school: Prospects for the future	John I. Goodlad	Ralph W. Tyler	6 members: national-, state-, and local-level educators	Questionnaires and observations in 38 schools across the country	8 years	September 1983
A study of high schools	National Association of Secondary School Principals and the Commission of Educational Issues of the National Association of Independent Schools	Theodore R. Sizer	Study team of educators and education researchers	Field studies of 14 public and private high schools	3 years	January 1984
A nation prepared: Teachers for the 21st century	Task Force on Teaching as a Profession, Carnegie Forum on Education and the Economy	Lewis M. Branscomb	14 members, National panel of leaders from business, higher education, professional associations, governors, legislators, chief state school officers, and policy center directors	Existing data bases, expertise of panel members	1 year	May 1986

TABLE 20.1 (*Continued*)

Title	Sponsor/ Author	Chair(s)	Representation of Task Force Members	Data Bases Utilized	Time Frame of Study	Date of Release
Holmes Report	Consortium of selected colleges of education	Judith Lanier	13 Deans of education at state universities, one education college president	Primarily philosophical	3 years	1986
Time for results	National Governors Association	Lamar Alexander	Governors of 50 states	State initiatives, existing reports	1 year	1986
First lessons	William J. Bennett, secretary, U.S. Department of Education	N/A	Author and study group of 21 distinguished Americans	Author's distillation of study group input, previous studies	1 year	1986
James Madison High	William J. Bennett, secretary, U.S. Department of Education	N/A	Single authors	none	1 year	1988

Source: This table is a modification and update of a table by the Northeast Regional Exchange, 1983.

charges were continually heard that the high school diploma was meaningless; the data from the National Assessment of Educational Progress showed that many 17-year-olds did not possess "higher-order" intellectual skills; the curriculum offerings in high schools were characterized as "homogenized," "diluted," and "diffuse." Thus, it is not surprising that the attention of many of the commissions and task forces was directed at secondary education. However, many of the reports' recommendations extend downward and clearly affect elementary education. For example, proposals to increase the length of the school day and year as well as proposals for merit pay affect education at all grade levels.

The Political Dimension of the Reports

The eight reports that relied exclusively on existing data are quintessential political documents. The panels that prepared the reports had the political agenda of returning education to the limelight and of building a consensus on the need for reform. They wanted to stimulate debate about the state of our schools; in the case of the Carnegie Forum's Task Force on Teaching as a Profession *(A nation prepared)* and the Holmes Group's report *(Tomorrow's teachers)* on the preparation of teachers, the primary aim was to describe what needed to be done to change the schools or teacher preparation. The reports were meant to be a clarion call for reform. In this they were successful. Education became front-page news and the reports helped to rally support for change at local, state, and federal levels.

To achieve this political objective, however, evidence was used selectively to buttress arguments that our schools were in trouble. Data that might have softened the impact of the negative portrait of schools was ignored. Box 20.1 includes two excerpts that illustrate the ominous picture painted in order to get the media and the general public to pay attention. One could look at many of the indicators used by these groups, such as test scores, and conclude that our schools were in fact doing a creditable job. However, the various commissions and task forces chose to ignore contradictions in the indicators in order to shock policy-makers into action and the public into accepting the need for reform (Stedman & Smith, 1983).

An illuminating example of how indicators were actually used selectively to inform the reports is provided by the Twentieth Century Fund Task Force report, *Making the grade.* It opens with the following gloomy assertion: "The nation's public schools are in trouble. By almost every measure . . . the performance of our schools falls far short of expectations" (1983, p. 3). However, in a commissioned background paper, published as an appendix to the report, a review that examined all the available indicators, including test scores, concluded that "Nothing in these data permits the conclusion that educational institutions have deteriorated badly" (Peterson, 1983, p. 59). It would seem that the task force did not take cognizance of its own commissioned paper in its zeal for reform.

Another example of the political use of numbers is to be found in the report of the National Commission on Excellence in Education (NCEE), *A*

If an unfriendly foreign power had attempted to impose on America the mediocre educational performance that exists today, we might well have viewed it as an act of war. As it stands, we have allowed this to happen to ourselves. We have even squandered the gains in student achievement made in the wake of the *Sputnik* challenge. Moreover, we have dismantled essential support systems which helped make those gains possible. We have, in effect, been committing an act of unthinking, unilateral educational disarmament.[1]

Alarming numbers of young Americans are ill-equipped to work in, contribute to, profit from and enjoy our increasingly technological society. Far too many emerge from the Nation's elementary and secondary schools with an inadequate grounding in mathematics, science and technology. As a result, they lack sufficient knowledge to acquire the training, skills and understanding that are needed today and will be even more critically needed in the 21st century. This situation must not continue—improved preparation of all students in the fields of mathematics, science and technology is essential to the maintenance and development of our Nation's economic strength, to its military security, to its continued commitment to the democratic ideal of an informed and participating citizenry and to fulfilling personal lives for its people.[2]

Source: [1]NCEE, *A nation at risk,* p. 5. [2]National Science Board Commission on Precollege Education in Mathematics, Science, and Technology, *Educating Americans for the 21st century,* p. 1.

nation at risk. The NCEE used data from the studies of the International Association for the Evaluation of Educational Achievement (IEA) to argue that American students perform worse than students in other countries. In using national averages on tests to arrive at their negative assessment, they over-looked the fact that a much smaller proportion of children in the other countries reach the terminal year of high school than in the United States. Simply put, foreign schools are more selective than are American schools. For example, in 1970, the year in which the data used by NCEE were collected, only 9 percent of German youth, compared to 75 percent of American youth, reached the last year of high school (Stedman & Smith, 1983). Thus, when NCEE used the IEA high school data, it was comparing apples and oranges. Nonetheless, the commission concluded that secondary school performance in the United States in all curricular areas measured by the IEA was far below that found in foreign schools.

A quite different picture emerges when we examine the achievement levels of the top 9 percent of students in countries that participated in the IEA studies. The results of a more carefully drawn comparison show that 11 of 17 countries fell *below* the United States average in science; all of 14 foreign countries fell *below* the United States average in reading comprehension; all of 9 countries were *below* the United States average in literature; and 6 out of 7 countries fell below the United States in civic education (Stedman & Smith, 1983).

The NCEE also used data from the National Assessment of Educational Progress (NAEP). The NAEP can be considered the nation's report card in that it continually monitors what American youngsters know and can do and reports the results to the American people. There were bright spots from the NAEP that the NCEE chose to overlook in its gloomy picture. For example, NAEP data show that in the past ten years there has been a dramatic gain in basic skill scores among black students, disadvantaged students, and lower

A main concern of the reform reports was that educational achievement in the United States was falling behind that of other industrialized countries.

achievers. Further, reading and mathematics scores have gone up or remained the same for all students except 17-year-olds, for whom scores have remained the same. Science scores for low achievers have gone up; however, scores for high achievers have dropped at all age levels (LaPointe, 1984).

This is *not* to deny that there are problems in certain curriculum areas or that our schools are not as good as they could be. Quite the contrary! For example, the NAEP data show that youngsters have poorly developed problem-solving skills in mathematics and a weakness in higher-order skills, such as inferential reading (LaPointe, 1984). The point to keep in mind, however, is that the picture of American education is not nearly as terrible across the board as the NCEE and other groups have painted it.

There is no denying that the political approach of shocking policymakers into demanding education reform has been successful. There are few educators or informed citizens who are not aware of the reform proposals for American education. The print and TV media have covered the reform movement extensively. As a result, the United States is witnessing an impressive renewal of support for public education. However, you should keep in mind the political nature of the arguments used by the various groups when you read the reform reports.

Not only was there a political motivation behind the selected use of data in the national reports, there were also interesting political dynamics in the reform movement itself at the state level. For example:

1. Governors were very active in pushing educational reform. They sometimes set up state-level commissions. Many made education a priority issue on their political agenda and in their political campaigns.
2. Legislatures dominated the reform process, often setting up their own study groups and enacting extensive reform legislation.
3. The business community was active in supporting educational reform.
4. Teachers, administrators, school boards, and state departments of education did not initiate or shape reform.
5. The national reports helped develop a momentum for change that

helped governors, legislatures, and the business community to get support from the public for their state-level proposals (Fuhrom, 1984).

Thus, the politics of reform at the state level were ideal. Governors and state legislatures, with the support of the business community, formed the political coalition necessary to enact reform legislation. The national reports generated support and gave their work credibility. As long as education remains in the forefront as a hot political issue, the chances for reform being enacted and enforced remain excellent.

Common Beliefs in the Reports

The reports share three common beliefs about education, which we shall briefly discuss in this section.

1. Educational reform is necessary for the United States to regain its competitive economic edge in the world.

A key factor impelling the reform movement was the perceived need to respond to the economic recession America was experiencing. Underlying many of the reports' proposals was the belief that reforming our educational system would restore the economic edge in world commerce that America had once enjoyed but somehow lost. Once that edge was regained, education would help the nation to maintain it. Box 20.2 contains a typical excerpt that captures this basic economic, competitive belief about the power of education that underlies most of the reports.

Statements of this kind clearly show that the various commissions and task forces saw the driving force behind educational reform as economic—our very standard of living was at stake. The assumption underlying this belief was that other nations were outpacing us economically because they were simply smarter and had a better-educated work force. To regain its former preeminence, the United States would have to enlarge its pool of well-educated people through the reform of its educational system.

Whether the implementation of the specific reforms proposed in the various reports will give the United States an economic edge or ensure its competitiveness worldwide is certainly open to question. There are many economic and structural factors that are unrelated to education (for example, pay scale of workers, new plants and technologies, costs of energy, and working conditions) that affect the worldwide competitiveness of many products. Also, it is a fact that some underdeveloped or developing countries with educational systems inferior to ours produce products that compete successfully with similar American products (Hacker, 1984).

A theme closely related to the emphasis on restoring our economic competitive edge in world markets through better education is that our schools need to prepare people for a high-tech future. Spurred by increasing domestic and international economic competition, industry in the United States was, at the time these study groups were working, in the process of moving toward computer-based automation in a major way (Office of Technology Assessment,

Pett Peeves by Joel Pett

"Pile of blocks? I was thinking of it as a long-overdue first step toward training the leaders of tomorrow, into whose hands will fall the awesome task of restoring America's faltering global competitiveness."

Source: Phi Delta Kappan, 1987, p. 493.

1982). This trend was recognized and the reports stressed the need for placing a premium on literacy in the areas of technology and information.

In many of the reports this need was simply translated into recommendations for greater emphasis on mathematics and science in the schools. However, a singular emphasis on these subjects to the exclusion of more generalized and transferable skills is detrimental to society. It is clear that, because of developments in high technology, society can expect lifelong retraining to become the norm for many people (Office of Technology Assessment, 1982). This is because in a rapidly advancing technological society skills and information requirements shift rapidly. Therefore, the schools, rather than simply putting more emphasis on mathematics and science, should give people the more generalized skills of thinking clearly and being adaptable to change when they encounter it (Stedman & Smith, 1983).

Whatever the pros and cons of the economic and competitive and technological arguments, they were persuasive and very powerful in generating widespread support for school reform.

   2. There should be a more rigorous approach to learning.

All the reports agree on the need for more rigorous instructional programs. While there is some variation in the specific curricular areas empha-

---

BOX 20.2 Excerpts from the Economic/Competitive Argument

The world is indeed one global village. We live among determined, well-educated, and strongly motivated competitors. We compete with them for international standing and markets, not only with products but also with the ideas of our laboratories and neighborhood workshops. America's position in the world may once have been reasonably secure with only a few exceptionally well-trained men and women. It is no longer.

   The risk is not only that the Japanese make automobiles more efficiently than Americans and have government subsidies for development and export. It is not just that the South Koreans recently built the world's most efficient steel mill, or that American machine tools, once the pride of the world, are being displaced by German products. It is also that these developments signify a redistribution of trained capability throughout the globe. Knowledge, learning, information, and skilled intelligence are the

new raw materials of international commerce and are today spread throughout the world as vigorously as miracle drugs, synthetic fertilizers, and blue jeans did earlier. If only to keep and improve on the slim competitive edge we still retain in world markets, we must dedicate ourselves to the reform of our educational system for the benefit of all—old and young alike, affluent and poor, majority and minority. Learning is the indispensable investment required for success in the "information age" we are entering.[1]

   The world is changing fast. Technological know-how is spreading throughout the world—along with the knowledge that such skills and sophistication are the basic capital of tomorrow's society. Already the quality of our manufactured products, the viability of our trade, our leadership in research and development, and our standards of living are strongly challenged. Our children could

BOX 20.2 (*Continued*)

be stragglers in a world of technology. We must not let this happen; America must not become an industrial dinosaur. We must not provide our children a 1960 education for the 21st century world.[2]

[The schools] are charged with training increasing percentages of the nation's youth, including large numbers of hard-to-educate youngsters, to improved levels of competency so that they can effectively enter a labor market in which employers are currently demanding both technical capability and the capacity to learn new skills.[3]

Today, however, our faith in change—and our faith in ourselves as the world's supreme innovators—is being shaken. Japan, West Germany and other relatively new industrial powers have challenged America's position on the

leading edge of change and technical invention. In the seventies, productivity in manufacturing industries grew nearly four times as fast in Japan and twice as fast in West Germany and France, as in the United States. The possibility that other nations may outstrip us in inventiveness and productivity is suddenly troubling Americans. Communities all over the United States are depressingly familiar now with what the experts call *technological*, or *structural*, unemployment: joblessness that occurs because our workers, our factories and our techniques are suddenly obsolete.[4]

Moreover, a technologically advanced society is subject to radical changes in the production of goods and services. These changes in turn require a work force that is prepared for flexible and intelligent adjustment to novel demands for skill and comprehension.[5]

Source: [1]NCEE, *A nation at risk,* pp. 6, 7; [2]National Science Board, *Educating Americans for the 21st century,* p. v; [3]Twentieth Century Task Force, *Making the grade,* p. 4; [4]Task Force on Education for Economic Growth, *Action for excellence,* p. 13; [5]Adler, *Paideia problems and possibilities,* p. 6.

sized, most reports call for more mathematics, English, science, and foreign languages for students. The reports stress the need for more homework, more instructional time, and safe and orderly schools. The reports on the reform of teacher training call for a much heavier emphasis on liberal arts courses.

The assumption that we need a more rigorous instructional program in our schools flows from a belief that there has been a serious decline in academic performance. This decline, as measured by test scores, was linked in many people's minds to what was seen as the undisciplined "funsie-wunsie" open-education philosophy of the 1960s (Kilpatrick, 1977). As we saw above, whether this characterization is valid or not, the argument is emotionally and rhetorically convincing for many people. The various study groups translated the agreement on the need for a more rigorous instructional program into specific recommendations that we shall discuss when we consider recommendations concerning the curriculum.

3. Academic excellence and quality are inseparable from equity.

All the reports stress the need for academic excellence, and all agree that it should not be achieved at the expense of equity. The excerpts displayed in Box 20.3 capture the essence of this ideal of attaining excellence and equity.

The language of the reports is clearly egalitarian rather than elitist. Academic excellence is for all students, not a small chosen few. This egalitarian emphasis coming from such nationally influential groups has been a powerful stimulus to the education community to set high expectations for all students. Holding high expectations for all students is a hallmark that distinguishes successful schools from less successful ones.

BOX 20.3 Excellence and Equity

We do not believe that a public commitment to excellence and educational reform must be made at the expense of a strong public commitment to the equitable treatment of our diverse population. The twin goals of equity and high-quality schooling have profound and practical meaning for our economy and society, and we cannot permit one to yield to the other either in principle or in practice. To do so would deny young people their chance to learn and live according to their aspirations and abilities. It also would lead to a generalized accommodation to mediocrity in our society on the one hand or the creation of an undemocratic elitism on the other.[1]

The Commission has found that virtually every child can develop an understanding of mathematics, science and technology if appropriately and skillfully introduced at the elementary, middle, and secondary levels.

The Nation should reaffirm its commitment to full opportunity and full achievement by all. Discrimination, and the lingering effects thereof, due to race, gender, and other such irrelevant factors, must be eradicated completely from the American educational system. "Excellence and elitism are not synonymous."[2]

In proposing new federal measures to stimulate national interest in improving the quality of public education, we urge that they not come at the expense of children from low-income families or of children suffering from one or another disability.[3]

Source: [1]NCEE, *A Nation at risk*, p. 13; [2]National Science Board, *Educating Americans for the 21st century*, p. vii; [3]Twentieth Century Task Force, *Making the grade*, p. 15.

There are, however, problems in this egalitarian approach that are not adequately addressed in the reports. Andrew Hacker discusses some of them:

> *A panel addressing a general audience cannot conclude that the nation's work force needs, say, 25 million people with sophisticated skills, and then propose that we provide such training for only that number. The democratic ideology dictates that algorithmic thinking must reach rural Wyoming and inner Chicago. The panelists omit saying that what they are proposing is both unprecedented and radical. Equal opportunities for everyone may be our accepted rhetoric. However, as a practical matter, we have never sought to close the gaps between different classes of schools. At best, some cities have special public schools that permit students from modest backgrounds to press ahead. By the same token, state and municipal universities have offered talented students a similar chance. However, the fact remains that high quality schooling, as defined by the educators themselves, at best reaches about a third of young Americans. Nor is this solely a matter of spending money. Expanding the number of people with comparable qualifications can threaten those in comfortable positions. We can already see this happening with the impending oversupply of lawyers and physicians (Hacker, 1984, p. 35).*

Some of the reports implicitly back away from a strict egalitarianism in their specific recommendations. For example, the NCEE proposes tracking students when it calls for placement and grouping guided by academic progress. It also suggests alternative schools for disruptive pupils. *Educating Americans for the 21st century* calls for the establishment of separate secondary schools that specialize in math and science. *Making the grade* suggests providing scholarships to attend small-scale academies for students who cannot succeed in public schools. It is not at all clear what would happen to poor disadvantaged minority and inner-city students if such proposals were implemented. One must also ask how many of these students would be enrolled in the secondary schools specializing in mathematics and science or how many would win scholarships to the proposed small academies. Or would these be primarily the preserve of the middle class (Hacker, 1984)?

Critics have also pointed out that, despite their egalitarian rhetoric, the reports fail to address adequately the serious problems facing disadvantaged poor, minority, and inner-city students. The dropout problem facing our schools receives little attention (Stedman & Smith, 1983). The debilitating social conditions facing many students—poor housing, poor diet, broken homes, etc.—are also, for the most part, ignored (Boyer, 1984). However, despite the problems facing these students, and the sometimes dreadful conditions of the schools they attend, everyone agrees that the strategy is not to set lower standards for them, thus perpetuating the destructive two-track system, but to recognize that the school is not an isolated institution. Schools cannot do the job alone; true reform must involve other institutions in our society (Boyer, 1984).

The emphasis on excellence and quality contained in the reports signals a very important shift in American education. It is a shift away from the heavy emphasis on equality of opportunity, traditionally one of the primary goals for our schools. Shifting the focus to excellence provides the schools with an exciting challenge, but it also carries with it the danger that traditional efforts on behalf of the poor and educationally disadvantaged may be deemphasized (Stedman & Smith, 1983). As you read the reports and evaluate recommendations made in your state, you need to keep in mind the tension between balancing excellence and equity.

Another issue that receives little attention in the reports is how programs emphasizing excellence with equity would be financed. In fact, there is very little talk about money at all. The reason for this omission is probably political; detailed discussion of the cost of implementing many of the recommendations can easily undercut the enthusiasm for reform that the reports are designed to generate. The reports, however, do raise serious financial issues. Raising teacher salaries, merit pay proposals, and lengthening the school day or school year, to name but a few, will of necessity cost money. Where will the money come from? Can we afford such changes?

The American Association of School Administrators tried to estimate the fiscal impact of just two reforms on 28 school districts—increasing starting teacher salaries to $18,720 and increasing the school day to seven hours and the school year to two hundred days. The financial impact of these reforms would vary enormously across school districts. For example, the budget of the West Point municipal school district in Mississippi would have to be increased by almost 61 percent, while the Caswell County schools in North Carolina would experience a comparatively modest increase of only 10 percent. Across all 28 districts, the average increase would amount to 27 percent.

Given the huge federal deficits and limited money available at state and

"As you all know, funding responsibilities are shifting back to local governments."

Source: Phi Delta Kappan, 1983, p. 13.

local levels, whether or not enough money can be found to meet the challenges set forth in the reform proposals remains to be seen. The federal, state, and local share of the cost of implementing the proposed reforms raises complex policy questions that will be in the forefront of political debate for years to come. How they are resolved will affect you throughout your entire teaching career.

The Reports' Recommendations

In this section we shall describe the major recommendations contained in the reports. We have divided the recommendations into those dealing with the curriculum and testing, teachers, school management and organization, and school and community relationships. Although we discuss these four categories of recommendations separately, they are, of course, clearly related to one another. For example, proposed changes in the curriculum have implications for teacher preparation and for school organization.

Recommendations Concerning the Curriculum and Testing

In discussing recommendations concerning the curriculum, it is helpful to separate *The Paideia Proposal* and *Horace's compromise*, which endorses the *Paideia* curriculum, from the rest of the reports. *The Paideia Proposal* stands alone in that it offers a radically new definition of the curriculum. The remaining reports define the basic curriculum in more traditional ways in terms of how much English, mathematics, science, and so forth, a student should take in order to graduate.

The word *paideia* (pay-dee-a) is from the Greek word *pais, paidos,* meaning the upbringing of a child. It is related to the words *pedagogy* and *pediatrics.* Mortimer Adler indicates that in an extended sense *paideia* is the equivalent of the Latin word for humanities and thus signifies the general learning that should be the possession of all human beings. *The Paideia Proposal* is an attempt to articulate the nature of this general learning.

The Paideia Proposal describes a one-track system of public schooling for the entire 12 years. It has the same three major objectives for all students, without exception. The first relates to the development of personal growth or self-improvement—mental, moral, and spiritual. The second objective is that students have adequate preparation for discharging the duties and responsibilities of citizenship. The final objective is to give students the basic skills that are common to all work in our society so they can earn a living.

To achieve these objectives three distinct, but interconnected, modes of teaching and learning are proposed for all students. The three modes are shown in Table 20.2. Each column in the table describes the goals of the column, the teaching-learning mode used to achieve the goal (means), and the required courses of study that span the 12 years of school (areas, operations, and activities).

The first row of Table 20.2 describes the goals; it is self-explanatory. The "means," or type of instruction, row is not, however, as self-evident. Column one deals with the acquisition of knowledge; therefore, the means row for column one stresses didactic instruction, that is, the traditional mode of "teaching by telling." The means include lectures, demonstrations, and also student use of textbooks and other instructional material. The second column deals with the development of skills; instruction focuses on *showing* students how to do certain things rather than telling them how. This is done by coach-

TABLE 20.2 Paideia's Three Modes of Learning and Teaching

	1	2	3
Goals	Acquisition of organized knowledge	Development of intellectual skills—skills of learning	Enlarged understanding of ideas and values
Means	Didactic instruction; lectures and responses; textbooks and other aids	Coaching, exercises, and supervised practice	Maieutic or socratic questioning and active participation
Areas, operations, and activities	Language, literature, and the fine arts; mathematics and natural science; history, geography, and social studies	Reading, writing, speaking, listening; calculating; problem-solving; observing, measuring, estimating; exercising critical judgment	Discussion of books (not textbooks) and other works of art and involvement in artistic activities (e.g., music, drama, visual arts)

Note: The three columns do not correspond to separate courses, nor is one kind of teaching and learning necessarily confined to any one class.
Source: Adler, 1982, p. 23.

ing, training, drilling, and practice. The third column has as its goal enlarged understanding and therefore involves the Socratic mode of teaching. The Socratic mode is also called *maieutic* (may-u-tic) because it helps students bring ideas to birth. Instruction involves asking questions, leading discussions, and helping students understand or appreciate concepts. Students must be active participants if this mode of teaching and learning is to be effective. The courses of study and subject matter described across the bottom row in Table 20.2 are required of all students. The only elective permitted is the choice of a foreign language.

   The Paideia Proposal has been criticized as being impractical, insensitive to individual differences, and oblivious to the "nonacademic" student's interests and motivation. Adler addresses these concerns in *Paideia problems and possibilities* when he argues that everyone is willing to agree that some students can be given the type of education described in *Paideia*. It is only when the plan is extended from *some* to *all* students that criticisms are heard. He goes on to argue that the older, easier, and safer approach of giving the type of education described in *The Paideia Proposal* to only some students has left unresolved the problem of giving all students equal opportunity. Adler claims that his proposals are not utopian and do not go beyond the bounds of the possible; they simply have never been tried. Hence, arguments raised against them are without empirical foundation of any kind (Adler, 1983).

   Everyone who has examined *The Paideia Proposal* would probably agree that its implementation would involve a radical restructuring of our educational system. Further, the specific details of the curriculum would have to be left to local districts. Theodore Sizer points out that *Paideia* "is not a detailed One Best Curriculum, but rather a set of principles, a framework, and a process" (Sizer, 1984b, p. 109). In using the *Paideia* principles, a school must craft the details of the program in ways appropriate to the community. Several communities are presently experimenting with the *Paideia* approach (Adler, 1983). It will be interesting to watch these experiments as they unfold, and you should try to keep abreast of their progress. Will Adler or his critics be proved right?

   RECOMMENDATIONS ABOUT GOALS Like *The Paideia Proposal*, the remaining reports call for a clarification of the mission, or goals of our schools. John Goodlad and Ernest Boyer are the most explicit in this regard. Boyer, for example, recommends that

   ● Every high school should establish clearly stated goals—purposes that are widely shared by teachers, students, administrators, and parents.
   ● School goals should focus on the mastery of language, on a core of common learning, on preparation for work and further education, and on community and civic service (Boyer, 1983, p. 301).

   Goodlad presents a list of goals that is broken down into (1) academic goals, which include mastery of basic skills and intellectual development; (2) vocational goals that prepare students for a world of work; (3) social, civic, and cultural goals that include interpersonal understanding, citizenship participation, enculturation; and (4) moral and ethical character and personal goals, which subsume emotional and physical well-being, creativity, aesthetic expression, and self-realization (Goodlad, 1984). Goodlad's goal categories closely resemble the three goals of *The Paideia Proposal.*

The remaining reports are not as detailed as those of Goodlad, Boyer, or Adler, but all refer to the need to reexamine goals. *First lessons* calls for the elementary schools first and foremost to provide students with the fundamental skills with which to manage a lifetime of learning. The NCEE calls for developing the talent of all to their fullest. The Commission of the National Science Board calls for providing all our youth with a level of education in mathematics, science, and technology that is not only of the highest quality in the world but that reflects the needs of our nation. Further, the various commissions all support the economic goal of the schools, so that the country will be provided with a trained work force that can help it compete successfully in world markets. Personal fulfillment and self-realization receive little attention in the reports of the various national commissions. As we have seen, their emphasis clearly is on economic and technological preparation.

Statements of goals are broader and more visionary than specific educational objectives. The aim or purpose of a goal statement is to excite the imagination and give people something they want to work for. Goal statements ultimately have to be translated into specific school programs, curricula, and instruction. If the goals are narrowly economic or technological in nature, programs will ultimately reflect this kind of vision. If the goals encompass academic, vocational, and personal outcomes, programs will reflect this broader vision. The emphasis in most of the national reports seems to be on a narrow economic and technological mission for our schools.

RECOMMENDATIONS ABOUT THE CURRICULUM All the reports agree that students should follow a common core curriculum. There is, however, no unanimity on what constitutes this core. The NCEE describes its core as the five "new basics." To graduate, all students would be required to take four years of English, three years of mathematics, three years of science, three years of social studies, and a half year of computer science. For college-bound students, two years of a foreign language are highly recommended. The only new "basic" subject is computer science; the remaining four are old standbys. The NCEE does spell out the number of years students should study each of these basics, and this new time prescription has played a large role in reforming graduation standards in many states.

High school puts heavy emphasis on mastering the English language, with writing as the key to this mastery. Boyer argues that clear writing leads to clear thinking, and vice versa. The core curriculum in *High school* is much broader than that of the NCEE, encompassing 12 areas of study. However, the overlap in certain areas is evident. It includes the study of literature, United States history, Western civilization, non-Western civilization, science and the natural world, technology, mathematics, foreign language (for all students, not just the college bound), the arts, civics, health, and work. *High school*, like *The Paideia Proposal*, would eliminate the vocational education track as we currently know it.

Making the grade, like *High school*, stresses proficiency in English, recommending that federal funds now going to bilingual programs be used to teach non-English-speaking children how to speak, read, and write in English. This recommendation is controversial. In dissenting from it, one commission member argued that, while all students must learn English, bilingual programs are essential if we are to provide a healthy learning environment for children of limited English-speaking ability. Further, he argues that the academic achievements of limited-English-speaking children will be significantly greater if the children's native language skills are maintained and improved. Debate over bilingual programs continues. Ultimately, the fate of bilingual education will be resolved on the basis of which value system prevails. If federal funds were withdrawn, as recommended in *Making the grade*, it would be a serious, if not fatal, blow to such programs.

James Madison High School would eliminate a "cafeteria-style" curriculum and replace it with strict traditional academic requirements and fewer electives. Literature would be tougher each year, with an emphasis on "classic" works, and there would be an increased emphasis on writing and speaking. A research paper would be required in the twelfth grade. The curriculum is designed to give students a firm grounding in the European and American past. Three years of mathematics and science are required, with electives in each of these areas in grade 12. The complete four-year plan is shown in Figure 20.1. Secretary Bennett is clear that adding required courses is not a panacea; the content and quality of the courses are what will make the difference. In a press conference he said, "It makes a difference whether you read Henry James or a Batman comic book."

Not surprisingly, the curriculum recommendations of the Commission of the National Science Board, in its report *Educating Americans for the 21st century*, center almost exclusively on mathematics and science. Similarly, the curriculum recommendations of the College Board Commission in *Academic preparation for college* describe those courses needed by students who intend to go to college.

First lessons calls for the elementary school to "assume as its most sublime and most solemn responsibility the task of teaching every child to read" (Bennett, 1986, p. 21). It then goes on to call for emphases on writing, mathematics, science, and social studies in grades K through 3; and history, geography, and civics in grades 4 through 8. Cultural literacy, the arts, foreign languages, health and physical education, and computer education round out Bennett's program for the elementary grades.

The curriculum recommendations found in the reports of the various national study groups contain little that is new. Most schools already teach the "core" subjects described in the reports. *First lessons* calls for foreign languages in the elementary grades, which is a notable exception. What *is* new is that many of the reports call for *all* students to pursue this core. Further, most of the reports recommend that students take various subjects for longer periods of time than they do at present.

The two reports clearly break new ground in their curriculum recommendations concerning teacher preparation. Both call for a bachelor's degree in the arts and sciences as a prerequisite for the professional study of teaching. The Holmes proposals have proved to be controversial. For example, there is

FIGURE 20.1 James Madison High School Four-Year Curriculum Plan

Subject	1st Year	2nd Year	3rd Year	4th Year
English	Introduction to Literature	American Literature	British Literature	Introduction to World Literature
Social Studies	Western Civilization	American History	Principles of American Democracy (*1 semester*) and American Democracy & the World (*1 semester*)	
Mathematics	Three years required from among the following courses: Algebra I, Plane and Solid Geometry, Algebra II, Trigonometry, Statistics and Probability (*1 semester*), Pre-Calculus (*1 semester*), and Calculus AB or BC			
Science	Three years required from among the following courses: Astronomy/Geology, Biology, Chemistry, and Physics or Principles of Technology			
Foreign Language	Two years required in a single language from among offerings determined by local jurisdictions		────── ELECTIVES ──────	
Physical Education/Health	Physical Education/Health 9	Physical Education/Health 10		
Fine Arts	Art History (*1 semester*) Music History (*1 semester*)			

Source: James Madison High School

no empirical basis for advocating a bachelor's degree in arts and science for elementary teachers or for locating teacher preparation courses after the bachelor's degree. For example, many European countries prepare their teachers in three years. Further, the economic impact on students of added tuition costs has not been dealt with. It remains to be seen whether, or to what degree, the Holmes curriculum is adopted.

Perhaps of greater importance than the appropriateness of any particular "core" subject area is the question of how classes and instruction should be organized so as to ensure that students acquire the skills embodied in the proposed curricula (Stedman & Smith, 1983). With the exception of *A place called school, Horace's compromise,* and *The Paideia Proposal,* however, the reports have little to say about instructional and organizational problems beyond advocating more homework, more time in school, and more testing of students. How students are helped to master the "new" core subjects is left to educators to figure out. The reports do not deal with this issue, because it is hard, if not impossible, to legislate specific instructional approaches.

RECOMMENDATIONS ABOUT TESTING Previously, we discussed the growing use of test results as an administrative device to implement policy. The recommendation concerning testing contained in *A nation at risk* illustrates this trend:

> *Standardized tests of achievement (not to be confused with aptitude tests) should be administered at major transition points from one level of schooling to another and particularly from high school to college or work. The purposes of these tests would be to: (a) certify the student's credentials; (b) identify the need for remedial intervention; and (c) identify the opportunity for advanced or accelerated work. The tests should be administered as part of a nationwide (but not federal) system of state and local standardized tests (NCEE, 1983, p. 28).*

Among other things, the commission is calling for a system of certification examinations run by an agency external to the local school district—most likely the individual state departments of education.

While the Twentieth Century Fund Task Force has no specific recommendations on testing, the ECS Task Force on Education for Economic Growth recommends periodic testing of general achievement and specific skills, with promotion based on mastery, not on age. The promotion recommendation is ambiguous; it could be interpreted as saying that mastery is determined by test success. And what agency should do the recommended testing? On this point the task force is diplomatically noncommital.

Ernest Boyer is more explicit. He recommends a new Student Achievement and Advisement Test (SAAT). The SAAT presumably would be built and administered by an external agency—the College Entrance Examination Board. (Many of you sat for the CEEB's scholastic aptitude tests in order to meet college entrance requirements.) The goals of the SAAT would be, first, to evaluate the academic achievement of students on the core curriculum studied, and second, to provide advice in making decisions about work and third-level education. While the recommendation does not explicitly call for the SAAT to be used for certification or admission purposes, the potential for this use clearly exists (Boyer, 1983).

The Paideia Proposal calls for testing, but testing that is essentially different from that recommended in other reports. Testing under a *Paideia* curriculum would be squarely in the hands of the local education agencies; in fact, the tests would be designed and administered by teachers. Further, *The Paedeia Proposal* calls for examinations in the fuller sense of the term: direct rather than indirect measures of student outcomes that go well beyond the usual multiple-choice format. The examinations should not involve merely regurgitating textbook or course material, an ever-present danger associated with the external examinations proposed in other reports.

If we contrast the *Paideia Proposal* treatment of testing with that contained in other reports, we are faced with a clear philosophical, not technical, position concerning the role and function of testing in the American system of education. These essentially philosophical issues have not received sufficient attention in these reports or in the testing community.

Recommendations Concerning Teachers

All the reports recognize that a key to reforming the schools is the improvement of the quality of those who teach in them. As a result, most reports focus on how to attract and retain quality teachers. It is interesting to note, however, that with the exception of *A place called school, Horace's compromise,* and *The Paideia Proposal,* the reports have little to say about teaching or pedagogy itself. Most of the recommendations concern teachers rather than teaching; they deal with recruitment and preservice training, compensation, in-service training and working conditions, and certification standards.

RECOMMENDATIONS CONCERNING RECRUITMENT AND PRESERVICE TRAINING A nation at risk and *Action for excellence* call for incentives such as grants, loans, and scholarships to attract outstanding students to prepare for the teaching profession. Many of the reports recommend that students wishing to enter teaching be carefully screened before admission to training programs, and that, at the end of their program, they demonstrate competencies in the academic disciplines in which they wish to teach.

While all the reports call for a strong liberal arts background for all teachers, there is disagreement on how this should be accomplished. *A nation at risk* and *The Paideia Proposal* call for fewer "professional" or methods courses for preservice teachers. This would make more time available for a stronger academic, liberal arts preparation. *High school,* the *Holmes report,* and *A nation prepared* recommend a four-year liberal arts education followed by a fifth year of professional study. *A place called school* is alone in calling for a greater variety of methods courses to equip teachers to deal with different types of students. However, it also suggests that closer links be formed between arts and science faculties and the faculties of schools of education so that content and subject matter will be more closely related to methods of teaching.

To solve the immediate and serious shortage of mathematics and science teachers, *A nation at risk* would open up teaching to qualified individuals with strong mathematics and science backgrounds who otherwise lacked the usual requirements for teacher certification. *Educating Americans for the 21st century* also recommends that school districts draw on industry, colleges and universities, the government, and retired mathematicians and scientists for assistance in meeting the critical shortage in mathematics and science teachers. Further, the report calls for exploring higher pay for people in mathematics and science than for those teaching in other areas in order to compete for, and retain, high-quality candidates. Changing certification requirements and paying mathematics and science teachers more than their peers in other subjects are both, needless to say, highly controversial proposals.

RECOMMENDATIONS CONCERNING COMPENSATION, IN-SERVICE TRAINING, AND WORKING CONDITIONS The recommendations that deal with compensation have three major thrusts: to make teaching (1) more competitive with other professions, (2) market-sensitive, and (3) performance-based.

First, there seems to be a consensus that teachers should be paid more than they are at present, perhaps in return for a longer school day and year. The proposal assumes that it is low pay that keeps many people from entering the profession. If that is so, teaching salaries should be raised to a level competitive with that of business and industry, at least at entry level.

Second, many of the reports call for the establishment of career ladders for teachers. This would provide a mechanism for teachers to move up in both salary and status without having to abandon the classroom.

Third, many of the reports suggest that salary be determined partly on the basis of merit or performance. This proposal is perhaps the most controversial of the three. It assumes that some teachers perform better than others and that superior performance can be identified and rewarded.

Several of the reports call for in-service training during the year and in the summer, which would be designed to help teachers stay up to date in their subject areas and to learn new ways to deliver instruction. Some reports also call for lighter teaching loads and for more time for planning (Boyer, 1983; Goodlad, 1984).

RECOMMENDATIONS CONCERNING TEACHER CERTIFICA-TION Several of the reports call for revamping present teacher certification requirements. Changes suggested include making it easier for liberal arts graduates to become licensed and instituting a written examination as part of the certification procedure. About half the states have now adopted the requirement of an examination.

The two reports dealing with reforms in teacher education *(Tomorrow's teachers* and *A nation prepared)* call for new tests or other assessment techniques to certify teachers. *A nation prepared* calls for a National Board for Professional Teaching Standards. This board would issue, on the basis of some form of assessment and examination, two certificates: a teacher's certificate and an advanced teacher's certificate. The report describes these certificates in this way:

> *The first would establish a high entry level standard for teachers. The second would be an advanced standard, signifying the highest level of competence as a teacher and possession of the qualities needed for leadership in the schools. Certificates at both levels would be specific to subjects taught and grade ranges and could be endorsed on examination for other areas of specialization. In time, the board would establish standards for recertification comparable to those that exist in other professions (Carnegie Forum, 1986, p. 66).*

Work on prototype assessment devices is under way at Stanford University under the direction of Professor Lee Shulman. The task is a very difficult one and will require time and extensive validation.

Alternatives to teacher testing have been suggested in some state reports. These include

1. Raising standards for admission to teacher education
2. Strengthening the institutional accreditation process
3. Supervised internships
4. Continuing on-the-job supervised training
5. Reforming teacher education
6. Lengthening preservice education by adding a fifth year (Vlaanderen, 1983)

As preservice teachers you need to keep abreast of recommendations in your state that will affect your salary, working conditions, and certification. There is great variation among states and the requirements are changing rapidly as recommendations of various state commissions and study groups are implemented.

Recommendations Concerning School Management

A number of recommendations in the reports deal with school management or the organization of schools. These recommendations can be grouped under the headings of school leadership, organization and management, and time.

SCHOOL LEADERSHIP High school, Horace's compromise, A place called school, The Paideia Proposal, and *Action for excellence* all recognize the importance of the principal in creating a climate for effective education. Hence, they advocate strengthening the role of the principal in running the school.

Despite agreement on the importance of the principal, there are some disagreements on specific aspects of the role. For example, in a *Paideia* school, the principal should "be a notably competent and dedicated teacher, with much classroom experience" (Adler, 1982 p. 64). He or she should be the "head teacher." John Goodlad, on the other hand, would create a new position of "head teacher" or "instructional leader" distinct from the principal. He argues that developing and maintaining a first-rate school, as well as carrying out ongoing planning and administrative chores, are a full-time job for any principal. So too, a head teacher's responsibilities as a role model and helper for teachers, as well as an instructional monitor, constitute a full-time job. Hence the recommendation that the positions be separated. Goodlad's new head-teacher position fits in very nicely with the career ladder idea recommended in other reports (Goodlad, 1984).

ORGANIZATION AND MANAGEMENT Although a number of the reports *(A place called school, Horace's compromise,* and *The Paideia Proposal)* call for radical changes in the way schools and school systems are organized, there is little consensus about how these changes should be brought about.

A place called school would divide schooling into four phases based on age: phase 1, ages 4 through 7, would replace the second year of nursery school and kindergarten and the first three grades of elementary school; phase 2, ages 8 through 11, would replace the present grades 4 through 8; and phase 3, ages 12 through 15, would replace the present grades 9 through 12. Under this plan, what presently takes 14 years to accomplish would be completed in 12.

In *A place called school,* all the proposed levels would be organized vertically rather than horizontally. That is, there would be nongraded units of 100 students or fewer that encompass the complete age span of that particular level. A cluster of teachers would stay with this nongraded unit for the entire phase. Such a reorganization would be contrary to the proposal in *A nation at risk* that grading should be by achievement level rather than by age.

Theodore Sizer, in *Horace's compromise,* also proposes a radical change in the way schools are presently structured. He argues that school systems currently (1984) constitute a hierarchical bureaucracy—"governance" flows from the top to the bottom. As states become more involved in education, this top-to-bottom bureaucracy will expand and education will become even more centralized than it is now. The report sees the following defects as being inherent in this top-down organization of schools:

1. It overlooks special local conditions, particularly important school-by-school differences in teachers, pupils, administrators, and parents.

2. Large, complex units like schools need simple ways of describing themselves so things that are easily counted, measured, or quantified become the only forms of quality.

3. Rules and schedules for teachers and pupils are set up and then are rigidly adhered to.

4. Centralized planning requires a high level of specificity. Once regulations, job descriptions, and licensure and collective bargaining agreements are made specific, it is hard to be adaptable or to change practices.

5. Hierarchical bureaucracy stifles initiative at the base, and in schools teachers constitute this base.

To eliminate these perceived defects, *Horace's compromise* proposes a decentralization of the system. Power and decision making would shift from the central office to the local school. In this context, the decentralized organization of the Catholic school system is cited as a model that could be followed (see Chapter 6). The report argues that a shift to decentralization would allow teachers and principals to adapt their schools to the needs and learning styles of their students. Greater authority at the base should act as an incentive to attract and hold good people.

The politics of implementing the types of reorganization suggested in these reports would be difficult, to say the least. Reorganization would reduce the power of certain groups, and therefore would be quite threatening. The decentralization proposed in *Horace's compromise* flies in the face of the trend toward greater centralization and accountability that presently enjoys widespread political support. It is interesting to note that the various national commissions avoided making recommendations about the restructuring or radical reorganization of our schools.

TRACKING High school, A place called school, The Paideia Proposal, and *Horace's compromise* all recommend that tracking be eliminated. On the other hand, *A nation at risk* and *Action for excellence* call for tracking by achievement rather than by age. We saw earlier that tracking proposals can vitiate the dual goal of excellence and equity.

TIME Three of the reports *(A nation at risk, Educating Americans for the 21st century,* and *Action for excellence)* call for extending the school day and/or the school year. There are two reasons behind such recommendations. First, European and Japanese students have longer school days and a longer school year (up to 220 days, compared to 180 days in the United States). It is assumed that increasing the amount of time spent in school would increase American achievement levels relative to those of European and Japanese students. Second, lengthening the school year is a proposal that is amenable to legislation. It is something concrete that can be mandated and therefore is attractive to policymakers. Not surprisingly, a number of state legislatures have mandated increases in either the school day or the school year.

The important issue regarding time is what is done with it, rather than the sheer quantity available. Schools must first consider how to maximize the use of the time that is presently available. If the school day or year is increased, schools will have to figure out how to best spend the additional time.

Recommendations Concerning School and Community Relationships

One major recommendation common to many of the reports is that a partnership be formed between the schools and the business community. The thrust of this recommendation is that the schools use the resources and personnel of the business community to help them in certain subject areas—primarily mathematics, science, and technology. Further, such a union would provide work-study opportunities for students and eventual employment opportunities. The reports are silent on the mechanics of such a partnership. There is a danger that involving the business community more closely in the schools could lead to an emphasis on corporate values to the detriment of social responsibility (Stedman & Smith, 1983).

All but one of the reports *(Academic preparation for college)* discuss the appropriate roles of the federal government in improving education. There is agreement that it should continue to provide support for special student groups, such as those from disadvantaged backgrounds, those with disabilities, and those with limited proficiency in English. There is also agreement that the federal government should fund research on education and collect basic statistics and information. Five reports *(A nation at risk, Educating Americans for the 21st century, High school, America's competitive challenge,* and *A nation prepared)* recommend that the federal government fund efforts to attract good people to the teaching profession.

All the reports call for state governments to become actively involved in school reform and develop state plans for education. This clearly has already happened.

CONCLUSION

The effects of the reform reports will continue to be felt long after you enter teaching. The reports mark a watershed in the history of American education. They have helped to create a new nationwide optimism about education, about our schools, and about teaching.

Specific reforms that affect the curriculum, teachers, school organizations, and school and community relationships vary widely among states and among local districts. You need to keep yourself informed about reform proposals that affect you directly while you are in preservice and once you enter the profession. You should not fear these changes; rather, you should be able to evaluate them carefully and critically. You should look on the positive climate created by the reform proposals as providing a range of opportunities to become a better teacher, better paid and more respected than at any time in our nation's history.

QUESTIONS AND ACTIVITIES

1. Do you agree or disagree with the major points made in *The Paideia Proposal?* What are some of the obstacles schools must overcome in order to implement Adler's suggestions?
2. Do you agree or disagree with the recommendations of *High school* and *The Paideia Proposal* that vocational education be eliminated?
3. Which of the many recommendations made by the reports do you think would have the greatest impact on education if implemented?
4. Contact your state department of education and request copies of any recent reports dealing with education reform. What parts of the reports have become policy? What effect, if any, have they had on schools?
5. What role should business and industrial organizations play in public school education?
6. What do you think of the proposal that all teachers be required to have a bachelor's degree in an arts and science subject. If this were to go into effect next year, how would it affect you?
7. You have now completed this textbook and have a general understanding of the issues facing American education. If you were to testify before a commission on excellence in education, what would be your suggestions for improving education?

REFERENCES

Note: Asterisks before citations indicate major reform reports or books on reform with which you should be familiar.

Adams, R. S., & Biddle, B. J. (1970). *Realities of teaching: Exploration with videotape.* New York: Holt, Rinehart and Winston.

Adler, M. J. (1977). *Reforming education in America: The schooling of a people and their education beyond schooling.* Boulder, CO: Westview Press.

*Adler, M. J. (1982). *The Paideia Proposal. An educational manifesto.* New York: Macmillan.

*Adler, M. J. (1983). *Paideia problems and possibilities: A consideration of questions raised by the Paideia Proposal.* New York: Macmillan.

Airasian, P. (1979). A perspective on the uses and misuses of standardized tests. *NCME Measurement in Education, 10* (3), 1–12.

American Association of Colleges of Teacher Education. (1972). *No one model American. A statement of multicultural education.* Washington, DC: AACTE.

American Association of School Administrators. (1982). *Time on task: Using instructional time more effectively.* Arlington, VA: AASA.

American Psychological Association, Committee to Develop Joint Technical Standards for Educational and Psychological Testing (1985). *Joint standards for educational and psychological tests.* Washington, DC: APA.

American School Counselors Association. (1981). The practice of guidance and counseling by school counselors: ASCA role statement. *School Counselor, 29,* 9–10.

Anastasi, A. (1958). *Differential psychology. Individual and group differences in behavior.* New York: Macmillan.

Anastasi, A. (1961). *Psychological testing* (2nd ed.). New York: Macmillan.

Anastasi, A. (1982). *Psychological testing* (5th ed.). New York: Macmillan.

Anrig, G. (1986). Teacher education and teacher testing: The rush to mandate. *Phi Delta Kappan, 67,* 447–451.

Areen, J., & Jencks, C. (1971). Education vouchers: A proposal for diversity and choice. *Teachers College Press, 72,* 327–335.

Argyle, M. (1972). *The psychology of interpersonal behaviour.* Harmondsworth, Middlesex, England: Penguin.

Argyle, M. (1975). *Bodily communication.* London: Methuen.

Argyle, M., Furnham, A., & Graham, J. A. (1981). *Social situations.* Cambridge, England: Cambridge University Press.

Ariès, P. H. (1965). *Centuries of childhood* (Robert Baldick, Trans.). New York: Random House. (Original work published 1960)

Arons, S. (1985, October 16) The great secular-humanism debate reveals a truth about public schooling. *Education Week,* pp. 18, 24.

Arons, S., & Lawrence, C. (1982). The manipulation of consciousness: A first amendment critique of schooling. In R. E. Everhart (Ed.), *The public school monopoly.* Cambridge, MA: Ballinger.

Atkins, J. M. (1979). Education accountability in the United States. *Educational Analyses,* 5–21.

Austin, G. R. (1981). Exemplary schools and their identification. *New Directions for Testing and Measurement,* No. 10, 31–48.

Ausubel, D. (1960). The use of advanced organizers in the learning and retention of meaningful verbal material. *Journal of Educational Psychology, 51,* 267–272.

Bailyn, B. (1960). *Education in the forming of American society.* New York: Vintage Books.

Baird, L. (1977). *The elite schools: A profile of prestigious independent schools.* Lexington, MA: Lexington Books.

Bane, M. J., & Jencks, C. (1976). Five myths about IQ. In N. J. Block & G. Dworken (Eds.), *The IQ controversy: Critical readings.* New York: Random House.

Barnes, D. (1973). *Language in the classroom. Educational studies: A second level course. Language and learning block 4.* Bletchley, Buckinghamshire, England: Open University Press.

Barr, A., & Feigenbaum, A. (1982). *The handbook of artificial intelligence* (Vol. 2). Los Altos, CA: William Kaufmann.

Barro, S. M. (1970). An approach to developing accountability measures for the public schools. *Phi Delta Kappan, 52,* 196–205.

Beck, M. D., & Stetz, F. P. (1979, April). *Teachers' opinions of standardized test use and usefulness.* Paper presented at the meeting of the American Educational Research Association, San Francisco.

Becker, H. J., & Sterling, C. W. (1987). Equity in school computer use: National data and neglected considerations. *Journal of Educational Computer Research, 3,* 289–312.

Bell, T. H. (1983). *Congressionally-mandated study of school finance.* A final report to Congress from the Secretary of Education: Vol. 2. Private elementary and secondary education. Washington, DC: U.S. Department of Education.

Bell, T. H. (1984). American education at a crossroads. *Phi Delta Kappan, 65,* 531–533.

Bem, D. J., & Allen, A. (1974). On predicting some of the people some of the time: The search for cross-situational consistencies in behavior. *Psychological Review, 81,* 506–520.

Bem, D. J., & Funder, D. C. (1978). Predicting more of the people more of the time: Assessing the personality of situations. *Psychological Review, 85,* 485–501.

*Bennett, W. J. (1986). *First lessons: A report on elementary education in America.* Washington, DC: U.S. Department of Education.

Bennett, W. J. (1988). *James Madison High School: A*

curriculum for American students. Washington, DC: U.S. Department of Education.

Berliner, D. C. (1979). Tempus educare. In P. L. Peterson & H. J. Walberg (Eds.), *Research on teaching: Concepts, findings, and implications.* Berkeley, CA: McCutchan.

Berliner, D. C. (1983). The executive who manages classrooms. In B. J. Fraser (Ed.), *Classroom management.* Bentley, Australia: Western Australian Institute of Technology.

Bernstein, B. (1971). *Primary socialization, language and education. Class, codes and control.* London: Routledge & Kegan Paul.

Bestor, A. (1955). *The restoration of learning.* New York: Knopf.

Bestor, D. K. (1977). *Aside from teaching English, what in the world can you do?* Seattle, WA: University of Washington Press.

Bickel, W. E. (1983). Effective schools: Knowledge, dissemination, inquiry. *Educational Researcher, 12* (4), 3–5.

Binder, F. M. (1974). *The age of the common school, 1830–1865.* New York: Wiley.

Block, J. H., & Burns, R. B. (1976). Mastery learning. In L. S. Shulman (Ed.), *Review of research in education* (Vol. 4). Itasca, IL: Peacock.

Block, N. J., & Dworkin, G. (Eds.). (1976). *The IQ controversy: Critical readings.* New York: Pantheon.

Bloom, B. S. (1964). *Stability and change in human characteristics.* New York: Wiley.

Bloom, B. S. (1976). *Human characteristics and school learning.* New York: McGraw-Hill.

Bloom, B. S. (1981). *All our children learning. A primer for parents, teachers, and other educators.* New York: McGraw-Hill.

Bloom, B. S. (1984). The 2-sigma problem: The search for methods of group instruction as effective as one-to-one tutoring. *Educational Researcher, 13*(6), 4–16.

Bloom, B. S. (Ed.). (1985).

Developing talent in young people. New York: Ballantine.

Bloom, B. S., Engelhart, M. D., Furst, E. J., Hill, W. H., & Krathwohl, D. R. (1956). *Taxonomy of educational objectives. The classification of educational goals: Handbook 1. Cognitive domain.* New York: McKay.

Bloom, B. S., Hastings, J. T., & Madaus, G. F. (1971). *Handbook on formative and summative evaluation of student learning.* New York: McGraw-Hill.

Bloom, B. S., Madaus, G. F., & Hastings, J. T. (1981). *Evaluation to improve learning.* New York: McGraw-Hill.

Borg, W. R. (1966). *Ability grouping in the public schools.* Madison, WI: Demba Educational Research Services.

Borko, H., & Niles, J. A. (1987). Descriptions of teacher planning: Ideas for teachers and researchers. In V. Richardson-Koehler (Ed.), *Educators' handbook. A research perspective.* New York: Longman.

Boyd, J. (1945). *The Declaration of Independence.* Princeton, NJ: Princeton University Press.

*Boyer, E. L. (1983). *High school: A report on secondary education in America.* New York: Harper & Row.

Boyer, E. L. (1984). Reflections on the Great Debate of '83. *Phi Delta Kappan, 65,* 525–530.

Brandt, R. (1982). Overview: The new catechism for school effectiveness. *Educational Leadership, 40,* 3.

Bremner, R. H. (1970). *Children and youth in America: A documentary history: Vol. 1. 1600–1865.* Cambridge, MA: Harvard University Press.

Brimer, A., Madaus, G. F., Chapman, B., Kellaghan, T., & Wood, R. (1978). *Sources of difference in school achievement.* Slough: NFER Publishing Co.

Brookhover, W., Beady, C., Flood, P., Schweitzer, J., & Wisenbaker, J. (1979). *Schools, social systems, and student achievement: Schools can make a difference.* New York: Praeger.

Brophy, J. E. (1981). Teacher praise:

A functional analysis. *Review of Educational Research, 51,* 5–32.

Brophy, J. E. (1986). Teacher influences on student achievement. *American Psychologist, 41,* 1069–1077.

Brophy, J. E., & Good, T. L. (1970). Teachers' communication of differential expectations for children's classroom performance: Some behavioral data. *Journal of Educational Psychology, 61,* 365–374.

Brophy, J. E., & Good, T. L. (1974). *Teacher-student relationships: Causes and consequences.* New York: Holt, Rinehart and Winston.

Brophy, J. E., & Good, T. L. (1986). Teacher behavior and student achievement. In M. Wittrock (Ed.), *Handbook of research on teaching* (3rd ed.). New York: Macmillan.

Broverman, I. K., Broverman, D. M., Clarkson, F. E., Rosenkrantz, P., & Vogel, S. R. (1970). Sex-role stereotypes and clinical judgments of mental health. *Journal of Consulting Psychology, 34,* 1–7.

Brown, J. S., & Burton, R. R. (1978). Diagnostic models for procedural bugs in basic mathematical skills. *Cognitive Science, 2,* 155–192.

Brown, R. (1965). *Social psychology.* New York: Free Press.

Bruner, J. S. (1964). Some theories on instruction illustrated with reference to mathematics. In E. R. Hilgard (Ed.), *Theories of learning and instruction: The sixty-third yearbook of the National Society for the Study of Education, Part 1.* Chicago: University of Chicago Press.

Bruner, J. S. (1965). *The process of education.* Cambridge, MA: Harvard University Press.

Bruner, J. S. (1966). *Toward a theory of instruction.* Cambridge, MA: Belknap Press.

Buchner, C. (1984, February 15). Survey shows 30 states have adopted teacher competency tests. *Education Week,* p. 12.

Burnes, D. W., Palaich, R. M., McGuinness, A., & Flakus-Mosqueda, P. (1983). Leadership in elementary/secondary education. In *State governance of education: 1983* (Report No. EG-83-1).

Denver: Education Commission of the States.

*Business-Higher Education Forum (1983). *America's competitive challenge: The need for a national response.* Washington, DC: Author.

Butts, R. F. (1974). The public school: Assaults on a great idea. In A. Kopan & H. Walberg (Eds.), *Rethinking educational equality.* Berkeley, CA: McCutchan.

Cameron, B. H., Underwood, K. E., & Fortune, J. C. (1988). Politics and power: How you are selected and elected to lead this nation's schools. *American School Board Journal, 175*(1), 17–21.

Cameron, D. (1984). The most effective tool in promoting excellence. *Community and Junior College Journal, 54,* 5.

Campbell, R. F. (1971). Accountability and stone soup. *Phi Delta Kappan, 53,* 176–178.

Campbell, R. F., Cunningham, L. L., Nystrand, R. O., & Usdan, M. D. (1985). *The organization and control of American schools* (5th ed.). Columbus, OH: Merrill.

Campbell, R. F., & Newell, L. J. (1985). History of administration. In T. Husen & T. N. Postlethwaite (Eds.), *The international encyclopedia of education. Research and studies.* New York: Pergamon.

*Carnegie Forum on Education and the Economy: Task Force on Teaching as a Profession. (1986). *A nation prepared: Teachers for the 21st century.* New York: Carnegie Corporation.

Carter, R. S. (1952). How valid are marks assigned by teachers? *Journal of Educational Psychology, 43,* 218–228.

Caruso, J. J. (1977, November). Phases in student teaching. *Young Children, 33,* 57–63.

Case, C. W., Lanier, J. C., & Miskel, C. G. (1986). The Holmes Group Report: Impetus for gaining professional status for teaching. *Journal of Teacher Education, 37*(4), 36–43.

Castetter, W. B. (1981). *The personnel function in educational administration* (3rd ed.). New York: Macmillan.

Cattell, R. B. (1971). *Abilities. Their structure, growth, and action.* Boston: Houghton Mifflin.

Cazden, C. B. (1971). Evaluation of learning in preschool education: Early language development. In B. S. Bloom, J. T. Hastings, & G. F. Madaus (Eds.), *Handbook on formative and summative evaluation of student learning.* New York: McGraw-Hill.

Chambers, S. M., & Clarke, V. A. (1987). Is inequity cumulative? The relationship between disadvantaged group membership and students' computing experience, knowledge, attitudes and intentions. *Journal of Educational Computing Research, 3,* 495–518.

Chen, M. (1986). Gender and computers: The beneficial effects of experience on attitudes. *Journal of Educational Computing Research, 2,* 265–282.

Cisneros, G. M., & Rosser, B. (1981). A model educational quality act—holding schools accountable. In J. F. Schwartz & M. S. Garet (Eds.), *Assessment for accountability.* Report of a study panel to the Ford Foundations and the National Institute of Education. Cambridge, MA: Massachusetts Institute of Technology.

Clark, C. M., & Elmore, J. S. (1979). *Teacher planning in the first weeks of school* (Research Series No. 56). East Lansing, MI: The Institute for Research on Teaching.

Cohen, D. K. (1987). Educational technology, policy, and practice. *Educational Evaluation and Policy Analysis, 9,* 153–170.

Cohen, E. G. (1972). Sociology and the classroom: Setting the conditions for teaching-student interaction. *Review of Educational Research, 42,* 441–452.

Cohen, S. S. (1974). *A history of colonial education, 1607–1766.* New York: Wiley.

Coleman, J. S. (1961). *The adolescent society.* New York: Free Press.

Coleman, J. S. (1968). The concept of equality of educational opportunity. *Harvard Educational Review, 38,* 7–22.

Coleman, J. S. (Chairman). (1974). *Youth: Transition to adulthood.* Report of the Panel on Youth of the President's Science Advisory Committee. Chicago: University of Chicago Press.

Coleman, J. S. (1975). What is meant by 'an equal educational opportunity'? *Oxford Review of Education, 1,* 27–29.

Coleman, J. S. (1987). Families and schools. *Educational Researcher, 16*(6), 32–38.

Coleman, J. S., Campbell, E. Q., Hobson, C. J., McPartland, J., Mood, A. M., Weinfeld, F. D., & York, R. L. (1966). *Equality of educational opportunity.* Washington, DC: Office of Education, U.S. Department of Health, Education and Welfare.

Coleman, J. S., & Hoffer, T. (1987). *Public and private high schools: The impact of communities.* New York: Basic Books.

Coleman, J. S., Hoffer, T., & Kilgore, S. (1982). *High-school achievement: Catholic and private schools compared.* New York: Basic Books.

*College Entrance Examination Board (1983). *Academic preparation for college: What students need to know and to be able to do.* New York: CEEB.

Collins, D. W. (1985). Teaching concepts. In D. M. Purdom & G. E. Fardig (Eds.), *Florida Teacher Performance Development Program.* (Learning Package 9). Tallahassee: State of Florida Department of Education.

Conant, J. B. (1959). *The American high school today.* New York: McGraw-Hill.

Confrey, J. (1987). Mathematics learning and teaching. In V. Richardson-Hoehler (Ed.), *Educators' handbook. A research perspective.* New York: Longman.

Cooley, W. W., & Lohnes, P. R. (1976). *Evaluation research in education.* New York: Wiley.

Coons, J. E., & Sugarman, S. D. (1978). *Education by choice.* Berkeley, CA: University of California Press.

Cooper, M., & Leiter, M. (1980). Teachers on testing. In C. B. Stalford (Ed.), *Testing and evaluation in schools: Practitioners' views.* Washington,

DC: National Institute of Education, U.S. Department of Education.

Copeland, W. (1977). *The nature of the relationship between cooperating teacher behavior and student teacher classroom performance* (ERIC Document Reproduction Service, No. ED 137 271). Paper presented at the annual meeting of the American Educational Research Association, New York.

Copperman, P. (1980). *The literacy hoax: The decline of reading, writing and learning in the public schools and what we can do about it.* New York: Morrow.

Covington, M. V., Crutchfield, R. S., Davies, L., & Olton, R. M. (1974). *The productive thinking programme: A course in learning to think.* Columbus, OH: Merrill.

Cremin, L. A. (1964). *The transformation of the school. Progressivism in American education 1876–1957.* New York: Vintage Books.

Cremin, L. A. (1965). *The genius of American education.* New York: Vintage Books.

Cresswell, A. M., & Murphy, M. J. (1980). *Teachers, unions, and collective bargaining in public education.* Berkeley, CA: McCutchan.

Cronbach, L. J. (1964). *Essentials of psychological testing* (2nd ed.). New York: Harper & Row.

Cronbach, L. J. (1967). How can instruction be adapted to individual differences? In R. M. Gagre (Ed.), *Learning and individual differences.* Columbus, OH: Merrill.

Cuban, L. (1983). How did teachers teach, 1890–1980? *Theory into Practice, 22,* 159–165.

Cuban, L. (1984). *How teachers taught: Constancy and change in American classrooms 1890–1980.* New York: Longman.

Cuban, L. (1986). *Teachers and machines: The classroom use of technology since 1920.* New York: Teachers College Press.

Cubberley, E. P. (1934). *Public education in the United States.* Boston: Houghton Mifflin.

Cunningham, L., & Hentges, J. T. (1982). *The American school superintendency: A summary report.* Washington, DC: American Association of School Administrators.

Cuttance, P. (1980a). The influence of schooling on student academic outcomes: A critical assessment of findings produced in the neo-classical paradigm of schooling effects research. *Canadian and International Education, 9,* 43–70.

Cuttance, P. (1980b). Do schools consistently influence the performance of their students? *Educational Review, 32,* 267–280.

Dearman, N., & Plisko, V. (1979). *The condition of education, 1979 edition.* Washington, DC: U.S. Government Printing Office.

Deaux, K. (1984). From individual differences to social categories: Analysis of a decade's research on gender. *American Psychologist, 39,* 105–116.

Deese, J. (1958). *The psychology of learning.* New York: McGraw-Hill.

DeMott, B. (1984, July 8). Did the 1960s damage fiction? *New York Times Book Review,* pp. 1, 26–27.

Deutsch, M. (1963). The disadvantaged child and the learning process: Some social, psychological and developmental considerations. In A. H. Passow (Ed.), *Education in depressed areas.* New York: Teachers College Bureau of Publications.

Devaney, K. (1980). Ingredients of teachers centers' uniqueness. In *What makes teachers' centers unique as inservice? Three views.* (Contract No. 400-80-0103). Washington, DC: National Institute of Education.

Dewey, J. (1916). *Democracy and education.* New York: Macmillan.

Dewey, J. (1938). *Experience and education.* New York: Collier.

Doyle, W. (1983). Academic work. *Review of Educational Research, 53,* 159–199.

Doyle, W. (1986). Classroom organization and management. In M. C. Wittrock (Ed.), *Handbook of research on teaching* (3rd ed.). New York: Macmillan.

Doyle, W., & Carter, K. (1987). Choosing the means of instruction. In V. Richardson-Koehler (Ed.), *Educators' handbook. A research perspective.* New York: Longman.

Dreeben, R. (1967). The contribution of schooling to the learning of norms. *Harvard Educational Review, 37,* 211–237.

Dreeben, R. (1968). *On what is learned in school.* Reading, MA: Addison-Wesley.

Dreeben, R. (1973). The school as a workplace. In R. M. W. Travers (Ed.), *Second handbook of research on teaching.* Chicago: Rand McNally.

DuBois, P. H. (1970). *A history of psychological testing.* Boston: Allyn & Bacon.

Duffy, R. (1981). *Survey of state aid to private schools.* Unpublished data, U.S. Catholic Reference.

Duncan, M. G. (1971, January). An assessment of accountability: The state of the art. *Educational Technology, II,* 27–30.

Dunn, R. (1984). Learning style: State of the science. *Theory into Practice, 23,* 10–19.

Dweck, C. S. (1975). The role of expectations and attributions in the alleviation of learned helplessness. *Journal of Personality and Social Psychology, 31,* 674–685.

Dyer, H. (1973). *How to achieve accountability in the public schools.* Bloomington, IN: Phi Delta Kappan Educational Foundation.

Eaker, R. (1984). High expectations and student achievement. *Effective School Report, 2,* 1–4.

Ebel, R. (1972). What are schools for? *Phi Delta Kappan, 54,* 3–7.

Edmonds, R. (1979). Some schools work and more can. *Social Policy, 9,* 28–32.

Edmonds, R. (1982). Programs of school improvement: An overview. *Educational Leadership, 40,* 4–11.

Education Commission of the States (1983). *A summary of major reports on education.* Denver: ECS.

Education Commission of the States Clearinghouse Notes No. 5. (1988, January). Education Commission of the States, 1860 Lincoln Street, Suite 300, Denver, CO.

Education Week (1988, February 3).

The fiercest competition. *Education Week*, pp. 1, 13. (Reported by B. Rodman)

Educational Policies Commission. (1944). *Education for ALL American youth.* Washington, DC: National Education Association.

Educational Research Service. (1979). *Merit pay for teachers.* Arlington, VA: Educational Research Service.

Educational Research Service. (1987). *Salaries paid to professional personnel in public schools, 1986–1987: Part 2 of National Survey of Salaries and Wages in Public Schools.* Arlington VA: Educational Research Service.

Educational Testing Service. (1973). *Making the classroom: A guide for teachers.* Princeton, NJ: Educational Testing Service.

Edwards, N. (1971). District organization and control. In *The courts and public schools.* Chicago: University of Chicago Press.

Eiden, L. J., & Grant, W. V. (1979). *Education in the United States: Statistical highlights through 1977–78.* Washington, DC: National Center for Education Statistics, U.S. Department of Health, Education and Welfare.

Ephron, D. (1978). *How to eat like a child.* New York: Viking.

Epstein, N. (1977). *Language, ethnicity, and the schools: Policy alternatives for bilingual-bicultural education.* Washington, DC: Institute for Educational Leadership, George Washington University.

Erickson, D. (1981, April). *Effects of public money on social climates in private schools: A preliminary report.* Paper presented at the meeting of the American Educational Research Association, Los Angeles.

Erickson, D. (1983). *Private schools in contemporary perspective.* Stanford, CA: Stanford University Institute for Research on Educational Finance and Governance.

Erickson, D., MacDonald, L., & Manley-Casimir, M. (1979). *Characteristics and relationships in public and independent schools.* San Francisco: Center for Research on Private Education.

Erickson, D., & Nault, R. (1980). *Effects of public money on Catholic schools in Western Canada: Exploring interviews.* A final report to the Spencer Foundation. San Francisco: Center for Research on Private Education.

Farr, R., & Tulley, M. A. (1985). Do adoption committees perpetuate mediocre textbooks? *Phi Delta Kappan, 66,* 467–471.

Feistritzer, C. E. (1983). *The condition of teaching: A state by state analysis.* Lawrenceville, NJ: Princeton University Press.

Feistritzer, C. E. (1988). *Profile of school administrators in the United States.* Washington, DC: National Center for Education Information.

Fenton, E. (1967). *The new social studies.* New York: Holt, Rinehart and Winston.

Ferguson, G. A. (1954). On learning and human ability. *Canadian Journal of Psychology, 8,* 95–112.

First, J., & Mezzell, M. H. (1980). *Everybody's business: A book about school discipline.* Columbia, SC: Southeastern Public Education Program, American Friends Service Committee.

Fiske, E. B. (1984). Noted educator foresees resurgence in teaching. *The New York Times,* pp. C2, C11.

Flavell, J. H. (1973). *The developmental psychology of Jean Piaget.* New York: Van Nostrand.

Forbes, J. (1984). *Comparison of recommendations from selected education reform reports.* (CRS-3). Washington, DC: Congressional Research Service, Library of Congress.

Frank (Pseud). (1975, February 6). The St. Crohane's Letters. *Education Times* (Dublin, Ireland), p. 3.

Fredericksen, N. (1981). Information for use on school accountability. In J. F. Schwartz & M. S. Garet (Eds.), *Assessment for accountability.* Report of a study panel to the Ford Foundation and the National Institute of Education. Cambridge, MA: Massachusetts Institute of Technology.

Fredrickson, R. H. (1982). *Career information.* Englewood Cliffs, NJ: Prentice-Hall.

Friedman, M. (1973, September 23). The voucher idea. *New York Times Magazine.*

Fuhram, S. (1984). The excellence agenda: States respond. *Educational Horizons, 62,* 48–51.

Gage, N. L. (1978). *The scientific basis of the art of teaching.* New York: Teachers College Press.

Gage, N. L. (1985). *Hard gains in the soft sciences. The case of pedagogy.* Bloomington, IN: Phi Delta Kappa Center on Evaluation, Development and Research.

Gagné, R. M. (1970). *The condition of learning* (2nd ed.). New York: Holt, Rinehart and Winston.

Gagné, R. M., & Dick, W. (1983). Instructional psychology. In M. R. Rosenweig & L. W. Porter (Eds.), *Annual review of psychology (Vol. 34).* Palo Alto, CA: Annual Reviews Inc.

Gallagher, J. J. (1975). *Teaching the gifted child.* Boston: Allyn & Bacon.

Gallagher, J. J., Weiss, P., Oglesby, K., & Thomas, T. (1983). *The status of gifted talented education: United States surveys of needs, practices, and policies.* Ventura, CA: Ventura County Superintendent's Office.

Gallup, A. M. (1985a). The 17th annual Gallup poll of the public's attitude toward the public schools. *Phi Delta Kappan, 64,* 37–50.

Gallup, A. M. (1985b). The Gallup poll of teachers' attitudes toward the public schools. Part 2. *Phi Delta Kappan, 66,* 323–330.

Gallup, A. M., & Clark, D. L. (1987). The 19th annual Gallup poll of the public's attitudes toward the public schools. *Phi Delta Kappan, 69,* 17–30.

Gardner, E. (1982). Uses and misuses of standardized aptitude and achievement tests. In A. K. Wigdor & W. R. Garner (Eds.), *Ability testing: Uses, consequences, and controversies.* Part 2: Documentary section. Washington, DC: National Academy Press.

Gardner, H. (1983). *Frames of mind: The theory of multiple intelligences.* New York: Basic Books.

Garms, W. I. (1983, April). Commentary: Striking a balance between individual choice and the interests of the State. *Education Week,* p. 24.

Garner, W. T., & Hannaway, J. (1981). Private schools: The client connection. In M. E. Manley-Casimir (Ed.), *Family choice in schooling: Issues and dilemmas.* Lexington, MA: Lexington Books.

Gauthier, W. J. (1983). *Instructionally effective schools: A model and a process* (Monograph No. 1). Hartford, CT: State of Connecticut, Department of Education.

Getzels, J. W. (1985). Creativity and human development. In T. Husén & T. N. Postlethwaite (Eds.), *The international encyclopedia of education* (Vol. 2). New York: Pergamon.

Getzels, J. W., & Dillon, J. (1973). The nature of giftedness and the education of the gifted. In R. Travers (Ed.), *Second handbook of research on teaching.* Chicago: Rand McNally.

Getzels, J. W., & Jackson, P. W. (1962). *Creativity and intelligence.* New York: Wiley.

Getzels, J. W., & Thelan, H. A. (1960). The classroom group as a unique social system. In N. B. Henry (Ed.), *The dynamics of instructional groups.* Fifty-ninth Yearbook of the National Society for the Study of Education, Part 2. Chicago: NSSE.

Geyer, A., Slyck, L., Thigpen, N., & Wilson, N. (1985). Using time efficiently. In G. E. Fardig, & D. M. Purdom (Eds.), *Florida Teacher Performance Development Program.* (Learning Package 13). Tallahassee, FL: State of Florida Department of Education.

Glaser, R. (1977). *Adaptive education: Individual diversity and learning.* New York: Holt, Rinehart and Winston.

Glaser, R., & Reynolds, J. (1964). Instructional objectives and programmed instruction. A case study. In C. M. Lindvall (Ed.),

Defining educational objectives. Pittsburgh: University of Pittsburgh Press.

Glickman, C. D. (1987). Good and/or effective schools: What do we want? *Phi Delta Kappan, 68*(8), 622–624.

Good, T. L., & Brophy, J. E. (1973). *Looking in classrooms.* New York: Harper & Row.

Good, T. L., & Brophy, J. E. (1977). *Educational psychology. A realistic approach.* New York: Holt, Rinehart and Winston.

Good, T. L., & Brophy, J. E. (1986). School effects. In M. C. Wittrock (Ed.), *Handbook of research and teaching* (3rd ed.). New York: Macmillan.

Good, T. L., & Marshall, S. (1984). Do students learn more in heterogeneous or homogeneous groups? In P. L. Peterson, L. C. Wilkinson, & M. Hallinan (Eds.), *The social context of instruction. Group organization and group processes.* New York: Academic Press.

Good, T. L., & Stipek, D. J. (1983). Individual differences in the classroom: A psychological perspective. In G. D. Fenstermacher & J. J. Goodlad (Eds.), *Individual differences and the common curriculum.* Eighty-second Yearbook of the National Society for the Study of Education, Part 1. Chicago: NSSE.

*Goodlad, J. I. (1984). *A place called school. Prospects for the future.* St. Louis: McGraw-Hill.

Goodlad, J. I., & Rehage, K. (1962). Unscrambling the vocabulary of school organization. *National Education Association Journal, 51,* 34–36.

Goodman, L. (1982). *Alternative careers for teachers, librarians, and counselors.* New York: Monarch Press.

Gordan, R. A. (1983). *School administration and supervision.* Dubuque, IA: Brown.

Gordon, H. (1923). *Mental and scholastic tests among retarded children.* Education Pamphlet No. 44. London: Board of Education.

Goslin, D. (1963). *The search for ability.* New York: Russell Sage.

Gould, S. J. (1981). *The mismeasure of man.* New York: Norton.

Gradisnik, A. (1980). Bilingual education. In F. M. Grittner (Ed.), *Learning a second language.* Seventy-ninth Yearbook of the National Society for the Study of Education, Part 2. Chicago: NSSE.

Graham, P. A. (1974). *Community and class in American education, 1865–1918.* New York: Wiley.

Graham, P. A. (1987). Black teachers: A drastically scarce resource. *Phi Delta Kappan, 69,* 598–605.

Gratiot, M. (1979, April). *Why parents choose non-public schools: Comparative attitudes and characteristics of public and private school consumers.* Paper presented at the meeting of the American Educational Research Association, San Francisco.

Graudbard, S. R. (1981). Preface to the issue, America's schools: Portrait and perspectives. *Daedalus, 110*(4), V–XVI.

Greeley, A. (1980). *Minority students in Catholic secondary schools.* Washington, DC: Report to National Center for Educational Statistics.

Green, R. L., Hoffman, L. T., Morse, R. J., Hayes, M. E., & Morgan, R. F. (1964). *The educational status of children in districts without public schools.* (Co-operative Research Project No. 2321). Washington, DC: Office of Education, U.S. Department of Health, Education and Welfare. Lansing: Michigan State University.

Green, T. F. (1980). *Predicting the behavior of the educational system.* Syracuse, NY: Syracuse University Press.

Grimsley, R. (1983). *Jean-Jacques Rousseau.* Totowa, NJ: Barnes & Noble.

Gronlund, N. E. (1981). *Measurement and evaluation in testing* (4th ed.). New York: Macmillan.

Guilford, J. P. (1956). The structure of the intellect. *Psychological Bulletin, 53,* 267–293.

Guilford, J. P. (1967). *The nature of human intelligence.* New York: McGraw-Hill.

Gumbert, E. G., & Spring, J. H. (1974). *The superschool and the superstate: American education in the twentieth century, 1918–1970.* New York: Wiley.

Gump, P. V. (1969). Intra-setting analysis: The third grade classroom as a special but instructive place. In E. Williams & H. Rausch (Eds.), *Naturalistic viewpoints in psychological research.* New York: Holt, Rinehart and Winston.

Gutek, G. L. (1986). *Education in the United States. An historical perspective.* Englewood Cliffs, NJ: Prentice-Hall.

Guyton, E., & Farokhi, E. (1987). Relationship among academic performance, basic skills, subject matter knowledge, and teaching skills of teacher education graduates. *Journal of Teacher Education, 38*(5), 37–42.

Hacker, A. (1984, April 12). The schools flunk out. *The New York Review,* pp. 35–40.

Hallinan, M. (1984). Summary and implications. In P. L. Peterson, L. C. Wilkinson, & M. Hallinan (Eds.), *The social context of instruction. Group organization and group processes.* New York: Academic Press.

Hambleton, R. K., & Eignor, D. R. (1978). *A practitioner's guide to criterion-referenced test development, validation, and test score usage.* Laboratory of Psychometric and Evaluative Research Report No. 70. Amherst: University of Massachusetts, School of Education.

Hambleton, R. K., Eignor, D. R., & Swaminathan, H. (1978). *Criterion referenced test development and validation methods.* Amherst: University of Massachusetts, AERA Precision Materials Laboratory of Psychometric and Evaluation Research.

Haney, W., Madaus, G. F., & Kreitzer, A. (1987). Charms talismanic: Testing teachers for the improvement of American education. In E. Rothkopf (Ed.), *Review of research in education* (Vol 14). Washington, DC: American Educational Research Association.

Hartford, B. S. (1982). Issues in bilingualism: A view to the future. In B. Harford, A. Valdman, & C. R. Foster (Eds.), *Issues in*

international bilingual education. New York: Plenum.

Hartley, D. (1978). Teachers' definitions of boys and girls: Some consequences. *Research in Education, 20,* 23–35.

Hawkins, D. (1973). What it means to teach. *Teachers College Record, 75*(1), 7–16.

Heibert, E. H. (1983). The examination of ability grouping for reading instruction. *Reading Research Quarterly, 18,* 231–255.

Henry, J. (1957). Attitude organization in elementary school classrooms. *American Journal of Orthopsychiatry, 27,* 117–123.

Henry, J. (1971). *Essays on education.* New York: Penguin.

Hewett, F. M., & Forness, S. R. (1984). *Education of special learners.* Boston: Allyn & Bacon.

Hilgard, E. R. (1958). *Theories of learning.* New York: Appleton-Century-Crofts.

Hirst, P. H. (1967). Public and private values and religious educational content. In T. R. Sizer (Ed.), *Religion and public education.* Boston: Houghton Mifflin.

Hirst, P. H., & Peters, R. S. (1970). *The logic of education.* London: Routledge & Kegan Paul.

Hobbes, T. (1651). *Leviathan.* (Available in many editions)

Hodgkinson, H. L. (1982). What's still right with education. *Phi Delta Kappan, 64,* 231–235.

Hodgson, G. (1973). Do schools make a difference? *Atlantic Monthly, 231,* 35–46.

Holmes, E. G. A. (1911). *What is and what might be: A study of education in general, and elementary in particular.* London: Constable.

*Holmes Group Executive Board. (1986). *Tomorrow's teachers: A report of the Holmes Group.* East Lansing, MI: Holmes Group.

Holt, J. (1964). *How children fail.* Marshfield, MA: Pitman.

Holt, J. (1981). *Teach your own.* New York: Delacorte/Seymour Lawrence.

Houts, P. L. (1975). Standardized testing in America. *National Elementary Principal, 54*(6), 2–3.

Hubner, K. (1983). *Critique of*

scientific reason (P. R. Dixon Jr. & H. M. Dixon, Trans.). Chicago: University of Chicago Press.

Hunter, M. (1979). Teaching in decision making. *Educational Leadership, 37*(1), 62–67.

Hutchins, R. (1936). *The higher learning in America.* New Haven: Yale University Press.

Hutchins, R. (1953). *The conflict in education in a democratic society.* Westport, CT: Greenwood Press.

Hyde, J. S. (1981). How large are cognitive gender differences? A meta-analysis using w^2 and *d.* *American Psychologist, 36,* 892–901.

Jackson, G., & Cosca, C. (1974). The inequality of educational opportunity in the southwest: An observation study of ethnically mixed classrooms. *American Educational Research Journal, 11,* 219–229.

Jackson, P. W. (1968). *Life in classrooms.* New York: Holt, Rinehart and Winston.

Jackson, P. W. (1969). *Technology and the teacher. The schools and the challenge of innovation.* Supplementary Paper No. 23, Committee for Economic Development, New York, 127–154.

Jackson, P. W. (1986). *The practice of teaching.* New York: Teachers College Press.

Jackson, S. E., & Maslach, C. (1982). After-effects of job related stress: Families as victims. *Journal of Occupational Behavior, 3,* 63–77.

James, T. (1982). *Public versus non-public education in historical perspective.* Stanford, CA: Stanford University Institute for Research on Educational Finance and Governance.

Johnson, D. W., Johnson, R. T., Holubec, E. J., & Roy, P. (1984). *Circles of learning: Cooperation in the classroom.* Alexandria, VA: Association for Supervision and Curriculum Development.

Joseph, P. B., & Green, N. (1986). Perspectives on reasons for becoming teachers. *Journal of Teacher Education, 37*(6), 28–33.

Jung, R. (1982). *Nonpublic school students in Title I ESEA programs: A question of "equal" service.* Washington, DC: Advanced Technology.

Kagan, J., & Messer, S. B. (1975). A reply to "Some misgivings about the Matching Familiar Figures Test as a measure of reflection-impulsivity." *Developmental Psychology, 11,* 224–248.

Kamin, J., & Erickson, D. (1981, April). *Parent choice of schooling in British Columbia: Preliminary findings.* Paper presented at the meeting of the American Education Research Association, Los Angeles.

Kane, P. R. (1987). Public or independent schools: Does where you teach make a difference? *Phi Delta Kappan, 69,* 286–289.

Karmos, A. H., & Jacko, C. M. (1977). The role of significant others during the student teaching experience. *Journal of Teacher Education, 28*(5), 51–55.

Katona, G. (1940). *Organizing and memorizing.* New York: Columbia University Press.

Katz, M. (1968). *The irony of early school reform.* Cambridge, MA: Harvard University Press.

Kellaghan, T. (1977). *The evaluation of an intervention programme for disadvantaged children.* Slough, England: NFER Publishing Co.

Kellaghan, T., Madaus, G. F., & Airasian, P. W. (1982). *The effects of standardized testing.* Boston: Kluwer-Nijhoff.

Kilpatrick, J. (1977, June 28). Teaching by the book pays off. *Denver Post.*

Kisiel, M. (1980). *Design for change: A guide to new careers.* New York: New Viewpoints/Vision Books.

Klitgaard, R. D., & Hall, G. R. (1975). Are there unusually effective schools? *Journal of Human Resources, 10,* 90–106.

Kogan, N., & Wallach, M. A. (1964). *Risk taking: A study in cognition and personality.* New York: Holt, Rinehart and Winston.

Kohlberg, L. (1969). Stage and sequence: The cognitive-developmental approach to socialization. In D. A. Goslin (Ed.), *Handbook of socialization theory and research.* Chicago: Rand McNally.

Kohlberg, L. (1975). The cognitive-developmental approach to moral education. *Phi Delta Kappan, 56,* 670–678.

Krathwohl, D. R., Bloom, B. S., & Masia, B. B. (1964). *Taxonomy of educational objectives: The classification of educational goals. Handbook 2. Affective domain.* New York: McKay.

Kraushaar, O. F. (1972). *American nonpublic schools: Patterns of diversity.* Baltimore: Johns Hopkins University Press.

Kraushaar, O. F. (1976). *Private schools: From the puritans to the present.* Bloomington, IN: Phi Delta Kappa.

Kulik, J., Kulik, C., & Cohen, P. (1979). Research on auto-tutorial instruction: A meta-analysis of comparative studies. *Research in Higher Education, 11,* 321–341.

Lampe, P. (1973). *Comparative study of the assimilation of Mexican-Americans: Parochial schools vs. public schools.* Ph.D. dissertation, Louisiana State University, Baton Rouge, LA.

Land, M. L. (1985). Vagueness and clarity in the classroom. In T. Husen & T. N. Postlethwaite (Eds.), *International encyclopedia of education: Research and studies.* Oxford: Pergamon.

LaPointe, A. E. (1984). The good news about American education. *Phi Delta Kappan, 65,* 663–667.

Lasley, T. J., & Wayson, W. W. (1982). Characteristics of schools with good discipline. *Educational Leadership, 40,* 28–37.

Lauro, D. R. (1982). Teacher evaluation: The union's point of view. *CEDR Quarterly, Phi Delta Kappan, 15,* 19–22.

Lefcourt, H. M. (1976). *Locus of control: Current trends in theory and research.* New York: Halstead.

Lennon, R. (1978). Perspectives on intelligence testing. *Measurement in Education, 9*(2), 1–8.

Lerner, B. (1981). Vouchers for literacy: Second chance legislation. *Phi Delta Kappan, 63,* 252–254.

Levenson, H. (1981). Differentiating among internality, powerful others, and change. In H. M.

Lefcourt (Ed.), *Research with the locus of control construct: Vol 1. Assessment methods.* New York: Academic Press.

Levin, H. M. (1974). A conceptual framework for accountability in education. *School Review, 82,* 363–391.

Levine, D., Lachowicz, H., Oxman, K., & Tangeman, A. (1972). The home environment of students in a high achieving inner-city parochial school and a nearby public school. *Sociology of Education, 45,* 435–445.

Lewis, E. G. (1981). *Bilingualism and bilingual education.* New York: Pergamon.

Lieberman, M. (1956). *Education as a profession.* Englewood Cliffs, NJ: Prentice-Hall.

Lieberman, M. (1981). Teacher bargaining: An autopsy. *Phi Delta Kappan, 63,* 231–234.

Lightfoot, S. L. (1983). *The good high school: Portraits of character and culture.* New York: Basic Books.

Lipsitz, J. (1981). Educating the early adolescent. *American Education, 17,* 38–42.

Lipsitz, J. (1982). Schools that succeed in teaching the early adolescent. *Education Digest, 47*(8), 26–30.

Little, J. W. (1982). The effective principal. *American Education, 18*(7), 38–42.

Little, J. W. (1987). Teachers as colleagues. In Richardson-Koehler (Ed.), *Educators' handbook: A research perspective.* New York: Longman.

Lloyd, A. L. (1967). *Folk song in England.* London: Lawrence & Wishart.

Lortie, D. C. (1975). *Schoolteacher: A sociological study.* Chicago: University of Chicago Press.

Lortie, D. C. (1986). Teacher status in Dade county: A case of structural strain? *Phi Delta Kappan, 67,* 568–575.

Luiten, J., Ames, W., & Ackerson, G. (1980). A meta-analysis of the aspects of advance organizers on learning and retention. *American Educational Research Journal, 17,* 211–218.

Lukowski, S., & Piton, M. (1980). *Strategy and tactics for getting a government job.* Washington, DC: Potomac Books.

Lunneborg, P. W., & Wilson, V. M. (1982). *To work: A guide for women college graduates.* Englewood Cliffs, NJ: Prentice-Hall.

Maccoby, E. E., & Jacklin, C. N. (1974). *The psychology of sex differences.* Stanford, CA: Stanford University Press.

MacDonald-Ross (1973). Behavioral objectives: A critical review. *Instructional Science, 2,* 1–52.

MacKenzie, D. E. (1983). Research for school improvement: An appraisal of some recent trends. *Educational Researcher, 12*(14), 5–17.

Madaus, G. F. (Ed.) (1983). *The courts, validity and minimum competency testing.* Boston: Kluwer-Nijhoff.

Madaus, G. F. (1985). Test scores as administrative mechanisms in educational policy. *Phi Delta Kappan, 66,* 611–617.

Madaus, G. F. (1988). Testing and the curriculum: From compliant servant to dictatorial monster. In L. Tanner (Ed.), *Critical issues in curriculum: The 1988 NSSE Yearbook.* Chicago: University of Chicago Press.

Madaus, G. F., Airasian, P. W., & Kellaghan, T. (1980). *School effectiveness: A reassessment of the evidence.* New York: McGraw-Hill.

Madaus, G. F., & Elmore, R. (1973). Testimony submitted to the Education and Labor Committee of the House of Representatives on Bill HR 5163. Cambridge, MA: Huron Institute, Harvard University (mimeographed).

Madaus, G. F., & Greaney, V. (1985). The Irish experience in competency testing: Implications for American education. *American Journal of Education, 93,* 268–294.

Madaus, G. F., Kellaghan, T., Rakow, E. A., & King, D. J. (1979). The sensitivity of measures of school effectiveness. *Harvard Educational Review, 49,* 207–230.

Madaus, G. F., & Pullin, D. (1987). Teacher certification tests: Do they really measure what we need to know? *Phi Delta Kappan, 69*(1), 31–37.

Madaus, G. F., & Rippey, R. M. (1966). Zeroing in on the STEP writing test: What does it tell a teacher? *Journal of Educational Measurement, 3,* 19–25.

Madsen, D. L. (1974). *Early national education 1776–1830.* New York: Wiley.

Mansfield, R. S., & Busse, T. V. (1981). *The psychology of creativity and discovery: Scientists and their work.* Chicago: Nebon-Hall.

Marland, S. P. (1972). *Education of the gifted and talented:* Report to the Congress of the United States by the U.S. Commissioner of Education, and background papers submitted to the U.S. Officer of Education. Washington, DC: U.S. Government Printing Office.

Marler, C. D. (1975). *Philosophy and schooling.* Boston: Allyn & Bacon.

Marsh, H. W., Smith, I. D., & Barnes, J. (1983). Multitrait-multimethod analyses of the self-description questionnaire: Student-teacher agreement on multidimensional ratings of student self-concept. *American Educational Research Journal, 20,* 333–357.

McCandless, B. R., Roberts, A., & Starnes, T. (1972). Teachers' marks, achievement test and scores, and aptitude relations with respect to social class, race and sex. *Journal of Educational Psychology, 63,* 153–159.

McCarthy, M. M., & Cameron, N. H. (1981). *Public school law: Teachers' and students' rights.* Boston: Allyn & Bacon.

McCormack-Larkin, M., & Kritek, W. J. (1982). Milwaukee's project RISE. *Educational Leadership, 40,* 16–21.

McDonald, F. J. (1973). The criteria for accountability: Pupil or professional performance. *Journal of Educational Evaluation, 4,* 6.

McKenna, B. (1982). Teacher evaluation: A teacher organization perspective. *CEDR Quarterly, Phi Delta Kappan, 15,* 14–17.

McLaughlin, B. (1978). *Second-language acquisition in childhood.* Hillsdale, NJ: Erlbaum.

McNeil, J. D. (1977). *Curriculum: A comprehensive introduction.* Boston: Little, Brown.

McNeil, L. M. (1988). Contradictions of control, Part 2. Teachers, students, and curriculum. *Phi Delta Kappan, 69,* 432–438.

Mergendoller, J. R., & Marchman, V. A. (1987). Friends and associates. In V. Richardson-Koehler (Ed.), *Educators' handbook. A research perspective.* New York: Longman.

Merton, R. K. (1948). The self-fulfilling prophecy. *Antioch Review,* Summer, 193–210.

Messick, S., & Associates. (1976). *Individuality in learning.* San Francisco: Jossey-Bass.

Miles, M. B., & Kaufman, T. (1985). A directory of programs. In R. M. J. Kyle (1985), *Reaching for excellence: An effective schools sourcebook.* Washington, DC: U.S. Government Printing Office.

Millerson, G. (1964). *The qualifying associations.* London: Routledge & Kegan Paul.

Millman, J. (Ed.). (1981). *Handbook of teacher education.* Beverly Hills, CA: Sage.

Mirga, T. (1988, January 20). Court upholds censorship of student press. *Education Week,* pp. 1, 28.

Mizell, M. Hayes. (1981). Citizens' model for accountability: How people try to make schools work for their children. In J. F. Schwartz & M. S. Garet (Eds.), *Assessment for accountability.* Report of a study panel to the Ford Foundation and the National Institute of Education. Cambridge: Massachusetts Institute of Technology.

Moore, T. W. (1982). *Philosophy of education. An introduction.* Boston: Routledge & Kegan Paul.

Morphet, E. L., Johns, R. L., & Reiler, T. (1982). *Educational organization and administration.* Englewood Cliffs, NJ: Prentice-Hall.

Morris, V. C., Crowson, R. L., Porter-Gehrie, C., & Hurwitz, E. (1984). *Principals in action.* Columbus, OH: Merrill.

Morrison, J., & Hodgkins, B. (1971). Research note: The effectiveness of Catholic schools: A comparative analysis. *Sociology of Education, 44,* 119–131.

Moss, M. H. (1973). *Deprivation and disadvantage?* Bletchley, Buckinghamshire, England: Open University Press.

Mosteller, F., & Moynihan, D. P. A. (1972). A pathbreaking report. In F. Mosteller & D. P. Moynihan (Eds.), *On equality of educational opportunity.* New York: Vintage Books.

Moumoto, K., Gregory, J., & Butler, P. (1973). Notes on the Context for Learning. *Harvard Educational Review, 43,* 245–257.

Murphy, J. T., & Cohen, K. (1974, Summer). Accountability in education—the Michigan experience. *The Public Interest.* No. 30, 53–87.

Murphy, J. F., Weil, M., Hallinger, P., & Mitman, A. (1983). Translating high expectations into school policies and classroom practices. *Educational Leadership, 40,* 22–26.

Myers, R. E., & Torrance, P. E. (1966). *Plots, puzzles, and ploys.* Boston: Ginn.

National Association of Elementary School Principals. (1984). *The education almanac, 1984–1985: Facts and figures about our nation's system of education.* Reston, VA: NAESP.

National Association of Elementary School Principals. (1985). *The education almanac, 1985–1986. Facts and figures about our nation's system of education.* Reston, VA: NAESP.

National Center for Education Statistics. (1982). *The condition of education: A statistical report.* Washington, DC: U.S. Government Printing Office.

National Center for Education Statistics. (1982). *Digest of education statistics 1982.* Washington, DC: U.S. Department of Education.

*National Commission on Excellence in Education. (1983). *A nation at risk: The imperative for educational reform.* Washington, DC: U.S. Government Printing Office.

National Council of Teachers of English. (1975). *Commonsense and*

testing in English. Urbana, IL: NCTE.

National Education Association. (1972). *Report of the Task Force on Corporal Punishment.* Washington, DC: NEA.

National Education Association. (1987). *Handbook.* Washington, DC: NEA.

*National Governors' Association. (1986). *Time for results: The Governors 1991 report on education.* Washington, DC: NGA.

National School Boards Association. (1977). *Standardized achievement testing.* (Research Report 1977-1). Washington, DC: NSBA.

*National Science Board Commission on Precollege Education in Mathematics, Science and Technology. (1983). *Educating Americans for the 21st century.* Washington, DC: National Science Foundation.

Nault, R. L., & Vchitelle, S. (1981). School choice in the public sector: A case study of parental decision making. In M. E. Manley-Casimir (Ed.), *Family choice in schooling: Issues and dilemmas.* Lexington, MA: Lexington Books.

NCWC Brief, Memorandum on the impact of the First Amendment to the Constitution upon federal aid to education. (1981). *Georgetown Law Review, 50,* 431–439.

Neill, S. B. (1978). *The competency movement.* AASA Critical Issues Report. Sacramento, CA: Education News.

Nevin, D., & Bills, R. E. (1976). *The schools that fear built.* Washington, DC: Acropolis Books.

Non-Catholic Christian schools growing fast. (1983, April 13). *The New York Times.*

Northeast Regional Exchange. (1983). *Education under study: An analysis of recent major reports.* Chelmsford, MA: Northeast Regional Exchange.

Odden, A., & Augenblick, J. (1981, January). School policy makers view school finance in the 1980s. *Education Digest,* pp. 13–15.

Office of Technology Assessment. (1982). *Information technology and its impact on American education.* Washington, DC: OTA.

Oja, S. N., & Ham, M. C. (1984). A

cognitive-developmental approach to collaborative action research with teachers. *Teachers College Record, 86,* 171–192.

O'Leary, K. D., & O'Leary, S. G. (1977). *Classroom management: The successful use of behavior modification* (2nd ed.). New York: Pergamon.

Ornstein, A. C. (1982). Curriculum contrasts: A historical overview. *Phi Delta Kappan, 63,* 404–408.

Otto, L. B., Call, V. R., & Spenner, K. I. (1981). *Design for a study of entry into careers.* Lexington, MA: Lexington Books.

Palardy, J. M. (1969). What teachers believe—What children achieve. *Elementary School Journal, 69,* 370–374.

Palker, P. (1980, May/June). Tenure: Do we need it? *Teacher, 97,* 40.

Papert, S. (1980). *Mindstorms: Children, computers and powerful ideas.* New York: Basic Books.

Parnes, S. J., Noller, R. B., Biondi, A. M. (1977). *Guide to creative action* (rev. ed.). New York: Scribner.

Passow, A. H. (Ed.). (1970). *Deprivation and disadvantage: Nature and manifestations.* Hamburg: UNESCO Institute for Education.

Passow, A. H., & Elliott, D. L. (1968). The nature and needs of the educationally disadvantaged. In A. H. Passow (Ed.), *Developing programs for the educationally disadvantaged.* New York: Teachers College Press.

Patton, M. Q. (1975). Understanding the gobbledygook: A people's guide to standardized test results and statistics. In V. A. Perrone & M. D. Cohen (Eds.), *Testing and evaluation: New views.* Washington, DC: Association for Childhood Education.

Persell, C. (1977). *Education and inequality: The roots and results of stratification in America's schools.* New York: Free Press.

Peterson, P. E. (1983). Background paper commissioned by the Twentieth Century Fund Task Force on Federal Elementary and Secondary Education Policy. In Twentieth Century Fund, *Making the grade. Report of the Twentieth Century Fund Task Force on*

Federal Elementary and Secondary Education Policy. New York: Twentieth Century Fund.

Piaget, J., & Inhelder, B. (1969). *The psychology of the child.* London: Routledge & Kegan Paul.

Pintrich, P. R., Cross, D. R., Kozma, R. B., & McKeachie, W. J. (1986). Instructional psychology. In M. R. Rosenweig & L. W. Porter (Eds.), *Annual review of psychology* (Vol. 37). Palo Alto, CA: Annual Reviews Inc.

Pipho, C. (1984). Stateline: A year of transition for educators. *Phi Delta Kappan, 65,* 661–662.

Pipho, C., & Hadley, C. (1984). State activity—minimum competency testing. *Clearinghouse Notes.* Denver: Education Commission of the States.

Pittman, N. L., & Pittman, T. S. (1979). Effects of amount of helplessness training and internal-external locus of control on mood and performance. *Journal of Personality and Social Psychology, 37,* 39–47.

Porter, A. C. (1983). The role of testing in effective schools. *American Education, 19,* 25–28.

Postman, N. (1981). The day our children disappear. *Phi Delta Kappan, 62,* 382–386.

Power, E. J. (1982). *Philosophy of education. Studies in philosophies, schooling, and educational policies.* Englewood Cliffs, NJ: Prentice-Hall.

Purdom, D. M., & Fardig, G. E. (1985). Specifying student behavior. In D. M. Purdom, & G. E. Fardig (Eds.), *Florida Teacher Performance Development Program.* (Learning Package 14). Tallahassee: State of Florida Department of Education.

Purkey, S. C., & Smith, M. S. (1982). Too soon to cheer? Synthesis of research on effective schools. *Educational Leadership, 40,* 64–69.

Purkey, S. C., & Smith, M. S. (1983). Effective schools: A review. *The Elementary School Journal, 83,* 425–452.

Quintero, A. (1981). Accountability and education: An outline of a model for promoting democracy and learning. In J. F. Schwartz & M. S. Garet (Eds.), *Assessment for accountability.* Report of a study panel to the Ford Foundation and the National Institute of Education. Cambridge: Massachusetts Institute of Technology.

Quintilian, M. F. The duties of a schoolmaster. In C. M. Fuess & E. S. Basford (Eds.), (1947). *Unseen harvests: A treasury of teaching.* New York: Macmillan.

Ravitch, D. (1983). *The troubled crusade. American education 1945–1980.* New York: Basic Books.

Reissman, F. (1962). *The culturally deprived child.* New York: Harper & Row.

Renzulli, J. S., Reis, S. M., & Smith, L. H. (1981). *The revolving door identification model.* Mansfield Center, CT: Creative Learning Press.

Richardson Foundation. (1985). *A national investigation of educational opportunities for able learners.* Austin: University of Texas Press.

Richardson-Koehler, V. (Ed.). (1987). *Educators' handbook. A research perspective.* New York: Longman.

Rippa, S. A. (1969). *Educational ideas in America. A documentary history.* New York: McKay.

Rippa, S. A. (1980). *Education in a free society: An American history* (4th ed.). New York: Longman.

Rist, R. C. (1970). Student social class and teacher expectations: The self-fulfilling prophecy in ghetto education. *Harvard Educational Review, 40,* 411–451.

Rist, R. C. (1977). On understanding the process of schooling: The contribution of labeling theory. In J. Karabel & A. H. Habey (Eds.), *Power and ideology in education.* New York: Oxford University Press.

Rosenbaum, J. E. (1984). The social organization of instructional grouping. In P. L. Peterson, L. C. Wilkinson, & M. Hallinan (Eds.), *The social context of instruction. Group organization and group processes.* New York: Academic Press.

Rosenfield, P., Lambert, N. M., & Black, A. (1985). Desk arrangement effects on pupil classroom behavior. *Journal of Educational Psychology, 77,* 101–108.

Rosenshine, B. V. (1980). How time is spent in elementary classrooms. In C. Denham & A. Lieberman (Eds.), *Time to learn.* Washington, DC: National Institute for Education.

Rosenshine, B. V., & Furst, N. (1973). The use of direct observation to study teaching. In R. M. W. Travers (Ed.), *Second handbook of research on teaching.* Chicago: Rand McNally.

Rosenshine, B. V., & Stevens, R. (1986). Teaching functions. In M. Wittrock (Ed.), *Handbook of research on teaching* (3rd ed.). New York: Macmillan.

Rosenthal, R., & Jacobson, L. (1968). *Pygmalion in the classroom. Teacher expectation and pupil intellectual development.* New York: Holt, Rinehart and Winston.

Rutter, M. (1983). School effects on pupil progress: Research findings and policy implications. *Child Development, 54,* 1–29.

Rutter, M., Maughan, B., Mortimore, P., Ouston, J., & Smith, A. (1979). *Fifteen thousand hours: Secondary schools and their effects on children.* Cambridge, MA: Harvard University Press.

Sanders, D. (1983). *Computers today.* New York: McGraw-Hill.

Schwab, R. L. (1983). Teacher burnout: Moving beyond psychobabble. *Theory into Practice, 22*(1), 21–26.

Schwab, R. L., & Iwanicki, E. F. (1982). Perceived role conflict, role ambiguity and teacher burnout. *Education Administration Quarterly, 18,* 60–74.

Schwab, R. L., Jackson, S., & Schuler, R. (1986). Educator burnout: Source and consequences. *Educational Research Quarterly, 7,* 5–17.

Schwartz, J. L. (1977). A is to B as C is to anything at all: The illogic of IQ tests. In P. Houts (Ed.), *The myth of measurability.* New York: Hart.

Schwartz, J. F., & Garet, M. S. (Eds.) (1981). *Assessment for accountability.* Report of a study panel to the Ford Foundation and the National Institute of

Education. Cambridge, MA: Massachusetts Institute of Technology.

Seeley, D. S. (1979). Reducing the confrontation over teacher accountability. *Phi Delta Kappan, 61,* 248–251.

Seligman, M. E. P. (1973). *Helplessness: On depression, development, and death.* San Francisco: Freeman.

Shanber, A. (1986, November 14). No way to grade teachers. *St. Louis Post Despatch,* p. 36.

Shane, H. G. (1960). Grouping in the elementary school. *Phi Delta Kappa, 61,* 313–319.

Shavelson, R. J., Hubner, J. J., & Stanton, G. C. (1976). Self-concept: Validation of construct interpretations. *Review of Educational Research, 46,* 407–441.

Shavelson, R. J., Webb, N. M., & Burstein, L. (1986). Measurement of teaching. In M. C. Wittrock (Ed.), *Handbook of research on teaching* (3rd ed.). New York: Macmillan.

Shulman, L. S. (1986). Paradigms and research programs in the study of teaching: A contemporary perspective. In M. Wittrock (Ed.), *Handbook of research on teaching* (3rd ed.). New York: Macmillan.

Silverman, H., & Shearer, A. P. (1985). Using questioning techniques. In G. E. Fardig & G. E. Purdom (Eds.), *Florida Performance Development Program.* (Learning Package 5). Tallahassee: State of Florida Department of Education.

Singer, J. D., & Butler, J. A. (1987). The education of all handicapped children act: Schools as agents of social reform. *Harvard Educational Review, 57,* 125–152.

Sizer, T. R. (1964). *The age of the academies.* New York: Teachers College Press.

*Sizer, T. R. (Ed.). (1984a). *Horace's compromise. The dilemma of the American high school.* Boston: Houghton Mifflin.

Sizer, T. R. (1984b). Appendix III. In M. J. Adler, *Paideia problems and possibilities. A consideration of questions raised by the Paideia Proposal.* New York: Macmillan.

Sjöstrand, W. (1973). *Freedom and equality.* Stockholm: Almqvist & Wiksell.

Skinner, B. F. (1953). *Science and human behavior.* New York: Macmillan.

Skinner, B. F. (1954). The science of learning and the art of teaching. *Harvard Educational Review, 24,* 86–97.

Slavin, R. E. (1983). *Cooperative learning.* New York: Longman.

Slavin, R. E. (1987). Ability grouping and student achievement in elementary schools: A best-evidence synthesis. *Review of Educational Research, 57,* 293–336.

Smith, F. (1986). *Insult to intelligence: The bureaucratic invasion of our classrooms.* New York: Arbor House.

Smith, M. S. (1976). Discussion: Evaluation of educational programs. In C. C. Abt (Ed.), *The evaluation of social programs.* Beverly Hills, CA: Sage.

Smith, S. D. (1987). Computer attitudes of teachers and students in relationship to gender and grade level. *Journal of Educational Computing Research, 3,* 479–499.

Snow, R. E. (1969). Unfinished *Pygmalion. Contemporary Psychology, 14,* 197–199.

Snow, R. E., & Lohman, D. F. (1984). Toward a theory of cognitive aptitude for learning from instruction. *Journal of Educational Psychology, 76,* 347–376.

Snyder, T. D. (1987). *Digest of education statistics, 1987.* Washington, DC: U.S. Government Printing Office.

Somers, R. (1969). *Personal space: The behavioral basis of design.* Englewood Cliffs, NJ: Prentice-Hall.

Southeastern Public Education Program. (1978). A citizen's introduction to minimum competence programs for students. Columbia, SC: American Friends Service Committee.

*Southern Regional Education Board. (1983). *Meeting the need for quality: Action in the south.* Atlanta: SREB.

Spearman, C. (1927). *The abilities of man.* New York: Macmillan.

Spencer, H. (1891). *Education: Intellectual, moral and physical.* London: Williams and Norgate.

Sroufe, L. A. (1970). A methodological and philosophical critique of intervention-oriented research. *Developmental Psychology, 2,* 140–145.

Stake, R. E. (1973). School accountability law. *Journal of Educational Evaluation, 4*(2), 1–3.

Staub, S. E. (1981). Compulsory unionism and the demise of education. *Phi Delta Kappan, 83,* 235–236.

Stebbins, R. (1975). *Teachers and meaning: Definitions of classroom situations.* Leiden, Netherlands: E. J. Bull.

Stedman, L. C., & Smith, M. (1983). Recent reform proposals for American education. *Contemporary Education Review, 27,* 85–104.

Stern, J. D. (1987). *The condition of education: A statistical report.* Washington, DC: Office of Educational Research and Improvement, U.S. Department of Education.

Sternberg, R. J. (1982). Reasoning, problem solving, and intelligence. In R. J. Sternberg (Ed.), *Handbook of human intelligence.* New York: Cambridge University Press.

Sternberg, R. J. (1985). *Beyond IQ: A triarchic theory of human intelligence.* New York: Cambridge University Press.

Sternberg, R. J. (1986a). Teaching critical thinking, Part 2: Possible solutions. *Phi Delta Kappan, 67,* 277–280.

Sternberg, R. J. (1986b). The future of intelligence testing. *Educational Measurement Issues and Practice, 5*(3), 19–22.

Strang, R. (1958). The nature of giftedness. In N. B. Henry (Ed.), *The fifty-seventh yearbook of the National Society for the Study of Education, Part II: Education for the gifted.* Chicago: NSSE.

Stufflebeam, D. L. (1987). Joint committee to develop standards for evaluation of educational personnel. *Education Leadership, 44*(7), 61.

Sullivan, P. J. (1983). *Comparing

efficiency between public and private schools. Stanford, CA: Stanford University Institute for Research on Educational Finance and Goverance.

Swetz, F. J. (1978). *Socialist mathematics education.* Southampton, PA: Burgundy Press.

Sykes, G. (1983). Contradictions, errors, and promises unfulfilled: A contemporary account of the status of teaching. *Phi Delta Kappan, 65,* 87–93.

Tannenbaum, A. (1983). *Gifted children: Psychological and educational perspectives.* New York: Macmillan.

Tannenbaum, A. (1985). The rights of the gifted child. In V. Greaney (Ed.), *The rights of children.* New York: Irvington.

*Task Force on Education for Economic Growth. (1983). *Action for excellence: A comprehensive plan to improve our nation's schools.* Denver: Education Commission of the States.

*Task Force on Education for Economic Growth. (1984). *Action in the states.* Denver: Education Commission of the States.

Taylor, I. A. (1975). An emerging view of creative actions. In I. A. Taylor & J. W. Getzels (Eds.), *Perspectives in creativity.* Chicago: Aldine.

Taylor, R. (Ed.) (1980). *The computer in the school: Tool, tutor, tutee.* New York: Teachers College Press.

Terman, L. M., & Associates. (1925). *Genetic studies of genius: Vol. 1. Mental and physical traits of a thousand gifted children.* Stanford, CA: Stanford University Press.

Thiessen, E. J. (1981). Religious freedom and educational pluralism. In M. E. Manley-Casimir (Ed.), *Family choice in schooling: Issues and dilemmas.* Lexington, MA: Lexington Books.

Thomas, W. I., & Thomas, D. S. (1932). *The child in America.* New York: Knopf.

Thorndike, R. L. (1968). Review of "Pygmalion in the classroom." *American Educational Research Journal, 5,* 708–711.

Torshen, K. P. (1977). *The mastery approach to competency-based education.* New York: Academic Press.

Tittle, C. K. (1981). *Career and family: Sex roles and adolescent life plans.* Beverly Hills, CA: Sage.

Toong, H., & Gupta, A. (1982). Personal computers. *Scientific American, 247*(6), 87–107.

Torrance, E. P. (1974). *Torrance tests of creative thinking: Directions manual and scoring guide.* Columbus, OH: Personnel Press.

Turner, W. (1979). *Reasons for enrollment in religious schools: A case study of three recently established fundamentalist schools in Kentucky and Wisconsin.* Unpublished doctoral dissertation, University of Wisconsin, Madison.

Twentieth Century Fund Task Force on Federal Elementary and Secondary Education Policy. (1983). *Making the grade: Report of the Twentieth Century Fund Task Force on Federal Elementary and Secondary Education Policy.* New York: Author.

Tyack, D. B. (1974). *The one best system. A history of American urban education.* Cambridge, MA: Harvard University Press.

Tyler, L. (1974). *Individual differences: Abilities and motivational directions.* Englewood Cliffs, NJ: Prentice-Hall.

Tyler, L. (1978). *Individuality: Human possibilities and personal choice in the psychological development of men and women.* San Francisco: Jossey-Bass.

Tyler, R. W. (1949). *Basic principles of curriculum and instruction.* Chicago: University of Chicago Press.

Upchurch, R. L., & Lockhead, J. (1987). Computers and higher order thinking skills. In V. Richardson-Koehler (Ed.), *Educators' handbook: A research perspective.* New York: Longman.

U'Ren, M. (1971). The image of women in textbooks. In V. Gornick & B. Moran (Eds.), *Women in sexist society.* New York: Basic Books.

U.S. Bureau of Education (1918). Cardinal principles of secondary education. Washington, DC: U.S. Government Printing Office.

U.S. Department of Education. (1983). State boards of education. In *Educational governance in the states: A status report on state boards of education, chief state school officers, and state education agencies* (Publication No. 1983-381-054: 103). Washington, DC: U.S. Government Printing Office.

U.S. Department of Education. (1984). *The condition of bilingual education in the nation, 1984.* Washington, DC: U.S. Department of Education.

Uzzell, L. (1985). Vouchers and hope. *Educational Freedom, 18*(2), 1–6.

Valente, W. (1986). *Law in the schools.* Columbus, OH: Merrill.

Vernon, P. E. (1961). *The structure of human abilities* (2nd ed.). London: Methuen.

Vlaanderen, R. B. (1983). Testing for teacher certification. *ECS Issuegram* (Issue No. 7). Denver: Education Commission of the States.

Walberg, H. J. (1975). Psychological theories of educational individualization. In H. Talmage (Ed.), *Systems of individualized education.* Berkeley, CA: McCutchan.

Waller, W. (1967). *The sociology of teaching.* New York: Wiley.

Walton, S. (1983, December 7). State's reform efforts increase as focus of issues shifts. *Education Week,* p. 5.

Warren, D. R. (1978). A past for the present. In D. R. Warren (Ed.), *History, education, and public policy.* Berkeley, CA: McCutchan.

Weiler, H. N. (1982). Education, public confidence, and the legitimacy of the modern state: Do we have a crisis? *Phi Delta Kappan, 64,* 9–14.

Weinstein, C. E., & Mayer, R. E. (1986). The teaching of learning strategies. In M. C. Wittrock (Ed.), *Handbook of research on teaching* (3rd ed.). New York: Macmillan.

Weinstein, R. S. (1986). The teaching of reading and children's awareness of teacher expectations.

In T. E. Raphael (Ed.), *Contexts of school-based literacy.* New York: Random House.

West, E. G. (1981). Choice of monopoly in education? *Policy Review, 15,* 103–117.

Whipple, G. M. (Ed.). (1925). *Adapting the schools to individual difference.* Twenty-fourth Yearbook of the National Society for the Study of Education, Part 2. Chicago: NSSE.

Whitty, G., & Young, N. (1976). *Explorations in the politics of school knowledge.* Nafferton, Humberside, England: Nafferton Books.

Wigdor, A. K., & Garner, W. R. (1982). Part 1: Report of the Committee on Ability Testing, Assembly of Behavioral and Social Sciences National Research Council. In A. K. Wigdor & W. R. Garner (Eds.), *Ability testing: Uses, consequences, and controversies.* Washington, DC: National Academy Press.

Wiley, D. E., & Blaunstein, P. (Eds.). (1983). *State boards of education: Quality leadership.* Alexandria, VA: National Association of State Boards of Education.

Wiley, D. E., & Harneschfeger, A. (1974). Explosion of a myth: Quality of schooling and exposure to instruction, major educational vehicles. *Educational Researcher, 3*(4), 7–12.

Wingo, G. M. (1965). *The philosophy of American education.* Lexington, MA: Heath.

Wise, A. (1979). *Legislated learning.* Berkeley, CA: University of California Press.

Witkin, H. A., & Goodenough, D. R. (1981). *Cognitive styles: Essence and origins—Field dependence and independence.* New York: International Universities Press.

Witkin, H. A., Moore, C. A., Goodenough, D. R., & Cox, P. W. (1977). Field-dependent and field-independent cognitive styles and their educational implications. *Review of Educational Research, 47,* 1–64.

Wittrock, M. C. (Ed.) (1986). *Handbook of research on teaching* (3rd ed.). New York: Macmillan.

Witty, P. A. (1958). Who are the gifted? In N. B. Henry (Ed.), *The fifty-seventh yearbook of the National Society for the Study of Education, Part II: Education for the gifted.* Chicago: NSSE.

Wolfle, D. L. (Ed.) (1969). *The discovery of talent.* Cambridge, MA: Harvard University Press.

Woodworth, R. S. (1963). *Contemporary schools of psychology.* London: Methuen.

Woolfolk, A. E., & Brooks, D. M. (1983). Nonverbal communication in teaching. In E. W. Gordon (Ed.), *Review of research in education 10.* Washington, DC: American Educational Research Association.

Wynn, R. (1981). The relationship of collective bargaining and teacher salaries, 1960 to 1980. *Phi Delta Kappan, 63,* 237–242.

Yinger, R. J. (1978). *A study of teacher planning: Description and a model of preactive decision making* (Research Series No. 19). East Lansing, MI: Institute for Research on Teaching.

Yudof, M. G., et al. (1982). *Educational policy and the law.* Berkeley, CA: McCutchan.

Zambrano, A. L., & Entine, A. D. (1976). *A guide to career alternatives for academics.* New Rochelle, NY: Change Magazine Press.

Zimpher, N. L., de Voss, G. G., & Nott, D. L. (1980). A closer look at university student teacher supervision. *Journal of Teacher Education, 31*(4), 11–15.

PICTURE CREDITS

Note: Page numbers appear in boldface.

Chapter 1: **7** Bettmann Archive. **15** National Portrait Gallery, Smithsonian Institution. **16** New York Public Library Picture Collection. **29** New York Public Library Picture Collection. **33** National Portrait Gallery, London. **35** New York Public Library Picture Collection.

Chapter 2: **39** Bettmann Archive. **48** National Portrait Gallery, Smithsonian Institution. **52** Bettmann Archive.

Chapter 3: **57** © Sandra Weiner/The Image Works. **64** Yves De Braine/Black Star. **76** National Library of Medicine. **77** Sybil Shelton/Monkmeyer Press Photos.

Chapter 4: **85** © Sandra Johnson/The Picture Cube. **98** David Strickler/Monkmeyer Press Photos.

Chapter 5: **109** © Harvey R. Phillips/Click/Chicago. **126** Paul Conklin/Monkmeyer Press Photos. **122** © Vivienne della Grotta 1987/Photo Researchers.

Chapter 6: **130** © Suzanne Szasz/Photo Researchers. **132** Glynne Robinson Betts © 1981/Photo Researchers.

Chapter 7: **145** © Spencer C. Grant III/Photo Researchers. **160** © Renee Lynn/Photo Researchers. **165** Photo courtesy of The Norman Rockwell Museum at Stockbridge, MA. Printed by permission of the Estate of Norman Rockwell, © 1964 Estate of Norman Rockwell. **166** © Steve Takatsuno/The Picture Cube.

Chapter 8: **177** © Michal Heron 1980/Woodfin Camp & Associates. **185** © Bruce Roberts/Photo Researchers. **204** UPI/Bettmann Newsphotos.

Chapter 9: **210** © 1980 Will McIntyre/Photo Researchers. **218** © Robert Kalman/The Image Works. **220** © Sam C. Pierson, Jr., 1982/Photo Researchers.

Chapter 10: **233** © Elizabeth Crews/Stock, Boston. **238** © Elizabeth Crews/Stock, Boston. **248** David Strickler/Monkmeyer Press Photos. **251** Paul Conklin/Monkmeyer Press Photos.

Chapter 11: **255** © Leif Skoogfors/Woodfin Camp & Associates. **257** © Elizabeth Crews/Stock, Boston. **264** Judith D. Sedwick/The Picture Cube. **273** © Michal Heron 1981/Woodfin Camp & Associates.

Chapter 12: **281** © Chester Higgins, Jr./Photo Researchers. **286** © Elizabeth Hamlin/Stock, Boston. **290** Jean-Claude Lejeune/Stock, Boston. **293** Mimi Forsyth/Monkmeyer Press Photos.

Chapter 13: **307** © David M. Grossman/Photo Researchers. **309** © Michal Heron 1981/Woodfin Camp & Associates.

Chapter 14: **337** © Dan Chidester/The Image Works. **345** © Shelley Rotner/Omni-Photo Communications. **346** David S. Strickler/The Picture Cube.

Chapter 15: **357** © Elaine Rebman 1985/Photo Researchers. **362** © Phyllis Graber Jensen/Stock, Boston. **380** © Vivienne della Grotta 1987/Photo Researchers.

Chapter 16: **383** Janice Fullman/The Picture Cube. **398** Karen R. Preuss © 1984/Taurus Photos. **402** © Barbara Rios/Photo Researchers.

Chapter 17: **407** © David Burnett 1983/Contact/Woodfin Camp & Associates.

411 Courtesy of IBM.   **417** © Alan Carey/The Image Works.   **415** Hugh
Rogers/Monkmeyer Press Photos.

Chapter 18:   **428** UPI/Bettmann Newsphotos.

Chapter 19:   **448** © Elaine Rebman 1986/Photo Researchers.

Chapter 20:   **476** Wide World Photos.   **485** © Michal Heron/Woodfin Camp &
Associates.

INDEX

Note: *Italicized* page numbers indicate material in figures and boxes.

Ability, 258–265, 322–323, 399
Ability tests, 455–456
*Academic preparation for college:
    What students need to know
    and be able to do* (Education
    Equality Project), 479, *480,* 496,
    504
Academies, 49, 133–134
Accountability, 429–447
    expectations for programs of,
        434–437
    mechanisms of, 442–446
    questions about, 437–442
    reasons for demands for, 429–434
Accountability laws, 150–151
Achievement
    ability and, 263–265
    and accountability programs,
        435
    and cognitive style, 265–268
    decline in student, 432–433
    equality of, 36
    impact of school attendance on,
        388–389
    and locus of control, 268
    and self-concept, 269–270
    and teaching methods, 59–61
Achievement tests, 59, 75–77,
        457–461, 463, 473–474
    criterion-referenced, 460–461
    norm-referenced, 457–460
    recommendations concerning
        reform of, 497–498
*Action for excellence: A
    comprehensive plan to improve
    our nation's schools* (Task Force
    on Education for Economic
    Growth), *480, 489,* 499, 501,
    503
Action research, 190
Active learning, and cognitive
    development theory, 65
Adler, Mortimer, 492, 494, 495
Administration. *See also* Principal;
    School boards; Superintendent
    accountability of, 439, 441, 442
    college, 222–223
    reform of role of, 54–55, 501–502
    uses of standardized tests by, 463
Administrators, organizations of,
    100
Advertising, careers in, 227
Affective objectives, 340
Airasian, P., *466*
Allergic reactions, 321
*America's competitive challenge:
    The need for a national
    response* (Business-Higher
    Education Forum), *480,* 504

American Federation of Teachers
    (AFT), 87, 100, 172, 188,
    190–193, *195,* 201–202, 429
American School Counselors
    Association (ASCA), 125–128
American Standard Code for
    Information Interchange
    (ASCII), 409
Analog computers, 408
Apprenticeships, 42
Aptitude tests, 76, 456–457
Argyle, M., *302*
Ariès, Philippe, 41
Aristotle, 14, 15, 17–18, 29, 34
Arons, S., 140–141
Art, 332, 333
Arts, careers in, 228–229
Assembly, freedom of, 160–161
Assistant principal, *219*
Assistant superintendents, 117–122
Associationism, 67–68
Attendance
    and achievement, 388–389
    compulsory, 136, 148–149
    records of, 378–379
Attention of students, 339
Auditory information, 267
Augustine, Saint, 22–23
Authority, 19–20, 78, 288

Back-to-basics movement, 23
Bankruptcy/receivership legislation,
    96
Barnes, D. W., *95, 359*
BASIC, 421
Behavior control model, 343
Behaviorist movement, 60, 70–72
Behavior modification, 70–72
Bennett, William, 99
Bias, test, 466–467
Bible, 41–44, 46
Bicultural students, 237–240, *241,*
    496
Bilingual students, 237–240, *241,*
    496
Binder, F. M., *47*
Binet, Alfred, 76, 258–259, 455
Block grants, 98–99
Bloom, Benjamin, 74, 275–276, 334,
    399
Board of education, state, 94–95,
    110–113, 188
Bonds, school, 104
Boyer, Ernest, 494, 495, 498
Branching, 273
Brophy, Jere, *314, 366,* 367–368
Brown v. Board of Education, 55,
    164–165
Bruner, Jerome, 69–70

Buckley amendment, 152
Budgets
    assistant superintendent for
        finance and budget, 121–122
    and electronic spreadsheets,
        414–415
    and local school board, 90
Bulletin boards, 319–320
Burnout, teacher, 204–206
Business manager, 121–122
Byte, 410

*Cardinal principles of secondary
    education,* 52
Career ladders, 199, 500
Carnegie unit, 96
Caruso, J. J., 186
Categorical aid, 98–99, 104
Catholic schools, 131–132, 135, 138,
    139, 141, 503
Cattell, James McKeen, 257–258
Cautiousness, 267
Cazden, C. B., *370*
Central processing unit (CPU),
    410–411
Centuries of Childhood (Ariès), 41
Certification, teacher, 169–170, 433
    and in-service education, 189–190,
        201
    recertification, 201
    recommendations concerning
        reform of, 500–501
    tests for, 186–188, 474
Chief state school officer (CSSO),
    94–95, 112–113
Child development, 61–67
    cognitive, 62–67, 388–389
    physical, 62
    theories of, 61–62
Civil Rights Act (1964), 165, 385
Classroom, 77–79
    and cooperative learning, 79
    curriculum planning at level of,
        325–328
    establishing rules of, 288–289,
        315–317
    grouping for instruction in,
        273–274, 321–323, 332–334,
        399, 467
    handling complexity of, 297–304
    as intellectually stimulating
        environment, 318–320
    planning for safety in, 320–321
    planning physical environment of,
        309–312
    planning psychological
        environment of, 312–318
    roles in, 78–79
    uses of standardized tests in, 462

Classroom lessons, 338–355
  evaluation in. *See* Evaluation of
    students
  general structure of, 338–347
  mastery learning, 275–276,
    347–348, 399–403
  motivation and, 349–350
  tests in, 368–379
  types of, 342, 350–354
Classroom mobility, 53, 54
COBOL, 420
Cognitive development, 62–67
  impact of school attendance on,
    388–389
  Kohlberg's moral thinking and
    reasoning, 65–67
  Piaget's stages of, 63–67
Cognitive objectives, 340
Cognitive style, 265–268
Cohen, E. G., 298
Coleman, James S., 36–37, 268,
    385–386
Coleman Report, 385–388, 391, 431
Collective bargaining, 90–91, 100,
    119, 170, 192, 201–203, 396,
    433
Colleges, career alternatives to
    teaching in, 221–223
Collins, D. W., *350*
Colonial America, 42–43, 132–134,
    429–430
Comenius, John Amos, 22, 40
Commercial groups, 102–103,
    503–504
Commission on the Reorganization
    of Secondary Education, 52
Committee of Ten, 50, 52
Common schools, 46–49, 51
Community colleges, 223
Compensatory education programs,
    236–237
Competition
  and educational vouchers,
    443–444
  and grades, 360
  and private schools, 141–143
Compulsory attendance, 136,
    148–149
Compulsory education, 42–43, 51–52
Computer-assisted instruction,
    72–74, 274
Computer-based job banks, 208
Computers, 408–427
  applications for, 414–416
  basics of using, 408–413
  careers in, 227
  future of, in education, 424–426
  problems of using, 422–424
  programming, 420–422
  as tutors, 416–420
Confidence, 313, 432–434

Confidentiality, of student records,
    151–153, 169
Conservative organizations, 102
Construct, 451
Construct validity, 451
Content area subjects, 328–329
Content domain, 450
Content validity, 451
Continuing education, 223, *224*
Contracts of teachers, 170, 171, 201
Contract tenure, 201
Control, in accountability programs,
    435–436
Convergent thinking, 271
Cooperative learning, 79
Corporal punishment, 156–157
Cost-benefit analysis, 468
Creationism, 149
Creativity, 270–272
Criterion domain, 452
Criterion-referenced tests, 460–461
Criterion-related validity, 452
Cuban, Lawrence, *20, 21, 49, 328,*
    425
Culture
  and bicultural students, 237–240,
    241, 496
  and liberal education, 21–25, 50,
    184
  transmission of, 21–25
Curriculum
  in academies, 49
  assistant superintendent for,
    117–118
  and child development theory,
    62
  and cognitive development
    theory, 63–67
  common school, 48
  and department chairperson,
    124–125
  hidden, 286–289
  high school, 50, 52
  influence of commercial interests
    on, 102–103
  influence of tests on, 467
  planning of, 323–328
  and progressive education, 27–28
  recommendations concerning
    reform of, 495–497
  state requirements for, 149
  and subject structuralism, 24–25

Data base management software,
    415–416
Day care, 12–13, 214
Deans, college, 222–223
Decentralization, 503
Degrees of Reading Power (DRP),
    461
Democracy, 28, 30–32, 35, 44–45

DeMott, Benjamin, 478
Department chairperson, 124–125,
    217
Department of Education, U.S., 99,
    100
Derived score, 458
Descartes, René, 15
Desegregation, 164–165
Developmental lessons, 350, *351*
Dewey, John, 13, *14*, 16–19, 26–28,
    32, 52–54, 60, 291
Diagnostic evaluation, 361–362
Digital computers, 408–409
Direct aid, 104
Directed-study lessons, *353*, 354
Director of personnel, 118–119
Disadvantaged students, 234–237
Discipline
  in effective schools, 401–403
  establishing routine for, 317–318
  legal issues concerning, 153–157
  procedural due process protection
    in, 158
  role of principal in, 394, 402
Discovery learning model, 343
Discrimination, 163–169
  and extracurricular activities,
    149–150
  sex, 165–166, 250–252
  and special-needs students,
    166–169
Discussion lessons, 350–351, *352*
District superintendent, 54, 89,
    116–117
Divergent thinking, 271
Domain-referenced tests, 460–461
Drill-and-practice software, 416–418
Drilling, 68
Due process of law, 153–155, 158
Dunn, R., *242*
Dyer, H., *441*

Eaker, R., *367*
Early childhood education, 214–215
Economic Opportunity Act (1964),
    55
ECS Task Force on Education for
    Economic Growth, 498
Edmonds, Ronald, 394–395
Educating Americans for the 21st
    century: A report to the
    American people and the
    National Science Board
    (National Science Board
    Commission), *480, 488–489,*
    490–491, 496, 500, 503, 504
Education
  aim of, 10–11
  characteristics of, 10
  defined, 9–12
  early compulsory, 42–43, 51–52

history of. *See* History of
  education
nature of, 8–12
philosophy of. *See* Philosophy of
  education
purpose of, 11–12, 23, 29
schooling versus, 12–13
social sciences in. *See* Social
  sciences in education
and society, 28–37
Educational games, 420
Educational policy
  and federal government, 86, 94,
    96–99
  and local districts, 86–93
  and local school board, 90
  and nongovernmental groups, 87,
    99–103, 503–504
  and state board of education,
    110–113
  and state education agency, 94
  and state governments, 86, 94–96
  use of tests in setting, 469–475
Educational vouchers, 142, *143*,
  443–444
Education Amendments (1972),
  165–166
Education Commission of the States
  (ECS), 87
Education Consolidation and
  Improvement Act (1981), 98,
  236–237
Education for All Handicapped
  Children Act (Public Law
  94-142) (1975), 97–98, 120, 152,
  167, 214, 245–249, 256, 442
Educationists, 32–33, 48
Effective schools, 384–404
  characteristics of, 391–403
  debate concerning, 384–387
  efficacy of, *393*, 396–399
  meaning of, 387–391
Efficiency
  concerns for lack of, 434
  of educational programs, 434
  of effective schools, *393*, 399–403
Eiden, L. J., *50, 53*
Eignor, D. R., 370–372, *373–376*
Electronic spreadsheet software,
  414–416
Elementary and Secondary
  Education Act (1965), 55, 56,
  97, 137, 239
Elementary schools, 50
  ability grouping in, 399
  bulletin boards in, 319
  and common school movement,
    46–49, 51
  costs of providing, 93, 103
  function of guidance counselors
    in, 126–127

learning centers in, 318–319
organization of, 91
positions for specialists in, 215
and progressivism, 52–54
report cards in, 380
"touch and look" tables, 319
use of time in, 400–401
Émile (Rousseau), 25–26
Emotional development, 12, 25–26
Empiricist tradition, 15
Enlightenment, 25–26, 34–35, 44–45
Enrichment, 243–245
Enrollment
  in Catholic schools, 135
  in public versus private schools,
    132, *133*
  secondary school, 51–52
Environment, 79–81
Ephron, D., 303–304
Equality of educational opportunity,
  33–37, 55–56, 234–253
  for bicultural and bilingual
    students, 237–240, *241*, 496
  and computer use, 423
  definitions of, 35–37
  federal legislation for, 97–98
  and financial issues, 104–107
  and gender stereotyping, 250–252
  link with academic excellence,
    489–492
  origins of, 33–35
  and school effectiveness debate,
    384–387
  for students from disadvantaged
    backgrounds, 234–237
  for students with handicapping
    conditions, 245–250
  for talented and gifted students,
    240–245
Essentialism, 23, 24, 53
Evaluation of curriculum, 325
Evaluation lessons, 354, *355*
Evaluation of students, 358–381
  during classroom lesson, 345–346
  constructing a classroom test for,
    368–378
  formal and informal, 358–361
  functions of classroom, 361–363
  moral dimension of, 284–285, 361,
    365
  record keeping for, 378–381, 415
  teachers' expectations and,
    363–368
  and unintended outcomes,
    294–296
Evaluation of teachers, 119,
  192–195, *196–198*. *See also*
  Accountability
  and department chairperson, 124
  by peers, 289–290
  techniques of, 193–194

Evaluation specialists, 219–221, 226,
  227
Expectations, 363–368
  for accountability programs,
    434–437
  and effective schools, 396–399
  of public for schools, 430
  steps in the expectancy process,
    364–367
  for teachers, 285–290
Experimental studies of learning, 70
Expert-judgment method, of
  identifying effective schools, 389
Expression, freedom of, 159–160
External locus of control, 268, 269
Extracurricular activities, 149–150,
  165–166
Eye contact, 302, 312

Fairness, 283–285, 312–313
Family
  accountability of, 439
  importance of, 385–387, 389–391
  role of, 12
  and role of children, 41
  and selection of private school,
    138–140, 142–143
  socioeconomic status of, 79–81,
    234–237
Family Educational Rights and
  Privacy Act (Buckley
  amendment), 152
Fardig, G. E., *316–317*
Federal government, 96–99
  accountability of legislators, 440
  aid to private schools, 137
  careers in, 228
  court system, *148*
  Department of Education (ED),
    99, 100
  educational legislation, 97–99. *See
    also specific legislation*
  and educational reform, 504
  financial aid programs, 56
  laws governing schools, 147, 148
  role of, in education, 45
Fees, school, 150
Field dependence, 266
Field independence, 266
Field theory, 68–69
Financial aid, 55
Financial issues, 103–107. *See also*
  Taxation
  assistant superintendent for
    finance and budget, 121–122
  concerning computers, 422
  costs of education, 93, 103, 434
  and educational reform, 491–492
  and federal legislation programs,
    97–99
  and private schools, 136–138, 162

Financial issues (*Continued*)
  salaries of teachers, 195–199,
    445–446
  and state governments, 96, 101,
    104–107
  and test-based funding, 470
First lessons, 99, 479, *482*, 495,
  496
Flakus-Mosqueda, P., *95*
Floppy disks, 409
Formative evaluation, 193, 362–363
Forness, S. R., *249*
FORTRAN, 420
Frank (Pseud.), 303
Franklin, Benjamin, 45
Froebel, Friedrich, 18, 19, 60
Full-state funding plans, 105
Fundamentalist Christian schools,
  131–132, 135, 139, 141
Furniture, classroom, 310–312

Gagne, R. M., 72–74
Gallup, A. M., *292*
Galton, Francis, 257
Game software, 420
Gardner, H., *262*
Gauthier, W. J., *387*, 395
Gender, 212, 250–252, 423
Gesell, Arnold, 62
Geyer, A., *330–331*
Gifted students, 240–245
Glaser, R., *73*
Goals
  of effective schools, 395–396
  local district, 89–90
  recommendations concerning
    reform of, 494–495
  of teachers, 290–294
Good, Thomas, *366*, 367–368
*Good high school: Portraits of
  character and culture*
  (Lightfoot), 479, *480*
Goodlad, John, 494–495, 502
Goss v. *Lopez*, 154
Government. *See also* Federal
  government; State government
  importance of education to, 44–45
  role of, in education, 45
Grade-equivalent (GE), 458–459,
  464–465
Grading, 359–360
  in effective schools, 398
  moral dimension of, 284
  record keeping for, 379
  report cards, 379–381
  and tracking system, 333–334
Gradisnik, A., *241*
Grant, W. V., *50, 53*
Grouping, 272–274, 321–323,
  332–334, 399, 467, 503
Guaranteed tax base plans, 106

Guidance counselors, 54, 120,
  125–128, 218–219, *220*
Guided practice, 344

Hacker, Andrew, 490
Hall, G. Stanley, 62
Hallinger, P., *397*
Hambleton, R. K., 370–372, *373–376*
Handicapping conditions, 245–250
  and discrimination, 166–169
  programs for students with,
    247–250
  Public Law 94-142, 97–98, 120,
    152, 167, 214, 245–249, 256,
    442
  types of, 246–247
Head Start, 55, 214, 236–237, 269,
  386
Health careers, 225
Hebrew schools, 131
Helvetius, Claude-Adrien, 60
Henry, J., *289*, 293, 295
Herbart, Johann, 18–19
Hewett, F. M., *249*
Hidden curriculum, 286–289
Hidden knowledge, of teacher,
  299–301
*High school: A report on secondary
  education in America* (Carnegie
  Foundation for the
  Advancement of Teaching), 479,
  480, 495, 499, 501, 503, 504
High schools. *See also* Secondary
  education
  ability grouping in, 399
  bulletin boards in, 319–320
  and educational reform, 479–483
  enrollment in, 52
  function of guidance counselors
    in, 127–128
  organization of, 93
  and progressivism. 52–54
  report cards in, 380
  specialists in, 215–221
Hilgard, E. R., 70, *71*
Hirst, Paul, 140
History of education, 39–56
  in colonial America, 42–43,
    132–134, 429–430
  in Europe, 40–42
  in the nineteenth century, 41–42,
    46–51, 134–135
  during Revolutionary period,
    43–45, 133–134
  in the twentieth century, 51–56
Hobbes, Thomas, 34, 60
Holmes, E. G. A., 395–396
Holmes Report, 184, 479, *482*, 483,
  496–497, 499
Holt, J., *304*
Home, influence of, 79–81

Home instruction, 137, 149
Homework, 398
Horizontal organization, 324
Hubner, J. J., *270*
Human resource departments, 226
Hume, David, 15, 16

Idealist tradition, 15
Illiteracy, *50*
Immigrants, 51, 237–240
Impulsivity, 266
Incentive programs, 198–199, 436
Independent practice, 344–345
Individualized education plans
  (IEP), 73–74, 120, 248–250,
  274–276, 354
Industrialization, and progressivism,
  52–54
Industrial Revolution, 41
Information in lessons, 342–343
Inhelder, Barbara, 65
Injuries, 321
Input, computer, 409–410
Input variables, 385
In-service training, 189–190, 201,
  500
Instructional clarity, 343
Insurance
  careers in, 227
  for teachers, 172
Integrated circuits (IC), 411
Intelligence, 258–265
  and achievement, 263–265
  and cognitive style, 265–268
  as single or plural ability, 260–263
  tests of, 67–68, 76, 258–260, 264,
    455–456
Interest of students, 339
Internal locus of control, 268, 269
International Association for the
  Evaluation of Educational
  Achievement (IEA), 484
Interviewing, 207, *208*

Jackson, P. W., *360, 361*
Jacobson, L., 364
James Madison High School
  (Bennett), 99, 479, *482*, 496
Jefferson, Thomas, 30–32, 45
Junior high schools, 91–93, 127

Keyboards, computer, 409
Kinesthetic information, 267
Knowledge
  as a pragmatic skill, 18
  nature of, 14–17
  and need for institution devoted
    to education, 40–42
  types of, 17–18
Kohlberg, Laurence, 65–67
Kritek, W. J., *393*

Language development, 63
Lasley, T. J., *402, 403*
Latin grammar schools, 43, 45, 49, 133
Lauro, D. R., *195*
Lawrence, C., 140–141
Leadership
  of effective schools, 393–396
  recommendations concerning reform of, 501–502
Learned helplessness, 268–269
Learning
  as an active process, 19, 20
  as a passive process, 18–20
  strategies for, 74–75
Learning centers, 318–319
Learning theory, 67–75
  associationism, 67–68
  behavior modification, 70–72
  contemporary studies, 72–75
  experimental studies with animals, 70
  structuralism, 68–70
Legal issues, 146–172
  discipline, 153–157
  discrimination, 163–169, 250–252
  employment of teachers, 169–171
  First Amendment guarantees, 159–161
  and private schools, 133–137
  procedural due process protections, 158
  religion, 161–162
  school attendance and programs, 148–151
  sources of laws governing schools, 147–148
  student records, 151–153
  tort liability, 171–172
Lemonade Stand (software), 419–420
Lesson planning, 328–334. *See also* Classroom lessons
  scheduling in, 329–332
  and type of subject matter, 328–329
  and within-class grouping, 332–334
Liberal arts, 21–25, 50, 184
Life patterns, 213
Lighting, classroom, 310–311
Lipsitz, Joan, 394
Lloyd, A. L., 296
Local district, 87–93
  and accountability programs, 436
  assistant superintendents, 117–122
  department chairperson, 124–125, *217*
  and educational policy, 86–93
  and financing of education, 88–90, 103

guidance counselors and other support staff, 54, 120, 125–128, 218, 219, *220*
principal. *See* Principal
rise of administration and, 54–55
role of, in education, 45
school administrative structure within, 91–93
school board, 89–91, 113–116, 439–442
secondary education and, 49–51
superintendent, 54, 89, 116–117
Local education authority (LEA), 88–89, 96, 101, 114–115
  and chief state school officer, 94–95, 112
  and federal block grants, 98–99
  and reform of education funding, 104–107
  tests and shifts in power from, 474–475
Locke, John, 15, 18, 22, 34–35, 40, 44, 51, 61
Locus of control, 268
Logic, 22
LOGO, 421–422, 426

Machine language, 409, 420
McCormack-Larkin, M., *393*
McGuinness, A., *95*
McKenna, B., *193, 194*
MacKenzie, D. E., *393*
Making the grade (Twentieth Century Fund Task Force), *481, 483, 489, 490,* 491, 495–496
Management theory, 54–55
Mann, Horace, 46–48, 61, 67
Marx, Karl, 32–33
Marxism, 18
Massachusetts School Law (1647), 42, *43*
Master teacher, 199
Master Type (software), 420
Mastery criterion, 460–461
Mastery learning, 275–276, 347–348, 399–403
Materials selection, 342
Mathematics, 22, 31, 251–252, 332, 488, 491
  bias in, 33
  programs for gifted in, 244
  subject structuralism in, 24–25
Maximum-competency achievement tests, 473–474
Mayer, R. E., 74–75
Media, careers in, 228–229
Memory, computer, 410
Mentor teachers, 184–186
Merchandising, careers in, 227
Merit pay programs, 445–446
Merton, Robert, 363–364

Microcomputers. *See* Computers
Middle schools, 91–93, 127
Minimum-competency testing (MCT) programs, 442, 443, 470–473
Minimum foundation plans, 105
Minority groups
  advocate groups for, 102
  bicultural and bilingual students from, 237–240, *241*
  in Coleman Report, 431
  on local school boards, 114
  and office of superintendent, 117
  in private schools, 138
  teachers from, 181–183
Mitman, A., *397*
Modeling, 344
Monitoring, of educational programs, 434–435
Monitors, computer, 411–412
Moral aspects of teaching, 282–289, 361, 365
Moral judgment, 23
Morrill Act (1862), 97
Motivation, 339, 349–350, 359–360
Motor skills, 12
Mueller v. *Allen*, 136
Murphy, J. F., *397*
Music, 332, 333

National Assessment of Educational Progress (NAEP), 251–252, 483–485
National Commission on Excellence in Education (NCEE), 30, 399–400, 432, 477, 483–485, 495
National Council for the Accreditation of Teacher Education (NCATE), 101
National Defense Education Act (NDEA) (1958), 56, 97
National Education Association (NEA), 87, 100, 172, 188, 190–193, *194,* 201–202, 429
Nationalism, 29–30
National School Boards Association (NSBA), 100–101
National Teachers Examination (NTE), 187
Nation at risk: The imperative for educational reform (National Commission on Excellence in Education), 30, 477, *481,* 483–485, *488, 490,* 497–500, 502–504
Nation prepared: Teachers for the 21st century (Task Force on Teaching as a Profession), 184, 479, *481,* 483, 499–501, 504
Neatness in classroom, 310
Negligence, 171–172

Nongovernmental groups, 87, 99–103, 430–431, 503–504. *See also* Professional associations
Nonverbal cues, 301–302
Norm group, 455, 457
Norm-referenced tests, 457–460

Objective-referenced tests, 460–461
Objectives
  of classroom lesson, 339–342
  of mastery learning, 348
Objective tests, 454–455
Objectivity, of knowledge, 14–17, 20
Operating system of computer, 409
Oral questioning, by teacher, 347
Organization
  of elementary schools, 91
  of high schools, 93
  of junior high schools, 91–93
  of private schools, 137–138
  recommendations for reform of, 502
Outlier method, of identifying effective schools, 389–390
Output, computer, 411–412

Paideia Proposal: An educational manifesto (Adler), 479, *481, 489,* 492–495, 497, *498,* 499, 501–503
Palaich, R. M., *95*
Parents
  accountability mechanisms for, 442–443
  accountability of, 439
  associations for, 101
Parent-Teacher Association (PTA), 101
Parker, Francis W., 48, 52
Pascal, 421
Percentage equalizing plans, 106
Percentile rank, 458
Perennialism, 23–24
Performance, teaching as, 296–297
Performance contracting, 444–445, 470
Permanent records, 378
Personal development, 25–28
Personality tests, 76
Personnel departments, 226
Pestalozzi, Johann, 61
Petty schools, 133
Philosophy of education, 7–37
  nature of education, 8–12
  nature of knowledge in, 14–17
  nature of the learner and of learning in, 18–19
  objective approach in, 21–25
  organization of knowledge in, 17–18
  personal development approach in, 25–28

role of student and, 19
role of teacher and, 19
schooling and, 12–13
society's needs and, 28–37
Physical development, 62
Physical education, 332
Physical sciences. *See* Science
Piaget, Jean, 60, 63–67
Place called school: Prospects for the future (Goodlad), 479, *481,* 497–503
Placement agencies, 208–209
Planning
  of classroom as stimulating environment, 318–320
  curriculum, 323–328
  and grouping for instruction, 321–323
  lesson, 328–334
  of physical environment of classroom, 309–312
  of psychological environment of classroom, 312–318
  of a safe classroom, 320–321
Plato, 9, 12–15, 17, 21, 29, 34, 40, 257
Plessy v. *Ferguson,* 55
Plyler v. *Doe,* 164
Practice, 344–345
Practice lessons, 351–352
Practice teaching, 185–186
Pragmatism, 16–17, 18, 20, 26
Praise, 313, *314*
Preactive teaching, 308–309. *See also* Planning
Preschool programs, 12–13, 55, 214–215, 236–237, 269, 386
Preservice training, 183–186, 499–500
Press, 397
Principal, 54, 122–123
  accountability of, 439, 441, 442
  high school, 93
  hiring of teachers by, 396
  job announcements for, *218, 219*
  recommendations concerning reform of role of, 501–502
  role in effective schools, 393–394, 402
Printers, computer, 412, *413*
Printing press, 40–42
Privacy, of student records, 151–153, 169
Private schools, 131–144
  academies, 49, 133–134
  choice of, 139–140
  in colonial America, 42–43
  current state of, 131–132
  and educational vouchers, 142, *143,* 443–444
  government aid to, 137
  historical origins of, 132–135

and issue of competition, 141–143
and issue of religion and values in education, 140–141
Latin grammar school, 43, 45, 49, 133
legal issues concerning, 135–137
organization of, 137–138
students of, 138–139
types of, 131
Problem solving, 272
Procedural due process, 158
Procedure of lessons, 342–343
Processing, computer, 410–411
Professional associations, 87, 100, 172, 190–192, 201–202, *221,* 227, 429
Professional development, 189–190, 201, 390, 500
Professors, college, 222–223
Program budgeting, 54
Programmed instruction, 72–73, 274
Programming, computer, 420–422
Progressive education, 26–28, 32, 52–54
Protestant Reformation, 16, 42, 134–135
Psychologists, 54, 120–121, 128, 218–219, *220*
Psychomotor objectives, 340
Psychosexual development, 12
Public education, 34–37
  in colonial America, 42–43
  common school movement, 46–49
  elementary. *See* Elementary schools
  and equal educational opportunity, 51, 55–56
  high schools. *See* High schools
  need for institution of, 40–42
  role of government in, 45
Public Law 94-142, 97–98, 120, 152, 167, 214, 245–249, 256, 442
Public service, careers in, 228
Publishing careers, 225, *226*
Pull-out class, 243
Punishment
  and accountability programs, 436–437
  in effective schools, 401–403
  grades as, 359–360
  informal evaluation in, 360–361, 365
  and learned helplessness, 268–269
  legal issues concerning, 156–157
  moral dimension of, 284
Pupil weighting system, 106
Purdom, D. M., *316–317*
Puritans, 42
Pygmalion in the classroom (Rosenthal and Jacobson), 364

Quality in education, 55–56. *See also* Effective schools
Questions
 in standardized tests, 453–455
 of students, 298
 of teachers, 347
Quincy system, 48
Quintilian, 282, *283*

Race discrimination, 164–165
Random-access memory (RAM), 410
Rationalist tradition, 15
Rational model, 343
Raw scores, 457–458
Reading, 42–43, 332
Read-only memory (ROM), 410
Realist tradition, 15
Record keeping. *See* Student records
Recruitment of teachers, 206–209, 396. *See also* Staffing
 and assistant superintendent for personnel, 118–119
 recommendations for reform of, 499–500
Reduction in force (RIF), 118, 207
Reflection, 266
Reform, educational, 477–504. *See also* Equality of educational opportunity
 background to the reports on, 478
 common beliefs in reports on, 486–492
 common school movement, 46–49, 51
 and criticisms of schools, 432–434
 of educational administration, 54–55, 501–502
 and funding through equalization, 104–107
 of the 1960s and 1970s, 53–54
 political dimension of reports on, 483–486
 profile of reports on, 479–483
 progressivism, 26–28, 32, 52–54
 public secondary schools, 49–51
 recommendations of reports on, 492–504
 and state involvement in education, 96
 in teacher training, 184–186
Reform, social, 32–37, 44–45
Regional high schools, 93
Regulations
 imposing, 288–289
 need for, 287–288
Rehabilitation Act (1973), 167–169
Reliability, test, 452–453, 463–464
Religion, 22, 23
 in colonial America, 42
 and common schools, 46
 and curriculum, 149

legal issues concerning, 161–162
 and private schools, 131–132, 135, 138, 139, 141, 503
Renaissance, 15–16, 22
Report cards, 379–381, 398
Research specialists, 219–221
Résumé, 208
Review, 339, 346
Review lessons, 353
Revolutionary period, 43–45, 133–134
Reward systems
 in effective schools, 398
 grading in, 359–360
 informal evaluation in, 360–361, 365
 and standardized test results, 469, 470, 474
Reynolds, J., *73*
Rice, Joseph Mayer, 67
Risk taking, 267
Rodriguez v. *San Antonio Independent School District*, 105
Roles, 212
 of students, 19–21, 24, 78–79
 of teachers, 19–20, 24, 78–79
Rosenthal, R., 364
Rousseau, Jean-Jacques, 19, 25–26, 44, 60
Rules, 155–156, 287–289, 315–317
Russia, 30, 55–56

Safety, classroom, 320–321
Salaries, teacher, 195–199, 445–446, 500
Sanctions
 grades as, 359
 informal evaluation in, 360–361, 365
 and standardized test results, 469, 470, 474
Scheduling, 329–332
Scholastic ability tests, 455–456
School board associations, 100–101
School boards, 54
 local district, 89–91, 113–116, 439–442
 state, 94–95, 110–113, 188
School bonds, 104
School fees, 150
Schooling, 9–10
 education and, 12–13
 and equality of educational opportunity, 33–37
 need for institution of, 40–42
 public, 34–37
School organization. *See* Organization
Science, 15–17, 22, 31, 32, 332, 488, 491
 influence on social sciences, 58–61

and national interests, 30, 55–56, 97
 programs for gifted in, 244
 subject structuralism in, 24–25
Scientific management, 54–55, 429
Searches of students, 157
Seat work, 401
Secondary education, 34, 36. *See also* High schools
 and common school movement, 46–49
 costs of providing, 93, 103
 growth of enrollment in, 51–52
 Latin grammar school, 43, 45, 49, 133
 in the nineteenth century, 47–51
Secular humanism, 135, 141
Segregation, 55
Selection questions, 453–454
Self-concept, 269–270
Sensory knowledge, 14–15
Sensory mode preference, 267–268
Serrano v. *Priest*, 104–105
Sex discrimination, 165–166, 250–252
Shared purposefulness, 394–395
Shavelson, R. J., *270*
Simulation software, 419–420
Sizer, Theodore, 502
Skill subjects, 332
Skinner, B. F., 70–72, 274
Slyck, L., *330–331*
Social class. *See* Socioeconomic status
Social development, 11, 12
Socialism, 32–33
Social mobility, 51
Social sciences in education, 57–81
 child development theory, 61–67, 388–389
 classroom as a social system, 77–79
 learning theory, 67–75
 relationship of home and school, 79–81
 and rise of scientific method, 58–61
 testing methods, 75–77. *See also* Tests, standardized
Social studies, 244, 332
Social workers, 128
Society, education and, 28–37
Socioeconomic status, 80
 and equality of educational opportunity, 51, 55–56
 and school performance, 80–81
 students with disadvantaged, 234–237
Software, computer, 414–420, 423–424
Special education, 55, 120, 214, *215, 216*

Special-interest groups. *See* Nongovernmental groups
Specialists, 91, 93, 119–121, 125–128, 211–229
Specialization of roles, 54
Spelling tests, 67
Spencer, Herbert, 11
Spock, Benjamin, 62
Spreadsheet software, 414–416
Sputnik, 30, 55–56, 97, 241
Stability, classroom, 313–318
Staff development, 396
Staffing. *See also* Recruitment of teachers
  assistant superintendent for personnel, 118–119
  and local school board, 90–91
  and teacher organizations, 100
Stake, Robert, 435
Standardized tests. *See* Tests, standardized
Stanton, G. C., *270*
State department of education (SDE), 95–96
State education agency (SEA), 94–96
  and federal block grants, 98–99
  tests and shift in power from, 474–475
State government, 94–96
  accountability of legislators, 440
  careers in, 228
  changes in control and, 96
  chief state school officer (CSSO), 94–95, 112–113
  in common school movement, 46–49, 51
  court system, *148*
  and educational reform, 504
  and financing of education, 96, 104–107
  laws governing schools, 147, 148
  and regional high schools, 93
  role of, in education, 45
  school board, 94–95, 110–113, 188
  state department of education (SDE), 95–96
  state education agency (SEA), 94–96, 98–99, 474–475
  and taxpayer associations, 101
  test requirements of, 449
Stereotypes, gender, 212, 250–252
Sternberg, Robert, 261–263, 265
Structuralism, 68–70
Student-centered instruction, *21*
  in common school movement, 48–49, 51
  and middle school structure, 92–93
  and progressive education, 26–28, 32, 52–54
  Rousseau's views of, 25–26

Student records, 169, 378–381
  attendance, 378–379
  data base management programs for, 415–416
  grades, 379
  legal issues concerning, 151–153
  medical, 320
  permanent, 378
  report cards, 379–381, 398
  spreadsheet programs for, 415
Students
  ability of, 258–265, 322–323, 399
  accountability of, 438, 441, 442
  bicultural and bilingual, 237–240, *241*, 496
  cognitive styles of, 265–268
  creativity of, 270–272
  from disadvantaged backgrounds, 234–237
  and ethical/moral relationship with teacher, 283–284
  evaluation of. *See* Evaluation of students
  and gender stereotyping, 212, 250–252
  with handicapping conditions. *See* Handicapping conditions
  individual differences of, 256–277
  individualized programs for, 73–74, 120, 248–250, 274–276, 354
  learned helplessness of, 268–269
  learning strategies of, 74–75
  locus of control of, 268
  questions of, 298
  roles of, 19–21, 24, 78–79
  selection and grouping of. *See* Grouping
  self-concept of, 269–270
  talented and gifted, 240–245
Study of high schools (Sizer), 479, *481*, 502–503
Subject structuralism, 24–25
Substantive due process, 155
Substitute teachers, 299–301
Summary of lesson, 346
Summative evaluation, 193, 363, 437
Superintendent
  accountability of, 439, 441, 442
  assistant, 117–122
  job announcement for, *219*
  local district, 54, 89, 116–117
  state, 94–95, 112–113
Supply-type questions, 453, *454*
Swaminathan, H., 370–372
Symbolic representation, 63

Talented and gifted students, 240–245
Tannenbaum, A., *244*

Taxation, 41–43, 45, 50
  deduction for education expenses, 136
  and local education authorities, 88–89, 104–107, 114–115
  taxpayer groups, 101
Tax credits, 142–143
Taylor, Frederick, 54
Teacher-centered instruction, *20*, 21–25
Teacher centers, 189–190
Teachers, 178–209
  accountability of, 437–438, 441, 442
  burnout of, 204–206
  career alternatives for, 211–229
  career decision of, 206
  certification of. *See* Certification
  classroom roles of, 78–79
  collective bargaining by, 90–91, 100, 119, 170, 192, 201–203, 396, 433
  demographics of, 181–183
  and department chairperson, 124–125, *217*
  evaluation of. *See* Evaluation of teachers
  expectations of, 363–368
  finding a job and, 206–209
  goals of, 290–294
  incentive programs for, 198–199, 436
  individualized instruction by, 73–74, 120, 248–250, 274–276, 354
  institutional expectations for, 286–290
  legal issues in employment of, 169–171
  merit pay programs for, 445–446
  methods of, 59–61
  and moral dimension of teaching, 282–289, 361, 365
  preservice training for, 183–186, 499–500
  professional associations of, 87, 100, 172, 188, 190–192, 201–202, 227, 429
  professional development programs for, 189–190, 201, 390, 500
  profession of, 178–181
  public confidence in, 433
  recommendations concerning, 498–501
  recruitment of, 206–209, 396, 499–500
  reduction in force (RIF), 118, 207
  role of, 19–20, 24, 78–79
  salaries of, 195–199, 445–446, 500
  and social context of teaching, 296–304

societal expectations for, 285–286
style of, 59–61
substitute, 299–301
tenure of, 171, 200–201
training of, in computer use, 423
and unintended outcomes of
  teaching, 294–296
Technology, 31–32, 55–56, 97, 241,
  486–488. *See also* Computers
Temperature, classroom, 311
Tenure, 171, 200–201
Test-based funding, 470
Test battery, 449
Test bias, 466–467
Testing specialists, 219–221
Test reliability, 452–453, 463–464
Tests, classroom, 368–379
Tests, standardized, 59, 120,
  449–475
  achievement. *See* Achievement
    tests
  aptitude, 76, 456–457
  characteristics of, 450–453
  criticisms of, 465–469
  decline in scores, 432–433
  and employment of teachers, 226,
    227
  history of development of, 75–77
  intelligence, 67–68, 76, 258–260,
    264, 455–456
  kinds of, 453–461
  legal issues concerning, 150–151
  to measure school effectiveness,
    391
  minimum-competency, 442, 443,
    470–473

and misuse of test results, 463–465
  personality, 76
  recommendations concerning
    reform of, 497–498
  spelling, 67
  for teacher certification, 186–188,
    474
  use of, in schools, 461–463
  use of, in setting educational
    policy, 469–475
Test validity, 451, 452
Textbooks, and educational policy,
  102–103
Theory of instruction, 69–70
Thigpen, N., *330–331*
Thorndike, Edward Lee, 67–68
Time, use of, 343, 399–401, 503
Time for results (National Governors
  Association), *482*
Time on-task, 343, 399–401
Title XI, Education Amendments
  (1972), 165–166
Tomorrow's teachers, 184
Torshen, K. P., 347–348
Tort liability, 171–172
"Touch and look" tables, 319
Tracking, 273, 322–323, 332–334,
  399, 467, 503
Training
  as career alternative to teaching,
    224–226
  preservice, 183–186, 499–500
  programmed learning in, 72–73,
    274
  vocational, 52, 53
Trait, 451

Transfer-of-training, 67–69
Transportation expenses, 106–107
Tutorial software, 418–419
Twentieth Century Fund Task
  Force, 498

Unintended outcomes, 294–296
Universities, career alternatives to
  teaching in, 221–223
University Council on Educational
  Administration (UCEA), 101

Validity, test, 451, 452
Values, 285–286
Verbal cues, 301–302
Vertical organization, 324–325
Visual information, 267
Vocational training, 52, 53
Voucher system, 142, *143*, 443–444

Waller, W., *285, 298, 300*
Wayson, W. W., *402, 403*
Weil, M., *397*
Weinstein, C. E., 74–75
Wertheimer, Max, 68–69
Wilson, N., *330–331*
Women
  advocate groups for, 102
  on local school boards, 114
  and office of superintendent, 117
  as teachers, 181
Word-processing software, 414, 416
Workshops, 189
Writing, 224, 225, 416, 455, 495

Yinger, R. J., *326–327*